GERLYVER KERNEWEK KEMMYN

An Gerlyver Kres

KERNEWEK - SOWSNEK

SOWSNEK - KERNEWEK

CORNISH – ENGLISH

ENGLISH – CORNISH

DICTIONARY

Dr Ken George

Kesva an Taves Kernewek

© Cornish Language Board, 2000
ISBN 0 907064 79 5

The publication of this book has been supported by a donation from H.R.H. the Duke of Cornwall.

First edition   October 1998   1000 copies
Reprinted with minor corrections   May 2000

FOREWORD TO THE FIRST EDITION

The *Gerlyver Kres* was planned as one of three versions of the *Gerlyver Kernewek Kemmyn*. The full Cornish – English version *(Gerlyver Meur)* was published in 1993, and all copies have been sold. The source-files used to produce this work have been revised, and new software has written by the editor to produce English – Cornish as well as Cornish – English dictionaries. The *Gerlyver Kres* contains both in one volume, but without the detailed etymologies and notes found in the full version. The revision of the source-files means, however, that a new edition of the *Gerlyver Meur* is almost ready. It has become increasingly clear that the editing of a dictionary is a never-ending task, and that further editions will be produced in the future.

The production of an English – Cornish version means that more attention has had to be paid to the meanings of words; Ray Edwards and Keith Syed have helped greatly in this respect. Indeed, the help of many other Cornish speakers is gratefully acknowledged, especially the following: George Ansell, Wella Brown, Pol Hodge, Julyan Holmes, Jowann Richards, Graham Sandercock and Tony Snell.

Dr Ken George
Bosprenn
October 1998

FOREWORD TO THE SECOND EDITION

This is essentially a reprint of the first edition, but since a new ISBN has been assigned, it must be described as a new edition. The number of explanatory pages in the first edition was restricted in order to keep the total number of pages to 320. No such restriction applies here, and a section on spelling and pronunciation is therefore included.

M. Everson has criticized *Gerlyver Kres* on superficial grounds, but as the publisher of a different dictionary of Cornish, he can hardly be regarded as impartial. He considers the following to be unconventional:
(a)   the use of different fonts for Cornish and English;
(b)   using + (instead of -) for indicating "add-on" plural endings;
(c)   using angle brackets for distinguishing homographs
The editor of *Gerlyver Kres* regards all of these features as improvements.

What is of greater concern is that a few words were omitted from the first edition, e.g. **ri** 'to give'; these words were present in the source-files, so that their omission in the dictionary was due to an error in the software. This error has now been traced to one of the four linked programs used to produce the dictionary, and corrected. Lawrence Rule, Sheila Williams and Chris Wilson are among the sharp-eyed speakers who spotted the omissions.

The opportunity has been taken to add a few more new words.

Dr Ken George
Bosprenn
May 2000

LAYOUT

General

Arial type is used for Cornish words, and Times Roman for English words. The abbreviations used for parts of speech are as follows:

adj.	adjective	*num.*	number
adv.	adverb	*phr.*	phrase
art.	article	*place*	name of a place
coll.	collective noun	*plur.*	plural noun
conj.	conjunction	*pref.*	prefix
dual	dual noun	*prep.*	preposition
f.	feminine	*pron.*	pronoun
int.	interjection	*ptl.*	verbal particle
m.	masculine	*suff.*	suffix
n.	noun	*v.*	verb
name	name of a person		

Cornish – English section

The source-files include practically all the words found in the corpus of traditional Cornish, and many more words introduced into Cornish in the twentieth century, especially by R. Morton Nance. Over one thousand more words have been added since the publication of the *Gerlyver Meur* in 1993. Some English loan-words in the traditional corpus, such as **onderstondya**, have not found favour with Cornish speakers, and have been omitted.

Head-words are printed in **Large Arial Bold** type, except for prefixes and suffixes, which are printed in Large Arial type. Homographs are distinguished by a reference within angled brackets; e.g. **bras**<big> and **bras**<plot>. The head-word is followed by an abbreviation indicating its part of speech. Many nouns have their plural form shown using + where suffixes are added (e.g. **dydh +yow** for **dydhyow**) or – where letters are replaced (e.g. **kiger −oryon** for **kigoryon**). There is a tendency to replace the English plural ending +ys by a Cornish ending such as **+ow**. In cases where **+ys** is attested in the traditional texts, but **+ow** is not, both endings are given. Collective nouns, which are already plural, have their singulative shown; e.g. **gwydh** *c.* **+enn** 'trees'. Phrases are printed in **Arial Bold** type. The English meanings are printed in Times Roman type.

English – Cornish section

Apart from the exception described below, this is intended to be a mirror-image of the Cornish – English section, because both have been prepared from the same source-files. The English head-words are in **Large Times Roman Bold**, and English phrases and amplifications in Times Roman. The same set of abbreviations is used for the part of speech. Cornish meanings are printed in **Arial Bold** type. A few English loan-words, (e.g. perysshya), omitted from the Cornish – English section, are however, included in the English – Cornish section (printed in light Arial type), because no suitable alternatives have yet been found for them. If any reader has ideas for such alternatives, please inform the editor.

SPELLING AND PRONUNCIATION

Four different spelling systems were used for writing traditional Cornish; those of Old, Middle and Late Cornish, and that of Edward Lhuyd. Only the last of these was reasonably fixed, and only the last attempted seriously to indicate the pronunciation. In the twentieth century, Jenner's orthography and Nance's Unified Cornish were fixed, but their links to the pronunciation were tenuous.

Since sound-recording apparatus had not been invented at the time when Cornish was spoken traditionally, we have no direct evidence of how it was pronounced. The nearest that we can get to its pronunciation is the description made by Edward Lhuyd during his visit to Cornwall in 1701. This applies to the Late Cornish phase, and because the sounds of Cornish (like those of any other language) changed with time, it is not applicable to the Middle Cornish phase on which the revived language is based. Otherwise we have to rely on the interpretation of the written texts. During the 1980s, the editor of this dictionary carried out an extensive study of the historical phonology of Cornish, and his recommended pronunciation, given below, was intended to approximate that of the traditional language c.1500.

Nance's orthography, known as Unified Cornish, was improved so as to fit the pronunciation more closely, and to be more phonemic. A phonemic orthography is one in which each phoneme (contrastive sound-unit) is represented by a unique grapheme (letter or group of letters). Using such an orthography, one can work out what the phonemes are from the written word. To determine the pronunciation then depends on knowing the way in which each phoneme is pronounced (its realization), which may vary according to its position in an utterance. The near one-to-one relationship between writing and sound enables learners of Cornish to acquire a fairly accurate pronunciation with ease and speed. The orthography is most phonemic when applied to stressed syllables; in unstressed syllables it is sometimes partly etymological.

The improved spelling (as used in this dictionary) and recommended pronunciation, known as *Kernewek Kemmyn*, were adopted in principle by the Cornish Language Board in July 1987. They have been criticized by N. Williams in his book *Cornish Today*, but his criticisms are largely unfounded, as shown by Paul Dunbar and the present editor in their reply *Kernewek Kemmyn – Cornish for the 21st Century*.

Vowels

LENGTH OF VOWELS

Vowels in traditional Cornish had three possible lengths, depending on the stress and by the nature of the following consonants, according to the following rules:

(a)   In unstressed syllables, all vowels were short.

(b)   In stressed syllables, vowels were short before consonant groups (except /sp/, /st/ and /sk/) and double consonants.

(c)   In stressed syllables, vowels were fully long in monosyllables and of mid-length in polysyllables before single consonants and the consonantal groups /sp/, /st/ and /sk/.

These rules applied until the seventeenth century, and are therefore appropriate for *Kernewek Kemmyn* (George, 1997). *(N. Williams has tried to argue that the breakdown of the rules, which he terms the prosodic shift, occurred before the date of the earliest Middle Cornish texts, perhaps c.1250, but his arguments are untenable).*

The length of vowels in most words may be determined from the spelling in *Kernewek Kemmyn*. *(No other Cornish spelling system has this valuable property; in Unified Cornish and in N. Williams' revision thereof, the length of vowels has to be learned separately for each individual word).*

STRESSED VOWELS

The vocalic system of Cornish was most fully developed in stressed vowels. It had the nine phonemes /i, ɪ, ɛ, a, ɔ, o, u, œ, y/, which are represented in *Kernewek Kemmyn* by the nine graphemes <i, y, e, a, o, oe, ou, eu, u>. *(N. Williams does not recognize /o/, though the evidence for it is abundant, and he has even tried to block publication of such evidence).*

The recommended pronunciations are as follows:

i   /i/   When long, as *ee* in English *beet,* or preferably even closer, like French /i/;   when of mid-length or short, the same sound appropriately reduced in duration.

y   /ɪ/   When short, as *i* in English *bit,* i.e. [ɪ];   when of mid- or full length, the same sound extended appropriately.

e   /ɛ/   When short, as *e* in English *bet,* i.e. [ɛ̞];   when of mid- or full length, the same sound extended appropriately.

a   /a/   When short, [a], which is the sound of *a* as heard in the English dialect of east Cornwall in words like *bat;*   when of mid- and full length, the same sound extended appropriately.

o   /ɔ/   When long, [Oː], which is similar to that of *ough* in English *bought,* but closer;   when short, [O], which is similar to that of *o* in English *pot,* but closer;   when of mid-length, between [Ọ] and [O].

oe   /o/   When of full or mid-length, this is a close back rounded vowel, [oː] or [oˑ] according to length: this sound does not occur in standard English, but is found in French in the words *eau* 'water' and *haut* 'high', which are homophones.   When short, the vowel is unrounded to [ɤ], which is similar to *u* in English *but, cut,* but closer.

ou   /u/   When long, as *oo* in English *boot,* i.e. [uː];   when of mid-length and short, the same sound appropriately shortened.

eu   /œ/   The basic sound is [œ], which does not occur in English;   as *eu* in the French word *peur* 'fear', with appropriate length.

u   /y/   This sound does not occur in English, but is represented by *u* in the French word *tu* 'thou'.   It may be approximated by saying [iː] (e.g. *ee* in English *beet)* with rounded lips.

UNSTRESSED VOWELS

The inventory of unstressed vowels in Middle Cornish was smaller than that for stressed vowels; three of the nine stressed vowels had no unstressed counterparts:

(a) unstressed /œ/ had been reduced to [ɛ], which is shown by the change *–uc, -oc* to *–ek* in place-names; i.e. the contrast between /œ/ and /ɛ/ was neutralized;

(b) unstressed /i/ was realized as [ɪ], at least in syllables ending in a consonant; i.e. the contrast between /i/ and /ɪ/ was neutralized;

(c) unstressed /y/ was realized as [ɪ], at least in syllables ending in a consonant; i.e. the contrast between /y/ and /ɪ/ was neutralized.

Kernewek Kemmyn recognizes (a) in its spelling, but cases of (b) and (c) are spelled according to the original historical phoneme before the neutralization took place, viz. <i> and <u> rather than <y>. These are etymological rather than phonemic spellings, but they are justified on the grounds of being able to distinguish in writing wordslike **gwelis** 'I saw' and **gwelys** 'seen'. Both of these are pronounced with the short vowel [ɪ]. The recommendations for pronouncing unstressed vowels are therefore similar to those for pronouncing stressed vowels, with the exceptionsthat **i, y** and **u**, when representing unstressed vowels in words ending in a consonant, may all be pronounced [ɪ].

The word **dhe** 'to' is pronounced like the English definite article *the;* i.e. **e** stands for the schwa vowel [ə].

Semi-vowels

y   /j/   As *y* in English *yes,* i.e. [j].

w   /w/   As *w* in English *way,* i.e. [w].

Consonants

STRESSED CONSONANTS

p   /p/   As *p* in English *pit, taper, keep.*

pp   /pp/   An extended [p]; as *p P* in English *tap Peter.*

t   /t/   An alveolar [t], as *t* in English *tea, later, beet.*

tt   /tt/   An extended [t]; as *t t* in English *a bit tired.*

k   /k/   [k]; as *k* in English *kit, taken, beak.*

kk   /kk/   An extended [k]; as *ck c* in English *sick cat.*

b   /b/   [b]; as *b* in English *bit, tuba, cube,* except when unvoiced to [p] in sandhi (i.e. in combination with other consonants).

d   /d/   [d]; as *d* in English *dog, laden, road.* In sandhi, it may be unvoiced to [t].

g   /g/   [g]; as *g* in English *gap, tiger, vague,* except when unvoiced to [k] in sandhi.

f   /f/   *f* as in English *fat.*

ff   /ff/   An extended [f], e.g. as *ff* in English *half fed.*

v   /v/   [v], as *v* in English *vat, river, cave,* except when unvoiced to [f] in sandhi.

th   /θ/   [θ], as *th* in English *thin, pithy, breath.*

tth   /θθ/   An extended [θ], as *th th* in English *he hath thought.*

dh   /ð/   [ð], as *th* in English *thither, weather, breathe.*

gh /x/ In final position, and in the group /xt/, this is pronounced [x]. This sound is not found in English, except in careful pronunciations of loan-words, e.g. *ch* in *loch*. It is the voiceless velar spirant written as *ch* in German *Achtung, Bach*. Between vowels, and in the groups /lx/ and /rx/ between vowels, it is pronounced [ɦ]. This is the sound of *h* in English *aha,* and is slightly different from that of *h* in initial position.

ggh /xx/ An extended [x].

h /h/ [h], as *h* in English *hat.*

s This stands for the two different sounds [s], as *s* in English *sat,* and its voiced counterpart [z], as *z* in English *zip*. Since <s> was used for both sounds in Middle Cornish (as it is in English), it is difficult to determine the circumstances in which each sound applies. **s** is usually [z], except:

(a) at the beginning of an utterance (absolute initial), e.g. *sa'bann* 'stand up';

(b) at the end of an utterance (absolute final) after /n/ or /l/, e.g. *war-nans* 'downwards';

but [z] was found in Late Cornish even in these environments. The grapheme **s** is also used in loan-words from French like *plas* and *gras,* though in Middle Cornish, the sound of *s* in these words was evidently different from that in native words; it may have been the affricate [ts].

ss /ss/ A lengthened [s].

sh /ʃ/ [ʃ], as *sh* in English *ship.*

ch /tʃ/ [tʃ], as *ch* in English *church.*

j /dʒ/ [dʒ], as *g* in English *ginger.*

m /m/ [m], as *m* in English *mad, homing, dame.*

mm /mm/ A doubled [m], as *mm* in English *Mummy.*

n /n/ [n], as *n* in English *nut, tenor, seen.*

nn /nn/ A doubled [n].

l   /l/   A clear [l], as *l* in English *late*.

ll   /ll/   As [l] but longer; similar to *ll* in English *filling*, but more like *ll* in Italian *bello*.

r   /r/   A voiced alveolar roll, sounded in all phonetic environments.

rr   /rr/   As [r], but longer in duration.

UNSTRESSED CONSONANTS

These are pronounced the same as the stressed consonants, except that **mm**, **nn**, **ll** and **rr** are reduced to [m, n, l, r] respectively.

VARIATIONS

The pronunciation of traditional Cornish was not static, but like that of all languages, changed slowly with time. Some of the changes took two centuries or more to complete. *Kernewek Kemmyn* recognizes in its spelling the results of the following changes:

1.	Unrounding of unstressed /œ/ to /ɛ/	**e**
2.	Assibilation of /d/ to [z] in certain environments	**s**
3.	Lowering of unstressed /e/ to /a/	**a**

but in the following, the spelling represents the situation before the change:

4.	Diphthongization of [-yː] to [-ɪʊ]	**u**
5.	Unrounding of stressed /œ/ to /ɛ/	**eu**
6.	Lowering of unstressed /ɔ/ to /a/	**o**
7.	Pre-occlusion of [mm, nn] to [bm,dn]	**mm, nn**
8.	Unrounding of [yː] to [iː]	**u**
9	Raising of [oː] to [uː]	**oe**

There is an element of anachronism here, since (4) probably occurred before (3).

Kernewek Kemmyn distinguishes /y/ and /ɪʊ/ finally in stressed open syllables; thus **du** 'black' is pronounced [ˈdyː] and **Dyw** 'God' is pronounced [ˈdɪʊ]. The fact that, in Middle Cornish the word for 'God' was often spelled *du*, suggests that the distinction had been lost, as pointed out by N. Williams.

In Middle Cornish, words in the following groups were spelled with <-e> and pronounced [-ɛ], whereas in **Kernewek Kemmyn** (following Nance) they are spelled with <-a> and pronounced [-a]:

		MIDDLE CORNISH		KERNEWEK KEMMYN
(i)	a large number of verbal nouns, e.g.	*tenne*	'to pull'	**tenna**
(ii)	prepositions with 3rd pl. endings, e.g.	*ynne*	'in them'	**ynna**
(iii)	loan-words with *-é* in Modern French, e.g.	*pyte*	'pity'	**pyta**
(iv)	3rd sg. endings in some tenses, e.g.	*ese*	'was'	**esa**
(v)	where a final consonant had been lost, e.g.	*kerense*	'love'	**kerensa**

Thus in unstressed final open syllables, Middle Cornish distinguished between /ɛ/ and /a/, but **Kernewek Kemmyn** does not make this distinction.

TECHNICAL

Since a new version of word-processing software seems to come out every other year, there is great merit in keeping the source-files for any word-processing project in a format which is independent of that software. Thus the basic data for *Gerlyver Kernewek Kemmyn* are kept in eight ASCII source-files, which are accessed using programs written in FORTRAN 77 by the editor. The program used to produce *Gerlyver Meur* was converted for the first edition of *Gerlyver Kres* to produce output suitable for use with Word 97, instead of LATEX, as the word-processing package.

In addition, three other programs were written to invert the Cornish-English dictionary into an English-Cornish one. GLSK1 extracts from the source-files those fields of relevance to the English - Cornish section, notably the Cornish word, English meaning, and code for part of speech. GLSK2 then scans the results eight times, extracting data for each of eight fascicules in the section. These data are sorted using Microsoft Word into English alphabetical order. GLSK3 then appends codes which denote the type and size of font to be used; these codes are interpreted by a macro in Word to produce the text. The separate headers for each page then had to added by hand.

Using just one set of source-files has the advantage that only one amendment has to be made every time information is added to the dictionary. It does mean, however, that the English-Cornish section is essentially an inversion of the Cornish-English section, rather than being designed *ab initio* as an English-Cornish dictiionary. It is intended in future editions to reconcile this conflict by using the principles of a relational data-base.

BIBLIOGRAPHY

GEORGE, K.J. (1986)   *The pronunciation and spelling of revived Cornish.*   Cornish Language Board, Saltash.

GEORGE, K.J. (1993)   *Gerlyver Kernewek Kemmyn – an Gerlyver Meur.*   Cornish Language Board, Saltash.

GEORGE, K.J. (1997)   'Mid-length vowels in Cornish'. *J. Celt. Linguistics,* **6**, 125-136.

DUNBAR, P. and GEORGE, K.J. (1997)   ***Kernewek Kemmyn:*** *Cornish for the twenty-first century.*   Cornish Language Board, Saltash.

RANN GYNSA

KERNEWEK – SOWSNEK

PART ONE

CORNISH - ENGLISH

A

a<goes> *v.* goes (part of irreg. vb.)
a<if> *conj.* if
a<of> *prep.* of, from
a<VP> *ptl.* (vbl. ptl.)
A *int.* O
-a<AJ> *suff.* (superlative ending)
-a<FN> *suff.* (fem. abst. noun ending from nouns and adjectives)
-a<VN> *v.* (VN ending)
a-ban *conj.* since
a-barth *prep.* for the sake of, beside, in the name of, along with; **a-barth Dyw** by God
abas *m.* **+ow** abbot
abases *f.* **+ow** abbess
abatti *m.* **+ow** abbey
abel *adj.* able, capable, fit
a-bell *adv.* afar
aber *m.* **+yow** river-mouth
Aberfal *place* Falmouth
Aberplymm *place* Plymouth
a-berth *prep.* within
a-berthek *adj.* intrinsic
a-bervedh *adv.* inside, indoors, aboard
a-ble *adv.* whence, from what place
abosteledh *coll.* apostles, apostolate
abostol *m.* **abesteli** apostle
abostolek *adj.* apostolic
a-boynt *adj.* punctual *adv.* promptly, with alacrity
Abram *name* Abraham
abrans *m.* **+ow**, *dual* **dewabrans** eyebrow
abransek *adj.* bushy-browed
a-brys *adv.* early, timely, on time, in good time
abusya *v.* abuse
a-byla *adv.* whence
acheson *m.* **+yow**, **+ys** occasion, cause, motive, reason
a-dal *prep.* opposite, facing, fronting

Adam *name* Adam
adamant *m.* **+ow**, **+ys** diamond
aden *f.* **+yow** binding board of a book
a-denewenn *adv.* aside, sideways, to one side
a-der *prep.* without, outside, except *adv.* not, rather than; **hi a'th kar a-der my** she loves you not me, she loves you rather than me
a-derdro *adv.* all around
a-dermyn *adv.* in time, on time, punctually
a-dhann *prep.* from under, from beneath
a-dhedro *adv.* about, round about
a-dheghow *adv.* on the right hand
a-dheghowbarth *adv.* on the South side
a-dhelergh *adv.* behind, aft, abaft, in arrears; **a-dhelergh dhe** *prep.* abaft
a-dherag *prep.* before, beforehand, in front of
a-dhesempis *adv.* suddenly, immediately, forthwith
a-dhevis *adj.* exact
a-dhewis *adj.* optional *adv.* optionally
a-dhia *prep.* from, since; **a-dhia Nadelik** since Christmas
a-dhifun *adv.* awake
a-dhihwans *adv.* immediately
a-dhistowgh *adv.* immediately
a-dhiwar *prep.* from on, from over
a-dhiwar-leur *adv.* up from the ground
a-dhiwedhes *adj.* late, recent
a-dhiworth *prep.* from
adhves *adj.* ripe, mellow
adhvesi *v.* ripen
adhvetter *m.* ripeness
adhyskans *m.* education
adhyski *v.* educate
adhyskonieth *f.* pedagogy

1

adla *m.* **adlyon** rogue

-adow *suff.* (abst. n. ending associated with verbs)

a-dre *adv.* from home, away

a-dreus *adv.* across, indirectly, transversely; **kewsel a-dreus** answer back, talk at cross-purposes

a-dro *adv.* around; **a-dro dhe** about, concerning, approximately

a-droes *adv.* on foot, afoot

a-dryv *adv.* behind

afia *v.* affirm

afina *v.* adorn, decorate, garnish

afinans *m.* decoration, garnish

afydhya *v.* assure, confirm, affirm

aga *pron.* their

a'ga *phr.* of their

a-gammow *adj.* progressive *adv.* progressively

agan *pron.* our

a'gan *phr.* of our

agas *pron.* your

a'gas *phr.* of your

agenn *f.* stomach (of animal)

a-gettep *adv.* respectively

ages *conj.* than

a-gevres *adj.* serial *adv.* serially

agh<fie> *int.* fie, ugh

agh<race> *f.* **+ow** offspring, race (ethnic)

aghel *adj.* racial

agha *m.* awe, dread

aghskrif *m.* **+ow** pedigree, genealogy

aghskrifer *m.* **-oryon** genealogist

a-gledh *adv.* on the left hand

a-gledhbarth *adv.* on the north side

ago-marghogyon *f.* knightly service, feudal tenure

agrowsenn *f.* **+ow**, *coll.* **agrows** hip (plant), dog-rose

a-gynnik *adj.* tentative *adv.* tentatively

a-gynsow *adv.* lately, recently, just now

aha *int.* aha

ahanan *adv.* hence, from us, of us

ahanas *adv.* from thee, of thee

ahanav *adv.* from me, of me

ahanowgh *adv.* from you, of you

ahas *adj.* bitter, severe, hateful

ahwer *m.* sorrow, distress, trouble; **heb ahwer** *adv.* readily

ahwesydh *m.* **+es** skylark (bird), lark

a-hys *adv.* full length, outstretched, from end to end

a-is *adv.* below, lower

a-ji *adv.* inside, within; **a-ji dhe** *prep.* inside, within

akont *m.* **+ys**, **+ow** account, reckoning; **akont arghow** deposit account; **akont kesres** current account; **akont kreun** deposit account; **akont poll** current account

akontieth *f.* accountancy

akontya *v.* count, reckon, esteem

akontyans *m.* **+ow** reckoning

akontydh *m.* **+yon** accountant

akord *m.* agreement, harmony (abst.), reconciliation; **gans unn akord** with one accord

akordya *v.* agree, harmonize (abst.), reconcile; **akordya orth** agree with; **akordya y golonn gans** agree with

akordyans *m.* agreement

akwitya *v.* pay off, absolve (of a debt), discharge

akwityans *m.* receipt, absolution (of a debt)

alabaster *m.* alabaster

alamand *m.* **+ow**, **+ys** almond

alann *coll.* coltsfoot

alargh *m.* **elergh** swan

Alban *place* Scotland *m.* **+yon** Scotsman

Albanek *adj.* Scottish, Scots

2

Albanes *f.* **+ow** Scotswoman
alemma *adv.* hence, from here;
  alemma rag henceforward
alena *adv.* thence, from there; **alena rag** thenceforward
a-lemmyn *adj.* current (as in current affairs), present
a-les *adv.* abroad, apart, widely, outstretched
alhwedh *m.* **+ow** key
alhwedha *v.* lock
alhwedh-know *f.* **alhwedhow-know** spanner, wrench (U.S.)
alhwedh-korkynn *m.*
  alhwedhow-korkynn corkscrew
alhwedhor *m.* **+yon** treasurer
alinya *v.* align
alkan *m.* metal, tin
Alman *m.* **+yon** German
Almanes *f.* **+ow** German
Almayn *place* Germany
Almaynek *adj.* German *m.* German language
aloes *plur.* aloes
alow **+enn** water-lilies
alowans *m.* allowance
als<cliff> *f.* **+yow** cliff
als<joint> *m.* joint
altenn *f.* **+ow** razor
alter *f.* **+yow** altar
altrewan *f.* step-mother
altrow *m.* **+yon** step-father
alusen *f.* **+ow** alms, charity (gift of money)
aluseneth *f.* **+ow** charity (body)
alusener *m.* **-oryon** almoner
alusenji *m.* **+ow** almshouse
alyon *m.* **+s** foreigner, alien
alymona *m.* alimony
am *pron.* my
a'm *phr.* of my
amal *m.* **emlow** edge, border, side, rim

amalek *adj.* peripheral
amalogneth *f.* peripherality
amalven *m.* **amalveyn** kerb-stone
amanenn *m.* **+ow** butter
amanenna *v.* butter
amari *m.* **+ow**, **+s** cupboard, locker; **amari gweli** bedside cabinet
amaya *v.* dismay, perplex, bewilder
a'm beus *phr.* I have
ambos *m.* **+ow** promise, contract, covenant; **ambos demmedhyans** engagement (to marry); **ambos surheans** insurance policy
ambosa *v.* promise; **ambosa orth nebonan** promise to someone
amendya *v.* make amends, atone, set right
amendys *plur.* amends
amiral *m.* **+yon** admiral
amkan *m.* **+ow** goal, objective, aim; **war amkan** *adv.* at random
amm *m.* **+ow** kiss
amma *v.* kiss N.B. Takes **dhe**, e.g. **amm dhymm !** 'kiss me !'
ammeth *f.* agriculture
ammetha *v.* farm
ammok *m.* defence
amontieth *f.* computing
amontya *v.* count, compute, estimate; **ny amont** *phr.* there's no point in, it's no good
amovya *v.* perturb, agitate, startle
amser *f.* **+yow** tense (of verb)
amseryow *plur.* period (menstrual)
amyttya *v.* admit, acknowledge, concede
amyttyans *m.* admittance
an *art.* the
a'n<of the> *phr.* of the
a'n<him> *phr.* him, it (obj.)
an- *pref.* un-
anabel *adj.* incapable
anadhves *adj.* unripe, immature
anall *f.* breath

anannedhadow *adj.* uninhabitable
anav *m.* **+es** slow-worm, blindworm
andhemmedhys *adj.* unmarried
androw *m.* afternoon
androweyth *m.* afternoon-time
anedha *adv.* from them, of them
anedhi *adv.* from her, of her
anella *v.* breathe
anerys *adj.* untilled, fallow (unploughed)
anes *adj.* troubled, wearied *m.* uneasiness
aneth *adj.* amazing *m.* **+ow** marvel, wonder, adventure; **leverel anethow** *v.* tell tales; **gul aneth a** *v.* wonder at
anewnder *m.* iniquity
anfel *adj.* naive
anfeus *f.* ill luck, misery, misfortune
anfeusi *m.* disaster
anfeusik *adj.* unfortunate, unlucky *m.* **-igyon** wretch
anfeyth *adj.* infertile
anfeythter *m.* infertility
anfur *adj.* unwise, imprudent
anfurneth *f.* imprudence
angus *m.* anguish
anhedhek *adv.* incessantly, without respite
anhun *m.* insomnia
anhwek *adj.* harsh, unpleasant
anhwekter *m.* roughness
ankablus *adj.* not guilty, innocent
ankar *m.* **ankrys** anchorite, recluse, hermit
ankarji *m.* **+ow** hermitage
ankemmeradow *adj.* unacceptable
ankempenn *adj.* untidy
anken *m.* **+yow** misery, grief, trouble
ankenek *m.* penance *adj.* penitential
ankensi *adj.* grievous
ankenya *v.* inflict grief
ankevi *v.* forget

ankombra *v.* bother, hamper, embarrass
ankombrynsi *m.* embarrassment
ankompes *adj.* uneven
ankor *m.* **+yow** anchor
ankorva *f.* anchorage
ankorya *v.* anchor
ankoth *adj.* unknown, strange, outlandish
ankothvos *m.* unknown thing
ankov *m.* forgetfulness, oblivion
ankovva *f.* forgetfulness
ankow *m.* Death (personified)
ankredor *m.* **+yon** unbeliever, pagan; **ankredor mor** Viking
ankres *m.* disquiet, distress
ankresya *v.* disturb
ankrysadow *adj.* unbelievable, incredible
ankryjyk *adj.* unbelieving
annawel *f.* tempest, hurricane
annedh *f.* **+ow** dwelling, habitation
annedhadow *adj.* habitable
annedhi *v.* inhabit
annedhyas *m.* **-ysi** inhabitant
annia *v.* tire, weary, vex, annoy, aggrieve
annown *m.* underworld, Hades, abode of the dead
anodho *adv.* from him, of him
anorak *m.* **anoragow** anorak
anperfeyth *adj.* imperfect
anpossybyl *adj.* impossible
anreyth *adj.* abnormal
anreythenn *f.* **+ow** abnormality (specific)
anreythter *m.* **+ow** abnormality (abst.)
-ans *suff.* **-ansow** (abst. n. ending)
ansans *adj.* unholy, profane, impious
ansansoleth *f.* impiety, profanity
anserghek *adj.* independent
anserghogeth *f.* independence
ansoedhogel *adj.* unofficial

anstrethys *adj.* unstructured, informal

ansurneth *f.* **+ow** uncertainty

antell *f.* **antylli** snare, trap, inveiglement

antemna *m.* **antemnow** anthem

anteythi *adj.* incapable, inert, without normal faculties

antryghadow *adj.* unbeatable, invincible, impregnable

antowlek *adj.* casual (of labour)

anusadow *adj.* unusual

anvab *adj.* childless

anvabas *m.* childlessness, sterility

anvarwel *adj.* immortal

anvarwoleth *f.* immortality

anven *adj.* weak

anvenowgh *adj.* infrequent

anvlas *m.* tastelessness, insipidity

anvlasus *adj.* insipid, bland, tasteless

anvodh *m.* unwillingness, reluctance; **a'y anvodh** *adv.* against his will

anvodhek *adj.* reluctant

anvodhogeth *f.* reluctance

anvri *m.* disrespect; **gul anvri dhe** *v.* show disrespect to

anwan *f.* **+yow** anvil

anweladow *adj.* invisible

anweladewder *adj.* invisibility

anwirvos *m.* unreality

anwiw *adj.* unfit, unworthy, inappropriate, unseemly, unsuitable

anwiwder *m.* unworthiness

anwodhvos *adj.* unknown *m.* unknown thing

anwoes *m.* chill, cold

anwoesek *m.* chilly, apt to catch cold

anwoesi *v.* catch cold

anwoheladow *adj.* unavoidable, inevitable

anyagh *adj.* unwell, infirm, unhealthy, unfit (out of condition)

apa *m.* **appys** ape, monkeyish person,

aparel *m.* outfit, gear (clothes)

apert *adj.* obvious, evident, open

aperya *v.* injure, harm, impair

apoyntya *v.* fix, nominate, ordain

appla *adj.* more able

apposya *v.* examine (of knowledge), test by questions

apposyans *m.* examination, test

apron *m.* **+yow** apron

ar *m.* ploughed land, tilth

ar- *pref.* before, facing, beside

Arab *m.* **Arabyon** Arab

Arabek *adj.* Arabic *m.* Arabic language

Arabi *place* Arabia

arader *m.* **ereder** plough

aradror *m.* **+yon** ploughman

aradow *adj.* arable

a-rag *prep.* before, in front of, in the presence of

arall *adj.* other, another

aras *v.* plough

aray *m.* order, array, arrangement

araya *v.* arrange, prepare, set in order

arbenniger *m.* **-oryon** specialist

arbennigi *v.* specialize

arbennik *adj.* special; **yn arbennik** especially, specially

arbennikter *m.* speciality, specialism

arbrevi *v.* experiment

arbrisya *v.* evaluate

arbrov *m.* **+ow** experiment

ardh *m.* **+ow** high place, height

ardhek *adj.* lofty

ardhynya *v.* seduce

areth *f.* oration, declamation, speech, lecture, address (talk)

arethor *m.* **-oryon** orator, lecturer, public speaker

arethva +ow *f.* rostrum, platform

arethya *v.* make a speech, harangue

argel *f.* **+yow** retreat, sequestered place

argeles *v.* sequester

argemmynn *m.* **+ow** advertisement, notice

argemmynna *v.* advertise

argerdh *m.* **+ow** process

argerdhes *v.* process

argerdhell *f.* **+ow** processor

argh *f.* **+ow** coffer, chest, bin, ark (e.g. of covenant); **argh vona** money box

arghadow *m.* **+yow** command, order (command), commandment; **arghadow dre bost** mail order

arghadow-mona *m.* **arghadowyow-mona** money-order

arghadow-post *m.* **arghadowyow-post** postal order, money order (U.S.)

arghans *m.* silver, money, finance; **arghans byw** quicksilver, mercury; **arghans tiogeth** housekeeping (money)

arghansek *adj.* financial *f.* **-egi** ground rich in silver

arghanser *m.* **-oryon** financier, banker

arghansereth *f.* finance

arghanswas *m.* **-wesyon** bank clerk

arghantell *f.* silvery stream

arghantti *m.* **+ow** bank (for money)

arghas *m.* **+ow** fund, bursary

argh-dillas *f.* **arghow-dillas** chest of drawers

arghdrewydh *m.* **+yon** archdruid

arghdyagon *m.* **+yon** archdeacon

arghel *m.* **+edh** archangel

arghena *v.* put shoes on, shoe

arghenas *m.* footwear, shoes

arghepskop *m.* **-epskobow** archbishop

arghepskobeth *m.* archbishopric

arghjevan *m.* arch-fiend

argh-lyvrow *f.* **arghow-lyvrow** book-case

arghoferyas *m.* **-ysi** high priest

arghpedrevan *m.* **+es** dinosaur

argoll *m.* danger of loss, perdition

argovrow *m.* dowry

argya *v.* reason; **argya orth nebonan** argue with someone

argyans *m.* argument

arloedh *m.* **arlydhi** lord, master

arloedhes *f.* **+ow** lady, mistress

arloedhesedh *m.* ladyship

arloettes *m.* lordship, jurisdiction

arnewa *v.* damage by weather

arnow *m.* storm damage

arnowydh *adj.* modern

aros *m.* **+yow** poop, stern-deck

art *m.* **+ow**, **+ys** art

arta *adv.* again, once more, on a future occasion

artweyth *m.* artwork

arv *f.* **+ow** weapon, arm; **arvow bywoniethek** *plur.* biological weapons; **arvow kymyk** chemical weapons; **arvow nuklerek** nuclear weapons

arva *v.* arm

arval *m.* grist, toll (of flour)

arvedh *v.* affront, harass, browbeat

arvek *adj.* armed *m.* **arvogyon** armed man

arveth *m.* hire, employment, wages *v.* hire, employ

arvethesik *m.* **-igyon** employee, hireling

arvethor *m.* **+yon** employer

arvethores *f.* **+ow** employer

arvji *m.* **+ow** arsenal

arvor *m.* coastland, coast

arvorek *adj.* coastal

arwask *m.* oppression

arwaska *v.* oppress

arwodhvos *v.* to be aware

arwoedh *f.* **+yow** sign, symbol, emblem, armorial device; symptom

arwoedha *v.* signal, signify, make a sign

arwoedhek *adj.* symbolic, emblematic

arwoedh-fordh *f.* **arwoedhyow-fordh** road-sign

arwoedhik *m.* **-igow** badge

arwoedhogeth *f.* symbolism

arwoedhor *m.* **+yon** signalman

arwystel *m.* pledge

arys *m.* stubble, arable field after reaping and before ploughing

as- *pref.* re-

-as<-ful> *suff.* **-asow** -ful

-as<VN> *v.* (VN ending)

-as<33> *v.* (3rd sg. pret. ending)

a's<her> *phr.* her, it (obj.)

a's<them> *phr.* them

asektour *m.* **+s** executor

asenn *f.* **+ow** rib, spoke of wheel, stave of barrel

asennek *adj.* ribbed

askall *coll.* **+enn** thistles

askallek *adj.* thistly

askell *f.* **eskelli** wing, fin, naker shell

askell-dro *f.* helicopter

askell-groghen eskelli-kroghen *m.* bat (mammal)

askellek *adj.* winged

askloesenn *f.* **+ow,** *coll.* **askloes** chip, splinter

askloesi *v.* chip, splinter

askloetti *m.* **+ow** chip-shop

askorr *m.* offspring, produce; **askorr lethek** dairy produce

askorrans *m.* production

askorras *m.* product

askorrer *m.* **-oryon** producer

askorn *m.* **eskern** bone

askornek *adj.* bony

askra *f.* bosom, fold forming pocket

askrifa *v.* ascribe

askus *m.* **+yow** excuse

askusya *v.* excuse

aslamm *m.* **+ow** rebound

aslamma *v.* rebound

asow *coll.* **+enn** ribs

asper *adj.* grim, harsh, stern

aspia *v.* espy, observe, spy; **aspia orth** spy on, look at

aspier *m.* **-oryon** scout, spy, observer

aspiyas *m.* **aspiysi** spy

asrann *f.* **+ow** department; **Asrann an Kyrghynnedh** Department of the Environment; **Asrann Garyans** Department of Transport; **Asrann Genwerth** Department of Trade; **Asrann Yeghes** Department of Health

ass *int.* how

assa *int.* how

assay *m.* **+s** attempt, essay, rehearsal

assaya *v.* try

assentya *v.* agree, acquiesce, consent; **assentya gans** take the side of

assentyans *m.* assent

assoylya *v.* solve, absolve (of sins)

astel *v.* discontinue, suspend, cease, break off *m.* strike (suspension of work)

astel-ober strike, stoppage of work

astel-omladh *m.* cease-fire

astelyer *m.* **-yoryon** striker

astell *f.* **estyll** board (timber), plank, splint, shingle; **astell an oeles** mantelpiece

astell-dhelinyans *f.* drawing-board

astell-omborth *f.* **estyll-omborth** seesaw

astiveri *v.* make up for, compensate, pour back

astiveryans *m.* compensation

astranj *adj.* strange, foreign

Asvens *m.* Advent
asver *v.* restore (fig.)
asvlas *m.* aftertaste
aswa *f.* **+ow** gap, breach, pass; **gul aswa** *v.* make a gap
aswek *adj.* gapped
aswels *m.* revived pasture, new growth of grass
aswonn *v.* know (persons or places), recognize, acknowledge, realize, be familiar with
aswonnans *m.* **+ow** acknowledgement
aswonnvos *m.* knowledge, acquaintance
asyn *m.* **-es** donkey, ass
asynik *m.* **-igow** foal (of an ass)
atal *coll.* rubbish, mine-waste, trash (U.S.), garbage (U.S.)
atalgyst *f.* **+yow** dustbin, trash can (U.S.), garbage can (U.S.)
a'th<of thy> *phr.* of thy
a'th<thee> *phr.* thee
atom *m.* **+ow** atom
atomek *adj.* atomic
attal *m.* repayment, recompense
attamya *v.* broach, make a first cut or bite in, meddle with
attendya *v.* notice, pay attention, take note of
attent *m.* attempt, experiment, endeavour
attes *adj.* comfortable, at ease
atti *m.* spite, malice, animosity
attyli *v.* repay, recompense
a-ugh *prep.* above, over, aloft
-av *v.* (1st sg. pres. ind. ending)
aval *m.* **+ow** apple
aval-bryansenn *m.* larynx
aval-dor *m.* **avalow-dor** potato
avalenn *f.* **+ow** apple-tree
avalennek *f.* **-egi** orchard
aval-gwlanek *m.* **avalow-gwlanek** peach

aval-kerensa *m.* **avalow-kerensa** tomato
aval-paradhis *m.* **avalow-paradhis** grapefruit
aval-sabenn *m.* **avalow-sabenn** fir-cone, pine cone (U.S.)
avalwydhenn *f.* **+ow**, *coll.* **avalwydh** apple-tree
avanenn *f.* **+ow**, *coll.* **avan** raspberry
a-vann *adv.* aloft, above, overhead
a-varr *adv.* early
avel *adv.* like, as
aventurya *v.* speculate, make a venture
a-ves *adj.* outside, away
avi<envy> *m.* envy, jealousy, ill-will; **perthi avi orth** *v.* to envy
avi<liver> *m.* liver; **avi glas** gizzard
avis *m.* advice, opinion, consideration
avisya *v.* observe, note, make known
avisyans *m.* **+ow** notice
avlan *adj.* unclean
avlavar *adj.* dumb, mute, speechless
avleythys *adj.* hardened, obdurate *m.* **+yon** ruffian, hard man, tough nut, hard-bitten fellow
avlymm *adj.* obtuse
a-vodh *adj.* voluntary *adv.* voluntarily
avodya *v.* leave, go away get out, escape, withdraw
avon *f.* **+yow** river
avond *int.* avaunt, begone
avonsya *v.* promote, advance, exalt, progress
avonsyans *m.* promotion, advancement
a-vorow *adv.* tomorrow
avoutrer *m.* **-oryon**, **+s** adulterer
avoutres *f.* **+ow** adulteress
avoutri *m.* adultery
avowa *v.* avow, confess, acknowledge
avoweson *m.* advowson

avoydya *v.* avoid, shun
a-wartha *adv.* above, aloft, on top
awedh *f.* **+yow** watercourse
awel *f.* **+yow** wind, gale, weather;
awel glor breeze
a-wel *adj.* visible; **a-wel dhe** *adv.*
before the eyes of, in sight of
awelek *adj.* windy
awen<jaw> *f.* jaw, mandible
awen<muse> *f.* inspiration, muse,
genius, poetic imagination
awenek<jawed> *adj.* jawed
awenek<poetic> *adj.* poetic,
creative, imaginative
aweni *v.* inspire
aweyl *f.* **+ys, +yow** gospel
aweyla *v.* evangelise
aweylek *adj.* evangelical
aweyler *m.* **+s** evangelist
awgrym *m.* mathematics
awtorita *m.* authority
awtour *m.* **+s** author
a-woeles *adv.* below, lower, at the
bottom
awos *conj.* because, though, for the
sake of, in spite of *m.* account;
awos Krist *phr.* for Christ's sake;
awos mernans because of death,
though I die; **awos neb tra** for
anything; **awos peryll** because of
danger, at any risk; **awos tra** for
anything, at all costs; **war neb 'wos**
on any account
a-wosa *adv.* after, afterwards
awotta *int.* behold
ay *int.* hey, hi
a'y<of her> *phr.* of her, of its
a'y<of his> *phr.* of his, of its; **a'y**
oes *adv.* ever; **a'y wosa** afterwards
ayr *m.* air
ayrborth *m.* **+ow** airport
ayrbost *m.* airmail
ayrek *adj.* airy
ayrell *f.* ventilator
ayrella *v.* ventilate

ayrellans *m.* ventilation
ayrewnans *m.* air-conditioning
ayrgylgh *m.* atmosphere
ayrgylghyek *adj.* atmospheric
ayrlorgh *f.* **+ow, -lergh** aerial
aysel *m.* vinegar
ayselek *adj.* vinegary

B (mutations V, P, F)

baban *m.* **+es** baby
babi *m.* **+ow** baby
bacheler *m.* **+s** bachelor, junior,
young man
badh<bath> *m.* bath
badh<boar> *m.* **+es** boar
badhya *v.* bathe
badus *adj.* lunatic, moonstruck
bagas *m.* **+ow** group, bunch, troop;
bagas ilewydhyon orchestra
bagas-gwari *m.* **bagasow-**
gwari play-group
bagasik *m.* **-igow** batch
bagel *f.* **baglow** crozier, crook,
pastoral staff
bagh<cell> *f.* **+ow** cell (small
room), dungeon, nook
bagh<hook> *f.* **+ow** hook, fetter,
crook
bagha *v.* trap
baglek *adj.* crooked (crook-shaped)
bakken *m.* bacon
bal *m.* **+yow** mine, area of tin-
working
balek *adj.* jutting *m.* **balogow**
projection
ball<plague> *f.* plague, pest
ball<spot> *m.* white spot on forehead
ballek *m.* bow-net
balyer *m.* **+yow, +s** barrel
banadhel *coll.* **banadhlenn**
broom flowers, besom
banadhlek *f.* **-egi** broom-brake

banana *m.* **+s** banana

band *m.* band (musical); **band brest** brass band

baner *m.* **+yow** flag, banner; **baner-es** flag of convenience

baneror *m.* **+yon** standard-bearer

bankenn *f.* **+ow** bank (topographical)

bann *m.* **+ow** height, prominent place

banna *m.* **bannaghow** drop, bit, jot; **ny welav banna** *phr.* I can't see a bit

bannek *adj.* peaked, prominent

bannya *v.* read banns

bannys *plur.* banns

banow *f.* **bynewi** sow (pig)

bara *m.* bread; **bara an gog** sorrel; **bara barlys** barley bread; **bara byghan** roll (bread); **bara goell** leavened bread; **bara gwaneth** wheaten bread; **bara gwynn** white bread; **bara heb goell** unleavened bread; **bara heydh** barley bread; **bara kales** ship's biscuit; **bara kann** white bread; **bara kergh** oaten bread; **bara segal** rye bread; **bara toes** underbaked bread

baramanenn *m.* sandwich

barbar *m.* **+yon** barbarian

barbarus *adj.* barbarous

bardh *m.* **berdh** bard, poet; **Bardh Meur** Grand Bard

bardhek *adj.* bardic

bardhes *f.* **+ow** bard, poet

bardhonek *adj.* poetic *m.* **-ogow** poem

bardhonieth *f.* poesy, poetry

bargen *m.* **+yow** bargain

bargen-tir *m.* **bargenyow-tir** farm, holding of land

bargenya *v.* bargain

bargesi *v.* hover

bargos *m.* **bargesyon** buzzard

barkado *m.* **+s** bulk of pilchards

barlenn *f.* **+ow** lap

barlenna *v.* hold in lap

barlys *coll.* **+enn** barley corn

barr<bar> *m.* **+ys** bar (of door), tribunal, judge's seat

barr<top> *m.* **+ow** summit, climax; branching bough

barras *m.* **+ow** crisis

barrek *adj.* twiggy

barrenn *f.* **+ow** small branch, twig

barthusek *adj.* wondrous, wonderful, marvellous

barv *f.* **+ow** beard; **barv gwydh** lichen

barvek *adj.* bearded

barver *m.* **-oryon** barber

barvus *adj.* bearded *m.* **+i** codfish

bas *adj.* shallow *m.* shoal (topographical)

basa *v.* stun

basar *m.* bazaar, jumble sale, rummage sale (U.S.)

basdhowr *m.* shallow ford

basnet *m.* **+ow** helmet, basinet (headgear); **basnet diogeledh** safety helmet

bason *m.* **+yow**, **+ys** large basin

baster *m.* shallowness

basya *v.* grow shallow, abate

batalyas *v.* fight

batel *f.* **+yow** battle

bath *m.* **+ow** coin

batha *v.* coin

bathor *m.* **+yon** coiner

batt *m.* **+ys** bat (cricket), cudgel

batti *m.* **+ow** mint (for money)

batri *m.* **+ow** battery

bay *m.* **+ow** kiss

baya *v.* kiss

bayli *m.* bailiff

baywydh *f.* **+enn** bay-trees

bedh *m.* **+ow** grave, sepulchre, tomb; **bedh men** sarcophagus, stone-built tomb

bedha *v.* dare, venture, presume

bedhas *m.* **+ow** venture

bedhek *adj.* daring, venturesome, presumptious

bedhyas *m.* **-ysi** challenger

bedhygla *v.* bellow, roar, low (of cows)

begel *m.* **+yow** navel, hillock, knob

begh *m.* **+yow** burden, load

beghus *adj.* burdensome, oppressive

beghya *v.* burden, oppress, load, impose upon

begi *v.* bray

begya *v.* beg

begyer *m.* **+s, -yoryon** beggar

bejeth *f.* **+ow** face, surface

bel *m.* war

belaber *m.* swift runner, sprinter

beler *coll.* **+enn** water-cress

belerek *adj.* cressy *f.* **-egi** cress-bed

ben<base> *m.* **+yow** stump, base, foot

ben<FN> *f.* woman; **hy ben** the other (f.)

benewenn *f.* **+ow** wench, little woman

benfis *f.* benefice

bengorfonieth *f.* gynaecology

bengorfydh *m.* **+yon** gynaecologist

bennath *f.* **+ow** blessing, benediction; **benna'sywes** *phr.* may blessing follow; **benna'tyw** God's blessing;

bennesik *adj.* blessed

bennesikter *m.* blessedness

benniga *v.* bless, hallow

bennigys *adj.* blessed

benow *adj.* female, feminine (grammatical gender)

ben'vas *f.* goodwife, housewife

benyn *f.* **+es** woman, wife; **benyn bries** bride; **benyn nowydh** bride; **benyn jentyl** gentlewoman, lady

benyna *v.* consort with women

benynek *adj.* womanly

benynreydh *f.* female, woman

benynses *m.* womanhood

benyn-vas *f.* goodwife, housewife

beol *m.* tub

ber *m.* **+yow** roasting spit

bera *v.* flow

berdh *plur.* bards

bern<care> *m.* care (solicitude), concern, interest; **ny vern** *phr.* it does not matter, it is of no concern

bern<heap> *m.* heap, rick, stack

bernya *v.* pile up, stack

berr<shank> *f.* **+ow** shank, calf (of leg)

berr<short> *adj.* short, brief

berr-anall *m.* asthma

berrder *m.* brevity

berrgamm *adj.* crook-shanked, bandy-legged, bow-legged

berrhe *v.* shorten, abbreviate, abridge

berrheans *m.* **+ow** abbreviation

berrskrif *m.* **+ow** summary

berrskrifa *v.* summarize

berri *m.* fatness, grossness, obesity

berrik *adj.* plump, obese, gross (fat)

berrwel *m.* short-sight, myopia

berya *v.* transfix, spit, run through

besont *m.* **besons** bezant

besowenn *f.* **+ow,** *coll.* **besow** birch-tree

best *m.* **+es** beast, animal

besydh *m.* baptism

besydhven *m.* font

besydhya *v.* baptise

besydhyans *m.* christening

besydhyer *m.* **-oryon** baptist

betysenn *f.* **+ow,** *coll.* **betys** beet (plant); **betys rudh** beetroot

beudhi *v.* drown

beudhowr *m.* filthy water

bever *m.* **+s** beaver

bewin *m.* beef

Bibel *m.* Bible

biblek *adj.* biblical**

bibyn-bubyn *m.* **bibynes-bubyn** shrimp
bilen *adj.* villainous *adv.* horribly
bileni *f.* villainy, vileness, ill-treatment
bilienn *f.* **+ow**, *coll.* **bili** pebble
bis *f.* **+yow** vice (tool)
blam *m.* blame, fault
blamya *v.* blame, censure, find fault with
blas *m.* taste, smell, relish
blasa *v.* taste, smell, relish
blesyon *plur.* flavouring
bleujenn *f.* **+ow**, *coll.* **bleujyow** flower, bloom, blossom; **bleujenn an gog** bluebell; **bleujenn fosow** wallflower; **bleujenn ster** aster
bleujennik *m.* floweret, floret
bleujyow *plur.* flowers
bleujyowa *v.* bloom, blossom, flower
bleujyowek *adj.* flowery *f.* **-egi** flower-bed
bleus *m.* **+yow** flour; **bleus bleujyow** pollen; **bleus fin** fine flour; **bleus heskenn** sawdust
bleusek *adj.* floury, farinaceous
blew *coll.* hair
blewek *adj.* hairy, shaggy
blewenn *f.* **+ow**, *coll.* **blew** a hair; **blewenn an lagas** eyelash
bleydh *m.* **+es**, **+i** wolf
bleydhek *adj.* abounding in wolves
bleydhes *f.* she-wolf
bleyn *m.* **+yow** tip (end), point, peak, forefront
bleynya *v.* sharpen, point, precede
blin *adj.* soft
bloedh *m.* year of age, age (in years)
bloedhweyth *m.* year's time
blogh *adj.* hairless, bald, close-shaven
bloghhe *v.* make bald
bloghter *m.* baldness
blojon *m.* **+s** bludgeon

blonegek *adj.* greasy, lardy
blonek *m.* fat, grease, lard
bludh *adj.* tender, delicate, soft
bludhhe *v.* tenderize
bludhik *adj.* delicate
bludhya *v.* soften, weaken, enervate
blydhen *f.* **blydhynyow** year
blydhenyek *adj.* yearly, annual
boba *m.* fool, simpleton, small calf
bodh *m.* will, inclination, consent
bodhar *adj.* deaf
bodhara *v.* become deaf
bodharek *m.* **-ogyon** deaf person
bodharhe *v.* deafen
bodharses *m.* deafness
bodhek *adj.* voluntary *m.* **-ogyon** volunteer
bodhenn *f.* corn-marigold
boekka *m.* **+s** hobgoblin, imp, scarecrow; **boekka du** bugbear; **boekka gwynn** ghost
boel *f.* **+yow** axe
boelik *m.* **-igow** hatchet
boemm *m.* **+yn** blow, thump, bump
boemmenn *f.* **+ow** blow, buffet, stroke
boes *m.* food, meal, fodder; **boes Pask** feast of Passover; **boes soper** supper
boesa *v.* feed
boessa *m.* large round earthenware pot, large salting-pot
boesti *m.* **+ow** restaurant, eating-house
bogalenn *f.* **+ow** vowel
bogh<buck> *m.* buck, billy-goat, he-goat
bogh<cheek> *f.* **+ow**, *dual* **diwvogh** cheek (Anat.)
bogh-diank *m.* scapegoat
boghek *adj.* big-cheeked
boghes *adj.* few, little *m.* little; **boghes venowgh** *adv.* seldom

boghosek *adj.* poor, indigent, destitute *m.* **-ogyon** pauper

boghosekhe *v.* impoverish

boghosogneth *f.* poverty, destitution, want

boghvlew *coll.* whiskers

Bohemi *place* Bohemia

bokla *v.* buckle

bokler *m.* **+s** buckler, small shield

boks<blow> *m.* **+ow** box (blow)

boks<container> *m.* **+ys** box (container)

boks<tree> *m.* box (tree)

boksas *m.* **+ow** flurry of blows, fisticuffs

boksusi *v.* box, cuff, slap, punch; boxing

bokyl *m.* **boklow, boklys** buckle

bold *adj.* bold, daring

bolder *m.* audacity, boldness, presumption

bolgh<gap> *m.* **+ow** gap, pass (topographical), breach

bolgh<pods> *coll.* **+enn** rounded seed-pods, capsules, bolls

bolgha *v.* breach

boll *adj.* transparent, translucent, gauzy

bolla<bowl> *m.* **bollow, bollys** bowl, small basin

bolla<bull> *m.* **bollys** papal bull

bollenn *f.* **+ow** light-bulb, bulb

bolonjedh *m.* will, wish

bolonjedhek *adj.* willing

bond *m.* band (strip)

bondenn *f.* **+ow** tyre

bond-hatt *m.* **bondow-hatt** hat-band

bond-ros *m.* **bondow-ros** tyre

bones *v.* be

boni *f.* hatchet

bonk *m.* **+ys** bump, knock, bang

bonkya *v.* knock, tap

bonkyer *m.* **-oryon** cooper, barrel-maker

bonngors *m.* **+es** bittern

bonni *m.* cluster, clump, bunch of ore

bonnik *m.* **-iges** meadow pipit

bonus *m.* bonus

bora<dawn> *m.* dawn, morn, daybreak

bord *m.* board (timber), table-top; **bord du** blackboard; **bord hornella** ironing-board

boreles *m.* daisy

borr *adj.* fat *f.* protuberance, paunch

Borlewen *f.* Venus (as morning "star"), north-east

bos<abode> *f.* **+ow** abode, dwelling-place

bos<bush> *m.* **+ow** bush

bos<VN> *v.* be, become, abide, exist; **na yll bos** impossible

bosek *adj.* bushy *f.* **-egi** bushy place

bost *m.* **+ow** boast, brag

boster *m.* **-oryon** boaster

bostya *v.* boast

bosva *f.* existence

Bosvenegh *place* Bodmin

botasenn *f.* **+ow**, *coll.* **botas** boot (footwear); **botas palvek** flippers

botell *m.* **+ow** bottle

boteller *m.* **-oryon** butler

botellya *v.* bottle

both *f.* **+ow** hump, boss (stud), nave (of wheel)

bothenn *m.* hump, swelling, lump

bothek *adj.* hump-backed, bossed *m.* **-oges** blind-fish, pout-fish; **-ogyon** hunchback

bothell *f.* blister

botler *m.* **+s** butler, wine-server, tankard-bearer

boton *m.* **+yow** button

botonya *v.* button

bounds *plur.* tin-bounds, miner's claim

bour *m.* embankment
bownder *f.* **+yow** lane
bowji *m.* **+ow** cow-house, cowshed
bowlann *f.* **+ow** cow-fold
brag *m.* malt
braga *v.* brew
bragas *m.* bragget, mix of ale and mead
bragji *m.* **+ow** brewery, malthouse
brager *m.* **-oryon** brewer, maltster
bragva *f.* malthouse
bragya *v.* bluster, menace, threaten
bragyer *m.* **+s** braggart
brall *m.* **+ow** dent
brallya *v.* dent
bramm *m.* **bremmyn** fart
bramma *v.* fart
bran *f.* **brini** crow; **bran dre brini tre** rook; **bran loes** hooded crow; **bran Marghas Yow** hooded crow; **bran vras** raven
branell *m.* **+ow** frame for the moulding of a wooden plough
bras<big> *adj.* big, great, large, huge *m.* **+yon** great man
bras<plot> *m.* plot, conspiracy
brasa *v.* plot
braser *m.* **-oryon** plotter, conspirator
brashe *v.* magnify
braskamm *m.* **+ow** stride
braskamma *v.* stride
brassa *adj.* bigger
braster *m.* greatness, size
brastereth *f.* greatness (abst.)
brastir *m.* **+yow** continent
brath *m.* **+ow** bite
bratha *v.* bite
brathki *m.* **-keun** biting dog, savage cur
brathles *m.* pimpernel
brav *adj.* fine, grand
bravder *m.* finery, bravery
braysya *v.* braise

bre *f.* **+ow** hill
breder *plur.* brothers
brederedh *m.* brotherhood, brethren
bregh *f.* **+ow**, *dual* **diwvregh** arm (limb)
breghas *f.* **+ow** armful,
breghel *m.* **bregholow** sleeve
breghellik *m.* **-igow** bracelet
bregholek *adj.* sleeved
bregh-rosell *f.* rotor-arm
breghwisk *m.* brassard, armband
breghyek *adj.* having arms
bremmyn *plur.* farts
brenn *m.* **+ow** hill
brennik *coll.* **-igenn** limpets
brennva *f.* conning tower
brennya *v.* direct, con (direct a vessel), give directions
brennyas *m.* **-ysi** look-out, officer on watch
bresel *f.* **+yow** dispute, strife, war
breselek *adj.* warlike
breseli *v.* make war
breselyer *m.* **-yoryon** warrior
breselyas *m.* **-ysi** warrior (professional)
brest *m.* brass
Breten *place* Britain; **Breten Veur** Great Britain; **Breten Vyghan** Brittany
Breton *m.* **+yon** Breton (man)
Bretonek *m.* Breton (language) *adj.* Breton
Bretones *f.* **+ow** Breton (woman)
breus *f.* **+ow** judgment, verdict, criticism, adjudication, doom
breusi *v.* judge, sentence
breuslys *f.* **+yow** assize-court, court of law
breusverk *m.* **+ow** criterion
breusyas *m.* **-ysi** judge, adjudicator, critic
breusydh *m.* **+yon** judge, referee

brew *adj.* broken, injured, bruised *m.*
+yon bruise
brewgik *m.* mincemeat, hash
brewi *v.* break, crush, crumble, mash, bruise
brewliv *f.* grindstone
brewvann *v.* soreness, inflammation
brewyon *coll.* **+enn** crumbs, bits, fragments
breyn *adj.* rotten
breyna *v.* rot
breynder *m.* rot
bri *f.* esteem, value, credit, worth, importance, reputation; **gul vri a** *phr.* take account of, esteem
bri'el *m.* **br'yli** mackerel
briallenn *f.* **+ow**, *coll.* **brialli** primrose
brialli *coll.* primroses
brilu *coll.* **+enn** roses
brini *plur.* crows
brith *adj.* streaked, striped, variegated *coll.* **+enn** freckles
britha *v.* dapple, mottle
brithek *adj.* dappled
brithel *m.* **brithyli** mackerel
brithenn *f.* **+ow**, *coll.* **brith** tartan
brithennek *adj.* freckled
brithweyth *m.* mosaic
bro *f.* **+yow** country, land
brocha *m.* **brochys** brooch, clasp
broder *m.* **breder** brother; **broder da** brother-in-law; **broder dre lagha** brother-in-law
broenn *coll.* **+enn** rushes
broennek *adj.* rushy *f.* **-egi** rush-grown marsh
brogh *m.* **+es** badger
brogha *v.* fume, fuss, fret
bronn *f.* **+ow**, *dual* **diwvronn** breast; **+ow** hill; **ri bronn** suckle
bronna *v.* suckle give the breast
bronnlenn *f.* **+ow** bib
bronnvil *m.* **+es** mammal

brons *m.* bronze
bros<hot> *adj.* extremely hot *m.*
+ow great heat, stew, thick broth
bros<sting> *m.* **+ow** sting, prick, stimulus, sharp point
brosa *v.* sting, prick, goad
brosweyth *m.* embroidery
brosya *v.* stitch, embroider
brosyer *m.* **-oryon** stitcher, embroiderer
brosyores *f.* **+ow** stitcher, embroideress
brottel *adj.* frail, brittle, fickle
brow *f.* **+yow** handmill, quern
browagh *m.* terror
broweghi *v.* terrorize
broweghyades *f.* **+ow** terrorist (female)
broweghyas *m.* **-ysi** terrorist (male)
brows *coll.* crumbled material
browsi *v.* crumble
browsyon *coll.* **+enn** crumbs, fragments; **browsyon bara** breadcrumbs
broylya *v.* broil
brunyon *plur.* groats (meal), oatmeal
bryansenn *f.* throat, windpipe, gullet
brybour *m.* **+s** vagabond, pilferer, vagrant
brygh *adj.* variegated, speckled, brindled, freckled *f.* **+i** mote, smallpox, pox; **brygh almaynek** German measles, rubella; **brygh rudh** measles; **brygh yar** chicken pox
bryjyek *adj.* convective
bryjyon *m.* boiling, seething, convection *v.* boil; **bryjyon yn kosel** stew
brykedhenn *f.* **+ow**, *coll.* **brykedh** apricot
brykk *m.* **+ow**, **+ys** brick
bryntin *adj.* noble, splendid

brys<mind> *m.* **+yow** mind, intention, way of thinking

brys<womb> *m.* womb

brysonieth *f.* psychology

brysoniethel *adj.* psychological

Brython *m.* **+yon** Briton, Brythonic Celt

Brythonek *adj.* Brittonic, Brittonic Celtic

bryton *m.* thrift (plant), sea-pink

bryv *f.* **+yow** bleating of sheep

bryvya *v.* bleat

bual *m.* **+yon** buffalo, bison, wild ox

bualgorn *m.* **-gern** bugle-horn, hunting-horn

buan *adj.* quick, lively, fast (speedy)

bubenn *f.* **+ow** lamp-wick

budh *m.* profit, gain

budhadewder *adj.* profitability

budhadow *adj.* profitable

budhek *adj.* victorious

budhogel *adj.* victorious

budhogoleth *f.* victory

budhrann *f.* **+ow** dividend

budhynn *m.* **+yow** meadow

bugel *m.* **+edh** herdsman; **bugel deves** shepherd; **bugel gever** goatherd; **bugel gwarthek** cowherd; **bugel lodhnow** neatherd, cowherd; **bugel mogh** swineherd

bugelek *adj.* pastoral, bucolic

bugeles *f.* **+ow** shepherdess

bugelya *v.* guard animals

bugh *f.* **+es** cow

bughik-Dyw *f.* **bughesigow-Dyw** ladybird

bughkenn *m.* cowhide

bughwas *m.* **-wesyon** cowboy

bulhorn *m.* **+es** snail

bulugenn *f.* **+ow**, *coll.* **buluk** earthworm

buorth *m.* **+ow** cattle-yard

burjes *m.* **burjysi** burgher, citizen, townsman

burjesek *adj.* bourgeois

burjeseth *f.* bourgeoisie

burjesti *m.* **+ow** guildhall, town-hall

burjestra *f.* borough

burm *coll.* barm, yeast

burow *m.* bureau; **Burow an Yethow Nebes Kewsys** Bureau for Lesser-Used Languages

busel *coll.* cattle-dung; **busel vergh** horse-dung

bush *m.* **+ys** crowd, mass

bushel *m.* **+s** bushel

but *m.* **+ys** butt (target for archery)

bydh *adv.* ever; **bydh moy** any more, still more, nor yet; **bydh pan** whenever; **bydh well** any better

bydhlas *adj.* evergreen

byghan *adj.* small, little

byghanhe *v.* reduce, make smaller

byjyon *m.* **+s** dung-hill, midden

bykken *adv.* ever, always

bynari *adv.* for ever

bynitha *adv.* ever, for evermore

bynk *f.* **+yow** platform, bench

bynner *adv.* never

byrla *v.* hug, embrace

bys<digit> *m.* **bysyes** finger, digit; **bys bras** thumb; **bys byghan** little finger; **bys bysow** ring finger, fourth finger; **bys kres** middle finger; **bys rag** forefinger; **bys troes** toe

bys<until> *prep.* until, as far as, up to; **bys di** *adv.* thither; **bys may** until; **bys nevra** evermore; **bys omma** up to this point; **bys pan** until; **bys vykken** for ever, perpetually; **bys vynari** evermore; **bys vynytha** for ever; **bys yn** unto, all the way to

bys<world> *m.* **+ow** world; **a'n bys** *adj.* worldly

bysaj *f.* face

bysi *adj.* busy, occupied, diligent; **bysi yw dhyn** *phr.* it is necessary for us, we must

byskoen *f.* **+yow** thimble;
 byskoen arghans silver thimble;
 byskoen mes acorn cup
byskweth *adv.* ever
bysmer *m.* infamy, scandal,
 contempt; **gul bysmer dhe** *phr.*
 bring into contempt
bysna *m.* warning to evildoers
bysow *m.* **bysowyer** ring (for
 finger)
bystel *f.* gall, bile
bysya *v.* finger
bysyel *adj.* digital
bytakyl *m.* **bytaklys** binnacle
bythkweth *adv.* ever
byttegyns *adv.* nevertheless, yet,
 however
byttele *adv.* never, any, the less
byttiwedh *adv.* to the end, after all
byttiwettha *adv.* nevertheless
byttydh *adv.* ever
byw<alive> *adj.* alive, quick, active;
 yn fyw alive
byw<flesh> *m.* living flesh; **byw an
 lagas** pupil (of the eye)
bywa *v.* live; **bywa orth** live on
bywbodradow *adj.* biodegradable
bywder *m.* liveliness, activity
bywedh *m.* **+ow** life-style
bywek *adj.* lively
bywekhe *v.* animate
bywekheans *v.* animation
bywhe *v.* quicken, bring to life
bywnans *m.* **+ow** life
bywonieth *f.* biology
bywoniethek *adj.* biological
bywonydh *m.* **+yon** biologist
bywva *f.* **+ow** habitat

CH (mutation J)

chal *m.* jowl
chalenj *m.* **+ys** challenge, claim

chalenjya *v.* challenge, claim,
 demand as a right
challa *m.* **challys** jawbone,
 mandible
chambour *m.* **+yow** bedroom,
 chamber
chambour-gwiska *m.* dressing-
 room, changing-room
chambourlen *m.* **+s** chamberlain
chanj *m.* **+yow** change
chanjya *v.* change, alter
chansel *m.* chancel
chansler *m.* **-oryon** chancellor
chapel *m.* **+yow** chapel
chaplen *m.* **+s** chaplain
chapon *m.* **+s** capon
chappenn *f.* cap
chaptra *m.* **chapters** chapter
charet *m.* **+ys, +ow** chariot
charj *m.* **+ys** charge, care,
 responsibility; **charj servisyow**
 service charge
charjya *v.* charge
chartour *m.* **+s** charter, deed of
 freehold
chas *m.* open hunting-ground
chast *adj.* chaste
chastya *v.* chastise, restrain, chasten
chastyta *m.* chastity
chasya *v.* chase, drive, hunt, go
 hunting
chatel *coll.* cattle, chattels, capital
 (money)
chayn *m.* **+ys** chain
chaynya *v.* chain
chayr *m.* **+ys** chair (eccl.), seat, chair
 (professorial)
chekk *m.* **+ys** cauldron, crock, open
 kettle, large boiling-pan; **chekk
 kyfeyth** preserving pan
chekkenn *f.* **+ow** cheque;
 chekkenn igor blank cheque
chekker *m.* **chekkres** stonechat
chekkya *v.* check
cheni *coll.* china-ware

chenon *m.* **+s** canon
chenonri *m.* canonry
cher *m.* mien, demeanour, state of mind
chershya *v.* caress, treat kindly
cherub *m.* **cherubim** cherub
cherya *v.* cheer (gladden), cheer up
cheryta *m.* charity
chett *m.* **+ys** young person
chevalri *m.* knighthood, chivalry, order of knights
chevisya *v.* borrow
chi *m.* **chiow** house, building; **Chi an Arlydhi** House of Lords; **Chi an Gemmynyon** House of Commons; **chi annedh** dwelling-house; **Chiow an Senedh** Houses of Parliament; **chi dolli** doll's house; **chi drog-vri** brothel; **chi forn** bake-house; **chi gwari** gaming-house, casino; **chi gweder** greenhouse; **Chi Gwynn** White House; **chi hwel** work-shop; **chi hwytha** blowing-house; **chi marghas** market-house; **chi pobas** bake-house; **chi melin** mill-house; **chi miles** cattle-shed, cowshed; **chi tiek** farm-house
chigokk *f.* **+es** house-martin
chofar *m.* **+s** hotplate, chafing-dish
chogha *m.* **choghys** jackdaw
choklet *m.* chocolate
chons *m.* **+yow** chance, luck, fortune, lot; **chons da** good luck
chonsya *v.* chance
chorl *m.* **+ys** churl
churra-nos *m.* nightjar, goatsucker (U.S.)
chyf *adj.* chief
chyffar *m.* bargain, chaffer
chylla *m.* **chyllys** lamp-chill
chymbla *m.* **chymblow**, **chymblys** chimney

D (mutations DH, T)

da<doe> *f.* doe
da<good> *adj.* good, wholesome, of full measure; in-law; **da yw genev** *phr.* I like, I enjoy
dader *m.* goodness
dadhel *f.* **dadhlow** argument, dispute, discussion
dadhelva *f.* **+ow** debate, discussion, argument
dadhla *v.* argue
dadhlor *m.* **+yon** debater, advocate, orator
daffar *m.* apparatus, equipment, provision, plant (equipment); **daffar lymm** cutlery; **daffar medhel** software
dager *m.* **dagrow** tear (weeping), drop (of fluid)
dagrenn *f.* **+ow** tear (weeping),
dagrewi *v.* weep, shed tears
dagyer *m.* **+s** dagger
dalgh *m.* **+ow** capacity, content, volume (spatial)
dalghasell *f.* **+ow** capacitor, condenser
dalghedh *m.* **+ow** volume (quantity in physics)
dalghenn *f.* **+ow** hold, grasp, grip; **kavoes dalghenn yn** *phr.* take hold of, get a grip on; **settya dalghenn yn** take hold of, get a grip on
dalghenna *v.* hold, grasp, seize, retain
dall *adj.* blind, without sight *m.* **dellyon** blind man
dalla *v.* blind
dalles *f.* **+ow** blind woman
dalleth *m.* start, commencement, origin *v.* begin, originate
dallether *m.* **-oryon** beginner
dallethvos *m.* origin, genesis
dallhe *v.* blind, dazzle
dama<dame> *f.* **damys** dame

dama<mother> *f.* **damyow**
mother; **dama dha,**; **dama dre lagha** mother-in-law; **dama kiogh** jacksnipe; **dama'n hern** allis shad; **dama goth** black bream

damaj *m.* damage, injury, harm

dama-wynn *f.* grandmother

dampnya *v.* condemn, damn

dampnyans *m.* damnation, condemnation

damsel *f.* **+s** damsel, miss

danjer *m.* difficulty, reluctance

dannvon *v.* send, dispatch, report; **dannvon warlergh** send for; **dannvon a** send in order to;

dannvonadow *m.* instructions

dans *m.* **dens** tooth, tine; **dans a-rag** front tooth, incisor; **dans a-dhelergh** back tooth, molar

dans-lew *m.* dandelion

dar *int.* what, eh, why

darader *m.* **-oryon** doorkeeper

daras *m.* **+ow** door; **daras a-rag** front door; **daras a-dhelergh** back door

daras-tro *m.* **darasow-tro** revolving door

darbar *m.* preparation, contrivance, equipment, provision

darbarer *m.* **-oryon** assistant

darbari *v.* prepare, supply, make ready

dargan *f.* **+ow** prediction, forecast, prophecy

dargana *v.* predict, forecast, prophesy

darganadow *adj.* predictable

dargenyas *m.* **-ysi** seer

darleverel *v.* foretell, forecast, predict

darn *m.* **+ow** bit, piece, part, fragment

darnas *m.* **+ow** portion, fraction

daromres *m.* oscillation, traffic *v.* frequent, haunt, come and go

darsywya *v.* prosecute

darsywyas *m.* **-ysi** prosecutor

darva *f.* **+ow** oak-place

darvos *m.* **+ow** event, happening *v.* happen

darwar *int.* be forewarned, beware

darwarnya *v.* forewarn

darwes *coll.* **+enn** ring-worm

das- re-

das *f.* **deys** stack, rick; **das woera** haystack

dasa *v.* stack

dasannedhi *adj.* resettle

dasfurvya *v.* reform

dasfurvyans *m.* reformation; **An Dasfurvyans** The Protestant Reformation

daskavoes *v.* recover

daskemmeres *v.* retake, regain

dasknias *v.* ruminate, chew the cud

daskorr *v.* yield, give up, return to giver, give back *m.* rebate

daskorrans *m.* restitution

daslea *v.* relocate

daslenki *v.* gulp, swallow down

dasleverel *v.* repeat, resay, restate

dasordena *v.* reorganize

daspobla *v.* repopulate

daspren *m.* redemption, ransom

dasprena *v.* redeem, ransom, buy back

dasprenans *m.* redemption

dasprenyas *m.* **-ysi** redeemer, re-buyer

daspryntya *v.* reprint

dasredya *v.* re-read

dasseni *v.* echo, reverberate, resound

dassenyans *m.* reverberation

dasserghi *v.* rise again

dasserghyans *m.* resurrection

dassevel *v.* rebuild, set back up

dasskrif *m.* **+ow** copy

dasskrifa *v.* copy, write again

dasson *m.* **+yow** echo

dastalleth *m.* re-start *v.* re-start

dastesedha *v.* re-adjust
dastewynnya *v.* reflect (of light), shine back
dastineythi *v.* regenerate
dastineythyans *m.* regeneration
dastisplegyans *m.* re-development
dastrehevel *v.* rebuild, raise again
dastreylya *v.* retranslate
dastyllans *m.* +ow re-publication
dastyllo *v.* re-publish
dasunya *v.* reunite
dasunyans *m.* +ow reunion
dasvywa *v.* revive, live again
dasvywnans *m.* revival
daswaynya *v.* reclaim
daswel *m.* +yow review
dasweles *v.* review
daswerth *f.* +ow resale
daswul *v.* remake, restore
daswrians *m.* +ow re-creation, copy
davas *f.* **deves** sheep
Davydh *name* David
de *adv.* yesterday
de- *pref.* (intensive prefix)
debatya *v.* dispute, wrangle, contend
deboner *adj.* affable, kind, gracious
debron *m.* itch, tickling, urge
debreni *v.* itch, tickle
dedhewi *v.* promise
dedhewadow *m.* promise
dedhwi *v.* lay eggs
defendya *v.* erase, defend, prohibit; **defendya dhe-ves** expunge
defens *m.* defence, resistance
defia *v.* defy, challenge
defola *v.* defile, pollute, violate
defolans *m.* pollution
defowt *m.* default, defect, failure
deg *num.* +ow ten
dega *m.* tithe
degblydhen *f.* -blydhynyow decade

degedhek *adj.* decimal
degea *v.* close, enclose, shut
degemmeres *v.* receive, take possession of, accept
degemmerva *f.* reception room
deges *adj.* closed
degevi *v.* pay tithes
deghesenn *f.* +ow missile
deghesi *v.* fling, cast, hurl
deghow *adj.* right (opposite to left), right hand *m.* South
deghowles *f.* southernwood
degi *v.* carry
degoedh *v.* it behoves, is due, is fitting
degoedha *v.* be appropriate
degplek *adj.* tenfold
degre *m.* **degrys** degree, rank, station
degrena *v.* shudder, shiver, tremble
degves *num.* tenth
degynsow *adv.* recently, just now
degynsywa *v.* threaten, impend, menace
dehelghya *v.* chase along, hurry
dehengeugh *m.* ancestor, great-great-grandfather
dehweles *v.* return, come back, atone
dehwelans *m.* forgiveness, atonement; return
dekkweyth *adj.* ten times
del *coll.* +enn leaves
dela *f.* **deledhow** yardarm
delatya *v.* postpone, delay; **delatya an termyn** kill time
delergh *m.* rear, stern, after part
deleva *v.* yawn
delghyas *m.* -ysi tenant
delghyaseth *f.* tenancy
delinya *v.* draw (as in art), portray, delineate
delinyans *m.* +ow drawing, delineation

delit *m.* delight, pleasure, fun

delivra *v.* deliver, release, set free; **delivra dhe** deliver to; **delivra diworth** deliver from

delk *m.* necklet

dell *adv.* as, so, since, how, in as much as; **dell hevel** as it seems; **dell grysav** as I believe

delledh *v.* it behoves, is suitable, is fitting

dellni *m.* blindness

dellyon *plur.* blind men

delow *m.* **+yow** statue

delya *v.* put forth leaves

delyek *adj.* leafy

delyow *plur.* leaves

delyowa *v.* collect leaves, sweep up leaves

delyowek *adj.* leafy

demma *m.* **demmys** dime (U.S.)

demmas *m.* good man, saint

demmedhi *v.* marry

demmedhyans *m.* **+ow** wedding, marriage

den *m.* **tus** human being, man, person; **den an klogh** sexton, bellringer; **den ankoth** stranger; **den Dyw** saint; **den hen** elder; **den jentyl** gentleman; **den koskor** retainer, servant; **den mor** seaman; **den nowydh** bridegroom; **den skattys** bankrupt; **den yowynk** youth; **den y'n bys** nobody

dena *v.* suck

denagha *v.* deny, retract, disown, refuse

dendil *v.* earn, gain, deserve

denel *adj.* human

denewes *f.* heifer

denladh *m.* manslaughter

denledhyas *m.* **-ysi** assassin, hit-man, murderer

densa *m.* good man

densek *adj.* toothy, jagged *m.*

densoges hake; **densek dowr** pike (fish)

densel *v.* bite

denses *m.* mankind, humanity

denseth *m.* humanity

denti *adj.* dainty, fastidious, fussy

denvydh *m.* nobody

der *prep.* through, by means of

-der *suff.* (masc. abst. noun ending)

derag *prep.* before, in the presence of, in front of N.B. Combines with pers. pronouns as **deragov, deragos, deragdho, derygdhi, deragon, deragowgh, deragdha.**

deray *m.* **+s** disarray, disorder, confusion

deraylya *v.* scold, brawl

dergh *adj.* bright

derivador *m.* **+yon** reporter, announcer

derivadow *m.* account (report), information

derivas *m.* report *v.* relate, tell, state, report; **derivas orth** relate to

dernik *m.* fragment, little bit

derow<oaks> *coll.* oak-trees

derow<start> *m.* beginning, start, commencement

dervynn *v.* demand, require, request

derwek *adj.* abounding in oaks *f.* **-egi** place abounding in oaks

derwenn *f.* **+ow,** *coll.* **derow** oak-tree

desedha *v.* situate, fit, locate, dispose, set in place

desedhans *m.* situation, setting (location)

desedheger *m.* **-oryon** commissioner

desedhek *m.* **desedhogow** commission (group of persons); **Desedhek an Vilvlydhen** Millennium Commission; **Desedhek an Oryon** Boundary Commission

desempis *adj.* instant, sudden, immediate *adv.* immediately, forthwith, at once; **koffi desempis** instant coffee

deserth *adj.* precipitous, very steep

desevos *v.* suppose, expect, speculate

desin *m.* **+yow** design, drawn plan

desinor *m.* **+yon** designer

desinores *f.* **+ow** designer

desinieth *f.* design (as a subject)

desinya *v.* design

desir *m.* **+ys** desire, request

desirya *v.* desire

desk *m.* **+ow, +ys** desk

deskerni *v.* snarl, gnash; **deskerni orth** snarl at

deskernus *adj.* surly

deskrifa *v.* describe

deskrifans *m.* **+ow** description

desper *m.* despair

despit *m.* despite, defiance; **yn despit dhe** *conj.* despite, in spite of

despitya *v.* spite, insult, worry

desta *v.* witness, testify, certify

destna *v.* destine

destrypya *v.* strip

desygha *v.* dry up, desiccate

deur *v.* matters, is of interest; **ny'm deur** *phr.* it does not matter to me, it does not concern me, I don't care

deuv *m.* **+yon** son-in-law

devar *m.* duty, what is due, what is incumbent

devedhyans *m.* origin, arrival, genealogical descent

devedhys *adj.* come

devera *v.* drip, dribble, trickle, shed tears

deveras *m.* dripping (fat)

deverel *adj.* watery

deves *plur.* sheep (pl.)

devesik *f.* **-igow** lamb

devessa *v.* chase sheep

devetti *m.* **+ow** sheep-cot

devis *m.* **+yow** device, fancy, notion

devisya *v.* devise, plan, contrive

devnydh *m.* **+yow** material, stuff, makings, ingredient; **gul devnydh a** *v.* use, make use of

devnydhya *v.* use

devnydhyer *m.* **-yoryon** consumer, user

devones *v.* come

devorya *v.* devour

devos *m.* **+ow** custom, rite, ceremony

devosel *adj.* ritual, customary

devrek *adj.* watery

devri *adv.* seriously, indeed, verily, certainly, truly

devyder *m.* **-oryon** sheep-worrier

devynn *m.* **+ow** extract, quotation, citation

devynna *v.* extract, quote, cite

dew *num.* two (m.)

dewabrans *dual* eyebrows

dewana *v.* penetrate, permeate

dewanus *adj.* penetrable, permeable

dewblek *adj.* double, twofold

dewblekhe *v.* duplicate

dewblekhes *adj.* duplicated

dewbries *m.* married couple

dewdhek *num.* twelve

dewdhegves *num.* twelfth

dewdhen *m.* couple, pair, man and woman

dewdhorn *dual* fists

dewdroes *dual* feet

dewfrik *dual* nostrils

dewgens *num.* forty

dewgorn *dual* horns

dewgroch *dual* pair of crutches

dewi *v.* burn, blaze, flare, kindle (intrans.)

Dewi *name* David

dewis *m.* choice, selection *v.* choose

dewisek *adj.* choosy, fastidious

dewisyans *m.* **+ow** election, choosing

dewisyas *m.* **-ysi** elector

dewlagas *dual* eyes

dewlin *dual* knees

dewlysi *m.* devilry, diabolical influence

Dewnens *place* Devon

dewraga *v.* gush

dewufern *dual* ankles

dew-ugens *num.* forty, two-score

dewweder *dual* spectacles

dewynn *m.* **+ow** ray (e.g. of light), beam (radiation)

dewynnek *adj.* glittering

dewynnya *v.* glitter, twinkle, radiate, shine

deyn *m.* **+ys** dean

deynji *m.* **+ow** deanery

deynieth *f.* deanery

deys *plur.* ricks, haystacks

dha *pron.* thy

dh'aga *phr.* to their

dh'agan *phr.* to our

dh'agas *phr.* to your

dhe *prep.* to, for, at; **dhe'n leur** *adv.* down; **dhe wari** *adj.* free (liberated); **dhe wir** *adv.* in truth, really, verily, truly

dhe-denewen *adv.* sidelong

dhedha *prep.* to them

dhedhi *prep.* to her

dhe-dre *adv.* home, homewards, back

dhe-hys *adv.* at length

dhejy *pron.* thou (emphatic)

dhe'm *phr.* to my

dhe'n *phr.* to the

dhe'th *phr.* to thy

dherag *prep.* before

dhe-ves *adv.* away

dhe-wir *adv.* in truth forsooth, verily

dhe-woeles *adv.* to the bottom, down below

dhi *adv.* thither, to that place

dhis *prep.* to thee

dhiso *prep.* to thee

dhiworth *prep.* from

dhodho *prep.* to him

dh'ow *phr.* to my

dh'y *phr.* to his, to her, to its

dhy'hwi *prep.* to you

dhy'hwyhwi *prep.* to you

dhymm *prep.* to me

dhymmo *prep.* to me

dhyn *prep.* to us

dhywgh *prep.* to you

di *adv.* thither, to that place

diagha *m.* tranquillity *adj.* unalarmed

dial *m.* vengeance, retribution; **tyli dial war** *phr.* wreak vengeance on

diala *v.* avenge, wreak vengeance

dialar *adj.* without grief

dialhwedh *m.* key (for unlocking) *adj.* unlocked

dialhwedha *v.* unlock

dialhwedhik *m.* **-igow** little key

dialloes *adj.* powerless, impotent, unable, incapable

dialor *m.* **+yon** avenger

dianall *adj.* breathless, out of breath

diank *m.* escape *v.* escape, run away

diannedh *adj.* homeless

diannedhder *m.* homelessness

diarghen *adj.* barefoot

diaskellek *adj.* wingless

diaskorna *v.* bone (remove bones)

diarv *adj.* unarmed

dibarow *adj.* odd (of numbers), unmatched, unique, unequalled, unlike others *adv.* separately

dibarth *f.* separation, parting, segregation

dibenn *adj.* headless, endless

dibenna *v.* behead, lop, crop (truncate), execute (by beheading)

dibennans *m.* **+ow** beheading

dibenner *m.* **-oryon** executioner

diber *m.* **dibrow** saddle

diberth *v.* separate, part, disperse; depart

diberthva *f.* separation

diblans *adj.* distinct, separate, clear *adv.* distinctly

dibobel *adj.* depopulated, deserted

dibobla *v.* depopulate

diboblans *m.* depopulation

diboltra *v.* dust

dibowes *adj.* restless

dibra *v.* saddle

dibreder *adj.* irresponsible, thoughtless, heedless, careless

dibrer *m.* -**oryon** saddler

dibygans *adj.* insolvent, improvident

dibyganseth *f.* insolvency

dibyta *adj.* pitiless

didakla *v.* dismantle

diderghi *v.* uncoil

didhan *adj.* amusing, funny, pleasing *m.* amusement, entertainment

didhana *v.* amuse, entertain, charm

didhanus *adj.* amusing, entertaining

didhena *v.* wean

didheurek *adj.* interesting

didhevnydh *adj.* useless

didhynnargh *adj.* inhospitable, unwelcome

didhysk *adj.* untaught, inexpert

dido *adj.* roofless

didoll *adj.* tax-free

didre *adj.* homeless

didros *adj.* silent, noiseless

diegi *m.* sloth, laziness

diek *adj.* lazy, idle, slothful

diekter *m.* laziness

dielvenna *v.* analyse

dielvennans *m.* +**ow** analysis

dien *adj.* complete, entire, whole; **yn tien** *adv.* completely

dieneth *f.* completeness

dienora *v.* dishonour

dieskis *adj.* barefoot

difasya *v.* deface, mar, disfigure

difastya *v.* unfasten

difenn *m.* ban, forbidding, interdiction, prohibition *v.* forbid, ban, prohibit; **difenn orth nebonan a wul neppyth** *phr.* forbid someone to do something; **Dyw difenn** God forbid

difennadow *m.* prohibition

difenner *m.* -**oryon** defendant

difeudhi *v.* quench, extinguish (a flame), put out a fire

difeyth *m.* wasteland, waste, desert *adj.* waste

difeythtir *m.* +**yow** desert

difeythya *v.* lay waste

difres *v.* relieve, protect, save *m.* relief, benefit

difresyas *m.* -**ysi** protector

difresyades *f.* +**ow** protectress

difresyans *m.* relief; **difresyans toll** tax relief

difreth *adj.* feeble, powerless, lacking in energy

difrethter *m.* feebleness

difun *adj.* awake, wake up

difuna *v.* awaken

difunedh *m.* sleeplessness

difunell *f.* alarm clock

difyga *v.* fail, cease, grow less

difygas *m.* +**ow** deficit

difygyek *adj.* defective

difyk *m.* **difygyow** failure, eclipse, defect

digabester *adj.* unchained, at liberty, unconstrained

digamma *v.* straighten out

digelmi *v.* untie, detach, solve a problem

digemmyska *v.* sort, unravel

digemusur *adj.* asymmetrical

digennertha *v.* discourage, demoralize

digeredh *adj.* excused

digeredhi *v.* excuse

digesson *adj.* discordant, unharmonious

digeudh *adj.* carefree, merry

digevelsi *v.* disjoint

digloes *adj.* exposed, without shelter, shut out

dignas *adj.* unnatural, unkindly

digodennell *f.* decoder

digolm *m.* solution

digolonn *f.* faintheartedness, discouragement *adj.* fainthearted

digommol *adj.* cloudless

digompes *adj.* irregular

digompoester *m.* **+yow** irregularity

digonfortya *v.* discourage

digosk *adj.* sleepless, insomniac

digreft *adj.* inexpert, unskilled, artless

digresenni *v.* decentralize, devolve

digresennans *m.* devolution

digressya *v.* decrease

digressyans *m.* decrease

digudh *adj.* unconcealed

diguv *adj.* unkind

dihares *v.* apologize *m.* **+ow** apology

dihaval *adj.* dissimilar, different

dihedh *m.* cause for regret; **dihedh yw dhymm** *phr.* I am reluctant

dihevelebi *v.* alter, deform, disfigure

dihevelepter *m.* difference, dissimilarity

dihwans *adv.* eagerly, quickly, incontinently (unrestrainedly)

dihynsas *m.* **+ow** diversion (of road)

dilea *v.* remove, delete, expunge

diles *adj.* profitless, useless

dileshya *v.* unleash

dilestra *v.* disembark

diliw *adj.* colourless

dillas *coll.* **+enn** clothes, clothing, dress, raiment; **dillas diogeledh** safety clothing; **dillas gweli** bedclothes

dillasenn *f.* **dillas**, *coll.* **dillas** garment

dillasi *v.* clothe

dillasva *f.* **+ow** wardrobe

dilughell *f.* **+ow** demister

dilughya *v.* demist

din *m.* fort

dinamm *adj.* immaculate, spotless

dinamma *v.* remove blemish

dinan *m.* small fort

dinas *m.* fort, earthwork, hill-fort

dinatur *adj.* unnatural

diner *m.* **+ow** penny

dinerenn *f.* **+ow** penny-piece

dinerth *adj.* powerless, lacking in energy

dinertha *v.* neutralize

dinewi *v.* pour, shed, flow

dineythi *v.* give birth, beget, generate

dineythyans *m.* **+ow** birth, generation (as a process)

Dintagell *place* Tintagel

diogel *adj.* certain, secure

diogeledh *m.* security, safety

diogeli *v.* secure, insure

diras *adj.* graceless, profane

direson *adj.* irrational

direwl *adj.* irregular, unruly, disorderly, obstreperous

dirolya *v.* unroll

diruska *v.* peel, flay, scrape off skin

disakra *v.* profane, commit sacrilege

disakrans *m.* profanation, sacrilege

disarva *v.* disarm

disarvans *m.* disarmament

disawor *adj.* unsavoury, noisome, repulsive

disedha *v.* unseat

disel *m.* diesel

disenor *m.* dishonour, disgrace

disenora *v.* dishonour

diserri *v.* appease, relent

dises *m.* **+ys** disease, disquiet, inconvenience

disesya *v.* vex, molest
disevel *v.* upset, dismantle, trip up, cause to fall
diskan *f.* second part in singing duet; **kan ha diskan** singing duet
diskant *m.* descant, second part in plain-song
diskarga *v.* unload, discharge
diskevelsi *v.* dislocate
diskians *m.* ignorance *adj.* ignorant, foolish, witless
disklerya declare
diskleryans *m.* declaration
disklosya *v.* disclose
diskolya *v.* decarbonize
diskonfortya *v.* discourage
diskont *m.* **+ow** discount
diskontya *v.* discount
diskortes *adj.* impolite, rude
diskrassyes *adj.* unfavoured, disgraced, out of grace
diskryjyans *m.* unbelief
diskryjyk *adj.* unbelieving *m.* -**ygyon** unbeliever, infidel, agnostic, sceptic
diskrysi *v.* disbelieve
diskudha *v.* discover, uncover, reveal, disclose
diskudhans *m.* **+ow** discovery
diskwedhes *v.* show, exhibit
diskwedhyans *m.* show, exhibition, demonstration
diskwitha *v.* relax, repose, rest
dislel *adj.* disloyal
dislen *adj.* unfaithful, faithless
disliw *adj.* discoloured
dismaylya *v.* unwrap, unswathe
dismygi *v.* guess, invent, find out
dismyk *m.* guess, find
dismygriv *m.* **+ow** estimate (numerical)
dismygriva *v.* estimate a numerical value
disobaya *v.* disobey

disobayans *m.* disobedience
dison *adj.* soundless, noiseless *adv.* forthwith, straightway, immediately without another word
disordyr *m.* disorder
dispal *adj.* scot-free
displegya *v.* unfold, develop, explain
displegyans *m.* **+ow** development, explanation
displesour *m.* **+s** displeasure
displesya *v.* displease
displesyans *m.* displeasure
displetya *v.* display, unfurl
displetyans *m.* display
displewyas *v.* splay, stretch apart
dispresya *v.* despise, decry, neglect
disprevi *v.* disprove
disputya *v.* argue, discuss; **disputya orth** dispute with
disranna *v.* divide mathematically
dissent *m.* dissent
dissentya *v.* dissent
dissentyans *v.* nonconformity
dissentyer *m.* -**oryon** dissenter, nonconformist
dissernya *v.* discern
distag *adj.* detached, untethered, unattached
distaga *v.* detach, untether; sever, secede
distagadow *adj.* detachable
distagas *m.* **+ow** detachment
distempra *v.* ruffle, upset
distowgh *adv.* immediately, suddenly, straight away
distrui *v.* destroy, undo, ruinate
distruyans *m.* destruction, mass destruction
distyr *adj.* insignificant, meaningless, of no account
diswar *adj.* rash, unwary, reckless
diswruthyl *v.* undo
diswrys *v.* undone

diswul *v.* undo, spoil, ruin
diswuthyl *v.* undo
disya *v.* dice meat
disygha *v.* quench thirst, refresh
divagla *v.* release (from trap)
divedhow *adj.* sober
diveghya *v.* unburden, unload, disburden
di'velebi *v.* alter
diveri *v.* pour
divers *adj.* various
diveth *adj.* shameless, unabashed
divlam *adj.* blameless, irreproachable
divlas *adj.* distasteful, disgusting, disgraceful
divlasa *v.* be disgusted with, offend, be ashamed of
divoemmell *m.* bumper of car
divoetter *m.* starvation, famine
divotonya *v.* unbutton
divres *m.* **+ow** exile, expatriate, banished person
divroa *v.* exile, banish
divynya *v.* chop, dissect, mince, cut up
diw *num.* two (f.)
diwar *prep.* from on top of
diwarr *dual* legs
diwbedrenn *dual* buttocks, posterior, hindquarters
diwedh *m.* end, finish, outcome
diwedha *v.* end, finish, conclude
diwedhes *adj.* late
diwedhva *f.* ending
diwedhyn *adj.* unbending, rigid, stiff
diwedhynder *m.* rigidity, stiffness
diwen *dual* jaws
diweres *adj.* helpless
diwern *adj.* dismasted, mastless
diwernya *v.* dismast
diwes *m.* **diwosow** drink, draught
diwessa *v.* go drinking, booze
diwettha *adj.* later, last
diweyth *adj.* unemployed

diweythieth *f.* unemployment
diwgell *dual* testicles
diwglun *dual* hips, loins
diwiska *v.* undress, unclothe
diwith *adj.* unprotected
diwiver *m.* radio, wireless
diwla *dual* hands
diwleuv *dual* hands
diwloneth *dual* kidneys
diwoesa *v.* bleed (trans.), draw blood from
diworth *prep.* from N.B. Combines with pers. pronouns as **diworthiv, diworthis, diworto, diworti, diworthyn, diworthowgh, diworta.**; **d'wor' an nos** *adv.* by night; **diworth an myttin** in the morning
diwotti *m.* **+ow** public house, alehouse
diwri *adj.* seamless
diwros *f.* **+ow** bicycle
diwrosa *m.* cycling *v.* cycle, bicycle
diwrosya *v.* go on a bicycle tour
diwskoedh *dual* shoulders
diwskovarn *dual* ears
diwvogh *dual* cheeks
diwvordhos *dual* thighs
diwvregh *dual* arms
diwvronn *dual* breast
diwvronner *m.* brassiere, bra
diwweus *dual* lips
diwweyth *adv.* twice
diwyethek *adj.* bilingual
diwyethogeth *f.* bilingualism
diwysek *adj.* earnest, zealous, conscientious, industrious, diligent
diwysogneth *f.* industry (hard work), diligence
diwysyans *m.* **+ow** industry (manufacture)
diwysyansek *adj.* industrial
diyskynna *v.* descend, go down, dismount
diyskynnyas *m.* **-ysi** descendant

27

doen *v.* carry, transport, bear (support)

does *adj.* dense (physically)

doester *m.* **+yow** density (in physics)

doeth *adj.* civilized, prudent, discreet *m.* **+yon** sage

doethter *m.* prudence

dohajydh *m.* afternoon, noon to sunset

dohajydhweyth *adv.* in the afternoon

dojel *m.* young pollack

doktour *m.* **+s** doctor (title)

doktourieth *f.* doctorate, doctor's degree

dol *m.* dole, welfare payment

dolli *f.* **+ow** doll

dolos *v.* pretend, give out falsely, dissemble

domhwel *v.* overthrow, subvert, overturn

domhwelans *m.* revolution (political)

domhwelus *adj.* subversive, revolutionary

dones *v.* come

dons *m.* **+yow** dance; **donskledha** sword-dance; **dons meyn** stone circle

donsya *v.* dance

donsyer *m.* **-oryon** dancer

donsyores *f.* **+ow** dancer

dor *m.* ground, soil, earth; **an dor** the ground, the soil; **an nor** the world

dorge *m.* **+ow** earth hedge, earthwork

dorgell *f.* **+ow** cellar

dorgi *m.* **dorgeun** terrier

dorgrys **+yow** *m.* earthquake

dorhys *m.* geographical latitude

dorhysel *adj.* latitudinal

dorles *m.* geographical longitude

dorlesel *adj.* longitudinal

dorn *m.* **+ow**, *dual* **dewdhorn** *m.* hand (when used as an instrument), fist; haft; **dre gildhorn** *adj.* backhanded

dorna *v.* thump, thrash, beat, punch

dornas *m.* **+ow** fistful, handful

dornla *m.* **dornleow** handle, handhold

dornlyver *m.* handbook

dornskrif *m.* **+ow** manuscript

dornskrifa *v.* write by hand

dornva *f.* **dornvedhi** span (unit of length), hand-breadth

doronieth *f.* geography

doroniethel *adj.* geographical

dororieth *f.* geology

dororydh *m.* **+yon** geologist

dorvagh *f.* dungeon

dorydh *m.* **+yon** geographer

dos *v.* come; **dos erbynn** meet with; **dos ha** happen to, occur, come to; **dos ha bos** become

dotya *v.* dote, act like a fool, become witless

dour *adv.* scrupulously, stringently, rigorously

doust *m.* dust, chaff

doustlenn *f.* **+ow** duster

dout *m.* **+ys** doubt, dread, fear; **na borth dout** *phr.* don't be afraid

doutya *v.* doubt, fear

dov *adj.* tame, gentle, domestic, pet

dova *v.* tame

dovedh *m.* tameness

dover *m.* **-oryon** tamer; **dover lewyon** lion tamer

dovhe *v.* tame, domesticate

down *adj.* deep, profound

downans *m.* **+ow** deep valley

downder *m.* **+yow** depth, profundity

downhe *v.* deepen

downvor *m.* ocean, deep sea

dowr *m.* **+ow** water, urine (fig.), river

dowra *v.* water
dowran *m.* watering-place, oasis
dowrargh *m.* **+ow** cistern, water-tank
dowrbons *m.* **+ow** aqueduct
dowrek *adj.* watery *f.* **-egi** watery place
dowrer *m.* watering-can
dowrergh *m.* slush
dowrfols *m.* **+yow** leak
dowrgi *m.* **dowrgeun** otter
dowrgleudh *m.* **+yow** canal, open drain
dowrhe *v.* water, irrigate
dowrhyns *m.* **+yow** watercourse
dowrla *m.* watering-place
dowrlamm *m.* **+ow** waterfall
dowrlann *f.* **+yow** waterside
dowrles *m.* pond-weed
dowrva *f.* **+ow** watering-place
dowrvargh *m.* **-vergh** hippopotamus
dowryar *f.* **-yer** coot
dragon *f.* **+es** dragon
dral *m.* scrap, fragment
dralya *v.* break into bits
dramasek *adj.* dramatic
dramm *f.* **+ow** swathe
drayl *m.* drag
draylell *f.* **+ow** sleigh
draylya *v.* drag
draylyer *m.* **-oryon** trailer, hanger-on
dre *prep.* through, by means of; **dre vras** *adv.* for the most part, generally
dredhi *adv.* thereby
drefenn *conj.* because, on account of
dregynn *m.* mischief, harm, injury
drehedhes *v.* reach, attain
drehedhyans *m.* **+ow** attainment
drehevel *v.* build (trans.), raise, erect, edify, lift up; rise, arise, rise up

drehevyans *m.* **+ow** building, edifice, erection
drem *m.* lamentation, keening
dremas *m.* saint, good man
dren *m.* **dreyn** thorn, prickle, spine, bone (of fish)
drenek *adj.* thorny, barbed *m.* **-ogyon** spur-dog (fish)
dres *prep.* beyond, over, past, above, besides, through the course of
dresniver *adj.* redundant
dresnivereth *f.* redundancy
drewydh *m.* **+yon** druid
drewydhek *adj.* druidical
drewydhieth *f.* druidism
dreyn *coll.* **+enn** thorns
dreynek *f.* **-egi** spinney, thicket
dreyngoes *m.* **+ow** spinney
dreys *coll.* **+enn** brambles
dreysek *adj.* brambly *f.* **-egi** bramble patch
dreyskoes *m.* **+ow** bramble thicket
dri *v.* bring, take with one, persuade
drog *adj.* bad, wicked; naughty *m.* evil, harm, hurt, ill, vice
drog-atti *m.* epilepsy
drogedh *m.* evil, vice, malice
drog-ger *m.* infamy
drog-gerys *adj.* infamous
drog-gras *m.* revenge
droglamm *m.* **+ow** accident, misadventure, adversity
drogober *m.* **+ow** misdeed, crime
drogoberer *m.* **-oryon** evil-doer, criminal, miscreant
drogwas *m.* **-wesyon** rogue, knave
drokoleth *f.* ill-treatment, wrong, ill-deed
drokpenn *m.* **+ow** headache
drok-pes *adj.* ill-pleased
drokpolat *m.* **+ys** rascal
drokter *m.* vice, harm
droktra *m.* evil

droktro *f.* unkind action
drolla *m.* **drollow** tale, story, play having a folk-tale plot
droppya *v.* drop
drudh *adj.* precious, cherished
drumm *m.* **+ow** ridge
drushya *v.* thresh
drushyer *m.* **+yoryon** thresher
drylsi *m.* monotonous noise
dryppynn *m.* **+ow** little drop
du<black> *adj.* black, sombre, dark
du<ended> *adj.* ended, finished, overspent
Du *m.* November
duder *m.* blackness, darkness
dug *m.* **+ys** duke
duges *f.* **+ow** duchess
dugeth *f.* duchy
dughan *m.* grief, sorrow, suffering; **kemmeres dughan** *phr.* be sorry
dughanhe *v.* grieve
duhe *v.* blacken
dur *m.* steel
durya *v.* endure, last
duryadow *adj.* long-lasting, durable, sempiternal
dustuni *m.* **dustuniow** witness, testimony, reference (for character)
dustunia *v.* testify, bear witness
dustunians *m.* **+ow** testimonial
dustunier *m.* **-oryon** referee (for character), witness (person)
dy- *pref.* (intensive prefix)
dy' *m.* day (abbr.); **dy' Fenkost** Pentecost; **dy' Gwener** Friday; **dy' Halann** first day of month; **dy' Lun** Monday; **dy' Lun Mus** Maze Monday; **dy' Mergher** Wednesday; **dy' Meurth** Tuesday; **dy' Sadorn** Saturday; **dy' Sul** Sunday; **dy' Yow** Thursday; **dy' Yow Hablys** Maundy Thursday
dyagon *m.* **+yon** deacon, levite
dyantell *adj.* dangerous, unstable, ready to fall

dybri *v.* eat
dydh *m.* **+yow** day, date; **an jydh** the day; **y'n jydh ma** today; **dydh da** good day
dydh-degea *m.* closing date
dydh-tardh *m.* daybreak
dydhweyth *adv.* by day, in the daytime *f.* **+yow** day's time
dydhya *v.* date (e.g. a document)
dyegrys *adj.* shocked, terrified, trembling
dyenn *m.* **+ow** cream; **dyenn rew** ice cream; **dyenn molys** clotted cream
dyenna *v.* form cream
dyennek *adj.* creamy
dyerbynna *v.* meet, encounter
dyewa *v.* pant, gasp, be out of breath
dyffra *v.* differ
dyffrans *m.* **+ow** difference *adj.* different
dyghtya *v.* prepare, serve, treat, manage, trim, appoint, provide, deal with
dyghtyans *m.* treatment
dyghtyer *m.* -**yoryon** manager
dy'goel *m.* **+yow** feast-day, holiday, vacation (U.S.); **dy'goel Deys** harvest-home; **dy'goel kemmyn** bank holiday; **dy'goel Mighal** Michaelmas; **dy'goel soedhogel** official holiday; **dy'goel Stoel** Epiphany
dy'goelya *v.* go on holiday
dy'gweyth *m.* **+yow** working day, weekday
dygynsete *m.* day before yesterday
dyji *m.* **+ow** small cottage
dyjynn *m.* **+ow** little piece
dyllans *m.* **+ow** publication
dyller *m.* -**oryon** publisher
dyllo<lively> *adj.* lively
dyllo<VN> *v.* emit, issue, publish, release
dynamo *m.* **+yow** dynamo

dynyta *m.* dignity
dynnargh *m.* greeting, welcome
dynnerghi *v.* greet, welcome, salute
dynya *v.* entice, allure, coax, lure
dyowl *m.* **dywolow** devil; **an jowl** the devil
dyowles *f.* **+ow** she-devil
dyowlek *adj.* devilish, diabolical
dyppa *m.* **dyppys** small pit
dyskador *m.* **+yon** teacher
dyskadores *f.* **+ow** teacher
dyskans *m.* **+ow** lesson, knowledge, instruction
dyskansek *adj.* scholastic
dyskas *m.* teaching, doctrine, moral
dyskevres *m.* **+ow** syllabus
dyski *v.* learn, train, educate, teach, instruct; **dyski gans** learn from; **dyski dhe Beder kana** train Peter to sing
dyskybel *m.* **dyskyblon** disciple, adherent, pupil, follower
dyskys *adj.* learned
dyth *m.* **+ow** recitation, dictum
dythya *v.* recite
dyw *m.* **+ow** god
Dyw *m.* God; **durdadhejy** *phr.* good day; **durdadhy'hwi** good day; **durdallodhy'hwi** thank you; **durnostadha** good night; **dursoenno dhis** God bless thee; **Dyw genes** goodbye; **Dyw gweres** God speed
dywes *f.* **+ow** goddess
dywolow *plur.* devils; **an dhywolow** the devils
dywses *m.* deity, godhead

E

e' *pron.* him, it
eal *m.* yoke-ox, beast
ebel *m.* **ebelli** colt, foal

ebil *m.* **+yow** bolt, nail, peg, stopper, electrical pin; **ebil prenn** peg (wooden); **ebil horn** nail, bolt (iron), peg
ebilyer *m.* **+ow** plug (electrical)
ebrenn *f.* sky, firmament, welkin
Ebrow *f.* Hebrew
Ebryl *m.* April
eder *v.* one is
-edh *suff.* (abst. noun ending from aj.)
edhel *coll.* **edhlenn** poplar-trees, aspen-trees
edhen *f.* **ydhyn** bird, wild fowl
-edhes *suff.* (abst. noun ending)
edhlek *f.* **-egi** poplar-grove
edhomm *m.* **+ow** need, want
edhommek *adj.* needy *m.*
    edhommogyon needy person
edhommva *f.* **+ow** service-station
edrega *m.* regret
edregus *adj.* repentant, regretful
edrek *m.* regret, remorse, repentance; **edrek a'm beus** *phr.* I regret; **kavoes edrek** *v.* repent
eev *pron.* him (emphatic), it (emphatic)
efan *adj.* spacious, wide, broad *adv.* evidently
efander *m.* space (in general), latitude (abst.)
efanvos *m.* space (Astron.)
effeyth *m.* effect; **effeyth chi gweder** greenhouse effect
effeythus *adj.* effective
eghan *int.* alas, heigho
eghek *m.* **eghogyon** salmon
eghel *f.* **+yow** axle
eghenn *f.* sort, variety, kind, species; utmost; **dres eghenn** *adv.* exceedingly
eghwa *m.* afternoon-evening
egin *m.* **+yow** sprout, shoot
egina *v.* germinate, shoot (of plants)

eglos *f.* **+yow** church; **Eglos Vesydhyek** Baptist Church; **Eglos an Vethodysi** Methodist Church

eglosyek *adj.* ecclesiastic

ehwias *v.* ride forth, raid on horseback

Ejyp *place* Egypt

-ek<AJ> *suff.* (aj. ending from noun); **-egi** (fem. noun ending denoting place); **-ogyon** (masc. noun from aj.)

-ek<VN> *suff.* (VN ending)

el *m.* **eledh** angel

-el<AJ> *suff.* (adj. ending)

-el<VN> *suff.* (VN ending)

elek *adj.* big-browed, jutting *m.* **eleges** red gurnard

elen *f.* **+es** fawn

elergh *plur.* swans

elester *coll.* **elestrenn** yellow irises, sedges, flags

elestrek *f.* **-egi** flag-bed, bed of yellow irises

elgeth *f.* **+yow** chin

eli *m.* **+ow** ointment, salve, balm

elia *v.* anoint

elik *m.* **eledhigow** cherub, little angel

elin *m.* **+yow**, *dual* **dewelin** elbow; **+yow** angle; **elin avlymm** obtuse angle; **elin lymm** acute angle; **elin pedrek** right angle

elinek *adj.* angular

-ell<dim.> *suff.* (dim. ending)

-ell<tool> *suff.* (fem. agency noun ending)

ellas *int.* alas, alack

elow *coll.* **+enn** elm-trees

elowek *f.* **+egi** elm-grove

els *m.* **+yon** step-son

elses *f.* **+ow** step-daughter

elvenn *f.* **+ow** element, spark

elvennek *adj.* elementary

elvennell *f.* **+ow** sparkler (firework)

emlow *plur.* edges

emperes *f.* **+ow** empress

emperour *m.* **+s** emperor

emperoureth *f.* empire; **Emperoureth Romanek** Roman Empire

emskemunya *v.* excommunicate, ban, curse

ena *adv.* there, then, at that place or time

enebi *v.* oppose

enebieth *f.* opposition

enep *m.* **enebow** surface, face, page (of book)

enev *m.* **+ow** soul

eneworres *m.* point of death

ennwydh *coll.* **+enn** ash-trees

eno *adv.* yonder, there

enor *m.* **+ys** honour

enora *v.* honour

enos *adv.* yonder, distant but visible

enowi *v.* light up

ensampel *m.* **-plow, -plys** example, instance; **rag ensampel** for example, for instance, e.g.

entent *m.* **+ys** purpose, intention

entra *v.* enter

envi<foe> *m.* enemy, foe

envi<ill-will> *m.* ill-will, grudge, envy

envius *adj.* envious

enyal *adj.* desolate, deserted

enyval *m.* **+es** animal, beast; **enyval dov** pet

eos *f.* **+ow** nightingale

eosik *f.* little nightingale

epskobeth *f.* **+ow** bishopric

epskop *m.* **epskobow** bishop

epystyl *m.* **epystlys** epistle

er<eagle> *m.* **+yon** eagle

er<for> *prep.* for, by, on account

er<temple> *m.* **+yow** temple (head)

-er *suff.* (agency noun ending)

erba *m.* **erbys** herb
erber *m.* **+ow** kitchen-garden, arbour
erberjour *m.* quartermaster
erbynn *prep.* against, in readiness for, by the time that N.B. Combines with pers. pronouns as **er ow fynn, er dha bynn, er y bynn, er hy fynn, er agan pynn, er agas pynn, er aga fynn.** Replaced by *warbyn* from *TH.* onwards.; **erbynn Nadelik** by Christmas
erbys *m.* **+yow** economy, thrift (saving money)
erbysek *adj.* economical, thrifty
erbysi *v.* save (amass money), economize, retrench
erbysieth *f.* economics
erbysiethek *adj.* economic
erbysyas *m.* **-ysi** miser
erbysydh *m.* **+yon** economist
erbysyon *plur.* savings
ereder *plur.* ploughs
erell *plur.* others
eres *f.* **+ow** heiress
erewi *plur.* acres
ergh *coll.* snow
erghek *adj.* snowy
erghenn *f.* **+ow,** *coll.* **ergh** snowflake
erghi *v.* command, order, require, bid; **erghi dhe Damsin dos tre** order Tamsin to come home
erghlaw *m.* sleet
ergila *v.* recoil
ermin *m.* ermine
erita *v.* inherit
ermit *m.* hermit
erna *conj.* till, until
ernag *conj.* till, until
erow *f.* **erewi** acre
erowhys *m.* **+ow** furlong
errya *v.* err
ertach *m.* heritage, birthright; **Ertach Kernewek** Cornish Heritage

erthygel *m.* **erthyglow** article (of text)
ervin *coll.* **+enn** turnips
ervira *v.* decide, settle, resolve
ervirans *m.* **+ow** decision
ervys *v.* armed
erwir *adj.* pious, devout
erys *ptl.* ploughed
es<ease> *m.* comfort, convenience *adj.* easy
es<PV> *v.* thou wast
es<than> *conj.* than N.B. Combines with pers. pronouns as **esov, esos, esso, essi, eson, esowgh, essa.** See also **ages.**
-es<FN> *suff.* **-esow** (fem. ending)
-es<MN> *suff.* (abst. noun ending)
-es<PL> *suff.* (pl. ending)
-es<VN> *suff.* (VN ending)
esa *v.* was
esedh *f.* **+ow** seat, throne N.B. 'in a sitting posture' translates as **a'm esedh, a'th esedh, a'y esedh, a'gan esedh, a'gas esedh, a'ga esedh,** depending on the person.
esedha *v.* sit down
esedhva *f.* **+ow** seat, siege, sitting-room
esedhvos *m.* **+ow** eisteddfod, session
esel *m.* **eseli** member (part of body), limb, one of a society
eseleth *f.* membership
eseliek *adj.* lanky, long-limbed
esen *v.* I was, we were
esens *v.* they were
eses *v.* thou wast
esewgh *v.* you were
-esigeth *suff.* (noun ending)
-esik *suff.* (vbl. adj. ending)
eskar *m.* **eskerens** enemy, foe
eskarek *adj.* hostile
eskarogeth *f.* hostility
eskeas *v.* exclude
eskeans *m.* **+ow** exclusion
eskelli *plur.* wings

eskelmi *v.* indemnify, exclude

esker *f.* **+yow**, *dual* **diwesker** leg, knee (ship-building)

eskerdh *m.* **+ow** expedition, exodus, walk-out

eskern *plur.* bones

eskeul *f.* **+yow** escalator

eskeulya *v.* escalate

eskis *f.* **+yow** shoe; **eskis sport** **eskisyow sport** trainer (shoe)

eskolm *m.* **+ow** indemnity

eson *v.* we are

esons *v.* they are

esos *v.* thou art

esov *v.* I am

esow *m.* dearth, privation, want, need

esowgh *v.* you are

esowi *v.* deprive

esperthi *v.* export

esplegya *v.* evolve

esplegyans *m.* evolution

Essa *place* Saltash

Est<August> *m.* August

Est<East> *adj.* East *m.* East

estenna *v.* extract

ester *coll.* **+enn** oysters

estewlel *v.* eject, expel, throw out

estrek *f.* **-egi** oyster-bed

estren *adj.* strange, alien *m.* **+yon** stranger, alien, foreigner

estrenes *f.* **+ow** stranger

estrenyek *adj.* foreign

estriger *m.* **-oryon** absentee

estrik *m.* absence

estyll *coll.* boards; **+enn** shelf

estyllenn *f.* **+ow**, *coll.* **estyll** shelf

esya<AJ> *adj.* easier

esya<VN> *v.* ease, make easy

etegves *num.* eighteenth

etek *num.* eighteen

eth<went> *v.* went

eth<8> *num.* eight

-eth *suff.* (abst. noun ending, f.)

ethenn *f.* **+ow** odour, scent, vapour, steam

ethenna *v.* evaporate, vaporize

ethgweyth *adv.* eight times

ethnek *adj.* ethnic

eth-ugens *num.* eight score

ethves *num.* eighth

eur *f.* **+yow** hour, time, o'clock; **y'n eur ma** *adv.* now, at this time, presently; **y'n eur na** then, at that time

euro *m.* **+yow** euro (currency)

Europa *f.* Europe

Europek *adj.* European

Eurosenedh *m.* European Parliament

euryador *m.* timetable

euryor *f.* watch (timepiece)

eus *v.* is

euth *m.* dread, horror, terror

euthek *adj.* dreadful, horrible, terrible *adv.* dreadfully, horribly, terribly

euthekter *m.* dread

euthvil *m.* **+es** monster

euver *adj.* futile, useless; frivolous

euveredh *m.* futility, uselessness; inanity

euvergryjyans *m.* superstition

euvergryjyk *adj.* superstitious

ev *pron.* he, him, it

eva *v.* drink, sip, sup

Eva *name* Eve

evor *coll.* hogweed

evredh *adj.* crippled, mutilated, disabled *m.* **+yon** cripple

evredhder *m.* **+yow** disability

evredhek *adj.* crippled *m.* **-ogyon** cripple, handicapped man, disabled man

evredhes *f.* **+ow** cripple, handicapped woman, disabled woman

Evrek *place* York

evr'ek *adj.* crippled

-evy *pron.* me
ewgh *v.* you were
ewik *f.* **ewiges** hind, doe
ewin *m.* **+es** finger-nail, talon, claw;
ewin kennin clove of garlic
ewinek *adj.* clawed, having long
finger-nails
ewingarn *m.* hoof
ewinrew *m.* numbness
ewl *f.* **+ow** craving, strong desire
ewn *adj.* correct, just, straight, proper
ewna *v.* correct
ewnadow *adj.* correctable
ewnans *m.* **+ow** correction,
amendment
ewnder *m.* **+yow** equity, justice,
legal right
ewnhe *v.* repair, mend, fix (U.S.)
ewnheans *m.* **+ow** repair, mend
ewnhynsek *adj.* just, upright
ewnhynseth *f.* integrity
ewn-hys *adj.* of the right length
ewnter *m.* **ewntres** uncle
ewyn *coll.* **+enn** froth, foam,
effervescence, head (on a glass of
beer)
ewynek *adj.* frothy, foamy,
effervescent
ewyni *v.* froth, effervesce
eyl *adj. pron.* one of two
eyla *v.* second
eylenn *f.* **+ow** second (of time)
eyles *m.* liver-fluke, sundew
eyn *plur.* lambs
Eynda *f.* India
Eyndek *adj.* Indian *m.*
Eyndogyon Indian (man)
Eyndoges *f.* **+ow** Indian (woman)
eyrin *coll.* **+enn** sloes
eythin *coll.* **+enn** gorse, prickles
eythinek *f.* **-egi** furze-brake

F

faborden *m.* **+yon** bass (Mus.)
fagel *f.* **faglow** flame, inflammation
fagel-las *f.* gastritis
fagel-vryansenn *f.* laryngitis
fagla *v.* inflame
faglenn *f.* **+ow** torch, flashlight
(U.S.)
falgh *f.* **fylghyer** scythe
falghas *v.* scythe, mow
falghun *m.* **-es** falcon
falghunieth *f.* falconry
falghuner *m.* **-oryon** falconer
fall *m.* failure, fault, deficiency
falladow *m.* failure
fals<fals> *adj.* false, treacherous *m.*
false person
fals<scythe> *f.* **+yow** scythe
falsa *v.* scythe
falsuri *m.* falseness, insincerity, foul
play
famya *v.* starve (intrans.)
famyans *m.* starvation
fansi *m.* pleasure, delight, relish
fantasi *m.* fantasy
fara *m.* behaviour, conduct,
demeanour *v.* behave
fardell *m.* **+ow** bundle, package,
luggage
fardella *v.* package
farwel *int.* farewell, goodbye
fas *m.* **fassow** face, countenance
appearance; **gallas fassow** *phr.*
the game is up
faskor *m.* **+yon** fascist
faskorieth *f.* fascism
fast *adj.* firm, fast (fixed) *adv.* firmly
fasta *v.* become fastened
faster *m.* stability
fasthe *v.* fasten, tie together, make
firm
fastya *v.* tighten
fasya *v.* pretend

fatell *adv.* how

fatla *adv.* how; **fatla genes ?** how are you ?

fav *coll.* **+enn** beans

favera *v.* favour (esteem), treat leniently; resemble

favour *m.* **+s** favour, appearance

fay *m.* faith

fayntys *m.* feigning, pretence, hypocrisy

faytour *m.* **+s** vagabond, impostor, swindler

fekla *v.* fawn, flatter; pretend

fekyl *adj.* false, flattering, perfidious; **fekyl cher** hypocritical

fel *adj.* cunning, wily, crafty

felder *m.* cunning

felgh *f.* spleen

fell *adj.* cruel, fierce, grim

felon *m.* **+s** felon

felsys *adj.* split

felyon *plur.* fools

fenester *f.* **-tri** window

fenestri *plur.* windows

fenna *v.* overflow

fennva *f.* flood-plain

fenogel *f.* fennel

fenten *f.* **fentynyow** spring (water), fountain, surface well

fer<fair> *m.* **+yow** fair, market

fer<leg> *f.* **+ow** shank, leg

ferdhynn *m.* **+ow** farthing

fergh *plur.* forks

ferla *m.* **-leow** fairground

fernoeth *adj.* barelegged

ferror *m.* **+yon** farrier, blacksmith

fesont *m.* **fesons** pheasant

fest<feast> *m.* **+ow** feast, banquet

fest<very> *adv.* very, extremely, indeed; **fest yn ta** very well

fesya *v.* drive away, put to flight, chase off

fetha *v.* defeat, beat, conquer, vanquish, overcome

fethus *adj.* luxurious, beautiful, well-formed, richly adorned

feusik *adj.* fortunate, lucky

feyth *adj.* fertile, fruitful

feythter *m.* fertility, fruitfulness

fi *int.* fie, disdain

fia<fie> *v.* cry fie on, despise, decry, disdain

fia<flee> *v.* flee; **fia dhe'n fo** take flight

fienasow *plur.* grief, anxiety, solicitude

figbrenn *m.* **+yer** fig-tree

figur +ys *m.* figure (shape),

figys *coll.* **+enn** figs

fin<AJ> *adj.* delicate, refined; **fin gonedhys** faultlessly wrought

fin<end> *f.* **+yow** end

finek *adj.* final

finfos *f.* **+ow** boundary-dyke

finwedh *f.* end, limit, cessation

finwedha *v.* limit

finwedh-doeth *f.* speed-limit

fiol *f.* **+yow** vial, shallow cup

fion *coll.* **+enn** narcissi

fisegieth *f.* physics

fisegydh *m.* **+yon** physicist

fisek *f.* medical science, physic

fisment *m.* **fismens** countenance (face), appearance, complexion

fistena *v.* hasten, make haste, hurry

fit *m.* **+ys** match (game), bout

Flamanek *adj.* Flemish *m.* Flemish language

flamm *m.* **+ow** flame

flammgoes *m.* spurge

flammya *v.* flame

flappya *v.* flap

flatter *m.* **-oryon** deceiver (male), wheedler

flattores *f.* **+ow** deceiver (female)

flattra *v.* wheedle, beguile, delude

fleghes *plur.* children

fleghigel *adj.* infantile

fleghik *m.* **fleghesigow** infant, little child

fler *m.* **+yow** bad smell, stench, stink, fetor

flerya *v.* stink, smell

flerynsi *m.* stench, fetidness foulness (of stink)

flerys *adj.* stinking, fetid, frowzy *m.* stinkard

flogh *m.* **fleghes** child, young person

floghel *adj.* childlike, childish, puerile

flogh-gwynn *m.* **fleghes-wynn** grandchild

flogholeth *f.* childhood, infancy

floghva *f.* **+ow** nursery (for children), kindergarten

floghwith *m.* child-care

florenn<tin> *f.* fine mealy tin

florenn<lock> *f.* **+ow** lock (of door)

floukenn *f.* soft ground

flour<deck> *m.* deck

flour<FN> *adj.* perfect, eminent *f.* **+ys** flower

flourenn *f.* **+ow** fine specimen

flour-rag *m.* forecastle, fo'c'sle, prow

flownenn *f.* **+ow** pert girl, hussy

flows *m.* nonsense, idle talk, waffle

flowsa *v.* waffle, talk nonsense

flynt *m.* flint

fo *m.* flight, retreat

foen *m.* new-mown hay

foenek *f.* **+egi** hayfield

fog *f.* **+ow** hearth, furnace, blowing-house; focus

foger *m.* **-oryon** stoker

fol *adj.* foolish, crazy, wild, mad *m.* **felyon** madman, fool

folenn *f.* **+ow** page (of book), sheet of paper, piece of metal foil; **folenn arghansek** bank-note, bill (U.S.); **folenn bobas** baking-foil; **folenn ober** work-sheet

folennik *m.* **-igow** leaflet

foles *f.* **+ow** mad woman

folhwarth *m.* giggle

folhwerthin *v.* giggle

foli *m.* folly

folneth *f.* folly, foolishness

fols *m.* **+yow** split, cleft, rift, schism, fissure

folsa *v.* split, cleave, rive

fondya *v.* found, institute, establish, lay foundations

fondyans *m.* **+ow** foundation, institute, establishment

fondyer *m.* **-oryon** founder

fordh *f.* **+ow** road, way, manner; **fordh dhall** no through road, cul-de-sac; **fordh unnlergh** single-track road

fordh-a-dro *f.* roundabout (for traffic), traffic circle (U.S.), rotary (U.S.)

fordh-dhall *f.* **fordhow-dall** blind alley, cul-de-sac, no through road, dead end

fordh-dhibarth *f.* road-junction (T or Y)

fordh-dremen *f.* by-pass (road)

fordh-entra *f.* **fordhow-entra** entrance drive,, entrance

fordh-lan *f.* **fordhow-glan** thoroughfare, freeway

fordhlett *m.* **+ow** road-block

fordh-veur *f.* **fordhow-meur** main road, highway

forgh *f.* **fergh** fork (tool), prong

forlya *v.* whirl

form *m.* **+ys** bench

forn *f.* **+ow** oven, kiln, stove

forn-doemma *f.* **fornow-toemma** boiler (for domestic heating)

forner *m.* **-oryon** tender of oven, firer of pots

fornes *f.* **+yow** furnace

forn-gorrdonn *f.* **fornow-korrdonn** microwave oven

fornya *v.* bake, tend a kiln

fors *m.* force, strength; **na fors** *phr.* no matter; **ny res dhyn fors** it need not matter to us; **ny wrav fors** I don't care;

fortun *m.* **+yow** fortune, chance, luck

fortunya *v.* chance

fos *f.* **+ow** wall, rampart, dyke

fosskrif *coll.* **+enn** graffiti

fosynn *f.* little wall

fow<beech> *coll.* **+enn** beech-trees

fow<cave> *f.* **+ys** cave, den

fowek *f.* **-egi** beech-grove

fowesik *m.* **-igyon** fugitive, runaway

Fowydh *place* Fowey

fowt *m.* **+ow** lack, fault, scarcity

fow-wydh *coll.* **+enn** beech-trees

fram *m.* **+ow** framework

fram-kerdhes *m.* walking-frame, zimmer frame, walker (U.S.)

framweyth *m.* structure, framework

framya *v.* frame, arrange, contrive

franchis *m.* franchise

frank *adj.* free, at liberty

frankedh *m.* freedom, liberty

frankmason *m.* **+s** freemason

frappya *v.* beat, knock, rap

frega *v.* tear up, rip, tatter, shred

fregell *v.* shredder

fregys *m.* tatterdemalion, raggedy person (U.S.)

fres *m.* freight

fresk *adj.* fresh

freth *adj.* fluent, eloquent; eager

frethter *m.* fluency, eloquence; eagerness

freudh *m.* commotion, brawl, violence

freudha *v.* fray out

freudhek *adj.* violent

freudhi *v.* brawl, commit violence

fria *v.* fry

frias *m.* **+ow** fry-up

frig *m.* **+ow**, *dual* **dewfrik** nostril

Frisek *m.* Frisian language

froeth *coll.* **+enn** fruit (in general)

fronn *f.* **+ow** brake (curb), restraint

fronna *v.* brake, restrain, curb

fronnow-gober *plur.* wage restraints

fros *m.* **+ow** stream, tumult current (flow); **fros goes** haemorrhage

frosa *v.* stream, gush

froslamm *m.* **+ow** cascade

frosva *f.* **+ow** flume

frows *m.* fraud

frowsus *adj.* fraudulent

frut *m.* **+ys** fruit (in general)

Frynk *place* France *m.* **+yon** Frenchman

Frynkek *adj.* French *m.* French language

Frynkeger *m.* **-oryon** French-speaker

Frynkes *f.* **+ow** Frenchwoman

fuelenn *f.* wormwood

fug *adj.* sham, fictitious, phoney, fake *m.* feint, swindle

fugieth *f.* fiction

fugya *v.* feign, fake, play unfairly

fukhanow *m.* **-henwyn** pseudonym, false name, nom-de-plume

fumado *m.* salted pilchard, sardine

fun *f.* **+yow** cable, long rope

funenn *f.* **+ow** string, cord

fur *adj.* wise, cautious, discreet

furneth *f.* wisdom, discretion

furv *f.* **+ow** form, shape, figure, mould (for casting)

furvya *v.* form, shape, figure, mould (for casting)

furvyer *m.* **furvyoryon** creator

fust *f.* **+ow** club (weapon), bludgeon, flail, truncheon

fusta *v.* thrash, whip, beat with a club

fustwarak *f.* **-waregow** crossbow

fydh *f.* faith, trust, reliance

fydhya *v.* trust, confide, hope, have faith in

fydhyans *m.* trust, faith, confidence

fyll *m.* **+ow** fiddle (Mus.), violin

fyllel *v.* fail; **fyllel a** fail to; **fyllel dhe** lack, be lacking to

fyller *m.* **-oryon** fiddler (Mus.), violinist

fyllores *f.* **+ow** violinist

fyllya *v.* fiddle

fylm *m.* film (cinema, T.V., video); **fylm bras** feature film

fylmya *v.* film (shoot a film)

fynngel *f.* **fynnglow** furrow

fynngla *v.* use a crook for catching sand-eels, hoe

fynngler *m.* crook for catching sand-eels

fynni *f.* bent coarse grass; **fynni veur** tussock grass

fyrv *adj.* firm, steadfast

fyrvder *m.* firmness

fysk *adj.* impulsive, impetuous, hasty *m.* rush, haste, hurry

fyski *v.* rush, hasten, hurry, make haste

fysla *v.* fidget

fyslek *adj.* fussy, fidgetty *m.* **-ogyon** fidget

fyttya *v.* make ready

G (mutations W, K, H)

gahen *f.* henbane

gaja *m.* **gajys** forfeit, security, pledge

gal *m.* **+yon** villain, outcast, criminal

galar *m.* **+ow** grief, sorrow, affliction

galari *v.* grieve, lament, mourn

galargan *f.* **+ow** elegy, dirge

galarwisk *m.* mourning-dress

gallina *m.* **gallinys** guinea-fowl

galloes *m.* power, ability, might *v.* be able

galloesek *adj.* powerful, mighty, potent

galow *m.* invitation, call, summons, appeal

galwenn *f.* **+ow** call; **galwenn bellgows** telephone call

galwesiges *f.* **+ow** professional (woman)

galwesigeth *f.* **+ow** vocation, calling, profession

galwesik *adj.* professional *m.* **-igyon** professional (man)

galweyth *m.* **+yow** crime

gam *m.* game (object of hunt)

ganow *m.* **+ow** mouth; **der anow** oral, spoken, verbal (spoken); **orth ganow** *adv.* face to face

ganowas *m.* mouthful

ganowek *adj.* big-mouthed, gaping

gans *prep.* with, by; **gans henna** *conj.* moreover

gansa *prep.* with them

ganso *prep.* with him

garan *f.* **+es** crane

garek *m.* gar-fish

gargasenn *f.* **+ow** gullet, glutton, guzzler

gargett *m.* **+ow** garter

garlont *f.* **+ow** garland, wreath, band (strip)

garm *f.* **+ow** shout, outcry

garma *v.* shout, cry out

garow *adj.* rough, rugged, coarse

garowder *m.* roughness

garr *f.* **+ow**, *dual* **diwarr** leg, stem, stalk

garrek *adj.* leggy

garrenn *f.* **+ow** shank, calf (of leg)

garrgamm *adj.* crook-shanked, bow-legged

garrgamma *v.* straddle
garros *m.* rough promontory
garrvoth *f.* **+ow** collar stud
garth<enclosure> *m.* **+ow**
enclosure, yard, garden
garth<ridge> *m.* **+ow** ridge,
promontory
garth-gwari *m.* **garthow-gwari**
playground
garthow *plur.* ox-goad
garwa *adj.* rougher
gas *m.* **+ow** gas
gasa *v.* leave, abandon, renounce,
leave off; let, permit, allow; **gasa
yn-mes** omit, leave out
gasadow *m.* balance of account
gas-dor *m.* natural gas
gast *f.* **gesti** bitch, whore
gava *v.* forgive, pardon, remit; **gava
dhe** forgive; **gav dhymm** excuse
me, pardon me
gavel *f.* **+yow** grasp, hold, capacity
gaver *f.* **gever** goat; **gaver hal**
snipe; **gaver vor** lobster
gavrewik *f.* **-iges** antelope
gedya *v.* guide, conduct, direct
gedyans *m.* guidance, clue
gedyer *m.* **-oryon** guide, leader
gel *f.* **+es** leech
geler *f.* **+yow** bier, coffin
gelforn *f.* **+ow** forge
gell *adj.* light brown, tawny, fawn-
coloured, tan; **gell kesten** chestnut
brown
Gelligesow *plur.* Brownies
gellik *adj.* brownish
gellrudh *adj.* auburn, russet brown
gelvin *m.* **+es** beak, bill (of bird)
gelvinek *adj.* long-beaked *m.*
gelvinogyon curlew
gelwel *v.* call, summon
gelwys *adj.* called
gemm *m.* **+ow** gem
gemmweyth *m.* jewellery

gen *f.* **+yow**, *dual* **diwen** jaw
genen *prep.* with us
genes *prep.* with thee
genesigeth *f.* time of birth
genesigva *f.* birthplace
genesik *adj.* native-born, natural,
aboriginal *m.* **-igyon** native,
aborigine
genev *prep.* with me
genn *m.* **+ow** chisel, iron wedge
genna *v.* chisel, wedge
genowgh *prep.* with you
gensi *prep.* with her; **ha gensi** *adv.*
what's more, withal
genva *f.* **+ow** horse's bit
Genver *m.* January
genynn *m.* **+ow** gene
genynnegieth *f.* genetics
genynnek *adj.* genetic
genys *adj.* born
ger *m.* **+yow** word, saying, report
gerda *m.* fame, reputation
gerdhyghtyer *m.* word-processor
gerenn *f.* **+ow** single word
gerennek *adj.* voluble, verbose
gerlyver *m.* **-lyvrow** dictionary
gerlyvrynn *m.* **+ow** glossary
gerva *f.* **+ow** vocabulary
gerya *v.* patter, prate, babble, gabble,
be verbose; repute; **geryes da** *adj.*
famous, well spoken of
geryel *adj.* verbal (concerned with
words)
ges *m.* jeer, mockery, satire; joke
gesigow *plur.* left-overs
gesya *v.* jeer, mock, jest, tell jokes
gesyer *m.* **gesyoryon** jester,
joker; comic, comedian
gesys *v.* left (remaining)
gevel *f.* tongs, pincers, snuffers;
gevel know nutcrackers
gevelhorn *f.* iron tongs
geveligow *plur.* pliers
gevell *m.* **+yon** twin (male)

gevella *v.* twin
gevellans *m.* **+ow** twinning
gevelles *f.* **+ow** twin (female)
gevellji *m.* **+ow** semi-detached house
gever *pron.* goats
gevrik *f.* **-igow** young goat, spider-crab, red gurnard
gevyans *m.* forgiveness, pardon, remission
gew *m.* **+ow** woe, grief, misery
gik *m.* smallest thing
gil *m.* guile, deceit, duplicity; **heb gil** *adv.* sincerely
gilles *coll.* lovage
gilotin *m.* guillotine
giow *coll.* **+enn** sinews, tendons
gis *m.* fashion, custom, manner, style
gis-leveryans *m.* pronunciation
gis-skrifa *m.* style (literary)
gitar *m.* guitar
gitarydh *m.* **+yon** guitarist
glan *adj.* clean, innocent, clear *adv.* completely, quite; **gyllys glan** *phr.* completely gone
glander *m.* purity, chastity; cleanliness, propriety
glanhe *v.* clean, clear
glann *f.* **+ow** bank (of river), brink, waterside; **glann gales** hard shoulder
glanyth *adj.* clean, neat, tidy
glanythter *m.* cleanliness, neatness, tidiness
glas<blue> *adj.* blue, green (of plants), light grey
glas<maw> *m.* maw, stomach
glasa *v.* green (of plants), flourish, put forth leaves
glasenn *f.* **+ow** greensward, verdure
glasneth *f.* verdure, greenness
glasrudh *adj.* purple, violet (colour)
glastan *f.* **+enn** evergreen oak-trees
glastonn *m.* greensward
glastir *m.* **+yow** verdant ground

glaswas *m.* **-wesyon** stripling, greenhorn (U.S.)
glavor *m.* slobber, drivel
glaveri *v.* slobber, drivel
glaw *m.* rain
glawji *m.* **+ow** shelter
glawlenn *f.* **+ow** umbrella
glena *v.* cling, stick, affix; **glena orth** stick to, adhere
glenus *adj.* adhesive
glenysenn *f.* **+ow** sticker
glesin *m.* **+yow** lawn, grassy plot
glesni *m.* greenness
glesyjyon *m.* grass-plot
glew *adj.* sharp, translucent, penetrating
glin *m.* **+yow**, *dual* **dewlin** knee
gloes *f.* **+ow** pang, anguish, spasm
gloesa *v.* hurt (intrans.), smart
glori *m.* glory
gloryus *adj.* glorious
glos *coll.* **+enn** dried cow-dung used as fuel
glotni *m.* gluttony
glow<bright> *adj.* bright
glow<coal> *coll.* **+enn** coal
glowbrenn *m.* charcoal
glow-wydh *f.* wood for charcoal
glow-wydhek *f.* charcoal burners' wood
glowek *f.* **+egi** coal-heap, coalfield, place abounding in coal
glowji *m.* **+ow** coal-shed, coal-house
glus *m.* **+ow** glue, paste, birdlime
glusa *v.* stick, glue, paste
glusek *adj.* sticky
glusles *coll.* **+enn** campions
gluth *m.* dew
gluthboynt *m.* dewpoint
gluthvelhwenn *f.* **+ow** slug
glyb *adj.* wet, damp, moist
glybor *m.* wetness, moisture, damp
glybya *v.* wet
glydh *m.* chickweed

glynn *m.* **+ow** large valley, glen
glyttra *v.* glitter
gnas *f.* **+ow** nature, quality, character
go *int.* woe
go- *pref.* sub-
gobalas *v.* skim (in mining)
gobans *m.* **+ow** hollow (small), re-entrant (small)
gober *m.* **gobrow** reward, pay (income), salary, wage, emolument; **gober dilavur** unemployment benefit
gobra *v.* pay wages to, reward, remunerate
gobrena *v.* hire
gobrenans *m.* **+ow** tenancy, lease
gobrener *m.* **-oryon** hirer, tenant
godegh *m.* lair, retreat, holt
godenow *m.* hole in ground
goderri *v.* interrupt, break the force of
godewl *adj.* dusky
godh *f.* **+ow** mole
godhalla *v.* dazzle
godhav *v.* suffer, endure, tolerate, bear
godhen *m.* **godhnow** sole (of foot), tread (of tyre)
godhes *m.* sediment, dregs, tea-leaves
godhevel *v.* suffer, tolerate, bear (endure)
godhevus *adj.* passive
godhevyans *m.* suffering
godhevyades *f.* **+ow** patient (female), sufferer (female)
godhevyas *m.* **-ysi** patient (male), sufferer (male)
godhnow *plur.* soles
godhonieth *f.* science
godhoniethek *adj.* scientific
godhonydh *m.* **+yon** scientist
godhor<mole> *f.* mole
godhor<PV> *v.* it is known

godhvos *m.* knowledge, ability *v.* know, have knowledge of, be able
godolgh *m.* knoll
godolghynn *m.* small tump, small knoll
godoemm *adj.* lukewarm
godorr *m.* **+ow** interruption
godra *v.* milk
godramm *m.* cramp
godreghi *v.* trim
godrek *m.* cow's first milk
godrev *f.* **+i** small farm, hamlet
godrevedh *f.* third day hence
godriga *v.* stay for a short time, visit
godriger *m.* **-oryon** visitor
godrik *m.* **-igow** short stay, visit
godroeth *m.* rennet
godroetha *v.* curdle with rennet
godros *v.* threaten, menace, scold *m.* **+ow** menace, threat
goedh<goose> *f.* **+ow** goose
goedh<wild> *adj.* wild, fierce, uncultivated
goedhan *m.* **+es** moth
goedhel *m.* **goedhyli** thicket
Goedhel *m.* **Goedhyli** Gael, Irishman
goedhgennin *coll.* saffron
goedhik *m.* **-igow** gosling
goedhvil *m.* **+es** wild beast, wild animal
goel<feast> *m.* **+yow** feast, fair; **goel ilow** concert
goel<sail> *m.* **+yow** sail, veil, wall-hanging
goel<vigil> *m.* **+yow** vigil, watch, revel, wake
goelann *f.* **+es** gull, seamew
goeldheys *m.* harvest home
goeles *m.* **+ow** bottom, base, lowest part
goelesenn *f.* petticoat, underskirt, slip (woman's undergarment)
goell *m.* yeast

Goelowann *m.* Midsummer
goelva *f.* **+ow** look-out place
goelya<feast> *v.* feast
goelya<sail> *v.* sail
goelyas *v.* keep watch *f.* night watch
goemmon *m.* seaweed
goen<down> *f.* **+yow** downland, unenclosed pasture, moor (upland); **Goen Brenn** *place* Bodmin Moor
goen<sheath> *f.* sheath, scabbard
goenbluv *coll.* cotton-grass
goendi *m.* **+ow** moor-house
goer *v.* knows
goera *m.* hay; **goera glas** silage
goes *m.* blood, gore, blood-line
goesa *v.* bleed, make bloody
goesegenn *f.* **+ow** black-pudding
goesek *adj.* bloodstained, bloody
goeth<pride> *m.* pride, haughtiness, vainglory
goeth<stream> *f.* **+ow** stream, watercourse; conduit, canal, pipeline, channel
goethek *f.* **-egi** place abounding in streams
goethel *adj.* watery *m.* watery ground
goethus *adj.* proud, haughty
go-ev *int.* woe to him
gogell *f.* **+ow** pulpit, little cell
gogerdher *m.* **-oryon** toddler
gogerdhes *v.* toddle
goghi *coll.* **+enn** wasps
gogo *f.* cave
gogosk *m.* nap, doze
gogoska *v.* nap, doze
gogledh *f.* North
gogrys *m.* suspicion
goheles *v.* shun, avoid, be shy of
gohelfordh *f.* **+ow** diversion (of road), alternative route
gohelus *adj.* shy, retiring
gohydh *f.* **+ow** daughter-in-law
gokki *adj.* foolish, silly, stupid, absurd *m.* **+es** foolish person,

gokkineth *f.* folly, foolishness, stupidity, absurdity
golans *m.* **+ow** small valley
goleder *f.* **goledrow** incline
goleski *v.* singe, char, smoulder
goleyth *m.* roast meat, collop
golghi *v.* wash, bathe; **golghi an lestri** *phr.* wash the dishes
golghva *f.* **+ow** bathroom, wash-place, washroom (U.S.)
golghva-gerri *f.* **golghvaow-kerri** car-wash
golghyon *plur.* slops, suds, hogwash
goli *m.* **+ow** wound, sore, ulcer
golia *v.* wound, hurt
gologhas *m.* adoration, worship, prayer
gologva *f.* outlook
golok *f.* sight, vision, look
golow *adj.* bright, brilliant *m.* **+ys** light; **golow dydh** daylight
golowbrenn *m.* **+yer** lamp-post
golowder *m.* glory, radiance, brightness
golowek *adj.* luminous
golowi *v.* illuminate (with light), shine, lighten
golowji *m.* **+ow** light-house
golowlester *m.* **-lestri** lamp
golowylyon *plur.* spangles, tinsel, sequins
golowyjyon *m.* radiance
gols *m.* head of hair
golusek *adj.* rich, affluent *m.* **golusogyon** rich man
golusogneth *f.* affluence
golvan *m.* **+es** sparrow
gon *m.* gown, robe, monk's habit
gonador *m.* **+yon** sower
gonedhys *adj.* worked, wrought
gonis *m.* work, service *v.* work, toil, labour; **Gonis Yeghes** Health Service; **Gonis Yowynkneth** Youth Service

gonisek *m.* -ogyon servant, workman

gonisogeth *f.* culture, service; gonisogeth tir agriculture

gonisogethek *adj.* cultural

gonisyas *m.* -ysi civil servant

gonn<gun> *m.* +ys, +ow gun

gonn<PV> *v.* I know

gonn-jynn *m.* gonnow-jynn machine-gun

gonysyas *m.* -ysi workman

gor *adj.* broody (of hen), *m.* suppuration, pus

gor- *pref.* over-

gorambos *m.* +ow bond (promise)

gorboellek *adj.* mad, irrational, out of one's senses

gordevi *v.* overgrow, luxuriate

gordevyans *m.* overgrowth, luxuriance

gordhiwedh *m.* conclusion *adv.* definitely, finally

gordhroglamm *m.* +ow catastrophe

gordhroglammek *adj.* catastrophic

gordhya *v.* worship, adore, honour

gordhyans *m.* worship, adoration, honour, glory

gordhyllo *v.* sack (dismiss), fire, expel, terminate employment of

gordoemma *v.* overheat

gordoll *m.* super tax

gorenn *f.* +ow abscess

goresek *v.* jog

goreseger *m.* -oryon jogger (male)

goresegores *f.* +ow jogger (female)

gorewin *m.* +es dew-claw

gorewnter *m.* -tres great-uncle

gorfals *adj.* superabundant, profuse

gorfalster *m.* superabundance, surfeit, glut, profusion

gorfenn *m.* end, finish, conclusion

gorfenna *v.* finish, conclude, terminate, come to an end

gorgath *m.* +es tom-cat

gorge *m.* +ow low hedge

gorgeredh *f.* +ow crack-down

gorgemmerys *adj.* obsessed

gorgi *m.* male dog

gorgudha *v.* overlap

gorhan *f.* +ow incantation, enchantment

gorhana *v.* enchant

gorharga *v.* overload

gorhel *m.* -holyon ship, vessel, ark

gorhel-tan *m.* gorholyon-tan steam-boat

gorhemmynn *v.* command, order (command) *m.* +ow command, order, commandment, injunction

gorhemmynnadow *m.* greetings, commandments

gorhengeugh *m.* +yon remote ancestor, great-great-great-grandfather

gorhenyas *m.* -ysi enchanter

gorher *m.* +yow cover, lid; paten

gorheras *m.* covering, horse-cloth, roof of mouth

gorheri *v.* cover, put a lid on, hide

gorholedh *m.* requisition, demand, request

gori *v.* suppurate, fester; hatch

gorlanow *m.* high water

gorlanwes *m.* repletion

gorlewin *f.* the West

gorleythenn *f.* +ow, *coll.* gorleyth sole (fish)

gorlostenn *f.* +ow, *coll.* gorlost earwig

gorm *adj.* brown, dun

gormel *v.* praise, laud

gormeula *m.* praise, triumph, glory

gormeuledha *v.* triumph

gormeuledhek *adj.* triumphant

goroker *m.* compound interest

gorow *adj.* male, masculine (grammatical gender)

gorowra *v.* gild over, cover with gold leaf

gorra *v.* put, place, set; **gorra a-denewen** put aside, reserve; **gorra arghans dhe** invest; **gorra nebonan** take someone, give a lift to someone; **gorra yn** insert

gorrans *m.* **+ow** lift (in car), ride (U.S.)

gorreydh *m.* male

gorsav *m.* **+ow** station (railway or bus), standstill; **gorsav yn-dann dhor** underground station, subway station (U.S.)

gorsedh *f.* **+ow** meeting of bards, throne

gorth *adj.* opposed, contrary, stubborn, perverse *pref.* anti-

gorthdhelenn *f.* **+ow** counterfoil, stub (of ticket)

gorthenep *m.* **-ebow** reverse side, opposite side

Gortheren *m.* July

gorthfagh *m.* **+ow** barb

gorthkenter *f.* **-kentrow** rivet

gorthkentrewi *v.* rivet

gorthkrist *m.* antichrist

gorthkryjyk *m.* **-kryjygyon** heretic

gorthkryjyans *m.* **+ow** heresy

gorthpoes *m.* **+ow** counterweight, counterbalance, counterpoise

gorthpoesa *v.* counterbalance

gorthpoynt *m.* counterpoint (music)

gorthrew *m.* anti-freeze

gorthroghya *v.* immerse, plunge under water

gorthsaym *adj.* greaseproof

gorthsedhi *v.* countersink

gorthter *m.* opposition stubbornness

gorthugher *m.* evening

gorthugherweyth *adv.* in the evening

gorthwenon *m.* antidote

gorthwyns *m.* **+ow** head-wind

gorthyp *m.* **gorthybow** answer, reply, response

gorthybi *v.* answer, reply, counter, respond; **gorthybi orth** answer

gorti *m.* **gwerti** husband, man of the house

gortos *v.* await, wait for, remain, stay; **gortos nebonan** wait for someone

gorughel *adj.* sublime, supreme

goruvel *adj.* obsequious

gorvarghas *f.* **+ow** supermarket

gorvarthys *adj.* stupendous

gorveghya *v.* overload

gorvodrep *f.* **gorvodrebedh** great-aunt

gorvynn *m.* **+ow** ambition, aspiration

gorwedha *v.* lie down

gorwedhva *f.* **+ow** couch, lair

gorwel *m.* **+yow** horizon

gorweles *v.* oversee

gorwelyek *adj.* horizontal

gorwir *adj.* surreal

gorwitha *v.* mind, be very careful

gorwoelyas *v.* monitor *m.* **-ysi** monitor

gorwul *v.* do strictly, overdo

gorylla *m.* **gorylles** gorilla

gos *v.* it is known

goskes *m.* shade, shelter, cover

goskeusek *adj.* shady, sheltered, shadowed

goskeusi *v.* shelter, shade, put under cover

goskeuswydh *coll.* **+enn** shady trees

goskotter *m.* shade

goslowes *v.* listen, pay attention; **goslowes orth** listen to

goslowyas *m.* **-ysi** hearer

goslowysi *plur.* audience

gossen *f.* rust, ferruginous earth

gossenek *adj.* rusty

gosseni *v.* rust, go rusty

gostyth *adj.* liable, susceptible; obedient, submissive, subservient

gostythter *m.* susceptibility

gotrel *m.* furniture, household goods

gour *m.* **gwer** man (as opposed to woman), adult male person, husband; **gour pries** bridegroom, groom (at a wedding)

gourel *adj.* masculine, manly, virile

gourhys *m.* **+ow** fathom

gouroleth *f.* masculinity, manliness, virility

gov *m.* **+yon** smith, blacksmith

govedhow *adj.* tipsy

govel *f.* **+i** smithy

govelya *v.* forge

govenek *m.* hope

gover *m.* **+ow** brook, stream, rivulet, creek (U.S.)

goverek *adj.* snuffling, snivelling

goverik *m.* **-igow** streamlet

governans *m.* **+ow** government

governour *m.* **+s** governor

governya *v.* govern, rule, regulate

govijyon *m.* sorrow, care (worry), regret

govis *m.* regard, account; **a'm govis** *phr.* on my account, because of me

govryjyon *v.* simmer, parboil

go-vy *int.* woe is me

govynn *m.* question *v.* ask, question; **govynn orth** ask of; **govynn diworth** ask of

govynnadow *m.* request, enquiry

govynnek *m.* **-egi** questionnaire

govynnva *f.* **+ow** enquiry office, information booth (U.S.)

gow *m.* **+yow** lie, untruth, falsehood; **heb wow** *adv.* certainly

gowek *adj.* lying *m.* **gowogyon** liar

gowl *f.* **+ow** fork (Y-shape), bifurcation; crotch

gowlek *adj.* forked

gowleveryas *m.* **-ysi** inveterate liar, teller of lies

gowli *m.* **+ow** false oath, perjury

gowlia *v.* forswear oneself, commit perjury

gownagh *adj.* sterile *f.* calfless cow

goyeyn *adj.* cool

grabalyas *v.* grapple, clutch, cling

grabel *m.* **grablow**, **grablys** grappling iron, grapnel, grappling hook (U.S.)

gradh *m.* **+ow** step, grade, degree, stair

gradhesiges *f.* **+ow** graduate (female)

gradhesik *m.* **-igyon** graduate (male)

graffya *v.* graft

graghell *f.* pile, heap

gral *m.* grail

gramasek *adj.* grammatical

gramer *m.* (Latin) grammar

gramm *m.* **+ow** gram

grappa *m.* **grappys**, **grappow** grape

gras *m.* **grassys**, **grassow** thanks, gratitude; grace

grassa *v.* thank, give thanks for; **grassa dhe nebonan** thank someone

grassyes *adj.* gracious, pious

grastal *m.* gratuity, tip (money)

gravath *m.* **+ow** barrow (vehicle), stretcher (for carrying), litter; **gravath-diwla** *m.* hand-barrow, handcart (U.S.); **gravath-ros** *m.* wheel-barrow

gravedh *m.* gravity (in physics)

gravya *v.* engrave

gravyans *m.* **+ow** engraving

gravyer *m.* **-yoryon** engraver, sculptor

gre\<herd\> *f.* **+ow** herd, stud (animals), flock

gre\<rank\> *m.* **+ys** rank, status, position

gredi *m.* cattle-shed

gredhya *v.* graduate

greg *m.* cackling

grega *v.* cackle

Greka *m.* Greek language *m.* **Grekys** Greek

grelynn *f.* **+ow** pond for livestock

greun *coll.* **+enn** grain (as a mass)

greunaval *m.* **+ow** pomegranate

greunji *m.* **+ow** granary, grange, barn

greuv *m.* face, front of body

grev *m.* **+ow** grief; **heb grev** *phr.* no bother, no worries, no problem

grevons *m.* complaint (medical), grievance

grevya *v.* grieve, trouble, aggrieve; **grevya dhe nebonan** trouble someone

Grew *m.* Greek language

grija *m.* starry ray

gris *m.* **+yow**, **+ys** stair, step

grogys *m.* **+yow** belt, girdle; **grogys diogeledh grogysyow diogeledh** safety-belt

grogysa *v.* gird, girdle

grogys-gwynsell *m.* **grogysyow-gwynsell** fan-belt

grolyek *adj.* craking, cracked-voiced *m.* **-ogyon** craker, complainer

grommya *v.* growl, rumble, roar

grond *m.* ground, foundation, base

grondya *v.* found, base, lay foundations

gronn *m.* mass (heap), bundle, bunch; **gyllys yn gronn** *phr.* huddled up

gronna *v.* bundle

gronnedh *m.* **+ow** mass (in physics)

gront *m.* **+ow**, **+ys** grant, leave, permission

grontya *v.* grant, award, accord

grot *m.* **+ys** groat (silver coin worth one sixtieth of a pound)

grow *coll.* gravel, grit, coarse sand

growan *m.* granite

growanek *adj.* granitic *f.* **-egi** granite outcrop

growdir *m.* gravelly subsoil, scouring sand

growedh *m.* lying posture

growedha *v.* lie down, recline

growek *f.* **-egi** gravel pit

growgleudh *m.* **+yow** gravel pit

grows *coll.* **+enn** gooseberries

growynn *coll.* **+enn** gravel, grit (stone)

growynnek *adj.* gravelly *f.* **-egi** gravel-pit

grudh *f.* jaw, cheek (Anat.)

grug *m.* **+ow** heather, ling

grugek *adj.* heathery *f.* **+egi** heath

grugloen *m.* **+yow** heather-bush

grugyar *f.* **-yer** partridge

grugyerik *f.* **-igow** young partridge

gryghias *v.* neigh, whinny

gryll *m.* **+es** cricket (insect), spider-crab

gryllya *v.* chirp

gryllyans *m.* chirping

grysel *adj.* grisly, frightful

grysla *v.* grin, snarl, show one's teeth

gul *v.* do, make, perform, accomplish; **gul dhe** cause to; **gul ges a** make fun of, mock, ridicule; **gul glaw** rain; **gul orth** do about

gusigenn *f.* **+ow** bladder, blister

gustel *m.* riot, mutiny

gustla *v.* riot

gwag *adj.* empty, void, vacant

gwagel *f.* **+es** great skua

gwagla *m.* **-leow** vacancy, hiatus

gwagva *f.* **+ow** vacuum, void

gwahalyeth *m.* **+ow** peer (nobleman), satrap (Persian official of high rank)

gwakter *m.* emptiness
gwalader *m.* leader
gwalgh *m.* glut, satiety, repletion
gwalgha *v.* satiate, cloy, stuff
gwall *m.* **+ow** mischance, neglect, defect, accident; **dre wall** *adv.* accidentally
gwan *f.* **+yow** stab, prick, piercing
gwana *v.* stab, sting, prick, puncture, pierce
gwanas *m.* **+ow** puncture
gwandra *v.* wander, roam, rove, stray
gwandrek *adj.* wandering, peripatetic
gwandryas *m.* **-ysi** wanderer, rover, roamer
gwaneth *coll.* **+enn** wheat
gwanethek *f.* **-egi** wheatfield
gwanettir *m.* **+ow** wheatland
gwann *adj.* weak, frail, feeble; immoral *m.* **+yon** weakling
gwannder *m.* weakness, feebleness, frailty
gwannegredh *m.* weakness, infirmity, frailty
gwannhe *v.* weaken, dilute, grow feeble
gwann-ober *m.* **+ow** misdeed
gwann-wikor *m.* **+yon** bad trader
gwann-wre'ti *f.* adulteress
gwar *adj.* chaste
gwara *coll.* merchandise, commodities, goods; **gwara devnydhyoryon** consumer goods
gwarak *f.* **-egow** bow, arc, arch
gwareger *m.* **-oryon** archer, bowman
gwari *v.* play *m.* **+ow** game, play, fun; **gwari mildamm** jigsaw puzzle
gwari-dall *m.* **gwariow-dall** lottery, raffle
gwariek *adj.* playful
gwariell *f.* **+ow** toy
gwarier *m.* **-oryon** player, actor

gwari-kan *m.* **gwariow-kan** opera
gwariores *f.* **+ow** actress
gwari-sagh *m.* **gwariow-sagh** raffle
gwari-sebon *m.* soap-opera
gwariva *f.* **+ow** theatre
gwarnya *v.* warn, notify, caution
gwarnyans *m.* **+ow** warning, proclamation, notification
gwarr *f.* **+ow** nape, curve
gwarrgromm *adj.* stooping
gwarrgromma *v.* stoop
gwarrlenn *f.* **+ow** shawl
gwartha *m.* summit, top *adj.* upper, higher
gwarthegva *f.* **+ow** cattle-yard
gwarthek *coll.* horned cattle
gwarthevya *v.* dominate
gwarthevyades *f.* **+ow** suzeraine
gwarthevyas *m.* **-ysi** overlord, suzerain
gwarthol *f.* **-yow** stirrup
gwas *m.* **gwesyon** servant, apprentice, follower; fellow, man, guy (U.S.)
gwas-hwel *m.* **gwesyon-hwel** workman
gwask *f.* press, stress; **An Wask** The Press
gwaska *v.* squeeze, press, compress, oppress
gwaskedh *m.* stress (quantity in physics), compression
gwaskubyllenn *f.* **+ow** squeegee mop
gwastas *adj.* flat, smooth
gwastya *v.* lay waste
gwav *m.* **+ow** winter
gwavi *v.* winter, hibernate pass the winter
gwavos *f.* **+ow** winter dwelling
gwaya *v.* move (intransitive), stir
gwayadow *adj.* mobile
gwayn *m.* gain, profit, advantage

gwaynya *v.* gain, win, profit, procure

gwaytya *v.* take care, mind, be sure to; hope, expect

gwaytyans *m.* expectation

gweder *m.* **gwedrow**, *dual* **dewweder** glass

gweder-gwlan *m.* fibre-glass

gweder-mires *m.* **gwedrow-mires** mirror, looking-glass

gwedhow *adj.* widowed, bereft of wife or husband *m.* **+yon** widower

gwedhra *v.* wither

gwedhwes *f.* **+ow** widow

gwedhyn *adj.* pliable, flexible, supple

gwedhynder *m.* flexibility, suppleness

gwedrenn *f.* **+ow** tumbler, drinking glass

gwedrennas *m.* **+ow** glassful

gwel\<field\> *m.* **+yow** field, prospect

gwel\<rods\> *coll.* **+enn** rods, poles, shafts, wands

gwel\<sight\> *m.* **+yow** sight, view, appearance

gwelenn *f.* **gwelynni**, *coll.* **gwel** rod, pole, shaft, wand

gwelenn-byskessa *f.* **gwelynni-pyskessa** fishing rod

gwelenn-dhornigell *f.* **gwelynni-dornigell** crankshaft

gwelenn-gala *f.* **gwelynni-kala** straw

gwelenn-skubell *f.* **gwelynni-skubell** broom-stick

gweles *v.* see, behold, perceive

gwelesigeth *f.* **+ow** vision (apparition)

gwelgyst *f.* **+yow** video-cassette

gwelhevin *coll.* aristocrats, ruling class, leading people

gweli *m.* **+ow** bed, layer, stratum; **gweli kala** straw bed; **gweli pluv** feather bed

gweli-dydh *m.* settee

gwelivedhes *f.* **+ow** midwife

gwelivos *m.* childbed

gwell *adj.* better; **gwell yw genev** I prefer

gwella *adj.* best

gwellhe *v.* improve; **gwellha dha jer** cheer up

gwellheans *m.* **+ow** improvement

gwels *coll.* **+enn** grass

gwelsek *adj.* grassy *f.* **-egi** grass-plot

gwelsigow *plur.* scissors

gwelsow *plur.* shears, clippers

gwelsowas *m.* fertility

gwelstir *m.* **+yow** grassland

gwelv *f.* **-ow** lip

gwelva *f.* **-ow** view-point, belvedere, point of view

gwelvek *adj.* thick-lipped

gwelvenn *f.* **+ow** lip

gwelynni *plur.* rods

gwenen *coll.* **+enn** bees

Gwener *f.* Venus; **dy' Gwener** Friday; **Gwener an Grows** Good Friday

gwenn *m.* anus

gwennel *f.* **gwennili** swallow (bird), weaver's shuttle

gwennenn *f.* **+ow** blister, wen, sore

gwennogenn *f.* **+ow** wart

gwenon *m.* poison, venom

gwenonek *adj.* poisonous, venomous

gwenonriyas *m.* **-riysi** poisoner

gwenton *m.* spring (season)

gwer *plur.* husbands, men (as opposed to women)

gweres\<help\> *v.* help, aid, assist *m.* help, assistance, aid; **gweres a lagha** legal aid;

gweres<soil> *m.* +ow soil, ground, mould

gwerin *f.* populace, folk, proletariat common people; **Yeth an Werin** informal gathering at which Cornish is spoken

gwerinel *adj.* democratic

gwerinieth *f.* +ow democracy

gweriniethor *m.* +yon democrat

gwerison *m.* reward

gwern<CN> *coll.* +enn alder-trees, alder-swamp, marsh

gwern<mast> *f.* +ow mast

gwernek *adj.* marshy *f.* -egi aldergrove

gwerrya *v.* make war

gwers *f.* +yow verse; **gwers meythrin** nursery-rhyme

gwersieth *f.* versification

gwerth *f.* sale (the event)

gwertha *v.* sell

gwerthas *m.* +ow sale (act of selling)

gwerthbris *m.* +yow sale price

gwerther *m.* -oryon salesman, vendor

gwerthevin *m.* primate (cleric)

gwerthji *m.* +ow shop

gwerthores *f.* +ow saleswoman, vendor

gwerthys *f.* +ow shuttle

gweskel *v.* beat, knock, hit, strike

gwesper *m.* +ow evensong, vespers

gwest *f.* lodging

gwester *m.* -oryon guest

gwesti *m.* +ow guest-house

gwestores *f.* +ow guest

gwestyas *m.* -ysi lodger

gwestyades *f.* +ow lodger

gwesyon *plur.* servants

gweth *adj.* worse

gwethhe *v.* worsen, deteriorate

gwethter *m.* deterioration

gwettha *adj.* worst

gweus *f.* +yow, *dual* **diwweus** lip (human)

gwevya *v.* wave, flourish (of a sword)

gwewenn *f.* heel

gweylgi *f.* ocean

gweyth<occasion> *f.* +yow occasion (time)

gweyth<work> *m.* work

gweytha *v.* work, exploit, set to work

gweythor *m.* +yon worker, workman; **gweythor arghans** silversmith; **gweythor kober** coppersmith; **gweythor chi** housebuilder

gweythres *m.* deed, action, function

gweythresek *m.* -ogyon executive

gweythresel *adj.* functional

gweythva *f.* +ow factory

gwia *v.* weave, knit, twine

gwiader *m.* -oryon weaver, spider

gwiadores *f.* +ow weaver

gwias *m.* +ow web, texture, woven cloth; **gwias kevnis** spider's web

gwiasedh *m.* +ow texture

gwiasva *f.* +ow web-site

gwiber *m.* poor-cod

gwibes *coll.* +enn gnats

gwibesek *adj.* infested by gnats

gwibessa *v.* waste time

gwig *f.* +ow village

gwigh<CN> *coll.* +enn periwinkles

gwigh<squeak> *m.* +yow squeak

gwighal *v.* squeak

gwikor *m.* +yon trader, businessman, chandler; peddler, hawker

gwin *m.* wine; **gwin fellys** vinegar

gwinbrenn *m.* +yer vine, grapevine

gwinji *m.* +ow vinery

gwinlann *f.* +ow vineyard

gwinreun *coll.* +enn grapes

gwinwask *f.* **+ow** wine-press
gwinwedrenn *f.* wine-glass
gwinwel *coll.* **+enn** maple-trees
gwir *adj.* true, real, right *m.* **+yow**
right, truth, fact, justice; **gwir
bryntya** copyright; **gwir dremen**
right of way
gwirbryntyans *m.* copyright
gwirder *m.* truth
gwires *f.* **gwirosow** liquor, drink
ardent alcoholic spirits
gwirhaval *adj.* likely
gwirhevelep *adj.* plausible
gwirhevelepter *m.* plausibility,
verisimilitude
gwirleveryas *m.* **-ysi** teller of the
truth
gwirotti *m.* **-ow** kiddleywink, dive
(U.S.)
gwirvos *m.* reality
gwir-vreus *m.* justice
gwiryon *adj.* righteous, genuine, just,
true
gwiryonedh *m.* truth
gwiryonses *m.* sincerity,
authenticity
gwiryow *plur.* rights; **gwiryow
kemmyn** civil rights
gwis *f.* **+i** sow (pig)
gwisk *m.* dress (clothes), husk, pod;
gwisk horn armour
gwiska *v.* dress, clothe, wear; coat,
line
gwiskas *m.* **+ow** layer of clothing,
coating, covering, raiment, outfit
(clothes)
gwiskti *m.* **+ow** vestry
gwith *m.* custody, care (keeping)
gwitha *v.* keep, reserve, preserve,
retain, be sure to; **gwitha orth**
guard against; **gwitha rag** guard
from, protect from; **gwitha war**
guard against
gwithlann *f.* **+ow** reserve (of land)
gwithti *m.* museum

gwithva *f.* **+ow** storehouse, depot,
reserve; **gwithva natur** nature
reserve
gwithyades *f.* **+ow** guardian,
warden
gwithyades-chi *f.*
gwithyadesow-chi
housekeeper (female)
gwithyas *m.* **gwithysi** guard,
guardian, warden, keeper;
gwithyas kres, *m.* **gwithysi gres**
policeman; **gwithyas milva** zoo-
keeper; **gwithyas tan** fireman;
gwithyas tren guard (of train)
gwithyans *m.* preservation,
stewardship
gwius *adj.* winding, intricate, tortuous
gwiver *coll.* **gwivrenn** wire
gwiw *adj.* fit, worthy, proper,
appropriate, suitable, meet, fitting
gwiwder *m.* **+yow** worthiness,
suitability
gwiwer *m.* **-ow** squirrel
gwlan *coll.* wool; **gwlan koton**
cotton-wool
gwlanek *adj.* woolly *m.* jersey;
gwlanogow
gwlanenn *f.* **+ow** flannel
gwlas *f.* **+ow** country, land; **Gwlas
an Hav** *place* Somerset
gwlasek *adj.* pertaining to a country,
political
gwlaskarer *m.* **-oryon** patriot
gwlaskerensa *f.* patriotism
gwlaskor *f.* **-kordhow** kingdom,
realm
gwlesik *m.* leader
gwlygh *adj.* wet, damp, moist
gwlygha *m.* wetness, moisture
gwlyghi *v.* soak
gwragedh *plur.* wives
gwragh *f.* **+es** witch, hag; **gwragh
oeles** wood-louse
gwrannenn *f.* wren

gwreg *f.* **gwragedh** wife, matron, woman

gwregel *adj.* feminine, womanly

gwregoleth *f.* femininity

gwrekk *m.* **+ys** wreck

gwres *f.* heat, ardour

gwresek *adj.* ardent

gwresenn *f.* fertile ground

gwre'ti *f.* housewife

gwreydh *coll.* **+enn** roots

gwreydhya *v.* root, take root

gwreydhyel *adj.* radical

gwreydhyow *plur.* roots

gwri *m.* **+ow** stitch, seam, join, thin seam of ore

gwriador *m.* **+yon** stitcher

gwriadores *f.* **+ow** seamstress

gwrians *m.* **+ow** action, deed, creation, manufacture

gwrias *v.* sew, stitch

gwrier *m.* maker, creator

gwrug *v.* did, made

gwruthyl *v.* create

gwryghon *coll.* **+enn** sparks

gwrynya *v.* wrestle, hug, squeeze

gwrynyer *m.* **-yoryon** wrestler

gwrys<done> *adj.* done

gwrys<crystal> *m.* **+ow** crystal

gwryth *f.* deeds, performance, service

gwrythyans *m.* performance

gwrythyer *m.* **-oryon** performer

gwydenn *f.* loop, noose, bight (of rope)

gwydh *coll.* **+enn** trees

gwydhboell *m.* chess

Gwydhel *m.* **Gwydhyli** Gael, Goidelic Celt, Irishman

Gwydhelek *adj.* Gaelic, Goidelic Celtic *m.* Gaelic language

Gwydheleger *m.* **-oryon** Gaelic speaker

Gwydheles *f.* **+ow** Irishwoman, Gael

gwydhek *adj.* wooded *f.* **-egi** woodland

gwydhlann *f.* **+ow** plantation (of trees)

gwydhvos *coll.* **+enn** honeysuckle, woodbine

gwydhyel *adj.* wooded

gwydhyow *m.* video

gwydhyv *m.* **+yow** bill-hook, hedging-bill

gwyg *coll.* **+enn** tares, bindweed, climbing weed

gwyll *m.* **+yow** vagrant, robber

gwylles *coll.* field gentian

gwyls *adj.* wild, savage, fierce

gwylvos *m.* wilderness, wild forest land

gwylter *m.* hunting-dog, large greyhound, mastiff

gwynk *m.* wink (of eye)

gwynkya *v.* wink

gwynn *adj.* white, blessed, fair (in colour)

gwynnder *m.* whiteness, brightness

gwynndonn *f.* ley land

gwynnek *adj.* whitish, hoar *m.* **-oges** whiting

gwynnel *v.* wriggle, writhe, squirm, struggle

Gwynngala *m.* September

gwynnhe *v.* whiten, ripen (of corn)

gwynnrew *m.* numbness

gwynnrudh *adj.* pink

gwynnvys *m.* bliss *adj.* blessed, fortunate

gwyns<wind> *m.* **+ow** wind, breath; **gwyns a-dro** whirlwind, tornado

gwyns<winze> *f.* **+ys** winze, windlass, winch

gwyns-ethenn *f.* steam-driven winch

gwynsa *v.* winnow

gwynsek *adj.* windy

gwynsell *f.* **+ow** fan (appliance)

gwynsella *v.* fan, winnow
gwyr *adj.* green
gwyrdh *adj.* green
gwyrgh *adj.* virginal, innocent, chaste
gwyrghes *f.* **+i** virgin, maid, maiden
gwyrwels *coll.* growing grass
gwystel *m.* **gwystlow** pledge, surety; pawn, hostage, collateral (U.S.)
gwystel-tir *m.* **gwystlow-tir** land mortgage
gwystla *v.* pledge
gwyth *f.* vein
gwythi *coll.* **+enn** veins, blood-vessels
gwythiek *adj.* bloodshot, veined
gyglet *m.* wanton person
gyki *v.* peep
gyllys *adj.* gone
gyrr *m.* gripes
gyth *m.* complaint
gyw *m.* **+ow** spear, lance, javelin
gywa *v.* spear
gywik *m.* **-igow** lancet

H

ha<and> *conj.* and (before consonants), while, then, and so
ha<IJ> *int.* ha
habadoellya *m.* row (disturbance)
habadrylsi *m.* row (disturbance)
hag *conj.* and (before vowels)
ha'ga *phr.* and their
ha'gan *phr.* and our
ha'gas *phr.* and your
hager *adj.* ugly, hideous, foul; **hager awel** *f.* bad weather; **hager dowl** *m.* rotten luck; **hager ober** crime
hakkra *adj.* uglier
hakkya *v.* hack, hew, chop, slash; **hakkya dhe demmyn** hack to pieces

hakney *m.* **+s** ambling nag, hack (horse)
hakter *m.* ugliness, cruelty, danger
hal *f.* **halow** moor, marsh, streamwork for tin
halya *v.* haul, hoist
ha'm *phr.* and my
hamster *m.* **+s** hamster
ha'n *phr.* and the
hanaf *m.* **+ow** cup, beaker
hanafas *m.* **+ow** cupful
hanas *m.* **+ow** sigh, murmur
hanasa *v.* sigh, murmur, speak under one's breath
hanasenn *f.* **+ow** sigh
handla *v.* handle, stroke, pat
haneth *adv.* tonight, this evening
hanow *m.* **henwyn** name, noun
hansel *m.* **+yow** breakfast
hansli *m.* **-livyow** brunch
hanter *m.* half
hanterdiner *m.* halfpenny
hanterdydh *m.* midday, noon
hanterkans *num.* **+ow** fifty
hanterkylgh *m.* **+yow** semicircle
hanternos *f.* midnight
hanwesik *m.* **-igyon** nominee
hanwesigeth *f.* **+ow** nomination
happ *m.* **+ys** chance, fortune, luck
happriv *m.* random number
happwari *v.* gamble
happya *v.* chance, happen
harber *m.* **+ys** refuge, shelter, lodging
hardh *adj.* bold, hardy
hardhder *m.* boldness, audacity
harfyll *m.* **+ow** fiddle (Mus.)
harfyller *m.* **-oryon** fiddler (Mus.)
harfyllores *f.* fiddler (Mus.)
harow<IJ> *int.* help
harow<MN> *m.* harrow
harth *m.* **+ow** bark (of a dog), baying (of a hound)
hartha *v.* bark

has *coll.* **+enn** seed, sperm, progeny
hasa *v.* sow, run to seed
hasek *adj.* seedy *f.* **-egi** seed-plot, seedbed
haslett *m.* **+ow** contraceptive
hast *m.* haste, hurry
hastenep *m.* haste
hatt *m.* **+ow, +ys** hat
ha'th *phr.* and thy
hav *m.* **+ow** summer
haval *adj.* similar, resembling; **haval dhe** similar to; **bos haval dhe** *v.* resemble
havalder *m.* **+yow** similarity
havar *m.* summer-fallow
havarel *adj.* fallow in summer
havas *m.* summer-time
havek *adj.* summery
havi *v.* pass the summer
havos *f.* summer dwelling, shieling
havrek *f.* **-egi** arable land
Havren *place* Severn
havyades *f.* **+ow** summer visitor, summer tourist
havyas *m.* **-ysi** summer visitor, summer tourist
ha'w *phr.* and my
hay *f.* enclosure
ha'y *phr.* and his
ha'y *phr.* and her
hayl *int.* hail (greeting)
haylya *v.* hail (greet)
-he *v.* (VN ending)
heb *prep.* without, lacking, not counting; **heb fordh** *adj.* trackless; **heb kost** free of charge; **heb wow** *adv.* truly
hebask *adj.* calm, quiet, sedate, peaceful; **Keynvor Hebask** *m.* Pacific Ocean
hebaska *m.* quietude, soothing, solace
hebaskhe *v.* soothe, sedate, pacify
hebaskheans *m.* sedation

hebleth *adj.* easy to weave, flexible, supple
hedh *int.* stop, halt *m.* **+ow** full-stop
hedhadow *adj.* attainable, accessible
hedhes *v.* reach, attain; fetch
hedhi *v.* stop (intrans.), cease, pause, rest, halt
hedhyw *adv.* today
hedorr *adj.* fragile, easily breakable
hedra *conj.* while, as long as
Hedra *m.* October
hedro *adj.* fickle, easily changeable
hedrogh *adj.* cuttable
hegar *adj.* amiable, kindly, affectionate, affable
hegas *adj.* hateful, repulsive
hegoel *adj.* credulous, trustful, superstitious
hegoeledh *m.* credulity, superstition
hegos *adj.* ticklish
hel<AJ> *adj.* bountiful, generous, munificent, liberal (with money)
hel<hall> *f.* **+yow** hall, parlour; **hel an dre** town-hall
helder *m.* generosity, hospitality, liberality, munificence, bounty
helergh *adj.* late, in the rear
helerghi *v.* track, detect
helerghyas *m.* **-ysi** detective, sleuth, tracker
helgh *m.* hunt
helghi *v.* hunt, go hunting
helghva *f.* **+ow** hunting-ground, chase (for hunting)
helghwisk *m.* hunting-dress
helghya *v.* hunt, chase, pursue, go hunting
helghyas *m.* **-ysi** hunter (professional), persecutor
helghyer *m.* **-oryon** hunter
helgi *m.* **-geun** hound
helgik *m.* game (meat)
helik *coll.* **-igenn** willows, osiers

helik-lowarth *m.* **+ow** willow-garden

hell *adj.* tardy, slow, reluctant

heller *m.* **helloryon** wild-natured individual

Hellys *place* Helston

hellys *f.* **+yow** old court

helvargh *m.* **-vergh** hunter (horse)

hembronk *v.* lead, conduct, bring

hembrenkyas *m.* **-ysi** leader, conductor

hemm *pron.* this (m.)

hemma *pron.* this one (m.)

hen *adj.* old, long-standing

hen- *pref.* ancient

henavek *adj.* senior; **-ogyon** elder

henbyth *m.* **+ow** antique

hendas *m.* **+ow** ancestor, forefather, grandfather

hender *m.* age, antiquity

hendhyskans *m.* archaeology

hendhyskyas *m.* **-ysi** archaeologist

hendi *m.* **+ow** ancient house

hendra *f.* home farm, family farm

henedh *m.* **+ow** generation (people in a family), descendants, posterity

henfordh *f.* ancient track

hengeugh *m.* **+yon** ancestor

hengov *m.* **+yow** tradition

hengovek *adj.* traditional

henhwedhel *m.* **-dhlow** legend

henji *m.* ancient house

henkyn *m.* iron peg

henlann *f.* old cemetery

henlavar *m.* **+ow** proverb

henn *pron.* that (m.)

henna *pron.* that one (m.)

henses *m.* antiquity

henvilonieth *f.* palaeozoology

henwel *v.* name, nominate

henwyn *plur.* names

henwys *v.* named

henys *m.* old age

hepken *adv.* only

hepkorr *v.* renounce, relinquish, surrender give up

hepkorrans *m.* renunciation

heptu *adj.* neutral

her<defiance> *m.* defiance, stubbornness, insistence

her<heir> *m.* heir

herdhya *v.* ram, push, shove

hern *coll.* **+enn** pilchards, sardines; **hernenn vyghan** *f.* **hern byghan** sprat; **hernenn wynn hern gwynn** herring

hernes *m.* harness

hernesya *v.* put on harness

hernyer *m.* **-oryon** ironmonger

herwydh *prep.* according to, in accordance with, on the authority of; **herwydh an lagha** *adj.* legitimate, lawful; **yn herwydh** adjoining

herya *v.* defy

hes *f.* **+ow** swarm, flock (of birds), school (of whales), shoal (of fish)

hesk<AJ> *adj.* milkless (of cow)

hesk<CN> *coll.* **+enn** sedges, saw-grass

heskenn *f.* **+ow**, *coll.* **hesk** sedge (one individual plant) *f.* **+ow** saw (tool); **heskenn gadon** chain saw; **heskenn vond** band saw; **heskenn warak** bow saw

heskenna *v.* saw

heski *v.* lose milk, dry up

heskynn *m.* marsh

hesp *m.* **+ow** hasp

hesya *v.* swarm, flock, shoal (of fish)

heudh *adj.* joyful, merry, glad

heudha *v.* be glad, be eased

heudhder *m.* joyfulness, rejoicing, happiness

heudhhe *v.* gladden, ease, make happy; be glad, be eased

heudhik *adj.* glad

hevelebi *v.* liken, make similar

hevelenep *m.* likeness

hevelep *adj.* like, similar *m.*
hevelebow likeness, resemblance, portrait

hevelepter *m.* likeness, similarity, image

heveli *v.* seem

hevis *m.* **+yow** shirt (rough), hair-shirt, blouse, smock, vest

hevisweyth *m.* smocking

hevlyna *adv.* this year

hevva *f.* swarming, flocking, shoaling

hewel *adj.* easily visible, obvious, manifest

heweres *adj.* helpful, auxiliary, ready to help

hewoel *adj.* vigilant

hewul *adj.* practicable

heydh *coll.* **+enn** barley

heydhek *f.* **-egi** barley-field

heyji *plur.* ducks

heyjik *m.* **-igow** duckling

heyl *m.* **+yow** estuary, river-mouth

heylynn *m.* **+ow** creek

hi *pron.* she, it, her (obj.)

hig *m.* **+ow** hook

higenn *f.* **+ow** hook

higenna *v.* hook

hik *m.* **+ow** hiccup

hikas *v.* hiccup

hin<border> *m.* **+yow** border

hin<climate> *f.* climate

hinonieth *f.* climatology

hir *adj.* long, tall, lengthy

hirbedrek *adj.* rectangular, oblong *m.* **hirbedrogow** rectangle, oblong

hirbellder *m.* long-distance

hirbenys *m.* long penance, long fast

hirbrena *v.* buy on hire purchase, rent-to-own (U.S.)

hirdrumm *m.* long ridge

hirder *m.* length, tedium

hireth *f.* longing, nostalgia, yearning

hirethek *adj.* longing, yearning, wistful, homesick

hirgernyas *m.* **-ysi** trumpeter

hirgorn *m.* **hirgern** trumpet

hirgrenn *adj.* cylindrical

hirgylgh *m.* **+yow** ellipse, oval

hirgylghyek *adj.* elliptical, oval

hirhe *v.* lengthen

hirlamma *v.* perform the long jump

hirneth *f.* long time

hiroes *m.* longevity, great age

hirwel *m.* long-sight, hypermetropia

hiryarth *f.* long ridge

ho *int.* ho, stop, halt

hoberjon *m.* habergeon, sleeveless coat of chainmail

hobi *m.* **+s** pony, cob, hobby

hod *m.* hood

hoelan *m.* salt; **hoelan koth** salt once used

hoelanedh *m.* salinity

hoelanek *adj.* salty, saline

hoelaner *m.* **-oryon** salter, salt-maker

hogan *m.* hawthorn

hogen *adv.* still, even, yet, perpetually

hogenn *f.* heap, pie, baked pastry

hogh *m.* **-es** pig, swine, hog

hoghwyw *m.* **+yow** boar-spear

hok *m.* **+ys** hawk

hokya *v.* hesitate, postpone, falter; **heb hokya** without further ado

holya *v.* follow, go after, come after

holyer *m.* **-oryon** follower

homm *pron.* this (f.)

homma *pron.* this one (f.), this woman

honan *m.* self, own; **y honan** *adv.* by himself, on his own; **y honan oll** all on his own

hond *m.* **hons** hound, dog (as term of abuse)

honn *pron.* that (f.)

honna *pron.* that one (f.), that woman
hons *adv.* yonder
hopys *coll.* **+enn** hops
hopysek *coll.* **+egi** hop-garden
hor'benn *m.* **+ow** battering-ram
hora *f.* **horys** whore
hordh *m.* **+es** ram
horn *m.* **hern** iron (metal); **horn margh** horse-shoe
hornek *adj.* ferric, like iron *f.* **-egi** iron-bearing ground
hornell *f.* **+ow** smoothing-iron, iron (appliance)
hornella *v.* iron, press
hornus *adj.* ferrous
hos<duck> *m.* **heyji** duck
hos<hoarse> *adj.* hoarse, husky
hos<hose> *coll.* **+enn** hose (clothing), stockings
hosanow *plur.* hose
hosi *v.* speak hoarsely
hosket *m.* **+ys** hogshead
hosyas *m.* hoarseness
hou *int.* hallo, hey, hi
Howl *m.* Sun, sunshine, sunlight
Howldrehevel *m.* Sunrise, east
Howldrevel *m.* Sunrise, east
howllenn *f.* **+ow** sunshade, parasol, awning
howlsedhes *m.* Sunset, west
howlsplann *m.* sunshine, sunlight
howlwedrow *plur.* sun-glasses
howlyek *adj.* sunny
howtyn *adj.* haughty
hudel *adj.* magical, enchanting, illusory
hudhygel *m.* soot, grime, smut
hudhyglek *adj.* sooty
huder *m.* **-oryon** magician, enchanter, sorcerer
hudores *f.* **+ow** magician, enchantress, sorceress
huk *f.* **+ys** riding-hood, hooded cloak
hulla *m.* nightmare

hun *m.* sleep, slumber
huna *v.* sleep, slumber
hunes *m.* sleep, slumber
huni *pron.* one
hunlev *m.* nightmare
hunros *m.* **+ow** dream, vision
hunrosa *v.* dream
hurlya *v.* hurl
hurlyas *m.* **-ysi** hurler
hus *m.* enchantment, charm, illusion
husa *v.* enchant, charm, beguile
huskosk *m.* hypnotism, mesmerism
hwaff *m.* **+ys** blow, whack, punch
hwannenn *f.* **+ow** flea
hwans *m.* **+ow** desire, longing, wish
hwansa *v.* desire, covet, long for, hanker after
hwansek *adj.* desirous, wishful, longing
hwansus *adj.* desirous
hwar *adj.* meek, gentle, mild, submissive, passive
hware *adv.* immediately, forthwith, at once, right away
hwarhe *v.* civilize, humanize, make gentler
hwarth *m.* laughter
hwarthus *adj.* laughable, comic, ridiculous, funny
hwarvedhyans *m.* **+ow** happening, event
hwarvedhys *adj.* happened, befallen, occurred, taken place, come to pass
hwarvos *v.* happen, befall, occur, take place, come to pass *m.* **+ow** happening, event
hwath *adv.* yet, still, again, once more; **hwath pella** furthermore; **na hwath** not yet, not either
hwatt *m.* **+ys** whack, slap, smack
hwedhel *m.* **hwedhlow** story, tale, fabrication, false report
hwedhlow *plur.* stories, nonsense, tattle, gossip

hwedner *m.* sixpence

hweg *adj.* sweet, dear, pleasant, pleasing, kind, gentle, nice; **+ow** darling

hwegenn *f.* **+ow** pet, darling, sweeting

hweger *f.* **hwegrow** mother-in-law

hwegh *num.* six

hweghkorn *m.* **+yow** hexagon

hweghmis *m.* semester

hwegh-ugens *num.* six score

hweghves *num.* sixth

hwegoll *adj.* darling, sweetest, kindest

hwegrew *m.* icing on cake

hwegrewi *v.* ice a cake

hwegron *m.* father-in-law

hwegynn *m.* **+ow** sweet

hwekter *m.* sweetness, pleasantness, kindness

hwel *m.* **+yow** work, mine-working; **hwelyow fordh** *plur.* road-works

hwelbark *m.* **+ow** industrial estate, industrial park (U.S.)

hweldro *m.* **+yow** revolution (in mechanics)

hwelros *f.* **+ow** flywheel

hwel-sten *m.* tin working

hwenn *coll.* **hwannenn** fleas

hwer *v.* happens

hwerow *adj.* bitter, sharp, harsh

hwerowder *m.* bitterness

hwerthin *v.* laugh; **hwerthin orth** laugh at

hwerydh *plur.* sisters

hwerik *f.* little sister

hwesker *coll.* **+enn** insects

hwetek *num.* sixteen

hwetegves *num.* sixteenth

hwettya *m.* whack, slap, smack

Hwevrer *m.* February

hwi *pron.* you (pl.), ye

hwib *f.* pipe (Mus.)

hwiban *f.* whistling (by mouth)

hwibana *v.* whistle (by mouth)

hwibanowl *f.* whistle (instrument)

hwibanor *m.* **+yon** whistler

hwibon *m.* stork

hwigenn *f.* crumb (of loaf), soft part of bread

hwil *m.* **+es** beetle, chafer

hwilas *v.* seek, search for, try; **hwilas neppyth orth nebonan** seek something from someone

hwilenn *f.* beetle, chafer; **+ow**

hwilessa *v.* catch beetles

hwilresek *m.* orienteering

hwilreseger *m.* **-oryon** orienteer

hwiogenn *f.* **+ow** dinner-cake made of pastry

hwistel *f.* **hwistlow** shrew (mouse)

hwithra *v.* examine, investigate, scrutinize, probe; carry out research; **hwithra orth** look at, examine; **hwithra war** gaze upon

hwithrans *m.* **+ow** research, investigation

hwithrer *m.* **-oryon** researcher, investigator

hwithrores *f.* **+ow** researcher, investigator

hwoer *f.* **hwerydh** sister

hwyflyn *adj.* roaring, blustering

hwyhwi *pron.* you (pl.), ye, yourselves

hwyja *v.* vomit, spue, throw up

hwymm-hwamm *adv.* capriciously, whimsically, slapdash, unsteadily, this way and that

hwynn *coll.* **+enn** weeds

hwynnek *adj.* weedy *f.* **hwynnegi** weed-patch

hwypp *m.* **+ys** whip

hwyppya *v.* whip

hwyrni *v.* hum, buzz, whirr, snore

hwyrnores *f.* **+ow** hornet

hwys *m.* sweat, perspiration

hwysa *v.* sweat, perspire

hwysti *m.* **+ow** sweat-shop

hwystra *v.* whisper

hwystrenn *f.* **+ow** whisper

hwyth *m.* **+ow** blast (of wind), blowing, puff, breath

hwytha *v.* blow, puff, breathe, blast (of wind), play (of a wind instrument)

hwythell *f.* **+ow** whistle, jet (of air)

hwythenn *f.* **+ow** bubble

hwythfi *v.* swell, bubble

hwythfians *m.* swelling, surge of sea

hy *pron.* her, its (f.)

hyg *f.* cheat, swindle

hyga *v.* cheat, tease

hyhi *pron.* her (emphatic), it (f., emphatic)

hyli *m.* brine, salt water, sea-water

hymna *m.* **hymnys** hymn

hynledan *m.* plantain, waybread

hyns *m.* **+yow** road, course, way, path; traffic lane; **hyns dall** blind alley,

hynsa *plur.* fellows, peers

hyns-horn *m.* **hynsyow-horn** railway

hyns-tira *m.* **hynsyow-tira** runway

hys *m.* length, extent

hys-ha-hys *adv.* end-to-end

I

i *pron.* they, them

-i<PL> *suff.* (pl. ending)

-i<VN> *v.* (VN ending)

idhyow *coll.* **+enn** ivy

idhyowek *adj.* ivy-clad *f.* **-egi** ivy-clad place

-ieth *suff.* (fem. abst. noun ending, from noun)

ifarn *m.* **+ow** hell

ifarnek *adj.* hellish

igerell *f.* **+ow** opener

igeri *v.* open, disclose, explain

igolenn *f.* **+ow** whetstone, hone

igor *adj.* open

-ik *suff.* **-igow** (dim. ending)

ilewydh *m.* **+yon** musician

ilow *f.* music, tune, melody

imaj *m.* **+ys** image

imajer *m.* **-oryon** sculptor, carver

imajri *m.* sculpture (in abst. sense), carving

-ir *v.* (impers. pres. ind. ending)

is *prep.* below, under

is- *pref.* lower, sub-, vice-

ischansler *m.* **+s** vice-chancellor

isel *adj.* low, lowly, modest, vulgar; soft (of sound)

iselder *m.* inferiority, lowliness, humility

iseldir *m.* **+yow** lowland

Iseldiryek *adj.* pertaining to the Netherlands, Dutch *m.* Dutch language,

Iseldiryow *plur.* Netherlands

iselhe *v.* lower, abase, degrade

iselheans *m.* lowering, abasement

iselvor *m.* low water

isframweyth *m.* infrastructure, substructure

iskaderyer *m.* vice-chairman

iskell *m.* clear broth, soup, pottage; **iskell kig** stock; **iskell pur** consomme

iskessedhek *m.* **-ogow** sub-committee

islavrek *m.* **-ogow** underpants

islywydh *m.* **+yon** vice-president

islonk *m.* abyss

ispann *m.* **+ow** lining of clothes

ispoynt *m.* **+ow** minimum

isos *adv.* downward, below

issavonek *adj.* sub-standard

isskrifennyas *m.* **-ysi** under-secretary

isstanchya *v.* under-seal

istewisyans *m.* **+ow** by-election
istitel *m.* **istitlow** subtitle
istitla *v.* subtitle
iston *m.* **+yow** line of harmony (e.g. tenor)
istorek *adj.* historical
istori *m.* **+ow** history
istorior *m.* **+yon** historian
istrovannel *adj.* sub-tropical
isyurl *m.* viscount
Italek *adj.* Italian *m.* Italian language
Itali *f.* Italy
-iv *v.* (1st sg. pres. subj. ending)
ivra *m.* darnel, rye-grass, tares
Iwerdhon *f.* Ireland
Iwerdhonek *adj.* Irish *m.* Irish language

J

jag *m.* **+ys** jag, jar (shock), jolt; **jag tredan** electric shock
jakk *m.* **+ow** car jack
jammes *adv.* never
Jamys *name* James
jardin *m.* garden
jarn *m.* garden
jayler *m.* **+s** gaoler
jelatin *m.* gelatine
jenevra *m.* gin (drink)
Jentil *m.* **+ys** Gentile
jentyl *adj.* gentle, pleasing, well-born *m.* **+s** well-born person
jentylys *m.* gentleness, grace
jerkynn *m.* jerkin, jacket short coat
jevan *m.* demon, fiend
jins *m.* jeans
jiraf *m.* **+es** giraffe
jist *m.* **+ys** joist, beam (timber), prop
jogler *m.* **-oryon**, **+s** juggler, buffoon, impostor
jolif *adj.* jolly, lively
Jori *name* George

jorna *m.* **jornyow** day
joust *m.* **+ys** joust
joustya *v.* joust
Jowann *name* John
jowdyn *m.* **+s** rascal, knave, vagrant
jowel *m.* **+ys** jewel
joweler *m.* **-oryon** jeweller
jowl *m.* devil
joy *m.* **joyys** joy
judo *m.* judo
junya *v.* join
juster *m.* **+s** justiciary
justis *m.* **+yow** justice (judge), magistrate
jy *pron.* thee
jydh *m.* day (after **an** or **unn**)
jynn *m.* **+ow**, **+ys** machine, engine, motor, gin (machine)
jynn-amontya *m.* **jynnow-amontya** computer
jynn-diwros *m.* **jynnow-diwros** motor-cycle, motor-bike
jynn-ebrenn *m.* **jynnow-ebrenn** aircraft, aeroplane
jynn-ethenn *m.* **jynnow-ethenn** steam-engine
jynn-glesin *m.* **jynnow-glesin** lawn-mower
jynn-golghi *m.* washing machine
jynn-keber *m.* beam-engine
jynn-krygh *m.* **jynnow-krygh** goffering-iron
jynnji *m.* **+ow** engine-house
jynn-mysi *m.* **jynnow-mysi** reaper (machine)
jynn-palas *m.* **jynnow-palas** excavator
jynn-pryntya *m.* **jynnow-pryntya** printer (machine)
jynn-rolya *m.* **jynnow-rolya** steam-roller
jynnskrifa *v.* type
jynn-skrifa *m.* **jynnow-skrifa** typewriter

jynn-tan *m.* **jynnow-tan** fire-engine

jynn-tenna *m.* **jynnow-tenna** tractor

jynn-toemma *m.* **jynnow-toemma** heater

jynnweyth *f.* machinery, mechanism

jynnweythek *adj.* mechanical

jynnweythor *m.* **+yon** engineer, mechanic

jynn-yskynn *m.* **jynnow-yskynn** lift (elevator)

K (mutations G, H)

kab *m.* **+ow** cab (of lorry)

kabel *m.* blame, censure, accusation

kabester *m.* **-trow** halter, noose, loop

kabla *v.* blame, censure, incriminate

kablus *adj.* guilty, blameworthy, culpable

Kablys *m.* Maundy; **dy' Yow Hablys** Maundy Thursday

kabol *m.* mix-up, medley, hotchpotch

kabolenn *f.* splashing stone

kaboler *m.* **-oryon** stirrer

kaboli *v.* stir, splash, mix

kabolva *f.* mix-up, medley, hotchpotch

kabynn *m.* **+ow** cabin

kacha *m.* **kachys** latch, door-catch

kachya *v.* catch, seize, snatch

kader *adj.* comely, beautiful, pretty

kaderya *v.* take the chair, preside

kaderyer *m.* **-oryon** chairman

kadon *f.* **+yow** chain, bond (link), trace

kador *f.* **+yow** chair, seat

kador-dreth *f.* **kadoryow-treth** deck-chair

kador-herdhya *f.* **kadoryow-herdhya** push-chair

kador-ros *f.* **kadoryow-ros** wheel-chair

kador-vregh *f.* **kadoryow-bregh** armchair

kagal *m.* dung of sheep or goats or rodents, clotted filth on fleece or clothing

kagla *v.* void excrement, spatter with filth

kaja *f.* daisy; **kaja velyn** corn-marigold; **kaja vras** ox-eye daisy

kala *coll.* straw (in bulk)

kala-gweli *coll.* straw bedding

kalamajina *m.* cuckoo ray

Kalann *m.* first of month, calends; **Kalann Genver** New Year's Day; **Kalann Gwav** All Hallows; **Kala' Hedra** first of October; **Kala' Me** May Day

kalavenn *f.* **+ow**, *coll.* **kala** straw

kalennik *m.* New Year's gift, Christmas box

kales *adj.* hard, difficult, severe

kalesenn *f.* **+ow** callosity; **kalesenn gig** tumour

kaleshe *v.* harden

kalesweyth *m.* hardware

kaletter *m.* hardness, difficulty

kalgh<lime> *m.* lime (mineral)

kalgh<MN> *m.* **+yow** penis

kalkar *m.* weever fish

kalkenn *f.* **+ow** father-lasher (fish)

kalkonieth *f.* science of calculation

kalkor *m.* **+yon** calculator (human), mathematician

kalkya<calculate> *v.* calculate

kalkya<caulk> *v.* caulk a ship

kalkyans *m.* **+ow** calculation (an individual)

kall<AJ> *adj.* cunning

kall<MN> *m.* tungstate of iron

kallder *m.* cunning

kallenn *f.* **+ow** iron ore

kalmynsi *m.* stillness, tranquillity, calm

kals *m.* heap, abundance; **kals meyn** heap of stones

kalter *f.* **+yow** kettle

kamera *m.* **+s** camera

kamm<bent> *adj.* bent, crooked, distorted, wrong *m.* **+ow** wrong, trespass; person who is morally crooked

kamm<step> *m.* **+ow** step, pace, a bit

kamma *v.* bend, curve, writhe

kammas *f.* bend, bay

Kammbronn *place* Camborne

kammder *m.* crookedness

kammdhavas *m.* sheep-track

kammdremena *v.* transgress (intrans.), trespass

kammdybi *v.* err in thought

kammdybyans *m.* **+ow** error, mistaken opinion

kammek *f.* **-ogow** rim, felloe (rim of wheel)

kammenn *f.* way *adv.* in no way, not at all, no-wise; **kammenn vydh** in no way at all

kammfydhwas *m.* **-wesyon** confidence trickster, conman (U.S.)

kammfydhweyth *m.* **+ow** confidence trick

kammgemmeryans *m.* mistake

kammgolm *m.* **+ow** granny-knot

kammgonvedhes *v.* misunderstand

kammgryjyans *m.* heresy

kammgryjyk *adj.* heretical *m.* **-jygyon** heretic

kammhynsek *adj.* unjust, unrighteous, malignant

kammhynseth *f.* injustice, wrong, injury

kammin *v.* grimace

kammleverel *v.* mispronounce

kammneves *f.* rainbow, spectrum

kammnevesel *adj.* spectral (of spectra)

kammomdhoen *v.* misbehave

kammskoedhek *adj.* crooked-shouldered

kammskrif *m.* mistake in writing,

kammskrifa *v.* make a mistake in writing, write wrongly, miswrite

kammva *f.* **+ow** stile

kammva-dro *f.* **kammvaow-tro** turnstile

kammvreusi *v.* misjudge

kammweyth *m.* misdeed, trespass, error

kammweythres *m.* misdeed, wrongdoing

kammwonis *v.* blunder, bungle *m.* blunder

kammworthybi *v.* reply impertinently, answer back

kammworthyp *m.* impertinence

kammwrians *m.* **+ow** misdeed, error

kammwul *v.* do ill, err, make a mistake

kamp *m.* **+ow**, **+ys** pleasure camp, bivouac

kamp-hav *m.* **kampow-hav** holiday camp, summer camp (U.S.)

kampoell *m.* **+ow** mention, comment

kampoella *v.* mention, refer

kampoellans *m.* **+ow** reference (e.g. in a letter)

kampoellys *adj.* mentioned, aforesaid

kampva *f.* **+ow** camp-site

kampya *v.* camp, encamp, bivouac

kampyer *m.* **-oryon** champion

kampyorieth *f.* championship

kams *f.* **+ow** surplice, alb

kan *f.* **+ow** song, poem; **kan werin** folk-song

kana *v.* sing, sound (of an instrument)

kanabyer *plur.* hemp-field

kanel *f.* **kanolyow** channel, canal, water-channel, inlet of sea; television channel

kanell *m.* spigot

kaner *m.* **-oryon** singer

kangour *m.* a hundred men

kangourou *m.* kangaroo

kanjon *m.* **+s** freak, abnormal person, wretch

kanker *m.* **kankres** crab, cancer, corrosion

kankweyth *adv.* a hundred times

kanmel *v.* laud, praise highly, eulogize

kanmeula *m.* eulogy

kann *adj.* bright white *m.* brightness, shine, fluorspar

kanna<bleach> *v.* bleach

kanna<can> *m.* **kannow** can, tin (container)

kanna-pobas *m.* baking tin, baking pan (U.S.)

kanna-rostya *m.* roasting-tin, roasting pan (U.S.)

kannas *f.* **+ow** messenger, ambassador, envoy

kanna-tesenn *m.* cake-tin, cake pan (U.S.)

kanna-torth *m.* loaf tin, bread pan (U.S.)

kannatti *m.* **+ow** embassy, mission-house

kanndir *m.* quartz

kanon *m.* **+yow** cannon

kanores *f.* **+ow** singer

kanou *m.* **+yow** canoe

kans *num.* **+ow** hundred; **kans bloedh** *phr.* hundred years old; **kans kolm** *m.* knotgrass

kansblydhen *f.* **kansblydhynyow** century, hundred years

kansewin *m.* **+es** orpine (plant)

kanspeuns *m.* hundred pound weight

kansplek *adv.* hundredfold

kanspoes *m.* hundredweight

kansrann *f.* **+ow** percentage, per cent

kanstell *f.* **+ow** basket

kanstroes *m.* centipede

kansves *num.* hundredth

kansvil *m.* **+yow** hundred thousand

kanter *m.* **kantrow** frame for fishing

kantol *f.* **+yow** candle, spark-plug; **kantol goer** wax tallow candle; **kantol soev** wax tallow candle

kantolbrenn *m.* **+yer** candle-stick

kantoler *m.* **+yow** chandelier, candelabrum

kanvas *m.* canvas

kapa *f.* cape (clothing)

kappa *m.* **kappow** cap

kapten *m.* **+yon** captain

kapyas *m.* writ of arrest, warrant for arrest

kar *m.* **kerens** kinsman, friend; **kar ogas** near relative

kara *v.* love, like, care for; **dell y'm kyrri** *adv.* please

karadow *adj.* beloved, loving, lovable *m.* loved one; **+yon**

karadewder *m.* lovableness, loving-kindness, amiability, fondness

karavan *m.* **+s** caravan, trailer (U.S.)

kardinal *m.* cardinal

karer *m.* **-oryon** boy-friend, lover

kares *f.* **+ow** girl-friend, lover

Karesk *place* Exeter

karetys *coll.* **+enn** carrots

karg *m.* **+ow** load, cargo, burden

karga *v.* load

karghar *m.* **+ow** fetter, shackle

karghara *v.* shackle, pillory, put in stocks

karghar-horn *m.* gyves, handcuffs

karghar-prenn *m.* stocks

karleyth *f.* **+ow** smooth ray, skate; **karleyth trylost** smooth ray

karn<hoof> *m.* **+ow** hoof; **karn kollan** knife-handle

karn<tor> *m.* **+ow** rock-pile, tor, cairn, underlying rock

karnedh *m.* **+ow** heap (of rocks)

karnedhek *adj.* rocky, abounding in cairns

karnek<hoofed> *adj.* hoofed

karnek<rocky> *adj.* rocky *f.* **-egi** rocky ground

karol *m.* **+yow** dance to sung music

karoli *v.* dance to sung music

karow *m.* **kerwys** stag; **karow ergh** reindeer

karpenter *m.* **-oryon** carpenter

karr *m.* **kerri** car, cart; **karr bonk** dodgem; **karr gobrena** hire car, rental car (U.S.); **karr kreslu** police car

karrak *m.* **+ys** carrack (great ship)

karrbons *m.* **+ow** cartbridge

karrdeyl *m.* manure

karregi *plur.* rocks

karrek *f.* **kerrek, karregi** rock; **karrek sans** rock altar

karrhyns *m.* **+yow** cart-track, carriageway, highway; **karrhyns dewblek** dual carriageway, divided highway (U.S.)

karrigell *f.* **+ow** trolley (e.g. in supermarket), caddy

karr-klavji *m.* **kerri-klavji** ambulance

karrji *m.* **+ow** garage, cart-house

karrostel *m.* **+yow** motel

karr-resek *m.* **kerri-resek** racing-car

karr-tan *m.* motor-car

karrvil *m.* **+es** carthorse

kartenn *f.* **+ow** card; **kartenn Nadelik** Christmas card

kartenn-bost *f.* **kartennow-post** post-card

kartenn-gresys *f.* **kartennow-kresys** credit-card

kartennik *m.* **-igow** small card

kartenn-vona *f.* **kartennow-mona** cash-card, ATM card (U.S.)

karth *m.* **+yon** purge, scouring, cleansing; **karth ethnek** ethnic cleansing

kartha *v.* scour, purge, cleanse, rid

karthprenn *m.* plough-staff

karthpib *m.* **+ow** sewer-pipe

karya *v.* cart, transport

karyans *m.* transport, carriage (act of carrying)

karyn *m.* carrion, carcase

kas<case> *m.* instance, case

kas<hate> *m.* hate, hatred, hostility; misery, wretchedness

kas<war> *f.* **+ow** battle, fight, war

kasa *v.* hate, abhor

kasadewder *m.* hatefulness

kasadow *adj.* hateful, detestable, repulsive

kasbeler *m.* wintercress

kasek *f.* **kasegi** mare; **kasek asyn** she-ass

kasek-koes *f.* **kasegi-koes** woodpecker

kasel *f.* **+yow** arm-pit, aisle underarm (U.S.)

kaskleudh *m.* **+yow** entrenchment, trench (for warfare)

kaskorn *m.* **kaskern** battle-horn

kaskyrgh *m.* **+ow** campaign

kaskyrghes *v.* campaign

kaslann *f.* battlefield

kaslys *f.* headquarters (military)

kaslu *m.* **+yow** regiment

kasor *m.* **-oryon** warrior

kaspoel *f.* battle-axe

kaspows *f.* coat of mail, bullet-proof jacket

kast *m.* **+ys** trick, dodge

kastell *m.* **kastylli** castle, fortress, hill-fort; village; tor; **kastell tewes** sand-castle

kastiga *v.* flog, thrash, castigate

kastik *m.* flogging, castigation

kasul *m.* chasuble

kasvargh *m.* **kasvergh** war-horse, charger (horse)

kaswydh *m.* thicket

kasyer *m.* large sieve

kath *f.* **kathes** cat; **kath helik** catkin; **kath vlewek** hairy caterpillar

kathes *f.* **+ow** she-cat

kathik *f.* **-igow** kitten

kathji *m.* **+ow** cattery

katholik *adj.* Catholic

kav *m.* **+yow** cave

kavanskeus *m.* evasion, subterfuge

kavanskeusa *v.* evade, shirk

kavas *m.* **+ow** vessel (container), can

kavasa *v.* can

kavoes *v.* get, find, acquire, procure, obtain; have; **kavoes dre nerth** extort

kavow *plur.* grief, trouble, sorrow

kawgh *m.* excrement, dung

kawgha *v.* void excrement, defecate

kawghbib *f.* **+ow** foul sewer

kawghla *m.* privy

kawghti *m.* **+ow** privy

kawghwas *m.* **-wesyon** filthy fellow

kaws *m.* cause

kawsya *v.* cause

kawser *m.* **-oryon** cause (person who causes something to happen)

kay *m.* **kayow** quay, wharf, platform (of railway station)

ke<go> *v.* go (impv.)

ke<hedge> *m.* **keow** hedge, fence, low wall of earth and stone; **bos war an ke** abstain (in a vote); **war an ke** abstaining (in a vote)

ke- *pref.* con-

keas *v.* hedge, enclose, shut; **keas mes** exclude, preclude

keber *f.* **kebrow** beam (timber), rafter, joist

kebrek *adj.* abounding in planks

kedhor *m.* pubic hair

kedhorieth *f.* puberty

kedhorva *f.* groin

kedhow *m.* mustard

kedrynn *f.* trouble, quarrel, dispute

kedrynna *v.* quarrel

keek *adj.* hedged

keffrys *adv.* also, likewise, moreover, too, as well

keffrysyas *m.* **-ysi** ally, confederate

keger *coll.* hemlock

keghik *m.* little cap

kegi *v.* cook

kegin<kitchen> *f.* **+ow** kitchen

kegin<jay> *f.* **+es** jay

kegin-geyn *f.* **+ow-keyn** scullery

keginer *m.* **-oryon** cook

keginieth *f.* cookery, cuisine

kegis *coll.* **+enn** hemlock, umbelliferous plant; **kegis hweg** celery

kegisek *adj.* abounding in hemlock *f.* **-egi** place abounding in hemlock

kegys *adj.* cooked

kehaval *adj.* similar, equal, corresponding *adv.* alike

keher *m.* **+ow** muscle, flesh

keherek *adj.* muscular

keheveli *v.* compare

kehys *adj.* of equal length; **kehys ha** *phr.* the same length as

kehysedh *m.* **+ow** extent, equator, equinoctial (celestial equator)

kekeffrys *adv.* also, alike, withal, as well

kekemmys *adv.* as many as, as much as *pron.* whoever, whatever

kel *adj.* hidden *m.* **+yow** hiding, shelter, bower; **yn-dann gel** *adv.* in secret

keladow *m.* concealment, secrecy, subterfuge

kelegel *m.* chalice

keler *coll.* **+enn** earthnuts, pignuts

keles *v.* hide, conceal, keep secret

kell *f.* **+ow** cell (Biol.); **+ow,** *dual* **diwgell** testicle

kellek *adj.* uncastrated

kellester *m.* flint

kelli<grove> *f.* **kelliow** grove, copse, holt

kelli<lose> *v.* lose, forfeit

kellian *f.* small grove

kellignowwydh *coll.* nut-grove

kelliwik *f.* **-igow** grove

kellyllik *f.* **-igow** penknife

kellynn *m.* duckweed

kelmi *v.* tie, bind, lash, knot; **kelmi orth** tie to

kelorn *m.* **kelern** bucket, pail

Kelt *m.* **+yon** Celt

Keltek *adj.* Celtic

kelyn *plur.* pups, puppies, whelps

kelynik *m.* little pup

kelynn *coll.* **+enn** holly-trees, holly; **kelynn byghan** butcher's broom; **kelynn Frynk** barberry; **kelynn mor** sea-holly; **kelynn treth** sea-holly

kelynnek *adj.* abounding in holly *f.* **-egi** holly-grove

kelyon *coll.* **+enn** flies; **kelyon kig** blowflies, bluebottles; **kelyon margh** horse flies, gadflies

kelyonek *adj.* full of flies, flyblown

Kembra *f.* Wales

Kembrek *adj.* Welsh *m.* Welsh language

Kembroes *f.* **+ow** Welshwoman

Kembro *m.* **+yon** Welshman

kemmeradewder *m.* acceptability

kemmeradow *adj.* acceptable

kemmeres *v.* take, receive; **kemmeres yn-mes** remove

kemmeryans *m.* reception

kemmyn *adj.* common, vulgar *m.* **+yon** commoner

kemmynegor *m.* **+yon** communist

kemmynegorek *adj.* communist

kemmynegores *f.* **+ow** communist

kemmynegoreth *f.* communism

kemmynieth *f.* community

kemmynn *m.* **+ow** bequest, legacy, endowment

kemmynna *v.* bequeath, endow, leave by will

kemmynnadow *m.* bequest

kemmynneth *f.* **+ow** commendation

kemmynnro *m.* **-rohow** legacy

kemmys *adj.* so much, so, as, as much as, as many as

kemmysk *m.* mixture, blend, alloy; miscellany, variety

kemmyska *v.* mix, mingle, blend

kemmyskreydh *adj.* hybrid

kempenn *adj.* neat, tidy, orderly

kempenna *v.* tidy, set in order

kempennses *m.* tidiness, neatness

kemper *m.* **+yow** junction of streams

kemusur *m.* symmetry, proportion *adj.* symmetrical, fitting

ken<cause> *m.* cause, reason, lawsuit

ken<other> *adj.* other, another, different, else *adv.* otherwise

kenans *m.* litigation

kenbrederedh *m.* confraternity

kenderow *m.* **kenderwi** cousin (male)

kendevryon *m.* meeting of waters

kendon *f.* debt, liability; **kavoes kendon** *v.* borrow

kendoner *m.* **-oryon** debtor

kendonores *f.* **+ow** debtor

kenedhel *f.* **-dhlow** nation
kenedhlegi *v.* nationalize
kenedhlek *adj.* national
kenedhloger *m.* **-oryon** nationalist
kenedhlogeth *f.* nationality
kenek *m.* ring-worm
keniterow *f.* **keniterwi** cousin (female)
keniver *adj.* as many, so many
kenkia *v.* contend
kenkidh *m.* **+yow** second home, imparked residence
kenlyther *m.* **+ow** covering letter
kenn *m.* skin, hide, peel
kenna *v.* coat with film
kennek *adj.* scummy
kennenn *f.* **+ow** film, cataract (on eye)
kennerth *m.* encouragement
kennertha *v.* encourage, boost
kennin *coll.* **+enn** garlic, ramsons; **kennin ewinek** garlic
kenninek *adj.* abounding in garlic *f.* **-egi** place abounding in garlic
kenow *m.* puppy
kensynsi *v.* keep hold of
kenter *f.* **kentrow** nail, spike;
kentevynn *m.* concrete
kentra *v.* nail, drive in a spike; **kentra orth** nail to
kentreni *v.* become maggoty
kentrek *adj.* spur-shaped
kentrevek *adj.* neighbouring *m.* **-ogyon** neighbour
kentreveth *f.* **+ow** neighbourhood
kentrevoges *f.* **+ow** neighbour
kentrevogeth *f.* neighbourliness
kentrewi *v.* nail with many nails
kentrik *f.* **-igow** tack (nail), small nail
kentrynn *m.* **+ow** spur (for boot)
kentrynna *v.* spur
kenwerth *m.* commerce, trade

kenwertha *v.* trade
kenwerthel *adj.* commercial
kenwerther *m.* **-oryon** tradesman
kenwystel *m.* **kenwystlow** bet, wager
kenwystla *v.* bet, wager
kenyades *f.* **+ow** professional female singer
kenyas *m.* **-ysi** professional male singer
kenys *m.* singing, sounding (of instruments), crowing (of cock)
kepar *adv.* in the same way, like, alike
ker<dear> *adj.* dear, costly, expensive, cherished
ker<fort> *f.* **+yow** fort, camp (earthwork), hill-fort
kera *v.* fortify (strengthen a defence-work)
kerdh *m.* **+ow** walk, expedition, journey
kerdher *m.* **-oryon** pedestrian, walker
kerdhes *v.* walk
kerdhin *coll.* **+enn** mountain-ash
kerdhva *f.* **+ow** footpath, promenade, parade
keredh *f.* rebuke, reproach, chastisement, reproof
keredhi *v.* rebuke, reproach, reprove, tell off
kerens *plur.* kinsmen, parents
kerensa *f.* love, charity, friendship, affection
kerensedhek *adj.* loving, beloved
keres *coll.* **+enn** cherries
keresik *adj.* dear *m.* **-igyon** sweetheart, darling, dear one
kergh *coll.* **+enn** oats
kerghdir *m.* oatlands
kerghek *f.* **-egi** oat-field
kerghwels *m.* oat-grass
kerghydh *f.* **+yon** heron
kern *plur.* horns

kerneth *f.* dearness, expensiveness

Kerneweger *m.* **-oryon** Cornish speaker

Kernewek *adj.* Cornish *m.* Cornish language; **Kernewek Dasserghys** Revived Cornish; **Kernewek Diwedhes** Late Cornish; **Kernewek Koth** Old Cornish; **Kernewek Kres** Middle Cornish

Kernewekhe *v.* Cornicize, make Cornish

Kernewes *f.* **+ow** Cornishwoman

kernik *f.* **-igow** little horn

Kernow *f.* Cornwall *m.* **+yon** Cornishman

kernyas *m.* **-ysi** horn-player, horner

kerrek *plur.* rocks

kersyek *adj.* abounding in reeds *f.* reed-bed; **-egi**

kert *m.* **+ow**, **+ys** lorry, cart, truck (U.S.); **kert torrva** breakdown lorry

kerth *f.* **+ow** property, possession

kervya *v.* carve

kerweyth *m.* fortification, earthwork

kerwys *plur.* stags

kerya *v.* cobble, make shoes, mend shoes

keryades *f.* **+ow** lover

keryas *m.* **-ysi** lover

keryn *f.* **+yow** tub, butt (container), open barrel

keryer *m.* **-oryon** shoemaker, cobbler

kes *adj.* hedged

kes- *pref.* co-

keschanj *m.* exchange

keschanjya *v.* exchange

keser *coll.* hail (weather)

keserenn *f.* **+ow**, *coll.* **keser** hailstone

keskalar *m.* **+ow** condolence

keskalari *v.* condole

keskan *f.* **+ow** concert

keskar *adj.* scattered *v.* disperse, scatter *m.* dispersion, scattering

keskelmi *v.* liaise; **keskelmi orth** liaise with

keskeltek *adj.* inter-Celtic

keskerdh *m.* organized walk, procession, march

keskerdher *m.* **-oryon** marcher (male)

keskerdhes *v.* walk together, march

keskerdhores *m.* **+ow** marcher (female)

keskewsel *v.* converse (speech)

keski *v.* exhort, admonish, tell off

kesklena *v.* cling together

keskodhevel *v.* sympathize, condole

keskolm *v.* liaison

keskolonn *adj.* unanimous, in accord

keskomunya *v.* communicate

keskomunyans *v.* **+ow** communication

keskorra *v.* collate, assemble (trans.), put together

keskoweth *m.* **+a** companion, associate

keskows *m.* **+ow** conversation

keskristyon *m.* **keskristonyon** fellow Christian

keskusulyans *m.* **+ow** conference; **keskusulyans barrek** summit conference

keslamm *m.* **+ow** coincidence

keslamma *v.* coincide

kesles *m.* mutual interest

keslinek *adj.* cognate, collateral

keslinel *adj.* collinear

keslowena *f.* congratulations

keslowenhe *v.* congratulate

kesoberi *v.* co-operate, collaborate

kesoberer *m.* **+yon** collaborator, co-worker

kesordena *v.* co-ordinate

kesordenor *m.* **+yon** co-ordinator

kespar *m.* **+ow** spouse, mate (married person)

kespoes *m.* equilibrium, poise

kesplegadow *adj.* compatible

kesreynya *v.* reign together

Kesroesweyth *m.* Internet

kessedhek *m.* **-sedhogow** committee

kesseni *v.* harmonize, accord

kessenyans *m.* harmony, euphony; agreement

kesskrifa *v.* correspond

kesskrifer *m.* **-oryon** correspondent

kesson *adj.* harmonious, euphonious; consistent

kessonenn *f.* **+ow** consonant

kessonennel *adj.* consonantal

kesstrif *m.* competition

kesstrivor *m.* **+yon** competitor

kesstrivya *v.* compete

kessydhya *v.* punish, chastise, castigate

kessydhyans *m.* punishment, retribution

kest *f.* **+ow** narrow-mouthed basket

kestav *m.* **+ow** contact

kestava *v.* contact

kesten *coll.* **+enn** chestnut-trees

kestya *v.* trick

kesunnses *m.* amalgam

kesunya *v.* unite, combine, merge

kesunyans +ow *m.* union, combination, merger; **kesunyans lavur** trade union

kesva *f.* **+ow** assembly, board (group of people); **Kesva an Taves Kernewek** Cornish Language Board; **kesva apposyans** examination board; **Kesva Tornyaseth Kernow** Cornwall Tourist Board

kesvywa *v.* live together, cohabit

kesvywnans *m.* living together, cohabitation

keswel *m.* **+yow** interview

kesweles *v.* interview

keswlasek *adj.* international

kesya *v.* unite

kesyewa *v.* yoke together

keth<same> *adj.* same, identical

keth<slave> *adj.* servile, subject, dependent *m.* **+yon** slave (male), serf, bondman

kethes *f.* **+ow** slave (female), bondmaid

kethneth *f.* slavery, servitude

kethsam *adj.* selfsame, identical

kethwas *m.* **-wesyon** bondman

kettell *adv.* as soon as

kettep *adj.* cach, every; **yn kettep penn** *phr.* everyone, everybody; **yn kettep poll** everyone, everybody; **yn kettep gwas** *phr.* to the last man

kettestenn *f.* **+ow** context

kettoeth *adv.* as soon as; **kettoeth ha'n ger** instantly

kettuel *adj.* parallel

keudh *m.* sorrow, grief, travail

keudhesik *adj.* sorry, contrite, repentant

keudhesigeth *f.* contrition, repentance, regret

keudhesikhe *v.* cause to repent

keudhi *v.* grieve, make sorry

keugh *m.* **+yon** grandfather

keun<dogs> *plur.* dogs

keun<reeds> *coll.* reeds, rushes

keunegenn *f.* **+ow** bog, reed-bed

keunek *f.* **-egi** reed-bed, marsh (reedy)

keunji *m.* **+ow** kennel (for several dogs), doghouse (U.S.)

keunys *coll.* **+enn** firewood, fuel

keunysek *adj.* abounding in firewood *f.* **-egi** place abounding in firewood

keunysenn *f.* **+ow,** *coll.* **keunys** piece of firewood, billet (piece of wood),

keunyser *m.* **-oryon** fuel-gatherer (male)

keunysores *f.* **+ow** fuel-gatherer (female)

keunyssa *v.* gather firewood

keur *m.* **+yow** choir

keurgan *f.* **+ow** chant, choral song

keus *m.* **+yow** cheese

keusveydh *m.* cheese whey

keuswask *f.* cheese-press; **An Geuswask** The Cheesewring

kevals *m.* **+yow** joint, articulation

kevambos *m.* **+ow** contract, covenant, treaty, agreement

kevammok *m.* battle, fight

kevannedhi *v.* occupy

kevar *m.* **+yow** joint-tillage

kevaras *v.* plough together

Kevardhu *m.* December

kevarghewi *v.* invest

kevarwoedh *m.* guidance, direction, information

kevarwoedha *v.* direct, guide, indicate

kevarwoedher *m.* **+yon** guide (male)

kevarwoedhores *f.* **+ow** guide (female)

kevarwoedhyades *f.* **+ow** director (female)

kevarwoedhyans *m.* guidance

kevarwoedhyas *m.* **-ysi** director (male)

kevelek *m.* **-oges** woodcock

kevelekka *v.* shoot woodcock

kevelin *m.* **+yow** cubit

kevnis *coll.* **+enn** spiders

kevoes *adj.* contemporary; **kevoes gans** of the same age as, contemporary with

kevoeth *m.* **+ow** power

kevoethek *adj.* powerful, mighty

kevogas *adj.* adjacent

kevradh *m.* **+ow** rate; **kevradh chanj** rate of exchange; **kevradh difyk** lapse-rate; **kevradh oker** rate of interest; **kevradh toll** rate of tax

kevrang *f.* **+ow** hundred (land unit)

kevrenn *f.* **+ow** share, dividend; fastening, link

kevrenna *v.* share, divide

kevrenner *m.* **-oryon** participator, shareholder

kevrennek *adj.* participating, associated *m.* **-ogyon** shareholder

kevres *m.* **+ow** series, sequence

kevresek *adj.* serial, sequential

kevresell *f.* **+ow** sequencer

kevri *v.* contribute

kevriv *m.* **+ow** score (in game)

kevriyas *m.* **kevriysi** contributor

kevrin *m.* **+yow** mystery, secret

kevrinek *adj.* mysterious, occult, secret

kevro *m.* **kevrohow** contribution

kevryllys *adj.* corrugated

kevysta *f.* seat

kevywi *m.* **+ow** party, feast

kevywya *v.* hold a party, feast together

kevywyas *m.* **-ysi** party-goer, table companion

kew *adj.* hollow *f.* **+yow** enclosure, hollow

kewar *adj.* correct, exact, precise; **yn kewar** exactly

kewargh *coll.* **+enn** hemp (plants), marijuana

kewarghlenn *f.* canvas

kewer *f.* weather

kewera *v.* fit, fulfil, keep a promise

keweras *m.* fulfilment, perfection

kewerder *m.* accuracy, correctness, precision

keweronieth *f.* meteorology

keweyth *m.* hedging

keworra *v.* add

keworrans *m.* **+ow** addition
keworransel *adj.* additional
kewsel *v.* speak, talk, converse;
kewsel orth speak to
kewydh *coll.* brushwood, hedging
keyn *m.* **+ow** back, ridge, keel;
keyn dorn back of hand; **keyn
lomm** bare-backed
keyndir *m.* **+yow** background
keyndreynek *m.* **-oges**
stickleback
keynek *adj.* strong-backed *m.* **-oges**
shad (fish)
keynres *m.* torrent, brook
keynvor *m.* ocean; **Keynvor
Atlantek** Atlantic Ocean; **Keynvor
Eyndek** Indian Ocean; **Keynvor
Hebask** Pacific Ocean
ki *m.* **keun** dog, hound
kib *f.* cup, receptacle
kibell *f.* **+ow** bath, tub
kibya *v.* snatch
kidell *m.* **+ow** stake-net
ki-deves *m.* **keun-deves**
sheepdog
kig *m.* **+yow** meat, flesh; **kig bewin**
beef; **kig mogh** pork; **kig yn
kneus** physically; **kig yar** chicken
meat
kiga *v.* grow flesh
kigbrenn *m.* **+yer** skewer
kiger *m.* **-oryon** butcher
kigereth *f.* butchery (trade)
kigliw *adj.* flesh-coloured
kikti *m.* **+ow** butcher's shop
kigver *m.* **+yow** fleshhook, skewer
kiji *m.* **+ow** kennel (for one dog)
kil<nook> *m.* **+yer** nook, recess,
back
kil<skittle> *m.* **+ys**, **+yow** skittle,
ninepin, bowling pin (U.S.)
kila<MN> *m.* companion, mate (pal);
y gila *pron.* the other (m.)
kila<VN> *v.* recede, draw back
kilans *m.* recession

kilbenn *m.* back of the head
kildenn *m.* retreat, recoil, withdrawal
kildenna *v.* pull back, retreat, recoil,
withdraw, reverse
kildhans *m.* **-dhens** molar tooth
kildro *f.* **+yow** backward turn, ruse
kilenn *f.* **+ow** nook
kilgi *m.* **kilgeun** coward, sneak
kilogramm *m.* **+ow** kilogram
kilweytha *v.* work backwards in
mine
kinyewel *v.* dine
kinyow *m.* **kinyewow** dinner
kiogh *f.* **+yon** snipe
kisya *v.* destroy, damage
klabytter *m.* **+s** bittern
klamder *m.* faint, numbness
klamdera *v.* faint, wilt, lose
consciousness
klapp *m.* chatter, gabble, babble;
syns dha glapp *phr.* hold thy
tongue
klappya *v.* chatter, gabble, babble,
jabber
klappyer *m.* **+s** chatterer, gabbler,
talkative person
klas *m.* **+ow**, **+ys** class, category
klasek *adj.* classic
klasya *v.* classify
klasyans *m.* **+ow** classification
klatter *m.* noisy chatter
klattra *v.* talk noisily, chatter, clatter
klav *adj.* sick, ill, sore *m.* **klevyon**
sick person; **klav diberthys**
separated leper
klavji *m.* **+ow** hospital
klavjior *m.* **+yon** male nurse
klavjiores *f.* **+ow** female nurse
klavor *m.* leprosy
klavorek *adj.* leprous *m.* **-ogyon**
leper
kledh *adj.* left (opposite of right) *m.*
North
kledha *m.* **kledhedhyow** sword;
kledha byghan dagger, poinard;

kledha kamm scimitar; **kledha kromm** cutlass; **kledha meur** claymore

kledh-barth *m.* North, northern side

kledhek *adj.* left-handed

kledher *coll.* **kledhrenn** hand-rail, rail

kledhevor *m.* **+yon** swordsman (amateur)

kledhevyas *m.* **-ysi** swordsman (professional)

kledhya *v.* wield a sword

klefni *m.* lameness

kleger *m.* **+ow** cliff, precipice, crag

klegerek *adj.* cliffed, precipitous, craggy

klegh *plur.* bells

kleghi *coll.* **+enn** icicles

kleghik *m.* little bell

kleghti *m.* **+ow** belfry

kleghtour *m.* **+yow** belfry, steeple

klem *m.* **+ys** defence, counterclaim

kler *adj.* pure, clear, spotless; evident

klerder *m.* clearness, clarity, transparency

klerfordh *f.* **+ow** clearway, expressway

klerhe *v.* clear, brighten; clarify

klerji *coll.* the learned, clergy

kleryon *m.* **+s** clarion

kleudh *m.* **+yow** ditch, trench, excavation

kleudhya *v.* dig a trench

kleves *m.* **+ow** illness, sickness, malady; **kleves an myghtern** scrofula; **kleves bras** leprosy; **kleves kogh** scarlet fever, scarlatina; **kleves meur** leprosy; **kleves seson** ague, malaria

kleys *m.* **+yow** trench, ditch

kloeregieth *f.* clerkship, ministry

kloerek *m.* cleric, clergyman, clerk

kloes *f.* **+yow** hurdle, fence, crate, trellis, lattice, rack, harrow

kloes-ayra *f.* **kloesyow-ayra** airing rack

kloes-kras *f.* **kloesyow-kras** toast-rack

kloes-platyow *f.* **kloesyow-platyow** plate-rack

kloes-syger *f.* **kloesyow-syger** drainer (rack)

kloesya *v.* harrow

klof *adj.* lame

klofi *v.* go lame

klog *f.* crag, cliff

klogh *m.* **klegh** bell; **klogh an eos** harebell; **klogh an marow** death knell; **klogh dybri** refectory bell; **klogh meur** church bell

kloghbrennyer *plur.* gallows

klok *m.* **+ys** cloak

klokk *m.* **+ow** clock

klokkweyth *m.* clockwork

klopenn *m.* **+ow** skull, numskull

kloppek *adj.* lame, limping *m.* **-ogyon** one who limps

kloppya *v.* limp, hobble

klor *adj.* mild, meek, modest

klorder *m.* mildness, modesty

klos *adj.* enclosed, closed, shut *m.* **+yow**, **+ys** enclosure, close, precinct

klosniver *m.* **+ow** quota

klout *m.* **+ys** clout, blow, patch; **klout bolghenn** tripe

kloutya *v.* patch

klow *m.* lock (of door)

kloyster *m.* **kloysters** cloister

klun *f.* **+yow**, *dual* **diwglun** hip, haunch

klus *m.* **+yow** heap, roost

klusya *v.* roost

klyji *m.* toffee

klyjya *v.* stick, clutch, cleave

klyket *m.* latch

klys *adj.* snug, cosy, sheltered

klysa *v.* make snug, shelter

klyswydh *coll.* **+enn** shelter-belt, sheltering trees
klyw *m.* sense of hearing
klywans *m.* hearing
klywes *v.* hear, feel; **klywes gans** hear from
klywwelyek *adj.* audio-visual
knakk *int.* snap *adv.* immediately
knegh *m.* **+yow** hillock, mound
kneus *coll.* **+enn** skin
knias *v.* gnaw
knouk *m.* **+ys** knock
knoukya *v.* knock
know *coll.* **+enn** nuts
knowa *v.* gather nuts
knowek *adj.* nutty *f.* **-egi** nut-grove
knowenn *f.* **+ow**, *coll.* **know** nut (Bot.); **knowenn basti** Brazil nut; **knowenn dhor** peanut, groundnut; **knowenn frynk** walnut;
knowwydhenn *f.* **+ow**, *coll.* **know** nut-tree
knyv *m.* **+ow** fleece
knyvyas *v.* shear
kober *m.* copper
koberenn *f.* **+ow** copper coin
koberweyth *m.* copperwork
kocha *m.* **kochow, kochys** coach, stage-coach, carriage (of train); **kocha dybri** dining-car
kodenn *f.* **+ow** code
kodh *f.* **+ow** pod, husk; **kodh fav** bean pod; **kodh pys** peasepod
koedh<fall> *m.* fall
koedh<PV> *v.* it behoves; **y koedh dhymm mos** *phr.* I ought to go, it behoves me to go
koedha *v.* fall, happen, befall
koeg *adj.* empty, worthless, vain *m.* **+yon** worthless person
koegas *m.* worthless person
koeglinas *f.* **+enn** dead-nettles
koel *f.* omen, belief

koela *v.* trust, lend, loan; **koela orth** trust, pay heed to
koelans *m.* **+ow** loan
koelyek *m.* **-ogyon** soothsayer, fortune-teller, diviner
koelyoges *f.* **+ow** soothsayer, fortune-teller, diviner
koen *f.* **+yow** late dinner
koena *v.* take late dinner
koer *coll.* **+enn** wax; **koer selya** sealing-wax
koera *v.* wax
koerenn *f.* **+ow**, *coll.* **koer** cake of wax
koes *m.* **+ow** wood (as trees), forest
koesek *adj.* woody
koesfinel *coll.* wild thyme
koeswik *f.* **-igow** forest
koesyorgh *m.* wild buck
kofer *m.* **kofrow, kofrys** coffer; **kofer bras** chest; **kofer horn** strong-box, safe
koffi *m.* coffee
koffiji *m.* **+ow** cafe, coffee-house
kofrik-erbys *m.* **-igow-erbys** money-box, piggy-bank
kofrynn *m.* **+ow** casket
kog<cuckoo> *f.* **+es** cuckoo
kog<cook> *m.* **+ow** cook
koger *m.* winding stream
koges *f.* cook
kogforn *f.* **+ow** cooker, cooking-stove
kogh<hood> *m.* **+ow** hood, crown (of hat), cover (of beehive), bonnet; hull
kogh<red> *adj.* blood-red, scarlet
koghynn *m.* **+ow** dug mine on a lode, coffin mine
kogrenn *f.* **+ow** meander
kogrenna *v.* meander
kok *m.* **kokow** fishing boat
koklys *coll.* **+enn** cockles
kokynn *m.* little boat

kolenn *f.* **+ow** coal of fire; **kolenn vyw** live coal; **kolenn leskys** burning coal; **kolenn varow** cinder
koler *m.* rage
kolera *m.* cholera
kolgh *m.* **+ow** point, spike
kolghes *f.* **+ow** quilt, bedspread, comforter (U.S.)
koll<hazel> *coll.* **+enn** hazel-trees
koll<loss> *m.* loss, damage, perdition
kollan *f.* **+ow** large sheath-knife
kollas *f.* hazlett, small group of hazel-trees
kollell *f.* **kellylli** knife; **kollell bleg** pen-knife, clasp-knife, pocket knife (U.S.); **kollell gamm** curved knife; **kollell gervya** carving knife; **kollell gravya** chasing-tool, scalpel
kollell-lesa *f.* octopus
kollenki *v.* swallow
kollenwel *v.* fulfil, fill, complete
kolles *m.* **+ow** loss
kollji *m.* **+ow** college, chapter of cathedral
kollva *f.* state of loss, destruction
kollwydh *coll.* **+enn** hazel-tree
kollwydhek *adj.* abounding in hazel-trees *f.* hazel-grove
kolm *m.* **+ow** knot, tie (link) bond; **kolm konna** necktie, tie (clothing); **kolm re** slip knot
kolmek *adj.* knotty
kolmenn *f.* **+ow** fastening
kolmer *m.* **-oryon** binder
kolmweyth *m.* knotwork
kolodhyonenn *f.* **+enn**, *coll.* **kolodhyon** bowel, gut, entrail, intestine
kolomm *f.* **+es** dove, pigeon; **kolomm koes** wood-pigeon
kolommenn *f.* **+ow**, *coll.* **kolommes** dove, pigeon
kolommji *m.* **+ow** dove-cote, pigeon-house, culverhouse
kolommyer *m.* **+s** dove-cote

kolonn *f.* **+ow** heart, courage; **kolonn drogh** broken heart
kolonnek *adj.* hearty, bold, kindly *m.* **-ogyon** friendly person
kolonnekter *m.* bravery, courage, boldness
kolonnenn *f.* **+ow** core (of apple, etc.)
koloven *f.* **+yow** column
kolpes *m.* **+ow** lever, fulcrum
kolpes-vaglenn *m.* **kolpesow-maglenn** gear-lever, gear-stick, gearshift (U.S.)
kolter *m.* **koltrow** coulter of plough
kolyn *m.* **kelyn** puppy, cub, whelp
komm *m.* **+ow** small valley, dingle
kommendya *v.* recommend, commend, introduce, present
kommol *coll.* **+enn** cloud (as a mass)
kommolek *adj.* cloudy, overcast
kommolenn *f.* **+ow**, *coll.* **kommol** individual cloud
kommol-sugra *coll.* candy-floss
kommynn *m.* dell
kompas *m.* circumference, extent
kompella *v.* compel
kompes *adj.* even, level, calm; **bos kompes gans** *phr.* be even with
komplek *adj.* complex, complicated
kompleth *adj.* complex, complicated, intricate
Komplin *m.* Compline
kompoesa *v.* make even, smooth, fit
kompoester *m.* evenness, equilibrium; propriety
komun *m.* communion; **Komun Sans** Holy Communion
komunya *v.* take the Sacrament, take Communion
komunyans *m.* communion; **Komunyans Sans** Holy Communion
koneri *m.* rabbit warren
konfessya confess *v.*

konfort *m.* comfort (spiritual), consolation, support, encouragement
konfortya *v.* console, comfort, support
konforter *m.* **+s** comforter
konin *m.* **+es** rabbit, coney
koningenn *m.* rabbit-skin
koninessa *v.* go rabbiting
konna *m.* **+ow** neck, narrow strip of land
konna-bregh *m.* wrist
konna-gwynn *m.* weasel
konna-tir *m.* **konnaow-tir** peninsula
konna-troes *m.* instep
konnar *f.* fury, rabies, rage
konnyk *adj.* clever *m.*
  konnygyon expert
konneryek *adj.* rabid, furious, mad (U.S.)
kons<causeway> *m.* **+ow** pavement, sidewalk (U.S.)
kons<FN> *f.* vagina
konsayt *m.* **+s** fancy, opinion, notion
konsel *m.* council; **Konsel Diogeledh** Security Council
konseler *m.* **-oryon** councillor
konsevya *v.* conceive
konshyans *m.* conscience
konsya *v.* pave
konter *adj.* contrary, opposite, cross *m.* **+s** cross lode
konternot *m.* counter-tenor
konteth *f.* **+ow** county, hundred of Cornwall N.B. Not to be used to describe Cornwall, which is a dukedom.
kontradia *v.* contradict, controvert
kontrari *adj.* contrary *adv.* otherwise *m.* opposer
kontraryus *adj.* opposed
kontrewaytya *v.* ambush
kontrolya *v.* order about, control
kontron *coll.* **+enn** maggots
kontronek *adj.* maggoty, flyblown

konvayour *m.* covered entrance, subway (underground walkway)
konvedhes *v.* understand, perceive, realize, comprehend
kop *m.* **+ys** cope, cloak
kopel *m.* **koplow** couple, pair
kopi *m.* **+ow** copy
kopia *v.* copy
kor<hedge> *m.* hedge, boundary
kor<turn> *m.* **+ow** turn, manner, style; shift (work); **war neb kor** *phr.* in some way
Korawys *m.* Lent
korbel *m.* **korblys** bracket
kordenn *f.* **kerdyn** string, cord
kordh *m.* **+ow** clan, tribe, extended family
kores *f.* **+ow** weir, enclosure of stakes to trap fish
korev *m.* **+ow** beer, ale
korf *m.* **+ow** body, person; **korf eglos** nave; **korf eskern** skeleton
korfek *adj.* corpulent, portly
korf-lagha *m.* constitution
korflann *f.* **+ow** churchyard
korfonieth *f.* anatomy (science)
korfwithyas *m.* **-ysi** bodyguard
kor' gwella *m.* strong ale
korhwyth *m.* **+ow** spiral, eddy
korkynn *m.* **+ow** cork (stopper)
korlann *f.* **+ow** fold, enclosure
korn<horn> *m.* **kern**, *dual*
  dewgorn horn (of animal); **kern** horn (musical); **korn eva** drinking horn; **korn tan** tinder box
korn<corner> *m.* **kernow** corner; **korn an oeles** chimney corner; **korn dowr** creek; **korn keunys** wood-corner; **korn tal** forehead
kornek *adj.* horned
kornell *f.* **+ow** nook, corner
kornet **+yow** *m.* nook
kornhwilenn *f.* **kernhwili** lapwing, peewit; **tyller kernhwili** *m.* lonely place

kornya *v.* butt, ram

korr *pref.* micro- *m.* **+yon** dwarf, pigmy

korrbibenn *f.* **+ow** capillary tube

korrbryv *m.* **+es** microbe, germ

korrdonner *m.* microwave oven

korres *f.* **+ow** dwarf, pigmy

korrgowser *m.* **+yow** microphone

korrik *m.* **-igow** midget

korrvagh *f.* nook

korrvarvus *m.* haddock

korryar *f.* **-yer** partridge

kors<course> *m.* moment, spell (period of time); course

kors<fen> *coll.* **+enn** reeds, fen, reed-grown bog

korsek *adj.* reedy *f.* **-egi** reed-bed

korsenn *f.* **+ow**, *coll.* **kors** reed, cable; **korsenn dredanek** electric cable

korswigenn *f.* **+ow**, *coll.* **korswik** guelder-rose, cranberry-bush

kortes *adj.* courteous, polite

kortesi *m.* courtesy, politeness, good manners

korwyns *m.* **+ow** whirlwind, tornado

kos *f.* itching, tickling

kosa *v.* itch, tickle, tingle

kosel *adj.* quiet, tranquil

koselhe *v.* quieten, pacify, soothe

kosk<FN> *f.* admonishment

kosk<sleep> *m.* sleep, mould (fungus), rot in timber

koska *v.* sleep, go mouldy, get dry rot

koskador *m.* **+yon** sleeper; **koskador desempis** one who falls asleep quickly

koskas *m.* sleep, doze, nap

koskles *m.* morphia, opium

koskor *coll.* retinue, dependants, household

koskti *m.* **+ow** dormitory

kosoleth *f.* quiet, stillness, tranquillity

kost *m.* **+ys** cost, expense, charge; **mos yn kost** go to expense

kosta *m.* incense, costmary, alecost (plant)

kostek *adj.* costly, expensive, pricey

kostenn *f.* **+ow** target, large shallow straw basket

kostenna *v.* target

kostow-mentons *plur.* maintenance costs

kostrel *m.* **+s** flask, flagon, decanter

kostya *v.* cost

kostyans *m.* cost

kota *m.* **kotow** coat; **kota arvow** coat-of-arms

koth<known> *adj.* familiar *m.* familiar friend

koth<old> *adj.* old, ancient, long untilled *m.* old man

kothenep *m.* antiquity (abst.)

kothenn *f.* undug subsoil

kothhe *v.* grow old

kothman *m.* **+s** comrade, friend

kothni *m.* old age

kothwas *m.* **-wesyon** old fellow, old guy

koton *m.* cotton

kott *adj.* short, brief

kotthe *v.* shorten

kottha *adj.* older, senior

koukow *f.* **+s** cuckoo

kourser *m.* charger (horse)

kov *m.* **+yow** memory, recollection; **perthi kov a** *v.* remember

kovadh *m.* remembrance, record

kovadhor *m.* **+yon** recorder

kovaytya *v.* covet

kovaytys *m.* greed, covetousness

kovhe *v.* remind, remember, commemorate

kovheans *m.* commemoration

kovia *v.* hatch, cherish, incubate

kovlyver *m.* **-lyvrow** register
kovnotenn *f.* **+ow** record (a single record), minute
kovnotyans *m.* **+ow** minute (a single record)
kovro *m.* **kovrohow** souvenir, keepsake, memento
kovskrifa *v.* register
kovskrifla *m.* **-leow** registry
kovskrifenn *f.* **+ow** register, archive
kovva<hideout> *f.* hiding place, hideout; concealment
kovva<remembrance> *f.* **+ow** remembrance, memory, recollection
kow *adj.* hollow *f.* **+yow** enclosure, hollow
kowa *v.* hollow
kowal *adj.* complete, entire, whole
kowann *f.* **+ow** owl
kowans *m.* excavation
kowas *f.* **kowasow** shower, rainstorm, blast (of rain); **kowas gwyns** gust, squall; **kowas niwl** thick mist
kowasek *adj.* showery
kowatti *m.* shelter
kowbal *m.* **+yow** ferry
kowbalhyns *m.* **+ow** ferry-crossing
kowbrenn *m.* **+yer** hollow tree
kowdarn *m.* **+s** cauldron
kowell *m.* **+ow** pannier basket; **kowell edhen** birdcage; **kowell gwenen** beehive; **kowell kankres** crab-pot; **kowell lesk** cradle
kowellik *m.* **-igow** sink-basket
kowesi *v.* shower
kowesik *adj.* hollowed
koweth *m.* **+a** male companion, friend, mate, fellow, peer
kowethas *m.* **+ow** society, association, fellowship; **Kowethas an Yeth Kernewek** Cornish Language Fellowship

kowethes *f.* **+ow** female companion, friend
kowethlyver *m.* **-lyvrow** manual, handbook
kowethya *v.* keep company, consort
kowethyades *f.* **+ow** colleague, partner, associate
kowethyadow *adj.* sociable
kowethyans *m.* fellowship, association, company
kowethyas *m.* **-ysi** colleague, partner, associate
kowfordh *f.* **+ow** tunnel, subway, underpass
kowgans *adj.* certain, sure
kowl<cabbage> *coll.* **+enn** cabbage (in general)
kowl<soup> *m.* **+ow** soup, broth, pottage
kowla *v.* curdle, clot, coagulate
kowldhrehevel *v.* finish building
kowlogneth *f.* gluttony
kowlek<FN> *f.* **-egi** cabbage plot
kowlek<AJ> *adj.* gluttonous *m.* **-ogyon** glutton
kowlennik *f.* **-igow** sprout (Brussels)
kowles *coll.* **+enn** curd, coagulation, jelly
kowlesenn *f.* **+ow**, *coll.* **kowles** clot
kowlik *m.* **-igow** sprout (Brussels)
kowlleski *v.* burn up, consume by fire, incinerate
kowlvleujenn *f.* **+ow** cauliflower, broccoli
kowlwul *v.* complete, accomplish, finish doing,
kownans *m.* **+ow** ravine
kowr *m.* **kewri** giant
kowrek *adj.* gigantic, enormous
kowres *f.* **+ow** giantess
kowrvargh *m.* **-vergh** camel
kows *v.* talk *m.* **+ow** speech, talk, discourse, speaking

kowsans *m.* manner of speech
kowses *m.* inward thought; **+yow** conscience, conviction
kowva *f.* **+ow** cavity
kowynn *m.* **+ow** mould (for casting)
koynt *adj.* strange, extraordinary, unusual odd (strange)
koyntys *f.* oddity, unusual thing
kraf *adj.* grasping, greedy, tenacious *m.* **+ow** grasp, grip; **krefyon** miser
krafa *v.* grasp, secure, stitch roughly
krafell *f.* **+ow** clutch (in car)
krag *coll.* **+enn** sandstone
kragh *adj.* scurvy, scabby *m. m.* **kreghi** scurf, scab
krakk *m.* **+ys** crack, snap; **krakk y gonna** *adj.* very steep
krakkya *v.* crack, snap
krakkya-konna *phr.* breakneck
krambla *v.* scramble, creep, climb
krammenn *f.* **+ow**, *coll.* **kramm** scab over sores
krampoetha *v.* beg for pancakes
krampoethenn *coll.* **+ow**, *coll.* **krampoeth** pancakes; **krampoeth mowesi** pennywort
kramvil *m.* **+es** reptile
kramya *v.* crawl, creep
krann *coll.* scrub, bracken
kranndir *m.* **+yow** scrubland
kras *adj.* parched, toasted *coll.* **+enn** toast (food)
krasa *v.* toast (food), parch
krasenn *f.* **+ow** piece of toast
kraster *m.* aridity
kravas *v.* scrape, scratch, claw
kravell *f.* **+ow** scraper, hoe
kravellas *v.* scrape mechanically, hoe
kraw *m.* **+yow** hole, perforation, socket; **kraw lagas** eye socket; **kraw naswydh** eye of needle
kraw-kolon *m.* colostomy

kreador *m.* creator
krebogh *adj.* wrinkled, withered
krefni *f.* avarice, greed
kreft *f.* **+ow** craft, occupation requiring manual skill
kreftor *m.* **+yon** craftsman, artificer, artisan
kreg *adj.* hoarse *m.* **+yon** hoarse person
kreghi *plur.* scurf
kreghyn *plur.* skins
kreghynva *f.* **+ow** tannery
kregi *v.* hang, suspend, depend
kregyans *m.* suspension
kregyar *f.* **-yer** landrail (bird)
krekter *m.* hoarseness
kren *m.* **+yow** tremble, shake, quake, shudder; **kren an leghow** fit of the ague
krena *v.* shake, tremble
krener *m.* **-oryon** quaker
krenn *adj.* round, circular
krennder *m.* roundness
krennwreydhenn *f.* **+ow**, *coll.* **krennwreydh** bulb (of plant)
krer *m.* **+yow** relic (of saint)
krerva *f.* **+ow** reliquary, shrine
kres<centre> *adj.* central *m.* centre (middle), waist
kres<faith> *f.* faith
kres<peace> *m.* peace
kresek *adj.* average *m.* **kresogow** average
kresenn *f.* **+ow** centre (building); **kresenn brenassa** shopping centre; **kresenn gemmynieth** community centre; **kresenn yowynkneth** youth centre
kreslu *m.* police, police force; **kreslu gustel** riot police
kressya *v.* increase, multiply, extend
kresva *f.* **+ow** centre (building)
kreswas *m.* centre (in rugby)
kresys *m.* credit, trust, confidence
kresysor *m.* **+yon** creditor

kresysores *f.* **+ow** creditor

kreun *m.* **+yow** reservoir, artificial pond, reserve (of money or materials); **kreun melin** mill-pool

kreunell *f.* **+ow** accumulator

kreuni *v.* accumulate, gather

kreupya *v.* creep

krev *adj.* strong, mighty, vigorous

krevder *m.* strength, might

krevenn *f.* **+ow** crust, scab

krevhe *v.* strengthen, make strong

krey *m.* chalk

kreyon *m.* **+yow** crayon

kreyth *coll.* **+enn** scar, cicatrice

kri *m.* **+ow** cry, call, clamour

kria *v.* cry

krib *f.* **+ow** comb, crest, reef (of rocks); **krib chi** ridge of a house

kriba *v.* split fragments

kribas *v.* comb

kribell *f.* **+ow** tassel, tuft

kribella *v.* tease out rope, form a tassel, tuft

kribenn *f.* **+ow** crest; **kribenn gulyek** cock's comb; **kribenn vel** honeycomb

kribya *v.* card wool

kribin *f.* wool-card

kribyon *plur.* combings

krier *m.* **-oryon** crier; **krier an dre** town crier

krin *adj.* dry, brittle, parched, withered, arid *m.* **+yon** dry stuff

krina *v.* become dry or brittle

krinder *m.* dryness

krindir *m.* arid land

kris<fold> *m.* **+yow** fold, wrinkle

kris<vigour> *m.* vigour

Krist *name* Christ

Kristones *f.* **+ow** Christian woman

Kristoneth *f.* Christianity

kristonhe *v.* christen

kristonya *v.* christen

Kristonyon *plur.* Christians

Kristyon *adj.* Christian *m.*

Kristonyon Christian man

kriv *adj.* raw (uncooked), unripe

krivder *m.* rawness (uncooked state)

kro *adj.* fresh (of food)

kroadur *m.* creature

kroch *m.* **+ow**, *dual* **dewgroch**, **+ys** crutch

krodhek *adj.* grumbling, carping, fault-finding

krodhvol *m.* **+yow** complaint

krodhvolas *v.* complain, grumble; **krodhvolas orth** complain at

kroeder *m.* **kroedrow** coarse sieve, riddle (strainer)

kroeder-kroghen *m.* hold-all

kroedra *v.* sift, winnow

kroen *m.* **+ow** thong, strap

kroenegynn *m.* **+ow** little toad; **kroenegynn hager du** ugly black little toad

kroenek *adj.* skinny *m.* **-ogow** toad; **kroenek du** dark toad; **kroenek ervys** tortoise; **kroenek melyn** light toad

kroenogas *v.* hop like a toad

kroener *m.* **-oryon** skinner, fellmonger (dealer in animal skins), currier (one who colours leather)

kroft *m.* **+ow** croft

krog *f.* **+ow** tug, hanging, suspension, tweak

krogbrenn *m.* **+yer** gallows

krogen *f.* **kregyn** shell, carapace, skull; **krogen an glin** knee-cap; **krogen an penn** skull

krogenn *f.* snare, springe, noose

krogenek *adj.* having a shell, thick-shelled

kroger *m.* **+yon** hangman

kroghen *f.* **kreghyn** skin, hide; **kroghen an lagas** eyelid; **kroghen fronn** brake-lining

kroghendanow *adj.* sensitive

krogla *m.* gibbet, hanging-place

kroglath *f.* **+ow** noose, springe

kroglenn *f.* **+ow** curtain, hanging; **kroglenn fos** wall-hanging

krokodil *m.* **+es** crocodile

krollya *v.* curl

kromm *adj.* curved, crooked, bent

kromma *v.* bend

krommbil *f.* gizzard

krommenn<bream> *f.* small bream

krommenn<sickle> *f.* sickle, curve, crescent; **krommenn eythin** furze-hook

krommlegh *f.* **+yow** cromlech, megalithic chamber-tomb

krommnen *m.* vaulted ceiling

kronk *m.* **+ys** thump, stroke bang (knock)

kronkya *v.* beat, thump, thrash

kropya *v.* penetrate, probe, crush inwards

krosser *m.* **+s** crozier-bearer

kroth *f.* belly, bird's crop

krothek *adj.* pot-bellied

kroust *m.* **+yow** picnic lunch, meal taken to work, snack

krow<gore> *m.* bloodshed, gore, death

krow<hut> *m.* **+yow** hut, shed, sty; **krow deves** sheep-cot;, sheep shed (U.S.); **krow gever** goat-shed; **krow goedhow** goose-house; **krow mogh** pigsty; **krow prenn** chalet; **krow yer** chicken-shed

krowd *m.* **+ys** violin, fiddle (Mus.)

krowder *m.* **-oryon** violinist, fiddler (Mus.)

krowdra *v.* loiter, idle

krowji *m.* **+ow** one-roomed cottage, cabin

krows *f.* **+yow** cross, rood; **krows eglos** transept

krowsek *adj.* cross-shaped, set crosswise; cross-tempered

krowseryow *plur.* crossword puzzle

krowsfordh *f.* **+ow** crossroads

krowshyns *m.* **+yow** crossroads

krowsik *f.* **-igow** little cross

krowsprenn *f.* **+yer** crucifix, crows-staff

krowsvaner *m.* cross flag

krowsya *v.* crucify

krug *m.* **+ow** mound, hillock, tumulus, barrow; **krug moryon** ant-hill

krugell *f.* **+ow** little mound

krugya *v.* pile up in a mound, put in a heap

krugynn *f.* **+ow** little mound

kruskynn *m.* **+ow** flagon, beer-jug stein (U.S.)

krygell *f.* cricket (insect), spider-crab

krygh *m.* **+yow** wrinkle, ripple, crinkle

krygha *v.* wrinkle, ripple, shrivel, crinkle

kryghlamm *m.* **+ow** somersault

kryghlemmel *v.* somersault

kryghylli *v.* jolt, rattle, shake

kryghyllyans *m.* concussion

kryjyans *m.* belief, faith, creed

kryjyk *adj.* believing, religious *m.* **kryjygyon** believer

kryllas *m.* rough hut, ruin of ancient dwelling

krys<quake> *m.* shaking, quivering, quaking

krys<shirt> *m.* **+yow** shirt, shift, chemise; **krys hwys** sweatshirt; **krys nos** nightshirt; **krys T** tee-shirt

kryshok *m.* **+ys** kestrel

krysi *v.* believe, have faith in; **krysi dhe nebonan** believe someone, have faith in someone; **krysi yn** believe in

kryspows *f.* jacket, waistcoat; **kryspows oferyas** cassock

kryswels *coll.* quaking-grass

krysya *v.* quiver

kryw *m.* weir

kub *m.* **+ow** cube
kudh *adj.* hidden, concealed, covert *m.* hiding place
kudha *v.* hide, conceal; **kudha rag** hide from
kudhans *m.* covering, concealment, cover (hiding-place)
kudhenn *f.* soft layer on hard rock
kudhlenn *f.* veil, cover (of a book); **kudhlenn fos** wall-hanging
kudhon *f.* wood-pigeon
kudynn *m.* **+ow** lock (of hair), skein; problem
kugol *m.* cowl, monk's hood; **kugol bardh** bard's hood
kuhudha *v.* accuse, denounce, tell tales about
kuhudhans *m.* accusation
kuhudhor *m.* **+yon** accuser, prosecutor
kuhudhyas *m.* **-ysi** accuser
kui *v.* foal
kul *adj.* narrow
kulder *m.* narrowness
kuldir *m.* **+yow** isthmus
kulvor *m.* strait
kulyek *m.* **kulyogyon** cock, cockerel, male bird; **kulyek goedh** gander; **kulyek gwyls** grouse; **kulyek Gyni** turkey-cock; **kulyek hos** drake
kulyek-gwyns *m.* weathercock
kulyek-kenys *m.* cockcrow
kulyek-reden *m.* grasshopper
kulyn *m.* chaff
kummyas *m.* permission, leave, licence, permit, clearance
kummyas-lywya *m.* **kummyasow-lywya** driving licence, driver's license (U.S.)
kuntell *v.* gather, pick (e.g. flowers), collect (trans.) *m.* **+ow** gathering, collection, meeting

kuntelles *m.* **+ow** gathering, meeting, assembly, congress; **Kuntelles Keltek** Celtic Congress
kuntellva *f.* **+ow** meeting-place, rendezvous
kuntellyans *m.* **+ow** gathering, meeting
kur *m.* care, cure, remedy
kurun *f.* **+yow** crown; **kurun spern** crown of thorns, hangover
kuruna *v.* crown
kurunans *m.* coronation
kurunik *f.* **-igow** coronet
kuryek -ogyon *m.* pimple, red spot on skin
kussynn *m.* **+ow** kiss, peck (small kiss)
kusul *f.* **+yow** advice, counsel, opinion
kusulya *v.* advise, counsel; **kusulya a** advise to
kusulyans *m.* **+ow** consultation
kusulyas *m.* **-ysi** consultant
kusulyek *adj.* advisory, consultative
kusulyer *m.* **-oryon** counsellor
kuv *adj.* dear, kind, loving *m.* **+yon** dear one; **kuv kolonn** dear heart, loved one, dearly beloved, sweetheart
kuva *m.* sawn-down barrel
kuvder *m.* kindness, clemency, lenience
kwakkya *v.* quack
kwallok *m.* **+s** hulking fellow
kwarel<pane> *m.* **+s** pane of glass
kwarel<claim> *m.* claim, demand
kwart *m.* **+ys** quart
kwartenn *f.* **+ow** quarter
kwarter *m.* **kwartrys** quarter
kwartron *m.* **+ys** quarter
kwartrona *v.* cut in quarters
kweth *f.* **+ow** cloth; **kweth lestri** dishcloth
kwetha *v.* clothe

kweth-leur *f.* **kwethow-leur**
floor-cloth

kweth-ponn *f.* **kwethow-ponn**
duster, dustcloth (U.S.)

kwethynn *m.* **+ow** napkin

kwilkyn *m.* **+yow** frog

kwit *adj.* free *adv.* completely,
deservedly

kwitya *v.* quit

kwoff *m.* repletion

kwoffi *v.* overeat, binge; swell up

kwyllenn *f.* **+ow** quill

kyf *m.* stump, root-stock, tree-trunk,
stub

kyfi *v.* confide in

kyfyans *m.* confidence, trust, reliance

kyfeyth *m.* **+yow** preserve, jam,
confection; **kyfeyth owraval**
marmalade

kyfeythya *v.* preserve

kyfeythyer *m.* **-yoryon**
confectioner

kygel *f.* **+yow** distaff

kyhwedhel *m.* **kyhwedhlow**
tidings, tale, rumour

kyhwedhla *v.* disseminate, talk
about

kykesow *plur.* Cornish heath

kylgh *m.* **+yow** circle, round, ring

kylghenn *f.* **+ow** circlet, circuit

kylghfordh *f.* **+ow** ring-road,
beltway (U.S.)

kylghigow *plur.* hoop-la

kylghya *v.* encircle

kylghyek *adj.* circular, round

kyllas *coll.* shale, slate

kyllik *coll.* **+enn** razor-shell, razor-
fish

kymygieth *f.* chemistry

kymyk *adj.* chemical

kymyst *m.* **+yon** chemist

kyn *conj.* though

kynbogh *m.* wether goat

kyner *m.* **-oryon** mourner

kyngel *f.* **kenglow** girdle

kyni *v.* lament, mourn, wail, bemoan

kynnik *v.* offer *m.* **-igow** offer,
proposal, proposition

kyns *adj.* former, previous *prep.*
before, ere *adv.* formerly, sooner,
rather; **kyns lemmyn** before now,
hitherto; **kyns skrif** *m.* first draft

kynsa *adj.* first

kynseghwa *m.* forenoon

kyns-hes *f.* first swarm

kynsistorek *adj.* prehistoric

kynsow *adv.* just now

kynth *conj.* though

kynvann *m.* lamentation, mourning

kynweres *m.* first aid

kynyav *m.* autumn, fall

kynyavos *m.* autumn dwelling

kyrghes *v.* fetch, bring, get

kyrghynn *m.* close environment,
surroundings, vicinity; **yn
kyrghynn** around, in the vicinity of;
y'm kyrghynn around me

kyrghynnedh *m.* **+ow**
environment

kyrghynnedhel *adj.* environmental

kyrghynnedhor *m.* **+yon**
environmentalist

kyst *f.* **+yow** box (container), chest

kystenn *f.* **+ow** small box;
kystenn liwyow paint-box

kyst-lyther *f.* **kystyow-lyther**
letter-box

kyst-vaglenn *f.* **kystyow-
maglenn** gear-box

kystven *f.* burial chamber in tumulus

kyttrin *m.* **+yow** bus, omnibus

kyttrinva *f.* bus-station, bus-stop

kywni *coll.* **+enn** moss, lichen,
mildew

kywnia *v.* become mossy, become
covered in mildew

kywniek *adj.* mossy

L

labol *adj.* brindled, striped

labydha *v.* stone, throw stones at

lader *m.* **ladron** thief, robber, pilferer, brigand

ladha *v.* kill, slay, murder, terminate, put to death; switch off

ladhva *f.* slaughter, murder

ladra *v.* steal, rob, pilfer, plunder

ladrans *m.* robbery (individual crime), larceny, theft

ladres *f.* **+ow** sluice

ladrynsi *m.* robbery (in general), larceny, theft

lafyl *adj.* lawful, permissible (legally)

lagas *m.* **+ow**, *dual* **dewlagas** eye *m.* patch of blue in clouded sky; **lagas du** black eye, spotted persicaria

lagasek *adj.* big-eyed *m.* **-ogyon** sharp-sighted one, big-eyed person

lagasenn *f.* **+ow** large ring for mooring

lagatta *v.* stare, gawk, gaze

lagatter<fish> *m.* **lagattres** blind fish

lagatter<starer> *m.* **-oryon** starer, goggler, gawker (U.S.)

lagenn *f.* **+ow** puddle, pond, slough

lagenna *v.* splash, bespatter

lagha *f.* **laghys, laghow** law, dogma

laghel *adj.* legal, lawful, permissible (legally)

laghenn *f.* **+ow** act (of law)

laghwas *m.* **-wesyon** solicitor's clerk, law clerk (U.S.)

laghyas *m.* **-ysi** solicitor, lawyer, attorney (U.S.)

laghyades *f.* **+ow** solicitor, lawyer, attorney (U.S.)

lagya *v.* splash

lagyar *f.* **-yer** moorhen

lakka *adj.* worse

lamm *m.* **+ow** leap, jump, bound; **war unn lamm** *adv.*; **yn unn lamm** at once, in a trice

lamma *v.* leap, jump, bound

lammleder *f.* precipice

lammlenn *f.* **+ow** parachute

lann *f.* **+ow** church-site, monastic close

lannergh *m.* **+i** clearing in a wood, glade

Lannstefan *place* Launceston

lanow *m.* high tide, fullness

lanwes *m.* abundance, flood stream

lappa *m.* **lappys** lappet, flap, fold

lappya *v.* leap, perform gymnastics

lappyer *m.* **-yoryon** acrobat, gymnast tumbler (U.S.)

lappyores *f.* **+ow** acrobat, gymnast

lapya *v.* lick, lap

larj *adj.* generous, liberal

larjes *m.* bounty, generosity

las<dram> *m.* **+ow** dram, liquor, alcohol

las<lace> *m.* **+ow, +ys** lace

lasek *adj.* alcoholic *m.* **-ogyon** alcoholic

lasogeth *f.* alcoholism

lash *m.* **+ys** lash, slash, stroke

last *m.* nastiness, loathsomeness, noisomeness

lastedhes *m.* filth, scum, vermin

lasvydh *m.* not a drop, nothing

lath *f.* **+ow** staff, rod, yard (measure)

lattha *m.* **latthys** lath

latthya *v.* latch

latti *m.* **+ow** slaughter-house, abattoir

latimer *m.* **+s** interpreter, Latin master

Latin *m.* Latin language

lavar *m.* **+ow** saying, speech, utterance; **lavar koth** proverb; **heb na hirra lavarow** *adv.* without further ado

lavasos *v.* venture, dare, permit

lavrek *m.* **lavrogow** trousers, breeches, pants (U.S.); **lavrek berr** shorts (clothing); **lavrek byghan** underpants

lavur *m.* labour, toil, work; **Parti Lavur** Labour Party; **lavur digreft** unskilled labour

lavurlu *m.* **+yow** work-force

lavurus *adj.* laborious, toilsome

lavurya *v.* labour, toil, work; travel

lavuryans *m.* toil

lavyn *m.* **+yon** sand-eel, launce

lawa *m.* praise; **dh'y lawa !** *phr.* praise him !

lawen *adj.* uncastrated

le<less> *adj.* less, lesser, smaller

le<place> *m.* **leow** place, situation, spot (location); **dhe bub le** *phr.* through traffic

led *m.* **+yow** lead (electrical)

ledan *adj.* wide, broad

ledanenn *f.* **+ow** plantain

ledanles *m.* plantain

leder *f.* **ledrow** slope, cliff

ledher *m.* leather

ledhrenn *m.* leather strap

ledhys *v.* killed, slain, murdered

ledra *v.* slope

ledras *m.* **+ow** gradient

ledrek *adj.* sloping

ledrynn *f.* ramp

ledrys *adj.* stolen

ledya *v.* lead, conduct

ledyer *m.* **ledyoryon** leader

leel *adj.* local

leg *adj.* lay, non-clerical *m.* **+yon** layman

legessa *v.* catch mice

legest *m.* **+i** lobster

legestik *m.* **-igow** langoustine

legh<rickets> *m.* rickets

legh<slab> *f.* **+yon** slab, tablet, flat stone

leghenn *f.* **+ow** slate, thin flat stone

leghven *m.* **-veyn** flagstone

lehe *v.* lessen, minify

lejek *f.* **lejegow** heifer

lekses *m.* laity

lel *adj.* loyal, faithful, trusty; **lel wonis** devotion

lelder *m.* loyalty, fidelity

lelduri *m.* loyalty

Lelyas *m.* **Lelysi** Loyalist

lemmel *v.* leap, jump, bound

lemmik *m.* **-igow** little drop

lemmyn *adv.* now, at present

len<AJ> *adj.* faithful, trusty

len<MN> *m.* stitch (of land), strip

lenduri *m.* sincerity, good faith

lenes *f.* **+ow** nun, ling-fish

lenji *m.* **+ow** nunnery

lenki *v.* swallow1

lenn *f.* **+ow** cloth, blanket, flannel; **lenn dhu** blind (curtain)

lenna *v.* read aloud

lennlyver *m.* lectionary

lenni *v.* veil, cover, clothe

lennor *m.* **+yon** reader

lennva *f.* **+ow** lectern

lent *adj.* slow

lenwel *v.* fill, replenish, endue; **lenwel a** fill with

lergh *m.* trace, track

les<plant> *m.* **+yow** plant, wort; **les an gog** marigold; **les densek** dandelion

les<profit> *m.* profit, advantage, benefit; **dhe les** *adj.* useful, interesting, worthwhile

les<width> *m.* width, breadth

lesa *v.* spread, unfold, expand

lesans *m.* spread

lesek *adj.* botanical

les-flogh *m.* **-fleghes** step-child

lesh *m.* **+ow** leash

les-hanow *m.* **-henwyn** nickname, alias

les-henwel *v.* nickname

les-hwoer *f.* **-hwerydh** step-sister
leshya *v.* leash hounds
leshyans *m.* licence
lesk *m.* **+ow** swing, oscillation, cradle
leska *v.* swing, rock
leskell *m.* **+ow** fluctuation
leskella *v.* fluctuate
leski *v.* burn
lesk-lovan *m.* **leskow-lovan** swing (plaything)
lesloes *m.* horehound
lesranna *v.* distribute
lesserghek *m.* burdock
lesta *v.* prevent, hinder
les-tas *m.* **+ow** step-father
lester *m.* **lestri** vessel (container or ship)
lester-sedhi *m.* **lestri-sedhi** submarine
lesterth *m.* feverfew
lestrier *m.* **+yow** dresser, plate-rack
les-vab *m.* **-vebyon** step-son
les-vamm *f.* **+ow** step-mother
les-vroder *m.* **-vreder** step-brother
les-vryjyon *v.* parboil
les-vyrgh *f.* **+es** step-daughter
leswedh *m.* **+ow** frying-pan; **leswedh fria-down** deep-fat frier
leth *m.* milk; **leth boesa** buzzy-milk, cow's first milk
lethegenn *f.* **+ow**, *coll.* **lethek** sow-thistle
lethek *adj.* milky *m.* **-egow** milky place
le'ti *m.* dairy
lett *m.* **+ow**, **+ys** hindrance, obstruction, check, blockage, barrier, impediment; **heb lett** incessantly
lettrys *adj.* literate, learned, lettered
lettya *v.* hinder, impede, prevent, block, obstruct; **lettya chekkenn** stop a cheque; **lettya rag** prevent from
letus *coll.* **+enn** lettuce

leugh *m.* **+i** calf
leughkenn *m.* calfskin
leughti *m.* **+ow** calf-house
leun *adj.* full; **leun a ras** full of grace
leunder *m.* fullness
leunhe *v.* fill
leur *m.* **+yow** floor, ground, storey
leurlenn *f.* **+ow** carpet
leusik *adj.* on heat
leuv *f.* **+yow**, *dual* **diwla**, **diwleuv** hand (in general)
leuvbann *m.* felt (material)
lev *m.* **+ow** voice, utterance, cry
leva *v.* cry out, shout
leven *adj.* smooth, even, level
levenhe *v.* smooth, level
leverel *v.* say, tell, relate, utter
leveryans *m.* **+ow** pronunciation
leveryas *m.* **-ysi** speaker, talker, teller (of tales)
levna *v.* smooth, level, press (of clothes)
levrith *m.* sweet milk
Levyas *m.* **-ysi** Levite
lew *m.* **+yon** lion
lewes *f.* **+ow** lioness
lewik *m.* **lewigow** lion cub
lewpard *m.* **+es** leopard
leys *m.* **+yow** mud, silt, alluvium, slime
leysyek *adj.* muddy *f.* **-egi** mire
leyth<humid> *adj.* humid, moist, flabby
leyth<fish> *f.* **+ow** flounder, flat-fish
leytha *v.* humidify, moisten, rot through damp
leythter *m.* humidity
li<lunch> *f.* **livyow** lunch(eon)
li<oath> *m.* **+ow** oath
lia *v.* take an oath
libel *m.* label

lien *m.* **+yow** napkin, kerchief, linen cloth; **lien dorn** handkerchief; **lien diwla** napkin; **lien konna** scarf; **lien gweli** sheet (for a bed), bed-sheet, bed-linen; **lien moes** table-cloth

liener *m.* **-oryon** draper

lies *pron.* many *adj.* many; **lies chi** many houses, a lot of houses; **meur a jiow** many houses, a lot of houses

liesek *adj.* multiple, various, plural

lieshe *v.* multiply

lieskenedhlek *adj.* multi-national

lieskweyth *adv.* often, many times

liesplek *m.* **-egow** plural

liesplekhe *v.* duplicate (a document)

liesskrifa *v.* photocopy, make copies of a document

liester *m.* multiplicity, variety, plurality

lieswregeth *f.* polygamy

liesyethek *adj.* polyglot *m.* **-ogyon** polyglot

lij *adj.* liege *m.* **+ys** liege

lili *m.* lily; **lili Korawys** daffodil

lim *m.* lime (mineral), cement

limaval *m.* **+ow** lime (fruit)

lin<fluid> *m.* **+yow** fluid, liquid, body-fluid; **lin sebon** detergent, washing-up liquid

lin<line> *m.* **+enn** line, thread

lin<linen> *coll.* **+enn** linen, flax

linaja *m.* lineage

linas *coll.* **+enn** nettles

linasek *f.* **-egi** nettle-bed

lindir *m.* **+yow** flax-land

linek *f.* **-egi** flax-field

linenn *f.* **+ow** line, string, thread; streak

linenna *v.* outline, sketch draw lines

linennans *v.* sketch,, line-drawing

linennell *f.* **+ow** straight-edge

linoges *m.* **+ow** linnet

linos *coll.* duckweed, green slime on stones

linyeth *f.* lineage, ancestry, progeny

lisiw *m.* washing-powder, lye

list *m.* **+ys** list for jousting

lith *m.* **+yow** limb, member (part of body)

liv<flood> *m.* **+ow** flood, deluge

liv<lunch> *f.* **+yow** lunch(eon)

liv<file> *f.* **+yow** file (tool), rasp

liva *v.* flood, inundate, swamp

livra *v.* liberate, set free, release

livrel *adj.* liberal (politically)

livreson *m.* liberation

LivWer *adj.* LibDem (i.e. Liberal Democrat)

livya<lunch> *v.* lunch

livya<file> *v.* file (to scrape)

liw *m.* **liwyow** colour, hue, complexion, tint; **liw bual** buff (colour)

liwek *adj.* coloured, hued, tinted; dyed

liwles *m.* woad

liwer *m.* **-oryon** dyer

liwya *v.* colour, dye

liwyans *m.* **+ow** picture, painting, colouring, coloration

lo *f.* **loyow** spoon, ladle, spatula

loas *f.* **+ow** spoonful

loas-te *f.* **+ow** teaspoonful

loas-veur *f.* **+ow** tablespoonful

lo-balas *f.* **loyow-balas** trowel

lo-de *f.* **loyow-te** teaspoon

loder *m.* **lodrow** stocking

lodhen *m.* **lodhnow** bullock, steer, beast

lodrik *m.* **-igow** sock

loer *f.* **+yow** Moon

loerek *adj.* lunatic, moonstruck *m.* **-ogyon** lunatic

loerel *adj.* lunar

loerell *f.* **+ow** artificial satellite

loergann *m.* moonlight

loes *adj.* grey, hoary, mouldy

loesedh *m.* greyness

loesik *adj.* greyish

loesles *m.* mugwort, wormwood
loesni *m.* greyness
loesrew *m.* hoar-frost
loeth *m.* tribe
log *f.* **+ow** cell (monastic)
logel *f.* **+ow** coffin
logh<lax> *adj.* lax, remiss, negligent
logh<pool> *m.* **+ow** lake (close to sea), pool, inlet of water
Logh *place* Looe
logos *coll.* **+enn** mice
logosek *adj.* abounding in mice
lok *m.* presence
lo-ledan *f.* **loyow-ledan** ladle
Lombardi *place* Lombardy
lomm<bare> *adj.* bare, nude, naked
lomm<drop> *m.* **+ow** drop
lommas *m.* **+ow** small bream
lommder *m.* nudity, bareness
lommenn *f.* **+ow** sip, sup
lommhe *v.* strip bare, denude
lo'n *m.* **+ow** bullock, steer
londer *m.* gutter
loneth *f.* **-i**, *dual* **diwloneth** kidney
lo'nji *m.* **+ow** bullock-house
lonk *m.* gully
lonklynn *m.* **+ow** whirlpool, vortex
lonktreth *m.* quicksand
lorden *m.* **+yon**, **+s** clown, galoot
lorel *m.* **+s** vagrant, rascal, bum (U.S.)
lorgh *f.* **+ow** staff (rod), pole, walking-stick
lorgh-resa *m.* **lorghow-resa** track-rod (mach.)
los *adj.* vile, soiled, squalid
losel *m.* **+s** rascal, vagrant, lout, bum (U.S.)
loselwas *m.* **-wesyon** tramp, hobo (U.S.)
losk *m.* burning, combustion, inflammation
loskvann *m.* burning, combustion
loskven *m.* brimstone, sulphur

loskvenek *adj.* sulphuric
loskvenus *adj.* sulphurous
loskvenydh *m.* **+yow** volcano
loskvenydhyek *adj.* volcanic
losni *m.* vileness
losonieth *f.* botany
losoniethel *adj.* botanical
losonydh *m.* **+yon** botanist
losow *coll.* **+enn** herbs
losowenn *f.* **+ow**, *coll.* **losow** herb; **losowenn an Hav** lily of the valley; **losowenn lagas** celandine; **losowenn Sen Yowann** St John's wort
losowek *adj.* herbal *f.* **-egi** herb garden, vegetable garden, kitchen-garden
losower *m.* **-oryon** herbalist
losowji *m.* **+ow** greenhouse
losow-kegin *plur.* vegetables
losow-mogh *coll.* hogweed
losowys *plur.* herbs
lost *m.* **+ow** tail, queue; **gul lost** *v.* queue, wait in line (U.S.)
lostek *adj.* big-tailed *m.* **-ogyon** fox
lostenn *f.* **+ow** skirt
lost-hes *f.* third swarm
lostledan *m.* **+es** beaver
Lostwydhyel *place* Lostwithiel
lostya *v.* queue, wait in line (U.S.)
loub *m.* slime, lubricant, lubricating oil
louba *v.* lubricate
Loundres *place* London
lovan *f.* **+ow** rope; **lovan tynn** tightrope
lovanenn *f.* **+ow** twine
lovaner *m.* **lovanyoryon** rope-maker, roper
lover *m.* **lovryon** leper
loverji *m.* **+ow** leper-hospital, lazar-house
lo-veur *f.* **loyow-meur** tablespoon

lovrek *adj.* leprous, scabby *m.*
-**ogyon** leper
lovryjyon *m.* leprosy
low *coll.* **lowenn** lice; **lowenn gi** dog-louse
lowarn *m.* **lewern** fox
lowarnek *adj.* abounding in foxes
lowarnes *f.* **+ow** vixen
lowarnik *m.* **lewernigow** fox-cub
lowarth *m.* **+yow** garden
lowartha *v.* garden
lowarther *m.* -**oryon** gardener
lowek *adj.* lousy
lowen *adj.* joyful, happy, glad
lowena *f.* joy, bliss, happiness
lowender *m.* mirth, jollity
lowenek *adj.* merry, glad, jolly
lowenhe *v.* rejoice, comfort, make glad
lowennan *m.* -**es** weasel
lower *adj.* many, much
lown<blade> *m.* **+yow** blade, sliver, lamina
lown<concourse> *m.* **+yow** concourse, open working area
lownek *adj.* laminated, flaky
lownya *v.* slice, cut, sliver, veneer; flake
lownyans *m.* **+ow** slice, veneer
lowr<enough> *adj.* enough *adv.* sufficiently, amply, in plenty
lowr<CN> *coll.* laurels
lowrwydh *coll.* **+enn** laurel-trees
lows<loose> *adj.* loose, slack, careless
lows<shoot> *m.* shoot, sprout
lowsedhes *m.* slackness, negligence, looseness
lowsel *v.* relax, untie, slacken, loosen
lowsya *v.* unloose, untie
lowta *m.* loyalty
lu *m.* **+yow** army, crowd, host; **lu diogeledh** security force; **lu lestri** fleet, navy

lugarn *m.* **lugern** lamp, lantern, light
lugarn-byghan *m.* **lugern-byghan** side-lamp
lugarnleyth *f.* **+es** brill
lugh *m.* sea-smoke, sea-mist
lughes *coll.* **+enn** lightning
lughesenn *f.* **+ow**, *coll.* **lughes** lightning stroke
lughesi *v.* flash
Lulynn *place* Newlyn
lurik *m.* breastplate
lus *coll.* **+enn** bilberries, whortleberries
lusek *adj.* abounding in bilberries
lusow *coll.* **+enn** ashes, embers
lusowek *adj.* ashy *f.* -**egi** ash-heap
lust *m.* **+ys** lust
lyenn *m.* literature, learning
lyennek *adj.* literary
lyfans *m.* **+es** toad
lyfansas *v.* hop like a toad
lyha *adj.* least, smallest, minimum
lymm *adj.* sharp (pointed), keen, acute
lymma *v.* sharpen, whet, hone
lymmaval *m.* **+ow** lemon
lymmder *m.* sharpness
lymna *v.* paint (of a picture), illuminate illustrate
lymnans *m.* **+ow** painting, picture, illustration
lymner *m.* -**oryon** artist, painter, illustrator
lynn *m.* **+ow** pond, pool, lake (inland)
lynnbysk *m.* -**buskes** carp (fish)
lynnek *adj.* abounding in ponds
lys *f.* **+yow** court, hall, palace; **lys an lagha** court of law
lyskannas *f.* **+ow** ambassador, diplomat
lyskannasedh *m.* diplomacy
lyskannasek *adj.* diplomatic
lyskannatti *m.* **+ow** embassy

Lyskerrys *place* Liskeard
lystenn *f.* **+ow** bandage, list, swaddling-band
lystenna *v.* bandage
lyswas *m.* **-wesyon** courtier
lyther *m.* **+ow** letter (epistle); **lyther apert** patent; **lytherow kresys** references (for potential employees), credentials
lytherdoll *m.* postage
lytherenn *f.* **+ow** letter (of alphabet)
lytherenna *v.* spell
lytherennans *m.* **+ow** spelling
lytherennek *f.* **-egi** alphabet
lytherennieth *f.* orthography
lytherva *f.* **+ow** post-office
lytherwas *m.* **-wesyon** postman
lyvenn *f.* **+ow** leaf (of paper), page (of book)
lyver *m.* **lyvrow** book; **lyver notennow** notebook
lyver-akontow *m.* **lyvrow-akontow** ledger, account book
lyver-dydhyow *m.* **lyvrow-dydhyow** calendar
lyverji *m.* **+ow** bookshop, bookstore (U.S.)
lyver-termyn *m.* **lyvrow-termyn** periodical, magazine
lyverva *f.* **+ow** library
lyverwerther *m.* **-oryon** bookseller
lyvrik *m.* **-igow** booklet
lyw *m.* **+yow** rudder, helm
lywya *v.* drive, steer, direct
lywyader *m.* **-oryon** pilot, steersman, helmsman
lywydh *m.* **+yon** director, president
lywyer *m.* **-yoryon** pilot, driver

M (mutations V, F)

ma<CJ> *conj.* so that

ma<this> *pron.* this
-ma *pron.* me
mab *m.* **mebyon** son, male child, boy; **mab bronn** mother's son; **mab an pla** (lit.) son of the plague; **Mebyon Kernow** Sons of Cornwall
mab-den *m.* mankind
mab-gov *m.* **mebyon-gov** smith's apprentice
mab-lyenn *m.* **mebyon-lyenn** cleric, clergyman
mab-meythrin *m.* foster-son
mabses *m.* boyhood
mab-wynn *m.* **mebyon-wynn** grandson
mabyar *f.* **-yer** pullet, chick young fowl
madama *f.* **madamys** madam, lady; ma'am, milady
madra *m.* groundsel
maga<as> *conj.* as; **maga ta** as well
maga<feed> *v.* feed, nourish, rear, raise (of children or animals),
magel *f.* **maglow** mesh, entanglement
mager *m.* **-oryon** breeder, rearer
magereth *f.* nurture, upbringing
maghtern *m.* **+yow** king, sovereign
maghteth *f.* **+yon** maid, maiden, maidservant
magla *v.* trap, ensnare, entangle; engage gear; **magla 'bann** change up (of gears), shift up (U.S.); **magla 'nans** change down (of gears), shift down (U.S.)
maglenn *f.* **+ow** trap, snare, mesh, gear (mech.); **maglenn dhelergh** reverse gear
magor *f.* **+yow** ruin
magores *f.* **+ow** wet nurse, breeder, rearer
Mahomm *name* Mahomet
mal *int.* pest
mala *v.* grind
malan *m.* devil

malbew *int.* plague take; **malbew damm** (expletive)

mall *m.* haste, eagerness, urgency, keenness; **mall yw genev** I am keen, I am in a hurry

mallart *m.* **-s** mallard

maler *m.* **-oryon** grinder

malow *coll.* **+enn** mallow

mamm *f.* **+ow** mother

mammel *adj.* maternal, motherly

mammeth *f.* **+ow** nursing mother

mamm-guv *f.* **mammow-kuv** great-grandmother

mammik *f.* mummy, mommy (U.S.)

mammoleth *f.* maternity, motherhood

mammskrif *m.* **+ow** original text, original manuscript

mamm-teylu *f.* matriarch, mistress of the house, materfamilias

mammveth *f.* **+ow** foster-mother

mammvro *f.* **+yow** motherland

mamm-wynn *f.* **mammow-gwynn** grandmother

mammyeth *f.* mother-tongue, native language

managh *m.* **menegh** monk

managhek *adj.* monastic

managhes *f.* **+ow** nun

managhti *m.* **+ow** monastery

manal *f.* **+ow** sheaf, rectorial tithes

manala *v.* put in sheaves, heap together

maneger *m.* **-oryon** glover

manek *f.* **manegow** glove; **manek plat** gauntlet

maner<manner> *f.* **+ow** custom, way, manner; **yn kepar maner** *adv.* similarly, likewise

maner<manor> *m.* manor

manerji *m.* **+ow** manor-house

mann *m.* nothing, nil *num.* zero *adv.* at all

mannbluv *coll.* fluff, down (fine feathers)

mannvlew *coll.* **+enn** fine hair

Manow *f.* Isle of Man

Manowek *adj.* Manx *m.* Manx language

mans *adj.* crippled, maimed *m.* **+yon** amputee, cripple

mantedh *coll.* stones (in body)

mantell *f.* **mantelli** cloak

mantell-nos *f.* **mantelli-nos** dressing-gown

mantol *f.* **+yow** balance, scales (for weighing)

manylya *v.* detail

manylyon *plur.* low-grade tin,, details, small particles

mappa *m.* **+ow** map

mar<if> *conj.* if, if only *m.* doubt; **mar pleg** please

mar<so> *adv.* so, as

mara *conj.* if

maras *conj.* if

marbel *m.* marble

marblenn *f.* **+ow** marble (sphere)

marchondis *m.* merchandise

marchont *m.* **-ons** merchant, trader, dealer

margarin *m.* margarine

margh *m.* **mergh** horse, stallion; **margh dall** blind man's buff; **margh kellek** stallion

marghador *m.* **+yon** marketeer, merchant

marghadores *f.* **+ow** marketeer, merchant

marghas *f.* **+ow** market; **marghas stokk** stock market

marghasa *v.* trade, market

marghasadow *adj.* marketable, saleable

marghasla *m.* market-place

marghasva *f.* **+ow** market-place

Marghasyow *place* Marazion

marghatti *m.* **+ow** market-house

marghboll *m.* **+ow** horse-pond

marghek *m.* **-ogyon** horseman, knight, soldier, cavalier rider (on horseback); **Marghek an Tempel** Knight Templar

marghes *plur.* horses

marghkenn *m.* horsehide

marghlergh *m.* **+ow** bridle-way

margh-leska *m.* **mergh-leska** rocking-horse

marghlynn *m.* **+ow** horse-pond

marghoges *f.* **+ow** horsewoman, rider

marghogeth *v.* ride

marghogieth *f.* horsemanship, knighthood, chivalry

margh-skrifa *m.* **mergh-skrifa** easel

marghti *m.* **+ow** stable

marghven *m.* **-veyn** mounting-block

marghvran *f.* **-vrini** raven

Maria *name* Mary; **Maria Wynn** Blessed Mary

marnas *conj.* unless, except, save

marner *m.* **marners**, **marnoryon** sailor, mariner

marow *adj.* dead *m.* deceased; **marow sygh** *adj.* stone dead

marowvor *m.* neap tide

mars *conj.* if

mar's *conj.* unless

martesen *adv.* perhaps, perchance, possibly, maybe

marth *m.* **+ow** wonder, astonishment, surprise

marthus *m.* **+yon** marvel, miracle, wonder

marthys *adj.* wonderful, marvellous, amazing, astounding *adv.* wonderfully, marvellously, amazingly, astoundingly

marwel *adj.* mortal, fatal

marwoleth *f.* mortality, fatality

marwystel *m.* **marwystlow** mortgage

marwystla *v.* mortgage

mas *adj.* good (morally)

ma's *conj.* unless

maskel *f.* **masklow** husk, pod

masken *m.* **+yow** bier

masoberer *m.* **-oryon** well-doer

mason *m.* **+s** mason

mata *m.* **matys** mate (pal), comrade, companion

mater *m.* **+s**, **+ow** matter, subject, affair; **mater tykkli** delicate matter

mater-redya *m.* reading-matter

materyel *adj.* material

materyoleth *f.* materialism

materyolethek *adj.* materialistic

Matthew *name* Matthew

maw *m.* boy, youth, servant

may *conj.* so that

maylya *v.* wrap, bind, swathe, envelop

maylyer *m.* **+s** envelope

mayn *adj.* average, mean *m.* **+ys** means, instrument, agency

mayner *m.* **-oryon** broker

maystri *m.* mastery, domination, control; **gul maystri orth** *phr.* exercise control over

mayth *conj.* so that (before vowels)

Me *m.* May

mebyl *m.* furniture

mebyon *plur.* sons, boys

medh *m.* mead (drink), hydromel

medhel *adj.* soft, tender, delicate

medhelder *m.* softness, delicacy, tenderness

medhelhe *v.* soften, weaken, enervate

medhelweyth *m.* software

medher *m.* **-oryon** speaker

medhes *v.* speak, say

medhow *adj.* drunk, intoxicated

medhwenep *m.* drunkenness, intoxication

medhwi *v.* intoxicate, get drunk

medhwynsi *f.* habitual drunkenness, alcoholism

medhygel *adj.* medical

medhygieth *f.* medicine (as science), remedy

medhyglynn *m.* metheglin, spiced mead

medhygneth *f.* medicine (as remedy),

medhygva *f.* **+ow** clinic, surgery (place), medical centre, doctor's office (U.S.)

medhyk *m.* **medhygyon** doctor, physician

medhyk-dens *m.* **medhygyon-dens** dentist

medra *v.* aim, notice, observe

medras *m.* **+ow** aim, aspiration

medyner *f.* **+yow** hinge

meghin *m.* bacon

megi *v.* smoke, smother, stifle

meginow *plur.* bellows

megyans *m.* culture, nutriment, sustenance

megys<choked> *v.* choked

megys<reared> *v.* reared

megys<smoked> *adj.* smoked

mel *m.* honey

mela *v.* gather honey

melder *m.* darling, sweetness, honey (U.S. endearment)

melek *adj.* honeyed, honey-yielding

melgennek *adj.* suave

meles *m.* red ochre, ruddle

melgowas *f.* **+ow** honeydew

melhwenn *f.* slug

melhwes *coll.* **+enn** snails

melhwesek *adj.* snail-like

melhwessa *v.* catch snails

melhwyoges *f.* tortoise

melin *f.* **+yow** mill

melin-sidhla *f.* bolting-mill

melin-wyns *f.* **melinyow-gwyns** windmill

melinji *m.* **+ow** mill-house

meliner *m.* **-yon** miller

mell *m.* **+ow** joint, articulation; **mell keyn** vertebra

mellek *adj.* jointed, articulated

mellya *v.* interfere, meddle, molest

mellyans *m.* interference, meddling, molestation

mellyon *coll.* **+enn** clover, violets; **mellyon melyn** bird's foot trefoil; **mellyon tryliw** viola (plant)

mellyonek *adj.* clovery *f.* **-egi** clover-patch

melon *m.* **+yow** melon

mels *plur.* wether sheep

melyas *v.* grind

melyn *adj.* yellow, tawny

melynder *m.* yellowness

melynek *m.* **-oges** goldfinch; **melynek eythin** yellowhammer

melynhe *v.* make yellow

melynik *adj.* jaundiced, yellowish

melys *adj.* insipid, very sweet

men<stone> *m.* **meyn** stone

men *adj.* strong, able, stalwart; **toeth men** *adv.* at full speed

men-bedh *m.* **meyn-bedh** gravestone

mendardh *coll.* saxifrage

men-du *m.* jet (mineral)

meneges *v.* mention, report, confess sins

menegh *plur.* monks

meneghi *m.* sanctuary, refuge, place of asylum

meneghiji *m.* **+ow** sanctuary

menegva *f.* **+ow** index

menek *m.* **-egow** mention, indication

menestrouthi *m.* instrumental music

mengleudh *m.* **+yow** quarry (stone-pit)

mengleudhya *v.* quarry

men-kov *m.* **meyn-kov** memorial stone

menhe *v.* petrify, turn to stone

menhir *m.* **-yon** long-stone, standing stone

meni *m.* household, crew, troop, set of chessmen, staff (group of workers)

menow *plur.* individual stones

menowgh *adv.* often, repeatedly, frequently

menowghder *m.* frequency

men-pobas *m.* **meyn-pobas** bakestone, griddle

menta *f.* mint (plant)

mentena *v.* maintain, abet, stand by

mentenour *m.* **-s** supporter

men-toemm *m.* **meyn-toemm** hotplate

mentons *m.* maintenance, upholding

menweyth *m.* masonry, stonework

menydh *m.* **+yow** mountain, hill

menydhek *adj.* mountainous

menydhyer *m.* **menydhyoryon** mountaineer

menyster *m.* **+yon, -trys** minister; **Menyster a-barth Fordhow;** Minister for Highways; **Menyster Estrenyek** Foreign Minister

menystra *v.* administer, serve

menystrans *m.* administration, ministry; **Menystrans Ammeth** Ministry of Agriculture

menystrer *m.* **-oryon** butler

meppik *m.* **-igow** small son

mer<marrow> *m.* bone-marrow

mer<mayor> *m.* **+yon** mayor

mera *v.* snivel

mer-boes *m.* **meryon-boes** steward

merdhin *m.* sea-fort

merek *adj.* snivelling *m.* **-ogyon** sniveller

meres *f.* **+ow** mayoress

mergh *plur.* horses; **an vergh** the horses

Mergher *m.* Wednesday, Mercury

merghik *m.* **-igow** pony

meri *adj.* merry, intoxicated, high; **maga feri avel hok** as high as a kite

merji *m.* **+ow** home of mayor

merk *m.* **+yow** mark

merk-post *m.* **merkyow-post** post-mark

merkya *v.* mark, observe

merkyl *m.* **merklys** miracle

mernans *m.* death; **gorra dhe vernans** *phr.* put to death

mersi *m.* mercy

mersiabyl *adj.* merciful

merther *m.* **+yon** saint's grave

mertherya *v.* martyr

mertherynsi *f.* martyrdom

merwel *v.* die, expire

Meryasek *name* (name of saint)

merys *m.* medlar

meryw *coll.* **+enn** juniper

mes<acorns> *coll.* **+enn** acorns

mes<but> *conj.* but

mes<field> *m.* **+yow** open field, open country

mesa *v.* gather acorns

meschons *m.* mischance

meschyvya *v.* injure, ruin

meschyf *m.* injury, harm, ruin

mesek *f.* cultivated land

meskel *coll.* **mesklenn** mussels

messach *m.* **messajys** message

messejer *m.* **+s** messenger

messent *adj.* musty

mester *m.* **mestrysi** master

Mester *m.* Mister, Mr

mestra *f.* **+ow** suburb

mestres *f.* **+ow** mistress

Mestres *f.* Mrs, Mistress; Ms; Miss (of adult women)

Mestresik *f.* Miss (of girls)

mestrevek *adj.* suburban
mestrogh-brys *m.* hysterectomy
mestronieth *f.* master's degree
mestrynses *m.* dominion, domination, mastery
meter *m.* **metrow** metre (unit)
meth<nurture> *m.* nurture, nourishing, feeding
meth<shame> *f.* **mothow** shame, failure, disgrace; **meth a'm beus** *phr.* I am ashamed; **kemmeres meth** be ashamed
methek *adj.* ashamed; **bos methek a** *phr.* be ashamed of
Metheven *m.* June
mether *m.* **-oryon** victualler, caterer
Methodek *adj.* Methodist
Methodyas *m.* **-ysi** Methodist
methus *adj.* shameful, ignominious
methya *v.* feed
metol *m.* metal
metregi *v.* metricate
metregieth *f.* metrication
metrek *adj.* metric
metya *v.* meet, encounter
metyans *m.* **+ow** meeting
meur *adj.* great, large, many; **meur a** many, a lot of; **meur ras** *phr.* thank you; **meur y golonn** *adj.* magnanimous
meuredh *m.* greatness, majesty, pomp, magnificence
meurgerys *adj.* beloved, much loved
meurgolonn *f.* magnanimity
meurhe *v.* magnify, make great
Meurth *m.* Tuesday, March, Mars
meurthwas *m.* **-wesyon** martian
meus *m.* thumb
meusva *f.* **meusvedhi** inch
meusya *v.* thumb a lift
-mevy *pron.* me (emphatic)
mewgh *m.* **+yow** bail, guarantee, warranty

mewghya *v.* stand bail, guarantee
mewghyer *m.* **-yoryon** guarantor, one who stands bail, bail-bondsman (U.S.)
mewl *m.* disgrace, reproach
meydh *m.* whey
meyl *m.* **+i** mullet
meylessa *v.* catch mullet
meyn *plur.* stones; **an veyn** the stones
meyndi *m.* stone-house
meynek *adj.* rocky *f.* **-egi** rocky place, rockery
meythrin *v.* rear, raise (of a child)
Mighal *name* Michael
migorn *m.* cartilage
mik *m.* squeak
mikenn *f.* malice, animosity
mil<animal> *m.* **+es** animal, wild beast
mil<1000> *m.* **+yow** thousand
milast *f.* **milisti** greyhound
milblek *adj.* thousandfold
mildir *m.* **+yow** mile
mildroes *m.* millipede
milgi *m.* **milgeun** greyhound
milgolm *m.* knotgrass
milhyntall *m.* maze, labyrinth
milliga *v.* curse
milus *adj.* brutal, beastly, bestial *m.* **milusyon** brute
milva *f.* **milvaow** zoo, menagerie
milvedhygieth *f.* veterinary science
milvedhyk *m.* **-ygyon** vet
milves *num.* thousandth
milvil *m.* **+yow** million
milvilwas *m.* **-wesyon** millionaire
milvloedh *phr.* thousand years old
milvlydhen *f.* **+yow** millennium
milwell *adj.* far better
milweth *adj.* far worse
milweyth *adv.* thousand times

min *m.* **+yow** face, lip, mouth; tip (end), edge, border; **syns dha vin** *phr.* shut your mouth

mindu *adj.* swarthy, blackavised

minfel *m.* yarrow, milfoil

mingamm *m.* **+ow** grimace

mingamma *v.* grimace

mingow *adj.* lying

minhwarth *m.* smile

minhwerthin *v.* smile

minrew *adj.* grey-bearded

minvlew *coll.* **+ynn** whiskers, moustache

minya *v.* nuzzle

minyek *adj.* long-muzzled, pointed *m.* **minyoges** long-nosed skate

miowal *v.* mew

mir *m.* appearance (of a person), look

mires *v.* look, behold, observe; **mires orth** look at, watch, regard; **mires war** look upon

mirewgh *int.* behold

mirji *m.* **+ow** observatory

mirour *m.* **+s** mirror

mis *m.* **misyow** month

mis-Du *m.* November

mis-Ebryl *m.* April

mis-Est *m.* August

mis-Genver *m.* January

mis-Gortheren *m.* July

mis-Gwynngala *m.* September

mis-Hedra *m.* October

mis-Hwevrer *m.* February

mis-Kevardhu *m.* December

miskweyth *m.* period of a month

mis-Me *m.* May

mis-Metheven *m.* June

mis-Meurth *m.* March

misyek *adj.* monthly

mita *m.* **mitys** mite

miter *m.* **+s** mitre

mo *m.* hour before dawn, dusk, twilight; **mo ha myttin** *adv.* by night and by day

modrep *f.* **modrebedh** aunt

moel *adj.* bald, bare

moelder *m.* baldness, bareness

moelhe *v.* make bald

moen<ore> *m.* ore

moen<thin> *adj.* slender, thin, slim

moendi *m.* mineral-house, building (for processing ore)

moenek *adj.* mineral *f.* **moenegi** ore-bearing ground

moengleudh *m.* **+yow** opencast mine-working

moes *f.* **+ow** table

mog *m.* smoke, fume, reek

moga *v.* choke

moggha *adj.* most

mogh *plur.* pigs, swine (pl.)

moghhe *v.* magnify

mogow *f.* **+yow** cave

mol *m.* **+yow** clot, hardened blood

mola<clot> *v.* clot

mola<mould> *v.* mould (for casting), knead

molas *m.* treacle, molasses

moldra *v.* murder, assassinate

moldrer *m.* **-oryon** murderer

molgh *f.* **+i** thrush; **molgh dhu** blackbird

molleth *f.* **mollothow** curse, malediction, imprecation; **molla'tyw** God's curse

mollethi *v.* curse, execrate

mollethyans *m.* **+ow** malediction

mollothek *adj.* cursed, accursed, execrable

mols *m.* **mels** wether sheep

mon *m.* dung, manure

mona *coll.* cash, money, change; **mona kemmyn** currency; **mona munys** small change

mones *v.* go

monesek *adj.* monetary

mong *f.* **+ow** mane

mongar *f.* horse-collar

mongarenn *f.* **+ow** horse-collar
mont *m.* mount
mor<CN> *coll.* **+enn** berries
mor<sea> *m.* **+yow** sea
mora *v.* put to sea
morast *f.* **moristi** blue shark
morbenn *m.* **+ow** mallet
morbrenn *m.* **+yer** bramble-bush
mordan *m.* phosphorescence
mordardh *m.* surf
mordardha *v.* surf
mordhos *f.* **-osow**, *dual*
  diwvordhos thigh; **mordhos**
  hogh ham
mordid *m.* tide
Mordir Nowydh *place* New
  Zealand
mordonn *f.* **+ow** wave (in sea), sea-
  wave
mordros *m.* sound of surf
mordryk *m.* low tide
mor-du *coll.* **morenn-dhu**
  blackberries
moredh *m.* regret, grief, sorrow,
  melancholy
moredhek *adj.* melancholy, pining,
  homesick
morek *adj.* maritime
morel *adj.* jet-black
moren *f.* **+yon** maiden; **moren**
  bries bridesmaid
morer *m.* **+es** erne (bird), sea-eagle
morgath *f.* **+es** skate
morgelynn *coll.* **+enn** sea-holly
morgi *m.* **morgeun** dogfish
morgowl *m.* sea-kale
morgowles *coll.* **+enn** jellyfish
morgroenek *m.* **-oges** blenny
morhesk *coll.* **+enn** marram grass,
  sandspire
morhogh *m.* **+es** porpoise, dolphin
morhwynnenn *f.* **+ow**, *coll.*
  morhwynn sand-hopper
morlader *m.* **-ladron** pirate

morlanow *m.* high tide
morlenwel *v.* rise (of tide)
morlu *m.* navy
mornader *f.* **mornadrys** lamprey
mornaswydh *f.* **+ow** pipe-fish
moronieth *f.* oceanography
morow *f.* morrow, following day
morrep *m.* sea-shore, sea-board,
  seaside, coast, seaward portion of a
  parish in Cornwall
morenn-rudh *f.* **morennow-**
  rudh, *coll.* **mor-rudh** raspberry
morsarf *f.* **morserf** sea-serpent
mortes *m.* **+ys** mortise
morthelik-ankow *m.*
  mortheligow-ankow death-
  watch beetle
morthol *m.* **+ow** hammer
mortholek *adj.* dinted, dented
mortholya *v.* hammer
mortholynn *m.* **+ow** tappet
morva *f.* **+ow** sea-marsh
morvanagh *m.* **-venegh** monk-
  fish
morvargh *m.* **-vergh** seahorse
morvelhwenn *f.* **+ow** sea-slug
morvil *m.* **+es** whale
morvleydh *m.* **+i** shark
morvoren *f.* **+yon** mermaid
morvran *f.* **-vrini** cormorant
morvugh *f.* **+es** walrus
morwas *m.* **-wesyon** seaman,
  matelot
morwels *coll.* grasswrack, sea-wrack
morwennol *f.* **-wennili** tern, sea-
  swallow
morwyrghes *f.* **+i** mermaid
moryon *coll.* **+enn** ants
mos *v.* go; **mos dres** exceed; **mos**
  erbynn meet with; **mos ha bos**
  become; **mos yn-rag** proceed,
  advance
mosegi *v.* stink
mosek *adj.* stinking

most *m.* **+yon** filth, impurity
mostedhes *m.* filth, dirt, defilement
mostya *v.* befoul, soil, dirty
mothow *plur.* indignities, breakdown, fiasco
mottys *plur.* motes
moutya *v.* moult, sulk, mope
movya *v.* move (spiritually), incite, arouse; **es y vovya** *adj.* nervous
movyans *m.* **+ow** movement
mowa *m.* **mowys** grimace
mowes *f.* **mowesi** girl
moy *adj.* more
moyha *adj.* most, maximum
Moyses *name* Moses
mujovenn *f.* ridge
mul *m.* **+yon** mule
mules *f.* **+ow** mule
munys *adj.* minute, little
mus *adj.* mad *m.* **+yon** madman
muskegi *v.* rave
muskogneth *f.* stupidity
muskok *m.* **-ogyon** madman, fool
muskokter *m.* madness
musur *m.* measure, moderation
musura *v.* measure, moderate
musurans *m.* **+ow** measurement
musurell *f.* **+ow** meter, gauge, measure (tool)
musurell-doeth *f.*
musurellow-toeth speedometer
musuryas *m.* **-ysi** surveyor (for map-making)
my *pron.* I, me
myghtern *m.* **+edh** king, sovereign, monarch
myghternans *m.* kingdom
myghternes *f.* **+ow** queen
myghternses *m.* sovereignty, kingship
mygli *v.* cool off, grow indifferent
mygyl *adj.* lukewarm, tepid
mygylder *m.* indifference
myjenn *m.* mite, pinch

myll *f.* **+es** corn-poppy, field poppy (U.S.)
mynchya *v.* play truant, play hookey (U.S.)
mynkek *m.* heather, ling
mynn *m.* **+ow** kid (goat), young goat
mynnenn *f.* **+ow** baby goat
mynnas *m.* wish, purpose, intent, intention
mynnes *v.* wish, want, intend, be willing to; **mynnes orth nebonan** require of someone
mynnik *m.* little kid (goat)
mynowes *m.* awl
myns *m.* size, amount, dimension, quantity *pron.* as many as, as much as, all who, whoever
mynsonieth *f.* geometry
mynster *m.* endowed church
mynstral *m.* **+s** minstrel
mynysenn *f.* **+ow** minute (of time)
myrgh *f.* **myrghes** daughter, girl, female child, young woman
myrghik *f.* **myrghesigow** little girl
myrr *m.* myrrh
myrtwydhenn *f.* **+ow**, *coll.*
myrtwydh myrtle-tree
myser *m.* **-oryon** reaper
mysi *v.* reap
mysk *m.* middle, midst; **y'ga mysk** among them; **y'gan mysk** among us; **y'gas mysk** among you
myska *v.* blend, mingle
myskemmeres *v.* mistake
myskemmeryans *m.* misunderstanding
myster *m.* craft, guild, trade
mysterden *m.* **+s** craftsman, member of trade-guild
mystrest *m.* mistrust
mystrestya *v.* mistrust, doubt
myswas *m.* **-wesyon** reaper
myttin *m.* **+yow** morning, forenoon *adv.* in the morning

myttinweyth *m.* forenoon, morning *adv.* during the morning

N

na<AV> *adv.* that, those
na<no> *int.* no
na<CJ> *conj.* that not
na<nor> *conj.* nor; **na fella** *adv.* no longer; **na hwath** not yet; **na ... na** neither ... nor
Nadelik *m.* Christmas
nader *f.* **nadres** viper, adder
nader-margh *f.* dragonfly
nadh *m.* hewing, chopping
nadha *v.* hew, chop
nag<CJ> *conj.* nor
nag<VP> *ptl.* that not
nagh *m.* denial, refusal
nagha *v.* deny, refuse, renounce, decline
nagonan *pron.* no-one, not one
nahen *adj.* any other, any more, otherwise (with neg.)
naker *m.* **nakrys** kettle-drum, timpano
nameur *adj.* many *adv.* many times, much (with neg.)
namm *m.* **+ow** defect, flaw, blemish, exception spot (pimple)
nammenowgh *adv.* seldom, rarely
nammna *adv.* almost, nearly, well nigh
nammnag *adv.* almost
nammnygen *adv.* just now
namoy *adj.* any more *adv.* again (with neg.)
naneyl *pron.* neither *conj.* neither; **naneyl ... na** neither ... nor
nans<now> *ptl.* now (in phrase); **nans yw** ago; **nans yw seythun** a week ago
nans<valley> *m.* **+ow** valley, dale
nappya *v.* nap

nas *f.* nature (character), disposition
naswydh *f.* **+yow** needle
nath *m.* **+es** puffin
natur *f.* nature, character
naturel *adj.* natural
natureth *f.* natural affection, human nature
naturor *m.* **+yon** naturalist
naw *num.* nine
nawmen *m.* knuckle bones
naw-ugens *num.* nine score
nawves *num.* ninth
neb *pron.* some *adj.* any; **neb le** anywhere; **neb lies** not many; **neb tyller** anywhere; **neb unn** a certain
nebes *m.* few, some *adj.* few *adv.* somewhat, a little; **mar nebes** so little; **nebes hir** somewhat long
nebonan *pron.* someone, anyone
nebreydh *adj.* neuter
nedh *coll.* **+enn** nits
nedha *v.* spin (of yarn), twist
nedher *m.* **-oryon** spinner
nedhores *f.* **+ow** spinner
negedhek *adj.* negative
negedhys *adj.* apostate *m.* **+yon** apostate, turncoat
neghys *v.* denied, rejected, renounced
negys *m.* **+yow** business, transaction; affair, errand; **negys orth** business with; **mones negys** *phr.* to go on an errand
negysya *v.* negotiate
negysydh *m.* **+yon** businessman, representative, negotiator
nell *m.* strength, power, force
nen *m.* **+yow** ceiling
nenbrenn *m.* **+yer** ridge-pole, roof-tree
nenlenn *f.* **+ow** canopy
nep-prys *adv.* sometime, at any time
nep-pell *adv.* at some distance
neppyth *pron.* something, anything

nep-tu *adv.* somewhere, anywhere; neutral

nerth *m.* +yow power, might, strength, force

nertha *v.* strengthen (a person), fortify (a person)

nerthek *adj.* powerful, mighty, potent, strenuous, robust

nerthegeth *f.* stamina

nerv *coll.* +enn nerves

nervenn *f.* +ow, *coll.* nerv nerve

nervus *adj.* nervous

nes *adj.* nearer; dos nes draw near, approach

nesa *v.* approach (intrans.), draw near

neshe *v.* approach

neshevin *plur.* kinsmen, next of kin

neskar *m.* neskerens near relative

nessa *adj.* nearest, next, second

nester *m.* proximity, nearness

-neth *suff.* (masc. abst. noun ending, from aj.)

neus *coll.* thread (in general)

neusa *v.* fray out, fringe

neusenn *f.* +ow, *coll.* neus thread (individual)

neusenna *v.* thread, embroider

neusynn *m.* +ow filament

neuvell *f.* +ow float (e.g. for fishing)

neuvella *v.* float

neuvelladow *adj.* buoyant; neuvelladow heptu neutrally buoyant

neuvwisk *m.* swimwear

neuvya *v.* swim

neuvyer *m.* -yoryon swimmer

nev *m.* +ow heaven

nevek *adj.* heavenly, celestial

neves *m.* sacred grove

nevesek *adj.* pertaining to a sacred grove

nevra *adv.* never (in neg. phrases), ever

new *f.* +yow trough, sink; new droghya dip (for sheep)

neweth *f.* immaturity

neyth *m.* +ow nest

neythi *v.* nest, build a nest

neythva *f.* +ow nesting-place

ni *pron.* we, us

-ni *suff.* (masc. abst. noun ending)

nij *m.* +ow flight

nija *v.* fly

nijys *adj.* air-borne

nisyta *m.* ignorance, folly

nith *f.* +ow niece

nivel *m.* +yow level, standard

niver *m.* +ow number

nivera *v.* count, reckon, number

niverenn *f.* +ow numeral

niverieth *f.* numeration

niveronieth *f.* arithmetic

niverus *adj.* numerous

niveryans *m.* counting, census, enumeration, count

niwl *m.* +ow mist, fog, haze

niwlek *adj.* misty

niwlenn *f.* +ow fog-bank

niwlgorn *m.* fog-horn

niwllaw *m.* drizzle

niwl-ster *m.* nebula

niwlrew *m.* hoar-frost

niwlwias *m.* +ow gauze

nobyl<AJ> *adj.* noble

nobyl<MN> *m.* noblys noble (coin)

noeth *adj.* naked, nude

noetha *f.* nakedness, nudity

nor *m.* world

Normanek *adj.* Norman

norter *m.* good manners, nurture

north *m.* North

north-est *m.* north-east

north-west *m.* north-west

norvys *m.* Earth

nos<night> *f.* **+ow** night, eve of
feast; **nos dha** goodnight; **dre
nos** *adv.* through the night
nos<token> *m.* **+ow** token
nos<yonder> *adv.* yonder
noskan *f.* **+ow** serenade
noswara *m.* contraband goods
nosweyth *adv.* at night *f.* **+yow**
night-time
noswikor *m.* **+yon** smuggler,
contrabandist
noswikorek *adj.* contraband
noswikorieth *f.* smuggling
notenn *f.* note
noter *m.* **-oryon** notary, solicitor
nothlenn *f.* **+ow** winnowing sheet
notha *v.* winnow
notya *v.* make known, remark, note
notyans *m.* **+ow** note
now *adv.* now (only in poetry)
nowedhys *m.* tidings, news
nown *m.* hunger, starvation
nownek *adj.* hungry
nownsegves *num.* nineteenth
nownsek *num.* nineteen
nowodhow *plur.* news, tidings;
hager nowodhow bad news; **yeyn
nowodhow** bad news
nowydh *adj.* new, fresh, novel;
nowydh flamm brand new
nowydha *v.* renew
nowydhadow *adj.* renewable
nowydhhe *v.* renew, renovate
nowydhses *m.* newness
noy *m.* **noyens** nephew
Noy *name* Noah
nuk *m.* back; **war nuk** *adv.* by return
nuklerek *adj.* nuclear
ny *ptl.* not
nyhewer *adv.* last night, yesterday
evening
nyni *pron.* us
nyns *ptl.* not

O

o *v.* was
obaya *v.* obey, submit, surrender
obayans *m.* obedience
ober *m.* **+ow** work, act, deed
oberenn *f.* **+ow** job, task, chore
(U.S.)
oberer *m.* **-oryon** worker, doer,
performer
obereth *f.* major work, deed, opus,
performance
oberi *v.* work, do, perform, operate
oberwas *m.* **-wesyon** workman
oberyans *m.* operation
oden *f.* kiln, furnace
oden-galgh *f.* lime-kiln
odor *m.* odour
odyt *m.* adit, aqueduct, water-channel
(from a mine)
oela *v.* weep, cry, lament (trans.)
oeles *f.* **+ow** hearth, fireplace
oelva *f.* weeping, wailing, lamentation
oen *m.* **eyn** lamb
oenes *f.* **+ow** ewe-lamb
oengenn *m.* lamb-skin
oenik *m.* **eynigow** lambkin, little
lamb
oer *adj.* excessively cold, freezing,
frigid
oerni *m.* frigidity
oerwyns *m.* **+ow** blizzard, icy wind
oes *m.* **+ow** age, period (of time);
Oes Brons Bronze Age; **Oes Men**
Stone Age
-oes *v.* (VN ending)
oesweyth *f.* **+yow** epoch, age
(period of time)
oferenn *f.* **+ow** mass (church
service), eucharist, religious service
oferenni *v.* celebrate mass
ofergugol *m.* chasuble
oferyas *m.* **oferysi** priest, celebrant
oferyasek *adj.* priestly, sacerdotal

offendya *v.* resist, offend, strive against

offens *m.* **+ys** offence, breach, opposition

offis *m.* **offisys** office (abst.), function, position

offra *v.* offer

offrynn *m.* **+ow** offering

offrynna *v.* offer up, sacrifice

ogas *adj.* near, close, adjoining *adv.* nearly, almost

ogatti *adv.* nearly, almost

-oges *suff.* (fem. noun ending, from aj.)

-ogeth *suff.* (fem. abst. noun ending)

ogh *int.* oh, ah, alas

oghen *plur.* oxen

-ogneth *suff.* (fem. abst. noun ending)

ojyon *m.* ox

oker *m.* interest (money), usury

okerer *m.* **-oryon** money-lender, usurer

ol *m.* **+ow** trace, track, print (e.g. of foot)

-oleth *suff.* (fem. abst. noun ending)

olew *m.* olive-oil

olewbrenn *m.* **-yer** olive-tree

olewenn *f.* **+ow** olive-tree

olewi *v.* anoint (with holy oil)

olifans *m.* **-es** elephant

oliv *m.* olive *coll.* **+enn** olive-trees

oll *adj.* all, every *adv.* wholly, entirely

ollgalloes *m.* omnipotence

ollgalloesek *adj.* almighty

ollsens *plur.* All Saints

ollvysel *adj.* global (of Earth)

om- *pref.* (reflexive prefix)

omaj *m.* homage

omajer *m.* **+s** vassal, retainer

omamendya *v.* correct oneself

omaskusya *v.* excuse oneself

omassaya *v.* test oneself, practise, rehearse

ombareusi *v.* prepare oneself

ombellhe *v.* distance oneself

omblegya *v.* submit, bow

omberthi *v.* balance, poise

omborth *adj.* balanced, poised

ombrederi *v.* ponder, reflect, consider

ombraysya show off

ombrena *v.* redeem oneself

ombrevi *v.* prove oneself

ombrofya *v.* offer oneself, stand as a candidate

ombrofyer *m.* **-oryon** candidate

omdenna *v.* withdraw, retire

omdewlel *v.* wrestle

omdhal *v.* quarrel, strive

omdhalgh *m.* **+ow** attitude

omdharbari *v.* prepare oneself

omdhaskorr *v.* capitulate, surrender

omdhihares *v.* excuse oneself

omdhiserri *v.* calm down

omdhisevel *v.* overbalance, stumble, trip and fall

omdhiskwedhes *v.* appear

omdhiskwedhyans *m.* **+ow** appearance (an appearance)

omdhiskwitha *v.* relax

omdhivas *adj.* bereft *m.* orphan (male)

omdhivasa *v.* orphan, bereave (of parents)

omdhivases *f.* orphan (female)

omdhivatti *m.* **+ow** orphanage

omdhivroa *v.* emigrate

omdhivroans *m.* **+ow** emigration

omdhiwiska *v.* undress oneself

omdhoen<behave> *v.* behave oneself

omdhoen<conceive> *v.* conceive (a child)

omdhrehevel *v.* raise oneself up

omdhyghtya *v.* look after oneself, order oneself

omdowl *m.* wrestling

omdowler *m.* **-oryon** wrestler

omervirans *m.* self-determination
omfolsadow *adj.* fissile
omgamma *v.* distort; **omgamma min** grimace; **omgamma orth** grimace at, make a face at
omgavoes *v.* be situated, find oneself
omgeles *v.* hide oneself, lurk
omgelli *v.* merge (intrans.)
omgemmyska *v.* mingle (oneself)
omgemmeres *v.* undertake, become responsible for
omgemmeryans *m.* **+ow** responsibility
omgerdh *m.* evolution
omgerdhes *v.* evolve
omglywans *m.* **+ow** feeling, sensation
omglywansel *adj.* sensual
omglywansus *adj.* sensuous
omglywes *v.* feel, sense
omgnoukya *v.* knock oneself
omgommendya *v.* introduce oneself
omgonfortya *v.* comfort oneself
omgonvedhes *v.* understand each other
omgregi *v.* hang oneself
omgudha *v.* hide oneself
omguntell *v.* meet, gather, collect (intrans.), assemble
omgusulya *v.* discuss
omgwetha *v.* dress, put on clothing
omgyfyans *m.* self-confidence
omherdhya *v.* obtrude, intrude
omhowla *v.* sunbathe
omhweles *v.* fall down, tip up, tip over
omhwithra *v.* examine oneself
omjershya *v.* be at ease
omjunya *v.* merge
omladh *v.* fight *m.* **+ow** fight
omladha *v.* kill oneself, commit suicide

omlesa *v.* spread (intrans.), expand
omlesans *m.* **+ow** expansion
omlet *m.* **+ow** omelette
omlettya *v.* stop oneself
omlowenhe *v.* rejoice, enjoy oneself
omlusek *adj.* self-adhesive
omma *adv.* here
omrewl *f.* autonomy, self-rule
omri *v.* surrender, dedicate
omrolya *v.* enrol
omsakrifia *v.* sacrifice oneself
omsav *m.* **+ow** movement (political), uprising
omsawya *v.* save oneself
omsedhi *v.* subside
omsettya *v.* set oneself, attack, raid
omsettyans *m.* **+ow** attack, raid
omsevel *v.* rise up
omsoena *v.* cross oneself
omsynsi *v.* hold oneself
omsywya *v.* follow, be consequent upon
omvedhwi *v.* get drunk
omvetya *v.* meet (one another)
omvodhek *adj.* self-indulgent, complaisant, wilful
omvodhya *v.* indulge oneself, be complaisant, be wilful
omwana *v.* stab oneself
omwen *v.* wriggle, writhe, wince
omweres *v.* take care of oneself; **omweres rag** protect oneself from
omweskel *v.* strike oneself
omwetha *v.* deteriorate, pine away
omwethhe *v.* deteriorate
omwiska *v.* dress oneself, put on clothing
omwitha *v.* keep oneself, guard oneself, be careful; **omwitha diworth** guard oneself from
omwodhvos *m.* consciousness, self-consciousness, self-awareness
omwolghi *v.* wash oneself
omwovynn *v.* wonder

omwul *v.* pretend, turn oneself into

omystynna *v.* extend (intrans.), stretch oneself

on *v.* we are

onan *num.* one *pron.* single person, single thing

onest *adj.* proper, seemly, decent

onester *m.* propriety, decency, decorum

ongel *m.* cabbage

-onieth *suff.* (fem. abst. noun ending, from noun), -ology

onn *coll.* **+enn** ash-trees

onnek *f.* **-egi** ash-grove

onyonenn *f.* **+ow**, *coll.* **onyon** onion

or<edge> *f.* **+yon** border, edge, boundary

or<is> *v.* one is

-or *suff.* **-oryon** (agency noun ending)

oratri *m.* **+s** oratory

ordena *v.* put in order, ordain, arrange, appoint, organize

ordenal *m.* **+ys** service-book

ordenans *m.* ordinance, control

ordenor *m.* **-yon** organizer

ordir *m.* **+yow** borderland, march (border district)

ordyr *m.* **ordyrs** religious order, rank

ordys *plur.* holy orders

-ores *suff.* **-oresow** (fem. agency noun ending)

organ *m.* **+s** organ (Mus.)

organek *adj.* organic

organydh *m.* **+yon** organist

orgelous *adj.* proud *m.* proud man

orrenn *f.* **+ow** bundle of thatch

ors *m.* **+es** bear (animal)

orses *f.* **+ow** she-bear

orsik *m.* **-igow** bear-cub, teddy-bear

orth *prep.* at, by

os *v.* thou art

ost *m.* **+ys** innkeeper

osta *phr.* you are, are you

ostel *f.* **+yow** lodging, hostel, hotel; **ostel yowynkneth** youth hostel

ostelri *m.* hostelry

ostes *f.* **+ow** hostess; **ostes ayr** air hostess

Ostrali *place* Australia

ostya *v.* lodge, stay (at a hotel, etc.)

ostyans *m.* hospitality, accommodation, board and lodging

o'ta *phr.* you are, are you

ott *int.* see, lo, behold; **ott ha** see how

otta *int.* behold, here is, there is; **ottahi** behold her; **ottahwi** behold you; **ottajy** behold thee; **ottani** behold us; **ottava** behold him; **ottavy** behold me; **ottensi** behold them

ottena *int.* look there

ottomma *int.* look here

oula *m.* **oulys** owl

oulya *v.* howl, bark, cry

oulyans *m.* howl

ouns *m.* **+yow** ounce; **ouns devrek** fluid ounce

our *m.* **+ys** hour, duration of one hour

out *int.* oh, out

outlayer *m.* **+s** outlaw

outray *m.* outrage, outrageous action

ov *v.* I am

ovydh *m.* **+yon** ovate

ow<-ing> *ptl.* -ing

ow<my> *adj.* my

-ow *suff.* (pl. ending)

owgh *v.* you are

own *m.* fear, dread, awe; **kemmeres own** *v.* take fright; **na borth own** don't be afraid

ownek *adj.* afraid *m.* **ownogyon** coward

ownekhe *v.* frighten

owr *m.* gold, money

owra *v.* gild

owraval *m.* **+ow** orange (fruit)

owrbysk *m.* **owrbuskes** goldfish

owrdynk *m.* **+es** goldfinch
owrek *adj.* golden *f.* **-egi** gold-mine
owrlin *m.* silk
owrer *m.* **-oryon** goldsmith
owth *ptl.* -ing
oy *m.* **+ow** egg; **ny dal oy** *phr.* it's absolutely worthless; **ny rov oy** I don't care a bit
oyl *m.* **oylys** oil

P (mutations B, F)

pab *m.* **+ow** pope
padell *f.* **+ow** pan
padell-bobas *f.* **padellow-pobas** baking-pan
padell-bonn *f.* **padellow-ponn** dust-pan
padell-dhorn *f.* **padellow-dorn** saucepan
padell-doemma *f.* **padellow-toemma** warming-pan
padell-fria *f.* **padellow-fria** frying-pan
padell-horn *f.* iron pan
padellik *f.* **-igow** saucer
pader *m.* **+ow** Lord's Prayer, pater, bead of rosary
padera *v.* repeat prayers
paderenn *f.* **+ow** single bead
pagan *m.* **+ys**, **+yon** pagan
paja *m.* **pajys** page (boy), lackey, serving-boy; **paja mergh** groom (for horses), stable-lad
pal *f.* **+yow** spade, shovel
palas *v.* dig, excavate
paler *m.* **-oryon** digger, shoveller, navvy
palfray *m.* palfrey, saddle-horse
pali *m.* velvet, brocade, glossy silk fabric
pall *m.* **+ow** mantle, pall

pallenn *f.* **+ow** blanket, covering (material); **pallenn vargh** horse-cloth
palm *m.* **+ow**, **+ys** palm-branch, palm-frond
palmer *m.* **-oryon** pilgrim (from the Holy Land), palmer
palmwydh *coll.* **+enn** palm-trees
palores *f.* **+ow** chough
pals *adj.* plentiful, numerous
palshe *v.* abound, multiply (intrans.)
palsi *m.* paralysis *m.* **palsyon** paralysed person
palster *m.* plenty, abundance
palsya *v.* paralyse
palv *f.* **+ow** palm (of hand)
palva *v.* caress, stroke
palvala *v.* grope, feel one's way
palvas *m.* **+ow** caress, stroke (of hand); **palvas kerensa** caress
palys *m.* **palesyow** palace
pan<when> *conj.* when
pan<what> *adj.* what
pana *adj.* what
panda *m.* **+s** panda
pandra *pron.* what
panes *coll.* **+enn** parsnip
pann *m.* **+ow** cloth, woven fabric
pannell *m.* **+ow** panel (of people)
panner *m.* **-oryon** draper
pann-ledan *m.* broad-cloth
pans *m.* **+ow** hollow, dingle, dell, re-entrant (large)
paper *m.* **+yow** paper; **paper gorthsaym** greaseproof paper; **paper paros** wallpaper; **paper skrifa** writing paper
paper-nowodhow *m.* newspaper
paperweyth *m.* paper-work
papynjay *m.* **+s** parrot
par<by> *prep.* by
par<as> *adv.* as, just as; **par dell yw** *phr.* just as it is

par<equal> *m.* **+ow** equal, mate, match (equal); sort, kind; **tus a'n par na** *phr.* such people

para<team> *m.* **parys** team, gang, squad; drove, flock

parabolenn *f.* **+ow** parable, parabola

paradhis *f.* paradise

parchemin *m.* parchment, vellum

pares *f.* **+ow** equal

pareusi *v.* prepare, make ready, cook

pargh *v.* endure, hold out, last

park *m.* **+ow** field, close, enclosure, park

park-kerri *m.* car-park, parking lot (U.S.)

parkya *v.* park, enclose

parkynn *m.* **+ow** small field

parledh *m.* **+ow** parlour

parlet *m.* prelate

paros *m.* **+yow** wall (interior), party wall

parow *adj.* even (of numbers)

parsel *m.* **+s** squad, band (group of people), set

part *m.* **+ys** share

parth *f.* **+ow** side, behalf

parti *m.* **+s, +ow** party (political), side (in a conflict), set of opponents

parya *v.* pair, couple

parys *adj.* ready, prepared; cooked

pas<cough> *m.* **+ow** cough

pas<pace> *m.* **+ys** pace, step

pasa *v.* cough

pas-garm *m.* whooping-cough

pask *m.* nourishment

Pask *m.* Easter; **Pask Byghan** Low Sunday

passya *v.* pass, surpass

passhyon *m.* passion

past *m.* paste; **past dens** tooth-paste

pastell *f.* **+ow** morsel, scrap

pastell-dir *f.* smallholding, allotment

pastell-vro *f.* district, constituency

pasti *m.* **+ow** pasty

pat *m.* pate

patatys *coll.* **+enn** potatoes

patron *m.* **+yow** pattern, example, model

paw *m.* **+yow** paw, claw (of crab), fluke (of anchor); hand (pejoratively)

pawa *v.* paw

pawgamm *adj.* club-footed

pawgenn *m.* **+ow** moccasin, slipper

payn *m.* **+ys** pain, torment, torture; **war bayn mernans** *phr.* on pain of death

paynes *f.* **+ow** peahen

paynt *m.* paint

payntya *v.* paint (a surface)

payntyer *m.* **payntyoryon** painter (of surfaces)

paynya *v.* torture, punish

payon *m.* **+es** peacock

payoni *v.* swagger, strut

pe *v.* pay, satisfy, pay for, settle accounts with

peber *m.* **-oryon** baker

peberynn *m.* **+ow** harbour-crab

peblys *adj.* populated

pebores *f.* **+ow** baker

pechya *v.* pierce

peder *num.* four (f.)

Peder *name* Peter

pedergweyth *adv.* four times

pedrek *adj.* square; **-ogow** square

pedrenn *f.* **+ow,** *dual* **diwbedrenn** haunch, buttock, hind-quarter

pedresyf *f.* newt, lizard

pedrevan *f.* **-es** lizard

pedrevanas *v.* creep on all fours, crawl

pedri *v.* rot, decay, fester, corrupt

pegh *m.* sin

pegha *v.* sin

peghador *m.* **+yon** sinner

peghadores *f.* **+ow** sinner

peghadow *m.* sinning, transgression
peghes *m.* peghosow sin, offence
pel *f.* +yow ball, sphere; pel an norvys globe
pel-ayr *f.* pelyow-ayr balloon
peldroes *f.* football, soccer
pelganstell *f.* basketball
pelikan *m.* +es pelican
pell *adj.* far, distant, long
pellbennti *m.* +ow tele-cottage
pellder *m.* +yow distance, great way
pellenn *f.* +ow ball, dumpling, lump, bullet
pellenni *v.* roll into a ball
pellennik *f.* -igow pill
peller *m.* -oryon remover of charms, white witch
pellgens *m.* midnight mass
pellgewsel *v.* telephone
pellgomunyans *m.* +ow telecommunication
pellgows *m.* telephony
pellgowser *m.* +yow telephone
pellhe *v.* send far away, expel, eject, banish
pellskrifa *v.* fax, telegraph
pellskrifenn *f.* +ow fax (message), telegram
pelvas *f.* baseball
pellweler *m.* telescope
pellwolok *f.* pellwologow television
pellyst *m.* +ow garment of fur, sheepskin coat
penans *m.* penance
Penkost *m.* Whitsuntide, Pentecost
penn *m.* +ow head, end, summit; Penn an Wlas *place* Land's End
penn-<chief> *pref.* chief
penn-<end> *pref.* end
penn-<one> *pref.* individual
pennardh *m.* +ow promontory
pennardhek *adj.* salient

penn-bagas *adj.* shock-headed
penn-barvus *m.* pennow-barvus three-bearded rockling
penn-bloedh *m.* pennow-bloedh anniversary, birthday
penn-blogh *m.* pennow-blogh shaven pate
penn-bras *m.* pennow-bras thick-head, fool
penn-broennenn *m.* pennow-broennenn rush-head (insult), fool
penn-bros *m.* pennow-bros fan (e.g. of sport), fanatic, hot-head
pennchambour *m.* +s master bedroom, main bedroom
penndaga *v.* perplex, bewilder, confuse
penndegys *adj.* perplexed, bewildered, confused
penn-diwglun *m.* hip, haunch
penn-dro *f.* giddiness, vertigo; rounders (disease of sheep), gid
penn-droppya *v.* nod
pennduenn *f.* +ow, *coll.* penndu bulrush
penn-du *m.* pennow-du blackhead
penndyskador *m.* +yon headmaster, head-teacher
penndyskadores *f.* +ow headmistress, head-teacher
penneglos *f.* +yow cathedral
pennek *adj.* big-headed
penn-elin *m.* elbow
pennfenten *f.* -tynyow head-spring, source (of stream)
pennfester *m.* halter, head-stall
penn-fol *adj.* panicky
pennfrosek *adj.* mainstream
penngarn *m.* +es gurnard; penngarn glas grey gurnard
penngasenn *f.* maw, stomach
penn-glas *m.* pennow-glas scabious (plant), horse's skull

pennglin *m.* **+yow** knee-cap
penn-glow *m.* coal-tit, titmouse
penngogh *m.* **+ow** hooded fur cloak
penngover *m.* **+yow** source (of stream)
penn-gwynn *adj.* white-headed *m.* **pennow-gwynn** penguin
penn-ha-min *m.* pin-game
pennhembrenkyas *m.* **pennhembrynkysi** general
pennjustis *m.* **+yow** chief justice
penn-kales *adj.* hard-headed, obstinate, stubborn
penn-kamm *adj.* wrong-headed, wrynecked
penn-kangour *m.* **pennow-kangour** centurion
pennkansbloedh *m.* centenary, centennial (U.S.)
pennklavjiores *f.* staff nurse, head nurse (U.S.)
pennklun *f.* **+yow** hip
penn-koeg *adj.* empty-headed
penn-kogh *adj.* broken pate
pennkostennow *plur.* key targets, primary targets
penn-kreghi *m.* **pennow-kreghi** scabby pate
pennlinenn *f.* **+ow** headline
pennlugarn *m.* **pennlugern** headlamp, headlight
penn-medhow *m.* **pennow-medhow** drunkard
pennmen *m.* **-meyn** cornerstone
pennmenyster *m.* **+yon** prime minister
penn-noeth *adj.* bare-headed
pennober *m.* **+ow** masterpiece, masterwork
pennoelva *f.* look-out place, observation post
penn-pali *m.* **pennow-pali** blue-tit

penn-pilus *m.* **pennow-pilus** punk
pennplas *m.* headquarters, chief seat
penn-pral *m.* **pennow-pral** skull of animal
pennpusorn *m.* **+ow** principal refrain in plain chant
penn-pyst *m.* **pennow-pyst** fool
pennrewler *m.* **-oryon** director
pennrynn *m.* **pennrynnow** headland, promontory
Pennrynn *place* Penryn
penn-sagh *m.* mumps
Pennsans *place* Penzance
pennser *m.* **+i** architect
pennseres *f.* **+ow** architect
pennserneth *f.* architecture (art of)
pennsernethel *adj.* architectural
pennseviges *f.* **+ow** princess
pennsevik *m.* **-igyon** prince
pennsevigyans *m.* nobility
pennsevigeth *f.* nobility, aristocracy
pennseythun *f.* **+yow** weekend
pennsoedhva *f.* **+ow** headquarters (e.g. of a company)
pennsita *f.* capital city
penn-skav *adj.* scatter-brained, hare-brained
pennskol *f.* **+yow** university, institution of higher education
pennskrif *m.* **+ow** editorial (article)
pennskrifer *m.* **-oryon** editor
penn-sogh *adj.* stupid slow-witted *m.* **pennow-sogh** dolt
penntan *m.* **+yow** back-log of fire
penntern *m.* chieftain
penn-teylu *m.* **pennow-teylu** head of family
pennti *m.* **+ow** cottage, cot (small house)
penntir *m.* **+yow** headland
Penntorr *place* Torpoint
penn-trydydh *m.* three days' end

pennvis *m.* **+yow** month's end
pennvlydhen *f.* **-vlydhynyow** year's end
penn-vyghternedh *m.* ruler of kings
pennwari *m.* **+ow** final (game)
pennweli *m.* **+ow** head-board (of a bed)
pennweythor *m.* **+yon** foreman
pennweythresek *m.* **-ogyon** chief executive
pennwisk *m.* head-dress, headgear
pennwlas *f.* **+ow** chief country
Pennwydh *place* Penwith
penn-yar *m.* **pennow-yar** harvest neck
pennynn *m.* **+ow** tadpole, remnant, residual
penn-ys *m.* **pennow-ys** ear of corn
penshyon *m.* **+ow** pension; **penshyon evredh** disability pension
penys *m.* penance *v.* do penance, fast
penytti *m.* **+ow** hermitage, anchorite's cell
per<pears> *coll.* **+enn** pears
per<crock> *m.* **+yow** crock (large jar)
perbrenn *m.* **+yer** pear-tree
perfeyth *adj.* perfect, entire
perghenn *m.* **+ow** owner; **foul y berghenn** worthless vagrant
perghenna *v.* own, claim
perghennogeth *f.* ownership, possession
perghennogi *v.* claim, appropriate
perghennek *m.* **-ogyon** owner, possessor
perghennieth *f.* ownership
pergherin *m.* **+yon** pilgrim
pergherinses *f.* pilgrimage
perlann *f.* **+ow** pear orchard
perl *m.* **+ys** pearl
perseth *m.* two-handled pot

persil *coll.* **+enn** parsley
person *m.* **+s** person
personel *adj.* personal
perth *f.* **-i** thicket, brake (vegetation), hedge of bushes
perthi *v.* bear (endure), endure, tolerate; **perthi orth** hold out against; **perthi kov** remember, recall; **perthi own** be afraid
perthyans *m.* endurance, patience, toleration, experience (something experienced)
pervedh *m.* interior
pervedhel *adj.* internal
pervers *m.* setback
peryll *m.* **+ow** danger, peril, risk
peryllus *adj.* dangerous, perilous, risky
peryllya *v.* incur risk, be endangered
pes<IJ> *int.* peace
pes<AV> *adv.* how many; **pes termyn** how long
pes<paid> *v.* paid; **pes da** pleased
pesek *adj.* decayed, rotten *m.* **pesogyon** rotter
peski *v.* graze (feed), fatten
peskweyth *adv.* how many times; **peskweyth may** *conj.* whenever, as often as
peswar *num.* four (m.)
peswara *num.* fourth
peswar-paw *m.* **+es** newt, lizard, ranatra (water-insect)
peswardhegves *num.* fourteenth
peswardhek *num.* fourteen
peswar-kornek *adj.* four-cornered
peswar-ugens *num.* eighty, four-score
pesya *v.* last, endure, continue; **ny besyav bones gwelys** *phr.* I cannot endure being seen
pethik *m.* smart blow
peub *pron.* all, everyone, everybody
peul *m.* **+yow** post, stake, pylon, pole; spire, steeple pile

peulge *m.* **+ow** palisade, railing
peulvan *m.* **+ow** pillar, standing stone
peuns *m.* **+ow** pound, pound weight
peur *m.* pasture
p'eur *adv.* when, at what time
peuri *v.* graze (feed), browse
peurla *m.* grazing-place
peurva *f.* grazing-place
peurwels *m.* grazing-place
piano *m.* **+s** piano
pib *f.* **+ow** pipe, flute; **an Bib** the Tube, the Underground; **pibow sagh** *plur.* bagpipes
piba *v.* pipe
pibell *f.* **+ow** pipe
pibenn *f.* **+ow** tube
pibenn-dhowr *f.* **pibennow-dowr** hose-pipe
pibenn-garth *f.* **pibennow-karth** sewer
pibenn-gawgh *f.* **pibennow-kawgh** foul sewer
piber *m.* **-oryon** piper
pibydh *m.* **+yon** piper
pies *coll.* **+enn** magpies
pig *m.* **+ow** point
piga *v.* prick, peck, sting
pigell *f.* pick
pigas *v.* prick, peck, sting
piger *m.* **+yow** goad, stimulant
pigellas *v.* use a pick
pigorn *m.* **pigern** peak, cone
pigornek *adj.* conical
pik *m.* **+ys** pike (weapon)
pil<arrowhead> **+ys** *m.* head of arrow
pil<heap> **+yow** *m.* pile, heap, hillock, mound
pil<rags> *coll.* rags; **+enn** rags, fringe, tatter; peel, coating
pilas *coll.* naked oats,, bald oats
pilek *adj.* heaped
pilenn *f.* **+ow**, *coll.* **pil** fringe

pilennek *adj.* fringed, ragged
pilya *v.* peel, strip
pilyek *adj.* useless *m.* **pilyogyon** useless person, spider-crab
pin *coll.* **+enn** pine
pinaval *m.* **+ow** pineapple
pinbrenn *m.* **+yer** pine-tree
pinta *m.* **+ow** pint
pisa *v.* urinate
pisas *m.* urine
pistyll *m.* **+ow** waterfall, spout
pistylla *v.* spout
pisva *f.* urinal
pith *adj.* greedy, avaricious, grasping, stingy
pithneth *f.* greed, avarice, cupidity
piw<own> *v.* own, possess, be entitled to; **an fleghes a biw an keun** the children own the dogs, the dogs belong to the children
piw<who> *pron.* who
piwas *m.* **+ow** reward, award; **ri piwas dhe** *v.* reward
piwpynag *pron.* whoever
pla *m.* **+ow** plague, pest, nuisance, anathema
plag *m.* **+ys** plague, visitation (of evil), affliction
plagya *v.* plague, afflict
planet *m.* **+ys**, **+ow** planet
plank *m.* **plenkys**, **+ow** plank, board (timber)
plans *m.* **+ow** plant
plansa *v.* plant
plas *m.* **plassow** place, mansion, stately home, country seat; place at table
plasenn *f.* **+ow** record, disc, recording (sound, etc.); **plasenn arghansek** compact disc
plaster *m.* plaster
plastra *v.* plaster
plat *m.* **+yow**, **+ys** plate, plate metal
plat-niver *m.* **platyow-niver** number-plate

platt *adj.* flat

plattya *v.* crouch, squat, cower

playn<AJ> *adj.* evident, plain (obvious)

playn<MN> *m.* **+ys** carpenter's plane

playnya *v.* plane

ple *adv.* where

pledya *v.* plead, advocate

pledyer *m.* **-oryon** pleader

pleg *m.* **+ow** bend, fold

plegadow *adj.* pleasing *m.* inclination

plegell *f.* **+ow** folder

pleg-mor *m.* **plegow-mor** bay, bight (of sea)

plegya *v.* bend, fold; **plegya dhe** be pleasing to; **plegya gans** be pleasing to; **plegya yn dor** bow down

plegyans *m.* tendency, bent, inclination

ple'ma *phr.* where is

plemmik *m.* **plemmigow** plummet

plen *adj.* plain *m.* **+ys** plain; **plen an gwari** playing-place, open-air theatre; **plen an varghas** market-place

plenkynn *f.* **+ow** board (timber), shingle, squared timber

plenta *m.* **plentys** plaint

plentya *v.* be plaintiff

plentyades *f.* **+ow** plaintiff (female)

plentyas *m.* **-ysi** plaintiff (male)

plepynag *conj.* wherever

plesour *m.* **+s** pleasure

plestrynn *m.* **+ow** small plaster, band-aid (U.S.)

plesya *v.* please

pleth *f.* **+ow** plait of hair, ridge of corn-mow

ple'th *phr.* where

pletha *v.* plait, braid, wattle

plethenn *f.* **+ow** plait of hair, braid, reel (dance); **plethenn onyon** string of onions

plether *m.* **-oryon** braider, plaiter

plethores *f.* **+ow** braider

plethweyth *m.* plaited work

plisk *coll.* husks, pods; **+enn**

pliskenna *v.* shell, husk

plit *m.* plight, predicament, condition

plomm *m.* lead (metal)

plommwedhek *adj.* vertical

plontya *v.* disseminate, propagate, implant

plontyans *m.* propaganda

plos *adj.* dirty, filthy, foul *m.* **+yon** foul person, foulness, defilement; **plos y daves** *adj.* foul-mouthed

plosegi *v.* get dirty

plosek *adj.* dirty *m.* **plosogyon** filthy fellow

plosedhes *m.* foulness, filth, rubbish

ploswas *m.* **ploswesyon** dirty fellow

ploumbrenn *m.* **+yer** plum-tree

ploumenn *f.* **+ow** plum

ploumsugen *m.* three-bearded rockling

ploumsugesenn *f.* three-bearded rockling

plowghya *v.* make a great splash

plustrenn *f.* mole on skin

pluv *coll.* **+enn** feathers

pluva *v.* grow feathers

pluvek *f.* **pluvogow** cushion, pillow

pluvenn *f.* **+ow**, *coll.* **pluv** pen, feather, quill; **pluvenn blomm** *f.* **pluvennow plomm** pencil

pluvynn *f.* **+ow** little feather

plynch *m.* **+ys** flinch; **war unn plynch** *adv.* in a twinkling

plynchya *v.* flinch

plyw *f.* **+ow** parish

plywek *adj.* parochial *m.*
  plywogyon parishioner
po *conj.* or
pobas *v.* bake
pobel *f.* **poblow** people, folk
pobla *v.* populate, people
poblans *m.* **+ow** population
poblek *adj.* public
poblus *adj.* populous
pochya *v.* trample wet soil
poder *adj.* rotten, decayed, corrupt
podh *m.* sheep-rot
podik *m.* jug; **podik oyl** oil can
podik-musura *m.* **-igow-musura** measuring jug
podin *m.* **+s** pudding; **podin bara** bread pudding; **podin Nadelik** Christmas pudding
podradow *adj.* perishable
podredhek *adj.* corrupt, festering
podredhes *m.* corruption, putridity, festering sore
podrek *adj.* corrupt, decayed, full of sores *m.* **podrogyon** depraved person
podrynn *m.* **+ow** rotter
poell *m.* intelligence, reason
poen *m.* **+ow** pain of spirit
poenvos *m.* trouble, vexation, misery
poenvosek *adj.* troubled, vexed, miserable
poenvotter *m.* state of trouble, state of misery
poenya *v.* run
poes *adj.* heavy, important; close, sultry *m.* **+ow** weight, pressure
poesa *v.* lean, weigh; **poesa war** accentuate
poesedh *m.* **+ow** weight (quantity in physics)
poesedhek *adj.* positive
poesek *adj.* important, weighty

poeslev *m.* **+ow** accent, emphasis, stress; **gans poeslev** emphatic
poesleva *v.* accentuate, emphasize, stress
poester *m.* heaviness, pressure on one's head before a thunderstorm breaks
poesyjyon *m.* oppression, drowsiness, heaviness
poeth *adj.* scorching, extremely hot
poetha *v.* heat
poethhe *v.* heat
poethter *m.* heat
poethvann *m.* extreme heat, scorching
pojer *m.* small bowl
pok *m.* **+yow** poke, push, shove
poken *conj.* or else, otherwise
poket *m.* **+ow** pocket
pokk *m.* **+ow** kiss
pokk *m.* **pokkys** pockmark
pokya *v.* poke, push, thrust
polat *m.* **+ys** fellow
politeger *m.* **-oryon** politician
politegieth *f.* politics
politek *adj.* political
poll<pool> *m.* **+ow** pool, pit, anchorage; **poll glow** coalpit; **poll goedh** goosepond; **poll greun** dammed-up pond; **poll growynn** gravel-pit; **poll heyji** duckpond; **poll hoelan** salt pond; **poll hyli** brine-pit; **poll kroenogow** toadpool; **poll lo'n** cattle pond; **poll lyfans** toadpool; **poll margh** horse-pond; **poll melin** millpond; **poll neuvya** swimming pool; **poll owr** gold-mine; **poll pennynnow** tadpole pond; **poll pri** claypit; **poll pri gwynn** china-clay pit; **poll ros** pit of water-wheel; **poll sten** tin-pit; **poll stronk** dirty pool; **poll tewes** sand-pit; **poll troyllya** whirlpool
poll<head> *m.* head, poll
pollenn *f.* **+ow** puddle, rock-pool, little pool

polltrigas *m.* gaiters, spatterdashes

Polonek *adj.* Polish *m.* Polish language

Poloni *place* Poland

pols *m.* **+yow** moment, instant, pulse, short time, short distance; **pols alemma** *adv.* a short distance away

polsa *v.* pulsate

polta *m.* a good while

polter *m.* powder, dust

polter-gonn *m.* gunpowder

pomp +yow pump; **pomp ayr** air-pump

pompya *v.* pump

pompyon *m.* **+s** pumpkin, gourd

pomster *m.* **+s** quack-doctor

pomstri *m.* quackery

ponn *m.* light flying dust

ponnek *adj.* dusty *f.* **-egi** dustheap

pons *m.* **+yow** bridge

ponsfordh *f.* **+ow** viaduct

ponsik *m.* **-igow** little bridge

ponsynn *m.* **+ow** little bridge

popa *m.* **popys** puffin

popet *m.* **+ow** doll, puppet

popti *m.* baker's shop, bake-house

poran *adv.* quite, exactly, rightly

porbugel *m.* bottle-nosed shark

porenn *f.* **+ow**, *coll.* **por** leek

porghell *m.* **+i** porker, vear, young pig

porghella *v.* farrow

porghellik *m.* **-igow** sucking-pig, piglet

porpos *m.* purpose, design, intent

porposya *v.* purpose

porres *adv.* urgently, absolutely, of necessity

pors *m.* **+ys** purse

port *m.* **+ys** porthole, entry port, cargo port

porth<cove> *m.* **+ow** cove, harbour, port

porth<gate> *m.* **+ow** gateway, entrance, porch

porther *m.* **-oryon** doorkeeper, janitor

Porthia *place* St Ives

porthores *f.* **+ow** porter

Porthpyran *place* Perranporth

portmantell *m.* **+ow** portmanteau

Portyngal *place* Portugal

Portyngalek *adj.* Portuguese *m.* Portuguese language

porvenn *f.* **+ow**, *coll.* **porv** rush

posna *v.* poison

possybyl *adj.* possible

post<mail> *m.* post (mail)

post<pole> *m.* **+ow** post (pole), column, pillar; **post arwoedh** sign-post

postvester *m.* **-vestrysi** post-master

pot *m.* **+yow** kick

pott *m.* **+ys**, **+ow** pot; **pott horn** iron pot; **pott pri** earthenware pot

pott-gwynn *m.* hasty-pudding

pott-mesenn *m.* acorn-cup

pott-te *m.* teapot

potya *v.* kick

pow *m.* **+yow** country, province, region; **Pow Chek** Czech Republic; **Pow Sows** England; **Pow Frynk** France; **Pow Grek** Greece

Powder *place* Powder (name of a hundred in Cornwall)

power *m.* **+s** power

powes *m.* rest, truce, repose *v.* rest, pause

powesva *f.* resting-place, state of rest

pows *f.* **+yow** coat, gown, frock, dress

poynt *m.* **+ys** point, item; **yn poynt da** *adj.* in good health

poyntya *v.* point

prag *adv.* why, wherefore, what for, how come

praga *adv.* why *m.* reason

praktis *m.* **+yow** practice

praktisya *v.* practise

pramm *m.* **+ow** pram

pras *m.* **+ow** meadow, common pasture; **pras goedh** goose-green

pratt *m.* **+ys** trick, prank; **gul pratt** play a trick

prays *m.* **+ys** praise

praysya *v.* praise

Predennek *adj.* British

preder *m.* **+ow** thought, meditation, worry, anxiety, care

prederi *v.* consider, reflect, think, ponder

prederus *adj.* careful, anxious, solicitous, worrying

prederyans *m.* **+ow** opinion

prederys *adj.* worried

predheges *v.* rant, make a noisy speech

predheger *m.* **-oryon** ranter, rabble-rouser

predhek *m.* rant

pregoth *m.* **+ow** sermon, formal speech

pregowtha *v.* preach

pregowther *m.* **-oryon** preacher

prena *v.* buy, purchase, redeem, pay for; **ty a'n pren** *phr.* you'll pay for it, you'll catch it

prenas *m.* **+ow** purchase

prenassa *v.* go shopping

prenedh *m.* atonement, expiation

prener *m.* **-oryon** buyer, purchaser

prenn *m.* **+yer** timber, wood (as timber), beam, sawn log

prenna *v.* bar, bolt, lock

prennweyth *m.* woodwork

prenores *f.* **+ow** buyer

prenyas *m.* **-ysi** buyer (professional), purchaser

presep *m.* **presebow** manger

presens *m.* presence

prest *adj.* readily, ever *adv.* quickly, continually, incessantly, always

previ *v.* prove, test, taste, try

prevyans *m.* **+ow** test, experiment

preydh *m.* prey, plunder, spoil

preydha *v.* prey on

preydher *m.* **-oryon** marauder, pirate; predator

pri *m.* clay, earth, mould (for casting); **pri gwynn** china-clay; **pri pib** pipe-clay

priek *f.* **priegi** clayey place

prienn *f.* **+ow** clayey place

pries *adj.* married *m.* **priosow** spouse

prileghenn *f.* **+ow** tile

priosel *adj.* matrimonial, conjugal

priosoleth *f.* state of marriage

pris *m.* **+yow** price, value, reputation; **a bris** *adj.* valuable; **a bris isel** cheap

prisner *m.* **+s, -oryon** prisoner (male)

prisnores *f.* **+ow** prisoner (female)

prison *m.* **+yow** prison

prisonya *v.* imprison

prisya *v.* price

prisyans *m.* pricing

priva *adj.* private, intimate, secret

privedh *adj.* secret, private

privedhyow *plur.* toilets, conveniences

privetter *m.* privacy

privyta *m.* private matter, secret matter

priweyth *m.* pottery

priweythor *m.* **+yon** clay-worker, potter

priweythva *f.* **+ow** clay-works, pottery

problem *m.* problem

professya *v.* profess

professor *m.* **+yon** professor

profoes *m.* **+i** prophet

profoesa *v.* prophesy

profya *v.* proffer, suggest, propose, offer

profyans *m.* offer, suggestion, proposal

programm *m.* computer program

pronter *m.* **+yon** priest, parson, clergyman, vicar

prontereth *f.* clergy, priesthood

pronterji *m.* **+ow** parsonage, rectory, vicarage

Protestant *m.* **-ans** Protestant

prouyt *int.* call to cattle

prov *m.* proof, test, trial; **gul prov** *v.* prove

provia *v.* procure, furnish, supply, provide

proviyas *m.* **-ysi** supplier, provider

prow *m.* gain, profit, benefit, advantage

prydydh *m.* **+yon** poet

prydydhes *f.* **+ow** poetess

prydydhi *v.* compose poetry

prydydhieth *f.* poetry

prydydhyek *adj.* poetic

pryerin *m.* pilgrim

prykk *m.* **+ow** point, degree, pitch

pryl *m.* tinstone

pryns *m.* **+ys** prince

prynses *f.* **+ow** princess

prynseth *f.* **+ow** principality

prynt *m.* **+ow** print

prynter *m.* **-oryon** printer (person)

pryntji *m.* **+ow** printing-office

pryntya *v.* print

pryntyans *m.* **+ow** print-run

prys *m.* **+yow** time, meal-time, season; **prys boes** meal-time; **prys gweli** bed-time; **prys mos** time to go; **y'n gwella prys** *adv.* fortunately; **yn gwettha prys** unfortunately, unluckily, unhappily

prysk *coll.* **+enn** bushes, thickets

pryskek *adj.* scrubby

pryskwydh *coll.* copse

prysweyth *m.* moment, instant, occasion (time)

pryv *m.* **+es**, **+yon** worm, creeping creature; **pryv del** caterpillar; **pryv malan** pipe-fish; **pryv nor** earthworm; **pryv owrlin** silkworm; **pryv prenn** woodworm

pryvenn *f.* **+ow** worm

pryves *plur.* worms, creeping creatures

pryvesek *adj.* wormy, verminous

pryvessa *v.* hunt vermin

pryvyon reptile vermin

pub *adj.* each, every; **puboll** all; **pub eur** *adv.* always; **pub eur oll** all the time; **pub termyn** always

puber *m.* pepper

pubonan *phr.* everyone, everybody

punyon *m.* gable

pup-prys *adv.* always

puptra *pron.* everything

pur<mucus> *m.* nasal mucus

pur<very> *adj.* pure, clean, absolute *adv.* very

puredh *m.* purity

purek *adj.* snotty, snivelling

purhe *v.* purify, absolve (of sins)

purheans *m.* purification, absolution (of sins)

purjya *v.* purge

purpur *adj.* purple

purra *adv.* thoroughly, very, fully

pursywya *v.* pursue

puskes *plur.* fish(es)

pusketti *m.* **+ow** aquarium

pusorn +ow *m.* bundle, bale, burden

pusornas *v.* bale, bundle together

puth *m.* **+ow** well (e.g. for water)

py *pron.* which, what

pych *m.* stab, thrust, piercing

pycher *m.* **+s** pitcher (jug)

pychya *v.* pierce, stab, transfix

pyffya *v.* puff, snort

pyffyer *m.* **-s** porpoise; *dial.* "piffer".

pyg *m.* pitch, tar

pygans *m.* wherewithal, livelihood, requisites, necessities, means

pygemmys *adv.* how much, how great

pyglenn *f.* **+ow** tarpaulin

pylla *v.* plunder, spoil, pillage

pyltya *v.* pelt

pyment *m.* spiced wine

pymp *num.* five

pympbys *m.* starfish

pympdelenn *f.* cinquefoil

pympes *num.* fifth

pymthegves *num.* fifteenth

pymthek *num.* fifteen

pynag *pron.* whoever, whatever

pynagoll *pron.* whosoever, whatsoever

pynakyl pynaklys *m.* pinnacle

pynchya *v.* pinch

pyneyl *pron.* which (of two)

pynn<pin> *m.* **+ow** pin, dowel, peg; **pynn meus** drawing pin

pynn<MN> *m.* lit. head

pynna *v.* pin together

pynsel *m.* artist's brush; **pynsel plomm** lead-pencil

pynser *m.* **+yow** pair of pincers

pypynag *pron.* whatever

pyraga *adv.* why

Pyran *name* Perran

pys *coll.* **+enn** peas

pysadow *m.* prayer, supplication, appeal

pyseul *pron.* whatever, how many, how much

pysi *v.* pray, entreat, beg; **pysi nebonan a wul neppyth** ask someone to do something; **pysi neppyth diworth nebonan** ask something from someone; **pysi rag** pray for; **pysi war Dhyw** pray to God; **my a'th pys** I pray thee, I prithee

pysk *m.* **puskes** fish

pyskador *m.* **+yon** fisherman

pyskek *f.* **-egi** fishing-ground

pyskessa *v.* fish

pysklynn *f.* **+ow** fish-pond

pystik *m.* **pystigow** hurt, injury

pystiga *v.* harm, hurt

pystigys *adj.* injured, hurt

pystri *m.* sorcery, witchcraft, magic

pystria *v.* work magic

pystrier *m.* **-oryon** sorcerer, magician

pystriores *f.* **+ow** sorceress

pyta *m.* pity; **kemmeres pyta orth** *phr.* have pity on

pyteth *f.* compassion

pytethus *adj.* compassionate, pitiful

pyth<thing> *m.* **+ow** thing, property, possession, asset; **an pyth** *conj.* that which; **pythow an bys** *plur.* worldly wealth

pyth<what> *pron.* what

pythow *plur.* riches, gear, possessions

pythyonenn *f.* **+ow,** *coll.* **pythyon** sheet of paper

pytt *m.* **+ys** pit, dungeon

R

rabmen *m.* granite gravel

rach *m.* heed, caution, care

radar *m.* radar

radell *m.* scree, clitter, loose stones

radyo *m.* **+yow** radio

rag *prep.* for, in order to, for the purpose of

rag- *pref.* fore-

ragarghas *m.* **+ow** booking, reservation

ragarveth *m.* **+ow** advance (of wages)

ragarwoedh *f.* **+yow** portent
ragbreder *m.* forethought
ragbren *m.* subscription
ragbrena *v.* subscribe
ragbrener *m.* **-oryon** subscriber
ragdal *m.* advance payment
ragdas *m.* **+ow** forefather
ragdha *prep.* for them
ragdho *prep.* for him
rager *m.* foreword
ragerghi *v.* book, reserve (e.g. a room)
raglavar *m.* **+ow** preface, foreword
raglenn *f.* **+ow** over-trousers
raglev *m.* **+ow** vote
ragleva *v.* vote
ragleverel *v.* say before;
    ragleverys *adj.* aforesaid, already mentioned
ragober *m.* **+ow** rehearsal
ragoberi *v.* rehearse
ragomogh *m.* hog
ragon *prep.* for us
ragos *prep.* for thee
ragov *prep.* for me
ragowgh *prep.* for you
ragown *m.* presentiment, foreboding
ragresegydh *m.* **+yon** precursor, predecessor
ragresek *v.* run before, predate
ragreser *m.* **-oryon** forerunner, harbinger
ragrestra *adj.* pre-arrange
ragsettya *adj.* prescribe
ragskeus *m.* **+ow** pretext
ragskrif *m.* preface
ragvlas *m.* foretaste
ragvreus *m.* prejudice
ragvreusi *v.* pre-judge, prejudicate
ragwel *m.* foresight
ragweles *v.* foresee
ragwir *m.* priority
ragworra *v.* set before, prefix
rahaya *v.* sneeze

rakan *m.* **+ow** garden rake
rakana *v.* rake
rakhanow *m.* **rakhenwyn** pronoun
rakhemma *conj.* wherefore
rakhenna *conj.* therefore
rakhenwel *v.* name before
rakhenwys *adj.* aforesaid
rakherdhya *v.* propel
rakherdhell *f.* **+ow** propeller
rakka *m.* **rakkow** amusing story, amusing tale
rakkeas *v.* preclude
rakker *m.* **-oryon** story-teller, raconteur
ralli *m.* rally (of cars, etc.)
rambla *v.* waddle
rann *f.* **+ow** part, share, portion, division
ranna *v.* part, divide, share, distribute
ranndal *m.* **+ow** dividend
ranndalas *m.* **+ow** instalment
ranndir *m.* region, district
ranndiryel *adj.* regional
ranndra *f.* suburb
rannji *m.* **+ow** apartment, flat
rannles *m.* **+ow** commission (money)
rannriv *m.* **+ow** fraction (math.)
rannvor *m.* **+yow** sea-area
rannvro *f.* **+yow** region
rannyeth *f.* **+ow** dialect
rannyethek *adj.* dialectal
ras *m.* **+ow** grace, blessing, virtue
rask *f.* **+ow** plane (tool)
raska *v.* plane
raskel *f.* **rasklow** spokeshave
rastell *f.* **restell** hayrake, grill, rack; grid; **rastell dhensek** rack (mach.); **rastell gras** toast-rack
rastella *v.* grill
rath *m.* **+es** rat
ratha *v.* scrape, rasp
rathell *f.* **+ow** grater, rasp

116

rathella *v.* grate
ravna *v.* plunder, ravage, violate
ravner *m.* **-oryon** marauder
ravshya *v.* entrance
ravshyans *m.* rapture, transport (of delight)
raw *f.* **+yow** strop, bond (cord)
re<by> *prep.* by (in oaths)
re<gives> *v.* gives
re<some> *pron.* some, persons, things, ones
re<too> *adv.* too, excessively *m.* too much, too many
re<VP> *ptl.* (perfective and optative particle)
rebellyans *m.* **+ow** rebellion
rech *m.* **+ys** hound
reden *coll.* **+enn** ferns, bracken
redenek *adj.* ferny *f.* **-egi** fernbrake
redik *coll.* **redigenn** radishes
redya *v.* read
redyans *m.* reading
redyer *m.* **-oryon** reader
redyores *f.* **+ow** reader
regydhenn *f.* **+ow**, *coll.* **regydh** ember, live coal
reken *m.* **reknow** bill, account, reckoning; **reken gwerth** bill of sale
rekenva *f.* **+ow** till (in shop), check-out
rekna *v.* reckon, count
reknell *f.* **+ow** calculator
rekord *m.* **+ys** record, witness, testimony
rekordya *v.* record, witness
rekordyans *m.* **+ow** recording (sound, etc.)
relystyon *plur.* low-grade tin
re'm *phr.* by my N.B. Also perfective ptl. + infixed pronoun
remedi *m.* solution, remedy; **nyns eus dhymmo remedi** *phr.* there's no way out

remenant *m.* **+s** remainder, residue, remnant
remm *m.* rheumatism
removya *v.* remove, move (trans.)
removyans *m.* removal
ren<by> *prep.* by (in oaths)
ren<PV> *phr.* we give, let us give
re'n<PH> *phr.* by the
re'n<VP> *phr.* (vbl. ptl. + infixed pronoun)
renk *m.* **+ow** rank
renkas *m.* **+ow** social class; **renkas kres** middle-class; **renkas ober** working-class
renki *v.* snore, snort, gurgle, croak
renka *v.* arrange, rank in order
renkyas *m.* **-ysi** snorer, snorter
rennyas *m.* **-ysi** carver (of meat), seneschal, steward
rennys *adj.* shared, divided
rent *m.* **+ow**, **+ys** revenue, income, rent
reowta *m.* dignity, respect, regard
repoblek *f.* republic
res<given> *v.* given
res<need> *m.* need, necessity; **a res** *adj.* essential; **res yw dhyn** *phr.* we must, it is necessary for us
res<run> *m.* race, course, running of water
res<row> *f.* **+yow** row (objects in a line), line
res<VP> *ptl.* (perfective and optative particle)
resa *v.* set in line, arrange
res-a-dro *m.* **resow-a-dro** roundabout (at fair)
resayt *m.* **+yow** recipe
resegva *f.* **+ow** course, career, orbit; **resegva jynn-diwros** motocross
resegydh *m.* **+yon** runner, racer
resek *v.* run (of liquids and people)
resell *f.* **+ow** cursor, cross-wire, cross-hairs
reski *m.* **reskeun** coursing hound

reskyon *plur.* shavings
resna *v.* reason
reson *m.* **+s** reason, logic, argument
reser *m.* **-oryon** runner, racer
resseva *v.* receive, accept
ressevans *m.* reception
rester *f.* **restri** arrangement
restorya *v.* restore, return, give back
restra *v.* arrange, make tidy, file (put in a drawer)
restrans *m.* organization (abst.)
restrenn *f.* **+ow** file (document)
restrennva *f.* **+ow** filing cabinet
restrer *m.* comb
restys *v.* roasted
resyas *m.* **+ow** rhythm
reudh *m.* upset, distress
reudhi *v.* upset, distress
reun<hair> *f.* coarse hair of mane
reun<seal> *m.* **+yon** seal (mammal)
rev *f.* **+ow** oar; **rev dhewbennek** paddle
revador *m.* **+yon** rower
revedh *adj.* strange, astounding *m.* **+ow** wonder
reverthi *f.* spring tide
revrons *m.* reverence, respect
revya *v.* row (a boat)
revyans *m.* rowing
rew<frost> *m.* frost, ice
rew<row> *m.* **+yow** row (objects in a line), succession, line; **yn rew** *adj.* mass
rewek *adj.* frosty
rewell *f.* freezer
rewi *v.* freeze
rewl *f.* **+ys** rule, order, regulation, management; **+ow**; **rewl voes** diet (as in "go on a diet")
rewlell *f.* **+ow** ruler (tool)
rewler *m.* **-oryon** ruler (head of state)
rewlerynn *m.* **+ow** regulator (elect.)

rewlya *v.* rule (trans.), regulate, control; **rewlya boes** diet
rewlyas *m.* **-ysi** ruler (head of state)
reydh *f.* sex
reydhel *adj.* sexual
reyn *m.* **+ys** reign
reynya *v.* reign
reynys *adj.* reigning
reyth *adj.* right, regular *m.* **+yow** right, law (act), order; **Reyth an Senedh** Act of Parliament
reythses *m.* equity
ri *v.* give, grant, render, present
rians *m.* **+ow** donation
ribin *m.* **+ow** strip, streak
rider ridrow *m.* sieve, riddle (strainer)
ridra *v.* sift, sieve
rim *m.* **+yow** rhyme
rimya *v.* rhyme
rin *m.* **+yow** secret, mystery
ris *coll.* rice
risenn *f.* **+ow**, *coll.* **ris** grain of rice
riv *m.* **+ow** number
riw *f.* slope
riyas *m.* **riysi** giver
ro *m.* **rohow** gift, present (offering), donation; **ro dhe Dhyw** oblation
roasek *adj.* gifted, talented
roes *f.* **+ow** net
roesenn *f.* **+ow** small net
roes-fardellow *f.* luggage-rack
roesweyth *m.* **+yow** network
roesweytha *v.* network
rogh *m.* **+ow** grunt
rogha<grunt> *v.* grunt
rogha<ray> *m.* **roghys** ray (fish), thornback
roghwerthin *v.* chortle
rol *f.* **+yow** roll, list; **rol negys** agenda
rolas *m.* **+ow** catalogue
rolbrenn *m.* **+yer** wooden roller, rolling-pin, reel (wooden)

rol-dhu *f.* blacklist
rolven *m.* **rolveyn** stone roller
rol-voes *f.* **rolyow-boes** menu
rolya *v.* roll
Rom *place* Rome
Roman *m.* **+yon** Roman
Romanek *adj.* Roman
romans *m.* novel, tale
romanseger *m.* **-oryon** romanticist
romansek *adj.* romantic
romansogeth *f.* romanticism
rond *adj.* round
ronk *adj.* hoarse, croaking *m.* snore, snort, croak
ronsyn *m.* nag, ass
ros<spur> *m.* **+yow** hill-spur, spur (topographic), promontory, moor
ros<roses> *coll.* **+enn** roses
ros<wheel> *f.* **+ow** wheel, circle; **ros dhensek** gear wheel; **ros dhowr** water wheel; **ros lywya** steering wheel; **ros nedha** spinning-wheel; **ros parys** spare wheel; **ros veur** big wheel
rosell *f.* **+ow** rotor, roulette wheel
rosella *v.* spin, whirl
roser *m.* **-oryon** stroller
rosla *m.* **-leow** cartrut
ros-rydh *f.* free-wheel
roskis *m.* **+yow** roller-skate
rostell *f.* **+ow** skate-board
rostya *v.* roast
rosva *f.* **+ow** promenade, avenue
rosvoes **+ow** trolley (for food)
roswydh *f.* ford
rosya *v.* stroll around
rosyas *m.* stroll, walk, roam
rosynn *m.* little promontory
roth *m.* **+ow** form, shape
roum *m.* **+ys** room (chamber),
router *m.* **+s** director, ruler, controller

routh *f.* **+ow** crowd, throng, multitude
routya *v.* direct, control, rule (trans.)
routyans *m.* direction (e.g. of a film)
rowedh *m.* importance
roy *v.* give (command)
rudh *adj.* red, scarlet
rudha *v.* redden, blush
rudhek *m.* **-ogyon** robin, redbreast
rudhik *adj.* reddish
rudhlas *adj.* purple
rudhloes *adj.* russet
rudhvelyn *adj.* orange (colour)
rugla *v.* rattle
ruglenn *f.* **+ow** rattle
run<hill> *f.* **+yow** hill
run<rune> *m.* **+yow** rune
runenn *f.* hillock
rusk *f.* **+enn** bark (of a tree), rind, peel
ruskek *adj.* rough-barked
Russek *adj.* Russian *m.* Russian language
Russi *place* Russia
ruta *m.* rue (herb)
rutya *v.* rub, apply friction
rutyans *m.* friction, rubbing
rutyer *m.* **+yow** rubber, eraser
ryal *adj.* royal, kingly, regal
ryalder *m.* pomp, magnificence
ryb *prep.* beside, by, close to, hard by
rybfordh *f.* **+ow** slip-road
rych *adj.* rich, sumptuous
rychedh *m.* richness (e.g. of a culture)
rychys *m.* wealth, riches
rydh *adj.* free, open, clear
rydhambos *m.* free hand, carte blanche
rydhhe *v.* set free, release
rydhses *m.* freedom, liberty
ryg *m.* **+yow** cattle wart
rygdhi *prep.* for her
ryjer *m.* inadequately castrated steer

ryll *f.* **+ow** cleft, furrow
rynk *f.* **+i** quail
rynn *m.* **+ow** point of land
rynni *v.* shiver
rypsav *m.* **+ow** lay-by
rys *f.* **+yow** ford
Rysoghen *f.* Oxford
Rysrudh *f.* Redruth
ryw *m.* ruler, king
rywvanes *f.* **+ow** queen
rywvaneth *f.* kingdom;
  Rywvaneth Unys United Kingdom

S

-s *suff.* (pl. ending)
sa'bann *phr.* stand up
sabenn *f.* **+ow**, *coll.* **sab** conifer,
  pine-tree, evergreen tree
Sabot *m.* Sabbath
sad *adj.* serious, constant, steadfast
Sadorn *m.* Saturday, Saturn (planet
  or god)
sadronenn *f.* **+ow**, *coll.* **sadron**
  drone (bee)
sadronenni *v.* buzz, drone
safron *m.* saffron
sagh *m.* **seghyer** bag, sack; **sagh
  bugh** udder; **sagh dyowl**
  demoniac
sagha *v.* put in a bag
saghlenn *m.* **+ow** sackcloth
saghwisk *f.* sackcloth (garments)
sakra *v.* consecrate, ordain
sakrament *m.* **+ys** sacrament
sakrifia *v.* sacrifice
sakrifis *m.* **+ow** sacrifice
salad *m.* salad
sall *adj.* salted
salla *v.* to salt
sallyour *m.* salt-cellar
salm *m.* **+ow** psalm
salmus *m.* shawm, oboe

salow *adj.* safe, healthy, well
  (healthy)
salusi *v.* salute
sampel *m.* **samplow** example,
  sample; **yn sampel** *phr.* for
  example, e.g.
sampla *v.* sample
sand *m.* **+ys** course (of meal), dish
  (food), mess (meal)
sandal *m.* **+yow**, **+ys** sandal
sans *adj.* holy, sacred *m.* **sens** saint
sansel *adj.* saintly, pious
sanses *f.* **+ow** saint (female)
sanshe *v.* sanctify
sansoleth *f.* saintliness, sanctity,
  holiness
sansolethus *adj.* sanctimonious
sarf *f.* **serf** serpent, snake
sarfek *adj.* serpentine
sarf-nija *f.* **serf-nija** kite (toy)
sarfven *m.* serpentine (rock)
Sarsyn *m.* **+s** Saracen, Moor
Sarsynek *adj.* Moorish
Satnas *name* Satan
sav *m.* stand, stance, erect posture
saven *f.* **savnow** geo, cleft, gully
savla *m.* **savleow** position,
  standpoint, status
savla-govynn *m.* **savleow-
  govynn** request-stop
savla-kyttrin *m.* **savleow-
  kyttrin** bus-stop
savon *f.* **+ow** standard
savonegi *v.* standardise
savonek *adj.* standard
saw<safe> *adj.* safe, sound, whole
  conj. except, unless
saw<load> *m.* **+yow** horseload
sawder *m.* safety, preservation,
  security
sawer *m.* **+yow** savour, flavour,
  taste
sawment *m.* **sawmens** salve
sawn *f.* **+yow** geo, cleft, gully

sawra *v.* savour, taste
sawrans *m.* seasoning, flavouring
sawrek *adj.* savoury, tasty
sawrenn *f.* **+ow** taste
sawrys *adj.* seasoned, flavoured
sawya *v.* save (from danger), rescue; preserve, heal
sawes *m.* health, soundness
saya *m.* light fine serge
saym *m.* pilchard-oil, train-oil
se *m.* **seow** throne, seat
sebon *m.* soap
sebon-les *f.* soapwort
seboni *v.* soap, lather (with soap)
sebonus *adj.* saponaceous, soapy
sedhek *adj.* sedentary *m.* **-ogow** tribunal
sedher *m.* **-oryon** diver, dipper (bird); **sedher downvor** deep-sea diver; **sedher meur** big dipper
sedhes *m.* sinking, setting
sedhi *v.* sink, dip, dive, submerge; set (of Sun)
seg *coll.* draff, brewer's grains
seghyer *plur.* bags, sacks
segi *v.* soak, steep
sel<base> *f.* **+yow** base, foundation
sel<seal> *f.* **+yow** seal, impression
selder *m.* cellar, basement
sellys *adj.* salted
selsigenn *f.* **+ow**, *coll.* **selsik** sausage
selven *m.* **selveyn** foundation stone
selvenek *adj.* fundamental, basic
Selwador *m.* Saviour
selwel *v.* save (from danger), rescue
selwyans *m.* salvation
Selwyas *m.* Saviour
selya<base> *v.* found, base, establish
selya<seal> *v.* seal
selyek *adj.* basic
semlant *m.* **-ns** appearance

sempel *adj.* simple, foolish; ordinary, plain
sempelhe *v.* simplify, make simple
sempledh *m.* simplicity
Sen *m.* Saint (as title)
sendal *m.* fine linen
senedh *m.* **+ow** synod, senate, parliament
senedher *m.* **-oryon** senator
seni *v.* sound (of an instrument), play, ring (of a bell)
Sen Ostell *place* St Austell
sens *plur.* saints
senser *m.* **+s** censer
sentri *m.* sanctuary
ser *m.* **+i** artificer, craftsman, artisan; **ser prenn** *m.* **seri prenn** carpenter; **ser men** *m.* **seri men** stone-mason, mason
serafyn *m.* seraph
seren *f.* requiem mass, mass for the dead
sergh *m.* affection, fondness, attachment (physical and emotional)
serghegenn *f.* **+ow**, *coll.* **serghek** goosegrass, cleaver (plant); **serghegenn vras** burdock
serghek *adj.* clinging, attached, dependent *m.* **-ogyon** dependant
serghi *v.* cling, be attached
serri *v.* anger, annoy, provoke, vex; **serri orth** be angry with
serrys *adj.* angry
sertan *adj.* certain *adv.* certainly
serth *adj.* steep, sheer, perpendicular
serthi *v.* rise straight up, rise sharply; stand upright
serthter *m.* steepness
servabyl *adj.* ready to serve, serviceable
servadow *adj.* provisional, serviceable
servis *m.* **+yow** service
servya *v.* serve

servyades *f.* waitress
servyas *m.* **-ysi** waiter, server, servant
servyour *m.* **+s** tray
-ses *suff.* (masc. abst. noun ending, from noun)
sesa *v.* seize, sequestrate, take seizin of a freehold
seson *m.* **+yow, +s** season, time, period (of time)
sesya *v.* seize, lay hold of
seth<arrow> *f.* **+ow** arrow
seth<jar> *m.* **+ow** large jar, crock
sethenn *f.* small arrow
sether *m.* **-oryon** archer, gannet, solan goose
sethik *f.* **-igow** dart
settya *v.* set, place, appoint; **settya orth** resist; **settya war** assault, attack; **ny settyav gwelenn gala** *phr.* I don't care a straw
settyans *m.* **+ow** setting (location)
seudh *m.* **+ow** depression (topographical),
seudhel *m.* **+yow** heel
seul *pron.* whoever
seu'l *m.* heel
seulabrys *adv.* formerly, already
seuladhydh *adv.* long since, formerly
sevel *v.* stand, rise, stay; raise up; **sevel orth** stand against, resist; **sevys a** *phr.* descended from
sevellek *f.* **-oges** redwing
sevelyek *m.* bystander
sevi *f.* **+enn** strawberries
sevia *v.* pick strawberries
seviek *f.* **-egi** strawberry-bed
sevur *adj.* severe, serious
sevureth *f.* seriousness, severity, gravity (abst.)
sevyans *m.* uprising
sewajya *v.* assuage, relieve, mitigate
sewen *adj.* successful, prosperous

sewena *f.* success, prosperity, welfare
seweni *v.* succeed, prosper, flourish
sewenyans *m.* success, prosperity
sewt *m.* colour of material, suit of cards
sewya *v.* sew, stitch
sewyades *f.* **+ow** seamstress
sewyas *m.* **-ysi** stitcher
Seys *m.* Englishman
seytegves *num.* seventeenth
seytek *num.* seventeen
seyth *num.* seven
seythblydhenyek *adj.* septennial
seythdelenn *f.* tormentil (herb)
seythgweyth *adv.* seven times
seythplek *adj.* sevenfold
seyth-ugens *num.* seven score
seythun *f.* **+yow** week
seythunyek *adj.* weekly
seythves *num.* seventh
shafta *m.* **-ys** mine-shaft
shakya *v.* shake, wag
sham *m.* shame, disgrace
shamya *v.* shame, humiliate, put to shame
shap *m.* **+ys** shape, form
shapya *v.* shape, form, fashion, model
sherewa *m.* **sherewys** rogue
sherewneth *f.* roguery
sherewynsi *m.* depravity
shora *m.* **shorys** fit, seizure
shyndya *v.* injure, hurt, ruin, harm
shyndys *adj.* injured, hurt, ruined, harmed
si<buzz> *m.* buzz, hiss
si<itch> *v.* fancy, itch, hanker
sia *v.* buzz, hiss
sians *m.* fancy, whim
sider *m.* cider
sidhel *m.* **sidhlow** filter, strainer
sidhla *v.* filter, strain, sift
sim *m.* **+es** monkey

sin *m.* **+ys, +yow** sign, mark, signal, symptom; **sin an grows** sign of the cross

sina *v.* sign, signal

sinell *f.* **+ow** signal

sinella *v.* signal

sira *m.* **sirys** sire, father; **sira da** father-in-law; **sira wynn** grandfather

sita *f.* **sitys** city

sivil *adj.* civil

sivilta *m.* civility

siw *m.* **+yon** bream

skajynn *m.* **+ow** vagabond, tramp

skala *m.* **+ys** saucer, dish (bowl)

skaldya *v.* scald, burn, inflame

skansek *adj.* scaly, flaky, laminated *m.* **-ogyon** scaly creature

skansenn *f.* **+ow,** *coll.* **skans** scale (of fish), flake

skant *adj.* scarce *adv.* scarcely, hardly

skantlowr *adv.* hardly, barely

skantlyn *m.* **+s** foot-rule, template, pattern

skapya *v.* escape, get away, slip out

skarf *m.* joint in timber, spline

skarfa *v.* scarf, spline

skath *f.* **+ow** boat

skath-hir *f.* **skathow-hir** longboat, barge

skath-kloes *f.* **skathow-kloes** raft

skath-revya *f.* **skathow-revya** rowing-boat

skath-roes *f.* **skathow-roes** seine-boat

skath-sawya *f.* **skathow-sawya** lifeboat

skath-tan *f.* **skathow-tan** motor-boat

skath-woelya *f.* **skathow-goelya** sailing-boat

skath-ynn *f.* **skathow-ynn** narrow-boat

skav *adj.* light, nimble, swift

skavder *m.* lightness

skavell *f.* **+ow** stool

skavell-droes foot-stool

skavell-groenek *f.* **skavellow-kroenek** toadstool, mushroom

skavhe *v.* lighten (reduce weight)

skaw *coll.* **-enn** elder-trees

skawenn-wragh *f.* **skawennow-gwragh,** *coll.* **skaw-gwragh** sycamore-tree

skenna *m.* **skennys, skennow** sinew, tendon

skennynn *m.* **+ow** tough bit of meat

skentel *adj.* learned, wise, knowledgeable

skentoleth *f.* knowledge, wisdom

skesya *v.* skate

sket *adv.* straightway, headlong

sketh *m.* **+ow** strip, tatter

skethenn *f.* **+ow** strip, tatter

skethenna *v.* shred, slice, tatter

skethennek *adj.* tattered, shredded

skether *m.* splinter, sliver

skethra *v.* lop, prune, chop

skethrek *adj.* tattered, splintered *m.* **-ogyon** tatterdemalion, ragged fellow

skethrenn *f.* **+ow** splinter, lopping

skethrik *m.* little splinter; **-igow**

skeul *f.* **+yow** ladder, scale; **skeul lovan** rope ladder

skeulya *v.* scale, climb by ladder

skeus *m.* **+ow** shadow

skeusek *adj.* shady, shadowy

skeusenn *f.* **+ow** photograph

skeusenner *m.* **-oryon** photographer

skeusennweyth *f.* photography

skeusi *v.* get away quickly, evade capture

skeuswydh *coll.* **+enn** privet

skevens *plur.* lungs, lights

skewyek *adj.* abounding in elder-trees

skewys *m.* place of elder-trees

skia *v.* ski

skians *m.* **+ow** knowledge, sense, science; **mes a'y skians** *adj.* out of his wits

skiansek *adj.* wise, intellectual *m.* **-ogyon** intellectual

skiber *f.* **+yow** barn, shed

skila *f.* **skilys** reason, cause *v.* be the cause of

skinenn *f.* **+ow** ear-ring

skit *m.* squirt, diarrhoea

skitell *f.* **+ow** syringe

skitya *v.* squirt, syringe, inject

skityans *m.* **+ow** injection

sklander *m.* slander, scandal

sklandra *v.* slander, defame

skochfordh *f.* **+ow** short-cut, alley, passage

skoedh *f.* **+ow**, *dual* **diwskoedh** shoulder

skoedhek *adj.* broad-shouldered

skoedh-lien *m.* priest's amice, linen shoulder-piece

skoedhya *v.* support, assist

skoedhyans *m.* support (abst.)

skoedhyer *m.* **-oryon** supporter

skoell *m.* **+yon** waste, neglect, carelessness; **tewel dhe skoell** *phr.* carelessly cast aside, treat wantonly

skoellva *f.* tip (for rubbish), dump

skoellya *v.* waste, squander; spill, pour; **skoellya a-les** disperse

skoellyek *adj.* wasteful *m.* **-ogyon** spendthrift, waster, wastrel

skoellyon *plur.* slops

skoes *m.* **+ow** shield, escutcheon; **skoes byw** human shield

skoeske *m.* **+ow** crash-barrier

skoestell *f.* **+ow** dashboard

skoeswas *m.* **-wesyon** shield-bearer, esquire

skogynn *m.* **+ow** fool, head of boiled mackerel

skol *f.* **+yow** school; **skol elvennek** elementary school; **skol gynsa** primary school; **skol nessa** secondary school, high school; **skol nos** night school; **skol ramer** grammar school; **skol Sul** Sunday school; **skol veythrin** nursery school

skoler *m.* scholar; **-oryon**

skolheygieth *f.* scholarship (learning)

skolheygses *m.* scholarship (learning)

skolheyk *m.* **skolheygyon** student

skolji *m.* **+ow** school-house

skolk *m.* **+yow** sneak

skolkya *v.* skulk, lurk, sneak

skolores *f.* **+ow** scholar

skolvester *m.* **skolvestri** schoolmaster

skombla *v.* defecate (of animals or birds)

skommow *plur.* wreckage

skommynn *m.* chip, splinter, kindling

skon *adv.* quickly, soon at once

skons *m.* fortress

skonya *v.* refuse, deny, withhold; **skonya a** abstain; **skonya a wul neppyth** refuse to do something

skor *m.* **+yow** score (in game)

skorja *m.* **+ys** scourge, whip, cat o' nine tails

skorjya *v.* scourge, thrash, whip

skorn *m.* mockery, slight, affront

skornya *v.* mock, ridicule

skorr *coll.* **+enn**, **+ow** branches, boughs, veins of ore

skorrek *adj.* branched

skorya *v.* score (in game)

skot *m.* **+ys** tavern score

skotter *m.* shelter

skoul *m.* kite (bird)

skout *f.* **+ys** hussy, skit (wanton girl)

skov *m.* rich tin-ore

skovarn *f.* **skovornow,** *dual* **diwskovarn** ear, handle of jar

skovarnek *adj.* long-eared, having handles *m.* **-ogyon** hare

skovenn *f.* ground rich in tin

skovva *f.* **+ow** shelter, refuge, shade tabernacle (dwelling-place)

skown *m.* **+yow** bench

skravinyas *v.* scratch, claw

skraw *m.* black-headed gull

skrawik *m.* **-igow** tern, black-headed gull

Skriba *m.* **Skribys** Scribe (Biblical)

skrif *m.* **+ow** writing, document, article (of text)

skrifa<VN> *v.* write

skrifa<MN> *m.* writing, inscription, writ

skrifenn *f.* **+ow** writing, article, document; **skrifenn a lagha** legal document

skrifennyades *f.* **+ow** secretary

skrifennyas *m.* **-ysi** secretary

skrifer +s, -oryon writer

skriflyver *m.* **skriflyvrow** notebook

skrifwas *m.* **-wesyon** scribe, clerk

skrifyas *m.* **-ysi** writer (professional), scribe

skrija *v.* cry out, screech

skrinva *f.* gnashing

skrogenn *f.* gallows-bird

skruth *m.* shudder, shock, shrug

skrutha *v.* shudder, be horrified

skruthus *adj.* shocking, horrible

skrynkya *v.* snarl, grimace; **skrynkya orth** make a grimace at

skryp *m.* **+ys** wallet

Skryptor *m.* **+s** Scripture

skuba *v.* sweep, brush

skubell *f.* **+ow** broom (implement)

skubellek *adj.* rubbishy, trashy (U.S.) *m.* **-ogyon** untidy person

skubelloges *f.* **+ow** untidy person

skubell-sugna *f.* **skubellow-sugna** vacuum-cleaner

skubell-wolghi *f.* **skubellow-golghi** mop

skubyllenn *f.* small brush, mop; **skubyllenn bast** pastry brush; **skubyllenn baynt** paint-brush; **skubyllenn dhens** tooth-brush

skubyon *coll.* sweepings

skudell *f.* **+ow** dish (bowl), soup-bowl

skudellas *f.* **+ow** dishful

skuthenn *m.* Manx shearwater

skward *m.* **+yow** tear, rip, rent, laceration

skwardya *v.* tear, rip, rend, lacerate

skwat *m.* crushing blow,

skwatya *v.* crush, hit, squash

skwier *m.* **+yon** esquire

skwir *m.* **+ys** standard (basis of comparison), set-square

skwith *adj.* tired, weary; **skwith marow** dead tired

skwitha *v.* tire

skwithans *m.* tiredness

skwithhe *v.* tire, weary make tired

skwithhes *adj.* wearied

skwithter *m.* fatigue, tiredness

skwithus *adj.* tiring, boring

skwych *m.* **+ys** jerk, twitch, spasm

skwychell *f.* **+ow** switch (electric)

skwychya *v.* jerk, twitch; switch; **skwychya yn fyw** switch on; **skwychya yn farow** switch off

skyll *coll.* **+enn** sprouts, shoots, eyes (of potato)

skyllwynn *adj.* whitish

skyrenn *f.* **+ow,** *coll.* **skyr** splinter

skyrmya *v.* fence (with swords)

slaba *m.* **slabow** kitchen-range

sley *adj.* clever, skilful

sleyneth *f.* skill, dexterity; cleverness

sloj *m.* **slejys** sledgehammer

slokkya *v.* entice

slynk *adj.* slippery *m.* **+ow** slide

slynkya *v.* slide, slip, creep

smat *adj.* hardy, rough *m.* **+ys** hardbitten fellow, tough guy

snell *adj.* quick, active *adv.* quickly

snod *m.* **+ow, +ys** ribbon, band (strip), tape, fillet

soda *m.* soda

soder *m.* solder

sodh *m.* sooth, truth

sodon *m.* **+ys** Sultan

sodra *v.* solder

soedh *f.* **+ow** office (job), occupation

soedha *v.* hold office, serve (in employment)

soedhek *m.* **-dhogyon** officer

soedhogel *adj.* official

soedhogoleth *f.* officialdom

soedhva *f.* **+ow** office (workplace), place of employment; **soedhva an post** post office; **soedhva govskrifa** register office; **soedhva greslu** police station

soegenn *f.* damp place

soen *m.* **-yow** charm, blessing

soena *v.* bless, charm

soenell *f.* **+ow** charm (item)

soev *m.* tallow, suet

sogh<AJ> *adj.* blunt, dull

sogh<MN> *m.* **+yow** ploughshare

sojet *m.* **+s** subject (e.g. of a king), liege; **sojet ankow** mortal

sokor *m.* succour, aid

sokra *v.* succour, relieve, aid

solas *m.* solace, relief

solempna *adj.* solemn

solempnya *v.* celebrate

solempnyta *m.* **-nytys** solemnity, ceremony

soler *m.* **+yow** loft, attic, upper floor

sols *m.* **+ow** shilling

somm *m.* sum, total

sommenn *f.* **+ow** sum, total

sommys *v.* flit, move about

somper *adj.* unequalled

son *m.* **+yow** sound (noise), noise; **gas dha son** *phr.* be quiet

songyst *f.* **+yow** audio-cassette

sononieth *f.* acoustics

sonskrif *m.* **+ow** sound-recording

sonskrifa *v.* record, make a soundrecording

sonsnod *m.* **+ow** audio-tape

soper *m.* supper

sopya *v.* sup

sordya *v.* arouse, stir up

sorn *m.* **+ow** nook, corner

sorr *m.* anger

sorrvann *m.* indignation

sort<hedgehog> *m.* **+es** hedgehog

sort<sort> *m.* **+ow** sort, kind

sortya *v.* sort

sos *m.* friend(s)

sosten *m.* sustenance, food, subsistence

sostena *v.* sustain

sotel *adj.* crafty, subtle

sotelneth *f.* sleight

Soth *m.* South

sotla *v.* subtilize

souba *v.* soak, steep, saturate

soubenn *f.* **+ow** soup, broth

soubenna *v.* break bread, sup

souder *m.* **-oryon, soudrys** soldier

sovran *adj.* sovereign *m.* sovereign

sovranedh *m.* sovereignty

sowdhan *m.* confusion, stupefaction, bewilderment; straying; **mos yn sowdhan** *v.* go astray

sowdhanas *v.* be confused;, stray; surprise

soweth *int.* alas

sowl *coll.* thatch
sowlek *adj.* stubbly *f.* **-egi** stubble field
sowlwoedh *f.* **+ow** stubble goose
sows *m.* **+ow** sauce
Sows *m.* **+on** Englishman, Saxon
Sowses *f.* **+ow** Englishwoman
sowsneger *m.* **-oryon** English speaker, anglophone
Sowsnek *adj.* English *m.* English language
sowsnekhe *v.* anglicize
sowsnekheans *m.* anglicization
sowser *m.* **+yow** saucer
sowter *m.* psalter
sowtri *m.* psaltery, zither
spadell *f.* **+ow** spatula
spadh *adj.* castrated, gelded, spayed
spadha *v.* castrate, geld, spay
spadhesik *m.* **-igyon** eunuch, castrato
spagetti *coll.* spaghetti
spal *m.* **+yow** fine (penalty), forfeiture
spala *v.* fine
spalyer *m.* **+s** mine labourer
sparbyl *m.* sparable, small headless wedge-shaped iron nail
sparya *v.* spare
sparyon *plur.* spares, spare parts
spas *m.* space, opportunity, room
spavenn *f.* lull, quiet interval
spavennhe *v.* lull
spavnell *f.* **+ow** lull
Spayn *place* Spain
Spaynek *adj.* Spanish *m.* Spanish language
spaynel *m.* **+s** spaniel
Spayner *m.* **-oryon** Spaniard
spedhas *coll.* **+enn** briars, brambles
spedhasek *f.* **-egi** briar-brake, bramble patch
spedya *v.* succeed, progress

spekkyar *f.* speckled hen
spena *v.* spend, use up
spens *m.* **+ow** larder, pantry
spenser *m.* **+s** butler
spern *coll.* **+enn** thorns
spernek *adj.* thorny *f.* **-egi** thornbrake
spernenn *f.* **+ow**, *coll.* **spern** thorn; **spernenn wynn** *f.* hawthorn; **spernenn dhu** *f.* blackthorn; **spernenn velyn** buckthorn, barberry
spiknard *m.* spikenard
spilgarn *m.* shag (bird), cormorant
spinach *m.* spinach
spis *m.* **+ys**, **+yow** spice
spiser *m.* **-oryon**, **+s** grocer, spicer
spisti *m.* **+ow** grocer's shop
spit *m.* spite, malice; **spit dhe** *conj.* in spite of, in despite of
spitus *adj.* spiteful, malicious
spitya *v.* spite
splann *adj.* shining, bright, splendid
splanna *v.* shine
splannder *m.* brightness
splannhe *v.* make bright, illuminate (with light)
splatt *m.* **+ow** plot (of ground)
splennyjyon *m.* brightness, luminosity
splettyar *f.* spotted hen
spong *m.* **+ow** sponge
spongya *v.* sponge
sport *m.* **+ow**, **+ys** sport, game (competition)
sportva *f.* **+ow** stadium
sportya *v.* sport, go hunting
sprall *m.* fetter, shackle, impediment
spralla *v.* fetter
sprallyer *m.* hobble
sprus *coll.* **+enn** kernels, pips
sprusek *adj.* pippy *f.* **-egi** seedbed
spyrys *m.* **+yon** spirit, fairy

spys *m.* period (of time); **a verr spys** *adv.* shortly

stag<fixed> *adj.* fixed, fastened *adv.* on the very spot *m.* tether, nightmare (in which one is fixed)

stag<mud> *m.* mud, mire

staga *v.* tether, fix, attach

stagell *f.* attachment (physical), tie (link), bond

stagen *m.* pond

stagsav *m.* **+ow** stand-off, deadlock, impasse

stall *m.* **+ow** stall; **stall tenna** shooting gallery

stall-marghas *m.* market-stall

stamp *m.* **+ys, +ow** postage-stamp

stampys *plur.* stamping-mill

stampya *v.* stamp

stanch *adj.* staunch, watertight

stanchura *v.* pay with pitch, seal

stanchynn *m.* **+ow** gasket

stank *m.* heavy tread, stamp (of foot)

stankya *v.* trample, stamp (with foot)

stark *adv.* fixedly

starn *f.* **+yow** framework, chassis, harness

stat *m.* **+ow, +ys** state (political), estate

statya *v.* convey an estate

sten *m.* tin (metal); **sten du** unsmelted tin; **sten gwynn** smelted tin

stenek *f.* **-egi** tin ground

stenor *m.* **+yon** tinner

stenus *adj.* containing tin, stannous

ster *coll.* **+enn, +ow** stars

sterenn *f.* **+ow,** *coll.* **ster** star; **sterenn lostek** comet

sterennek *adj.* starry

sterenni *v.* sparkle, twinkle, star (in film)

sterennik *f.* **-igow** little star, asterisk

stergann *m.* starlight

sterji *m.* **+ow** planetarium

sterlyn *adj.* sterling *m.* sterling

steronieth *f.* astronomy

steroniethek *adj.* astronomical

steronydh *m.* **+yon** astronomer

stervarner *m.* **-oryon** astronaut

stervya *v.* die of cold

steus *f.* **+ow** course (of study), series

steuv *m.* **+ow** warp

steuvi *v.* warp

stevell *f.* **+ow** room

stevell-dhybri *f.* **stevellow-dybri** dining-room

stevell-dhiskwedhyans *f.* exhibition hall

stevell-oberyans *f.* operating theatre, operating room (U.S.)

stevell-omwolghi *f.* **stevellow-omwolghi** bathroom

stevnik *f.* palate

stevya *v.* hasten

stif +ow *f.* jet, squirt

stifa *v.* squirt

stifek *m.* squid

stiwenn *m.* blow, slap

stiwenna *v.* slap

stlav *adj.* lisping *m.* **stlevyon** lisper

stlavedh *adj.* lisping

stlevi *v.* lisp

stlevyon *plur.* lispers

Stoel *m.* Epiphany

stoff *m.* goods, stuff, substance

stoffki *m.* **-keun** junkie, drug-addict

stoffya *v.* stuff

stokk *m.* **+ys, +ow** stump, stock; **y'n stokkys** *adv.* in the stocks

stokkynn *f.* **+ow** stub

stol *f.* **+yow** stole

stoppya *v.* stop (trans.), prevent, block

stoppyer *m.* **+s** stopper, plug

stos *m.* **+ow** gnat, gadfly

stoul *m.* timber frame in mine

stout *adj.* proud

straght *adj.* strict

stras *m.* **+ow** low ground, flat valley

strech *m.* **+ys** delay

strechya *v.* spin out time

stredh *f.* **+ow** stream, brook

strekys *f.* **strokosow** stroke, blow

strel *m.* **+yow** mat; **strel gweli** bedside mat

strelik *m.* **-igow** beer or table mat

stret *m.* **+ow, +ys** street

stretynn *m.* **+ow** alley, little street lane (in town),

streyl *f.* currycomb

streylya *v.* curry a horse

strif *m.* **+ow** strife

strifwerth *m.* **+ow** auction

strik *adj.* active, nimble *m.* hyphen

striver *m.* **-oryon** wrangler

strivya *v.* strive, contend

strivyans *m.* contention

striw *m.* **+yow** sneeze

striwi *v.* sneeze

strol *m.* mess (untidiness), litter (rubbish), garbage (U.S.)

strolgyst *f.* **+yow** litter-bin, garbage can (U.S.)

strolya *v.* make untidy, trash (U.S.)

strolyek *adj.* dirty, messy

stronk *adj.* dirty (of liquid) *m.* filth

stronka *v.* pollute water, befoul water

stroth *adj.* tight, strict, stringent

strotha *v.* squeeze, constrict, constrain; embrace

strus *m.* **+yow** ostrich

studh *m.* **+yow** state, condition, predicament

studhla *m.* **-leow** studio

studhva *f.* **+ow** study (room)

studhya *v.* study

studhyer *m.* **studhyoryon** student

studhyus *adj.* studious

stumm *m.* **+ow** bend, turning

stumma *v.* turn, bend, wind

stykkenn *f.* **+ow** stake, post

stykkenna *v.* stake

styl *m.* **+yow** beam (timber), rafter

styr *m.* **+yow** meaning, significance

styrya *v.* explain, mean, signify, define, expound

styryans *m.* **+ow** definition, explanation

suant *adj.* level, even

substans *m.* substance

sugal *coll.* **+enn** rye

sugaldir *m.* rye ground

sugalek *f.* **-egi** rye-field

sugen *m.* **+yow** juice, sap, essence; **sugen aval** apple-juice; **sugen froeth** fruit juice; **sugen limaval** lime-juice; **sugen owraval** orange-juice

sugna *v.* suck

sugnans *m.* suction

sugnus *adj.* succulent

sugra *m.* sugar *v.* sugar, sweeten with sugar

Sul *m.* **+yow** Sunday

Sulweyth *m.* Sunday (time) *adv.* on a Sunday

sur *adj.* sure *adv.* surely

surhe *v.* insure, assure, ensure, confirm

surheans *m.* insurance, assurance

surkot *m.* overcoat

surredi *adv.* most surely, verily, really

swaysya *v.* swing (e.g. one's arms, or a golf club)

swynnenn *f.* **+ow** swig, draught

sybwydh *coll.* **+enn** fir-trees, evergreen trees

syg *f.* attachment (physical), tie (link), leash, chain, bond, trace (of a harness)

sygenn *f.* attachment (physical), loop, cord for fastening

syger *adj.* oozing, sluggish, lazy, leaky, slow, idle

sygera *v.* ooze, idle, dawdle, drain away, leak slowly

sygerneth *f.* sluggishness, idleness, laziness, sloth

sygh *adj.* dry, parched, arid, waterless; withered

sygha *v.* dry, wipe

syghan *m.* dry place

syghborth *m.* **+ow** dry-dock

syghes *m.* thirst; **yma syghes dhymm** I am thirsty

syghla *m.* dry place

syghor *m.* drought, dryness

syghnans *m.* **+ow** streamless valley

syghtenow *m.* streamless valley

syghter *m.* drought, dryness

syghtir *m.* **+yow** dry land

syllabenn *f.* **+ow** syllable

Syllan *place* Scilly

sylli *f.* **+es** eel

symbal *m.* **+ys** cymbal

symfoni *m.* hurdy-gurdy

synaga *m.* **synagys** synagogue

synsas *m.* **+ow** contents, holding (financial)

synsell *f.* **+ow** clip (e.g. paper-clip)

synsi *v.* hold

synsyas *m.* **-ysi** holder

synthesek *adj.* synthetic

syrk *m.* **+ow** circus (show)

syrr *m.* **+ys** sir

syrra *m.* sir, sirrah

system *m.* **+ow** system

sythol *m.* **+s** dulcimer

sywya *v.* follow, result

sywyas *m.* **-ysi** follower, successor

sywyans *m.* **+ow** result, consequence

T (mutations D, TH)

tabour *m.* **+s**, **+yow** drum, tabor

tag *m.* choking, strangulation

taga *v.* choke, stifle, strangle, constrict

tagell *f.* **+ow** constriction, choker

tag-hir *m.* cuttlebone

takkya *v.* nail, fasten, affix; **takkya orth** nail to

takla *v.* furnish, array, deck

taklenn *f.* **+ow** item

taklow *plur.* material things

taksi *m.* **+ow** taxi

takya *v.* clap hands

tal *m.* **+yow** brow, forehead, temple; gable

talar *m.* headland (in field)

talas *m.* **+ow** payment

talbenn *m.* **+ow** knob

talek *adj.* big-browed *m.* **taloges** roach (fish), dace

taler *m.* **-oryon** payer; **taler toll** tax-payer

talesik *m.* **-igyon** payee

talgamm *adj.* sullen *m.* **+ow** scowl, frown

talgamma *v.* scowl, frown

talgell *f.* **+ow** pantry, buttery, store-cellar

talgh *m.* **telghyon** bran, grist

talik *m.* **taligow** garret, attic

tallyour *m.* **+s** serving-dish, trencher

tal-sogh *adj.* stupid, dull, blunt-witted

talverr *m.* **+es** skate (fish)

talvesa *v.* value, price

talvosogeth *f.* value, worth

talvos *v.* value

talvosek *adj.* valuable

Tamer *m.* Tamar (name of river)

tamm *m.* **temmyn** piece, bit, fragment; **tamm ha tamm** gradually, bit by bit

tan *m.* **+yow** fire; **gans tan** on fire

tanbellenn *f.* **+ow** bomb, shell (explosive); **tanbellenn gonnyk** smart bomb

tanbellenna *v.* bomb, bombard

tanbrenn *m.* **-yer** match (matchstick)

tanlester *m.* **-lestri** fire-ship

tank *m.* **tankow** tank; **tank puskes** fish tank

tanker *m.* **+yow** tanker; **tanker oyl** oil tanker

tann<by> *prep.* by

tann<take> *v.* take (impv.)

tanow *adj.* thin, rare, frugal, scarce

tanowder *m.* rarity, scarcity

tanowhe *v.* attenuate, diminish

tansys *m.* **+yow** bonfire, blaze

tantans *m.* courtship, wooing

tanter *m.* **-oryon** suitor, wooer

tanvaglenn *f.* **+ow** fire-grate

tanweyth *coll.* **+enn** fireworks

taper *m.* **taprys** wax candle

tapp *m.* **+ow**, **+ys** tap (e.g. of bath)

taran *f.* thunder

taranek *adj.* thundery, like thunder

taraner *m.* **-oryon** thunderer

tarder *m.* **terder** auger, drill

tardh *m.* **+ow** explosion, bang

tardha *v.* explode

tardhell *f.* **+ow** vent, loophole, outlet

tardra *v.* bore, drill, tap a barrel

tarena *v.* thunder, roar, bang

tarosvann *m.* **+ow** ghost, apparition, spectre

tarosvannus *adj.* ghostly, unreal, fantastic, spectral (of ghosts)

tarow *m.* **terewi** bull

tarow-hes *f.* second swarm

tas *m.* **+ow** father; **Tas Nadelik** Father Christmas

tasek *adj.* paternal, patronal *m.* **tasogyon** spiritual father, patron saint

tas-gwynn *m.* **tasow-wynn** grandfather

tasik *m.* daddy

tas-kuv *m.* **tasow-guv** great-grandfather

tasmeth *m.* **+ow** foster-father

tasoges *f.* patroness

tasogeth *f.* patronage

tasoleth *f.* paternity

tassens *plur.* holy fathers

tast *m.* taste

tastya *v.* taste

tava *v.* touch, stroke

tavell *f.* **+ow** probe

tavella *v.* probe

tavern *m.* **+yow** tavern

tavernor *m.* **+yon** innkeeper

taves *m.* **tavosow** tongue, language

tavethli *v.* broadcast

tavlinenn *f.* **+ow** tangent

tavol *coll.* **+enn** dock-plants

tavosa *m.* scold, jaw

tavosek *adj.* verbose, talkative; long-tongued *m.* **tavosogyon** chatterbox

tavoseth *f.* **+ow** idiom

taw *m.* silence, quiet; **taw taves** *phr.* keep quiet

tawesek *adj.* silent, taciturn

tawesigeth *f.* taciturnity

te *m.* tea

tebel *adj.* evil, wicked *m.* **+es** evil person

tebeldhyghtya *v.* abuse, treat badly

tebott *m.* **+ow** teapot

teg *adj.* fine, beautiful, pretty *adv.* quite, completely

tegenn *f.* **+ow** trinket, jewel; **tegenn Dyw** butterfly

tegh *m.* flight, retreat

teghes *v.* flee

tegynn *m.* **+ow** toy, trinket

tegys *v.* choked

tejy *pron.* thee (emphatic)

tekhe *v.* beautify

tekka *adj.* finer, prettier, more beautiful

tekkenn *f.* scrap, bit
tekst *m.* text
tekter *m.* beauty, finery
tell *plur.* holes
tellek *adj.* riddled, pockmarked *m.*
tellogyon ragamuffin
telli *v.* bore holes, drill holes
tellik *m.* **-igow** tiny hole
tellvolla *m.* **-vollow** colander
tellyas *m.* **-ysi** tax inspector
telynn *f.* **+ow** harp
telynnek *adj.* lyric
telynnya *v.* play a harp
telynnyer *m.* **+yon** harpist
telynnyores *f.* **+ow** harpist
temmik *m.* **temmigow** little bit, particle, mite
temmyn *plur.* pieces
tempel *m.* **templow** temple
templa *m.* **templys** temple
tempra *v.* tame, subdue, moderate, temper
tempredh *m.* **+ow** temperature
temprek *adj.* temperate
temprer *m.* **-oryon** tamer, moderator
tempter *m.* **-oryon** tempter
temptya *v.* tempt
temptyans *m.* temptation
tender *adj.* tender
tenewenn *m.* **tenwennow** side, flank
tenki *v.* destine
tenkys *f.* fate
tenn *m.* **+ow** pull, drag, tug, draught, wooden beam in tension, stretcher (wooden beam)
tenna *v.* pull, drag, haul; attract; shoot, draw, fire (a weapon); **tenna yn-mes** remove, extract
tenner *m.* **-oryon** puller, drawer (person)
tennik *f.* **-igow** ripple, wavelet
tennis *m.* tennis; **tennis moes** table-tennis
tennlester *m.* **-lestri** tug (boat)
tennroes *f.* **+ow** draw-net
tennstrif *m.* tug-of-war
tennva *f.* tension, drawing (pulling)
tennvargh *m.* **-vergh** draught-horse
tennven *m.* **tennveyn** magnet, lodestone
tennvenek *adj.* magnetic
tennvos *m.* attraction
tenor *m.* **+yon** tenor
tenow *m.* **+i** valley-bottom, low ground
ter *adj.* eager, insistent, urgent
-ter *suff.* (masc. abst. noun ending)
terder *m.* eagerness
terewi *plur.* bulls
tergravas *v.* scarify
terghi *v.* wreathe, coil
terghya *v.* rootle, root (of pigs)
tergoska *v.* doze
teri *v.* insist, be eager
terlemmel *v.* gambol, frisk
terlenki *v.* gulp
terlentri *v.* glisten, twinkle
termyn *m.* **+yow** time, term, period (of time); **a-dermyn**; **a dermyn dhe dermyn** *adv.* from time to time; **a verr dermyn** briefly, shortly; **an termyn eus passys** the past
termynek *adj.* dawdling, dilatory *m.* **-ogyon** time-waster
ternas *m.* kingdom, realm
ternija *v.* flutter, flit
ternoeth *adj.* half naked
ternos *adv.* next day, on the morrow, the day after; **ternos vyttin** tomorrow morning, on the following morning
ternwelenn *f.* **+ow** sceptre
terras *m.* **+ow** terrace

terri *v.* break, pick (e.g. flowers);
terri chi tear down a house; **terri
syghes** slake thirst
terroes *m.* havoc, destruction,
downfall
terroesa *m.* disaster, havoc
terroesus *adj.* disastrous
terroesva *f.* disaster area
terrys *adj.* broken
terthenn *f.* **+ow** fever, influenza, flu
terva *v.* make a tumult
tervans *m.* tumult, din
tervyajor *m.* **+yon** tourist
tervysk *m.* **+ow** muddle
tervyska *v.* muddle, muddle up
tes *m.* heat, warmth
tesa *v.* heat, warm in the sunshine
tesek *adj.* hot, sultry; hot-tempered,
irritable
tesogneth *f.* irritability
tesenn *f.* **+ow** cake; **tesenn
dhyenn** cream cake; **tesenn gales**
biscuit, cookie (U.S.); **tesenn
vyghan** bun
test *m.* **+ow** witness
testa *v.* bear witness
testament *m.* testament (Biblical);
Testament Koth Old Testament;
Testament Nowydh New
Testament
testenn *f.* **+ow** subject (of study)
testskrif *m.* **+ow** certificate,
testimonial
teth *f.* **+ow** teat
tethenn *f.* **+ow** teat
tetivali *int.* tut-tut, tush, nonsense
teudh *adj.* molten, melted, melting
teudher *m.* **-oryon** melter
teudhergh *m.* slush
teudherik *m.* **-igow** fuse
teudherigva *f.* **+ow** fuse-box
teudhi *v.* melt, smelt, thaw, fuse
teudhji *m.* **+ow** foundry
teudhla *m.* foundry

teudhlester *m.* **-lestri** crucible
teudhva *f.* **+ow** foundry
teuregonieth *f.* parasitology
teurek *coll.* **teuregenn** parasites,
bugs
tevesik *adj.* adult *m.* **-igyon** adult
(male)
tevesiges *f.* **+ow** adult (female)
tevi *v.* grow, shoot (of plants)
tevyans *m.* growth
tew *adj.* thick, fat, dense, impervious
tewal *adj.* dark, gloomy, murky
tewder *m.* thickness, fatness
tewedh *m.* storm
tewedha *v.* weather
tewedhans *v.* weathering
tewedhek *adj.* weather-beaten
tewel *v.* be silent, cease speaking,
hush
tewes *coll.* **+enn** sand
tewesek *adj.* sandy
tewhe *v.* thicken, fatten
tewl *adj.* dark, gloomy, murky, sombre
tewlder *m.* darkness
tewlel *v.* throw, cast, toss, fling;
tewlel prenn cast lots; **tewlel
towl** plan; **tewlel yn-mes** throw
out, eject, expel
tewlhe *v.* darken, become dark
tewlwolow *m.* half-light
tewlyjyon *m.* darkness
tewolgow *m.* darkness
tewynn *m.* **+ow** dune
tewynnek *adj.* duned
Tewynn Pleustri *place* Newquay
teyl *m.* manure
teylek *f.* **teylegi** dung-heap
teylu *m.* **+yow** family, household
teyr *num.* three (f.)
teyrgweyth *adv.* thrice
teyrros *f.* **+ow** tricycle
teythi *plur.* attributes, faculties,
abilities, qualities

teythyek *adj.* indigenous, local, home-grown, vernacular, aboriginal *m.* **teythyogyon** native, local, aborigine

ti<roof> *v.* roof, thatch, slate

ti<swear> *v.* swear *m.* **+ow** oath, imprecation; **bedhav y di** *phr.* I dare say

tid *m.* tide

tiek *m.* **tiogow, tiogyon** farmer, householder

tigenn *f.* **+ow** hand-bag, wallet

tiger *m.* **tigri** tiger

tigres *f.* **+ow** tigress

tim *m.* thyme

tin *f.* arse, posterior, rump

tingogh *m.* **+es** redstart

tinwynn *f.* **+yon** wheatear (bird)

tioges *f.* **+ow** farmer, countrywoman, housewife

tiogeth *f.* **+yow** household

tiogow *plur.* farmers

tiogyon *plur.* farmers

tior *m.* **+yon** thatcher, slater

tir *m.* **+yow** land, ground, territory; **tir meur** mainland

tira *v.* land, come ashore

tirans *m.* landing

tiredh *m.* country, land, territory

tirvusuryas *m.* **-ysi** land-surveyor

tirwel *m.* **+yow** landscape

titel *m.* **titlow, titlys** legal right, title

tiyas *m.* **tiysi** juror

tnow *m.* **-i** valley-bottom

to *m.* **tohow** roof

toch *m.* moment

tochya *v.* touch accidentally

toell *m.* deceit, fraud

toella *v.* deceive, cheat, fool

toeller *m.* **-oryon** deceiver (male)

toellores *f.* **+ow** deceiver (female)

toellwisk *m.* disguise

toellwiska *v.* disguise

toemm *adj.* warm, ardent

toemma *v.* warm

toemmder *m.* warmth, heat

toemmhe *v.* warm

toemmheans-kres *m.* central heating

toemmyjyon *m.* warmth

toes<dough> *m.* dough; **toes gwari** play dough

toes<tuft> *m.* **+ow** tuft, tassel, bunch

toesa *v.* knead

toesek *adj.* tufted

toeth *m.* haste, hurry, speed; **toeth bras** high speed; **toeth da** high speed, with alacrity

toethya *v.* hasten

tokyn *m.* **toknys, tokynyow** ticket, symptom, token; **tokyn mos-ha-dos** return ticket; **yn tokyn** *phr.* as a sign of, as a mark of

tokynva *f.* **+ow** ticket-office, booking office

toll<hole> *m.* **tell** hole, burrow

toll<tax> *f.* **+ow** tax, toll, duty

toll-annedh *f.* rate (on property), property tax

tollans *m.* taxation

toll-benn *f.* poll-tax

tollbons *m.* toll-bridge

tollborth *m.* **+ow** toll-gate

toll-boton *m.* **tell-boton** button-hole

toll-brenas *f.* purchase tax

toll-dhowr *f.* **tollow-dowr** water rate

toll-dir *f.* **tollow-tir** land tax

tollek *adj.* holed

toller *m.* **-oryon** tax collector

tollfordh *f.* **+ow** toll-road

toll-gevoeth *f.* wealth tax

tollgorn *m.* **tollgern** flute; **tollgorn sowsnek** recorder (Mus.)

tolli *v.* levy tax, tax

tollji *m.* **+ow** toll-house, customs-house

tollva *f.* **+ow** tax-office, toll-booth; **Tollva an Wlas** Inland Revenue

tollven *m.* **tollveyn** holed stone

toll-vernans *f.* death duty

toll-wober *f.* income tax

Tommas *name* Thomas

tommenn *f.* **+ow** earth-bank, dyke, dam; **tommenn ergh** snowdrift

ton *m.* **+yow** tune, melody; tone; **ton kerdh** march (tune)

tonlev *m.* intonation

tonn<ley> *coll.* **+enn** ley-land, turf

tonn<wave> *f.* **+ow** wave, billow

tonnas *m.* **+ow** ton, tonne

tonnek<flock> *m.* flock, crowd

tonnek<wavy> *adj.* wavy, rough (of sea)

tonnell *f.* **+ow** tun, keeve

tonnhys *m.* wavelength; **tonnhys kres** medium wave

tont *adj.* impudent, saucy, pert, cheeky, impertinent

tonteth *f.* impudence, cheek (rudeness), impertinence

tontya *v.* be cheeky

tonya *v.* intone, accentuate

topp *m.* **+ys** top, summit, peak

toppynn *m.* **+ow** tip (end)

tor' *m.* turn; **y'n tor' ma** *adv.* at this time

torgh<boar> *m.* **+es** boar, barrow pig

torgh<wreath> *f.* **tergh** wreath, neck-chain; torque, spring (coil)

torghedh *m.* torque (physical quantity)

torment *m.* **tormens** torment, torture

tormentor *m.* **+ys** tormentor, torturer

tormentya *v.* torment, torture

torn *m.* **+ow** turn, deed, tour; **torn da** good turn

tornyas *m.* **-ysi** tourist

tornyaseth *f.* tourism

torr<belly> *f.* **+ow** belly, stomach; womb

torr<break> *m.* **+ow** break, rupture, fracture

torr<tor> *f.* **+ow** tor

torras *m.* litter (of animals), bellyful

torrek *adj.* pot-bellied, big-bellied

torrgyngel *f.* cummerbund, horse's bellyband

torrleveryas *m.* **-ysi** ventriloquist

torr-men *m.* saxifrage

torrva *f.* **+ow** rupture, breach, breakdown; **torrva ambos** breach of contract; **torrva chi** burglary; **torrva demmedhyans** divorce

torth *f.* **+ow** loaf, large cake

torthell *m.* **+ow** small loaf, bun

toul *m.* **+ys, +ow** tool, implement

toul-lowarth *m.* **toulow-lowarth** garden tool

tour *m.* **+yow** tower, steeple; **tour korslynk** helter skelter; **tour routya** control tower

tourik *m.* **-igow** turret

towargh *coll.* **+enn** peat, turf (for burning)

towarghek *adj.* peaty *f.* **-egi** peat-bog, turbary

towarghweyth *m.* turfwork, turbary

towell *m.* **+ow** towel

towl *m.* **+ow** throw, plan, design

towlargh *m.* **+ow** budget

towlenn *f.* **+ow** programme, schedule; **towlenn ober** schedule of work, scheme of work

towlenna *v.* program

towlenner *m.* **-oryon** programmer

towlennores *f.* **+ow** programmer

towlgost *m.* **+ow** price quotation, estimate of cost

towl-howl *m.* sunstroke

towl-hys *m.* range (of missile etc.)

tra *f.* **+ow** thing, article (object); affair, fact

tragesort *m.* **+es** spider-crab

tramor *adj.* overseas, abroad

trank *m.* period (of time); **trank heb worfenn** *adv.* for ever and ever

traow *plur.* things (abst.)

transyek *m.* ecstasy, quandary, state of wonder or alarm

trapp *m.* **+ys** trap-stile

travalya *v.* walk far, travel, trudge

travel *m.* long walk, travel

travydh *f.* nothing, anything (in neg. phrases)

trayn *m.* **+ys** enticement, guile, allure

traynya *v.* entice, beguile, lure

trayson *m.* treason, treachery

trayta *v.* betray

traytour *m.* **+s** traitor

trayturi *m.* treachery

tre *f.* **trevow** farmstead, village, town; home

trebuchya *v.* trip, stumble; recoil

trebyl *m.* treble (Mus.), soprano

tredan *m.* electricity

tredanek *adj.* electric

tredaner *m.* **-oryon** electrician

tredanhe *adj.* electrify

tredanva *f.* power station, power plant

tredanva-wyns *f.* wind farm

tregeredh *f.* **+ow** mercy (loving kindness)

tregeredhus *adj.* merciful

tregeredhva *f.* mercy-seat

tregh *m.* **+ow** cut, chop, section, slice, tranch

tregher *m.* **-oryon** tailor, cutter

tregherieth *f.* tailoring

tregheriethek *adj.* sartorial

treghi *v.* cut, carve (of meat)

treghyas *m.* **-ysi** cutter

tregynn *m.* **+ow** drawer (in furniture)

tremadheves *m.* dance in a ring

tremen *m.* transit

tremena *v.* pass, exceed, die; **tremena dres** pass by, overtake

tremengummyas *m.* **+ow** passport

tremensorn *m.* **+ow** passing-place

tremenva *f.* passing-place

tremenvann *f.* passing away

tremenyas *m.* **-ysi** passer-by, traveller

tremenyans *m.* passing

tremm *f.* sight, look

tremmynn *m.* face, look, aspect

tren *m.* **+ow** railway train; **tren fres** goods train; **tren toeth bras (T.T.B.)** high speed train

tren-fardellow *m.* baggage-train

trenja *adv.* two days hence, on the day after tomorrow

trenk *adj.* acid, sharp (of taste or smell) acrid

trenkenn *f.* **+ow** acid

trenkhe *v.* acidify

trenkles *m.* rhubarb

trenkter *m.* acidity, sourness, sharpness (of taste)

tres *m.* **+ow** trace, track

tresa *v.* draw (as in art), trace

tresas *m.* **+ow** drawing, tracing

tresenn *f.* **+ow** trace (as in art), graph, chart

tresklenn *f.* **+ow**, *coll.* **treskel** missel-thrush

tresor *m.* **+yow**, **+ys** treasure

tresorva *f.* **+ow** treasury

tresorya *v.* treasure, keep with care

tressa *num.* third; **Tressa Bys** Third World

trest *m.* trust, expectation, reliance; **Trest Ertach Kernow** Cornwall Heritage Trust; **Trest Gwith-Yeghes** Healthcare Trust

tresya *v.* trace

tresyas *m.* **-ysi** draughtsman

tresyades *f.* **+ow** draughtswoman

treth<beach> *m.* **+ow** beach, strand, sea-shore

treth<ferry> *m.* **+yow** ferry, passage over water

tretha *v.* cross by a ferry, ferry

trethek *adj.* sandy

trethenn *f.* **+ow** sandy patch

trethes *m.* extreme heat

trethor *m.* **+yon** ferryman

trethyades *f.* **+ow** female passenger in ferry

trethyas *m.* **-ysi** male passenger in ferry

trettya *v.* trample, stamp (with foot)

treudhow *m.* threshold

treus *adj.* transverse, cross, wicked *m.* **+yon** nonsense

treus-heskenn *f.* **+ow** cross-saw

treusi *v.* cross, pass over

treusfurvya *v.* transform, transfigure

treusfurvyans *m.* **+ow** transformation

treusnija *v.* fly over, overfly

treuspass *m.* **+ow** trespass, transgression, offence

treuspassya *v.* trespass

treusperthi *v.* transport, transfer

treusplansa *v.* transplant

treuspluvek *f.* **-ogow** bolster

treusporth *m.* **+ow** transfer, transport

treusprenn *m.* **+yer** transom, cross-piece, cross-bar, perch (for birds)

treusskrif *m.* **+ow** transcription

treusskrifa *v.* transcribe

treuster *m.* **treustrow** cross-beam, cross-bar

treustroeth *m.* transfusion

treustroetha *v.* transfuse

treustrumm *m.* fish-bait

treusworra *v.* transfer

treusva *f.* **+ow** crossing-place, crossing; **treusva hyns-horn** level crossing on a railway

treusvysek *adj.* worldwide

treuswels *coll.* couch-grass

trev *f.* **+ow** farmstead

trevas *f.* **+ow** harvest, crop

trevbark *m.* **+ow** housing estate

treveglos *f.* **+yow** churchtown, village

trevek *adj.* urban

treven *plur.* homesteads

trevesik *m.* **-igyon** countryman, rustic

trevesiga *v.* settle (on new land)

trevesigel *adj.* colonial

trevesiges *f.* **+ow** countrywoman

trevesigeth *f.* colony, settlement

treveth<home> *f.* domicile, residence, homestead

treveth<occasion> *m.* occasion (time)

trevlu *m.* militia

trew *m.* saliva, spittle

trewa *v.* spit

treweythus *adj.* occasional, scarce

treweythyow *adj.* occasionally

trewyas *m.* sputum

treylouba *v.* stir

treylva *f.* change, transformation; turning-point

treylya *v.* turn, twist, convert, translate

treylyans *m.* **+ow** translation

treylyer *m.* **+yon** translator

treynya *v.* lag, hang back

treynas *m.* **+ow** tail-back (traffic)

treys *plur.* feet

tri *num.* three (m.)

tria *v.* try (in court)

trial *m.* **+s** trial (legal)

trig *m.* position

triga *v.* dwell, sojourn, abide, stay, remain, live (at a place)

trigas *m.* **+ow** stay
triger *m.* **-oryon** dweller, inhabitant, lodger
trigva *f.* **+ow** address (place), abode, country seat
trihans *num.* three hundred
trihorn *m.* **trihern** triangle
trihornek *adj.* triangular
trist *adj.* sad, mournful, gloomy
tristans *m.* sadness, sorrow
tristhe *v.* sadden
tristyns *m.* sadness, sorrow
tri-ugens *num.* sixty, threescore
tro *f.* **+yow** turn, circuit, twist; **war neb tro** *adv.* at some time
tro-askell *f.* **tro-eskelli** helicopter
trobel *m.* trouble
trobla *v.* trouble, vex, molest, bother
troblys *adj.* troubled
troboll *m.* **+ow** whirlpool
troboynt *m.* turning point
troe'lergh *m.* **+ow** footpath
troell *f.* **+ow** lathe
troen *m.* **-yow** nose, snout, point of land, trunk (of animal)
troengornvil *m.* **+es** rhinoceros
troenn ['trɔ·ɛn] *f.* **+ow** turn, caunter lode
troes<bird> *m.* starling
troes<foot> *m.* **treys**, *dual* **dewdroes** foot (Anat.); **treys** hilt (of sword)
troesenn *f.* starling
troesek *adj.* large-footed
troesell *f.* **+ow** pedal
troesella *v.* pedal
troes-hys *m.* foot (unit of length)
troesla *m.* **troesleow** treadle, pedal, foothold
troespons *m.* **+ow** footbridge
troessa *v.* pack, truss
troesya *v.* trudge, plod
troesyer *m.* **-oryon** peddler
troeth *m.* infusion, decoction

troetha *v.* infuse
trog *m.* **+ow** chest (box), coffin, case, trunk, boot (of car)
trogel *m.* earthly life; **yn trogel** *phr.* in the flesh
trogenter *f.* screw
trogentrell *f.* screw-driver
trogh *adj.* cut, wretched, cracked, broken *m.* **+ow** cut (incision)
trogh-bryansenn *m.* trachaeotomy
trogher *m.* **+yow** coulter of plough
troghva *f.* **+ow** cutting (e.g. on road)
troghya *v.* dip, plunge, immerse; **troghya deves** sheep-dipping
troghyer *m.* **-oryon** tucker
trog-tenna *m.* **trogow-tenna** drawer
trogylgh *m.* **+yow** circuit
troha *prep.* towards
trohag *adv.* towards
tromm *adj.* sudden, immediate, prompt
trommder *m.* suddenness
trompa *m.* **trompys** large trumpet, trump
trompet *m.* trumpet
trompour *m.* **+s** trumpeter
tron *m.* **+ys**, **+yow** throne
tros *m.* **+yow** noise, clamour, sound
trosek *adj.* noisy
troskenn *f.* scab
trova *f.* **+ow** circuit
trovann *m.* **+ow** tropic
trovannel *adj.* tropical
trovya *v.* find, discover
troweyth *f.* **+yow** cycle (of motion)
troyll *m.* **+yow** spin, ceilidh, fest-noz
troyllya *v.* spin around
tru *int.* alas, woe
truan *adj.* miserable, poor, wretched
truedh *m.* pity, mercy (compassion), compassion, pathos, sad state of affairs; **truedh a'm beus** *phr.* I

have pity; **kemmeres truedh** have pity,, have mercy

truedhek *adj.* piteous, compassionate, plaintive, pathetic

truesi *adj.* sad, serious, doleful

trufel *adj.* trifling

trufla *v.* trifle, dally, toy with

truflenn *f.* **+ow** trifle

trumm *m.* **+ow** ridge

trumach *m.* **trumajow, trumajys** sea-voyage

Truru *place* Truro

truth *m.* **+es** trout

trybedh<horn> *m.* **+ow** post-horn

trybedh<tripod> *m.* **+ow** tripod, brandise, trivet

trydhek *num.* thirteen

trydhegves *num.* thirteenth

trydydh *m.* period of three days

tryg *m.* low tide; **boes tryg** shore-gathered shellfish

trygh *adj.* superior, victorious, triumphant *m.* victory, triumph, conquest

trygher *m.* **-oryon** victor, conqueror

tryghi *v.* triumph, conquer, be victorious

trymis *m.* school term, quarter (of a year), three months

trymisyek *adj.* termly, quarterly

trymynsek *adj.* three-dimensional

trynn *f.* trouble, quarrel, fuss

trynses *f.* trinity; **An Drynses** The Trinity

trysa *num.* third

tu *m.* **+yow** direction, way, side; **tu ha** *prep.* towards; **heb tu** *adj.* neutral; **bos heb tu** *v.* abstain (in a vote)

tuba-rudh *m.* red gurnard

tuedh *m.* **+ow** trend, tendency

tummas *m.* **+ow** blow

turant *m.* **turans** tyrant, despot, ruler by force

turenn *f.* **+ow** turtle-dove

Turk *m.* **+ys, +yon** Turk

tus *plur.* people, persons, men (human beings)

tuttynn *m.* hassock

ty *pron.* thou

tybi *v.* suppose, fancy, imagine, think, hold an opinion

tybyans *m.* **+ow** opinion, thought, notion, idea

tygri *m.* kestrel

tykki-Dyw *f.* butterfly

tykkli *adj.* delicate, critical

tylda *m.* **tyldow, tyldys** tent, tabernacle

tyli *v.* owe, recompense; **y tal dhymm** I ought

tyller *m.* **+yow** place, spot (location)

tynk *m.* **+es** chaffinch

tynkyal *v.* tinkle, clink

tynn *adj.* tight, firm, intense, sharp, cruel, strict, taut

tynnder *m.* tension, tightness

tynnow *plur.* tights

tys-ha-tas *phr.* noisily, tit for tat

tysk *f.* **+ow** sheaf, mass (heap)

tyskenn *f.* **+ow** sheaf, bunch

tythya *v.* hiss, seethe, sizzle

U

ufern *m.* **+yow,** *dual* **dewufern** ankle

ugens *num.* twenty

ugensplek *adj.* twentyfold

ugensves *num.* twentieth

ughboynt *m.* **+ow** maximum

ughel *adj.* high, lofty, loud (of sound)

ugheldas *m.* **+ow** patriarch

ughelder *m.* **+yow** height, superiority

ugheldir *m.* **+yow** highland; **An Ugheldiryow** *phr.* The Highlands

ugheldiryek *adj.* highland

ughelgowser *m.* **+yow**
loudspeaker
ughelhe *v.* exalt, heighten
ughella *adj.* higher
ughelor *m.* **+yon** noble, prince
ughelvarr *coll.* **+enn** mistletoe
ughelver *m.* high sheriff
ughframweyth *m.* superstructure
ughlamma *v.* perform the high jump
ughos *adv.* upward(s)
ughradh *adj.* higher grade
ugh-sommys *m.* bat (mammal)
ughvarghas *f.* **+ow** hypermarket
unn *adj.* one, only, sole *art.* a, a
certain
unndav *m.* **unndevyon** bachelor
unnegves *num.* eleventh
unnek *num.* eleven
unnigedh *m.* solitude
unnik *adj.* only, single, unique
unnikter *m.* singularity, uniqueness
unnkorn *m.* **unnkern** unicorn
unnlagasek *adj.* one-eyed *m.*
cyclops
unnliw *adj.* monochrome
unnplek *adj.* singular (not plural)
unnrann *adj.* one-piece
unnros *f.* **+ow** unicycle
unnsel *adv.* only
unnses *m.* unity, unit
unnsyllabek *adj.* monosyllabic
unnver *adj.* agreed, unanimous; **bos
unnver** *v.* agree; **bos unnver
gans** *v.* be in accord with
unnveredh *m.* solidarity;
Unnveredh Kernewek Cornish
Solidarity
unnverhe *v.* reconcile, bring to same
opinion
unnverheans *m.* **+ow**
reconciliation, settlement, agreement,
accordance; **unnverheans gober**
wage-settlement
unnverhes *adj.* reconciled

unnweyth *adv.* once, only, even,
just, at all; **unnweyth a** *conj.* if
only
unnwoes *adj.* akin, of same blood,
related by blood
unnton *adj.* monotonous
unntoneth *f.* monotony
unya *v.* unite, amalgamate, unify
unyans *m.* union, alliance; **Unyans
Europek** European Union
unyent *m.* ointment, unguent, salve
unnyethek *adj.* monolingual
unys *adj.* united, unified;
Kenedhlow Unys United Nations
ura *v.* anoint, grease, lubricate,
besmear, baste
uras *m.* ointment, salve, unguent,
lubricant
urdh *f.* order (organization); **Urdh
Rudhvelyn** Orange Order
urdhas *m.* **+ow** hierarchy
urdhya *v.* ordain, initiate
urin *m.* urine
us<chaff> *coll.* chaff
us<use> *m.* use, custom, habit
us<yell> *m.* yell, hoot, shriek
-us *suff.* (aj. ending)
usa *v.* yell, hoot, shriek
usadow *m.* usage, habit *adj.* usual;
herwydh usadow *adv.* as usual,
habitually, according to custom
uskis *adj.* quick, nimble, fast (speedy)
adv. quickly
uskishe *v.* accelerate
uskisheans *m.* **+ow** acceleration;
uskisheans bryjyek convective
acceleration
uskitter *m.* **+yow** velocity
uskorn *m.* **-kern**
usi *v.* is
usya *v.* use
usyon *plur.* chaff, husks
usys *adj.* used, usual, habitual; worn
out; **dell yw usys** *adv.* habitually
uvel *adj.* humble

uvelder *m.* humility
uvelhe *v.* humble
uvelses *f.* humility

V

-va *suff.* **-vaow** (place-name ending), (fem. abst. noun, from noun)
vandal *m.* **+s** vandal
-vann *suff.* (masc. abst. noun ending)
varya *v.* alter, change, derange
varyes *adj.* insane, deranged
'vas *adj.* useful, suitable, of service
vayl *f.* veil
venja *v.* avenge
venjans *m.* vengeance
venim *m.* venom, poison
venimya *v.* poison, envenom
verb *f.* **+ow** verb
verbel *adj.* verbal (concerning verbs)
vertu *f.* **+s** courage, valour, virtue, authority
vertutys *plur.* virtues
-ves *suff.* **-vesow** (ordinal number ending)
vesta *m.* vest
vil *adj.* vile, dreadful, horrible
vilta *f.* vileness, baseness
visour *m.* mask
volt *m.* volt
voltedh *m.* voltage
votya *v.* vote
vu *m.* view, sight, appearance
vy<(obj.)> *pron.* me
vy<enclitic> *pron.* me
vyaj *m.* journey, venture, expedition, voyage; **hager vyaj** bad business
vyajya *v.* journey, travel, voyage
vydh *adj.* any (in neg. expressions)
vydholl *adv.* at all
vynitha *adv.* ever
vytel *m.* victuals, viands
vythkweyth *adv.* ever

W

waja *m.* **+ys** wage, salary
war<aware> *adj.* aware, wary, cautious; **bydh war** take care, look out, be cautious
war<on> *prep.* on, upon N.B. This is NOT pronounced like Eng. *war.*; **war dir** *adv.* on land, ashore; **war euryow** *adv.* now and then; **war fordh** *adv.* on the way; **war gamm** *adv.* gently; **war not** *adv.* simultaneously; **war nuk** *adv.* by return; **war skeus** on the pretext of; **war yew** *int.* onward
warbarth *adv.* together
war-bervedh *adv.* inwards
war-dhelergh *adv.* backwards
war-ji *adv.* homewards
war-lergh *prep.* after
warlyna *adv.* last year,
warn *adv.* on the (used only in numbers 21 to 30)
warnan *prep.* on us
war-nans *adv.* downwards
warnas *prep.* on thee
warnav *prep.* on me
warnedha *prep.* on them
warnedhi *prep.* on her
warnodho *prep.* on him
warnowgh *prep.* on you
war-rag *adv.* forwards
war-tu *prep.* towards
war-vann *adv.* upward(s)
war-woeles *adv.* down, towards the bottom
warya *v.* beware, take care, watch out
wassel *m.* wassail
wast *adj.* waste; **tus wast** *plur.* wasters, loafers, layabouts
wastya *v.* lay waste, squander
wel *int.* well
West *adj.* West *m.* West
wolkomm *adj.* welcome
wolkomma *v.* welcome
wondrys *adj.* wondrous

wordhi *adj.* worthy, deserving, honourable
wor'talleth *adv.* in the beginning
wor'taswerth *adj.* second-hand
wor'tiwedh *adv.* in the end, finally
wosa *prep.* after; **wosa hemma** *conj.* henceforth; **wosa henna** thenceforth
wostalleth *adv.* at first, in the beginning, to begin with
wostiwedh *adv.* at last
wrynch *m.* trick, deceit, subterfuge

Y

y<his> *pron.* his, its
y<VP> *ptl.* (vbl. ptl.)
ya *int.* yes
-ya *v.* (VN ending)
-yades *suff.* **-yadesow** (fem. agency noun ending)
yagh *adj.* healthy, sound, fit, well (not ill)
yaghhe *v.* cure
yaghus *adj.* healthful, healing, health-giving, wholesome
yalgh *f.* **+ow** purse
yalghas *m.* **+ow** disbursement
-yans *suff.* **-yansow** (masc. abst. noun ending)
yar *f.* **yer** hen; **yar Gyni** turkey; **yar wyls** hen-grouse
yarji *m.* **+ow** hen-house
-yas *suff.* **-ysi** (masc. agency noun ending)
-ydh *suff.* **-ydhyon** (masc. noun agency ending)
ydhna *m.* fowler
ydhnik *m.* young bird
ydhyl *adj.* feeble, weak, slight
ydhyn *plur.* birds
ye *int.* yea, affirmative
Yedhow *m.* **Yedhewon** Jew, Israelite

yedhowek *adj.* Jewish
Yedhowek *m.* Yiddish language
Yedhowes *f.* **+ow** Jewess
yeghes *m.* health; **yeghes da !** good health !
yeghesel *adj.* sanitary
yeghesweyth *m.* sanitation
-yek *suff.* (aj. ending)
-yel *suff.* (pl.n. and aj. ending)
yer *plur.* hens
-yer<MN> *suff.* **-yoryon** (masc. agency noun ending from VN in **-ya**)
-yer<PL> *suff.* (pl. ending)
yerik *f.* **-igow** chicken
yerghik *m.* **yerghesigow** fawn
yes *v.* confess (of sins), absolve, shrive
-yes *v.* (past ptcpl. ending)
yet *f.* **yetys**, **yetow** gate
yeth *f.* **+ow** language, way of speaking
yethador *m.* grammar (book)
yethonieth *f.* linguistics, philology
yethonydh *m.* **+yon** linguist, philologist
yethor *m.* **+yon** linguist, grammarian
yeth-plen *f.* prose
yeunadow *m.* yearning, craving
yeunek *adj.* craving, desirous
yeunes *m.* **+ow** yearning
yeuni *v.* yearn, crave; **yeuni warlergh** yearn after, long for
yeunogneth *f.* craving
yew *f.* **+ow** yoke
yewa *v.* yoke
yewgenn *m.* ferret, stoat, marten, polecat
yey *m.* ice
yeyn *adj.* cold
yeynder *m.* cold, chill
yeynell *f.* **+ow** refrigerator
yeynhe *v.* cool, chill
yeynyjyon *m.* cold
y'ga *phr.* in their

y'gan *phr.* in our

y'gas *phr.* in your

-yjyon *suff.* (masc. abst. noun ending, from aj.)

ylyn *adj.* limpid, transparent, clear, bright; nett

ylynder *m.* limpidity, clarity

y'm *phr.* in my

yma *v.* is, there is, there are; **yma genev** I have

yma'n *phr.* the {noun} is, the {noun} are

ymons *v.* they are

ymp *m.* **+s** graft

ympya *v.* graft

ympynnyon *plur.* brains

yn<in> *prep.* in, at (occasl.), to (occasl.), on (occasl.) Adjectival phrases with **yn** include: **yn kosk** *adj.* asleep; **yn tenn** taut. Adverbial phrases with **yn** include: **yn chi** *adv.* at home; **yn fas** properly; **yn fen** strongly; **yn herwydh** in the vicinity of; **yn hirbren** on hire purchase; **yn igor** openly; **yn kerdh** away; **yn kettella** just like that; **yn kettellma** just like this; **yn kettermyn** simultaneously; **yn rew** single file; **yn tre** at home; **yn y oes** ever; Prepositional phrases with **yn** include: **yn le** *prep.* in place of; **yn kever** about, concerning; **yn kyrghynn** around; **yn mysk** among. The following phrase acts as a verbal particle: **yn unn** *ptl.* -ing

yn<VP> *ptl.* -ly (adv. ptl.); **yn hwir** *adv.* truly, certainly, in fact; **yn pell** distantly; **yn sur** assuredly; **yn surredi** assuredly; **yn ta** well; **yn tien** completely, entirely; **yn teg** beautifully; **yn tevri** really

yn- *pref.* (adverbial prefix)

y'n<him> *phr.* him

y'n<in the> *phr.* in the; **y'n bys** *adv.* at all; **y'n dre** in town; **y'n for' ma** in this way; **y'n for' na** in that way; **y'n tor' ma** at this time

yn-bann *adv.* upward(s)

yn-dann *prep.* under N.B. Combines with pers. pronouns as **yn-dannov, yn-dannos, yn-danno, yn-danni, yn-dannon, yn-dannowgh, yn-danna**.

yndella *adv.* like that, similarly

yndellma *adv.* like this, in this way

ynflammya *v.* inflame

ynflammyans *m.* inflammation

yn-hons *adv.* yonder

ynjin *adj.* ingenious *m.* **+ys** engine

ynjinor *m.* **+yon** engineer

ynjinieth *f.* originality, ingenuity

ynjinores *f.* **+ow** engineer

ynjinorieth *f.* engineering

ynk *m.* ink

ynkleudhva *f.* cemetery

ynkleudhyas *m.* burial, interment *v.* bury, inter

ynkressya *v.* swell, increase, augment

ynkys *m.* incense

ynkyslester *m.* censer

yn-medh *v.* says, said, quoth

yn-mes *adv.* out, outside

ynn *adj.* narrow, slender, confined

-ynn *suff.* **-ynnow** (dim. ending)

ynna *prep.* in them

yn-nans *adv.* down

ynnder *m.* narrowness

yn-nes *adv.* closer, nearer

ynni<urge> *m.* **+ow** urge, pressure

ynni<PP> *prep.* in her

ynnia *v.* urge, incite, force, exhort

ynniadow *m.* urgency *adj.* urgent

ynno *prep.* in him

ynnon *prep.* in us

ynnos *prep.* in thee

ynnov *prep.* in me

ynnowgh *prep.* in you

yn-rag *adv.* forward, onward

yns *v.* they are

ynsi *pron.* they (emphatic), themselves

-**ynsi** *suff.* (masc. abst. noun ending)

yn-sol *int.* arise, up

ynter *prep.* between, among

yntra *prep.* between

yntredha *prep.* between them

yntredhon *prep.* between us

yntredhowgh *prep.* between you

ynwedh *adv.* also, likewise, as well

ynys *f.* **+ow** island, isolated place;
Ynys Wyth Isle of Wight

Ynys *m.* Shrovetide

ynysega *v.* insulate

ynysegans *m.* insulation

ynysek *f.* **-egi** archipelago;
Ynysek Syllan *place* Isles of Scilly

ynysekter *m.* isolation

yogort *m.* **+ow** yoghurt

-**yon** *suff.* (pl. ending)

yo'nk *adj.* young

yonker *m.* **+s** young man

-**yores** *suff.* -**yoresow** (fem. agency noun ending)

yorgh *f.* **+es** roedeer

yos *m.* pap, hasty-pudding

Yow *m.* Thursday

-**yow** *suff.* (pl. ending)

Yowann *name* John

yown *m.* **+es** bass (fish)

yowynk *adj.* young

yowynkhe *v.* rejuvenate, make young

yowynkneth *f.* youth

yowynkses *m.* youth

yr *adj.* fresh

yredi *adv.* readily, verily

ys *coll.* **+enn** corn; **ys brith** dredge-corn

-**ys**<MN> *suff.* (masc. abst. noun ending)

-**ys**<PL> *suff.* (pl. ending)

-**ys**<PV> *suff.* (past ptcpl. ending)

y's *phr.* her, they

ysasver *m.* harvest

ysek *adj.* rich in corn *f.* **-egi** cornfield

yskar *m.* sackcloth, bolting cloth

yskynna *v.* ascend, mount, climb

yskynnans *m.* ascent

ysla *m.* **ysleow** granary

yslann *f.* **+ow** rick-yard, mowhay

ysow *plur.* kinds of corn

Ysrael *place* Israel

ystynna *v.* extend

ystynnans *m.* **+ow** extension, supplement, appendix; **ystynnans lyennek** literary supplement

yth *ptl.* (vbl. ptl.)

y'th<in thy> *phr.* in thy

y'th<thee> *pron.* thee

ytho *conj.* therefore, then, so, well then, in that case

yttew *m.* **+i** firebrand, log

yurl *m.* **yurlys** earl, count (nobleman) governor of shire

yw *v.* is

ywin *coll.* **+enn** yew

RANN NESSA

SOWSNEK - KERNEWEK

PART TWO

ENGLISH - CORNISH

A

a *art.* **unn**; a certain **unn**
abaft *prep.* **a-dhelergh dhe:** *adv.*
  a-dhelergh
abandon *v.* **gasa**
abase *v.* **iselhe**
abasement *n.* **iselheans** *m.*
abate *v.* **basya**
abattoir *n.* **latti** *m.* **+ow**
abbess *n.* **abases** *f.* **+ow**
abbey *n.* **abatti** *m.* **+ow**
abbot *n.* **abas** *m.* **+ow**
abbreviate *v.* **berrhe**
abbreviation *n.* **berrheans** *m.*
  +ow
abet *v.* **mentena**
abhor *v.* **kasa**
abide *v.* **bos, triga**
abilities *plur.* **teythi**
ability *n.* **galloes** *m.*, **godhvos** *m.*
able *adj.* **abel, men**; more able
  appla: *v.* be able **galloes,**
  godhvos
abnormal *n.* abnormal person
  kanjon *m.* **+s:** *adj.* **anreyth**
abnormality *n.* (abst.) **anreyther**
  m. **+ow**; (specific) **anreythenn** *f.*
  +ow
aboard *adv.* **a-bervedh**
abode *n.* **trigva** *f.* **+ow, bos** *f.* **+ow**
aboriginal *adj.* **genesik, teythyek**
aborigine *n.* **genesik** *m.* **-igyon,**
  teythyek *m.* **teythyogyon**
abound *v.* **palshe**
about *prep.* **yn kever:** *adv.* **a-dro**
  dhe, a-dhedro; round about **a-**
  dhedro
above *prep.* **a-ugh, dres:** *adv.* **a-**
  vann, a-wartha
Abraham *name* **Abram**
abridge *v.* **berrhe**
abroad *adj.* (overseas) **tramor:** *adv.*
  (widely) **a-les**
abscess *n.* **gorenn** *f.* **+ow**

absence *n.* **estrik** *m.*
absentee *n.* **estriger** *m.* **-oryon**
absolute *adj.* **pur**
absolutely *adv.* **porres**
absolution *n.* (of a debt) **akwityans**
  m.; (of sins) **purheans** *m.*
absolve *v.* (of a debt) **akwitya**; (of
  sins) **assoylya, purhe, yes**
abstain *n.* (in a vote) **bos war an ke**
  m.: *v.* **skonya a**; (in a vote) **bos**
  heb tu
abstaining *n.* (in a vote) **war an ke**
  m.
absurd *adj.* **gokki**
absurdity *n.* **gokkineth** *f.*
abundance *n.* **kals** *m.*, **lanwes** *m.*,
  palster *m.*
abuse *v.* **abusya, tebeldhyghtya**
abyss *n.* **islonk** *m.*
accelerate *v.* **uskishe**
acceleration *n.* **uskisheans** *m.*
  +ow; convective acceleration
  uskisheans bryjyek *m.*
accent *n.* **poeslev** *m.* **+ow**
accentuate *v.* **poesa war,**
  poesleva, tonya
accept *v.* **degemmeres, resseva**
acceptability *n.* **kemmeradewder**
  m.
acceptable *adj.* **kemmeradow**
accessible *adj.* **hedhadow**
accident *n.* **droglamm** *m.* **+ow,**
  gwall *m.* **+ow**
accidentally *adv.* **dre wall**
accommodation *n.* **ostyans** *m.*
accomplish *v.* **gul, kowlwul**
accord *n.* with one accord **gans unn**
  akord *m.:* *adj.* in accord
  keskolonn: *v.* **grontya,**
  kesseni; be in accord with **bos**
  unnver gans
accordance *n.* **unnverheans** *m.*
  +ow: *prep.* in accordance with
  herwydh

according *prep.* according to
herwydh
account *n.* akont *m.* +ys, +ow,
awos *m.,* govis *m.,* reken *m.*
reknow; (report) derivadow *m.;*
account book lyver-akontow *m.*
lyvrow-akontow; current account
akont kesres *m.,* akont poll *m.;*
deposit account akont arghow *m.,*
akont kreun *m.: adj.* of no
account distyr: *prep.* on account
er: *conj.* on account of drefenn:
phr. on any account war neb 'wos;
on my account a'm govis; take
account of gul vri a
accountancy *n.* akontieth *f.*
accountant *n.* akontydh *m.* +yon
accumulate *v.* kreuni
accumulator *n.* kreunell *f.* +ow
accuracy *n.* kewerder *m.*
accurate *adj.* kewar
accursed *adj.* mollothek
accusation *n.* kabel *m.,*
kuhudhans *m.*
accuse *v.* kuhudha
accuser *n.* kuhudhor *m.* +yon,
kuhudhyas *m.* -ysi
acid *n.* trenkenn *f.* +ow: *adj.*
trenk
acidify *v.* trenkhe
acidity *n.* trenkter *m.*
acknowledge *v.* aswonn,
amyttya, avowa
acknowledgement *n.* aswonnans
m. +ow
acorn *n.* mesenn *f.* +ow *coll.* mes;
acorn cup byskoen mes *f.*
acorns *v.* gather acorns mesa
acoustics *n.* sononieth *f.*
acquaintance *n.* aswonnvos *m.*
acquiesce *v.* assentya
acquire *v.* kavoes
acre *n.* erow *f.* erewi
acrid *adj.* trenk
acrobat *n.* lappyer *m.* -yoryon,
lappyores *f.* +ow

across *adv.* a-dreus
act *n.* ober *m.* +ow; (of law)
laghenn *f.* +ow; Act of Parliament
Reyth an Senedh *m.*
action *n.* gweythres *m.,* gwrians
m. +ow
active *adj.* byw, snell, strik
activity *n.* bywder *m.*
actor *n.* gwarier *m.* -oryon
actress *n.* gwariores *f.* +ow
acute *n.* acute angle elin lymm *m.:*
adj. lymm
Adam *name* Adam
add *v.* keworra
adder *n.* nader *f.* nadres
addition *n.* keworrans *m.* +ow
additional *adj.* keworransel
address *n.* (place) trigva *f.* +ow;
(talk) areth *f.*
adhere *v.* glena orth
adherent *n.* dyskybel *m.*
dyskyblon
adhesive *adj.* glenus
adit *n.* odyt *m.*
adjacent *adj.* kevogas
adjoining *adj.* ogas, yn herwydh
adjudication *n.* breus *f.* +ow
adjudicator *n.* breusyas *m.* -ysi
administer *v.* menystra
administration *n.* menystrans *m.*
admiral *n.* amiral *m.* +yon
admit *v.* amyttya
admittance *n.* amyttyans *m.*
admonish *v.* keski
admonishment *n.* kosk *f.*
ado *v.* without further ado heb
hokya: *adv.* heb na hirra
lavarow
adoration *n.* gologhas *m.,*
gordhyans *m.*
adore *v.* gordhya
adorn *v.* afina
adorned *adj.* richly adorned fethus

adult *n.* (female) **tevesiges** *f.* **+ow**;
(male) **tevesik** *m.* **-igyon:** *adj.*
tevesik
adulterer *n.* **avoutrer** *m.* **-oryon,**
+s
adulteress *n.* **avoutres** *f.* **+ow,**
gwann-wre'ti *f.*
adultery *n.* **avoutri** *m.*
advance *n.* (of wages) **ragarveth** *m.*
+ow: *v.* **avonsya, mos yn-rag**
advancement *n.* **avonsyans** *m.*
advantage *n.* **les** *m.,* **gwayn** *m.,*
prow *m.*
Advent *n.* **Asvens** *m.*
adventure *n.* **aneth** *m.* **+ow**
adversity *n.* **droglamm** *m.* **+ow**
advertise *v.* **argemmynna**
advertisement *n.* **argemmynn** *m.*
+ow
advice *n.* **kusul** *f.* **+yow, avis** *m.*
advise *v.* **kusulya**; advise to
kusulya a
advisory *adj.* **kusulyek**
advocate *n.* **dadhlor** *m.* **+yon:** *v.*
pledya
advowson *n.* **avoweson** *m.*
aerial *n.* **ayrlorgh** *f.* **+ow, -lergh**
aeroplane *n.* **jynn-ebrenn** *m.*
jynnow-ebrenn
afar *adv.* **a-bell**
affable *adj.* **deboner, hegar**
affair *n.* **negys** *m.* **+yow, tra** *f.*
+ow, mater *m.* **+s, +ow**
affection *n.* **kerensa** *f.,* **sergh** *m.*
affectionate *adj.* **hegar**
affirm *v.* **afia, afydhya**
affirmative *int.* **ye**
affix *v.* **takkya, glena**
afflict *v.* **plagya**
affliction *n.* **galar** *m.* **+ow, plag** *m.*
+ys
affluence *n.* **golusogneth** *f.*
affluent *adj.* **golusek**
affront *n.* **skorn** *m.:* *v.* **arvedh**
afoot *adv.* **a-droes**

aforesaid *adj.* **kampoellys,**
ragleverys, rakhenwys
afraid *adj.* **ownek:** *v.* be afraid
perthi own; *phr.* don't be afraid **na**
borth own, na borth dout
aft *adv.* **a-dhelergh**
after *n.* after part **delergh** *m.:* *prep.*
war-lergh, wosa: *adv.* **a-wosa**;
after all **byttiwedh**
afternoon *n.* **dohajydh** *m.,*
androw *m.:* *adv.* in the afternoon
dohajydhweyth
afternoon-evening *n.* **eghwa** *m.*
afternoon-time *n.* **androweyth** *m.*
aftertaste *n.* **asvlas** *m.*
afterwards *adv.* **a-wosa, a'y wosa**
again *adv.* **arta, hwath**; (with neg.)
namoy
against *prep.* **erbynn:** *adv.* against
his will **a'y anvodh**
age *n.* **oes** *m.* **+ow, hender** *m.;* (in
years) **bloedh** *m.;* (period of time)
oesweyth *f.* **+yow**; Bronze Age
Oes Brons *m.;* great age **hiroes**
m.; Stone Age **Oes Men** *m.;* year
of age **bloedh** *m.:* *adj.* of the same
age as **kevoes gans**
agency *n.* **mayn** *m.* **+ys**
agenda *n.* **rol negys** *f.*
aggrieve *v.* **annia, grevya**
agitate *v.* **amovya**
agnostic *n.* **diskryjyk** *m.* **-ygyon**
ago *ptl.* **nans yw**; a week ago **nans**
yw seythun
agree *v.* **akordya, assentya, bos**
unnver; agree with **akordya orth,**
akordya y golonn gans
agreed *adj.* **unnver**
agreement *n.* **akord** *m.,*
akordyans *m.,* **kessenyans** *m.,*
kevambos *m.* **+ow,**
unnverheans *m.* **+ow**
agriculture *n.* **ammeth** *f.,*
gonisogeth tir *f.*
ague *n.* **kleves seson** *m.;* fit of the
ague **kren an leghow** *m.*

ah *int.* ogh
aha *int.* aha
aid *n.* gweres *m.*, sokor *m.;* first
aid kynweres *m.;* legal aid
gweres laghel *m.:* *v.* gweres,
sokra
aim *n.* amkan *m.* +ow, medras *m.*
+ow: *v.* medra
air *n.* ayr *m.;* air hostess ostes ayr
f.
air-borne *adj.* nijys
air-conditioning *n.* ayrewnans *m.*
aircraft *n.* jynn-ebrenn *m.*
jynnow-ebrenn
airmail *n.* ayrbost *m.*
airport *n.* ayrborth *m.* +ow
air-pump *n.* pomp ayr *m.*
airy *adj.* ayrek
aisle *n.* kasel *f.* +yow
akin *adj.* unnwoes
alabaster *n.* alabaster *m.*
alack *int.* ellas
alacrity *n.* with alacrity toeth da *m.:*
adv. a-boynt
alarm *n.* alarm clock difunell *f.;*
state of wonder or alarm transyek
m.
alas *int.* soweth, tru, eghan, ellas,
ogh
alb *n.* kams *f.* +ow
alcohol *n.* las *m.* +ow
alcoholic *n.* lasek *m.* -ogyon: *adj.*
lasek
alcoholism *n.* lasogeth *f.,*
medhwynsi *f.*
alder-grove *n.* gwernek *f.* -egi
alder-swamp *n.* gwern *coll.* +enn
alder-tree *n.* gwernenn *f.* gwern
alder-trees *n.* gwern *coll.* +enn
ale *n.* korev *m.* +ow; mix of ale and
mead bragas *m.;* strong ale kor'
gwella *m.*
alecost *n.* (plant) kosta *m.*
alehouse *n.* diwotti *m.* +ow
alias *n.* les-hanow *m.* -henwyn

alien *n.* estren *m.* +yon, alyon *m.*
+s: *adj.* estren
align *v.* alinya
alike *adv.* kepar, kehaval,
kekeffrys
alimony *n.* alymona *m.*
alive *adj.* byw, yn fyw
all *pron.* peub; all who myns: *adj.*
oll, puboll: *adv.* all the time pub
eur oll; at all mann, unnweyth
alley *n.* skochfordh *f.* +ow,
stretynn *m.* +ow; blind alley
fordh-dhall *f.* fordhow-dall,
hyns dall *m.*
alliance *n.* unyans *m.*
allotment *n.* pastell-dir *f.*
allow *v.* gasa
allowance *n.* alowans *m.*
alloy *n.* kemmysk *m.*
allure *n.* trayn *m.* +ys: *v.* dynya
alluvium *n.* leys *m.* +yow
ally *n.* keffrysyas *m.* -ysi
almighty *adj.* ollgalloesek
almond *n.* alamand *m.* +ow, +ys
almoner *n.* alusener *m.* -oryon
almost *adv.* ogas, nammna,
nammnag, ogatti
alms *n.* alusen *f.* +ow
almshouse *n.* alusenji *m.* +ow
aloes *plur.* aloes
aloft *prep.* a-ugh: *adv.* a-vann, a-
wartha
alphabet *n.* lytherennek *f.* -egi
already *adv.* seulabrys
also *adv.* keffrys, ynwedh,
kekeffrys
altar *n.* alter *f.* +yow; rock altar
karrek sans *f.*
alter *v.* chanjya, dihevelebi,
di'velebi, varya
always *adv.* bykken, pup-prys,
prest, pub eur, pub termyn
am *v.* I am esov, ov
amalgam *n.* kesunnses *m.*
amalgamate *v.* unya

amazing *adj.* **aneth, marthys**
amazingly *adv.* **marthys**
ambassador *n.* **kannas** *f.* **+ow,**
lyskannas *f.* **+ow**
ambition *n.* **gorvynn** *m.* **+ow**
ambulance *n.* **karr-klavji** *m.* **kerri-**
klavji
ambush *v.* **kontrewaytya**
amendment *n.* **ewnans** *m.* **+ow**
amends *plur.* **amendys:** *v.* make
amends **amendya**
amiability *n.* **karadewder** *m.*
amiable *adj.* **hegar**
amice *n.* priest's amice **skoedh-lien**
m.
among *n.* among them **y'ga mysk**
m.; among us **y'gan mysk** *m.;*
among you **y'gas mysk** *m.: prep.*
yn mysk, ynter, yntra
amount *n.* **myns** *m.*
amply *adv.* **lowr**
amputee *n.* **mans** *m.* **+yon**
amuse *v.* **didhana**
amusement *n.* **didhan** *m.*
amusing *adj.* **didhan, didhanus**
analyse *v.* **dielvenna**
analysis *n.* **dielvennans** *m.* **+ow**
anathema *n.* **pla** *m.* **+ow**
anatomy *n.* (science) **korfonieth** *f.*
ancestor *n.* **dehengeugh** *m.,*
hendas *m.* **+ow, hengeugh** *m.*
+yon; remote ancestor
gorhengeugh *m.* **+yon**
ancestry *n.* **linyeth** *f.*
anchor *n.* **ankor** *m.* **+yow:** *v.*
ankorya
anchorage *n.* **poll** *m.* **+ow,**
ankorva *f.*
anchorite *n.* **ankar** *m.* **ankrys**
ancient *adj.* **koth**
and *conj.* (before consonants) **ha;**
(before vowels) **hag;** and so **ha**
angel *n.* **el** *m.* **eledh;** little angel
elik *m.* **eledhigow**
anger *n.* **sorr** *m.: v.* **serri (orth)**

angle *n.* **elin** *m.* **+yow;** acute angle
elin lymm *m.;* right angle **elin**
pedrek *m.*
anglicization *n.* **sowsnekheans**
m.
anglicize *v.* **sowsnekhe**
anglophone *n.* **sowsneger** *m.*
-oryon
angry *adj.* **serrys:** *v.* be angry with
serri orth
anguish *n.* **angus** *m.,* **gloes** *f.* **+ow**
angular *adj.* **elinek**
animal *n.* **enyval** *m.* **+es, best** *m.*
+es, mil *m.* **+es;** wild animal
goedhvil *m.* **+es**
animate *v.* **bywekhe**
animation *v.* **bywekheans**
animosity *n.* **atti** *m.,* **mikenn** *f.*
ankle *n.* **ufern** *m.* **+yow** *dual*
dewufern
anniversary *n.* **penn-bloedh** *m.*
pennow-bloedh
announcer *n.* **derivador** *m.* **+yon**
annoy *v.* **serri, annia**
annual *adj.* **blydhenyek**
anoint *v.* **elia, ura;** (with holy oil)
olewi
anorak *n.* **anorak** *m.* **anoragow**
another *adj.* **arall, ken**
answer *n.* **gorthyp** *m.* **gorthybow:**
v. **gorthybi, gorthybi orth;**
answer back **treusworthybi**
ant *n.* **moryonenn** *f.* **+ow** *coll.*
moryon
antelope *n.* **gavrewik** *f.* **-iges**
anthem *n.* **antemna** *m.* **antemnow**
ant-hill *n.* **krug moryon** *m.*
anti- *pref.* **gorth**
antichrist *n.* **gorthkrist** *m.*
antidote *n.* **gorthwenon** *m.*
anti-freeze *n.* **gorthrew** *m.*
antiquary *n.* **antikwari** *m.*
antique *n.* **henbyth** *m.* **+ow**
antiquity *n.* **hender** *m.,* **henses**
m.; (abst.) **kothenep** *m.*

anus *n.* gwenn *m.*

anvil *n.* anwan *f.* +yow

anxiety *n.* preder *m.* +ow: *plur.*
fienasow

anxious *adj.* prederus

any *adj.* neb; (in neg. expressions)
vydh: *adv.* byttele

any more *adj.* namoy

anyone *pron.* nebonan

anything *n.* (in neg. phrases)
travydh *f.:* *pron.* neppyth: *phr.*
for anything awos neb tra, awos
tra

anywhere *adj.* neb le, neb tyller:
adv. nep-tu

apart *adv.* a-les

apartment *n.* rannji *m.* +ow

ape *n.* apa *m.* appys

apologize *v.* dihares

apology *n.* dihares *m.* +ow

apostate *n.* negedhys *m.* +yon:
adj. negedhys

apostle *n.* abostol *m.* abesteli

apostles *n.* abosteledh *m.*

apostolate *n.* abosteledh *m.*

apostolic *adj.* abostolek

apparatus *n.* daffar *m.*

apparition *n.* (ghost) tarosvann *m.*
+ow

appeal *n.* galow *m.,* pysadow *m.*

appear *v.* omdhiskwedhes

appearance *n.* gwel *m.* +yow,
favour *m.* +s, fisment *m.*
fismens, semlant *m.* -ns, vu *m.;*
(an appearance)
omdhiskwedhyans *m.* +ow; (of
a person) mir *m.*

appease *v.* diserri

appendix *n.* ystynnans *m.* +ow

apple *n.* aval *m.* +ow

apple-juice *n.* sugen aval *m.*

apple-tree *n.* avalenn *f.* +ow,
avalwydhenn *f.* +ow *coll.*
avalwydh

appoint *v.* dyghtya, ordena,
settya

apprentice *n.* gwas *m.* gwesyon;
smith's apprentice mab-gov *m.*
mebyon-gov

approach *adj.* dos nes: *v.*
neshe; (intrans.) nesa

appropriate *adj.* gwiw: *v.*
perghennogi; be appropriate
degoedha

approximately *adv.* a-dro dhe

apricot *n.* brykedhenn *f.* +ow *coll.*
brykedh

April *n.* Ebryl *m.,* mis-Ebryl *m.*

apron *n.* apron *m.* +yow

aquarium *n.* pusketti *m.* +ow

aqueduct *n.* dowrbons *m.* +ow,
odyt *m.*

Arab *n.* Arab *m.* Arabyon

Arabia *place* Arabi

Arabic *n.* Arabic language Arabek
m.: *adj.* Arabek

arable *adj.* aradow

arbour *n.* erber *m.* +ow

arc *n.* gwarak *f.* -egow

arch *n.* gwarak *f.* -egow

archaeologist *n.* hendhyskyas *m.*
-ysi

archaeology *n.* hendhyskans *m.*

archangel *n.* arghel *m.* +edh

archbishop *n.* arghepskop *m.*
-epskobow

archbishopric *n.* arghepskobeth
m.

archdeacon *n.* arghdyagon *m.*
+yon

archdruid *n.* arghdrewydh *m.*
+yon

archer *n.* gwareger *m.* -oryon,
sether *m.* -oryon

arch-fiend *n.* arghjevan *m.*

archipelago *n.* ynysek *f.* -egi

architect *n.* pennser *m.* +i,
pennseres *f.* +ow

architectural *adj.* pennsernethel

architecture *n.* (art of)
pennserneth *f.*
archive *n.* kovskrifenn *f.* +ow
ardent *adj.* toemm, gwresek
ardour *n.* gwres *f.*
are *v.* they are esons, ymons, yns;
we are eson; you are esowgh:
phr. are you o'ta; the {noun} are
yma'n
area *n.* open working area lown *m.*
+yow
argue *v.* dadhla, disputya; argue
with someone argya orth
nebonan
argument *n.* argyans *m.*, dadhel *f.*
dadhlow, dadhelva *f.* +ow,
reson *m.* +s
arid *n.* arid land krindir *m.:* *adj.*
sygh, krin
aridity *n.* kraster *m.*
arise *v.* drehevel: *int.* yn-sol
aristocracy *n.* pennsevigeth *f.*
aristocrats *n.* gwelhevin *m.*
arithmetic *n.* niveronieth *f.*
ark *n.* (e.g. of covenant) argh *f.* +ow;
(ship) gorhel *m.* -holyon
arm *n.* (limb) bregh *f.* +ow *dual*
diwvregh: *adj.* having arms
breghyek
arm *v.* arva; (weapon) *n.* arv *f.*
+ow
armband *n.* breghwisk *m.*
armchair *n.* kador-vregh *f.*
kadoryow-bregh
armed *n.* armed man arvek *m.*
arvogyon: *adj.* arvek: *v.* ervys
armful *n.* breghas *f.* +ow
armour *n.* gwisk horn *m.*
arm-pit *n.* kasel *f.* +yow
army *n.* lu *m.* +yow
around *n.* yn kyrghynn *m.;* around
me y'm kyrghynn *m.:* *prep.* yn
kyrghynn: *adv.* a-dro; all around
a-derdro
arouse *v.* movya, sordya

arrange *v.* restra, araya, framya,
ordena, renka, resa
arrangement *n.* aray *m.*, rester *f.*
restri
array *n.* aray *m.:* *v.* takla
arrears *adv.* in arrears a-dhelergh
arrival *n.* devedhyans *m.*
arrow *n.* seth *f.* +ow; head of arrow
pil *m.* +ys; small arrow sethenn *f.*
arse *n.* tin *f.*
arsenal *n.* arvji *m.* +ow
art *n.* art *m.* +ow, +ys: *v.* thou art
esos, os
article *n.* skrifenn *f.* +ow; (object)
tra *f.* +ow; (of text) erthygel *m.*
erthyglow, skrif *m.* +ow
articulated *adj.* mellek
articulation *n.* kevals *m.* +yow,
mell *m.* +ow
artificer *n.* kreftor *m.* +yon, ser *m.*
+i
artisan *n.* kreftor *m.* +yon, ser *m.*
+i
artist *n.* lymner *m.* -oryon
artist's *n.* artist's brush pynsel *m.*
artless *adj.* digreft
artwork *n.* artweyth *m.*
as *adj.* kemmys; as many keniver;
as many as kemmys; as much as
kemmys: *prep.* as far as bys:
conj. maga; as long as hedra; as
well maga ta: *adv.* avel, dell,
mar, par; as many as kekemmys;
as much as kekemmys; as soon as
kettell, kettoeth; as well keffrys,
kekeffrys; in as much as dell
ascend *v.* yskynna
ascent *n.* yskynnans *m.*
ascribe *v.* askrifa
ashamed *adj.* methek: *v.* be
ashamed of divlasa: *phr.* be
ashamed kemmeres meth; be
ashamed of bos methek a; I am
ashamed meth a'm beus
ashes *n.* lusow *coll.* +enn
ash-grove *n.* onnek *f.* -egi

ash-heap *n.* **lusowek** *f.* **-egi**
ashore *v.* come ashore **tira:** *adv.*
    war dir
ash-tree *n.* **ennwydhenn** *f.* **+ow**
    coll. **ennwydh, onnenn** *f.* **+ow**
    coll. **onn**
ashy *adj.* **lusowek**
aside *adv.* **a-denewenn**
ask *v.* **govynn;** ask of **govynn**
    orth, govynn diworth; ask
    someone to do something **pysi**
    nebonan a wul neppyth; ask
    something from someone **pysi**
    neppyth diworth nebonan
asleep *n.* one who falls asleep quickly
    koskador desempis *m.:* *adj.* **yn**
    kosk
aspect *n.* **tremmynn** *m.*
aspen-tree *n.* **edhlenn** *f.* **+ow** *coll.*
    edhel
aspiration *n.* **gorvynn** *m.* **+ow,**
    medras *m.* **+ow**
ass *n.* **asyn** *m.* **-es, ronsyn** *m.*
assassin *n.* **denledhyas** *m.* **-ysi**
assassinate *v.* **moldra**
assault *v.* **settya war**
assemble *v.* (intrans.) **omguntell;**
    (trans.) **keskorra**
assembly *n.* **kesva** *f.* **+ow,**
    kuntelles *m.* **+ow**
assent *n.* **assentyans** *m.*
asset *n.* **pyth** *m.* **+ow**
assist *v.* **gweres, skoedhya**
assistance *n.* **gweres** *m.*
assistant *n.* **darbarer** *m.* **-oryon**
assize-court *n.* **breuslys** *f.* **+yow**
associate *n.* **keskoweth** *m.* **+a,**
    kowethyades *f.* **+ow, kowethyas**
    m. **-ysi**
associated *adj.* **kevrennek**
association *n.* **kowethas** *m.* **+ow,**
    kowethyans *m.*
assuage *v.* **sewajya**
assurance *n.* **surheans** *m.*
assure *v.* **afydhya, surhe**

assuredly *adv.* **yn sur, yn surredi**
aster *n.* **bleujenn ster** *f.*
asterisk *n.* **sterennik** *f.* **-igow**
asthma *n.* **berr-anall** *m.*
astonishment *n.* **marth** *m.* **+ow**
astounding *adj.* **marthys, revedh**
astoundingly *adv.* **marthys**
astray *v.* go astray **mos yn**
    sowdhan
astronaut *n.* **stervarner** *m.* **-oryon**
astronomer *n.* **steronydh** *m.* **+yon**
astronomical *adj.* **steroniethek**
astronomy *n.* **steronieth** *f.*
asylum *n.* place of asylum **meneghi**
    m.
asymmetrical *adj.* **digemusur**
at *prep.* **dhe, orth;** (occasl.) **yn:**
    adv. at all **vydholl, y'n bys**
atmosphere *n.* **ayrgylgh** *m.*
atmospheric *adj.* **ayrgylghyek**
atom *n.* **atom** *m.* **+ow**
atomic *adj.* **atomek**
atone *v.* **amendya, dehweles**
atonement *n.* **dehwelans** *m.,*
    prenedh *m.*
attach *v.* **staga**
attached *adj.* **serghek:** *v.* be
    attached **serghi**
attachment *n.* (physical and
    emotional) **sergh** *m.;* (physical)
    stagell *f.,* **syg** *f.,* **sygenn** *f.*
attack *n.* **omsettyans** *m.* **+ow:** *v.*
    omsettya, settya war
attain *v.* **drehedhes, hedhes**
attainable *adj.* **hedhadow**
attainment *n.* **drehedhyans** *m.*
    +ow
attempt *n.* **assay** *m.* **+s, attent** *m.*
attention *v.* pay attention **attendya,**
    goslowes
attenuate *v.* **tanowhe**
attic *n.* **soler** *m.* **+yow, talik** *m.*
    taligow
attitude *n.* **omdhalgh** *m.* **+ow**

attorney (U.S.) *n.* **laghyas** *m.*
-**ysi, laghyades** *f.* **+ow**
attract *v.* **tenna**
attraction *n.* **tennvos** *m.*
attributes *plur.* **teythi**
auburn *adj.* **gellrudh**
auction *n.* **strifwerth** *m.* **+ow**
audacity *n.* **bolder** *m.*, **hardhder**
m.
audience *plur.* **goslowysi**
audio-cassette *n.* audio-cassette
songyst *f.* **+yow**
audio-tape *n.* **sonsnod** *m.* **+ow**
audio-visual *adj.* **klywwelyek**
auger *n.* **tarder** *m.* **terder**
augment *v.* **ynkressya**
August *n.* **Est** *m.*, **mis-Est** *m.*
aunt *n.* **modrep** *f.* **modrebedh**
Australia *place* **Ostrali**
authenticity *n.* **gwiryonses** *m.*
author *n.* **awtour** *m.* **+s**
authority *n.* **awtorita** *m.*, **vertu** *f.*
+s: *prep.* on the authority of
herwydh
autonomy *n.* **omrewl** *f.*
autumn *n.* **kynyav** *m.*
auxiliary *adj.* **heweres**
avail *v.* **avaylya**
avarice *n.* **krefni** *f.*, **pithneth** *f.*
avaricious *adj.* **pith**
avaunt *int.* **avond**
avenge *v.* **diala, venja**
avenger *n.* **dialor** *m.* **+yon**
avenue *n.* **rosva** *f.* **+ow**
average *n.* **kresek** *m.* **kresogow**:
adj. **kresek, mayn**
avoid *v.* **avoydya, goheles**
avow *v.* **avowa**
await *v.* **gortos**
awake *adj.* **difun**: *adv.* **a-dhifun**
awaken *v.* **difuna**
award *n.* **piwas** *m.* **+ow**: *v.*
grontya

aware *adj.* **war**: *v.* to be aware
arwodhvos
away *adj.* **a-ves**: *v.* get away
skapya; get away quickly **skeusi**;
go away **avodya**: *adv.* **a-dre,**
dhe-ves, yn kerdh; a short
distance away **pols alemma**
awe *n.* **own** *m.*, **agha** *m.*
awl *n.* **mynowes** *m.*
awning *n.* **howllenn** *f.* **+ow**
axe *n.* **boel** *f.* **+yow**
axle *n.* **eghel** *f.* **+yow**

B

babble *n.* **klapp** *m.*: *v.* **klappya,**
gerya
baby *n.* **baban** *m.* **+es, babi** *m.*
+ow
bachelor *n.* **bacheler** *m.* **+s,**
unndav *m.* **unndevyon**
back *n.* **keyn** *m.* **+ow, kil** *m.* **+yer,**
nuk *m.*; back of hand **keyn dorn**
m.; back of the head **kilbenn** *m.*:
adv. **dhe-dre**; answer back
kewsel a-dreus
background *n.* **keyndir** *m.* **+yow**
back-handed *adj.* **dre gildhorn**
backwards *adv.* **war-dhelergh**
bacon *n.* **bakken** *m.*, **meghin** *m.*
bad *n.* bad trader **gwann-wikor** *m.*
+yon: *plur.* bad news **hager**
nowodhow, yeyn nowodhow:
adj. **drog**
badge *n.* **arwoedhik** *m.* -**igow**
badger *n.* **brogh** *m.* **+es**
bag *n.* **sagh** *m.* **seghyer**: *v.* put in
a bag **sagha**
baggage-train *n.* **tren-fardellow**
m.
bagpipes *plur.* **pibow sagh**
bail *n.* **mewgh** *m.* **+yow**; one who
stands bail **mewghyer** *m.* -**yoryon**:
v. stand bail **mewghya**

bail-bondsman (U.S.) *n.*
mewghyer *m.* -yoryon
bailiff *n.* bayli *m.*
bake *v.* pobas, fornya
bake-house *n.* popti *m.*, chi forn
m., chi pobas *m.*
baker *n.* peber *m.* -oryon,
pebores *f.* +ow; baker's shop
popti *m.*
bakestone *n.* men-pobas *m.*
meyn-pobas
baking pan (U.S.) *n.* kanna-
pobas *m.*
baking-foil *n.* folenn bobas *f.*
baking-pan *n.* padell-bobas *f.*
padellow-pobas
balance *n.* mantol *f.* +yow;
balance of account gasadow *m.:* *v.*
omberthi
balanced *adj.* omborth
bald *adj.* moel, blogh: *v.* make
bald bloghhe, moelhe
baldness *n.* bloghter *m.*, moelder
m.
bale *n.* pusorn *m.* +ow: *v.*
pusornas
ball *n.* pel *f.* +yow, pellenn *f.* +ow:
v. roll into a ball pellenni
balloon *n.* pel-ayr *f.* pelyow-ayr
balm *n.* eli *m.* +ow
ban *n.* difenn *m.:* *v.* difenn,
emskemunya
banana *n.* banana *m.* +s
band *n.* (group of people) parsel *m.*
+s; (musical) band *m.;* (strip)
bond *m.*, garlont *f.* +ow, snod *m.*
+ow, +ys; brass band band brest
m.
bandage *n.* lystenn *f.* +ow: *v.*
lystenna
band-aid (U.S.) *n.* plestrynn *m.*
+ow
bandy-legged *adj.* berrgamm
bang *n.* (explosion) tardh *m.* +ow;
(knock) bonk *m.* +ys, kronk *m.*
+ys: *v.* tarena

banish *v.* divroa, pellhe
banished *n.* banished person divres
m. +ow
bank *n.* (for money) arghantti *m.*
+ow; (of river) glann *f.* +ow;
(topographical) bankenn *f.* +ow
banker *n.* arghanser *m.* -oryon
bank-note *n.* folenn arghansek *f.*
bankrupt *n.* den skattys *m.*
banner *n.* baner *m.* +yow
banns *plur.* bannys: *v.* read banns
bannya
banquet *n.* fest *m.* +ow
baptise *v.* besydhya
baptism *n.* besydh *m.*
baptist *n.* besydhyer *m.* -oryon;
Baptist Church Eglos Vesydhyek
f.
bar *n.* bar (of door) barr *m.* +ys: *v.*
prenna
barb *n.* gorthfagh *m.* +ow
barbarian *n.* barbar *m.* +yon
barbarous *adj.* barbarus
barbed *adj.* drenek
barber *n.* barver *m.* -oryon
barberry *n.* kelynn Frynk *coll.*,
spernenn velyn *f.*
bard *n.* bardh *m.* berdh, bardhes
f. +ow; Grand Bard Bardh Meur
m.; meeting of bards gorsedh *f.*
+ow
bardic *adj.* bardhek
bare *adj.* moel, lomm: *v.* strip bare
lommhe
bare-backed *n.* keyn lomm *m.*
barefoot *adj.* diarghen, dieskis
bare-headed *adj.* penn-noeth
barelegged *adj.* fernoeth
barely *adv.* skantlowr
bareness *n.* lommder *m.*, moelder
m.
bargain *n.* bargen *m.* +yow,
chyffar *m.:* *v.* bargenya
barge *n.* skath-hir *f.* skathow-hir

bark *n.* (of a dog) **harth** *m.* **+ow**; (of
a tree) **rusk** *f.* **+enn**:   *v.* **hartha,
oulya**
barley *n.* **heydh** *coll.* **+enn**;   barley
corn **barlys** *coll.* **+enn**
barley-field *n.* **heydhek** *f.* **-egi**
barm *n.* **burm** *coll.*
barn *n.* **skiber** *f.* **+yow, greunji** *m.*
+ow
barrel *n.* **balyer** *m.* **+yow, +s**;
open barrel **keryn** *f.* **+yow**;   sawn-
down barrel **kuva** *m.*
barrel-maker *n.* **bonkyer** *m.*
-oryon
barrier *n.* **lett** *m.* **+ow, +ys**
barrow *n.* (tumulus) **krug** *m.* **+ow**;
(vehicle) **gravath** *m.* **+ow**
base *n.* **goeles** *m.* **+ow, ben** *m.*
+yow, grond *m.,* **sel** *f.* **+yow**:   *v.*
grondya, selya
baseball *n.* **pelvas** *f.*
basement *n.* **selder** *m.*
baseness *n.* **vilta** *f.*
basic *adj.* **selvenek, selyek**
basin *n.* large basin **bason** *m.* **+yow,
+ys**;   small basin **bolla** *m.* **bollow,
bollys**
basinet *n.* (headgear) **basnet** *m.*
+ow
basket *n.* **kanstell** *f.* **+ow**;   large
shallow straw basket **kostenn** *f.*
+ow;   narrow-mouthed basket **kest**
f. **+ow**;   pannier basket **kowell** *m.*
+ow
basketball *n.* **pelganstell** *f.*
bass *n.* (fish) **yown** *m.* **+es**;   (Mus.)
faborden *m.* **+yon**
baste *v.* **ura**
bat *n.* (cricket) **batt** *m.* **+ys**;
(mammal) **askell-groghen** *m.*
eskelli-kroghen, ugh-sommys
m.
batch *n.* **bagasik** *m.* **-igow**
bath *n.* **badh** *m.,* **kibell** *f.* **+ow**
bathe *v.* **golghi, badhya**

bathroom *n.* **golghva** *f.* **+ow,
stevell-omwolghi** *f.* **stevellow-
omwolghi**
battering-ram *n.* **hor'benn** *m.*
+ow
battery *n.* **batri** *m.* **+ow**
battle *n.* **batel** *f.* **+yow, kas** *f.* **+ow,
kevammok** *m.*
battle-axe *n.* **kaspoel** *f.*
battlefield *n.* **kaslann** *f.*
battle-horn *n.* **kaskorn** *m.*
kaskern
bay *n.* **kammas** *f.,* **pleg-mor** *m.*
plegow-mor
baying *n.* (of a hound) **harth** *m.* **+ow**
bay-trees *n.* **baywydh** *f.* **+enn**
bazaar *n.* **basar** *m.*
be *v.* **bos, bones**
beach *n.* **treth** *m.* **+ow**
bead *n.* bead of rosary **pader** *m.*
+ow;   single bead **paderenn** *f.*
+ow
beak *n.* **gelvin** *m.* **+es**
beaker *n.* **hanaf** *m.* **+ow**
beam *n.* (radiation) **dewynn** *m.* **+ow**;
(timber) **jist** *m.* **+ys, keber** *f.*
kebrow, prenn *m.* **+yer, styl** *m.*
+yow;   wooden beam in tension
tenn *m.* **+ow**
beam-engine *n.* **jynn-keber** *m.*
bean *n.* **favenn** *f.* **+ow** *coll.* **fav**
bean pod *n.* **kodh fav** *f.*
bear *n.* (animal) **ors** *m.* **+es**
bear *v.* (endure) **godhav, perthi**;
(support) **doen**
bear (endure) *v.* **godhevel**
bear-cub *n.* **orsik** *m.* **-igow**
beard *n.* **barv** *f.* **+ow**
bearded *adj.* **barvek, barvus**
beast *n.* **enyval** *m.* **+es, best** *m.*
+es, eal *m.,* **lodhen** *m.* **lodhnow**;
wild beast **goedhvil** *m.* **+es, mil** *m.*
+es
beastly *adj.* **milus**

beat *v.* **dorna, frappya, gweskel, kronkya**; (defeat) **fetha**; beat with a club **fusta**

beautiful *adj.* **teg, fethus, kader**; more beautiful **tekka**

beautifully *adv.* **yn teg**

beautify *v.* **tekhe**

beauty *n.* **tekter** *m.*

beaver *n.* **bever** *m.* **+s, lostledan** *m.* **+es**

because *conj.* **awos, drefenn**: *phr.* because of danger **awos peryll**; because of death **awos mernans**; because of me **a'm govis**

become *v.* **bos, dos ha bos, mos ha bos**

bed *n.* **gweli** *m.* **+ow**; feather bed **gweli pluv** *m.;* straw bed **gweli kala** *m.*

bed-clothes *n.* **dillas gweli** *coll.*

bed-linen *n.* **lien gweli** *m.*

bedroom *n.* **chambour** *m.* **+yow**; main bedroom **pennchambour** *m.* **+s**; master bedroom **pennchambour** *m.* **+s**

bed-sheet *n.* **lien gweli** *m.*

bedside *n.* bedside mat **strel gweli** *m.*

bedspread *n.* **kolghes** *f.* **+ow**

bed-time *n.* **prys gweli** *m.*

bee *n.* **gwenenenn** *f.* **+ow** *coll.* **gwenenn**

beech-grove *n.* **fowek** *f.* **-egi**

beech-tree *n.* **fowenn** *f.* **+ow** *coll.* **fow, fow-wydhenn** *f.* **+ow** *coll.* **fow-wydh**

beef *n.* **bewin** *m.,* **kig bewin** *m.*

beehive *n.* **kowell gwenen** *m.*

beer *n.* **korev** *m.* **+ow**

beer-jug *n.* **kruskynn** *m.* **+ow**

beet *n.* (plant) **betysenn** *f.* **+ow** *coll.* **betys**

beetle *n.* **hwil** *m.* **+es, hwilenn** *f.;* death-watch beetle **morthelik-**

ankow *m.* **mortheligow-ankow**: *v.* catch beetles **hwilessa**

beetroot *n.* **betys rudh** *coll.*

befall *v.* **koedha, hwarvos**

befallen *adj.* **hwarvedhys**

before *prep.* **a-dherag, a-rag, kyns, derag, dherag**: *adv.* before now **kyns lemmyn**

beforehand *prep.* **a-dherag**

befoul *v.* **mostya**; befoul water **stronka**

beg *v.* **pysi, begya**

beget *v.* **dineythi**

beggar *n.* **begyer** *m.* **+s, -yoryon**

begin *v.* **dalleth**: *adv.* to begin with **wostalleth**

beginner *n.* **dallether** *m.* **-oryon**

beginning *n.* **derow** *m.:* *adv.* in the beginning **wor'talleth, wostalleth**

begone *int.* **avond**

beguile *v.* **flattra, husa, traynya**

behalf *n.* **parth** *f.* **+ow**

behave *v.* **fara**; behave oneself **omdhoen**

behaviour *n.* **fara** *m.*

behead *v.* **dibenna**

beheading *n.* **dibennans** *m.* **+ow**

behind *adv.* **a-dhelergh, a-dryv**

behold *v.* **gweles, mires**: *int.* **ott, otta, awotta, mirewgh**; behold her **ottahi**; behold him **ottava**; behold me **ottavy**; behold thee **ottajy**; behold them **ottensi**; behold us **ottani**; behold you **ottahwi**

behoves *v.* it behoves **degoedh, delledh, koedh**: *phr.* it behoves me to go **y koedh dhymm mos**

belfry *n.* **kleghti** *m.* **+ow, kleghtour** *m.* **+yow**

belief *n.* **kryjyans** *m.,* **koel** *f.*

believe *v.* **krysi**; believe in **krysi yn**; believe someone **krysi dhe nebonan**: *adv.* as I believe **dell grysav**

believer *n.* **kryjyk** *m.* **kryjygyon**

believing *adj.* **kryjyk**
bell *n.* **klogh** *m.* **klegh**; church bell **klogh meur** *m.;* little bell **kleghik** *m.;* refectory bell **klogh dybri** *m.*
bellow *v.* **bedhygla**
bellows *plur.* **meginow**
bellringer *n.* **den an klogh** *m.*
belly *n.* **torr** *f.* **+ow, kroth** *f.*
bellyband *n.* horse's bellyband **torrgyngel** *f.*
bellyful *n.* **torras** *m.*
belong *v.* the dogs belong to the children **an fleghes a biw an keun**
beloved *n.* dearly beloved **kuv kolonn** *m.:* *adj.* **karadow, kerensedhek, meurgerys**
below *prep.* **is:** *adv.* **a-woeles, a-is, isos**
belt *n.* **grogys** *m.* **+yow**
beltway (U.S.) *n.* **kylghfordh** *f.* **+ow**
belvedere *n.* **gwelva** *f.* **-ow**
bemoan *v.* **kyni**
bench *n.* **bynk** *f.* **+yow, form** *m.* **+ys, skown** *m.* **+yow**
bend *n.* **kammas** *f.,* **pleg** *m.* **+ow, stumm** *m.* **+ow:** *v.* **kamma, kromma, plegya, stumma**
benediction *n.* **bennath** *f.* **+ow**
benefice *n.* **benfis** *f.*
benefit *n.* **les** *m.,* **difres** *m.,* **prow** *m.*
bent *n.* **plegyans** *m.:* *adj.* **kamm, kromm**
bequeath *v.* **kemmynna**
bequest *n.* **kemmynn** *m.* **+ow, kemmynnadow** *m.*
bereave *v.* (of parents) **omdhivasa**
bereft *adj.* **omdhivas**; bereft of wife or husband **gwedhow**
berry *n.* **morenn** *f.* **+ow** *coll.* **mor**
beside *prep.* **a-barth, ryb**
besides *prep.* **dres**
besmear *v.* **ura**

besom *n.* (plant) **banadhlenn** *f.* **+ow** *coll.* **banadhel**
bespatter *v.* **lagenna**
best *adj.* **gwella**
bestial *adj.* **milus**
bet *n.* **kenwystel** *m.* **kenwystlow:** *v.* **kenwystla**
betray *v.* **trayta**
better *adj.* **gwell**; far better **milwell:** *adv.* any better **bydh well**
between *prep.* **yntra,** (before vowels) **ynter** ; between them **yntredha**; between us **yntredhon**; between you **yntredhowgh**
beware *v.* **warya:** *int.* **darwar**
bewilder *v.* **amaya, penndaga**
bewildered *adj.* **penndegys**
bewilderment *n.* **sowdhan** *m.*
beyond *prep.* **dres**
bezant *n.* **besont** *m.* **besons**
bib *n.* **bronnlenn** *f.* **+ow**
Bible *n.* **Bibel** *m.*
biblical *adj.* **biblek**
bicycle *n.* **diwros** *f.* **+ow:** *v.* **diwrosa**; go on a bicycle tour **diwrosya**
bid *v.* **erghi**
bier *n.* **geler** *f.* **+yow, masken** *m.* **+yow**
bifurcation *n.* **gowl** *f.* **+ow**
big *adj.* **bras**
big-bellied *adj.* **torrek**
big-browed *adj.* **elek, talek**
big-cheeked *adj.* **boghek**
big-eyed *n.* big-eyed person **lagasek** *m.* **-ogyon:** *adj.* **lagasek**
bigger *adj.* **brassa**
big-headed *adj.* **pennek**
bight *n.* (of rope) **gwydenn** *f.;* (of sea) **pleg-mor** *m.* **plegow-mor**
big-mouthed *adj.* **ganowek**
big-tailed *adj.* **lostek**
bilberry *n.* **lusenn** *f.* **+ow** *coll.* **lus:** *adj.* abounding in bilberries **lusek**

bile *n.* **bystel** *f.*

bilingual *adj.* **diwyethek**

bilingualism *n.* **diwyethogeth** *f.*

bill *n.* **reken** *m.* **reknow**; (of bird) **gelvin** *m.* **+es**; bill of sale **reken gwerth** *m.*

bill (U.S.) *n.* **folenn arghansek** *f.*

billet *n.* (piece of wood) **keunysenn** *f.* **+ow** *coll.* **keunys**

bill-hook *n.* **gwydhyv** *m.* **+yow**

billow *n.* **tonn** *f.* **+ow**

billy-goat *n.* **bogh** *m.*

bin *n.* **argh** *f.* **+ow**

bind *v.* **kelmi, maylya**

binder *n.* **kolmer** *m.* **-oryon**

bindweed *n.* **gwyg** *coll.* **+enn**

binge *v.* **kwoffi**

binnacle *n.* **bytakyl** *m.* **bytaklys**

biodegradable *adj.* **bywbodradow**

biological *adj.* **bywoniethek**

biologist *n.* **bywonydh** *m.* **+yon**

biology *n.* **bywonieth** *f.*

birch-tree *n.* **besowenn** *f.* **+ow** *coll.* **besow**

bird *n.* **edhen** *f.* **ydhyn**; young bird **ydhnik** *m.*

birdcage *n.* **kowell edhen** *m.*

birdlime *n.* **glus** *m.* **+ow**

birth *n.* **dineythyans** *m.* **+ow**; time of birth **genesigeth** *f.:* *v.* give birth **dineythi**

birthday *n.* **penn-bloedh** *m.* **pennow-bloedh**

birthplace *n.* **genesigva** *f.*

birthright *n.* **ertach** *m.*

biscuit *n.* **tesenn gales** *f.;* ship's biscuit **bara kales** *m.*

bishop *n.* **epskop** *m.* **epskobow**

bishopric *n.* **epskobeth** *f.* **+ow**

bison *n.* **bual** *m.* **+yon**

bit *n.* **banna** *m.* **bannaghow, tamm** *m.* **temmyn, brewyonenn** *f.* **+ow** *coll.* **brewyon, darn** *m.* **+ow, tekkenn** *f.;* not a bit **kamm**

m. **+ow**; bit by bit **tamm ha tamm** *m.;* horse's bit **genva** *f.* **+ow**; little bit **dernik** *m.,* **temmik** *m.*

temmigow: *phr.* I can't see a bit **ny welav banna**

bitch *n.* **gast** *f.* **gesti**

bite *n.* **brath** *m.* **+ow**: *v.* **bratha, densel**; make a first cut or bite in **attamya**

bitter *adj.* **ahas, hwerow**

bittern *n.* **bonngors** *m.* **+es, klabytter** *m.* **+s**

bitterness *n.* **hwerowder** *m.*

bivouac *n.* **kamp** *m.* **+ow, +ys**: *v.* **kampya**

black *adj.* **du**

blackavised *adj.* **mindu**

blackberry *n.* **morenn-dhu** *f.* **morennow-du** *coll.* **mor-du**

blackbird *n.* **molgh dhu** *f.* **–es du**

blackboard *n.* **bord du** *m.*

blacken *v.* **duhe**

blackhead *n.* **penn-du** *m.* **pennow-du**

blacklist *n.* **rol-dhu** *f.*

blackness *n.* **duder** *m.*

black-pudding *n.* **goesegenn** *f.* **+ow**

blacksmith *n.* **gov** *m.* **+yon, ferror** *m.* **+yon**

blackthorn *n.* **spernenn dhu** *f.*

bladder *n.* **gusigenn** *f.* **+ow**

blade *n.* **lown** *m.* **+yow**; (of grass) **gwelsenn** *f.* **gwels**

blame *n.* **blam** *m.,* **kabel** *m.:* *v.* **blamya, kabla**

blameless *adj.* **divlam**

blameworthy *adj.* **kablus**

bland *adj.* **anvlasus**

blanket *n.* **lenn** *f.* **+ow, pallenn** *f.* **+ow**

blast *n.* (of rain) **kowas** *f.* **kowasow**; (of wind) **hwyth** *m.* **+ow**: *v.* **hwytha**

blaze *n.* **tansys** *m.* **+yow**: *v.* **dewi**

bleach *v.* **kanna**
bleat *v.* **bryvya**
bleating *n.* bleating of sheep **bryv** *f.*
+yow
bleed *v.* **goesa**; (trans.) **diwoesa**
blemish *n.* **namm** *m.* **+ow**: *v.*
remove blemish **dinamma**
blend *n.* **kemmysk** *m.:* *v.*
kemmyska, myska
blenny *n.* **morgroenek** *m.* **-oges**
bless *v.* **benniga, soena**: *phr.* God
bless thee **dursoenno dhis**
blessed *name* Blessed Mary **Maria
Wynn**: *adj.* **gwynn, bennesik,
bennigys, gwynnvys**
blessedness *n.* **bennesikter** *m.*
blessing *n.* **bennath** *f.* **+ow, ras** *m.*
+ow, soen *m.* **-yow**: *phr.* God's
blessing **benna'tyw**; may blessing
follow **benna'sywes**
blind *n.* (curtain) **lenn dhu** *f.;* blind
fish **lagatter** *m.* **lagattres**; blind
man **dall** *m.* **dellyon**; blind man's
buff **margh dall** *m.;* blind woman
dalles *f.* **+ow**: *adj.* **dall**: *v.*
dalla, dallhe
blind-fish *n.* **bothek** *m.* **-oges**
blindness *n.* **dellni** *m.*
blindworm *n.* **anav** *m.* **+es**
bliss *n.* **lowena** *f.,* **gwynnvys** *m.*
blister *n.* **bothell** *f.,* **gusigenn** *f.*
+ow, gwennenn *f.* **+ow**
blizzard *n.* **oerwyns** *m.* **+ow**
block *v.* **lettya, stoppya**
blockage *n.* **lett** *m.* **+ow, +ys**
blood *n.* **goes** *m.;* hardened blood
mol *m.* **+yow**: *adj.* of same blood
unnwoes: *v.* draw blood from
diwoesa
blood-line *n.* **goes** *m.*
blood-red *adj.* **kogh**
bloodshed *n.* **krow** *m.*
bloodshot *adj.* **gwythiek**
bloodstained *adj.* **goesek**
bloody *adj.* **goesek**: *v.* make
bloody **goesa**

bloom *n.* **bleujenn** *f.* **+ow** *coll.*
bleujyow: *v.* **bleujyowa**
blossom *n.* **bleujenn** *f.* **+ow** *coll.*
bleujyow: *v.* **bleujyowa**
blouse *n.* **hevis** *m.* **+yow**
blow *n.* **boemm** *m.* **+yn,**
boemmenn *f.* **+ow, hwaff** *m.* **+ys,**
klout *m.* **+ys, stiwenn** *m.,* **strekys**
f. **strokosow, tummas** *m.* **+ow**;
crushing blow **skwat** *m.;* smart
blow **pethik** *m.:* *v.* **hwytha**
blowflies *n.* **kelyon kig** *coll.*
blowing *n.* **hwyth** *m.* **+ow**
blowing-house *n.* **chi hwytha** *m.,*
fog *f.* **+ow**
blows *n.* flurry of blows **boksas** *m.*
+ow
bludgeon *n.* **blojon** *m.* **+s, fust** *f.*
+ow
blue *adj.* **glas**
bluebell *n.* **bleujenn an gog** *f.*
bluebottles *n.* **kelyon kig** *coll.*
blue-tit *n.* **penn-pali** *m.* **pennow-
pali**
blunder *n.* **kammwonis** *m.:* *v.*
kammwonis
blunt *adj.* **sogh**
blunt-witted *adj.* **tal-sogh**
blush *v.* **rudha**
bluster *v.* **bragya**
blustering *adj.* **hwyflyn**
boar *n.* **badh** *m.* **+es, torgh** *m.* **+es**;
domestic boar **bora** *m.*
board *n.* (group of people) **kesva** *f.*
+ow; (timber) **astell** *f.* **estyll,
bord** *m.,* **plank** *m.* **plenkys, +ow,
plenkynn** *f.* **+ow**; binding board of
a book **aden** *f.* **+yow**; board and
lodging **ostyans** *m.;* Cornish
Language Board **Kesva an Taves
Kernewek** *f.;* Cornwall Tourist
Board **Kesva Tornyaseth
Kernow** *f.;* examination board
kesva apposyans *f.*
boar-spear *n.* **hoghwyw** *m.* **+yow**
boast *n.* **bost** *m.* **+ow**: *v.* **bostya**

boaster *n.* **boster** *m.* **-oryon**
boat *n.* **skath** *f.* **+ow;** fishing boat
kok *m.* **kokow;** little boat **kokynn**
m.
Bodmin *place* **Bosvenegh**
Bodmin Moor *place* **Goen Brenn**
body *n.* **korf** *m.* **+ow;** front of body
greuv *m.*
body-fluid *n.* **lin** *m.* **+yow**
bodyguard *n.* **korfwithyas** *m.* **-ysi**
bog *n.* **keunegenn** *f.* **+ow;** reed-
grown bog **kors** *coll.* **+enn**
Bohemia *place* **Bohemi**
boil *v.* **bryjyon**
boiler *n.* (for domestic heating) **forn-**
doemma *f.* **fornow-toemma**
boiling *n.* **bryjyon** *m.*
boiling-pan *n.* large boiling-pan
chekk *m.* **+ys**
bold *adj.* **kolonnek, bold, hardh**
boldness *n.* **bolder** *m.*, **hardhder**
m., **kolonnekter** *m.*
boll *n.* (seed-pod) **bolghenn** *f.* **+ow**
coll. **bolgh**
bolster *n.* **treuspluvek** *f.* **-ogow**
bolt *n.* **ebil** *m.* **+yow;** (iron) **ebil**
horn *m.:* *v.* **prenna**
bolting-mill *n.* **melin-sidhla** *f.*
bomb *n.* **tanbellenn** *f.* **+ow;** smart
bomb **tanbellenn gonnyk** *f.:* *v.*
tanbellenna
bombard *v.* **tanbellenna**
bond *n.* (cord) **raw** *f.* **+yow;** (link)
kadon *f.* **+yow, kolm** *m.* **+ow,**
stagell *f.*, **syg** *f.;* (promise)
gorambos *m.* **+ow**
bondmaid *n.* **kethes** *f.* **+ow**
bondman *n.* **keth** *m.* **+yon,**
kethwas *m.* **-wesyon**
bone *n.* **askorn** *m.* **eskern;** (of fish)
dren *m.* **dreyn:** *v.* (remove bones)
diaskorna
bone-marrow *n.* **mer** *m.*
bones *n.* knuckle bones **nawmen** *m.*
bonfire *n.* **tansys** *m.* **+yow**

bonnet *n.* **kogh** *m.* **+ow**
bonus *n.* **bonus** *m.*
bony *adj.* **askornek**
book *n.* **lyver** *m.* **lyvrow;** account
book **lyver-akontow** *m.* **lyvrow-**
akontow: *v.* **ragerghi**
book-case *n.* **argh-lyvrow** *f.*
arghow-lyvrow
booking *n.* **ragarghas** *m.* **+ow;**
booking office **tokynva** *f.* **+ow**
booklet *n.* **lyvrik** *m.* **-igow**
bookseller *n.* **lyverwerther** *m.*
-oryon
bookshop *n.* **lyverji** *m.* **+ow**
bookstore (U.S.) *n.* **lyverji** *m.* **+ow**
boost *v.* **kennertha**
boot *n.* (footwear) **botasenn** *f.* **+ow**
coll. **botas;** (of car) **trog** *m.* **+ow**
booze *v.* **diwessa**
border *n.* **amal** *m.* **emlow, hin** *m.*
+yow, min *m.* **+yow, or** *f.* **+yon**
borderland *n.* **ordir** *m.* **+yow**
bore *v.* **tardra;** bore holes **telli**
boring *adj.* **skwithus**
born *adj.* **genys**
borough *n.* **burjestra** *f.*
borrow *v.* **chevisya, kavoes**
kendon
bosom *n.* **askra** *f.*
boss *n.* (stud) **both** *f.* **+ow**
bossed *adj.* **bothek**
botanical *adj.* **lesek, losoniethel**
botanist *n.* **losonydh** *m.* **+yon**
botany *n.* **losonieth** *f.*
bother *v.* **ankombra, trobla:** *phr.*
no bother **heb grev**
bottle *n.* **botell** *m.* **+ow:** *v.*
botellya
bottom *n.* **goeles** *m.* **+ow:** *adv.* at
the bottom **a-woeles;** to the bottom
dhe-woeles; towards the bottom
war-woeles
bough *n.* **skorrenn** *f.* **+ow** *coll.*
skorr; branching bough **barr** *m.*
+ow

bound *n.* **lamm** *m.* **+ow**: *v.*
lamma, lemmel
boundary *n.* **kor** *m.*, or *f.* **+yon**;
Boundary Commission **Desedhek**
an Oryon *m.*
boundary-dyke *n.* **finfos** *f.* **+ow**
bountiful *adj.* **hel**
bounty *n.* **helder** *m.*, **larjes** *m.*
bourgeois *adj.* **burjesek**
bourgeoisie *n.* **burjeseth** *f.*
bout *n.* **fit** *m.* **+ys**
bow *n.* (arc) **gwarak** *f.* **-egow**
bow *v.* **omblegya**; bow down
plegya yn dor
bowel *n.* **kolodhyonenn** *f.* **+enn**
coll. **kolodhyon**
bower *n.* **kel** *m.* **+yow**
bowl *n.* **bolla** *m.* **bollow, bollys**;
small bowl **pojer** *m.*
bow-legged *adj.* **berrgamm,**
garrgamm
bowman *n.* **gwareger** *m.* **-oryon**
bow-net *n.* **ballek** *m.*
box *n.* (blow) **boks** *m.* **+ow**;
(container) **boks** *m.* **+ys, kyst** *f.*
+yow; (tree) **boks** *m.;* Christmas
box **kalennik** *m.;* money box **argh**
vona *f.;* small box **kystenn** *f.*
+ow; tinder box **korn tan** *m.:* *v.*
boksusi
boxing *v.* **boksusi**
boy *n.* **mab** *m.* **mebyon, maw** *m.*
boy-friend *n.* **karer** *m.* **-oryon**
boyhood *n.* **mabses** *m.*
bra *n.* **diwvronner** *m.*
bracelet *n.* **breghellik** *m.* **-igow**
bracken *n.* **krann** *coll.*, **reden** *coll.*
+enn
bracket *n.* **korbel** *m.* **korblys**
brag *n.* **bost** *m.* **+ow**
braggart *n.* **bragyer** *m.* **+s**
bragget *n.* **bragas** *m.*
braid *n.* **plethenn** *f.* **+ow**: *v.*
pletha

braider *n.* **plether** *m.* **-oryon,**
plethores *f.* **+ow**
brains *plur.* **ympynnyon**
braise *v.* **braysya**
brake *n.* (curb) **fronn** *f.* **+ow**: *v.*
fronna; *n.* (vegetation) **perth** *f.* **-i**
brake-lining *n.* **kroghen fronn** *f.*
bramble *n.* **spedhasenn** *f.* **+ow**
coll. **spedhas**; bramble patch
dreysek *f.* **-egi, spedhasek** *f.*
-egi; bramble thicket **dreyskoes**
m. **+ow**
bramble-bush *n.* **morbrenn** *m.*
+yer
brambles *n.* **dreys** *coll.* **+enn**
brambly *adj.* **dreysek**
bran *n.* **talgh** *m.* **telghyon**
branch *n.* **skorrenn** *f.* **+ow** *coll.*
skorr; small branch **barrenn** *f.*
+ow
branched *adj.* **skorrek**
brandise *n.* **trybedh** *m.* **+ow**
brass *n.* **brest** *m.*
brassard *n.* **breghwisk** *m.*
brassiere *n.* **diwvronner** *m.*
bravery *n.* **bravder** *m.*,
kolonnekter *m.*
brawl *n.* **freudh** *m.:* *v.* **deraylya,**
freudhi
bray *v.* **begi**
breach *n.* **aswa** *f.* **+ow, bolgh** *m.*
+ow, offens *m.* **+ys, torrva** *f.*
+ow; breach of contract **torrva**
ambos *f.:* *v.* **bolgha**
bread *n.* **bara** *m.;* barley bread **bara**
barlys *m.*, **bara heydh** *m.;*
leavened bread **bara goell** *m.;*
oaten bread **bara kergh** *m.;*
rye bread **bara segal** *m.;* soft part
of bread **hwigenn** *f.;*
underbaked bread **bara toes** *m.;*
unleavened bread **bara heb goell**
m.; wheaten bread **bara gwaneth**
m.; white bread **bara gwynn** *m.*,
bara kann *m.:* *v.* break bread
soubenna

bread pan (U.S.) *n.* **kanna-torth**
m.
breadcrumbs *n.* **browsyon bara**
coll.
breadth *n.* **les** *m.*
break *n.* **torr** *m.* **+ow**: *v.* **terri,**
brewi; break bread **soubenna**;
break into bits **dralya**; break off
astel; break the force of **goderri**
breakable *adj.* easily breakable
hedorr
breakdown *n.* **torrva** *f.* **+ow**:
plur. **mothow**
breakfast *n.* **hansel** *m.* **+yow**
breakneck *phr.* **krakkya-konna**
bream *n.* **siw** *m.* **+yon**; black bream
dama goth *f.;* small bream
krommenn *f.,* **lommas** *m.* **+ow**
breast *n.* **bronn** *f.* **+ow** *dual*
diwvronn: *v.* give the breast
bronna
breastplate *n.* **lurik** *m.*
breath *n.* **gwyns** *m.* **+ow, hwyth**
m. **+ow, anall** *f.:* *adj.* out of breath
dianall: *v.* be out of breath **dyewa**
breathe *v.* **hwytha, anella**
breathless *adj.* **dianall**
breeches *n.* **lavrek** *m.* **lavrogow**
breeder *n.* **mager** *m.* **-oryon,**
magores *f.* **+ow**
breeze *n.* **awel glor** *f.*
brethren *n.* **brederedh** *m.*
Breton *n.* (language) **Bretonek** *m.;*
(man) **Breton** *m.* **+yon**; (woman)
Bretones *f.* **+ow**: *adj.* **Bretonek**
brevity *n.* **berrder** *m.*
brew *v.* **braga**
brewer *n.* **brager** *m.* **-oryon**
brewery *n.* **bragji** *m.* **+ow**
briar *n.* **spedhasenn** *f.* **+ow** *coll.*
spedhas
briar-brake *n.* **spedhasek** *f.* **-egi**
brick *n.* **brykk** *m.* **+ow, +ys**
bride *n.* **benyn bries** *f.,* **benyn**
nowydh *f.*

bridegroom *n.* **den nowydh** *m.,*
gour pries *m.*
bridesmaid *n.* **moren bries** *f.*
bridge *n.* **pons** *m.* **+yow**; little
bridge **ponsik** *m.* **-igow, ponsynn**
m. **+ow**
bridle-way *n.* **marghlergh** *m.* **+ow**
brief *adj.* **berr, kott**
briefly *adv.* **a verr dermyn**
brigand *n.* **lader** *m.* **ladron**
bright *adj.* **golow, splann, dergh,**
glow, ylyn: *v.* make bright
splannhe
brighten *v.* **klerhe**
brightness *n.* **splannder** *m.,*
golowder *m.,* **gwynnder** *m.,* **kann**
m., **splennyjyon** *m.*
brill *n.* **lugarnleyth** *f.* **+es**
brilliant *adj.* **golow**
brimstone *n.* **loskven** *m.*
brindled *adj.* **brygh, labol**
brine *n.* **hyli** *m.*
brine-pit *n.* **poll hyli** *m.*
bring *v.* **dri, hembronk, kyrghes**
brink *n.* **glann** *f.* **+ow**
Britain *place* **Breten**; Great Britain
Breten Veur
British *adj.* **Predennek**
Briton *n.* **Brython** *m.* **+yon**
Brittany *place* **Breten Vyghan**
brittle *adj.* **brottel, krin**: *v.*
become dry or brittle **krina**
Brittonic *adj.* **Brythonek**
broach *v.* **attamya**
broad *adj.* **efan, ledan**
broadcast *v.* **tavethli**
broad-cloth *n.* **pann-ledan** *m.*
broad-shouldered *adj.* **skoedhek**
brocade *n.* **pali** *m.*
broccoli *n.* **kowlvleujenn** *f.* **+ow**
broil *v.* **broylya**
broken *n.* broken heart **kolonn**
drogh *f.:* *adj.* **brew, terrys,**
trogh; broken pate **penn-kogh**

broker *n.* **mayner** *m.* **-oryon**

bronze *n.* **brons** *m.*

brooch *n.* **brocha** *m.* **brochys**

broody *adj.* (of hen) **gor**

brook *n.* **gover** *m.* **+ow, keynres** *m.,* **stredh** *f.* **+ow**

broom *n.* (implement) **skubell** *f.* **+ow**; (plant) **banadhlenn** *f.* **+ow** *coll.* **banadhel**; butcher's broom **kelynn byghan** *coll.*

broom-brake *n.* **banadhlek** *f.* **-egi**

broom-stick *n.* **gwelenn-skubell** *f.* **gwelynni-skubell**

broth *n.* **kowl** *m.* **+ow, soubenn** *f.* **+ow**; clear broth **iskell** *m.;* thick broth **bros** *m.* **+ow**

brothel *n.* **chi drog-vri** *m.*

brother *n.* **broder** *m.* **breder**

brotherhood *n.* **brederedh** *m.*

brother-in-law *n.* **broder da** *m.,* **broder dre lagha** *m.*

brow *n.* **tal** *m.* **+yow**

browbeat *v.* **arvedh**

brown *adj.* **gorm**; chestnut brown **gell kesten**; light brown **gell**; russet brown **gellrudh**

Brownies *plur.* **Gelligesow**

brownish *adj.* **gellik**

browse *v.* (feed) **peuri**

bruise *n.* **brew** *m.* **+yon**: *v.* **brewi**

bruised *adj.* **brew**

brunch *n.* **hansli** *m.* **-livyow**

brush *n.* artist's brush **pynsel** *m.;* pastry brush **skubyllenn bast** *f.;* small brush **skubyllenn** *f.:* *v.* **skuba**

brushwood *n.* **kewydh** *coll.*

brutal *adj.* **milus**

brute *n.* **milus** *m.* **milusyon**

bubble *n.* **hwythenn** *f.* **+ow**: *v.* **hwythfi**

buck *n.* wild buck **koesyorgh** *m.*

bucket *n.* **kelorn** *m.* **kelern**

buckle *n.* **bokyl** *m.* **boklow, boklys**: *v.* **bokla**

buckler *n.* **bokler** *m.* **+s**

buckthorn *n.* **spernenn velyn** *f.*

bucolic *adj.* **bugelek**

budget *n.* **towlargh** *m.* **+ow**

buff *n.* (colour) **liw bual** *m.*

buffalo *n.* **bual** *m.* **+yon**

buffet *n.* **boemmenn** *f.* **+ow**

buffoon *n.* **jogler** *m.* **-oryon, +s**

bugbear *n.* **boekka du** *m.*

bugle-horn *n.* **bualgorn** *m.* **-gern**

bugs *n.* **teurek** *coll.* **teuregenn**

build *v.* (trans.) **drehevel**

building *n.* **chi** *m.* **chiow, drehevyans** *m.* **+ow**; (for processing ore) **moendi** *m.:* *v.* finish building **kowldhrehevel**

bulb *n.* (light) **bollenn** *f.* **+ow**; (of plant) **krennwreydhenn** *f.* **+ow** *coll.* **krennwreydh**

bull *n.* **tarow** *m.* **terewi**; papal bull **bolla** *m.* **bollys**

bullet *n.* **pellenn** *f.* **+ow**

bullock *n.* **lodhen** *m.* **lodhnow, lo'n** *m.* **+ow**

bullock-house *n.* **lo'nji** *m.* **+ow**

bulrush *n.* **pennduenn** *f.* **+ow** *coll.* **penndu**

bum (U.S.) *n.* **lorel** *m.* **+s, losel** *m.* **+s**

bump *n.* **bonk** *m.* **+ys, boemm** *m.* **+yn**

bumper *n.* bumper of car **divoemmell** *m.*

bun *n.* **tesenn vyghan** *f.,* **torthell** *m.* **+ow**

bunch *n.* **bagas** *m.* **+ow, gronn** *m.,* **toes** *m.* **+ow, tyskenn** *f.* **+ow**; bunch of ore **bonni** *m.*

bundle *n.* **fardell** *m.* **+ow, gronn** *m.,* **pusorn** *m.* **+ow**: *v.* **gronna**; bundle together **pusornas**

bungle *v.* **kammwonis**

buoyant *adj.* **neuvelladow**; neutrally buoyant **neuvelladow heptu**

burden *n.* **begh** *m.* **+yow, karg** *m.*
+ow, pusorn *m.* **+ow:** *v.* **beghya**
burdensome *adj.* **beghus**
burdock *n.* **lesserghek** *m.*,
serghegenn vras *f.*
bureau *n.* **burow** *m.;* Bureau for
Lesser-Used Languages **Burow an
Yethow Nebes Kewsys** *m.*
burgher *n.* **burjes** *m.* **burjysi**
burglary *n.* **torrva chi** *f.*
burial *n.* **ynkleudhyas** *m.*
burn *v.* **leski, dewi, skaldya;** burn
up **kowlleski**
burning *n.* **losk** *m.*, **loskvann** *m.*
burrow *n.* **toll** *m.* **tell**
bursary *n.* **arghas** *m.* **+ow**
bury *v.* **ynkleudhyas**
bus *n.* **kyttrin** *m.* **+yow**
bush *n.* **bos** *m.* **+ow, pryskenn** *f.*
+ow *coll.* **prysk**
bushel *n.* **bushel** *m.* **+s**
bushy *n.* bushy place **bosek** *f.* **-egi:**
adj. **bosek**
bushy-browed *adj.* **abransek**
business *n.* **negys** *m.* **+yow;** bad
business **hager vyaj** *m.;* business
with **negys orth** *m.*
businessman *n.* **gwikor** *m.* **+yon,
negysydh** *m.* **+yon**
bus-station *n.* **kyttrinva** *f.*
bus-stop *n.* **kyttrinva** *f.*, **savla-
kyttrin** *m.* **savleow-kyttrin**
busy *adj.* **bysi**
but *conj.* **mes**
butcher *n.* **kiger** *m.* **-oryon;**
butcher's shop **kikti** *m.* **+ow**
butchery *n.* (trade) **kigereth** *f.*
butler *n.* **boteller** *m.* **-oryon,
botler** *m.* **+s, menystrer** *m.*
-oryon, spenser *m.* **+s**
butt *n.* (container) **keryn** *f.* **+yow;**
(target for archery) **but** *m.* **+ys:** *v.*
kornya
butter *n.* **amanenn** *m.* **+ow:** *v.*
amanenna

butterfly *n.* **tykki-Dyw** *f.*, **tegenn
Dyw** *f.*
buttery *n.* **talgell** *f.* **+ow**
buttock *n.* **pedrenn** *f.* **+ow** *dual*
diwbedrenn
button *n.* **boton** *m.* **+yow:** *v.*
botonya
button-hole *n.* **toll-boton** *m.* **tell-
boton**
buy *v.* **prena;** buy back **dasprena;**
buy on hire purchase **hirbrena**
buyer *n.* **prener** *m.* **-oryon,
prenores** *f.* **+ow;** (professional)
prenyas *m.* **-ysi**
buzz *n.* **si** *m.:* *v.* **hwyrni,
sadronenni, sia**
buzzard *n.* **bargos** *m.* **bargesyon**
buzzy-milk *n.* **leth boesa** *m.*
by *prep.* **gans, orth, ryb, er, par,
tann;** (in oaths) **re, ren;** by
Christmas **erbynn Nadelik;** hard
by **ryb:** *phr.* by my **re'm;** by the
re'n
by-election *n.* **istewisyans** *m.*
+ow
by-pass *n.* (road) **fordh-dremen** *f.*

C

cab *n.* (of lorry) **kab** *m.* **+ow**
cabbage *n.* **ongel** *m.;* (in general)
kowl *coll.* **+enn;** cabbage plot
kowlek *f.* **-egi;** individual cabbage
kowlenn *f.* **+ow** *coll.* **kowl**
cabin *n.* **krowji** *m.* **+ow, kabynn** *m.*
+ow
cabinet *n.* bedside cabinet **amari
gweli** *m.*
cable *n.* **fun** *f.* **+yow, korsenn** *f.*
+ow; electric cable **korsenn
dredanek** *f.*
cackle *v.* **grega**
cackling *n.* **greg** *m.*
caddy *n.* **karrigell** *f.* **+ow**
cafe *n.* **koffiji** *m.* **+ow**

cairn *n.* **karn** *m.* **+ow**: *adj.*
abounding in cairns **karnedhek**
cake *n.* **tesenn** *f.* **+ow**; cake of wax
koerenn *f.* **+ow**; cream cake
tesenn dhyenn *f.;* large cake
torth *f.* **+ow**
cake pan (U.S.) *n.* **kanna-tesenn**
m.
cake-tin *n.* **kanna-tesenn** *m.*
calculate *v.* **kalkya**
calculation *n.* science of calculation
kalkonieth *f.*
calculator *n.* **reknell** *f.* **+ow**;
(human) **kalkor** *m.* **+yon**
calendar *n.* **lyver-dydhyow** *m.*
lyvrow-dydhyow
calends *n.* **Kalann** *m.*
calf *n.* **leugh** *m.* **+i**; (of leg) **berr** *f.*
+ow, garrenn *f.* **+ow**; small calf
boba *m.*
calf-house *n.* **leughti** *m.* **+ow**
calfskin *n.* **leughkenn** *m.*
call *n.* **galow** *m.,* **galwenn** *f.* **+ow,**
kri *m.* **+ow**; telephone call
galwenn bellgows *f.:* *v.* **gelwel**:
int. call to cattle **prouyt**
called *adj.* **gelwys**
calling (vocation) *n.* **galwesigeth** *f.*
+ow
callosity *n.* **kalesenn** *f.* **+ow**
calm *n.* **kalmynsi** *m.:* *adj.*
kompes, hebask: *v.* calm down
omdhiserri
Camborne *place* **Kammbronn**
camel *n.* **kowrvargh** *m.* **-vergh**
camera *n.* **kamera** *m.* **+s**
camp *n.* (earthwork) **ker** *f.* **+yow**;
holiday camp **kamp-hav** *m.*
kampow-hav; pleasure camp
kamp *m.* **+ow, +ys**; summer camp
(U.S.) **kamp-hav** *m.* **kampow-**
hav: *v.* **kampya**
campaign *n.* **kaskyrgh** *m.* **+ow**:
v. **kaskyrghes**
campions *n.* **glusles** *coll.* **+enn**
camp-site *n.* **kampva** *f.* **+ow**

can *n.* **kanna** *m.* **kannow**;
(container) **kavas** *m.* **+ow**; oil can
podik oyl *m.:* *v.* **kavasa**
canal *n.* **dowrgleudh** *m.* **+yow,**
goeth *f.* **+ow, kanel** *f.* **kanolyow**
cancer *n.* **kanker** *m.* **kankres**
candelabrum *n.* **kantoler** *m.*
+yow
candidate *n.* **ombrofyer** *m.*
-oryon: *v.* stand as a candidate
ombrofya
candle *n.* **kantol** *f.* **+yow**; wax
candle **taper** *m.* **taprys**; wax tallow
candle **kantol goer** *f.,* **kantol soev**
f.
candle-stick *n.* **kantolbrenn** *m.*
+yer
candy-floss *n.* **kommol-sugra** *coll.*
cannon *n.* **kanon** *m.* **+yow**
canoe *n.* **kanou** *m.* **+yow**
canon *n.* **chenon** *m.* **+s**
canonry *n.* **chenonri** *m.*
canopy *n.* **nenlenn** *f.* **+ow**
canticle *n.* **kantykyl** *m.*
canvas *n.* **kanvas** *m.,*
kewarghlenn *f.*
cap *n.* **chappenn** *f.,* **kappa** *m.*
kappow; little cap **keghik** *m.*
capable *adj.* **abel**
capacitor *n.* **dalghasell** *f.* **+ow**
capacity *n.* **dalgh** *m.* **+ow, gavel** *f.*
+yow
cape *n.* (clothing) **kapa** *f.*
capillary *n.* capillary tube
korrbibenn *f.* **+ow**
capital *n.* capital city **pennsita** *f.*
capital (money) *n.* **chatel** *coll.*
capitulate *v.* **omdhaskorr**
capon *n.* **chapon** *m.* **+s**
capriciously *adv.* **hwymm-**
hwamm
capsule *n.* **bolghenn** *f.* **+ow** *coll.*
bolgh
captain *n.* **kapten** *m.* **+yon**

car *n.* **karr** *m.* **kerri**; hire car **karr gobrena** *m.;* police car **karr kreslu** *m.*

carapace *n.* **krogen** *f.* **kregyn**

caravan *n.* **karavan** *m.* **+s**

carcase *n.* **karyn** *m.*

card *n.* **kartenn** *f.* **+ow**; ATM card (U.S.) **kartenn-vona** *f.* **kartennow-mona**; Christmas card **kartenn Nadelik** *f.;* small card **kartennik** *m.* **-igow**: *v.* card wool **kribya**

cardinal *n.* **kardinal** *m.*

care *n.* (cure) **kur** *m.;* (heed) **rach** *m.;* (keeping) **gwith** *m.;* (responsibility) **charj** *m.* **+ys**; (solicitude) **bern** *m.;* (worry) **govijyon** *m.,* **preder** *m.* **+ow**: *adj.* take care **bydh war**: *v.* care for **kara**; take care **gwaytya, warya**; take care of oneself **omweres**: *phr.* I don't care **ny'm deur, ny wrav fors**; I don't care a straw **ny settyav gwelenn gala**

career *n.* **resegva** *f.* **+ow**

carefree *adj.* **digeudh**

careful *adj.* **prederus**: *v.* be careful **omwitha**; be very careful **gorwitha**

careless *adj.* **dibreder, lows**

carelessness *n.* **skoell** *m.* **+yon**

caress *n.* **palvas** *m.* **+ow, palvas kerensa** *m.:* *v.* **chershya, palva**

cargo *n.* **karg** *m.* **+ow**

carp *n.* (fish) **lynnbysk** *m.* **-buskes**

car-park *n.* **park-kerri** *m.*

carpenter *n.* **karpenter** *m.* **-oryon, ser prenn** *m.* **seri prenn**

carpet *n.* **leurlenn** *f.* **+ow**

carping *adj.* **krodhek**

carrack *n.* (great ship) **karrak** *m.* **+ys**

carriage *n.* (act of carrying) **karyans** *m.;* (of train) **kocha** *m.* **kochow, kochys**

carriageway *n.* **karrhyns** *m.* **+yow**; dual carriageway **karrhyns dewblek** *m.*

carrion *n.* **karyn** *m.*

carrot *n.* **karetysenn** *f.* **+ow** *coll.* **karetys**

carry *v.* **doen, degi**

cart *n.* **karr** *m.* **kerri, kert** *m.* **+ow, +ys**: *v.* **karya**

cartbridge *n.* **karrbons** *m.* **+ow**

carte *n.* carte blanche **rydhambos** *m.*

carthorse *n.* **karrvil** *m.* **+es**

cart-house *n.* **karrji** *m.* **+ow**

cartilage *n.* **migorn** *m.*

cartrut *n.* **rosla** *m.* **-leow**

cart-track *n.* **karrhyns** *m.* **+yow**

carve *v.* **kervya**; (of meat) **treghi**

carver *n.* **imajer** *m.* **-oryon**; (of meat) **rennyas** *m.* **-ysi**

carving *n.* **imajri** *m.*

car-wash *n.* **golghva-gerri** *f.* **golghvaow-kerri**

cascade *n.* **froslamm** *m.* **+ow**

case *n.* **kas** *m.;* (box) **trog** *m.* **+ow**: *conj.* in that case **ytho**

cash *n.* **mona** *m.*

cash-card *n.* **kartenn-vona** *f.* **kartennow-mona**

casino *n.* **chi gwari** *m.*

casket *n.* **kofrynn** *m.* **+ow**

cassette *n.* audio-cassette **songyst** *f.* **+yow**; video-cassette **gwelgyst** *f.* **+yow**

cassock *n.* **kryspows oferyas** *f.*

cast *v.* **tewlel, deghesi**; cast lots **tewlel prenn**: *phr.* carelessly cast aside **tewlel dhe skoell**

castigate *v.* **kastiga, kessydhya**

castigation *n.* **kastik** *m.*

castle *n.* **kastell** *m.* **kastylli**

castrate *v.* **spadha**

castrated *adj.* **spadh**

castrato *n.* **spadhesik** *m.* **-igyon**

casual *adj.* (of labour) **antowlek**

cat *n.* kath *f.* kathes; cat o' nine
tails skorja *m.* +ys
catalogue *n.* rolas *m.* +ow
cataract *n.* (on eye) kennenn *f.*
+ow
catastrophe *n.* gordhroglamm *m.*
+ow
catastrophic *adj.*
gordhroglammek
catch *v.* kachya; catch beetles
hwilessa; catch mice legessa:
phr. you'll catch it ty a'n pren
category *n.* klas *m.* +ow, +ys
caterer *n.* mether *m.* -oryon
caterpillar *n.* pryv del *m.;* hairy
caterpillar kath vlewek *f.*
cathedral *n.* penneglos *f.* +yow
Catholic *adj.* katholik
catkin *n.* kath helik *f.*
cattery *n.* kathji *m.* +ow
cattle *n.* chatel *coll.;* horned cattle
gwarthek *coll.: plur.* bughes
cattle-dung *n.* busel *coll.*
cattle-shed *n.* chi miles *m.,* gredi
m.
cattle-yard *n.* buorth *m.* +ow,
gwarthegva *f.* +ow
cauldron *n.* chekk *m.* +ys,
kowdarn *m.* +s
cauliflower *n.* kowlvleujenn *f.*
+ow
caulk *v.* caulk a ship kalkya
cause *n.* acheson *m.* +yow, +ys,
kaws *m.,* ken *m.,* skila *f.* skilys;
(person who causes something to
happen) kawser *m.* -oryon; cause
for regret dihedh *m.: v.* kawsya;
be the cause of skila skilys; cause
to gul dhe; cause to repent
keudhesikhe
caution *n.* rach *m.: v.* gwarnya
cautious *adj.* fur, war; be cautious
bydh war
cavalier *n.* marghek *m.* -ogyon
cave *n.* fow *f.* +ys, gogo *f.,* kav *m.*
+yow, mogow *f.* +yow

cavity *n.* kowva *f.* +ow; small
cavity in rock fog *f.*
cease *v.* hedhi, astel, difyga
cease-fire *n.* astel-omladh *m.*
ceilidh *n.* troyll *m.* +yow
ceiling *n.* nen *m.* +yow; vaulted
ceiling krommnen *m.*
celandine *n.* losowenn lagas *f.*
celebrant *n.* oferyas *m.* oferysi
celebrate *v.* solempnya; celebrate
mass oferenni
celery *n.* kegis hweg *coll.*
celestial *adj.* nevek
cell *n.* (Biol.) kell *f.* +ow; (monastic)
log *f.* +ow; (small room) bagh *f.*
+ow; anchorite's cell penytti *m.*
+ow; little cell gogell *f.* +ow
cellar *n.* dorgell *f.* +ow, selder *m.*
Celt *n.* Kelt *m.* +yon; Brythonic
Celt Brython *m.* +yon; Goidelic
Celt Gwydhel *m.* Gwydhyli
Celtic *adj.* Keltek; Brittonic Celtic
Brythonek; Goidelic Celtic
Gwydhelek
cement *n.* lim *m.*
cemetery *n.* ynkleudhva *f.;* old
cemetery henlann *f.*
censer *n.* senser *m.* +s,
ynkyslester *m.*
censure *n.* kabel *m.: v.* blamya,
kabla
census *n.* niveryans *m.*
cent *n.* per cent kansrann *f.* +ow
centenary *n.* pennkansbloedh *m.*
centennial (U.S.) *n.*
pennkansbloedh *m.*
centipede *n.* kanstroes *m.*
central *adj.* kres
centre *n.* (building) kresenn *f.* +ow,
kresva *f.* +ow; (in rugby)
kreswas *m.;* (middle) kres *m.;*
community centre kresenn
gemmynieth *f.;* medical centre
medhygva *f.* +ow; shopping
centre kresenn brenassa *f.;*

youth centre **kresenn
yowynkneth** *f.*
centurion *n.* **penn-kangour** *m.*
pennow-kangour
century *n.* **kansblydhen** *f.*
kansblydhynyow
ceremony *n.* **devos** *m.* **+ow,
solempnyta** *m.* **-nytys**
certain *art.* a certain **unn**: *adj.*
diogel, kowgans, sertan; a
certain **neb unn**
certainly *adv.* **devri, yn hwir, heb
wow, sertan**
certificate *n.* **testskrif** *m.* **+ow**
certify *v.* **desta,** sertifia
cessation *n.* **finwedh** *f.*
chafer *n.* **hwil** *m.* **+es, hwilenn** *f.*
chaff *n.* **doust** *m.,* **kulyn** *m.,* **us**
coll.: plur. **usyon**
chaffer *n.* **chyffar** *m.*
chaffinch *n.* **tynk** *m.* **+es**
chafing-dish *n.* **chofar** *m.* **+s**
chain *n.* **chayn** *m.* **+ys, kadon** *f.*
+yow, syg *f.:* *v.* **chaynya**
chair *n.* **kador** *f.* **+yow**; (eccl.)
chayr *m.* **+ys**; (professorial) **chayr**
m. **+ys**: *v.* take the chair **kaderya**
chairman *n.* **kaderyer** *m.* **-oryon**
chalet *n.* **krow prenn** *m.*
chalice *n.* **kelegel** *m.*
chalk *n.* **krey** *m.*
challenge *n.* **chalenj** *m.* **+ys**: *v.*
chalenjya, defia
challenger *n.* **bedhyas** *m.* **-ysi**
chamber *n.* **chambour** *m.* **+yow**;
burial chamber in tumulus **kystven**
f.
chamberlain *n.* **chambourlen** *m.*
+s
chamber-tomb *n.* megalithic
chamber-tomb **krommlegh** *f.* **+yow**
champion *n.* **kampyer** *m.* **-oryon**
championship *n.* **kampyorieth** *f.*
chance *n.* **chons** *m.* **+yow, fortun**
m. **+yow, happ** *m.* **+ys**: *v.*
chonsya, fortunya, happya

chancel *n.* **chansel** *m.*
chancellor *n.* **chansler** *m.* **-oryon**
chandelier *n.* **kantoler** *m.* **+yow**
chandler *n.* **gwikor** *m.* **+yon**
change *n.* **chanj** *m.* **+yow, treylva**
f.; (money) **mona** *c.;* small change
mona munys *c.:* *v.* **chanjya,
varya**; change down (of gears)
magla 'nans; change up (of gears)
magla 'bann
changeable *adj.* easily changeable
hedro
changing-room *n.* **chambour-
gwiska** *m.*
channel *n.* **goeth** *f.* **+ow, kanel** *f.*
kanolyow; television channel
kanel *f.* **kanolyow**
chant *n.* **keurgan** *f.* **+ow**
chapel *n.* **chapel** *m.* **+yow**
chaplain *n.* **chaplen** *m.* **+s**
chapter *n.* **chaptra** *m.* **chapters**;
chapter of cathedral **kollji** *m.* **+ow**
char *v.* **goleski**
character *n.* **gnas** *f.* **+ow, natur** *f.*
charcoal *n.* **glowbrenn** *m.*
charge *n.* **kost** *m.* **+ys**;
(responsibility) **charj** *m.* **+ys**;
service charge **charj servisyow**
m.: *v.* **charjya**
charger *n.* (horse) **kasvargh** *m.*
kasvergh, kourser *m.*
chariot *n.* **charet** *m.* **+ys, +ow**
charity *n.* **kerensa** *f.,* **cheryta** *m.;*
(body) **aluseneth** *f.* **+ow**; (gift of
money) **alusen** *f.* **+ow**
charm *n.* **hus** *m.,* **soen** *m.* **-yow**;
(item) **soenell** *f.* **+ow**: *v.*
didhana, husa, soena
charms *n.* remover of charms **peller**
m. **-oryon**
chart *n.* **tresenn** *f.* **+ow**
charter *n.* **chartour** *m.* **+s**
chase *n.* (for hunting) **helghva** *f.*
+ow: *v.* **chasya, helghya**; chase
along **dehelghya**; chase off **fesya**
chasing-tool *n.* **kollell gravya** *f.*

chassis *n.* **starn** *f.* **+yow**
chaste *adj.* **chast, gwar, gwyrgh**
chasten *v.* **chastya**
chastise *v.* **chastya, kessydhya**
chastisement *n.* **keredh** *f.*
chastity *n.* **chastyta** *m.*, **glander**
m.
chasuble *n.* **kasul** *m.*, **ofergugol** *m.*
chattels *n.* **chatel** *coll.*
chatter *n.* **klapp** *m.*; noisy chatter
klatter *m.*: *v.* **klappya, klattra**
chatterbox *n.* **tavosek** *m.*
tavosogyon
chatterer *n.* **klappyer** *m.* **+s**
cheap *adj.* **a bris isel**
cheat *n.* **hyg** *f.*: *v.* **toella, hyga**
check *n.* **lett** *m.* **+ow, +ys**: *v.*
chekkya
check-out *n.* **rekenva** *f.* **+ow**
cheek *n.* (Anat.) **bogh** *f.* **+ow** *dual*
diwvogh, grudh *f.*; (rudeness)
tonteth *f.*
cheeky *adj.* **tont**: *v.* be cheeky
tontya
cheer *v.* (gladden) **cherya**; cheer up
cherya, gwellha dha jer
cheese *n.* **keus** *m.* **+yow**
cheese-press *n.* **keuswask** *f.*
Cheesewring *n.* The Cheesewring
An Geuswask *f.*
chemical *adj.* **kymyk**
chemise *n.* **krys** *m.* **+yow**
chemist *n.* **kymyst** *m.* **+yon**
chemistry *n.* **kymygieth** *f.*
cheque *n.* **chekkenn** *f.* **+ow**; blank
cheque **chekkenn igor** *f.*
cherish *v.* **kovia**
cherished *adj.* **ker, drudh**
cherry *n.* **keresenn** *f.* **+ow** *coll.*
keres
cherub *n.* **cherub** *m.* **cherubim,**
elik *m.* **eledhigow**
chess *n.* **gwydhboell** *m.*
chessmen *n.* set of chessmen **meni**
m.

chest *n.* **argh** *f.* **+ow, kofer bras**
m.; (box) **trog** *m.* **+ow**; (container)
kyst *f.* **+yow**; chest of drawers
argh-dillas *f.* **arghow-dillas**
chestnut-tree *n.* **kestenenn** *f.*
+ow *coll.* **kesten**
chew *v.* chew the cud **dasknias**
chick *n.* **mabyar** *f.* **-yer**
chicken *n.* **yerik** *f.* **-igow**; chicken
meat **kig yar** *m.*; chicken pox
brygh yar *f.*
chicken-shed *n.* **krow yer** *m.*
chickweed *n.* **glydh** *m.*
chief *n.* chief executive
pennweythresek *m.* **-ogyon**:
adj. **chyf**
chieftain *n.* **penntern** *m.*
child *n.* **flogh** *m.* **fleghes**; female
child **myrgh** *f.* **myrghes**; little
child **fleghik** *m.* **fleghesigow**;
male child **mab** *m.* **mebyon**
childbed *n.* **gwelivos** *m.*
child-care *n.* **floghwith** *m.*
childhood *n.* **flogholeth** *f.*
childish *adj.* **floghel**
childless *adj.* **anvab**
childlessness *n.* **anvabas** *m.*
childlike *adj.* **floghel**
chill *n.* **anwoes** *m.*, **yeynder** *m.*: *v.*
yeynhe
chilly *n.* **anwoesek** *m.*
chimney *n.* **chymbla** *m.*
chymblow, chymblys; chimney
corner **korn an oeles** *m.*
chin *n.* **elgeth** *f.* **+yow**
china-clay *n.* **pri gwynn** *m.*; china-
clay pit **poll pri gwynn** *m.*
china-ware *n.* **cheni** *m.*
chip *n.* **askloesenn** *f.* **+ow** *coll.*
askloes, skommynn *m.*: *v.*
askloesi
chip-shop *n.* **askloetti** *m.* **+ow**
chirp *v.* **gryllya**
chirping *n.* **gryllyans** *m.*
chisel *n.* **genn** *m.* **+ow**: *v.* **genna**

chivalry *n.* chevalri *m.*,
    marghogieth *f.*
chocolate *n.* choklet *m.*
choice *n.* dewis *m.*
choir *n.* keur *m.* +yow
choke *v.* moga, taga
choked *v.* megys, tegys
choker *n.* tagell *f.* +ow
choking *n.* tag *m.*
cholera *n.* kolera *m.*
choose *v.* dewis
choosing *n.* dewisyans *m.* +ow
choosy *adj.* dewisek
chop *n.* tregh *m.* +ow: *v.* divynya,
    hakkya, nadha, skethra
chopping *n.* nadh *m.*
chore (U.S.) *n.* oberenn *f.* +ow
chortle *v.* roghwerthin
chough *n.* palores *f.* +ow
Christ *name* Krist
christen *v.* kristonhe, kristonya
christening *n.* besydhyans *m.*
Christian *n.* Christian man Kristyon
    m. Kristonyon; Christian woman
    Kristones *f.* +ow; fellow Christian
    keskristyon *m.* keskristonyon:
    adj. Kristyon
Christianity *n.* Kristoneth *f.*
Christmas *n.* Nadelik *m.*
church *n.* eglos *f.* +yow; endowed
    church mynster *m.*
church-site *n.* lann *f.* +ow
churchtown *n.* treveglos *f.* +yow
churchyard *n.* korflann *f.* +ow
churl *n.* chorl *m.* +ys
cicatrice *n.* kreyth *coll.* +enn
cider *n.* sider *m.*
cinder *n.* kolenn varow *f.*
cinquefoil *n.* pympdelenn *f.*
circle *n.* kylgh *m.* +yow, ros *f.*
    +ow; stone circle dons meyn *m.*
circlet *n.* kylghenn *f.* +ow

circuit *n.* tro *f.* +yow, kylghenn *f.*
    +ow, trogylgh *m.* +yow, trova *f.*
    +ow
circular *adj.* krenn, kylghyek
circumference *n.* kompas *m.*
circus *n.* (show) syrk *m.* +ow
cistern *n.* dowrargh *m.* +ow
citation *n.* devynn *m.* +ow
cite *v.* devynna
citizen *n.* burjes *m.* burjysi
city *n.* sita *f.* sitys
civil *adj.* sivil
civility *n.* sivilta *m.*
civilize *v.* hwarhe
civilized *adj.* doeth
claim *n.* chalenj *m.* +ys, kwarel
    m.: *plur.* miner's claim bounds:
    v. chalenjya, perghenna,
    perghennogi
clamour *n.* tros *m.* +yow, kri *m.*
    +ow
clan *n.* kordh *m.* +ow
clap *v.* clap hands takya
clarify *v.* klerhe
clarion *n.* kleryon *m.* +s
clarity *n.* klerder *m.*, ylynder *m.*
clasp *n.* brocha *m.* brochys
clasp-knife *n.* kollell bleg *f.*
class *n.* klas *m.* +ow, +ys; social
    class renkas *m.* +ow
classic *adj.* klasek
classification *n.* klasyans *m.* +ow
classify *v.* klasya
clatter *v.* klattra
claw *n.* ewin *m.* +es; (of crab) paw
    m. +yow: *v.* kravas, skravinyas
clawed *adj.* ewinek
clay *n.* pri *m.*
clayey *n.* clayey place priek *f.*
    priegi, prienn *f.* +ow
claymore *n.* kledha meur *m.*
claypit *n.* poll pri *m.*
clay-worker *n.* priweythor *m.*
    +yon

clay-works *n.* priweythva *f.* +ow
clean *adj.* glan, pur, glanyth: *v.*
glanhe
cleanliness *n.* glander *m.*,
glanythter *m.*
cleanse *v.* kartha
cleansing *n.* karth *m.* +yon; ethnic
cleansing karth ethnek *m.*
clear *adj.* kler; (clean) glan;
(distinct) diblans; (free) rydh;
(transparent) ylyn: *v.* glanhe,
klerhe
clearance *n.* (permission) kummyas
m.
clearing *n.* clearing in a wood
lannergh *m.* +i
clearness *n.* klerder *m.*
clearway *n.* klerfordh *f.* +ow
cleave *v.* folsa, klyjya
cleaver *n.* (plant) serghegenn *f.*
+ow *coll.* serghek
cleft *n.* fols *m.* +yow, ryll *f.* +ow,
saven *f.* savnow, sawn *f.* +yow
clemency *n.* kuvder *m.*
clergy *n.* klerji *c.*, prontereth *f.*
clergyman *n.* pronter *m.* +yon,
kloerek *m.*, mab-lyenn *m.*
mebyon-lyenn
cleric *n.* kloerek *m.*, mab-lyenn *m.*
mebyon-lyenn
clerk *n.* kloerek *m.*, skrifwas *m.*
-wesyon; bank clerk arghanswas
m. -wesyon; solicitor's clerk
laghwas *m.* -wesyon
clerkship *n.* kloeregieth *f.*
clever *adj.* konnyk, sley
cleverness *n.* sleyneth *f.*
cliff *n.* als *f.* +yow, kleger *m.* +ow,
klog *f.*, leder *f.* ledrow
cliffed *adj.* klegerek
climate *n.* hin *f.*
climatology *n.* hinonieth *f.*
climax *n.* barr *m.* +ow
climb *v.* krambla, yskynna; climb
by ladder skeulya

cling *v.* glena, grabalyas, serghi;
cling together kesklena
clinging *adj.* serghek
clinic *n.* medhygva *f.* +ow
clink *v.* tynkyal
clip *n.* (e.g. paper-clip) synsell *f.*
+ow
clippers *plur.* gwelsow
clitter *n.* radell *m.*
cloak *n.* mantell *f.* mantelli, klok
m. +ys, kop *m.* +ys; hooded cloak
huk *f.* +ys; hooded fur cloak
penngogh *m.* +ow
clock *n.* klokk *m.* +ow
clockwork *n.* klokkweyth *m.*
cloister *n.* kloyster *m.* kloysters
close *n.* park *m.* +ow, klos *m.*
+yow, +ys; monastic close lann *f.*
+ow: *adj.* ogas, poes: *prep.*
close to ryb: *v.* degea
closed *adj.* deges, klos
closer *adv.* yn-nes
close-shaven *adj.* blogh
clot *n.* kowlesenn *f.* +ow *coll.*
kowles, mol *m.* +yow: *v.* kowla,
mola
cloth *n.* kweth *f.* +ow, pann *m.*
+ow, lenn *f.* +ow; bolting cloth
yskar *m.*; linen cloth lien *m.*
+ow; woven cloth gwias *m.* +ow
clothe *v.* gwiska, dillasi, kwetha,
lenni
clothes *n.* dillas *coll.* +enn
clothing *n.* dillas *coll.* +enn; layer
of clothing gwiskas *m.* +ow;
safety clothing dillas diogeledh
coll.: *v.* put on clothing
omgwetha, omwiska
cloud *n.* individual cloud
kommolenn *f.* +ow *coll.* kommol
cloudless *adj.* digommol
cloudy *adj.* kommolek
clout *n.* klout *m.* +ys
clove *n.* clove of garlic ewin kennin
m.
clover *n.* mellyon *coll.* +enn

clover-patch *n.* mellyonek *f.* -egi

clovery *adj.* mellyonek

clown *n.* lorden *m.* +yon, +s

cloy *v.* gwalgha

club *n.* (weapon) fust *f.* +ow

club-footed *adj.* pawgamm

clue *n.* gedyans *m.*

clump *n.* bonni *m.*

cluster *n.* bonni *m.*

clutch *n.* (in car) krafell *f.* +ow: *v.* grabalyas, klyjya

coach *n.* kocha *m.* kochow, kochys

coagulate *v.* kowla

coagulation *n.* kowles *coll.* +enn

coal *n.* glow *coll.* +enn; (one lump) glowenn *f.* glow; burning coal kolenn leskys *f.;* coal of fire kolenn *f.* +ow; live coal kolenn vyw *f.,* regydhenn *f.* +ow *coll.* regydh; place abounding in coal glowek *f.* +egi

coalfield *n.* glowek *f.* +egi

coal-heap *n.* glowek *f.* +egi

coal-house *n.* glowji *m.* +ow

coalpit *n.* poll glow *m.*

coal-shed *n.* glowji *m.* +ow

coal-tit *n.* penn-glow *m.*

coarse *adj.* garow

coast *n.* arvor *m.,* morrep *m.*

coastal *adj.* arvorek

coastland *n.* arvor *m.*

coat *n.* kota *m.* kotow, pows *f.* +yow; coat of mail kaspows *f.;* short coat jerkynn *m.;* sleeveless coat of chainmail hoberjon *m.:* *v.* gwiska; coat with film kenna

coating *n.* gwiskas *m.* +ow, pil *coll.* +enn

coat-of-arms *n.* kota arvow *m.*

coax *v.* dynya

cob *n.* hobi *m.* +s

cobble *v.* kerya

cobbler *n.* keryer *m.* -oryon

cock *n.* kulyek *m.* kulyogyon

cockcrow *n.* kulyek-kenys *m.*

cockle *n.* koklysenn *f.* +ow *coll.* koklys

code *n.* kodenn *f.* +ow

codfish *n.* barvus *m.* +i

coffee *n.* koffi *m.:* *adv.* instant coffee koffi desempis

coffee-house *n.* koffiji *m.* +ow

coffer *n.* argh *f.* +ow, kofer *m.* kofrow, kofrys

coffin *n.* geler *f.* +yow, logel *f.* +ow, trog *m.* +ow; coffin mine koghynn *m.* +ow

cognate *adj.* keslinek

cohabit *v.* kesvywa

cohabitation *n.* kesvywnans *m.*

coil *v.* terghi

coin *n.* bath *m.* +ow; copper coin koberenn *f.* +ow: *v.* batha

coinage *n.* coinage of tin koynach *m.*

coincide *v.* keslamma

coincidence *n.* keslamm *m.* +ow

coiner *n.* bathor *m.* +yon

colander *n.* tellvolla *m.* -vollow

cold *n.* anwoes *m.,* yeynder *m.,* yeynyjyon *m.;* apt to catch cold anwoesek *m.:* *adj.* yeyn; excessively cold oer: *v.* catch cold anwoesi

collaborate *v.* kesoberi

collaborator *n.* kesoberer *m.* +yon

collate *v.* keskorra

collateral *adj.* keslinek

collateral (U.S.) *n.* gwystel *m.* gwystlow

colleague *n.* kowethyades *f.* +ow, kowethyas *m.* -ysi

collect *v.* (intrans.) omguntell; (trans.) kuntell; collect leaves delyowa

collection *n.* kuntell *m.* +ow

college *n.* kollji *m.* +ow

collinear *adj.* keslinel

collop *n.* goleyth *m.*

colonial *adj.* **trevesigel**
colony *n.* **trevesigeth** *f.*
coloration *n.* **liwyans** *m.* **+ow**
colostomy *n.* **kraw-kolon** *m.*
colour *n.* **liw** *m.* **liwyow**; colour of
material **sewt** *m.:* *v.* **liwya**
coloured *adj.* **liwek**
colouring *n.* **liwyans** *m.* **+ow**
colourless *adj.* **diliw**
colt *n.* **ebel** *m.* **ebelli**
coltsfoot *n.* **alann** *coll.*
column *n.* **koloven** *f.* **+yow, post**
m. **+ow**
comb *n.* **krib** *f.* **+ow, restrer** *m.:* *v.*
kribas
combination *n.* **kesunyans** *m.*
+ow
combine *v.* **kesunya**
combings *plur.* **kribyon**
combustion *n.* **losk** *m.,* **loskvann**
m.
come *adj.* **devedhys**; come to pass
hwarvedhys: *v.* **dos, devones,**
dones; come after **holya**; come
and go **daromres**; come back
dehweles; come to **dos ha**; come
to pass **hwarvos**
comedian *n.* **gesyer** *m.*
gesyoryon
comely *adj.* **kader**
comet *n.* **sterenn lostek** *f.*
comfort *n.* **es** *m.;* (spiritual)
konfort *m.:* *v.* **konfortya,**
lowenhe; comfort oneself
omgonfortya
comfortable *adj.* **attes**
comforter *n.* **konforter** *m.* **+s**
comic *n.* **gesyer** *m.* **gesyoryon**:
adj. **hwarthus**
command *n.* **arghadow** *m.* **+yow,**
gorhemmynn *m.* **+ow**: *v.* **erghi,**
gorhemmynn
commandment *n.* **arghadow** *m.*
+yow, gorhemmynn *m.* **+ow**;
commandments
gorhemmynnadow *m.*

commemorate *v.* **kovhe**
commemoration *n.* **kovheans** *m.*
commencement *n.* **dalleth** *m.,*
derow *m.*
commend *v.* **kommendya**
commendation *n.* **kemmynneth** *f.*
+ow
comment *n.* **kampoell** *m.* **+ow**
commerce *n.* **kenwerth** *m.*
commercial *adj.* **kenwerthel**
commission *n.* (group of persons)
desedhek *m.* **desedhogow**;
(money) **rannles** *m.* **+ow**;
Boundary Commission **Desedhek**
an Oryon *m.;* Millennium
Commission **Desedhek an**
Vilvlydhen *m.*
commissioner *n.* **desedheger** *m.*
-oryon
commit *v.* **kommyttya**
committee *n.* **kessedhek** *m.*
-sedhogow
commodities *n.* **gwara** *m.*
common *adj.* **kemmyn**
commoner *n.* **kemmyn** *m.* **+yon**
commotion *n.* **freudh** *m.*
communicate *v.* **keskomunya**
communication *v.*
keskomunyans +ow
communion *n.* **komun** *m.,*
komunyans *m.;* Holy Communion
Komun Sans *m.,* **Komunyans**
Sans *m.:* *v.* take Communion
komunya
communism *n.* **kemmynegoreth**
f.
communist *n.* **kemmynegor** *m.*
+yon, kemmynegores *f.* **+ow**:
adj. **kemmynegorek**
community *n.* **kemmynieth** *f.*
compact *n.* compact disc **plasenn**
arghansek *f.*
companion *n.* **kila** *m.,* **keskoweth**
m. **+a, mata** *m.* **matys**; female
companion **kowethes** *f.* **+ow**; male

companion **koweth** *m.* **+a**; table
companion **kevywyas** *m.* **-ysi**
company *n.* **kowethyans** *m.:* *v.*
keep company **kowethya**
compare *v.* **keheveli**
compassion *n.* **pyteth** *f.,* **truedh** *m.*
compassionate *adj.* **pytethus,**
truedhek
compatible *adj.* **kesplegadow**
compel *v.* **kompella**
compensate *v.* **astiveri**
compensation *n.* **astiveryans** *m.*
compete *v.* **kesstrivya**
competition *n.* **kesstrif** *m.*
competitor *n.* **kesstrivor** *m.* **+yon**
complain *v.* **krodhvolas**; complain
at **krodhvolas orth**
complainer *n.* **grolyek** *m.* **-ogyon**
complaint *n.* **gyth** *m.,* **krodhvol** *m.*
+yow; (medical) **grevons** *m.*
complaisant *adj.* **omvodhek**: *v.*
be complaisant **omvodhya**
complete *adj.* **kowal, dien**: *v.*
kollenwel, kowlwul
completely *adv.* **glan, teg, yn tien,**
yn tien, kwit
completeness *n.* **dieneth** *f.*
complex *adj.* **komplek, kompleth**
complexion *n.* **liw** *m.* **liwyow,**
fisment *m.* **fismens**
complicated *adj.* **komplek,**
kompleth
Compline *n.* **Komplin** *m.*
comprehend *v.* **konvedhes**
compress *v.* **gwaska**
compression *n.* **gwaskedh** *m.*
compute *v.* **amontya**
computer *n.* **jynn-amontya** *m.*
jynnow-amontya
computer program *n.* **programm**
m.
computing *n.* **amontieth** *f.*
comrade *n.* **kothman** *m.* **+s, mata**
m. **matys**
con *v.* (direct a vessel) **brennya**

conceal *v.* **kudha, keles**
concealed *adj.* **kudh**
concealment *n.* **keladow** *m.,*
kovva *f.,* **kudhans** *m.*
concede *v.* **amyttya**
conceive *v.* **konsevya**; (a child)
omdhoen
concern *n.* **bern** *m.:* *phr.* it does
not concern me **ny'm deur**; it is of
no concern **ny vern**
concerning *prep.* **yn kever**: *adv.*
a-dro dhe
concert *n.* **goel ilow** *m.,* **keskan** *f.*
+ow
conclude *v.* **gorfenna, diwedha**
conclusion *n.* **gordhiwedh** *m.,*
gorfenn *m.*
concourse *n.* **lown** *m.* **+yow**
concrete *n.* **kentevynn** *m.*
concussion *n.* **kryghyllyans** *m.*
condemn *v.* **dampnya**
condemnation *n.* **dampnyans** *m.*
condenser *n.* **dalghasell** *f.* **+ow**
condition *n.* **plit** *m.,* **studh** *m.*
+yow
condole *v.* **keskalari,**
keskodhevel
condolence *n.* **keskalar** *m.* **+ow**
conduct *n.* **fara** *m.:* *v.* **hembronk,**
gedya, ledya
conductor *n.* **hembrenkyas** *m.*
-ysi
conduit *n.* **goeth** *f.* **+ow**
cone *n.* **pigorn** *m.* **pigern**
coney *n.* **konin** *m.* **+es**
confection *n.* **kyfeyth** *m.* **+yow**
confectioner *n.* **kyfeythyer** *m.*
-yoryon
confederate *n.* **keffrysyas** *m.* **-ysi**
conference *n.* **keskusulyans** *m.*
+ow; summit conference
keskusulyans barrek *m.*
confess *n.* **konfessya** *m.:* *v.*
avowa; (of sins) **yes**; confess sins
meneges

confide *v.* **fydhya,** confide in **kyfi**
confidence *n.* **fydhyans** *m.*,
   kresys *m.*, **kyfyans** *m.*
confined *adj.* **ynn**
confirm *v.* **afydhya, surhe**
confound *v.* konfondya
confraternity *n.* **kenbrederedh** *m.*
confuse *v.* **penndaga**
confused *adj.* **penndegys**: *v.* be
   confused **sowdhanas**
confusion *n.* **deray** *m.* **+s,**
   sowdhan *m.*
confute *n.* konviktya *m.*
congratulate *v.* **keslowenhe**
congratulations *n.* **keslowena** *f.*
congress *n.* **kuntelles** *m.* **+ow;**
   Celtic Congress **Kuntelles Keltek**
   m.
conical *adj.* **pigornek**
conifer *n.* **sabenn** *f.* **+ow** *coll.* **sab**
conjugal *adj.* **priosel**
conman (U.S.) *n.* **kammfydhwas**
   m. **-wesyon**
conning *n.* conning tower **brennva** *f.*
conquer *v.* **fetha, tryghi**
conqueror *n.* **trygher** *m.* **-oryon**
conquest *n.* **trygh** *m.*
conscience *n.* **konshyans** *m.*,
   kowses *m.* **+yow**
conscientious *adj.* **diwysek**
consciousness *n.* **omwodhvos** *m.*:
   v. lose consciousness **klamdera**
consecrate *v.* **sakra**
consent *n.* **bodh** *m.*: *v.* **assentya**
consequence *n.* **sywyans** *m.* **+ow**
consequent *v.* be consequent upon
   omsywya
consider *v.* **prederi, ombrederi**
consideration *n.* **avis** *m.*
consist *v.* konsystya
consistent *adj.* **kesson**
consolation *n.* konfort *m.*
console *v.* **konfortya**
consomme *n.* **iskell pur** *m.*

consonant *n.* **kessonenn** *f.* **+ow**
consonantal *adj.* **kessonennel**
consort *v.* **kowethya**
conspiracy *n.* **bras** *m.*
conspirator *n.* **braser** *m.* **-oryon**
constant *adj.* **sad**
constituency *n.* **pastell-vro** *f.*
constitution *n.* **korf-lagha** *m.*
constrain *v.* **strotha**
constrict *v.* **strotha, taga**
constriction *n.* **tagell** *f.* **+ow**
consultant *n.* **kusulyas** *m.* **-ysi**
consultation *n.* **kusulyans** *m.* **+ow**
consultative *adj.* **kusulyek**
consumer *n.* **devnydhyer** *m.* **-**
   yoryon
contact *n.* **kestav** *m.* **+ow**: *v.*
   kestava
contemporary *adj.* **kevoes;**
   contemporary with **kevoes gans**
contempt *n.* **bysmer** *m.*: *phr.*
   bring into contempt **gul bysmer**
   dhe
contend *v.* **debatya, kenkia,**
   strivya
content *n.* **dalgh** *m.* **+ow**: *adj*
   lowen
contention *n.* **strivyans** *m.*
contentious *adj.* **kavillek**
contents *n.* **synsas** *m.* **+ow**
context *n.* **kettestenn** *f.* **+ow**
continent *n.* **brastir** *m.* **+yow**
continually *adv.* **prest**
continue *v.* **pesya**
contraband *n.* contraband goods
   noswara *m.*: *adj.* **noswikorek**
contrabandist *n.* **noswikor** *m.*
   +yon
contraceptive *n.* **haslett** *m.* **+ow**
contract *n.* **ambos** *m.* **+ow,**
   kevambos *m.* **+ow;** breach of
   contract **torrva ambos** *f.*
contradict *v.* **kontradia**

contrary *adj.* **gorth, konter, kontrari**
contribute *v.* **kevri**
contribution *n.* **kevro** *m.* **kevrohow**
contributor *n.* **kevriyas** *m.* **kevriysi**
contrite *adj.* **keudhesik**
contrition *n.* **keudhesigeth** *f.*
contrivance *n.* **darbar** *m.*
contrive *v.* **devisya, framya**
control *n.* **maystri** *m.,* **ordenans** *m.;* control tower **tour routya** *m.:* *v.* **kontrolya, rewlya, routya:** *phr.* exercise control over **gul maystri orth**
controller *n.* **router** *m.* **+s**
controversy *n.* **kontroversita** *m.* **-sitys**
controvert *v.* **kontradia**
convection *n.* **bryjyon** *m.*
convective *adj.* **bryjyek**
convenience *n.* **es** *m.*
conveniences *plur.* (toilets) **privedhyow**
conversation *n.* **keskows** *m.* **+ow**
converse *v.* **kewsel;** (speech) **keskewsel**
convert *v.* **treylya**
convey *v.* convey an estate **statya**
conviction *n.* **kowses** *m.* **+yow**
cook *n.* **keginer** *m.* **-oryon, kog** *m.* **+ow, koges** *f.:* *v.* **kegi, pareusi**
cooked *adj.* **kegys, parys**
cooker *n.* **kogforn** *f.* **+ow**
cookery *n.* **keginieth** *f.*
cookie (U.S.) *n.* **tesenn gales** *f.*
cooking-stove *n.* **kogforn** *f.* **+ow**
cool *adj.* **goyeyn:** *v.* **yeynhe;** cool off **mygli**
cooper *n.* **bonkyer** *m.* **-oryon**
co-operate *v.* **kesoberi**
co-ordinate *v.* **kesordena**
co-ordinator *n.* **kesordenor** *m.* **+yon**

coot *n.* **dowryar** *f.* **-yer**
cope *n.* **kop** *m.* **+ys**
copper *n.* **kober** *m.;* copper coin **koberenn** *f.* **+ow**
coppersmith *n.* **gweythor kober** *m.*
copperwork *n.* **koberweyth** *m.*
copse *n.* **kelli** *f.* **kelliow, pryskwydh** *coll.*
copy *n.* **dasskrif** *m.* **+ow, daswrians** *m.* **+ow, kopi** *m.* **+ow:** *v.* **dasskrifa, kopia**
copyright *v.* **gwirbryntya:** *n.,* **gwirbryntyans** *m.*
cord *n.* **kordenn** *f.* **kerdyn, funenn** *f.* **+ow;** cord for fastening **sygenn** *f.*
core *n.* (of apple, etc.) **kolonnenn** *f.* **+ow**
cork *n.* (stopper) **korkynn** *m.* **+ow**
corkscrew *n.* **alhwedh-korkynn** *m.* **alhwedhow-korkynn**
cormorant *n.* **morvran** *f.* **-vrini, spilgarn** *m.*
corn *n.* **ys** *coll.* **+enn;** ear of corn **penn-ys** *m.* **pennow-ys:** *adj.* rich in corn **ysek**
corner *n.* **korn** *m.* **kernow, kornell** *f.* **+ow, sorn** *m.* **+ow;** chimney corner **korn an oeles** *m.*
cornerstone *n.* **pennmen** *m.* **-meyn**
cornet *n.* **tollgorn** *m.* **tollgern**
cornfield *n.* **ysek** *f.* **-egi**
Cornicize *v.* **Kernewekhe**
Cornish *n.* Cornish language **Kernewek** *m.;* Cornish Language Fellowship **Kowethas an Yeth Kernewek** *m.;* Cornish speaker **Kerneweger** *m.* **-oryon;** Late Cornish **Kernewek Diwedhes** *m.;* Middle Cornish **Kernewek Kres** *m.;* Old Cornish **Kernewek Koth** *m.;* Revived Cornish **Kernewek Dasserghys** *m.:* *adj.* **Kernewek:** *v.* make Cornish **Kernewekhe**

Cornishman n. Kernow m. +yon
Cornishwoman n. Kernewes f.
  +ow
corn-marigold n. bodhenn f.,
  kaja velyn f.
corn-poppy n. myll f. +es
Cornwall n. Kernow f.; Cornwall
  Tourist Board Kesva Tornyaseth
  Kernow f.
coronation n. kurunans m.
coronet n. kurunik f. -igow
corpulent adj. korfek
correct adj. ewn, kewar: v. ewna;
  correct oneself omamendya
correctable adj. ewnadow
correction n. ewnans m. +ow
correctness n. kewerder m.
correspond v. kesskrifa
correspondent n. kesskrifer m.
  -oryon
corresponding adj. kehaval
corrosion n. kanker m. kankres
corrugated adj. kevryllys
corrupt adj. podrek, poder,
  podredhek: v. pedri
corruption n. podredhes m.
cost n. kost m. +ys, kostyans m.:
  v. kostya
costly adj. ker, kostek
costmary n. kosta m.
costs plur. maintenance costs
  kostow-mentons: phr. at all
  costs awos tra
cosy adj. klys
cot n. (small house) pennti m. +ow
cottage n. pennti m. +ow; one-
  roomed cottage krowji m. +ow;
  small cottage dyji m. +ow
cotton n. koton m.
cotton-grass n. goenbluv coll.
cotton-wool n. gwlan koton coll.
couch n. gorwedhva f. +ow
couch-grass n. couch-grass
  treuswels coll.
cough n. pas m. +ow: v. pasa

coulter n. coulter of plough kolter m.
  koltrow, trogher m. +yow
council n. konsel m.; Security
  Council Konsel Diogeledh m.
councillor n. konseler m. -oryon
counsel n. kusul f. +yow: v.
  kusulya
counsellor n. kusulyer m. -oryon
count n. (census) niveryans m.;
  (nobleman) yurl m. yurlys: v.
  nivera, akontya, amontya,
  rekna
countenance n. (face) fisment m.
  fismens
counter v. gorthybi
counterbalance n. gorthpoes m.
  +ow: v. gorthpoesa
counterclaim n. klem m. +ys
counterfoil n. gorthdhelenn f.
  +ow
counterpoint n. (music)
  gorthpoynt m.
counterpoise n. gorthpoes m.
  +ow
countersink v. gorthsedhi
counter-tenor n. konternot m.
counterweight n. gorthpoes m.
  +ow
counting n. niveryans m.: prep.
  not counting heb
country n. bro f. +yow, gwlas f.
  +ow, pow m. +yow, tiredh m.;
  chief country pennwlas f. +ow;
  country seat plas m. plassow,
  trigva f. +ow; open country mes
  m. +yow: adj. pertaining to a
  country gwlasek
countryman n. trevesik m. -igyon
countrywoman n. tioges f. +ow,
  trevesiges f. +ow
county n. konteth f. +ow
couple n. dewdhen m., kopel m.
  koplow; married couple dewbries
  m.: v. parya
courage n. kolonn f. +ow,
  kolonnekter m., vertu f. +s

course *n.* hyns *m.* +yow, kors *m.*,
res *m.*, resegva *f.* +ow; (of meal)
sand *m.* +ys; (of study) steus *f.*
+ow
court *n.* lys *f.* +yow; court of law
breuslys *f.* +yow, lys an lagha *f.;*
old court hellys *f.* +yow
courteous *adj.* kortes
courtesy *n.* kortesi *m.*
courtier *n.* lyswas *m.* -wesyon
courtship *n.* tantans *m.*
cousin *n.* (female) keniterow *f.*
keniterwi; (male) kenderow *m.*
kenderwi
cove *n.* porth *m.* +ow
covenant *n.* ambos *m.* +ow,
kevambos *m.* +ow
cover *n.* gorher *m.* +yow, goskes
m.; (hiding-place) kudhans *m.;*
(of a book) kudhlenn *f.;* (of
beehive) kogh *m.* +ow: *v.*
gorheri, lenni; put under cover
goskeusi
covering *n.* gorheras *m.*, gwiskas
m. +ow, kudhans *m.;* (material)
pallenn *f.* +ow
covert *adj.* kudh
covet *v.* hwansa, kovaytya
covetousness *n.* kovaytys *m.*
cow *n.* bugh *f.* +es; calfless cow
gownagh *f.*
coward *n.* ownek *m.* ownogyon,
kilgi *m.* kilgeun
cowardice *n.* kowardi *m.*
cowboy *n.* bughwas *m.* -wesyon
cow-dung *n.* dried cow-dung used as
fuel glos *coll.* +enn
cower *v.* plattya
cow-fold *n.* bowlann *f.* +ow
cowherd *n.* bugel gwarthek *m.*,
bugel lodhnow *m.*
cowhide *n.* bughkenn *m.*
cow-house *n.* bowji *m.* +ow
cowl *n.* kugol *m.*
co-worker *n.* kesoberer *m.* +yon

cowshed *n.* bowji *m.* +ow, chi
miles *m.*
crab *n.* kanker *m.* kankres;
harbour-crab peberynn *m.* +ow;
spider-crab tragesort *m.* +es
crab-pot *n.* kowell kankres *m.*
crack *n.* krakk *m.* +ys: *v.* krakkya
crack-down *n.* gorgeredh *f.* +ow
cracked *adj.* trogh
cracked-voiced *adj.* grolyek
cradle *n.* kowell lesk *m.*, lesk *m.*
+ow
craft *n.* kreft *f.* +ow, myster *m.*
craftsman *n.* kreftor *m.* +yon,
mysterden *m.* +s, ser *m.* +i
crafty *adj.* fel, sotel
crag *n.* kleger *m.* +ow, klog *f.*
craggy *adj.* klegerek
craker *n.* grolyek *m.* -ogyon
craking *adj.* grolyek
cramp *n.* godramm *m.*
cranberry-bush *n.* korswigenn *f.*
+ow *coll.* korswik
crane *n.* garan *f.* +es
crankshaft *n.* gwelenn-
dhornigell *f.* gwelynni-dornigell
crash-barrier *n.* skoeske *m.* +ow
crate *n.* kloes *f.* +yow
crave *v.* yeuni
craving *n.* ewl *f.* +ow, yeunadow
m., yeunogneth *f.:* *adj.* yeunek
crawl *v.* kramya, pedrevanas
crayon *n.* kreyon *m.* +yow
crazy *adj.* fol
cream *n.* dyenn *m.* +ow; clotted
cream dyenn molys *m.:* *v.* form
cream dyenna
creamy *adj.* dyennek
create *v.* gwruthyl
creation *n.* gwrians *m.* +ow
creative *adj.* awenek
creator *n.* furvyer *m.* furvyoryon,
gwrier *m.*, kreador *m.*
creature *n.* kroadur *m.;* creeping
creature pryv *m.* +es, +yon

credentials *n.* lytherow kresys *m.*
credit *n.* brif., kresys *m.*
credit-card *n.* kartenn-gresys*f*
kartennow-kresys
creditor *n.* kresysor *m.* +yon,
kresysores*f.* +ow
credulity *n.* hegoeledh *m.*
credulous *adj.* hegoel
creed *n.* kryjyans *m.*
creek *n.* heylynn *m.* +ow, korn
dowr *m.*
creek (U.S.) *n.* gover *m.* +ow
creep *v.* slynkya, krambla,
kramya, kreupya; creep on all
fours pedrevanas
crescent *n.* krommenn*f.*
cress-bed *n.* belerek*f.* -egi
cressy *adj.* belerek
crest *n.* krib*f.* +ow, kribenn*f.* +ow
crew *n.* meni *m.*
cricket *n.* (insect) gryll *m.* +es,
krygell*f.*
crier *n.* krier *m.* -oryon; town crier
krier an dre *m.*
crime *n.* drogober *m.* +ow,
galweyth *m.* +yow, hager ober
m.
criminal *n.* drogoberer *m.* -oryon,
gal *m.* +yon
crinkle *n.* krygh *m.* +yow: *v.*
krygha
cripple *n.* evredhek *m.* -ogyon,
evredh *m.* +yon, evredhes*f.*
+ow, mans *m.* +yon
crippled *adj.* evredhek, evredh,
evr'ek, mans
crisis *n.* barras *m.* +ow
criterion *n.* breusverk *m.* +ow
critic *n.* breusyas *m.* -ysi, krytyk
m.
critical *adj.* tykkli
criticism *n.* breus*f.* +ow
croak *n.* ronk *m.*: *v.* renki
croaking *adj.* ronk

crock *n.* chekk *m.* +ys, seth *m.*
+ow; (large jar) per *m.* +yow
crocodile *n.* krokodil *m.* +es
croft *n.* kroft *m.* +ow
cromlech *n.* krommlegh*f.* +yow
crook *n.* bagel*f.* baglow, bagh*f.*
+ow; crook for catching sand-eels
fynngler *m.:* *v.* use a crook for
catching sand-eels fynngla
crooked *n.* person who is morally
crooked kamm *m.* +ow: *adj.*
kamm, kromm; (crook-shaped)
baglek
crookedness *n.* kammder *m.*
crooked-shouldered *adj.*
kammskoedhek
crook-shanked *adj.* berrgamm,
garrgamm
crop *n.* trevas*f.* +ow; bird's crop
kroth*f.:* *v.* (truncate) dibenna
cross *n.* krows*f.* +yow; little cross
krowsik*f.* -igow: *adj.* konter,
treus: *v.* treusi; cross by a ferry
tretha; cross oneself omsoena
cross-bar *n.* treusprenn *m.* +yer,
treuster *m.* treustrow
cross-beam *n.* treuster *m.*
treustrow
crossbow *n.* fustwarak*f.* -
waregow
cross-hairs *n.* resell*f.* +ow
crossing *n.* treusva*f.* +ow; level
crossing on a railway treusva
hyns-horn*f.*
cross-piece *n.* treusprenn *m.* +yer
cross-purposes *adv.* talk at cross-
purposes kewsel a-dreus
crossroads *n.* krowshyns *m.*
+yow, krowsfordh*f.* +ow
cross-saw *n.* treus-heskenn*f.*
+ow
cross-shaped *adj.* krowsek
cross-tempered *adj.* krowsek
cross-wire *n.* resell*f.* +ow
crosswise *adj.* set crosswise
krowsek

crossword *plur.* crossword puzzle
krowseryow
crotch *n.* **gowl** *f.* **+ow**
crouch *v.* **plattya**
crow *n.* **bran** *f.* **brini**; hooded crow
bran loes *f.*, **bran Marghas Yow**
f.
crowd *n.* **bush** *m.* **+ys, lu** *m.* **+yow**,
routh *f.* **+ow, tonnek** *m.*
crowing *n.* (of cock) **kenys** *m.*
crown *n.* **kurun** *f.* **+yow**; (of hat)
kogh *m.* **+ow**; crown of thorns
kurun spern *f.:* *v.* **kuruna**
crows-staff *n.* **krowsprenn** *f.* **+yer**
crozier *n.* **bagel** *f.* **baglow**
crozier-bearer *n.* **krosser** *m.* **+s**
crucible *n.* **teudhlester** *m.* **-lestri**
crucifix *n.* **krowsprenn** *f.* **+yer**
crucify *v.* **krowsya**
cruel *adj.* **fell, tynn**
cruelty *n.* **hakter** *m.*, **fellder** *m.*
crumb *n.* **brewyonenn** *f.* **+ow** *coll.*
brewyon, browsyonenn *f.* **+ow**
coll. **browsyon**; (of loaf)
hwigenn *f.*
crumble *v.* **brewi, browsi**
crumbled *n.* crumbled material
brows *coll.*
crush *v.* **brewi, skwatya**; crush
inwards **kropya**
crust *n.* **krevenn** *f.* **+ow**
crutch *n.* **kroch** *m.* **+ow** *dual*
dewgroch, +ys; pair of crutches
dewgroch
cry *n.* **lev** *m.* **+ow, kri** *m.* **+ow**: *v.*
kria, oulya; (weep) **oela**; cry fie
on **fia**; cry out **garma, leva, skrija**
crystal *n.* **gwrys** *m.* **+ow**
cub *n.* **kolyn** *m.* **kelyn**
cube *n.* **kub** *m.* **+ow**
cubit *n.* **kevelin** *m.* **+yow**
cuckoo *n.* **kog** *f.* **+es, koukow** *f.* **+s**
cudgel *n.* **batt** *m.* **+ys**
cuff *v.* **boksusi**
cuisine *n.* **keginieth** *f.*

cul-de-sac *n.* **fordh dhall** *f.*, **fordh-
dhall** *f.* **fordhow-dall**
culpable *adj.* **kablus**
cultivated *n.* cultivated land **mesek**
f.
cultural *adj.* **gonisogethek**
culture *n.* **gonisogeth** *f.*,
megyans *m.*
culverhouse *n.* **kolommji** *m.* **+ow**
cummerbund *n.* **torrgyngel** *f.*
cunning *n.* **felder** *m.*, **kallder** *m.:*
adj. **fel, kall**
cup *n.* **hanaf** *m.* **+ow, kib** *f.;*
shallow cup **fiol** *f.* **+yow**
cupboard *n.* **amari** *m.* **+ow, +s**
cupful *n.* **hanafas** *m.* **+ow**
cupidity *n.* **pithneth** *f.*
cur *n.* savage cur **brathki** *m.* **-keun**
curb *v.* **fronna**
curd *n.* **kowles** *coll.* **+enn**
curdle *v.* **kowla**; curdle with rennet
godroetha
cure *n.* **kur** *m.:* *v.* **yaghhe**
curl *v.* **krollya**
curlew *n.* **gelvinek** *m.*
gelvinogyon
currency *n.* **mona kemmyn** *m.*
current *n.* (flow) **fros** *m.* **+ow**: *adj.*
(as in current affairs) **a-lemmyn**
currier *n.* (one who colours leather)
kroener *m.* **-oryon**
curry *v.* curry a horse **streylya**
currycomb *n.* **streyl** *f.*
curse *n.* **molleth** *f.* **mollothow**;
God's curse **molla'tyw** *f.:* *v.*
emskemunya, milliga, mollethi
cursed *adj.* **mollothek**
cursor *n.* **resell** *f.* **+ow**
curtain *n.* **kroglenn** *f.* **+ow**
curve *n.* **gwarr** *f.* **+ow, krommenn**
f.: *v.* **kamma**
curved *adj.* **kromm**
cushion *n.* **pluvek** *f.* **pluvogow**
custody *n.* **gwith** *m.*

custom *n.* devos *m.* +ow, gis *m.*,
maner *f.* +ow, us *m.:* *adv.*
according to custom herwydh
usadow
customary *adj.* devosel
customs-house *n.* tollji *m.* +ow
cut *n.* (incision) trogh *m.* +ow;
(slice) tregh *m.* +ow: *adj.* trogh:
v. treghi, lownya; cut in quarters
kwartrona; cut up divynya; make
a first cut or bite in attamya
cutlass *n.* kledha kromm *m.*
cutlery *n.* daffar lymm *m.*
cuttable *adj.* hedrogh
cutter *n.* tregher *m.* -oryon,
treghyas *m.* -ysi
cutting *n.* (e.g. on road) troghva *f.*
+ow
cuttlebone *n.* tag-hir *m.*
cycle *n.* (of motion) troweyth *f.*
+yow: *v.* diwrosa
cycling *n.* diwrosa *m.*
cyclops *n.* unnlagasek *m.*
cylindrical *adj.* hirgrenn
cymbal *n.* symbal *m.* +ys
Czech *n.* Czech Republic Pow Chek
m.

D

dace *n.* talek *m.* taloges
daddy *n.* tasik *m.*
daffodil *n.* lili Korawys *m.*
dagger *n.* dagyer *m.* +s, kledha
byghan *m.*
dainty *adj.* denti
dairy *n.* le'ti *m.;* dairy produce
askorr lethek *m.*
daisy *n.* boreles *m.*, kaja *f.;* ox-eye
daisy kaja vras *f.*
dale *n.* nans *m.* +ow
dally *v.* trufla
dam *n.* tommenn *f.* +ow

damage *n.* koll *m.*, damaj *m.;*
storm damage arnow *m.:* *v.*
kisya; damage by weather arnewa
dame *n.* dama *f.* damys
damn *v.* dampnya
damnation *n.* dampnyans *m.*
damp *n.* glybor *m.;* damp place
soegenn *f.:* *adj.* glyb, gwlygh
damsel *n.* damsel *f.* +s
dance *n.* dons *m.* +yow; dance in a
ring tremadheves *m.;* dance to
sung music karol *m.* +yow: *v.*
donsya; dance to sung music
karoli
dancer *n.* donsyer *m.* -oryon,
donsyores *f.* +ow
dandelion *n.* dans-lew *m.*, les
densek *m.*
danger *n.* peryll *m.* +ow, hakter
m.; danger of loss argoll *m.*
dangerous *adj.* dyantell, peryllus
dapple *v.* britha
dappled *adj.* brithek
dare *v.* bedha, lavasos: *phr.* I
dare say bedhav y di
daring *adj.* bedhek, bold
dark *adj.* du, tewal, tewl: *v.*
become dark tewlhe
darken *v.* tewlhe
darkness *n.* tewlder *m.*, duder *m.*,
tewlyjyon *m.*, tewolgow *m.*
darling *n.* hwegenn *f.* +ow,
keresik *m.* -igyon, melder *m.:*
adj. hweg +ow, hwegoll
darnel *n.* ivra *m.*
dart *n.* sethik *f.* -igow
dashboard *n.* skoestell *f.* +ow
date *n.* dydh *m.* +yow; closing date
dydh-degea *m.:* *v.* (e.g. a
document) dydhya
daughter *n.* myrgh *f.* myrghes
daughter-in-law *n.* gohydh *f.*
+ow
David *name* Davydh, Dewi
dawdle *v.* sygera

dawdling *adj.* **termynek**
dawn *n.* **bora** *m.;* hour before dawn
mo *m.*
day *n.* **dydh** *m.* **+yow, jorna** *m.*
jornyow; (abbr.) **dy'** *m.;* day
before yesterday **dygynsete** *m.;*
day's time **dydhweyth** *f.* **+yow**;
first day of month **dy' Halann** *m.;*
following day **morow** *f.;* period of
three days **trydydh** *m.;* the day **an**
jydh *m.;* third day hence
godrevedh *f.;* three days' end
penn-trydydh *m.;* working day
dy'gweyth *m.* **+yow**: *adv.* by day
dydhweyth; by night and by day
mo ha myttin; next day **ternos**;
on the day after tomorrow **trenja**;
the day after **ternos**: *phr.* good day
durdadhejy, durdadhy'hwi
daybreak *n.* **bora** *m.,* **dydh-tardh**
m.
daylight *n.* **golow dydh** *m.*
daytime *adv.* in the daytime
dydhweyth
dazzle *v.* **dallhe, godhalla**
deacon *n.* **dyagon** *m.* **+yon**
dead *n.* abode of the dead **annown**
m.: adj. **marow**; stone dead
marow sygh
deadlock *n.* **stagsav** *m.* **+ow**
dead-nettles *n.* **koeglinas** *f.* **+enn**
deaf *n.* deaf person **bodharek** *m.*
-ogyon: *adj.* **bodhar**: *v.* become
deaf **bodhara**
deafen *v.* **bodharhe**
deafness *n.* **bodharses** *m.*
deal *v.* deal with **dyghtya**
dealer *n.* **marchont** *m.* **-ons**
dean *n.* **deyn** *m.* **+ys**
deanery *n.* **deynji** *m.* **+ow,**
deynieth *f.*
dear *n.* dear heart **kuv kolonn** *m.;*
dear one **keresik** *m.* **-igyon, kuv**
m. **+yon:** *adj.* **hweg, ker, kuv,**
keresik
dearness *n.* **kerneth** *f.*

dearth *n.* **esow** *m.*
death *n.* **mernans** *m.;* (personified)
ankow *m.;* (bloodshed) *n.* **krow** *m.*;
point of death **eneworres** *m.: v.*
put to death **ladha:** *phr.* **gorra**
dhe vernans
debate *n.* **dadhelva** *f.* **+ow**
debater *n.* **dadhlor** *m.* **+yon**
debt *n.* **kendon** *f.*
debtor *n.* **kendoner** *m.* **-oryon,**
kendonores *f.* **+ow**
decade *n.* **degblydhen** *f.*
-blydhynyow
decanter *n.* **kostrel** *m.* **+s**
decarbonize *v.* **diskolya**
decay *v.* **pedri**
decayed *adj.* **podrek, pesek,**
poder
deceased *n.* **marow** *m.*
deceit *n.* **gil** *m.,* **toell** *m.,* **wrynch** *m.*
deceive *v.* **toella**
deceiver *n.* (female) **flattores** *f.*
+ow, toellores *f.* **+ow**; (male)
flatter *m.* **-oryon, toeller** *m.*
-oryon
December *n.* **Kevardhu** *m.,* **mis-**
Kevardhu *m.*
decency *n.* **onester** *m.*
decent *adj.* **onest**
decentralize *v.* **digresenni**
decide *v.* **ervira**
decimal *adj.* **degedhek**
decision *n.* **ervirans** *m.* **+ow**
deck *n.* **flour** *m.: v.* **takla**
deck-chair *n.* **kador-dreth** *f.*
kadoryow-treth
declamation *n.* **areth** *f.*
declaration *n.* **diskleryans** *m.*
declare *adj.* **disklerya**
decline *v.* **nagha**
decoction *n.* **troeth** *m.*
decoder *n.* **digodennell** *f.*
decorate *v.* **afina**
decoration *n.* **afinans** *m.*

decorum *n.* onester *m.*

decrease *n.* digressyans *m.:* *v.* digressya

decry *v.* dispresya, fia

dedicate *v.* omri

deed *n.* ober *m.* +ow, gweythres *m.,* gwrians *m.* +ow, obereth *f.,* torn *m.* +ow; deed of freehold chartour *m.* +s; deeds gwryth *f.*

deep *adj.* down

deepen *v.* downhe

deface *v.* difasya

defame *v.* sklandra

default *n.* defowt *m.*

defeat *v.* fetha

defecate *v.* kawgha; (of animals or birds) skombla

defect *n.* defowt *m.,* difyk *m.* difygyow, gwall *m.* +ow, namm *m.* +ow

defective *adj.* difygyek

defence *n.* ammok *m.,* defens *m.,* klem *m.* +ys

defend *v.* defendya

defendant *n.* difenner *m.* -oryon

defiance *n.* despit *m.,* her *m.*

deficiency *n.* fall *m.*

deficit *n.* difygas *m.* +ow

defile *v.* defola

defilement *n.* plos *m.* +yon, mostedhes *m.*

define *v.* styrya

definitely *adv.* gordhiwedh

definition *n.* styryans *m.* +ow

deform *v.* dihevelebi

defy *v.* defia, herya

degrade *v.* iselhe

degree *n.* gradh *m.* +ow, degre *m.* degrys, prykk *m.* +ow; doctor's degree doktourieth *f.;* master's degree mestronieth *f.*

deity *n.* dywses *m.*

delay *n.* strech *m.* +ys: *v.* delatya

delete *v.* dilea

delicacy *n.* medhelder *m.*

delicate *adj.* medhel, bludh, bludhik, fin, tykkli

delight *n.* delit *m.,* fansi *m.*

delineate *v.* delinya

delineation *n.* delinyans *m.* +ow

deliver *v.* delivra; deliver from delivra diworth; deliver to delivra dhe

dell *n.* kommynn *m.,* pans *m.* +ow

delude *v.* flattra

deluge *n.* liv *m.* +ow

demand *n.* gorholedh *m.,* kwarel *m.:* *v.* dervynn; demand as a right chalenjya

demeanour *n.* cher *m.,* fara *m.*

demist *v.* dilughya

demister *n.* dilughell *f.* +ow

democracy *n.* gwerinieth *f.* +ow

democrat *n.* gweriniethor *m.* +yon

democratic *adj.* gwerinel

demon *n.* jevan *m.*

demoniac *n.* sagh dyowl *m.*

demonstration *n.* diskwedhyans *m.*

demoralize *v.* digennertha

den *n.* fow *f.* +ys

denial *n.* nagh *m.*

denied *v.* neghys

denounce *v.* kuhudha

dense *adj.* tew; (physically) does

density *n.* (in physics) doesedh *m.* +yow

dent *n.* brall *m.* +ow: *v.* brallya

dented *adj.* mortholek

dentist *n.* medhyk-dens *m.* medhygyon-dens

denude *v.* lommhe

deny *v.* nagha, denagha, skonya

depart *v.* diberth

department *n.* asrann *f.* +ow; Department of Health Asrann Yeghes *f.;* Department of the Environment Asrann an Kyrghynnedh *f.;* Department of

Trade **Asrann Genwerth** *f.;*
Department of Transport **Asrann
Garyans** *f.*
depend *v.* **kregi**
dependant *n.* **serghek** *m.* **-ogyon**
dependants *n.* **koskor** *m.*
dependent *adj.* **keth, serghek**
depopulate *v.* **dibobla**
depopulated *adj.* **dibobel**
depopulation *n.* **diboblans** *m.*
depot *n.* **gwithva** *f.* **+ow**
depraved *n.* depraved person
podrek *m.* **podrogyon**
depravity *n.* **sherewynsi** *m.*
depression *n.* (topographical) **seudh**
m. **+ow**
deprive *v.* **esowi**
depth *n.* **downder** *m.* **+yow**
derange *v.* **varya**
deranged *adj.* **varyes**
descant *n.* **diskant** *m.*
descend *v.* **diyskynna**
descendant *n.* **diyskynnyas** *m.*
-ysi
descendants *n.* **henedh** *m.* **+ow**
descended *phr.* descended from
sevys a
descent *n.* genealogical descent
devedhyans *m.*
describe *v.* **deskrifa**
description *n.* **deskrifans** *m.* **+ow**
desert *n.* **difeyth** *m.*, **difeythtir** *m.*
+yow
deserted *adj.* **dibobel, enyal**
deserve *v.* **dendil**, deservya
deservedly *adv.* **kwit**
deserving *adj.* **wordhi**
desiccate *v.* **desygha**
design *n.* **towl** *m.* **+ow, desin** *m.*
+yow, porpos *m.;* (as a subject)
desinieth *f.:* *v.* **desinya**
designer *n.* **desinor** *m.* **+yon,
desinores** *f.* **+ow**

desire *n.* **hwans** *m.* **+ow, desir** *m.*
+ys; strong desire **ewl** *f.* **+ow**: *v.*
desirya, hwansa
desirous *adj.* **hwansek, hwansus,
yeunek**
desk *n.* **desk** *m.* **+ow, +ys**
desolate *adj.* **enyal**
despair *n.* **desper** *m.*
despise *v.* **dispresya, fia,** despisya
despite *n.* **despit** *m.:* *conj.* **yn
despit dhe**; in despite of **spit dhe**
despot *n.* **turant** *m.* **turans**
destine *v.* **destna, tenki**
destitute *adj.* **boghosek**
destitution *n.* **boghosogneth** *f.*
destroy *v.* **distrui, kisya,
konsumya**
destruction *n.* **distruyans** *m.,*
kollva *f.,* **terroes** *m.*
detach *v.* **digelmi, distaga**
detachable *adj.* **distagadow**
detached *adj.* **distag**
detachment *n.* **distagas** *m.* **+ow**
detail *v.* **manylya**
details *plur.* **manylyon**
detect *v.* **helerghi**
detective *n.* **helerghyas** *m.* **-ysi**
detergent *n.* **lin sebon** *m.*
deteriorate *v.* **gwethhe,
omwetha, omwethhe**
deterioration *n.* **gwethter** *m.*
detestable *adj.* **kasadow**
develop *v.* **displegya**
development *n.* **displegyans** *m.*
+ow
device *n.* **devis** *m.* **+yow**; armorial
device **arwoedh** *f.* **+yow**
devil *n.* **dyowl** *m.* **dywolow, malan**
m.; the devil **an jowl** *m.:* *plur.* the
devils **an dhywolow**
devilish *adj.* **dyowlek**
devilry *n.* **dewlysi** *m.*
devise *v.* **devisya**
devolution *n.* **digresennans** *m.*

devolve *v.* digresenni
Devon *place* Dewnens
devotion *adj.* lel wonis
devour *v.* devorya
devout *adj.* erwir
dew *n.* gluth *m.*
dew-claw *n.* gorewin *m.* +es
dewpoint *n.* gluthboynt *m.*
dexterity *n.* sleyneth *f.*
diabolical *n.* diabolical influence dewlysi *m.: adj.* dyowlek
dialect *n.* rannyeth *f.* +ow
dialectal *adj.* rannyethek
diamond *n.* adamant *m.* +ow, +ys
diarrhoea *n.* skit *m.*
dice *v.* dice meat disya
dictionary *n.* gerlyver *m.* -lyvrow
dictum *n.* dyth *m.* +ow
did *v.* gwrug
die *v.* merwel, tremena; die of cold stervya
diesel *n.* disel *m.*
diet *n.* (as in "go on a diet") rewl voes *f.: v.* rewlya boes
differ *v.* dyffra
difference *n.* dihevelepter *m.,* dyffrans *m.* +ow
different *adj.* dihaval, dyffrans +ow, ken
difficult *adj.* kales
difficulty *n.* kaletter *m.,* danjer *m.*
dig *v.* palas; dig a trench kleudhya
digger *n.* paler *m.* -oryon
digit *n.* bys *m.* bysyes
digital *adj.* bysyel
dignity *n.* dynyta *m.,* reowta *m.*
dilatory *adj.* termynek
diligence *n.* diwysogneth *f.*
diligent *adj.* bysi, diwysek
dilute *v.* gwannhe
dime (U.S.) *n.* demma *m.* demmys
dimension *n.* myns *m.*
diminish *v.* tanowhe

din *n.* tervans *m.*
dine *v.* kinyewel
dingle *n.* komm *m.* +ow, pans *m.* +ow
dining-room *n.* stevell-dhybri *f.* stevellow-dybri
dinner *n.* kinyow *m.* kinyewow; late dinner koen *f.* +yow: *v.* take late dinner koena
dinner-cake *n.* dinner-cake made of pastry hwiogenn *f.* +ow
dinosaur *n.* arghpedrevan *m.* +es
dinted *adj.* mortholek
dip *n.* (for sheep) new droghya *f.: v.* sedhi, troghya
diplomacy *n.* lyskannasedh *m.*
diplomat *n.* lyskannas *f.* +ow
diplomatic *adj.* lyskannasek
dipper *n.* (bird) sedher *m.* -oryon; big dipper sedher meur *m.*
direct *v.* kevarwoedha, lywya, brennya, gedya, routya
direction *n.* tu *m.* +yow, kevarwoedh *m.;* (e.g. of a film) routyans *m.: v.* give directions brennya
director *n.* lywydh *m.* +yon, pennrewler *m.* -oryon, router *m.* +s; (female) kevarwoedhyades *f.* +ow; (male) kevarwoedhyas *m.* -ysi
dirge *n.* galargan *f.* +ow
dirt *n.* mostedhes *m.*
dirty *n.* dirty fellow ploswas *m.* ploswesyon; dirty pool poll stronk *m.: adj.* plos, plosek, strolyek; (of liquid) stronk: *v.* mostya; get dirty plosegi
disability *n.* evredhder *m.* +yow
disabled *n.* disabled man evredhek *m.* -ogyon; disabled woman evredhes *f.* +ow: *adj.* evredh
disarm *v.* disarva
disarmament *n.* disarvans *m.*
disarray *n.* deray *m.* +s
disaster *n.* anfeusi *m.,* terroesa *m.*

disastrous *adj.* **terroesus**
disbelieve *v.* **diskrysi**
disburden *v.* **diveghya**
disbursement *n.* **yalghas** *m.* **+ow**
disc *n.* (sound-recording) **plasenn** *f.*
  +ow; compact disc **plasenn**
  arghansek *f.*
discern *v.* **dissernya**
discharge *v.* **diskarga**; (of a debt)
  akwitya
disciple *n.* **dyskybel** *m.* **dyskyblon**
disclose *v.* **igeri, disklosya,**
  diskudha
discoloured *adj.* **disliw**
discontinue *v.* **astel**
discordant *adj.* **digesson**
discount *n.* **diskont** *m.* **+ow**: *v.*
  diskontya
discourage *v.* **digennertha,**
  digonfortya, diskonfortya
discouragement *n.* **digolonn** *f.*
discourse *n.* **kows** *m.* **+ow**
discover *v.* **diskudha, trovya**
discovery *n.* **diskudhans** *m.* **+ow**
discreet *adj.* **fur, doeth**
discretion *n.* **furneth** *f.*
discuss *v.* **disputya, omgusulya**
discussion *n.* **dadhel** *f.* **dadhlow,**
  dadhelva *f.* **+ow**
disdain *v.* **fia**: *int.* **fi**
disease *n.* **dises** *m.* **+ys**
disembark *v.* **dilestra**
disfigure *v.* **difasya, dihevelebi**
disgrace *n.* **meth** *f.* **mothow,**
  disenor *m.*, **mewl** *m.*, **sham** *m.*
disgraced *adj.* **diskrassyes**
disgraceful *adj.* **divlas**
disguise *n.* **toellwisk** *m.*: *v.*
  toellwiska
disgusted *v.* be disgusted with
  divlasa
disgusting *adj.* **divlas**
dish *n.* (bowl) **skala** *m.* **+ys, skudell**
  f. **+ow**; (food) **sand** *m.* **+ys**: *phr.*
  wash the dishes **golghi an lestri**

dishcloth *n.* **kweth lestri** *f.*
dishful *n.* **skudellas** *f.* **+ow**
dishonour *n.* **disenor** *m.*: *v.*
  dienora, disenora
disjoint *v.* **digevelsi**
dislocate *v.* **diskevelsi**
disloyal *adj.* **dislel**
dismantle *v.* **didakla, disevel**
dismast *v.* **diwernya**
dismasted *adj.* **diwern**
dismay *v.* **amaya**
dismount *v.* **diyskynna**
disobedience *n.* **disobayans** *m.*
disobey *v.* **disobaya**
disorder *n.* **deray** *m.* **+s, disordyr**
  m.
disorderly *adj.* **direwl**
disown *v.* **denagha**
dispatch *v.* **dannvon**
disperse *v.* **diberth, keskar,**
  skoellya a-les
dispersion *n.* **keskar** *m.*
display *n.* **displetyans** *m.*: *v.*
  displetya
displease *v.* **displesya**
displeasure *n.* **displesour** *m.* **+s,**
  displesyans *m.*
dispose *v.* **desedha**
disposition *n.* **nas** *f.*
disprove *v.* **disprevi**
dispute *n.* **bresel** *f.* **+yow, dadhel**
  f. **dadhlow, kedrynn** *f.*: *v.*
  debatya; dispute with **disputya**
  orth
disquiet *n.* **ankres** *m.*, **dises** *m.*
  +ys
disrespect *n.* **anvri** *m.*: *v.* show
  disrespect to **gul anvri dhe**
dissect *v.* **divynya**
dissemble *v.* **dolos**
disseminate *v.* **kyhwedhla,**
  plontya
dissent *n.* **dissent** *m.*: *v.*
  dissentya
dissenter *n.* **dissentyer** *m.* **-oryon**

dissimilar *adj.* **dihaval**
dissimilarity *n.* **dihevelepter** *m.*
distaff *n.* **kygel** *f.* **+yow**
distance *n.* **pellder** *m.* **+yow**; short
distance **pols** *m.* **+yow**: *v.* distance
oneself **ombellhe**: *adv.* a short
distance away **pols alemma**; at
some distance **nep-pell**
distant *adj.* **pell**: *adv.* distant but
visible **enos**
distantly *adv.* **yn pell**
distasteful *adj.* **divlas**
distinct *adj.* **diblans**
distinctly *adv.* **diblans**
distort *v.* **omgamma**
distorted *adj.* **kamm**
distress *n.* **ahwer** *m.*, **ankres** *m.*,
reudh *m.*: *v.* **reudhi**
distribute *v.* **lesranna, ranna**
district *n.* **pastell-vro** *f.*, **ranndir**
m.
disturb *v.* **ankresya**
ditch *n.* **kleudh** *m.* **+yow, kleys** *m.*
+yow
dive *v.* **sedhi**
dive (U.S.) *n.* **gwirotti** *m.* **-ow**
diver *n.* **sedher** *m.* **-oryon**; deep-
sea diver **sedher downvor** *m.*
diversion *n.* (of road) **dihynsas** *m.*
+ow, gohelfordh *f.* **+ow**
divide *v.* **kevrenna, ranna**; divide
mathematically **disranna**
divided *adj.* **rennys**
divided highway (U.S.) *n.*
karrhyns dewblek *m.*
dividend *n.* **budhrann** *f.* **+ow,**
kevrenn *f.* **+ow, ranndal** *m.* **+ow**
diviner *n.* **koelyek** *m.* **-ogyon,**
koelyoges *f.* **+ow**
division *n.* **rann** *f.* **+ow**
divorce *n.* **torrva demmedhyans**
f.
do *v.* **gul, oberi**; do about **gul orth**;
do ill **kammwul**; do strictly
gorwul; finish doing **kowlwul**

dock *n.* (plant) **tavolenn** *f.* **+ow** *coll.*
tavol
doctor *n.* **medhyk** *m.* **medhygyon**;
(title) **doktour** *m.* **+s**; doctor's
office (U.S.) **medhygva** *f.* **+ow**
doctorate *n.* **doktourieth** *f.*
doctrine *n.* **dyskas** *m.*
document *n.* **skrif** *m.* **+ow,**
skrifenn *f.* **+ow**; legal document
skrifenn laghel *f.*: *v.* make copies
of a document **liesskrifa**
dodge *n.* (trick) **kast** *m.* **+ys**
dodgem *n.* **karr bonk** *m.*
doe *n.* **da** *f.*, **ewik** *f.* **ewiges**
doer *n.* **oberer** *m.* **-oryon**
dog *n.* **ki** *m.* **keun**; (as term of abuse)
hond *m.* **hons**; biting dog **brathki**
m. **-keun**; male dog **gorgi** *m.*
dogfish *n.* **morgi** *m.* **morgeun**
doghouse (U.S.) *n.* **keunji** *m.* **+ow**
dog-louse *n.* **lowenn gi** *f.*
dogma *n.* **lagha** *f.* **laghys, laghow**
dog-rose *n.* **agrowsenn** *f.* **+ow**
coll. **agrows**
dole *n.* **dol** *m.*
doleful *adj.* **truesi**
doll *n.* **dolli** *f.* **+ow, popet** *m.* **+ow**
dolphin *n.* **morhogh** *m.* **+es**
dolt *n.* **penn-sogh** *m.* **pennow-**
sogh
domestic *adj.* **dov**
domesticate *v.* **dovhe**
domicile *n.* **treveth** *f.*
dominate *v.* **gwarthevya**
domination *n.* **maystri** *m.*,
mestrynses *m.*
domineer *v.* **lordya**
dominion *n.* **mestrynses** *m.*
donation *n.* **ro** *m.* **rohow, rians** *m.*
+ow
done *adj.* **gwrys**
donkey *n.* **asyn** *m.* **-es**
doom *n.* **breus** *f.* **+ow**
door *n.* **daras** *m.* **+ow**; back door
daras a-dhelergh *m.*; front door

daras a-rag *m.;* revolving door **daras-tro** *m.* **darasow-tro**

door-catch *n.* **kacha** *m.* **kachys**

doorkeeper *n.* **darader** *m.* **-oryon, porther** *m.* **-oryon**

dormitory *n.* **koskti** *m.* **+ow**

dote *v.* **dotya**

double *adj.* **dewblek**

doubt *n.* **mar** *m.,* **dout** *m.* **+ys:** *v.* **doutya, mystrestya**

dough *n.* **toes** *m.;* play dough **toes gwari** *m.*

dove *n.* **kolomm** *f.* **+es, kolommenn** *f.* **+ow** *coll.* **kolommes**

dove-cote *n.* **kolommji** *m.* **+ow, kolommyer** *m.* **+s**

dowel *n.* **pynn** *m.* **+ow**

down *n.* (fine feathers) **mannbluv** *coll.: adv.* **dhe'n leur, war-woeles, yn-nans;** down below **dhe-woeles**

downfall *n.* **terroes** *m.*

downland *n.* **goen** *f.* **+yow**

downward *adv.* **isos**

downwards *adv.* **war-nans**

dowry *n.* **argovrow** *m.*

doze *n.* **gogosk** *m.,* **koskas** *m.:* *v.* **gogoska, tergoska**

draff *n.* **seg** *coll.*

draft *n.* first draft **kyns skrif** *m.*

drag *n.* **drayl** *m.,* **tenn** *m.* **+ow:** *v.* **tenna, draylya**

dragon *n.* **dragon** *f.* **+es**

dragonfly *n.* **nader-margh** *f.*

drain *n.* open drain **dowrgleudh** *m.* **+yow:** *v.* drain away **sygera**

drainer *n.* (rack) **kloes-syger** *f.* **kloesyow-syger**

drake *n.* **kulyek hos** *m.*

dram *n.* **las** *m.* **+ow**

dramatic *adj.* **dramasek**

draper *n.* **panner** *m.* **-oryon, liener** *m.* **-oryon**

draught-horse *n.* **tennvargh** *m.* **-vergh**

draughtsman *n.* **tresyas** *m.* **-ysi**

draughtswoman *n.* **tresyades** *f.* **+ow**

draw *v.* (as in art) **delinya, tresa;** (drag) **tenna;** draw back **kila;** draw blood from **diwoesa;** draw lines **linenna**

draw near *v.* **nesa**

drawer *n.* **trog-tenna** *m.* **trogow-tenna;** (in furniture) **tregynn** *m.* **+ow;** (person) **tenner** *m.* **-oryon**

drawing *n.* **delinyans** *m.* **+ow, tresas** *m.* **+ow;** (pulling) **tennva** *f.*

drawing-board *n.* **astell-dhelinyans** *f.*

draw-net *n.* **tennroes** *f.* **+ow**

dread *n.* **own** *m.,* **agha** *m.,* **dout** *m.* **+ys, euth** *m.,* **euthekter** *m.*

dreadful *adj.* **euthek, vil**

dreadfully *adv.* **euthek**

dream *n.* **hunros** *m.* **+ow:** *v.* **hunrosa**

dredge-corn *n.* **ys brith** *coll.*

dregs *n.* **godhes** *m.*

dress *n.* **dillas** *coll.* **+enn, pows** *f.* **+yow;** (clothes) **gwisk** *m.:* *v.* **gwiska, omgwetha;** dress oneself **omwiska**

dresser *n.* **lestrier** *m.* **+yow**

dressing-gown *n.* **mantell-nos** *f.* **mantelli-nos**

dressing-room *n.* **chambour-gwiska** *m.*

dribble *v.* **devera**

drill *n.* **tarder** *m.* **terder:** *v.* **tardra;** drill holes **telli**

drink *n.* **diwes** *m.* **diwosow;** (spirits) **gwires** *f.* **gwirosow;** draught **diwes** *m.* **diwosow, swynnenn** *f.* **+ow:** *v.* **eva**

drinking *v.* go drinking **diwessa**

drip *v.* **devera**

dripping *n.* (fat) **deveras** *m.*

drive   duty

drive *n.* entrance drive **fordh-entra** *f.*
    fordhow-entra: *v.* **lywya,**
    chasya; drive away **fesya**; drive
    in a spike **kentra**
drivel *n.* **glavor** *m.:* *v.* **glaveri**
driver *n.* **lywyer** *m.* **-yoryon**
drizzle *n.* **niwllaw** *m.*
drone *n.* (bee) **sadronenn** *f.* **+ow**
    coll. **sadron:** *v.* **sadronenni**
drop *n.* **banna** *m.* **bannaghow,**
    lomm *m.* **+ow**; (of fluid) **dager** *m.*
    dagrow; little drop **dryppynn** *m.*
    +ow, lemmik *m.* **-igow**; not a drop
    lasvydh *m.:* *v.* **gasa dhe**
    goedha, droppya
drought *n.* **syghor** *m.,* **syghter** *m.*
drove *n.* **para** *m.* **parys**
drown *v.* **beudhi**
drowsiness *n.* **poesyjyon** *m.*
drug-addict *n.* **stoffki** *m.* **-keun**
druid *n.* **drewydh** *m.* **+yon**
druidical *adj.* **drewydhek**
druidism *n.* **drewydhieth** *f.*
drum *n.* **tabour** *m.* **+s, +yow**
drunk *adj.* **medhow**: *v.* get drunk
    medhwi, omvedhwi
drunkard *n.* **penn-medhow** *m.*
    pennow-medhow
drunkenness *n.* **medhwenep** *m.;*
    habitual drunkenness **medhwynsi** *f.*
dry *n.* dry land **syghtir** *m.* **+yow**;
    dry place **syghan** *m.,* **syghla** *m.;*
    dry stuff **krin** *m.* **+yon**: *adj.*
    sygh, krin: *v.* **sygha**; become
    dry or brittle **krina**; dry up
    desygha, heski
dry-dock *n.* **syghborth** *m.* **+ow**
dryness *n.* **krinder** *m.,* **syghor** *m.,*
    syghter *m.*
duchess *n.* **duges** *f.* **+ow**
duchy *n.* **dugeth** *f.*
duck *n.* **hos** *m.* **heyji**
duckling *n.* **heyjik** *m.* **-igow**
duckpond *n.* **poll heyji** *m.*
duckweed *n.* **kellynn** *m.,* **linos**
    coll.

due *n.* what is due **devar** *m.:* *v.* is
    due **degoedh**
duet *n.* second part in singing duet
    diskan *f.;* singing duet **kan ha**
    diskan *f.*
duke *n.* **dug** *m.* **+ys**
dulcimer *n.* **sythol** *m.* **+s**
dull *adj.* **sogh, tal-sogh**
dumb *adj.* **avlavar**
dump *n.* **skoellva** *f.*
dumpling *n.* **pellenn** *f.* **+ow**
dun *adj.* **gorm**
dune *n.* **tewynn** *m.* **+ow**
duned *adj.* **tewynnek**
dung *n.* **kawgh** *m.,* **mon** *m.;* dung
    of sheep or goats or rodents **kagal**
    m.
dungeon *n.* **bagh** *f.* **+ow, dorvagh**
    f., **pytt** *m.* **+ys**
dung-heap *n.* **teylek** *f.* **teylegi**
dung-hill *n.* **byjyon** *m.* **+s**
duplicate *v.* **dewblekhe**; (a
    document) **liesplekhe**
duplicated *adj.* **dewblekhes**
duplicity *n.* **gil** *m.*
durable *adj.* **duryadow**
dusk *n.* **mo** *m.*
dusky *adj.* **godewl**
dust *n.* **doust** *m.,* **polter** *m.;* light
    flying dust **ponn** *m.:* *v.* **diboltra**
dustbin *n.* **atalgyst** *f.* **+yow**
dustcloth (U.S.) *n.* **kweth-ponn** *f.*
    kwethow-ponn
duster *n.* **doustlenn** *f.* **+ow,**
    kweth-ponn *f.* **kwethow-ponn**
dustheap *n.* **ponnek** *f.* **-egi**
dust-pan *n.* **padell-bonn** *f.*
    padellow-ponn
dusty *adj.* **ponnek**
Dutch *n.* Dutch language **Iseldiryek**
    m.: *adj.* **Iseldiryek**
duty *n.* **devar** *m.;* (tax) **toll** *f.* **+ow**;
    death duty **toll-vernans** *f.*

191

dwarf *n.* **korr** *m.* **+yon, korres** *f.*
+ow
dwell *v.* **triga**
dweller *n.* **triger** *m.* **-oryon**
dwelling *n.* **annedh** *f.* **+ow;**
autumn dwelling **kynyavos** *m.;*
summer dwelling **havos** *f.;* winter
dwelling **gwavos** *f.* **+ow**
dwelling-house *n.* **chi annedh** *m.*
dwelling-place *n.* **bos** *f.* **+ow**
dye *v.* **liwya**
dyed *adj.* **liwek**
dyer *n.* **liwer** *m.* **-oryon**
dyke *n.* **fos** *f.* **+ow, tommenn** *f.*
+ow

E

e.g. *n.* **rag ensampel** *m.:* *phr.* **yn**
sampel
each *adj.* **kettep, pub**
eager *adj.* **freth, ter:** *v.* be eager
teri
eagerly *adv.* **dihwans**
eagerness *n.* **mall** *m.*, **frethter** *m.*,
terder *m.*
eagle *n.* **er** *m.* **+yon**
ear *n.* **skovarn** *f.* **skovornow** *dual*
diwskovarn; ear of corn **penn-ys**
m. **pennow-ys**
earl *n.* **yurl** *m.* **yurlys**
early *adv.* **a-varr, a-brys**
earn *v.* **dendil**
earnest *adj.* **diwysek**
ear-ring *n.* **skinenn** *f.* **+ow**
earth *n.* **dor** *m.*, **pri** *m.;* ferruginous
earth **gossen** *f.*
Earth *n.* **norvys** *m.*
earth-bank *n.* **tommenn** *f.* **+ow**
earthnut *n.* **kelerenn** *f.* **+ow** *coll.*
keler
earthquake *n.* **dorgrys** *m.* **+yow**
earthwork *n.* **dorge** *m.* **+ow,**
kerweyth *m.*

earthworm *n.* **bulugenn** *f.* **+ow**
coll. **buluk, pryv nor** *m.*
earwig *n.* **gorlostenn** *f.* **+ow** *coll.*
gorlost
ease *adj.* at ease **attes:** *v.* **esya,**
heudhhe; be at ease **omjershya**
eased *v.* be eased **heudha, heudhhe**
easel *n.* **margh-skrifa** *m.* **mergh-**
skrifa
easier *adj.* **esya**
East *n.* **Est** *m.*, **Howldrevel** *m.*,
Howldrehevel *m.:* *adj.* **Est**
Easter *n.* **Pask** *m.*
easy *adj.* **es:** *v.* make easy **esya**
eat *v.* **dybri**
eating-house *n.* **boesti** *m.* **+ow**
ecclesiastic *adj.* **eglosyek**
echo *n.* **dasson** *m.* **+yow:** *v.*
dasseni
eclipse *n.* **difyk** *m.* **difygyow**
economic *adj.* **erbysiethek**
economical *adj.* **erbysek**
economics *n.* **erbysieth** *f.*
economist *n.* **erbysydh** *m.* **+yon**
economize *v.* **erbysi**
economy *n.* **erbys** *m.* **+yow**
ecstasy *n.* **transyek** *m.*
eddy *n.* **korhwyth** *m.* **+ow**
edge *n.* **amal** *m.* **emlow, min** *m.*
+yow, or *f.* **+yon**
edifice *n.* **drehevyans** *m.* **+ow**
edify *v.* **drehevel**
editor *n.* **pennskrifer** *m.* **-oryon**
editorial *n.* (article) **pennskrif** *m.*
+ow
educate *v.* **dyski, adhyski**
education *n.* **adhyskans** *m.*
eel *n.* **sylli** *f.* **+es**
effect *n.* **effeyth** *m.;* greenhouse
effect **effeyth chi gweder** *m.*
effective *adj.* **effeythus**
effervesce *v.* **ewyni**
effervescence *n.* **ewyn** *coll.* **+enn**
effervescent *adj.* **ewynek**

egg *n.* oy *m.* **+ow**:   *v.* lay eggs
   dedhwi
Egypt *place* **Ejyp**
eh *int.* **dar**
eight *num.* **eth**:   *adv.* eight times
   ethgweyth
eighteen *num.* **etek**
eighteenth *num.* **etegves**
eighth *num.* **ethves**
eighty *num.* **peswar-ugens**
eisteddfod *n.* **esedhvos** *m.* **+ow**
either *adv.* not either **na hwath**
eject *v.* **estewlel, pellhe, tewlel**
   yn-mes
elbow *n.* **elin** *m.* **+yow** *dual*
   dewelin, penn-elin *m.*
elder *n.* **den hen** *m.:*   *adj.* **henavek**
   -ogyon
elder-tree *n.* **skawenn** *f.* **+ow** *coll.*
   skaw . place of elder-trees **skewys**
   m.:   *adj.* abounding in elder-trees
   skewyek
election *n.* **dewisyans** *m.* **+ow**
elector *n.* **dewisyas** *m.* **-ysi**
electric *n.* electric cable **korsenn**
   dredanek *f.;*   *adj.* **tredanek**
electrician *n.* **tredaner** *m.* **-oryon**
electricity *n.* **tredan** *m.*
electrify *adj.* **tredanhe**
elegy *n.* **galargan** *f.* **+ow**
element *n.* **elvenn** *f.* **+ow**
elementary *adj.* **elvennek**
elephant *n.* **olifans** *m.* **-es**
eleven *num.* **unnek**
eleventh *num.* **unnegves**
ellipse *n.* **hirgylgh** *m.* **+yow**
elliptical *adj.* **hirgylghyek**
elm-grove *n.* **elowek** *f.* **+egi**
elm-tree *n.* **elowenn** *f.* **+ow** *coll.*
   elow
eloquence *n.* **frethter** *m.*
eloquent *adj.* **freth**
else *adj.* **ken**
embankment *n.* **bour** *m.*

embarrass *v.* **ankombra**
embarrassment *n.* **ankombrynsi**
   m.
embassy *n.* **kannatti** *m.* **+ow,**
   lyskannatti *m.* **+ow**
ember *n.* **regydhenn** *f.* **+ow** *coll.*
   regydh
embers *n.* **lusow** *coll.* **+enn**
emblem *n.* **arwoedh** *f.* **+yow**
emblematic *adj.* **arwoedhek**
embrace *v.* **byrla, strotha**
embroider *v.* **brosya, neusenna**
embroiderer *n.* **brosyer** *m.*
   -oryon
embroideress *n.* **brosyores** *f.*
   +ow
embroidery *n.* **brosweyth** *m.*
emigrate *v.* **omdhivroa**
emigration *n.* **omdhivroans** *m.*
   +ow
eminent *adj.* **flour**
emit *v.* **dyllo**
emolument *n.* **gober** *m.* **gobrow**
emperor *n.* **emperour** *m.* **+s**
emphasis *n.* **poeslev** *m.* **+ow**
emphasize *v.* **poesleva**
emphatic *n.* **gans poeslev** *m.*
empire *n.* **emperoureth** *f.;*   Roman
   Empire **Emperoureth Romanek** *f.*
employ *v.* **arveth**
employee *n.* **arvethesik** *m.* **-igyon**
employer *n.* **arvethor** *m.* **+yon,**
   arvethores *f.* **+ow**
employment *n.* **arveth** *m.:*   *v.*
   terminate employment of **gordhyllo**
empress *n.* **emperes** *f.* **+ow**
emptiness *n.* **gwakter** *m.*
empty *adj.* **gwag, koeg**
empty-headed *adj.* **penn-koeg**
encamp *v.* **kampya**
enchant *v.* **gorhana, husa**
enchanter *n.* **gorhenyas** *m.* **-ysi,**
   huder *m.* **-oryon enchanting**
   adj. **hudel**

enchantment *n.* gorhan *f.* +ow,
hus *m.*
enchantress *n.* hudores *f.* +ow
encircle *v.* kylghya
enclose *v.* degea, keas, parkya
enclosed *adj.* klos
enclosure *n.* park *m.* +ow, garth
m. +ow, hay *f.*, kew *f.* +yow, klos
m. +yow, +ys, korlann *f.* +ow,
kow *f.* +yow; enclosure of stakes to
trap fish kores *f.* +ow
encounter *v.* dyerbynna, metya
encourage *v.* kennertha
encouragement *n.* kennerth *m.*,
konfort *m.*
end *n.* diwedh *m.*, penn *m.* +ow,
fin *f.* +yow, finwedh *f.*, gorfenn
m.; dead end fordh-dhall *f.*
fordhow-dall: *v.* diwedha;
come to an end gorfenna: *adv.*
from end to end a-hys; in the end
wor'tiwedh; to the end byttiwedh
endangered *v.* be endangered
peryllya
endeavour *n.* attent *m.*
ended *adj.* gorfennys, du
ending *n.* diwedhva *f.*
endless *adj.* dibenn
endow *v.* kemmynna
endowment *n.* kemmynn *m.* +ow
end-to-end *adv.* hys-ha-hys
endue *v.* lenwel
endurance *n.* perthyans *m.*
endure *v.* perthi, pesya, durya,
godhav, pargh: *phr.* I cannot
endure being seen ny besyav
bones gwelys
enemy *n.* envi *m.*, eskar *m.*
eskerens
energy *adj.* lacking in energy
difreth, dinerth
enervate *v.* bludhya, medhelhe
engage *v.* engage gear magla
engagement *n.* (to marry) ambos
demmedhyans *m.*

engine *n.* jynn *m.* +ow, +ys, ynjin
m. +ys
engineer *n.* jynnweythor *m.* +yon,
ynjinor *m.* +yon, ynjinores *f.*
+ow
engineering *n.* ynjinorieth *f.*
engine-house *n.* jynnji *m.* +ow
England *n.* Pow Sows *m.*
English *n.* English language
Sowsnek *m.;* English speaker
sowsneger *m.* -oryon: *adj.*
Sowsnek
Englishman *n.* Sows *m.* +on,
Seys *m.*
Englishwoman *n.* Sowses *f.* +ow
engrave *v.* gravya
engraver *n.* gravyer *m.* -yoryon
engraving *n.* gravyans *m.* +ow
enjoy *v.* enjoy oneself omlowenhe:
phr. I enjoy da yw genev
enormous *adj.* kowrek
enough *adj.* lowr
enquiry *n.* govynnadow *m.;*
enquiry office govynnva *f.* +ow
enrol *v.* omrolya
ensnare *v.* magla
ensure *v.* surhe
entangle *v.* magla
entanglement *n.* magel *f.* maglow
enter *v.* entra
entertain *v.* didhana
entertaining *adj.* didhanus
entertainment *n.* didhan *m.*
entice *v.* dynya, slokkya, traynya
enticement *n.* trayn *m.* +ys
entire *adj.* kowal, dien, perfeyth
entirely *adv.* oll, yn tien
entitled *v.* be entitled to piw
entrail *n.* kolodhyonenn *f.* +enn
coll. kolodhyon
entrance *n.* porth *m.* +ow, fordh-
entra *f.* fordhow-entra; covered
entrance konvayour *m.:* *v.*
ravshya
entreat *v.* pysi

entrenchment *n.* **kaskleudh** *m.*
+yow
enumeration *n.* **niveryans** *m.*
envelop *v.* **maylya**
envelope *n.* **maylyer** *m.* **+s**
envenom *v.* **venimya**
envious *adj.* **envius**
environment *n.* **kyrghynnedh** *m.*
+ow; close environment **kyrghynn**
m.; Department of the Environment
Asrann an Kyrghynnedh *f.*
environmental *adj.*
kyrghynnedhel
environmentalist *n.*
kyrghynnedhor *m.* **+yon**
envoy *n.* **kannas** *f.* **+ow**
envy *n.* **avi** *m.,* **envi** *m.:* *v.* to envy
perthi avi orth
epilepsy *n.* **drog-atti** *m.*
Epiphany *n.* **dy'goel Stoel** *m.,*
Stoel *m.*
epistle *n.* **epystyl** *m.* **epystlys**
epoch *n.* **oesweyth** *f.* **+yow**
equal *n.* **par** *m.* **+ow, pares** *f.* **+ow**:
adj. **kehaval**; of equal length
kehys
equator *n.* **kehysedh** *m.* **+ow**
equilibrium *n.* **kespoes** *m.,*
kompoester *m.*
equinoctial *n.* (celestial equator)
kehysedh *m.* **+ow**
equipment *n.* **daffar** *m.,* **darbar** *m.*
equity *n.* **ewnder** *m.* **+yow,**
reythses *m.*
erase *v.* **defendya**
eraser *n.* **rutyer** *m.* **+yow**
ere *prep.* **kyns**
erect *n.* erect posture **sav** *m.:* *v.*
drehevel
erection *n.* **drehevyans** *m.* **+ow**
ermine *n.* **ermin** *m.*
erne *n.* (bird) **morer** *m.* **+es**
err *v.* **kammwul, errya**; err in
thought **kammdybi**

errand *n.* **negys** *m.* **+yow**: *phr.* to
go on an errand **mones negys**
error *n.* **kammdybyans** *m.* **+ow,**
kammweyth *m.,* **kammwrians** *m.*
+ow
escalate *v.* **eskeulya**
escalator *n.* **eskeul** *f.* **+yow**
escape *n.* **diank** *m.:* *v.* **avodya,**
diank, skapya
escutcheon *n.* **skoes** *m.* **+ow**
especially *adj.* **yn arbennik**
espy *v.* **aspia**
esquire *n.* **skoeswas** *m.* **-wesyon,**
skwier *m.* **+yon**
essay *n.* **assay** *m.* **+s**
essence *n.* **sugen** *m.* **+yow**
essential *adj.* **a res**
establish *v.* **fondya, selya**
establishment *n.* **fondyans** *m.*
+ow
estate *n.* **stat** *m.* **+ow, +ys**; housing
estate **trevbark** *m.* **+ow**
esteem *n.* **bri** *f.:* *v.* **akontya**
estimate *n.* (numerical) **dismygriv**
m. **+ow**; estimate of cost **towlgost**
m. **+ow**; *v.* **amontya**; estimate a
numerical value **dismygriva**
estuary *n.* **heyl** *m.* **+yow**
ethnic *adj.* **ethnek**
eucharist *n.* **oferenn** *f.* **+ow**
eulogize *v.* **kanmel**
eulogy *n.* **kanmeula** *m.*
eunuch *n.* **spadhesik** *m.* **-igyon**
euphonious *adj.* **kesson**
euphony *n.* **kessenyans** *m.*
euro *n.* (currency) **euro** *m.* **+yow**
Europe *n.* **Europa** *f.*
European *n.* European Parliament
Eurosenedh *m.;* European Union
Unyans Europek *m.:* *adj.*
Europek
evade *v.* **kavanskeusa**; evade
capture **skeusi**
evaluate *v.* **arbrisya**
evangelical *adj.* **aweylek**

evangelise *v.* **aweyla**

evangelist *n.* **aweyler** *m.* **+s**

evaporate *v.* **ethenna**

evasion *n.* **kavanskeus** *m.*

eve *n.* eve of feast **nos** *f.* **+ow**

Eve *name* **Eva**

even *adj.* **kompes, leven, suant;**
(of numbers) **parow:** *v.* make even
kompoesa: *adv.* **unnweyth,**
hogen: *phr.* be even with **bos**
kompes gans

evening *n.* **gorthugher** *m.: adv.* in
the evening **gorthugherweyth;**
this evening **haneth**

evenness *n.* **kompoester** *m.*

evensong *n.* **gwesper** *m.* **+ow**

event *n.* **darvos** *m.* **+ow,**
hwarvedhyans *m.* **+ow, hwarvos**
m. **+ow**

ever *adj.* **prest:** *adv.* **bydh,**
bykken, bythkweth, nevra, a'y
oes, bynitha, byskweth,
byttydh, vynitha, vythkweyth,
yn y oes; for ever **bynari, bys**
vykken, bys vynytha; for ever
and ever **trank heb worfenn**

evergreen *n.* evergreen tree **sabenn**
f. **+ow** *coll.* **sab, sybwydhenn** *f.*
+ow *coll.* **sybwydh:** *adj.*
bydhlas

evermore *adv.* **bys nevra, bys**
vynari; for evermore **bynitha**

every *adj.* **kettep, oll, pub**

everybody *pron.* **peub:** *phr.* **yn**
kettep penn, yn kettep poll,
pubonan

everyone *pron.* **peub:** *phr.* **yn**
kettep penn, yn kettep poll,
pubonan

everything *pron.* **puptra**

evident *adj.* **kler, apert, playn**

evidently *adv.* **efan**

evil *n.* **drog** *m.,* **drogedh** *m.,*
droktra *m.;* evil person **tebel** *m.*
+es: *adj.* **tebel**

evil-doer *n.* **drogoberer** *m.* **-oryon**

evolution *n.* **esplegyans** *m.,*
omgerdh *m.*

evolve *v.* **esplegya, omgerdhes**

ewe-lamb *n.* **oenes** *f.* **+ow**

exact *adj.* **a-dhevis, kewar**

exactly *adj.* **yn kewar:** *adv.* **poran**

exalt *v.* **avonsya, ughelhe**

examination *n.* **apposyans** *m.*

examine *v.* **hwithra, hwithra orth;**
(of knowledge) **apposya;** examine
oneself **omhwithra**

example *n.* **ensampel** *m.* **-plow,**
-plys, patron *m.* **+yow, sampel**
m. **samplow;** for example **rag**
ensampel *m.: phr.* **yn sampel**

excavate *v.* **palas**

excavation *n.* **kleudh** *m.* **+yow,**
kowans *m.*

excavator *n.* **jynn-palas** *m.*
jynnow-palas

exceed *v.* **tremena, mos dres**

exceedingly *adv.* **dres eghenn**

except *prep.* **a-der:** *conj.* **marnas,**
saw: *v.* **ekseptya**

exception *n.* **namm** *m.* **+ow**

excessively *adv.* **re**

exchange *n.* **keschanj** *m.: v.*
keschanjya

exclude *v.* **eskeas, eskelmi, keas**
mes

exclusion *n.* **eskeans** *m.* **+ow**

excommunicate *v.* **emskemunya**

excrement *n.* **kawgh** *m.: v.* void
excrement **kawgha**

excuse *n.* **askus** *m.* **+yow:** *v.*
askusya, digeredhi; excuse me
gav dhymm; excuse oneself
omaskusya, omdhihares

excused *adj.* **digeredh**

execrable *adj.* **mollothek**

execrate *v.* **mollethi**

execute *v.* (by beheading) **dibenna**

executioner *n.* **dibenner** *m.*
-oryon

executive n. gweythresek m.
-ogyon; chief executive
pennweythresek m. -ogyon
executor n. asektour m. +s
exercise phr. exercise control over
gul maystri orth
Exeter place Karesk
exhibit v. diskwedhes
exhibition n. diskwedhyans m.
exhort v. keski, ynnia
exile n. divres m. +ow: v. divroa
exist v. bos
existence n. bosva f.
exodus n. eskerdh m. +ow
expand v. lesa, omlesa
expansion n. omlesans m. +ow
expatriate n. divres m. +ow
expect v. gwaytya, desevos
expectation n. gwaytyans m.,
trest m.
expedition n. kerdh m. +ow,
eskerdh m. +ow, vyaj m.
expel v. estewlel, pellhe, tewlel
yn-mes; (dismiss) gordhyllo
expense n. kost m. +ys; go to
expense mos yn kost m.
expensive adj. ker, kostek
expensiveness n. kerneth f.
experience n. (something
experienced) perthyans m.
experiment n. arbrov m. +ow,
attent m., prevyans m. +ow: v.
arbrevi
expert n. konnyk m. konnygyon
expiation n. prenedh m.
expire v. merwel
explain v. igeri, displegya, styrya
explanation n. displegyans m.
+ow, styryans m. +ow
explode v. tardha
exploit v. gweytha
explosion n. tardh m. +ow
export v. esperthi
exposed adj. digloes

expound v. styrya
expressway n. klerfordh f. +ow
expunge v. defendya dhe-ves,
dilea
extend v. kressya, ystynna;
(intrans.) omystynna
extension n. ystynnans m. +ow
extent n. hys m., kehysedh m.
+ow, kompas m.
extinguish v. (a flame) difeudhi
extort v. kavoes dre nerth
extract n. devynn m. +ow: v.
devynna, estenna, tenna yn-
mes
extraordinary adj. koynt
extremely adv. fest
eye n. lagas m. +ow dual
dewlagas; (of potato) skyllenn f.
+ow coll. skyll; black eye lagas
du m.; eye of needle kraw
naswydh m.: adv. before the eyes
of a-wel dhe
eyebrow n. abrans m. +ow dual
dewabrans
eyelash n. blewenn an lagas f.
eyelid n. kroghen an lagas f.

F

fabric n. woven fabric pann m. +ow
fabrication n. (tale) hwedhel m.
hwedhlow (manuf.) gwrians m.
face n. enep m. enebow, bejeth f.
+ow, bysaj f., fas m. fassow,
greuv m., min m. +yow,
tremmynn m.; appearance fas m.
fassow; countenance fas m.
fassow: v. make a face at
omgamma orth: adv. face to face
orth ganow
facing prep. a-dal
fact n. gwir m. +yow, tra f. +ow:
adv. in fact yn hwir
factory n. gweythva f. +ow

faculties *plur.* **teythi**: *adj.* without
normal faculties **anteythi**
fail *v.* **fyllel, difyga**; fail to **fyllel a**
failure *n.* **meth** *f.* **mothow, defowt**
m., **difyk** *m.* **difygyow, fall** *m.*,
falladow *m.*
faint *n.* **klamder** *m.:* *v.* **klamdera**
fainthearted *adj.* **digolonn**
faintheartedness *n.* **digolonn** *f.*
fair *n.* **fer** *m.* **+yow, goel** *m.* **+yow**:
adj. (in colour) **gwynn**
fairground *n.* **ferla** *m.* **-leow**
fairy *n.* **spyrys** *m.* **+yon**
faith *n.* **kryjyans** *m.*, **fay** *m.*, **fydh** *f.*,
fydhyans *m.*, **kres** *f.;* good faith
lenduri *m.:* *v.* have faith in
fydhya, krysi; have faith in
someone **krysi dhe nebonan**
faithful *adj.* **lel, len**
faithless *adj.* **dislen**
fake *adj.* **fug**: *v.* **fugya**
falcon *n.* **falghun** *m.* **-es**
falconer *n.* **falghuner** *m.* **-oryon**
falconry *n.* **falghunieth** *f.*
fall *n.* **koedh** *m.;* (autumn) **kynyav**
m.: *adj.* ready to fall **dyantell**: *v.*
koedha; cause to fall **disevel**; fall
down **omhweles**; trip and fall
omdhisevel
fallow *adj.* (unploughed) **anerys**;
fallow in summer **havarel**
Falmouth *place* **Aberfal**
false *n.* false person **fals** *m.:* *adj.*
fals, fekyl
falsehood *n.* **gow** *m.* **+yow**
falsely *adv.* **falslych**
falseness *n.* **falsuri** *m.*
falter *v.* **hokya**
fame *n.* **gerda** *m.*
familiar *adj.* **aswonnys, koth**: *v.*
be familiar with **aswonn**
family *n.* **teylu** *m.* **+yow**; extended
family **kordh** *m.* **+ow**; head of
family **penn-teylu** *m.* **pennow-
teylu**

famine *n.* **divoetter** *m.*
famous *adj.* **geryes da**
fan *n.* (appliance) **gwynsell** *f.* **+ow**;
(e.g. of sport) **penn-bros** *m.*
pennow-bros: *v.* **gwynsella**
fanatic *n.* **penn-bros** *m.* **pennow-
bros**
fan-belt *n.* **grogys-gwynsell** *m.*
grogysyow-gwynsell
fancy *n.* **devis** *m.* **+yow, konsayt**
m. **+s, sians** *m.:* *v.* **si**; (suppose)
tybi
fantastic *adj.* **tarosvannus**
fantasy *n.* **fantasi** *m.*
far *adj.* **pell**
farewell *int.* **farwel**
farinaceous *adj.* **bleusek**
farm *n.* **bargen-tir** *m.* **bargenyow-
tir**; family farm **hendra** *f.;* home
farm **hendra** *f.;* small farm **godrev**
f. **+i**; wind farm **tredanva-wyns** *f.:*
v. **ammetha**
farmer *n.* **tiek** *m.* **tiogow, tiogyon,
tioges** *f.* **+ow**
farm-house *n.* **chi tiek** *m.*
farmstead *n.* **tre** *f.* **trevow, trev** *f.*
+ow
farrier *n.* **ferror** *m.* **+yon**
farrow *v.* **porghella**
fart *n.* **bramm** *m.* **bremmyn**: *v.*
bramma
farthing *n.* **ferdhynn** *m.* **+ow**
fascism *n.* **faskorieth** *f.*
fascist *n.* **faskor** *m.* **+yon**
fashion *n.* **gis** *m.:* *v.* **shapya**
fast *n.* long fast **hirbenys** *m.:* *adj.*
(fixed) **fast**; (speedy) **buan, uskis**:
v. **penys**
fasten *v.* **takkya, fasthe**
fastened *adj.* **stag**: *v.* become
fastened **fasta**
fastening *n.* **kevrenn** *f.* **+ow,
kolmenn** *f.* **+ow**; cord for fastening
sygenn *f.*
fastidious *adj.* **denti, dewisek**

fat *n.* **blonek** *m.:* *adj.* **tew, borr**
fatal *adj.* **marwel**
fatality *n.* **marwoleth** *f.*
fate *n.* **tenkys** *f.*
father *n.* **tas** *m.* **+ow, sira** *m.* **sirys**;
Father Christmas **Tas Nadelik** *m.;*
spiritual father **tasek** *m.* **tasogyon:**
plur. holy fathers **tassens**
father-in-law *n.* **hwegron** *m.*, **sira**
da *m.*
father-lasher *n.* (fish) **kalkenn** *f.*
+ow
fathom *n.* **gourhys** *m.* **+ow**
fatigue *n.* **skwithter** *m.*
fatness *n.* **berri** *m.*, **tewder** *m.*
fatten *v.* **peski, tewhe**
fault *n.* **fowt** *m.* **+ow, blam** *m.*, **fall**
m.: *v.* find fault with **blamya**
fault-finding *adj.* **krodhek**
favour *n.* **favour** *m.* **+s:** *v.* (esteem)
favera
fawn *n.* **elen** *f.* **+es, yerghik** *m.*
yerghesigow: *v.* **fekla**
fawn-coloured *adj.* **gell**
fax *n.* (message) **pellskrifenn** *f.*
+ow: *v.* **pellskrifa**
fear *n.* **own** *m.*, **dout** *m.* **+ys:** *v.*
doutya
feast *n.* **kevywi** *m.* **+ow, fest** *m.*
+ow, goel *m.* **+yow;** feast of
Passover **boes Pask** *m.:* *v.*
goelya; feast together **kevywya**
feast-day *n.* **dy'goel** *m.* **+yow**
feather *n.* **pluvenn** *f.* **+ow** *coll.*
pluv; little feather **pluvynn** *f.*
+ow: *v.* grow feathers **pluva**
February *n.* **Hwevrer** *m.*, **mis-**
Hwevrer *m.*
feeble *adj.* **gwann, difreth, ydhyl:**
v. grow feeble **gwannhe**
feebleness *n.* **difrethter** *m.*,
gwannder *m.*
feed *v.* **boesa, maga, methya**
feeding *n.* **meth** *m.*
feel *v.* **klywes, omglywes;** feel
one's way **palvala**

feeling *n.* **omglywans** *m.* **+ow**
feign *v.* **fugya**
feigning *n.* **fayntys** *m.*
feint *n.* **fug** *m.*
fellmonger *n.* (dealer in animal
skins) **kroener** *m.* **-oryon**
felloe *n.* (rim of wheel) **kammek** *f.*
-ogow
fellow *n.* **gwas** *m.* **gwesyon,**
koweth *m.* **+a, polat** *m.* **+ys;**
filthy fellow **kawghwas** *m.*
-wesyon; hard-bitten fellow **smat**
m. **+ys;** hulking fellow **kwallok** *m.*
+s; old fellow **kothwas** *m.*
-wesyon
fellows *plur.* **hynsa**
fellowship *n.* **kowethas** *m.* **+ow,**
kowethyans *m.;* Cornish
Language Fellowship **Kowethas**
an Yeth Kernewek *m.*
felon *n.* **felon** *m.* **+s**
felt *n.* (material) **leuvbann** *m.*
female *n.* **benynreydh** *f.:* *adj.*
benow
feminine *adj.* **gwregel;**
(grammatical gender) **benow**
femininity *n.* **gwregoleth** *f.*
fen *n.* **kors** *coll.* **+enn**
fence *n.* **ke** *m.* **keow, kloes** *f.*
+yow: *v.* (with swords) **skyrmya**
fennel *n.* **fenogel** *f.*
fernbrake *n.* **redenek** *f.* **-egi**
ferns *n.* **reden** *coll.* **+enn**
ferny *adj.* **redenek**
ferret *n.* **yewgenn** *m.*
ferric *adj.* **hornek**
ferrous *adj.* **hornus**
ferry *n.* **kowbal** *m.* **+yow, treth** *m.*
+yow: *v.* **tretha**
ferry-crossing *n.* **kowbalhyns** *m.*
+ow
ferryman *n.* **trethor** *m.* **+yon**
fertile *n.* fertile ground **gwresenn** *f.:*
adj. **feyth**

fertility *n.* **feythter** *m.*, **gwelsowas** *m.*
fester *v.* **pedri, gori**
festering *adj.* **podredhek**
fest-noz *n.* **troyll** *m.* **+yow**
fetch *v.* **kyrghes, hedhes**
fetid *adj.* **flerys**
fetidness *n.* **flerynsi** *m.*
fetor *n.* **fler** *m.* **+yow**
fetter *n.* **bagh** *f.* **+ow, karghar** *m.*
+ow, sprall *m.:* *v.* **spralla**
fever *n.* **terthenn** *f.* **+ow**; scarlet fever **kleves kogh** *m.*
feverfew *n.* **lesterth** *m.*
few *n.* **nebes** *m.:* *adj.* **nebes, boghes**
fiasco *plur.* **mothow**
fibre-glass *n.* **gweder-gwlan** *m.*
fickle *adj.* **brottel, hedro**
fiction *n.* **fugieth** *f.*
fictitious *adj.* **fug**
fiddle *n.* (Mus.) **fyll** *m.* **+ow, harfyll** *m.* **+ow, krowd** *m.* **+ys**: *v.* **fyllya**
fiddler *n.* (Mus.) **fyller** *m.* **-oryon, harfyller** *m.* **-oryon, harfyllores** *f.*, **krowder** *m.* **-oryon**
fidelity *n.* **lelder** *m.*
fidget *n.* **fyslek** *m.* **-ogyon:** *v.* **fysla**
fidgetty *adj.* **fyslek**
fie *v.* cry fie on **fia:** *int.* **agh, fi**
field *n.* **park** *m.* **+ow, gwel** *m.* **+yow**; arable field after reaping and before ploughing **arys** *m.;* open field **mes** *m.* **+yow**; small field **parkynn** *m.* **+ow**
field poppy (U.S.) *n.* **myll** *f.* **+es**
fiend *n.* **jevan** *m.*
fierce *adj.* **gwyls, fell, goedh**
fifteen *num.* **pymthek**
fifteenth *num.* **pymthegves**
fifth *num.* **pympes**
fifty *num.* **hanterkans +ow**
fig *n.* **figysenn** *f.* **+ow** *coll.* **figys**

fight *n.* **kas** *f.* **+ow, kevammok** *m.*, **omladh** *m.* **+ow:** *v.* **batalyas, omladh**
fig-tree *n.* **figbrenn** *m.* **+yer**
figure *n.* (form) **furv** *f.* **+ow**; (shape) **figur** *m.* **+ys:** *v.* **furvya**
filament *n.* **neusynn** *m.* **+ow**
file *n.* (document) **restrenn** *f.* **+ow**; (tool) **liv** *f.* **+yow:** *v.* (put in a drawer) **restra**; (to scrape) **livya:** *adv.* single file **yn rew**
filing *n.* filing cabinet **restrennva** *f.* **+ow**
fill *v.* **kollenwel, lenwel, leunhe**; fill with **lenwel a**
fillet *n.* **snod** *m.* **+ow, +ys**
film *n.* **kennenn** *f.* **+ow**; (cinema, T.V., video) **fylm** *m.;* feature film **fylm bras** *m.:* *v.* (shoot a film) **fylmya**; coat with film **kenna**
filter *n.* **sidhel** *m.* **sidhlow:** *v.* **sidhla**
filth *n.* **lastedhes** *m.*, **most** *m.* **+yon, mostedhes** *m.*, **plosedhes** *m.*, **stronk** *m.;* clotted filth on fleece or clothing **kagal** *m.*
filthy *n.* filthy fellow **kawghwas** *m.* **-wesyon, plosek** *m.* **plosogyon:** *adj.* **plos**
fin *n.* **askell** *f.* **eskelli**
final *n.* (game) **pennwari** *m.* **+ow:** *adj.* **finek**
finally *adv.* **wor'tiwedh, gordhiwedh**
finance *n.* **arghans** *m.*, **arghansereth** *f.*
financial *adj.* **arghansek**
financier *n.* **arghanser** *m.* **-oryon**
find *n.* **dismyk** *m.:* *v.* **kavoes, trovya**; find oneself **omgavoes**; find out **dismygi**
fine *n.* (penalty) **spal** *m.* **+yow:** *adj.* **teg, brav:** *v.* **spala**
finer *adj.* **tekka**
finery *n.* **tekter** *m.*, **bravder** *m.*

finger *n.* **bys** *m.* **bysyes**; fourth
finger **bys bysow** *m.;* little finger
bys byghan *m.;* middle finger **bys
kres** *m.;* ring finger **bys bysow**
m.: *v.* **bysya**
finger-nail *n.* **ewin** *m.* **+es**: *adj.*
having long finger-nails **ewinek**
finish *n.* **diwedh** *m.,* **gorfenn** *m.:*
v. **gorfenna, diwedha**
finished *adj.* **gorfennys, du**
fir-cone *n.* **aval-sabenn** *m.*
avalow-sabenn
fire *n.* **tan** *m.* **+yow**; back-log of fire
penntan *m.* **+yow**; on fire **gans
tan** *m.:* *v.* (a weapon) **tenna**;
consume by fire **kowlleski**
firebrand *n.* **yttew** *m.* **+i**
fire-engine *n.* **jynn-tan** *m.*
jynnow-tan
fire-grate *n.* **tanvaglenn** *f.* **+ow**
fireman *n.* **gwithyas tan** *m.*
fireplace *n.* **oeles** *f.* **+ow**
firer *n.* firer of pots **forner** *m.* **-oryon**
fire-ship *n.* **tanlester** *m.* **-lestri**
firewood *n.* **keunys** *coll.* **+enn**;
piece of firewood **keunysenn** *f.*
+ow *coll.* **keunys;** place
abounding in firewood **keunysek** *f.*
-egi: *adj.* abounding in firewood
keunysek: *v.* gather firewood
keunyssa
fireworks *n.* **tanweyth** *coll.* **+enn**
firm *adj.* **fast, fyrv, tynn**
firmament *n.* **ebrenn** *f.*
firmly *adv.* **fast**
firmness *n.* **fyrvder** *m.*
first *n.* first of month **Kalann** *m.:*
adj. **kynsa:** *adv.* at first
wostalleth
fir-tree *n.* **sybwydhenn** *f.* **+ow**
coll. **sybwydh**
fish *n.* **pysk** *m.* **puskes:** *v.*
pyskessa
fish-bait *n.* **treustrumm** *m.*
fisherman *n.* **pyskador** *m.* **+yon**
fishing-ground *n.* **pyskek** *f.* **-egi**

fish-pond *n.* **pysklynn** *f.* **+ow**
fissile *adj.* **omfolsadow**
fissure *n.* **fols** *m.* **+yow**
fist *n.* **dorn** *m.* **+ow** *dual* **dewdhorn**
fistful *n.* **dornas** *m.* **+ow**
fisticuffs *n.* **boksas** *m.* **+ow**
fit *n.* **shora** *m.* **shorys**; fit of the
ague **kren an leghow** *m.:* *adj.*
(able) **abel**; (healthy) **yagh**;
(suitable) **gwiw:** *v.* **desedha,
kewera, kompoesa**
fitting *adj.* **gwiw, kemusur:** *v.* is
fitting **degoedh**
five *num.* **pymp**
fix *v.* **apoyntya**; (attach) **staga**
fix (U.S.) *v.* **ewnhe**
fixed *adj.* **stag**
fixedly *adv.* **stark**
flabby *adj.* **leyth**
flag *n.* **baner** *m.* **+yow**; (plant)
elestrenn *f.* **+ow** *coll.* **elester;**
cross flag **krowsvaner** *m.;* flag of
convenience **baner-es** *m.*
flag-bed *n.* **elestrek** *f.* **-egi**
flagon *n.* **kostrel** *m.* **+s, kruskynn**
m. **+ow**
flagstone *n.* **leghven** *m.* **-veyn**
flail *n.* **fust** *f.* **+ow**
flake *n.* **skansenn** *f.* **+ow** *coll.*
skans: *v.* **lownya**
flaky *adj.* **lownek, skansek**
flame *n.* **flamm** *m.* **+ow, fagel** *f.*
faglow: *v.* **flammya**
flank *n.* **tenewenn** *m.* **tenwennow**
flannel *n.* **gwlanenn** *f.* **+ow, lenn** *f.*
+ow
flap *n.* **lappa** *m.* **lappys:** *v.*
flappya
flare *v.* **dewi**
flash *v.* **lughesi**
flashlight (U.S.) *n.* **faglenn** *f.* **+ow**
flask *n.* **kostrel** *m.* **+s**
flat *n.* **rannji** *m.* **+ow:** *adj.*
gwastas, platt
flat-fish *n.* **leyth** *f.* **+ow**

flatter v. fekla
flattering adj. fekyl
flavour n. sawer m. +yow
flavoured adj. sawrys
flavouring n. sawrans m.: plur.
blesyon
flaw n. namm m. +ow
flax n. lin coll. +enn
flax-field n. linek f. -egi
flax-land n. lindir m. +yow
flay v. diruska
flea n. hwannenn f. +ow,
hwennenn f. hwenn
flee v. teghes, fia
fleece n. knyv m. +ow
fleet n. lu lestri m.
Flemish n. Flemish language
Flamanek m.: adj. Flamanek
flesh n. keher m. +ow, kig m.
+yow; living flesh byw m.: v.
grow flesh kiga: phr. in the flesh
yn trogel
flesh-coloured adj. kigliw
fleshhook n. kigver m. +yow
flexibility n. gwedhynder m.
flexible adj. gwedhyn, hebleth
flies n. horse flies kelyon margh
coll.: adj. full of flies kelyonek
flight n. fo m., nij m. +ow, tegh m.:
v. put to flight fesya; take flight fia
dhe'n fo
flinch n. plynch m. +ys: v.
plynchya
fling v. tewlel, deghesi
flint n. flynt m., kellester m.
flippers n. botas palvek f.
flit v. sommys, ternija
float n. (e.g. for fishing) neuvell f.
+ow: v. neuvella
flock n. para m. parys, tonnek m.;
(of animals) gre f. +ow; (of birds)
hes f. +ow: v. hesya
flocking n. hevva f.
flog v. kastiga
flogging n. kastik m.

flood n. liv m. +ow; flood stream
lanwes m.: v. liva
flood-plain n. fennva f.
floor n. leur m. +yow; upper floor
soler m. +yow
floor-cloth n. kweth-leur f.
kwethow-leur
floret n. bleujennik m.
flounder n. leyth f. +ow
flour n. bleus m. +yow; fine flour
bleus fin m.
flourish v. (of a sword) gwevya; (of
plants) glasa; (succeed) seweni
floury adj. bleusek
flow v. bera, dinewi
flower n. bleujenn f. +ow coll.
bleujyow, flour f. +ys: v.
bleujyowa
flower-bed n. bleujyowek f. -egi
floweret n. bleujennik m.
flowery adj. bleujyowek
flu n. terthenn f. +ow
fluctuate v. leskella
fluctuation n. leskell m. +ow
fluency n. frethter m.
fluent adj. freth
fluff n. mannbluv coll.
fluid n. lin m. +yow; fluid ounce
ouns devrek m.
fluke n. (of anchor) paw m. +yow
flume n. frosva f. +ow
fluorspar n. kann m.
flurry n. flurry of blows boksas m.
+ow
flute n. pib f. +ow, tollgorn m.
tollgern
flutter v. ternija
fly n. kelyonenn f. +ow coll.
kelyon: v. nija; fly over
treusnija
flyblown adj. kelyonek,
kontronek
flywheel n. hwelros f. +ow
foal n. ebel m. ebeli; (of an ass)
asynik m. -igow: v. kui

foam *n.* **ewyn** *coll.* **+enn**
foamy *adj.* **ewynek**
fo'c'sle *n.* **flour-rag** *m.*
focus *n.* **fog** *f.* **+ow**
fodder *n.* **boes** *m.*
foe *n.* **envi** *m.*, **eskar** *m.* **eskerens**
fog *n.* **niwl** *m.* **+ow**
fog-bank *n.* **niwlenn** *f.* **+ow**
fog-horn *n.* **niwlgorn** *m.*
foil *n.* piece of metal foil **folenn** *f.*
+ow
fold *n.* (bend) **pleg** *m.* **+ow**;
(enclosure) **korlann** *f.* **+ow**; (flap)
lappa *m.* **lappys**; (wrinkle) **kris** *m.*
+yow; fold forming pocket **askra**
f.: *v.* **plegya**
folder *n.* **plegell** *f.* **+ow**
folk *n.* **gwerin** *f.*, **pobel** *f.* **poblow**
folk-song *n.* **kan werin** *f.*
follow *v.* **sywya, holya, omsywya**
follower *n.* **gwas** *m.* **gwesyon,
dyskybel** *m.* **dyskyblon, holyer**
m. **-oryon, sywyas** *m.* **-ysi**
following *adv.* on the following
morning **ternos vyttin**
folly *n.* **foli** *m.*, **folneth** *f.*,
gokkineth *f.*, **nisyta** *m.*
fondness *n.* **karadewder** *m.*, **sergh**
m.
font *n.* **besydhven** *m.*
food *n.* **boes** *m.*, **sosten** *m.*
fool *n.* **fol** *m.* **felyon, boba** *m.*,
muskok *m.* **-ogyon, penn-bras**
m. **pennow-bras, penn-
broennenn** *m.* **pennow-
broennenn, penn-pyst** *m.*
pennow-pyst, skogynn *m.* **+ow**:
v. **toella**; act like a fool **dotya**
foolish *n.* foolish person **gokki** *m.*
+es: *adj.* **fol, gokki, diskians,
sempel**
foolishness *n.* **folneth** *f.*,
gokkineth *f.*
foot *n.* (Anat.) **troes** *m.* **treys** *dual*
dewdroes; (base) **ben** *m.* **+yow**;

(unit of length) **troes-hys** *m.*: *adv.*
on foot **a-droes**
football *n.* **peldroes** *f.*
footbridge *n.* **troespons** *m.* **+ow**
foothold *n.* **troesla** *m.* **troesleow**
footpath *n.* **troe'lergh** *m.* **+ow,
kerdhva** *f.* **+ow**
foot-rule *n.* **skantlyn** *m.* **+s**
foot-stool *n.* **skavell-droes** *f.*
footwear *n.* **arghenas** *m.*
for *prep.* **dhe, rag, er**; for her
rygdhi; for him **ragdho**; for me
ragov; for thee **ragos**; for them
ragdha; for us **ragon**; for you
ragowgh
forbid *v.* **difenn**: *phr.* forbid
someone to do something **difenn
orth nebonan a wul neppyth**;
God forbid **Dyw difenn**
forbidding *n.* **difenn** *m.*
force *n.* **nerth** *m.* **+yow, fors** *m.*,
nell *m.*; police force **kreslu** *m.*;
security force **lu diogeledh** *m.*: *v.*
ynnia
ford *n.* **roswydh** *f.*, **rys** *f.* **+yow**;
shallow ford **basdhowr** *m.*
foreboding *n.* **ragown** *m.*
forecast *n.* **dargan** *f.* **+ow**: *v.*
dargana, darleverel
forecastle *n.* **flour-rag** *m.*
forefather *n.* **hendas** *m.* **+ow,
ragdas** *m.* **+ow**
forefinger *n.* **bys rag** *m.*
forefront *n.* **bleyn** *m.* **+yow**
forehead *n.* **tal** *m.* **+yow, korn tal**
m.
foreign *adj.* **astranj, estrenyek**
foreigner *n.* **estren** *m.* **+yon,
alyon** *m.* **+s**
foreman *n.* **pennweythor** *m.* **+yon**
forenoon *n.* **myttin** *m.* **+yow,
kynseghwa** *m.*, **myttinweyth** *m.*
forerunner *n.* **ragreser** *m.* **-oryon**
foresee *v.* **ragweles**
foresight *n.* **ragwel** *m.*

forest *n.* koes *m.* +ow, koeswik
f.-igow
foretaste *n.* ragvlas *m.*
foretell *v.* darleverel
forethought *n.* ragbreder *m.*
forewarn *v.* darwarnya
forewarned *int.* be forewarned
darwar
foreword *n.* rager *m.*, raglavar *m.*
+ow
forfeit *n.* gaja *m.* gajys: *v.* kelli
forfeiture *n.* spal *m.* +yow
forge *n.* gelforn *f.* +ow: *v.*
govelya
forget *v.* ankevi
forgetfulness *n.* ankov *m.*,
ankovva *f.*
forgive *v.* gava, gava dhe
forgiveness *n.* dehwelans *m.*,
gevyans *m.*
fork *n.* (tool) forgh *f.* fergh; (Y-
shape) gowl *f.* +ow
forked *adj.* gowlek
form *n.* furv *f.* +ow, roth *m.* +ow,
shap *m.* +ys: *v.* furvya, shapya
former *adj.* kyns
formerly *adv.* kyns, seulabrys,
seuladhydh
forsooth *adv.* dhe-wir
forswear *v.* forswear oneself gowlia
fort *n.* din *m.*, dinas *m.*, ker *f.*
+yow; small fort dinan *m.*
forthwith *adv.* a-dhesempis,
desempis, dison, hware
fortification *n.* kerweyth *m.*
fortify *v.* (a person) nertha;
(strengthen a defence-work) kera
fortress *n.* kastell *m.* kastylli,
skons *m.*
fortunate *adj.* feusik, gwynnvys
fortunately *adv.* y'n gwella prys
fortune *n.* chons *m.* +yow, fortun
m. +yow, happ *m.* +ys
fortune-teller *n.* koelyek *m.*
-ogyon, koelyoges *f.* +ow

forty *num.* dewgens, dew-ugens
forward *adv.* yn-rag
forwards *adv.* war-rag
foster-father *n.* tasmeth *m.* +ow
foster-mother *n.* mammveth *f.*
+ow
foster-son *n.* mab-meythrin *m.*
foul *n.* foul person plos *m.* +yon;
foul play falsuri *m.*: *adj.* hager,
plos
foul-mouthed *adj.* plos y daves
foulness *n.* plos *m.* +yon,
plosedhes *m.*; (of stink) flerynsi
m.
found *v.* fondya, grondya, selya
foundation *n.* fondyans *m.* +ow,
grond *m.*, sel *f.* +yow; foundation
stone selven *m.* selveyn: *v.* lay
foundations fondya, grondya
founder *n.* fondyer *m.* -oryon
foundry *n.* teudhji *m.* +ow,
teudhla *m.*, teudhva *f.* +ow
fountain *n.* fenten *f.* fentynyow
four *num.* (f.) peder; (m.) peswar:
adv. four times pedergweyth
four-cornered *adj.* peswar-
kornek
four-score *num.* peswar-ugens
fourteen *num.* peswardhek
fourteenth *num.* peswardhegves
fourth *num.* peswara
Fowey *place* Fowydh
fowl *n.* wild fowl edhen *f.* ydhyn;
young fowl mabyar *f.* -yer
fowler *n.* ydhna *m.*
fox *n.* lowarn *m.* lewern, lostek *m.*
-ogyon: *adj.* abounding in foxes
lowarnek
fox-cub *n.* lowarnik *m.*
lewernigow
fraction *n.* darnas *m.* +ow; (math.)
rannriv *m.* +ow
fracture *n.* torr *m.* +ow
fragile *adj.* hedorr

fragment *n.* tamm *m.* temmyn, brewyonenn *f.* +ow *coll.* brewyon, browsyonenn *f.* +ow *coll.* browsyon, darn *m.* +ow, dernik *m.*, dral *m.*

frail *adj.* gwann, brottel

frailty *n.* gwannder *m.*, gwannegredh *m.*

frame *n.* frame for fishing kanter *m.* kantrow; frame for the moulding of a wooden plough branell *m.* +ow; timber frame in mine stoul *m.: v.* framya

framework *n.* fram *m.* +ow, framweyth *m.*, starn *f.* +yow

France *n.* Pow Frynk *m.: place* Frynk

franchise *n.* franchis *m.*

fraud *n.* frows *m.*, toell *m.*

fraudulent *adj.* frowsus

fray *v.* fray out freudha, neusa

freak *n.* kanjon *m.* +s

freckled *adj.* brithennek, brygh

freckles *n.* brith *coll.* +enn

free *n.* free hand rydhambos *m.: adj.* rydh, frank, kwit; (liberated) dhe wari; free of charge heb kost: *v.* set free delivra, rydhhe

freedom *n.* frankedh *m.*, rydhses *m.*

freemason *n.* frankmason *m.* +s

freeway *n.* fordh-lan *f.* fordhow-glan

free-wheel *n.* ros-rydh *f.*

freeze *v.* rewi

freezer *n.* rewell *f.*

freezing *adj.* oer

freight *n.* fres *m.*

French *n.* French language Frynkek *m.: adj.* Frynkek

Frenchman *n.* Frynk *m.* +yon

French-speaker *n.* Frynkeger *m.* -oryon

Frenchwoman *n.* Frynkes *f.* +ow

frequency *n.* menowghder *m.*

frequent *v.* daromres

frequently *adv.* menowgh

fresh *adj.* fresk, yr; (new) nowydh; (of food) kro

fret *v.* brogha

friction *n.* rutyans *m.: v.* apply friction rutya

Friday *n.* dy' Gwener *m.*, dy' Gwener *f.;* Good Friday Gwener an Grows *f.*

friend *n.* kar *m.* kerens, koweth *m.* +a, kowethes *f.* +ow, kothman *m.* +s; familiar friend koth *m.*

friend(s) *n.* sos *m.*

friendly *n.* friendly person kolonnek *m.* -ogyon

friendship *n.* kerensa *f.*

frier *n.* deep-fat frier leswedh fria-down *m.*

fright *v.* take fright kemmeres own

frighten *v.* ownekhe

frightful *adj.* grysel

frigid *adj.* oer

frigidity *n.* oerni *m.*

fringe *n.* pil *coll.* +enn, pilenn *f.* +ow *coll.* pil: *v.* neusa

fringed *adj.* pilennek

Frisian *n.* Frisian language Frisek *m.*

frisk *v.* terlemmel

frivolous *adj.* euver

frock *n.* pows *f.* +yow

frog *n.* kwilkyn *m.* +yow

from *prep.* a, dhiworth, diworth, a-dhia, a-dhiworth; from beneath a-dhann; from on a-dhiwar; from on top of diwar; from over a-dhiwar; from under a-dhann: *adv.* from her anedhi; from him anodho; from me ahanav; from thee ahanas; from them anedha; from us ahanan; from you ahanowgh

front *prep.* in front of a-dherag, a-rag, derag

fronting *prep.* a-dal

frost *n.* rew *m.*

frosty *adj.* rewek
froth *n.* ewyn *coll.* +enn: *v.* ewyni
frothy *adj.* ewynek
frown *n.* talgamm *m.* +ow: *v.*
  talgamma
frowzy *adj.* flerys
frugal *adj.* tanow
fruit *n.* (in general) froeth *coll.*
  +enn, frut *m.* +ys
fruitful *adj.* feyth
fruitfulness *n.* feythter *m.*
fry *v.* fria
frying-pan *n.* leswedh *m.* +ow,
  padell-fria *f.* padellow-fria
fry-up *n.* frias *m.* +ow
fuel *n.* keunys *coll.* +enn; dried
  cow-dung used as fuel glos *coll.*
  +enn
fuel-gatherer *n.* (female)
  keunysores *f.* +ow; (male)
  keunyser *m.* -oryon
fugitive *n.* fowesik *m.* -igyon
fulcrum *n.* kolpes *m.* +ow
fulfil *v.* kewera, kollenwel
fulfilment *n.* keweras *m.*
full *adj.* leun; full of grace leun a
  ras
fullness *n.* lanow *m.*, leunder *m.*
full-stop *n.* hedh *m.* +ow
fully *adv.* purra
fume *n.* mog *m.:* *v.* brogha
fun *n.* gwari *m.* +ow, delit *m.:* *v.*
  make fun of gul ges a
function *n.* gweythres *m.*, offis *m.*
  offisys
functional *adj.* gweythresel
fund *n.* arghas *m.* +ow
fundamental *adj.* selvenek
funny *adj.* didhan, hwarthus
fur *n.* garment of fur pellyst *m.* +ow
furious *adj.* konneryek
furlong *n.* erowhys *m.* +ow
furnace *n.* fog *f.* +ow, fornes *f.*
  +yow, oden *f.*

furnish *v.* provia, takla
furniture *n.* gotrel *m.*, mebyl *m.*
furrow *n.* fynngel *f.* fynnglow,
  ryll *f.* +ow
furthermore *adv.* hwath pella
fury *n.* konnar *f.*
furze-brake *n.* eythinek *f.* -egi
furze-hook *n.* krommenn eythin
  f.
fuse *n.* teudherik *m.* -igow: *v.*
  teudhi
fuse-box *n.* teudherigva *f.* +ow
fuss *n.* trynn *f.:* *v.* brogha
fussy *adj.* denti, fyslek
futile *adj.* euver
futility *n.* euveredh *m.*

G

gabble *n.* klapp *m.:* *v.* klappya,
  gerya
gabbler *n.* klappyer *m.* +s
gable *n.* tal *m.* +yow, punyon *m.*
gadflies *n.* kelyon margh *coll.*
gadfly *n.* stos *m.* +ow
Gael *n.* Goedhel *m.* Goedhyli,
  Gwydhel *m.* Gwydhyli,
  Gwydheles *f.* +ow
Gaelic *n.* Gaelic language
  Gwydhelek *m.;* Gaelic speaker
  Gwydheleger *m.* -oryon: *adj.*
  Gwydhelek
gain *n.* budh *m.*, gwayn *m.*, prow
  m.: *v.* gwaynya, dendil
gaiters *n.* polltrigas *m.*
gale *n.* awel *f.* +yow
gall *n.* bystel *f.*
gallery *n.* shooting gallery stall
  tenna *m.*
gallows *n.* krogbrenn *m.* +yer:
  plur. kloghbrennyer
gallows-bird *n.* skrogenn *f.*
galoot *n.* lorden *m.* +yon, +s
gamble *v.* happwari

gambol v. terlemmel
game n. gwari m. +ow;
(competition) sport m. +ow, +ys;
(meat) helgik m.; (object of hunt)
gam m.: phr. the game is up
gallas fassow
gaming-house n. chi gwari m.
gander n. kulyek goedh m.
gang n. para m. parys
gannet n. sether m. -oryon
gaoler n. jayler m. +s
gap n. aswa f. +ow, bolgh m. +ow:
v. make a gap gul aswa
gaping adj. ganowek
gapped adj. aswek
garage n. karrji m. +ow
garbage (U.S.) n. atal c., strol m.
garbage can (U.S.) n. atalgyst f.
+yow, strolgyst f. +yow
garden n. lowarth m. +yow, garth
m. +ow, jardin m., jarn m.: v.
lowartha
gardener n. lowarther m. -oryon
gar-fish n. garek m.
garland n. garlont f. +ow
garlic n. kennin coll. +enn, kennin
ewinek coll.; place abounding in
garlic kenninek f. -egi: adj.
abounding in garlic kenninek
garment n. dillasenn f. dillas coll.
dillas; garment of fur pellyst m.
+ow
garnish n. afinans m.: v. afina
garret n. talik m. taligow
garter n. gargett m. +ow
gas n. gas m. +ow; natural gas gas-
dor m.
gasket n. stanchynn m. +ow
gasp v. dyewa
gastritis n. fagel-las f.
gate n. yet f. yetys, yetow
gateway n. porth m. +ow
gather v. kuntell, kreuni,
omguntell; gather firewood
keunyssa

gathering n. kuntell m. +ow,
kuntelles m. +ow, kuntellyans m.
+ow; informal gathering at which
Cornish is spoken Yeth an Werin f.
gauge n. musurell f. +ow
gauntlet n. manek plat f.
gauze n. niwlwias m. +ow
gauzy adj. boll
gawk v. lagatta
gawker (U.S.) n. lagatter m.
-oryon
gaze v. lagatta; gaze upon hwithra
war
gear n. (mech.) maglenn f. +ow;
reverse gear maglenn dhelergh f.:
plur. pythow: v. engage gear
magla
gear (clothes) n. aparel m.
gear-box n. kyst-vaglenn f.
kystyow-maglenn
gear-lever n. kolpes-vaglenn m.
kolpesow-maglenn
gearshift (U.S.) n. kolpes-
vaglenn m. kolpesow-maglenn
gear-stick n. kolpes-vaglenn m.
kolpesow-maglenn
gelatine n. jelatin m.
geld v. spadha
gelded adj. spadh
gem n. gemm m. +ow
gene n. genynn m. +ow
genealogist n. aghskrifer m.
-oryon
genealogy n. aghskrif m. +ow
general n. pennhembrenkyas m.
pennhembrynkysi
generally adv. dre vras
generate v. dineythi
generation n. (as a process)
dineythyans m. +ow; (people in a
family) henedh m. +ow
generosity n. helder m., larjes m.
generous adj. hel, larj
genesis n. dallethvos m.
genetic adj. genynnek

genetics *n.* **genynnegieth** *f.*
genius *n.* **awen** *f.*
gentian *n.* field gentian **gwylles** *coll.*
Gentile *n.* **Jentil** *m.* **+ys**
gentle *adj.* **hweg, dov, hwar,**
   jentyl
gentleman *n.* **den jentyl** *m.*
gentleness *n.* **jentylys** *m.*
gentler *v.* make gentler **hwarhe**
gentlewoman *n.* **benyn jentyl** *f.*
gently *adv.* **war gamm**
genuine *adj.* **gwiryon**
geo *n.* **saven** *f.* **savnow, sawn** *f.*
   +yow
geographer *n.* **dorydh** *m.* **+yon**
geographical *adj.* **doroniethel**
geography *n.* **doronieth** *f.*
geologist *n.* **dororydh** *m.* **+yon**
geology *n.* **dororieth** *f.*
geometry *n.* **mynsonieth** *f.*
George *name* **Jori**
germ *n.* (microbe) **korrbryv** *m.* **+es**
German *n.* **Alman** *m.* **+yon,**
   Almanes *f.* **+ow**; German
   language **Almaynek** *m.:* *adj.*
   Almaynek
Germany *place* **Almayn**
germinate *v.* **egina**
get *v.* **kavoes, kyrghes**; get out
   avodya
ghost *n.* **tarosvann** *m.* **+ow,**
   boekka gwynn *m.*
ghostly *adj.* **tarosvannus**
giant *n.* **kowr** *m.* **kewri**
giantess *n.* **kowres** *f.* **+ow**
gibbet *n.* **krogla** *m.*
gid *n.* (disease of sheep) **penn-dro** *f.*
giddiness *n.* **penn-dro** *f.*
gift *n.* **ro** *m.* **rohow**; New Year's gift
   kalennik *m.*
gifted *adj.* **roasek**
gigantic *adj.* **kowrek**
giggle *n.* **folhwarth** *m.:* *v.*
   folhwerthin

gild *v.* **owra**; gild over **gorowra**
gin *n.* (drink) **jenevra** *m.;* (machine)
   jynn *m.* **+ow, +ys**
giraffe *n.* **jiraf** *m.* **+es**
gird *v.* **grogysa**
girdle *n.* **grogys** *m.* **+yow, kyngel**
   f. **kenglow**: *v.* **grogysa**
girl *n.* **mowes** *f.* **mowesi, myrgh** *f.*
   myrghes; little girl **myrghik** *f.*
   myrghesigow; pert girl
   flownenn *f.* **+ow**
girl-friend *n.* **kares** *f.* **+ow**
give *v.* **ri**; (command) **roy**; give
   back **daskorr, restorya**; give birth
   dineythi; give out falsely **dolos**;
   give up **daskorr, hepkorr**: *phr.*
   let us give **ren**; we give **ren**
given *v.* **res**
giver *n.* **riyas** *m.* **riysi**
gives *v.* **re**
gizzard *n.* **avi glas** *m.*, **krommbil** *f.*
glad *adj.* **lowen, heudh, heudhik,**
   lowenek: *v.* be glad **heudha,**
   heudhhe; make glad **lowenhe**
gladden *v.* **heudhhe**
glade *n.* **lannergh** *m.* **+i**
glass *n.* **gweder** *m.* **gwedrow;**
   drinking glass **gwedrenn** *f.* **+ow;**
   pane of glass **kwarel** *m.* **+s**
glasses (spectacles) *dual* **dewweder**
glassful *n.* **gwedrennas** *m.* **+ow**
glen *n.* **glynn** *m.* **+ow**
glisten *v.* **terlentri**
glitter *v.* **dewynnya, glyttra**
glittering *adj.* **dewynnek**
global *adj.* (of Earth) **ollvysel**
globe *n.* **pel an norvys** *f.*
gloomy *adj.* **tewal, tewl, trist**
glorious *adj.* **gloryus**
glory *n.* **glori** *m.*, **golowder** *m.*,
   gordhyans *m.*, **gormeula** *m.*
glossary *n.* **gerlyvrynn** *m.* **+ow**
glove *n.* **manek** *f.* **manegow**
glover *n.* **maneger** *m.* **-oryon**
glue *n.* **glus** *m.* **+ow**: *v.* **glusa**

glut *n.* gorfalster *m.*, gwalgh *m.*
glutton *n.* gargasenn *f.* +ow,
    kowlek *m.* -ogyon
gluttonous *adj.* kowlek
gluttony *n.* glotni *m.*, kowlogneth
    f.
gnash *v.* deskerni
gnashing *n.* skrinva *f.*
gnat *n.* gwibesenn *f.* +ow *coll.*
    gwibes, stos *m.* +ow: *adj.*
    infested by gnats gwibesek
gnaw *v.* knias
go *v.* ke, mos, mones; go after
    holya; go astray mos yn
    sowdhan; go away avodya; go
    down diyskynna: *phr.* to go on an
    errand mones negys
goad *n.* piger *m.* +yow: *v.* brosa
goal *n.* (aim) amkan *m.* +ow
goat *n.* gaver *f.* gever; baby goat
    mynnenn *f.* +ow; buck bogh *m.;*
    wether goat kynbogh *m.;* young
    goat gevrik *f.* -igow, mynn *m.*
    +ow
goatherd *n.* bugel gever *m.*
goat-shed *n.* krow gever *m.*
goatsucker (U.S.) *n.* churra-nos
    m.
god *n.* dyw *m.* +ow
God *n.* Dyw *m.:* *phr.* by God a-
    barth Dyw, God speed Dyw
    gweres
goddess *n.* dywes *f.* +ow
godhead *n.* dywses *m.*
goes *v.* (part of irreg. vb.) a
goffering-iron *n.* jynn-krygh *m.*
    jynnow-krygh
goggler *n.* lagatter *m.* -oryon
gold *n.* owr *m.:* *v.* cover with gold
    leaf gorowra
golden *adj.* owrek
goldfinch *n.* melynek *m.* -oges,
    owrdynk *m.* +es
goldfish *n.* owrbysk *m.*
    owrbuskes

gold-mine *n.* owrek *f.* -egi, poll
    owr *m.*
goldsmith *n.* owrer *m.* -oryon
gone *adj.* gyllys: *phr.* completely
    gone gyllys glan
good *n.* good man demmas *m.*,
    densa *m.*, dremas *m.:* *adj.* da;
    (morally) mas: *phr.* good day
    durdadhejy, durdadhy'hwi;
    good night durnostadha; it's no
    good ny amont
good &day *n.* dydh da *m.*
goodbye *int.* farwel: *phr.* Dyw
    genes
goodness *n.* dader *m.*
goodnight *n.* nos dha *f.*
goods *n.* gwara *c.*, stoff *m.;*
    consumer goods gwara
    devnydhyoryon *c.;* goods train
    tren fres *m.*
goodwife *n.* ben'vas *f.*, benyn-vas
    f.
goose *n.* goedh *f.* +ow; solan goose
    sether *m.* -oryon; stubble goose
    sowlwoedh *f.* +ow
gooseberry *n.* growsenn *f.* +ow
    coll. grows
goosegrass *n.* serghegenn *f.* +ow
    coll. serghek
goose-green *n.* pras goedh *m.*
goose-house *n.* krow goedhow *m.*
goosepond *n.* poll goedh *m.*
gore *n.* goes *m.*, krow *m.*
gorilla *n.* gorylla *m.* gorylles
gorse *n.* eythinenn *f.* +ow *coll.*
    eythin
gosling *n.* goedhik *m.* -igow
gospel *n.* aweyl *f.* +ys, +yow
gossip *plur.* hwedhlow
gourd *n.* pompyon *m.* +s
govern *v.* governya
government *n.* governans *m.* +ow
governor *n.* governour *m.* +s;
    governor of shire yurl *m.* yurlys
gown *n.* pows *f.* +yow, gon *m.*

grace *n.* gras *m.* grassys,
grassow, jentylys *m.,* ras *m.*
+ow: *adj.* full of grace leun a ras;
out of grace diskrassyes

graceless *adj.* diras

gracious *adj.* deboner, grassyes

grade *n.* gradh *m.* +ow: *adj.*
higher grade ughradh

gradient *n.* ledras *m.* +ow

gradually *n.* tamm ha tamm *m.*

graduate *n.* (female) gradhesiges
f. +ow; (male) gradhesik *m.*
-igyon: *v.* gredhya

graffiti *n.* fosskrif *coll.* +enn

graft *n.* ymp *m.* +s: *v.* graffya,
ympya

grail *n.* gral *m.*

grain *n.* (an individual) greunenn *f.*
+ow *coll.* greun; (as a mass)
greun *coll.* +enn

grains *n.* brewer's grains seg *coll.*

gram *n.* gramm *m.* +ow

grammar *n.* (book) yethador *m.*

grammarian *n.* yethor *m.* +yon

grammatical *adj.* gramasek

granary *n.* greunji *m.* +ow, ysla
m. ysleow

grand *adj.* brav

grandchild *n.* flogh-gwynn *m.*
fleghes-wynn

grandfather *n.* tas-gwynn *m.*
tasow-wynn, hendas *m.* +ow,
keugh *m.* +yon, sira wynn *m.*

grandmother *n.* dama-wynn *f.,*
mamm-wynn *f.* mammow-
gwynn

grandson *n.* mab-wynn *m.*
mebyon-wynn

grange *n.* greunji *m.* +ow

granite *n.* growan *m.;* granite
gravel rabmen *m.;* granite outcrop
growanek *f.* -egi

granitic *adj.* growanek

granny-knot *n.* kammgolm *m.*
+ow

grant *n.* gront *m.* +ow, +ys: *v.* ri,
grontya

grape *n.* grappa *m.* grappys,
grappow, gwinreunenn *f.* +ow
coll. gwinreun

grapefruit *n.* aval-paradhis *m.*
avalow-paradhis

grape-vine *n.* gwinbrenn *m.* +yer

graph *n.* tresenn *f.* +ow

grapnel *n.* grabel *m.* grablow,
grablys

grapple *v.* grabalyas

grappling *n.* grappling iron grabel
m. grablow, grablys

grappling hook (U.S.) *n.* grabel
m. grablow, grablys

grasp *n.* dalghenn *f.* +ow, gavel *f.*
+yow, kraf *m.* +ow: *v.*
dalghenna, krafa

grasping *adj.* kraf, pith

grass *n.* gwels *coll.* +enn; bent
coarse grass fynni *f.;* couch-grass
treuswels *coll.;* growing grass
gwyrwels *coll.;* new growth of
grass aswels *m.;* tussock grass
fynni veur *f.*

grasshopper *n.* kulyek-reden *m.*

grassland *n.* gwelstir *m.* +yow

grass-plot *n.* glesyjyon *m.,*
gwelsek *f.* -egi

grasswrack *n.* morwels *coll.*

grassy *n.* grassy plot glesin *m.*
+yow: *adj.* gwelsek

grate *v.* rathella

grater *n.* rathell *f.* +ow

gratitude *n.* gras *m.* grassys,
grassow

gratuity *n.* grastal *m.*

grave *n.* bedh *m.* +ow; saint's grave
merther *m.* +yon

gravel *n.* grow *coll.,* growynn *coll.*
+enn; (one lump) growenn *f.*
grow; gravel pit growek *f.* -egi,
growgleudh *m.* +yow

gravelly *n.* gravelly subsoil growdir
m.: *adj.* growynnek

gravel-pit *n.* growynnek *f.* -egi,
poll growynn *m.*
gravestone *n.* men-bedh *m.*
meyn-bedh
gravity *n.* (abst.) sevureth *f.;* (in
physics) gravedh *m.*
graze *v.* (feed) peski, peuri
grazing-place *n.* peurla *m.,*
peurva *f.,* peurwels *m.*
grease *n.* blonek *m.: v.* ura
greaseproof *adj.* gorthsaym
greasy *adj.* blonegek
great *n.* great man bras *m.* +yon:
adj. bras, meur: *v.* make great
meurhe: *adv.* how great
pygemmys
great-aunt *n.* gorvodrep *f.*
gorvodrebedh
great-grandfather *n.* tas-kuv *m.*
tasow-guv
great-grandmother *n.* mamm-
guv *f.* mammow-kuv
great-great-grandfather *n.*
dehengeugh *m.*
great-great-great-grandfather *n.*
gorhengeugh *m.* +yon
greatness *n.* braster *m.,* meuredh
m.; (abst.) brastereth *f.*
great-uncle *n.* gorewnter *m.* -tres
Greece *n.* Pow Grek *m.*
greed *n.* kovaytys *m.,* krefni *f.,*
pithneth *f.*
greedy *adj.* kraf, pith
Greek *n.* Greka *m.* Grekys; Greek
language Greka *m.,* Grew *m.*
green *adj.* gwyr, gwyrdh; (of
plants) glas: *v.* glasa
greenhorn (U.S.) *n.* glaswas *m.*
-wesyon
greenhouse *n.* chi gweder *m.,*
losowji *m.* +ow
greenness *n.* glasneth *f.,* glesni *m.*
greensward *n.* glasenn *f.* +ow,
glastonn *m.*
greet *v.* dynnerghi
greeting *n.* dynnargh *m.*

greetings *n.* gorhemmynnadow
m.
grey *adj.* loes; light grey glas
grey-bearded *adj.* minrew
greyhound *n.* milast *f.* milisti,
milgi *m.* milgeun; large greyhound
gwylter *m.*
greyish *adj.* loesik
greyness *n.* loesedh *m.,* loesni *m.*
grid *n.* rastell *f.* restell
griddle *n.* men-pobas *m.* meyn-
pobas
grief *n.* galar *m.* +ow, keudh *m.,*
anken *m.* +yow, dughan *m.,* gew
m. +ow, grev *m.* +ow, moredh *m.:*
plur. fienasow, kavow: *adj.*
without grief dialar: *v.* inflict grief
ankenya
grievance *n.* grevons *m.*
grieve *v.* dughanhe, galari,
grevya, keudhi
grievous *adj.* ankensi
grill *n.* rastell *f.* restell: *v.*
rastella
grim *adj.* asper, fell
grimace *n.* mingamm *m.* +ow,
mowa *m.* mowys: *v.* kammin,
mingamma, omgamma min,
skrynkya; grimace at omgamma
orth; make a grimace at skrynkya
orth
grime *n.* hudhygel *m.*
grin *v.* grysla
grind *v.* mala, melyas
grinder *n.* maler *m.* -oryon
grindstone *n.* brewliv *f.*
grip *n.* dalghenn *f.* +ow, kraf *m.*
+ow: *phr.* get a grip on kavoes
dalghenn yn, settya dalghenn
yn
gripes *n.* gyrr *m.*
grisly *adj.* grysel
grist *n.* arval *m.,* talgh *m.* telghyon
grit *n.* grow *coll.;* (one piece)
growenn *f.* grow; (stone)
growynn *coll.* +enn

groat *n.* (silver coin worth one sixtieth
of a pound) **grot** *m.* **+ys:** *plur.*
groats (meal) **brunyon**
grocer *n.* **spiser** *m.* **-oryon, +s**
grocer's *n.* grocer's shop **spisti** *m.*
+ow
groin *n.* **kedhorva** *f.*
groom *n.* (at a wedding) **gour pries**
m.; (for horses) **paja mergh** *m.*
grope *v.* **palvala**
gross *adj.* (fat) **berrik**
grossness *n.* **berri** *m.*
ground *n.* **dor** *m.,* **leur** *m.* **+yow, tir**
m. **+yow, grond** *m.;* (soil) **gweres**
m. **+ow;** fertile ground **gwresenn**
f.; ground rich in tin **skovenn** *f.;*
low ground **stras** *m.* **+ow, tenow**
m. **+i;** ore-bearing ground **moenek**
f. **moenegi;** soft ground **floukenn**
f.; the ground **an dor** *m.;* verdant
ground **glastir** *m.* **+yow**
groundnut *n.* **knowenn dhor** *f.*
groundsel *n.* **madra** *m.*
group *n.* **bagas** *m.* **+ow**
grouse *n.* **kulyek gwyls** *m.*
grove *n.* **kelli** *f.* **kelliow, kelliwik** *f.*
-igow; sacred grove **neves** *m.;*
small grove **kellian** *f.:* *adj.*
pertaining to a sacred grove
nevesek
grow *v.* **tevi;** grow flesh **kiga;** grow
less **difyga**
growl *v.* **grommya**
growth *n.* **tevyans** *m.*
grudge *n.* **envi** *m.*
grumble *v.* **krodhvolas**
grumbling *adj.* **krodhek**
grunt *n.* **rogh** *m.* **+ow:** *v.* **rogha**
guarantee *n.* **mewgh** *m.* **+yow:** *v.*
mewghya
guarantor *n.* **mewghyer** *m.*
-yoryon
guard *n.* **gwithyas** *m.* **gwithysi;**
(of train) **gwithyas tren** *m.:* *v.*
guard against **gwitha orth, gwitha**
war; guard animals **bugelya;**

guard from **gwitha rag;** guard
oneself **omwitha;** guard oneself
from **omwitha diworth**
guardian *n.* **gwithyas** *m.*
gwithysi, gwithyades *f.* **+ow**
guelder-rose *n.* **korswigenn** *f.*
+ow *coll.* **korswik**
guess *n.* **dismyk** *m.:* *v.* **dismygi**
guest *n.* **gwester** *m.* **-oryon,**
gwestores *f.* **+ow**
guest-house *n.* **gwesti** *m.* **+ow**
guidance *n.* **gedyans** *m.,*
kevarwoedh *m.,*
kevarwoedhyans *m.*
guide *n.* **gedyer** *m.* **-oryon;**
(female) **kevarwoedhores** *f.* **+ow;**
(male) **kevarwoedher** *m.* **+yon:**
v. **kevarwoedha, gedya**
guild *n.* **myster** *m.*
guildhall *n.* **burjesti** *m.* **+ow**
guile *n.* **gil** *m.,* **trayn** *m.* **+ys**
guillotine *n.* **gilotin** *m.*
guilty *adj.* **kablus;** not guilty
ankablus
guinea-fowl *n.* **gallina** *m.* **gallinys**
guitar *n.* **gitar** *m.*
guitarist *n.* **gitarydh** *m.* **+yon**
gull *n.* **goelann** *f.* **+es;** black-
headed gull **skraw** *m.,* **skrawik** *m.*
-igow
gullet *n.* **bryansenn** *f.,* **gargasenn**
f. **+ow**
gully *n.* **lonk** *m.,* **saven** *f.* **savnow,**
sawn *f.* **+yow**
gulp *v.* **daslenki, terlenki**
gun *n.* **gonn** *m.* **+ys, +ow**
gunpowder *n.* **polter-gonn** *m.*
gurgle *v.* **renki**
gurnard *n.* **penngarn** *m.* **+es;** grey
gurnard **penngarn glas** *m.;* red
gurnard **elek** *m.* **eleges, gevrik** *f.*
-igow, tuba-rudh *m.*
gush *v.* **dewraga, frosa**
gust *n.* **kowas gwyns** *f.*
gut *n.* **kolodhyonenn** *f.* **+enn** *coll.*
kolodhyon

gutter *n.* londer *m.*
guy (U.S.) *n.* gwas *m.* gwesyon;
old guy kothwas *m.* -wesyon
guzzler *n.* gargasenn *f.* +ow
gymnast *n.* lappyer *m.* -yoryon,
lappyores *f.* +ow
gymnastics *v.* perform gymnastics
lappya
gynaecologist *n.* bengorfydh *m.*
+yon
gynaecology *n.* bengorfonieth *f.*

H

ha *int.* ha
habergeon *n.* hoberjon *m.*
habit *n.* us *m.,* usadow *m.;* monk's
habit gon *m.*
habitable *adj.* annedhadow
habitat *n.* bywva *f.* +ow
habitation *n.* annedh *f.* +ow
habitual *adj.* usys
habitually *adv.* herwydh usadow,
dell yw usys
hack *n.* (horse) hakney *m.* +s: *v.*
hakkya; hack to pieces hakkya
dhe demmyn
haddock *n.* korrvarvus *m.*
Hades *n.* annown *m.*
haemorrhage *n.* fros goes *m.*
haft *n.* dorn *m.* +ow
hag *n.* gwragh *f.* +es
hail *n.* (weather) keser *coll.: v.*
(greet) haylya: *int.* (greeting) hayl
hail-stone *n.* keserenn *f.* +ow *coll.*
keser
hair *n.* blew *coll.;* a hair blewenn *f.*
+ow *coll.* blew; coarse hair of
mane reun *f.;* fine hair mannvlew
coll. +enn; head of hair gols *m.;*
plait of hair pleth *f.* +ow, plethenn
f. +ow; pubic hair kedhor *m.*
hairless *adj.* blogh
hair-shirt *n.* hevis *m.* +yow

hairy *adj.* blewek
hake *n.* densek *m.* densoges
half *n.* hanter *m.*
half-light *n.* tewlwolow *m.*
halfpenny *n.* hanterdiner *m.*
hall *n.* hel *f.* +yow, lys *f.* +yow;
exhibition hall stevell-
dhiskwedhyans *f.*
hallo *int.* hou
hallow *v.* benniga
Hallows *n.* All Hallows Kalann
Gwav *m.*
halt *v.* hedhi: *int.* hedh, ho
halter *n.* kabester *m.* -trow,
pennfester *m.*
ham *n.* mordhos hogh *f.*
hamlet *n.* godrev *f.* +i, penndra *f.*
hammer *n.* morthol *m.* +ow: *v.*
mortholya
hamper *v.* ankombra
hamster *n.* hamster *m.* +s
hand *n.* (in general) leuv *f.* +yow
dual diwla, diwleuv;
(pejoratively) paw *m.* +yow; (when
used as an instrument) dorn *m.* +ow
dual dewdhorn
hand-bag *n.* tigenn *f.* +ow
hand-barrow *n.* gravath-diwla *m.*
handbook *n.* dornlyver *m.,*
kowethlyver *m.* -lyvrow
hand-breadth *n.* dornva *f.*
dornvedhi
handcart (U.S.) *n.* gravath-diwla
m.
handcuffs *n.* karghar-horn *m.*
handful *n.* dornas *m.* +ow
handhold *n.* dornla *m.* dornleow
handicapped *n.* handicapped man
evredhek *m.* -ogyon;
handicapped woman evredhes *f.*
+ow
handkerchief *n.* lien dorn *m.*
handle *n.* dornla *m.* dornleow;
handle of jar skovarn *f.*

skovornow *dual* **diwskovarn:** *v.*
handla
handles *adj.* having handles
skovarnek
handmill *n.* **brow** *f.* **+yow**
hand-rail *n.* **kledher** *coll.*
kledhrenn
hang *v.* **kregi**; hang back **treynya**;
hang oneself **omgregi**
hanger-on *n.* **draylyer** *m.* **-oryon**
hanging *n.* **kroglenn** *f.* **+ow, krog**
f. **+ow**
hanging-place *n.* **krogla** *m.*
hangman *n.* **kroger** *m.* **+yon**
hangover *n.* **kurun spern** *f.*
hanker *v.* **si**; hanker after **hwansa**
happen *v.* **koedha, darvos +ow,**
happya, hwarvos; happen to **dos**
ha
happened *adj.* **hwarvedhys**
happening *n.* **darvos** *m.* **+ow,**
hwarvedhyans *m.* **+ow, hwarvos**
m. **+ow**
happens *v.* **hwer**
happiness *n.* **lowena** *f.*, **heudhder**
m.
happy *adj.* **lowen**: *v.* make happy
heudhhe
harangue *v.* **arethya**
harass *v.* **arvedh**
harbinger *n.* **ragreser** *m.* **-oryon**
harbour *n.* **porth** *m.* **+ow**
harbour-crab *n.* harbour-crab
peberynn *m.* **+ow**
hard *n.* hard man **avleythys** *m.*
+yon: *adj.* **kales**
hard-bitten *n.* hard-bitten fellow
avleythys *m.* **+yon, smat** *m.* **+ys**
harden *v.* **kaleshe**
hardened *adj.* **avleythys**
hard-headed *adj.* **penn-kales**
hardly *adv.* **skant, skantlowr**
hardness *n.* **kaletter** *m.*
hardware *n.* **kalesweyth** *m.*
hardy *adj.* **hardh, smat**

hare *n.* **skovarnek** *m.* **-ogyon**
harebell *n.* **klogh an eos** *m.*
hare-brained *adj.* **penn-skav**
harm *n.* **drog** *m.*, **damaj** *m.*,
dregynn *m.*, **drokter** *m.*, **meschyf**
m.: *v.* **aperya, pystiga, shyndya**
harmed *adj.* **shyndys**
harmonious *adj.* **kesson**
harmonize *v.* **kesseni**; (abst.)
akordya
harmony *n.* **kessenyans** *m.;*
(abst.) **akord** *m.;* line of harmony
(e.g. tenor) **iston** *m.* **+yow**
harness *n.* **hernes** *m.*, **starn** *f.*
+yow: *v.* put on harness **hernesya**
harp *n.* **telynn** *f.* **+ow**: *v.* play a
harp **telynnya**
harpist *n.* **telynnyer** *m.* **+yon,**
telynnyores *f.* **+ow**
harrow *n.* **harow** *m.*, **kloes** *f.*
+yow: *v.* **kloesya**
harsh *adj.* **anhwek, asper,**
hwerow
harvest *n.* **trevas** *f.* **+ow, ysasver**
m.; harvest home **goeldheys** *m.;*
harvest neck **penn-yar** *m.*
pennow-yar
harvest-home *n.* **dy'goel Deys** *m.*
hash *n.* **brewgik** *m.*
hasp *n.* **hesp** *m.* **+ow**
hassock *n.* **tuttynn** *m.*
haste *n.* **mall** *m.*, **toeth** *m.*, **fysk** *m.*,
hast *m.*, **hastenep** *m.:* *v.* make
haste **fistena, fyski**
hasten *v.* **fistena, fyski, stevya,**
toethya
hasty *adj.* **fysk**
hasty-pudding *n.* **pott-gwynn** *m.*,
yos *m.*
hat *n.* **hatt** *m.* **+ow, +ys**
hat-band *n.* **bond-hatt** *m.*
bondow-hatt
hatch *v.* **gori, kovia**
hatchet *n.* **boelik** *m.* **-igow, boni** *f.*
hate *n.* **kas** *m.:* *v.* **kasa**

hateful *adj.* **kasadow, ahas, hegas**
hatefulness *n.* **kasadewder** *m.*
hatred *n.* **kas** *m.*
haughtiness *n.* **goeth** *m.*
haughty *adj.* **goethus, howtyn**
haul *v.* **tenna, halya**
haunch *n.* **klun** *f.* **+yow** *dual* **diwglun, pedrenn** *f.* **+ow** *dual* **diwbedrenn, penn-diwglun** *m.*
haunt *v.* **daromres**
have *v.* **kavoes**; I have **yma genev**: *phr.* have pity on **kemmeres pyta orth**; I have **a'm beus**
havoc *n.* **terroes** *m.,* **terroesa** *m.*
hawk *n.* **hok** *m.* **+ys**
hawker *n.* **gwikor** *m.* **+yon**
hawthorn *n.* **hogan** *m.,* **spernenn wynn** *f.*
hay *n.* **goera** *m.;* new-mown hay **foen** *m.*
hayfield *n.* **foenek** *f.* **+egi**
hayrake *n.* **rastell** *f.* **restell**
haystack *n.* **das woera** *f.*
haze *n.* **niwl** *m.* **+ow**
hazel-grove *n.* **kollwydhek** *f.*
hazel-tree *n.* **kollenn** *f.* **+ow** *coll.* **koll, kollwydhenn** *f.* **+ow** *coll.* **kollwydh**; small group of hazel-trees **kollas** *f.:* *adj.* abounding in hazel-trees **kollwydhek**
hazlett *n.* **kollas** *f.*
he *pron.* **ev**
head *n.* **penn** *m.* **+ow, poll** *m.;* (on a glass of beer) **ewyn** *coll.* **+enn**; back of the head **kilbenn** *m.;* head of arrow **pil** *m.* **+ys**; head of family **penn-teylu** *m.* **pennow-teylu**; head of hair **gols** *m.*
head nurse (U.S.) *n.* **pennklavjiores** *f.*
headache *n.* **drokpenn** *m.* **+ow**
head-board *n.* (of a bed) **pennweli** *m.* **+ow**
head-dress *n.* **pennwisk** *m.*

headgear *n.* **pennwisk** *m.*
headlamp *n.* **pennlugarn** *m.* **pennlugern**
headland *n.* **pennrynn** *m.* **pennrynnow, penntir** *m.* **+yow**; (in field) **talar** *m.*
headless *adj.* **dibenn**
headlight *n.* **pennlugarn** *m.* **pennlugern**
headline *n.* **pennlinenn** *f.* **+ow**
headlong *adv.* **sket**
headmaster *n.* **penndyskador** *m.* **+yon**
headmistress *n.* **penndyskadores** *f.* **+ow**
headquarters *n.* **pennplas** *m.;* (e.g. of a company) **pennsoedhva** *f.* **+ow**; (military) **kaslys** *f.*
head-spring *n.* **pennfenten** *f.* **-tynyow**
head-stall *n.* **pennfester** *m.*
head-teacher *n.* **penndyskador** *m.* **+yon, penndyskadores** *f.* **+ow**
head-wind *n.* **gorthwyns** *m.* **+ow**
heal *v.* **sawya**
healing *adj.* **yaghus**
health *n.* **yeghes** *m.,* **sawes** *m.;* Department of Health **Asrann Yeghes** *f.;* good health ! **yeghes da** ! *m.:* *adj.* in good health **yn poynt da**
healthful *adj.* **yaghus**
health-giving *adj.* **yaghus**
healthy *adj.* **yagh, salow**
heap *n.* **kals** *m.,* **bern** *m.,* **graghell** *f.,* **hogenn** *f.,* **klus** *m.* **+yow, pil** *m.* **+yow**; (of rocks) **karnedh** *m.* **+ow**; heap of stones **kals meyn** *m.:* *v.* heap together **manala**; put in a heap **krugya**
heaped *adj.* **pilek**
hear *v.* **klywes**; hear from **klywes gans**
hearer *n.* **goslowyas** *m.* **-ysi**

hearing *n.* **klywans** *m.;* sense of hearing **klyw** *m.*

heart *n.* **kolonn** *f.* **+ow**; broken heart **kolonn drogh** *f.;* dear heart **kuv kolonn** *m.*

hearth *n.* **oeles** *f.* **+ow, fog** *f.* **+ow**

hearty *adj.* **kolonnek**

heat *n.* **toemmder** *m.*, **gwres** *f.*, **poethter** *m.*, **tes** *m.;* extreme heat **poethvann** *m.*, **trethes** *m.;* great heat **bros** *m.* **+ow**: *adj.* on heat **leusik**: *v.* **poetha, poethhe, tesa**

heater *n.* **jynn-toemma** *m.* **jynnow-toemma**

heath *n.* **grugek** *f.* **+egi**: *plur.* Cornish heath **kykesow**

heather *n.* **grug** *m.* **+ow, mynkek** *m.*

heather-bush *n.* **grugloen** *m.* **+yow**

heathery *adj.* **grugek**

heating *n.* central heating **toemmheans-kres** *m.*

heaven *n.* **nev** *m.* **+ow**

heavenly *adj.* **nevek**

heaviness *n.* **poester** *m.*, **poesyjyon** *m.*

heavy *adj.* **poes**

Hebrew *n.* **Ebrow** *f.*

hedge *n.* **ke** *m.* **keow, kor** *m.;* earth hedge **dorge** *m.* **+ow**; hedge of bushes **perth** *f.* **-i**; low hedge **gorge** *m.* **+ow**: *v.* **keas**

hedged *adj.* **keek, kes**

hedgehog *n.* **sort** *m.* **+es**

hedging *n.* **keweyth** *m.*, **kewydh** *coll.*

hedging-bill *n.* **gwydhyv** *m.* **+yow**

heed *n.* **rach** *m.:* *v.* pay heed to **koela orth**

heedless *adj.* **dibreder**

heel *n.* **seudhel** *m.* **+yow, seu'l** *m.*, **gwewenn** *f.*

he-goat *n.* **bogh** *m.*

heifer *n.* **denewes** *f.*, **lejek** *f.* **lejegow**

heigho *int.* **eghan**

height *n.* **ardh** *m.* **+ow, bann** *m.* **+ow, ughelder** *m.* **+yow**

heighten *v.* **ughelhe**

heir *n.* **er** *m.* **eryon**

heiress *n.* **eres** *f.* **+ow**

helicopter *n.* **askell-dro** *f.*, **tro-askell** *f.* **tro-eskelli**

hell *n.* **ifarn** *m.* **+ow**

hellish *adj.* **ifarnek**

helm *n.* **lyw** *m.* **+yow**

helmet *n.* **basnet** *m.* **+ow**; safety helmet **basnet diogeledh** *m.*

helmsman *n.* **lywyader** *m.* **-oryon**

help *n.* **gweres** *m.:* *adj.* ready to help **heweres**: *v.* **gweres**: *int.* **harow**

helpful *adj.* **heweres**

helpless *adj.* **diweres**

Helston *place* **Hellys**

helter *n.* helter skelter **tour korslynk** *m.*

hemlock *n.* **keger** *coll.*, **kegis** *coll.* **+enn**; place abounding in hemlock **kegisek** *f.* **-egi**: *adj.* abounding in hemlock **kegisek**

hemp *n.* (plants) **kewargh** *coll.* **+enn**

hemp-field *plur.* **kanabyer**

hen *n.* **yar** *f.* **yer**; spotted hen **splettyar** *f.*

henbane *n.* **gahen** *f.*

hence *adv.* **alemma, ahanan**; two days hence **trenja**

henceforth *conj.* **wosa hemma**

henceforward *adv.* **alemma rag**

hen-grouse *n.* **yar wyls** *f.*

hen-house *n.* **yarji** *m.* **+ow**

her *pron.* **hy**; (emphatic) **hyhi**: *phr.* **a's, y's**; and her **ha'y**; to her **dh'y**

her (obj.) *pron.* **hi**

herb *n.* erba *m.* erbys, losowenn
f. +ow *coll.* losow; herb garden
losowek *f.* -egi
herbal *adj.* losowek
herbalist *n.* losower *m.* -oryon
herbs *plur.* losowys
herd *n.* gre *f.* +ow
herdsman *n.* bugel *m.* +edh
here *adv.* omma; from here
alemma: *int.* here is otta
heresy *n.* gorthkryjyans *m.* +ow,
kammgryjyans *m.*
heretic *n.* gorthkryjyk *m.*
-kryjygyon, kammgryjyk *m.*
-gryjygyon
heretical *adj.* kammgryjyk
heritage *n.* ertach *m.;* Cornish
Heritage Ertach Kernewek *m.*
hermit *n.* ankar *m.* ankrys, ermit
m.
hermitage *n.* ankarji *m.* +ow,
penytti *m.* +ow
heron *n.* kerghydh *f.* +yon
herring *n.* hernenn wynn *f.* hern
gwynn
hesitate *v.* hokya
hew *v.* hakkya, nadha
hewing *n.* nadh *m.*
hexagon *n.* hweghkorn *m.* +yow
hey *int.* ay, hou
hi *int.* ay, hou
hiatus *n.* gwagla *m.* -leow
hibernate *v.* gwavi
hiccup *n.* hik *m.* +ow: *v.* hikas
hidden *adj.* kel, kudh
hide *n.* (skin) kenn *m.,* kroghen *f.*
kreghyn: *v.* kudha, keles;
(cover) gorheri; hide from kudha
rag; hide oneself omgeles,
omgudha
hideous *adj.* hager
hideout *n.* kovva *f.*
hiding *n.* kel *m.* +yow; hiding place
kovva *f.,* kudh *m.*
hierarchy *n.* urdhas *m.* +ow

high *n.* high place ardh *m.* +ow;
high speed toeth bras *m.,* toeth da
m.; high speed train tren toeth
bras (T.T.B.) *m.;* high water
gorlanow *m.:* *adj.* ughel;
(intoxicated) meri; as high as a kite
maga feri avel hok: *v.* perform
the high jump ughlamma
higher *adj.* gwartha, ughella
highland *n.* ugheldir *m.* +yow:
adj. ugheldiryek
Highlands *phr.* The Highlands An
Ugheldiryow
highway *n.* fordh-veur *f.*
fordhow-meur, karrhyns *m.*
+yow
hill *n.* bre *f.* +ow, bronn *f.* +ow,
menydh *m.* +yow, brenn *m.* +ow,
run *f.* +yow
hill-fort *n.* kastell *m.* kastylli,
dinas *m.,* ker *f.* +yow
hillock *n.* begel *m.* +yow, knegh
m. +yow, krug *m.* +ow, pil *m.*
+yow, runenn *f.*
hill-spur *n.* ros *m.* +yow
hilt *n.* (of sword) troes *m.* treys
him *pron.* ev, e'; (emphatic) eev:
phr. a'n, y'n
himself *adv.* by himself y honan
hind *n.* ewik *f.* ewiges
hinder *v.* lettya, lesta
hind-quarter *n.* pedrenn *f.* +ow
dual diwbedrenn
hindrance *n.* lett *m.* +ow, +ys
hinge *n.* medyner *f.* +yow
hip *n.* klun *f.* +yow *dual* diwglun,
penn-diwglun *m.,* pennklun *f.*
+yow; (plant) agrowsenn *f.* +ow
coll. agrows
hippopotamus *n.* dowrvargh *m.*
-vergh
hire *n.* arveth *m.:* *v.* arveth,
gobrena; buy on hire purchase
hirbrena: *adv.* on hire purchase
yn hirbren
hireling *n.* arvethesik *m.* -igyon

hirer *n.* gobrener *m.* -oryon
his *pron.* y: *phr.* and his ha'y; to his
dh'y
hiss *n.* si *m.:* *v.* sia, tythya
historian *n.* istorior *m.* +yon
historical *adj.* istorek
history *n.* istori *m.* +ow
hit *v.* gweskel, skwatya
hitherto *adv.* kyns lemmyn
hit-man *n.* denledhyas *m.* -ysi
ho *int.* ho
hoar *adj.* gwynnek
hoar-frost *n.* loesrew *m.*, niwlrew
m.
hoarse *n.* hoarse person kreg *m.*
+yon: *adj.* hos, kreg, ronk
hoarseness *n.* hosyas *m.*, krekter
m.
hoary *adj.* loes
hobble *n.* sprallyer *m.:* *v.*
kloppya
hobby *n.* hobi *m.* +s
hobby-horse *n.* hobihors *m.*
hobgoblin *n.* boekka *m.* +s
hobo (U.S.) *n.* loselwas *m.*
-wesyon
hoe *n.* kravell *f.* +ow: *v.* fynngla,
kravellas
hog *n.* hogh *m.* -es, ragomogh *m.*
hogshead *n.* hosket *m.* +ys
hogwash *plur.* golghyon
hogweed *n.* evor *coll.*, losow-
mogh *coll.*
hoist *v.* halya
hold *n.* dalghenn *f.* +ow, gavel *f.*
+yow: *v.* synsi, dalghenna;
hold in lap barlenna; hold oneself
omsynsi; hold out pargh; hold
out against perthi orth; keep hold
of kensynsi; lay hold of sesya:
phr. take hold of kavoes dalghenn
yn, settya dalghenn yn
hold-all *n.* kroeder-kroghen *m.*
holder *n.* synsyas *m.* -ysi

holding *n.* (financial) synsas *m.*
+ow; holding of land bargen-tir *m.*
bargenyow-tir
hole *n.* toll *m.* tell, kraw *m.* +yow;
hole in ground godenow *m.;* tiny
hole tellik *m.* -igow
holed *adj.* tollek
holiday *n.* dy'goel *m.* +yow; bank
holiday dy'goel kemmyn *m.;*
official holiday dy'goel
soedhogel *m.:* *v.* go on holiday
dy'goelya
holiness *n.* sansoleth *f.*
hollow *n.* kew *f.* +yow, kow *f.*
+yow, pans *m.* +ow; (small)
gobans *m.* +ow; hollow tree
kowbrenn *m.* +yer: *adj.* kew,
kow: *v.* kowa
hollowed *adj.* kowesik
holly *n.* kelynn *coll.* +enn: *adj.*
abounding in holly kelynnek
holly-grove *n.* kelynnek *f.* -egi
holly-tree *n.* holly-trees kelynn *coll.*
+enn
holt *n.* kelli *f.* kelliow, godegh *m.*
holy *plur.* holy orders ordys: *adj.*
sans
homage *n.* omaj *m.*
home *n.* tre *f.* trevow; second home
kenkidh *m.* +yow; stately home
plas *m.* plassow: *adv.* dhe-dre;
at home yn chi, yn tre; from home
a-dre
home-grown *adj.* teythyek
homeless *adj.* diannedh, didre
homelessness *n.* diannedhder *m.*
homesick *adj.* hirethek,
moredhek
homestead *n.* treveth *f.:* *plur.*
homesteads treven
homewards *adv.* dhe-dre, war-ji
hone *n.* igolenn *f.* +ow: *v.* lymma
honey *n.* mel *m.;* honey (U.S.
endearment) melder *m.:* *v.* gather
honey mela
honeycomb *n.* kribenn vel *f.*

honeydew *n.* melgowas *f.* +ow
honeyed *adj.* melek
honeysuckle *n.* gwydhvos *coll.*
+enn
honey-yielding *adj.* melek
honour *n.* enor *m.* +ys,
gordhyans *m.: v.* enora,
gordhya
honourable *adj.* wordhi
hood *n.* hod *m.*, kogh *m.* +ow;
bard's hood kugol bardh *m.;*
monk's hood kugol *m.*
hoof *n.* karn *m.* +ow, ewingarn *m.*
hoofed *adj.* karnek
hook *n.* bagh *f.* +ow, hig *m.* +ow,
higenn *f.* +ow: *v.* higenna
hoop-la *plur.* kylghigow
hoot *n.* us *m.: v.* usa
hop *v.* hop like a toad kroenogas,
lyfansas
hope *n.* govenek *m.: v.* gwaytya,
fydhya
hop-garden *n.* hopysek *f.* +egi
hops *n.* hopys *coll.* +enn
horehound *n.* lesloes *m.*
horizon *n.* gorwel *m.* +yow
horizontal *adj.* gorwelyek
horn *n.* (musical) korn *m.* kern; (of
animal) korn *m.* kern *dual*
dewgorn; drinking horn korn eva
m.; little horn kernik *f.* -igow
horned *adj.* kornek
horner *n.* kernyas *m.* -ysi
hornet *n.* hwyrnores *f.* +ow
horn-player *n.* kernyas *m.* -ysi
horrible *adj.* euthek, skruthus,
vil
horribly *adv.* euthek, bilen
horrified *v.* be horrified skrutha
horror *n.* euth *m.*
horse *n.* margh *m.* mergh; horse
flies kelyon margh *coll.;* horse's
bit genva *f.* +ow; horse's skull
penn-glas *m.* pennow-glas:

plur. horses marghes, mergh; the
horses an vergh
horse-cloth *n.* gorheras *m.*,
pallenn vargh *f.*
horse-collar *n.* mongar *f.*,
mongarenn *f.* +ow
horse-dung *n.* busel vergh *coll.*
horsehide *n.* marghkenn *m.*
horseload *n.* saw *m.* +yow
horseman *n.* marghek *m.* -ogyon
horsemanship *n.* marghogieth *f.*
horse-pond *n.* marghboll *m.* +ow,
marghlynn *m.* +ow, poll margh
m.
horse-shoe *n.* horn margh *m.*
horsewoman *n.* marghoges *f.*
+ow
hose *plur.* hosanow
hose-pipe *n.* pibenn-dhowr *f.*
pibennow-dowr
hospital *n.* klavji *m.* +ow
hospitality *n.* helder *m.*, ostyans
m.
host *n.* lu *m.* +yow
hostage *n.* gwystel *m.* gwystlow
hostel *n.* ostel *f.* +yow; youth
hostel ostel yowynkneth *f.*
hostelry *n.* ostelri *m.*
hostess *n.* ostes *f.* +ow
hostile *adj.* eskarek
hostility *n.* kas *m.*, eskarogeth *f.*
hot *adj.* tesek; extremely hot bros,
poeth
hotchpotch *n.* kabol *m.*, kabolva *f.*
hotel *n.* ostel *f.* +yow
hot-head *n.* penn-bros *m.*
pennow-bros
hotplate *n.* chofar *m.* +s, men-
toemm *m.* meyn-toemm
hot-tempered *adj.* tesek
hound *n.* ki *m.* keun, helgi *m.*
-geun, hond *m.* hons, rech *m.*
+ys; coursing hound reski *m.*
reskeun

hour *n.* eur *f.* **+yow, our** *m.* **+ys;** duration of one hour **our** *m.* **+ys**

house *n.* **chi** *m.* **chiow**; ancient house **hendi** *m.* **+ow, henji** *m.;* doll's house **chi dolli** *m.;* House of Commons **Chi an Gemmynyon** *m.;* House of Lords **Chi an Arlydhi** *m.;* Houses of Parliament **Chiow an Senedh** *m.;* public house **diwotti** *m.* **+ow;** semi-detached house **gevellji** *m.* **+ow;** White House **Chi Gwynn** *m.*

house-builder *n.* **gweythor chi** *m.*

household *n.* **teylu** *m.* **+yow, koskor** *c.,* **meni** *m.,* **tiogeth** *f.* **+yow;** household goods **gotrel** *m.*

householder *n.* **tiek** *m.* **tiogow, tiogyon**

housekeeper *n.* (female) **gwithyades-chi** *f.* **gwithyadesow-chi**

housekeeping *n.* (money) **arghans tiogeth** *m.*

house-martin *n.* **chigokk** *f.* **+es**

housewife *n.* **tioges** *f.* **+ow, ben'vas** *f.,* **benyn-vas** *f.,* **gwre'ti** *f.*

hover *v.* **bargesi**

how *adv.* **dell, fatell, fatla**; how are you ? **fatla genes ?**; how come **prag**; how great **pygemmys**; how long **pes termyn**; how many **pes**; how much **pygemmys:** *int.* **ass, assa**; see how **ott ha**

however *adv.* **byttegyns**

howl *n.* **oulyans** *m.:* *v.* **oulya**

huddled *phr.* huddled up **gyllys yn gronn**

hue *n.* **liw** *m.* **liwyow**

hued *adj.* **liwek**

hug *v.* **byrla, gwrynya**

huge *adj.* **bras**

hulking *n.* hulking fellow **kwallok** *m.* **+s**

hull *n.* **kogh** *m.* **+ow**

hum *v.* **hwyrni**

human *n.* human being **den** *m.* **tus:** *adj.* **denel**

humanity *n.* **denses** *m.,* **denseth** *m.*

humanize *v.* **hwarhe**

humble *adj.* **uvel:** *v.* **uvelhe**

humid *adj.* **leyth**

humidify *v.* **leytha**

humidity *n.* **leythter** *m.*

humiliate *v.* **shamya**

humility *n.* **iselder** *m.,* **uvelder** *m.,* **uvelses** *f.*

hump *n.* both *f.* **+ow, bothenn** *m.*

hump-backed *adj.* **bothek**

hunchback *n.* **bothek** *m.* **-ogyon**

hundred *n.* (land unit) **kevrang** *f.* **+ow;** a hundred men **kangour** *m.;* hundred of Cornwall **konteth** *f.* **+ow;** hundred pound weight **kanspeuns** *m.;* hundred thousand **kansvil** *m.* **+yow;** hundred years **kansblydhen** *f.* **kansblydhynyow:** *num.* **kans +ow;** three hundred **trihans:** *adv.* a hundred times **kankweyth:** *phr.* hundred years old **kans bloedh**

hundredfold *adv.* **kansplek**

hundredth *num.* **kansves**

hundredweight *n.* **kanspoes** *m.*

hunger *n.* **nown** *m.*

hungry *adj.* **nownek**

hunt *n.* **helgh** *m.:* *v.* **chasya, helghi, helghya**; hunt vermin **pryvessa**

hunter *n.* **helghyer** *m.* **-oryon;** (horse) **helvargh** *m.* **-vergh;** (professional) **helghyas** *m.* **-ysi**

hunting *v.* go hunting **chasya, helghi, helghya, sportya**

hunting-dog *n.* **gwylter** *m.*

hunting-dress *n.* **helghwisk** *m.*

hunting-ground *n.* **helghva** *f.* **+ow;** open hunting-ground **chas** *m.*

hunting-horn *n.* **bualgorn** *m.* **-gern**

hurdle *n.* **kloes** *f.* **+yow**

hurdy-gurdy *n.* symfoni *m.*
hurl *v.* deghesi, hurlya
hurler *n.* hurlyas *m.* -ysi
hurricane *n.* annawel *f.*
hurry *n.* toeth *m.*, fysk *m.*, hast *m.*;
I am in a hurry mall yw genev *m.*:
v. dehelghya, fistena, fyski
hurt *n.* drog *m.*, pystik *m.*
pystigow: *adj.* pystigys,
shyndys: *v.* golia, pystiga,
shyndya; (intrans.) gloesa
husband *n.* gour *m.* gwer, gorti *m.*
gwerti
hush *v.* tewel
husk *n.* gwisk *m.*, kodh *f.* +ow,
maskel *f.* masklow, pliskenn *f.*
+ow *coll.* plisk: *v.* pliskenna
husks *plur.* usyon
husky *adj.* hos
hussy *n.* flownenn *f.* +ow, skout *f.*
+ys
hut *n.* krow *m.* +yow; rough hut
kryllas *m.*
hybrid *adj.* kemmyskreydh
hydromel *n.* medh *m.*
hymn *n.* hymna *m.* hymnys
hypermarket *n.* ughvarghas *f.*
+ow
hypermetropia *n.* hirwel *m.*
hyphen *n.* strik *m.*
hypnotism *n.* huskosk *m.*
hypocrisy *n.* fayntys *m.*
hypocritical *adj.* fekyl cher
hysterectomy *n.* mestrogh-brys
m.

I

I *pron.* my
ice *n.* rew *m.*, yey *m.*; ice cream
dyenn rew *m.*: *v.* ice a cake
hwegrewi
icicle *n.* kleghienn *f.* +ow *coll.*
kleghi

icing *n.* icing on cake hwegrew *m.*
idea *n.* tybyans *m.* +ow
identical *adj.* keth, kethsam
idiom *n.* tavoseth *f.* +ow
idle *adj.* diek, syger: *v.* krowdra,
sygera
idleness *n.* sygerneth *f.*
if *conj.* mar, a, mara, maras, mars;
if only unnweyth a
ignominious *adj.* methus
ignorance *n.* diskians *m.*, nisyta
m.
ignorant *adj.* diskians
ill *n.* drog *m.*: *adj.* klav: *v.* do ill
kammwul
ill-deed *n.* drokoleth *f.*
illness *n.* kleves *m.* +ow
ill-pleased *adj.* drok-pes
ill-treatment *n.* bileni *f.*,
drokoleth *f.*
illuminate *v.* (of a picture) lymna;
(with light) golowi, splannhe
illusion *n.* hus *m.*
illusory *adj.* hudel
illustrate *v.* lymna
illustration *n.* lymnans *m.* +ow
illustrator *n.* lymner *m.* -oryon
ill-will *n.* avi *m.*, envi *m.*
image *n.* hevelepter *m.*, imaj *m.*
+ys
imagination *n.* poetic imagination
awen *f.*
imaginative *adj.* awenek
imagine *v.* tybi
immaculate *adj.* dinamm
immature *adj.* anadhves
immaturity *n.* neweth *f.*
immediate *adj.* desempis, tromm
immediately *adv.* a-dhesempis,
a-dhistowgh, desempis,
distowgh, a-dhihwans, dison,
hware, knakk
immerse *v.* gorthroghya, troghya
immoral *adj.* gwann

immortal *adj.* anvarwel
immortality *n.* anvarwoleth *f.*
imp *n.* boekka *m.* +s
impair *v.* aperya
imparked *n.* imparked residence
kenkidh *m.* +yow
impasse *n.* stagsav *m.* +ow
impede *v.* lettya
impediment *n.* lett *m.* +ow, +ys,
sprall *m.*
impend *v.* degynsywa
imperfect *adj.* anperfeyth
impertinence *n.* kammworthyp
m., tonteth *f.*
impertinent *adj.* tont
impertinently *v.* reply impertinently
kammworthybi
impervious *adj.* tew
impetuous *adj.* fysk
impiety *n.* ansansoleth *f.*
impious *adj.* ansans
implant *v.* plontya
implement *n.* toul *m.* +ys, +ow
implore *v.* konjorya
impolite *adj.* diskortes
importance *n.* bri *f.*, rowedh *m.*
important *adj.* poes, poesek
impose *v.* impose upon beghya
impossible *adj.* anpossybyl: *v.*
na yll bos
impostor *n.* faytour *m.* +s, jogler
m. -oryon, +s
impotent *adj.* dialloes
impoverish *v.* boghosekhe
imprecation *n.* molleth *f.*
mollothow, ti *m.* +ow
impregnable *adj.* antryghadow
impression *n.* sel *f.* +yow
imprison *v.* prisonya
improve *v.* gwellhe
improvement *n.* gwellheans *m.*
+ow
improvident *adj.* dibygans
imprudence *n.* anfurneth *f.*

imprudent *adj.* anfur
impudence *n.* tonteth *f.*
impudent *adj.* tont
impulsive *adj.* fysk
impurity *n.* most *m.* +yon
in *prep.* yn; in her ynni; in him
ynno; in me ynnov; in thee
ynnos; in them ynna; in us
ynnon; in you ynnowgh: *phr.* in
my y'm; in our y'gan; in the y'n;
in their y'ga; in thy y'th; in your
y'gas
inanity *n.* euveredh *m.*
inappropriate *adj.* anwiw
incantation *n.* gorhan *f.* +ow
incapable *adj.* anabel, anteythi,
dialloes
incense *n.* kosta *m.*, ynkys *m.*
incessantly *n.* heb lett *m.:* *adv.*
anhedhek, prest
inch *n.* meusva *f.* meusvedhi
incinerate *v.* kowlleski
incisor *n.* dans a-rag *m.*
incite *v.* movya, ynnia
inclination *n.* bodh *m.*, plegadow
m., plegyans *m.*
incline *n.* goleder *f.* goledrow
income *n.* rent *m.* +ow, +ys
incontinently *adv.* (unrestrainedly)
dihwans
inconvenience *n.* dises *m.* +ys
increase *v.* kressya, ynkressya
incredible *adj.* ankrysadow
incriminate *v.* kabla
incubate *v.* kovia
indeed *adv.* devri, fest
indemnify *v.* eskelmi
indemnity *n.* eskolm *m.* +ow
independence *n.* anserghogeth *f.*
independent *adj.* anserghek
index *n.* menegva *f.* +ow
India *n.* Eynda *f.*
Indian *n.* (man) Eyndek *m.*
Eyndogyon; (woman) Eyndoges
f. +ow: *adj.* Eyndek

indicate *v.* **kevarwoedha**
indication *n.* **menek** *m.* **-egow**
indifference *n.* **mygylder** *m.*
indifferent *v.* grow indifferent **mygli**
indigenous *adj.* **teythyek**
indigent *adj.* **boghosek**
indignation *n.* **sorrvann** *m.*
indignities *plur.* **mothow**
indirectly *adv.* **a-dreus**
indoors *adv.* **a-bervedh**
indulge *v.* indulge oneself
omvodhya
industrial *n.* industrial estate
hwelbark *m.* **+ow**: *adj.*
diwysyansek
industrial park (U.S.) *n.*
hwelbark *m.* **+ow**
industrious *adj.* **diwysek**
industry *n.* (hard work)
diwysogneth *f.;* (manufacture)
diwysyans *m.* **+ow**
inert *adj.* **anteythi**
inevitable *adj.* **anwoheladow**
inexpert *adj.* **didhysk, digreft**
infamous *adj.* **drog-gerys**
infamy *n.* **bysmer** *m.*, **drog-ger** *m.*
infancy *n.* **flogholeth** *f.*
infant *n.* **fleghik** *m.* **fleghesigow**
infantile *adj.* **fleghigel**
inferiority *n.* **iselder** *m.*
infertile *adj.* **anfeyth**
infertility *n.* **anfeythter** *m.*
infidel *n.* **diskryjyk** *m.* **-ygyon**
infirm *adj.* **anyagh**
infirmity *n.* **gwannegredh** *m.*
inflame *v.* **fagla, skaldya,
ynflammya**
inflammation *n.* **fagel** *f.* **faglow,
losk** *m.*, **ynflammyans** *m.:* *v.*
brewvann
influenza *n.* **terthenn** *f.* **+ow**
informal *adj.* **anstrethys**
information *n.* **derivadow** *m.*,
kevarwoedh *m.*

information booth (U.S.) *n.*
govynnva *f.* **+ow**
infrastructure *n.* **isframweyth** *m.*
infrequent *adj.* **anvenowgh**
infuse *v.* **troetha**
infusion *n.* **troeth** *m.*
ingenious *adj.* **ynjin**
ingenuity *n.* **ynjinieth** *f.*
ingredient *n.* **devnydh** *m.* **+yow**
inhabit *v.* **annedhi**
inhabitant *n.* **annedhyas** *m.* **-ysi,
triger** *m.* **-oryon**
inherit *v.* **erita**
inheritance *n.* **eretons** *m.*
inhospitable *adj.* **didhynnargh**
iniquity *n.* **anewnder** *m.*
initiate *v.* **urdhya**
inject *v.* **skitya**
injection *n.* **skityans** *m.* **+ow**
injunction *n.* **gorhemmynn** *m.*
+ow
injure *v.* **aperya, meschyvya,
shyndya**
injured *adj.* **brew, pystigys,
shyndys**
injury *n.* **damaj** *m.*, **dregynn** *m.*,
kammhynseth *f.*, **meschyf** *m.*,
pystik *m.* **pystigow**
injustice *n.* **kammhynseth** *f.*
ink *n.* **ynk** *m.*
in-law *adj.* **da**
inlet *n.* inlet of sea **kanel** *f.*
kanolyow; inlet of water **logh** *m.*
+ow
innkeeper *n.* **ost** *m.* **+ys, tavernor**
m. **+yon**
innocent *adj.* **glan, ankablus,
gwyrgh**
insane *adj.* **varyes**
inscription *n.* **skrifa** *m.*
insect *n.* **hweskerenn** *f.* **+ow** *coll.*
hwesker
insert *v.* **gorra yn**
inside *prep.* **a-ji dhe:** *adv.* **a-ji, a-
bervedh**

insignificant *adj.* distyr
insincerity *n.* falsuri *m.*
insipid *adj.* anvlasus, melys
insipidity *n.* anvlas *m.*
insist *v.* teri
insistence *n.* her *m.*
insistent *adj.* ter
insolvency *n.* dibyganseth *f.*
insolvent *adj.* dibygans
insomnia *n.* anhun *m.*
insomniac *adj.* digosk
inspiration *n.* awen *f.*
inspire *v.* aweni
installation *n.* stallashyon *m.*
instalment *n.* ranndalas *m.* +ow
instance *n.* ensampel *m.* -plow,
    -plys, kas *m.;* for instance rag
    ensampel *m.*
instant *n.* pols *m.* +yow,
    prysweyth *m.:* *adj.* desempis
instantly *adv.* kettoeth ha'n ger
instep *n.* konna-troes *m.*
institute *n.* fondyans *m.* +ow: *v.*
    fondya
institution *n.* institution of higher
    education pennskol *f.* +yow
instruct *v.* dyski
instruction *n.* dyskans *m.* +ow
instructions *n.* dannvonadow *m.*
instrument *n.* mayn *m.* +ys
insulate *v.* ynysega
insulation *n.* ynysegans *m.*
insult *v.* despitya
insurance *n.* surheans *m.*
insure *v.* diogeli, surhe
integrity *n.* ewnhynseth *f.*
intellectual *n.* skiansek *m.*
    -ogyon: *adj.* skiansek
intelligence *n.* poell *m.*
intend *v.* mynnes
intense *adj.* tynn
intent *n.* mynnas *m.,* porpos *m.*
intention *n.* brys *m.* +yow, entent
    m. +ys, mynnas *m.*

inter *v.* ynkleudhyas
inter-Celtic *adj.* keskeltek
interdiction *n.* difenn *m.*
interest *n.* (concern) bern *m.;*
    (money) oker *m.;* compound
    interest goroker *m.:* *v.* is of
    interest deur
interesting *adj.* dhe les,
    didheurek
interfere *v.* mellya
interference *n.* mellyans *m.*
interior *n.* pervedh *m.*
interlude *n.* ynterlud *m.*
interment *n.* ynkleudhyas *m.*
internal *adj.* pervedhel
international *adj.* keswlasek
Internet *n.* Kesroesweyth *m.*
interpreter *n.* latimer *m.* +s
interrupt *v.* goderri
interruption *n.* godorr *m.* +ow
interview *n.* keswel *m.* +yow: *v.*
    kesweles
intestine *n.* kolodhyonenn *f.* +enn
    coll. kolodhyon
intimate *adj.* priva
intonation *n.* tonlev *m.*
intone *v.* tonya
intoxicate *v.* medhwi
intoxicated *adj.* medhow, meri
intoxication *n.* medhwenep *m.*
intricate *adj.* gwius, kompleth
intrinsic *adj.* a-berthek
introduce *v.* kommendya;
    introduce oneself omgommendya
intrude *v.* omherdhya
inundate *v.* liva
inveiglement *n.* antell *f.* antylli
invent *v.* dismygi
invest *v.* gorra arghans dhe,
    kevarghewi
investigate *v.* hwithra
investigation *n.* hwithrans *m.*
    +ow

investigator *n.* **hwithrer** *m.*
-oryon, hwithrores *f.* **+ow**
invincible *adj.* **antryghadow**
invisibility *adj.* **anweladewder**
invisible *adj.* **anweladow**
invitation *n.* **galow** *m.*
inwards *adv.* **war-bervedh**
Ireland *n.* **Iwerdhon** *f.*
iris *n.* bed of yellow irises **elestrek** *f.*
-egi; yellow iris **elestrenn** *f.* **+ow**
coll. **elester**
Irish *n.* Irish language **Iwerdhonek**
m.: *adj.* **Iwerdhonek**
Irishman *n.* **Goedhel** *m.*
Goedhyli, Gwydhel *m.* **Gwydhyli**
Irishwoman *n.* **Gwydheles** *f.* **+ow**
iron *n.* (appliance) **hornell** *f.* **+ow**;
(metal) **horn** *m.* **hern**; iron ore
kallenn *f.* **+ow**: *adj.* like iron
hornek: *v.* **hornella**
iron-bearing *n.* iron-bearing ground
hornek *f.* **-egi**
ironing-board *n.* **bord hornella**
m.
ironmonger *n.* **hernyer** *m.* **-oryon**
irrational *adj.* **direson,**
gorboellek
irregular *adj.* **digompes, direwl**
irregularity *n.* **digompoester** *m.*
+yow
irreproachable *adj.* **divlam**
irresponsible *adj.* **dibreder**
irrigate *v.* **dowrhe**
irritability *n.* **tesogneth** *f.*
irritable *adj.* **tesek**
is *v.* **eus, usi, yma, yw**; one is
eder, or; there is **yma**: *phr.* the
{noun} is **yma'n**
island *n.* **ynys** *f.* **+ow**
isolated *n.* isolated place **ynys** *f.*
+ow
isolation *n.* **ynysekter** *m.*
Israel *place* **Ysrael**
Israelite *n.* **Yedhow** *m.* **Yedhewon**
issue *v.* **dyllo**

isthmus *n.* **kuldir** *m.* **+yow**
it *pron.* **ev, hi, e'**; (emphatic) **eev**;
(f., emphatic) **hyhi**: *phr.* (obj.) **a'n,**
a's
Italian *n.* Italian language **Italek** *m.*:
adj. **Italek**
Italy *n.* **Itali** *f.*
itch *n.* **debron** *m.*: *v.* **debreni,**
kosa, si
itching *n.* **kos** *f.*
item *n.* **poynt** *m.* **+ys, taklenn** *f.*
+ow
its *pron.* **y**; (f.) **hy**: *phr.* to its **dh'y**
ivy *n.* **idhyow** *coll.* **+enn**; ivy-clad
place **idhyowek** *f.* **-egi**: *adj.* ivy-
clad **idhyowek**

J

jabber *v.* **klappya**
jack *n.* car jack **jakk** *m.* **+ow**
jackdaw *n.* **chogha** *m.* **choghys**
jacket *n.* **jerkynn** *m.*, **kryspows** *f.*;
bullet-proof jacket **kaspows** *f.*
jacksnipe *n.* **dama kiogh** *f.*
jag *n.* **jag** *m.* **+ys**
jagged *adj.* **densek**
jam *n.* **kyfeyth** *m.* **+yow**
James *name* **Jamys**
janitor *n.* **porther** *m.* **-oryon**
January *n.* **Genver** *m.*, **mis-**
Genver *m.*
jar *n.* (shock) **jag** *m.* **+ys**; large jar
seth *m.* **+ow**
jaundiced *adj.* **melynik**
javelin *n.* **gyw** *m.* **+ow**
jaw *n.* **awen** *f.*, **gen** *f.* **+yow** *dual*
diwen, grudh *f.*, **tavosa** *m.*
jawbone *n.* **challa** *m.* **challys**
jawed *adj.* **awenek**
jay *n.* **kegin** *f.* **+es**
jealousy *n.* **avi** *m.*
jeans *n.* **jins** *m.*

jeer *n.* ges *m.*: *v.* gesya
jelly *n.* kowles *coll.* +enn
jellyfish *n.* morgowles *coll.* +enn
jerk *n.* skwych *m.* +ys: *v.*
skwychya
jerkin *n.* jerkynn *m.*
jersey *n.* gwlanek *m.*
jest *v.* gesya
jester *n.* gesyer *m.* gesyoryon
jet *n.* stif *f.* +ow; (mineral) men-du
m.; (of air) hwythell *f.* +ow
jet-black *adj.* morel
Jew *n.* Yedhow *m.* Yedhewon
jewel *n.* jowel *m.* +ys, tegenn *f.*
+ow
jeweller *n.* joweler *m.* -oryon
jewellery *n.* gemmweyth *m.*
Jewess *n.* Yedhowes *f.* +ow
Jewish *adj.* yedhowek
jigsaw *n.* jigsaw puzzle gwari
mildamm *m.*
job *n.* oberenn *f.* +ow
jog *v.* goresek
jogger *n.* (female) goresegores *f.*
+ow; (male) goreseger *m.* -
oryon
John *name* Yowann, Jowann
join *n.* (seam) gwri *m.* +ow: *v.*
junya
joint *n.* als *m.,* kevals *m.* +yow,
mell *m.* +ow; joint in timber skarf
m.
jointed *adj.* mellek
joint-tillage *n.* kevar *m.* +yow
joist *n.* jist *m.* +ys, keber *f.*
kebrow
joke *n.* ges *m.*
joker *n.* gesyer *m.* gesyoryon
jollity *n.* lowender *m.*
jolly *adj.* jolif, lowenek
jolt *n.* jag *m.* +ys: *v.* kryghylli
jot *n.* banna *m.* bannaghow
journey *n.* kerdh *m.* +ow, vyaj *m.*:
v. vyajya

joust *n.* joust *m.* +ys: *v.* joustya
jowl *n.* chal *m.*
joy *n.* lowena *f.,* joy *m.* joyys
joyful *adj.* lowen, heudh
joyfulness *n.* heudhder *m.*
judge *n.* breusyas *m.* -ysi,
breusydh *m.* +yon: *v.* breusi
judgment *n.* breus *f.* +ow
judo *n.* judo *m.*
jug *n.* podik *m.;* measuring jug
podik-musura *m.* -igow-musura
juggler *n.* jogler *m.* -oryon, +s
juice *n.* sugen *m.* +yow; fruit juice
sugen froeth *m.*
July *n.* mis-Gortheren *m.,*
Gortheren *m.*
jumble *n.* jumble sale basar *m.*
jump *n.* lamm *m.* +ow: *v.* lamma,
lemmel; perform the high jump
ughlamma; perform the long jump
hirlamma
junction *n.* junction of streams
kemper *m.* +yow
June *n.* Metheven *m.,* mis-
Metheven *m.*
junior *n.* bacheler *m.* +s
juniper *n.* meryw *coll.* +enn
junkie *n.* stoffki *m.* -keun
jurisdiction *n.* arloettes *m.*
juror *n.* tiyas *m.* tiysi
just *adj.* ewn, ewnhynsek,
gwiryon: *adv.* unnweyth; just as
par; just now nammnygen: *phr.*
just as it is par dell yw
justice *n.* gwir *m.* +yow, ewnder
m. +yow, gwir-vreus *m.;* (judge)
justis *m.* +yow; chief justice
pennjustis *m.* +yow
justiciary *n.* juster *m.* +s
justify *v.* justifia
jutting *adj.* balek, elek

K

kangaroo *n.* **kangourou** *m.*

keel *n.* **keyn** *m.* **+ow**

keen *n.* I am keen **mall yw genev**
m.: adj. **lymm**

keening *n.* **drem** *m.*

keenness *n.* **mall** *m.*

keep *v.* **gwitha;** keep hold of
kensynsi; keep oneself **omwitha;**
keep with care **tresorya**

keeper *n.* **gwithas** *m.* **gwithysi**

keepsake *n.* **kovro** *m.* **kovrohow**

keeve *n.* **tonnell** *f.* **+ow**

kennel *n.* (for one dog) **kiji** *m.* **+ow;**
(for several dogs) **keunji** *m.* **+ow**

kerb-stone *n.* **amalven** *m.*
amalveyn

kerchief *n.* **lien** *m.* **+yow**

kernel *n.* **sprusenn** *f.* **+ow** *coll.*
sprus

kestrel *n.* **kryshok** *m.* **+ys, tygri** *m.*

kettle *n.* **kalter** *f.* **+yow;** open kettle
chekk *m.* **+ys**

kettle-drum *n.* **naker** *m.* **nakrys**

key *n.* **alhwedh** *m.* **+ow;** (for
unlocking) **dialhwedh** *m.;* little
key **dialhwedhik** *m.* **-igow**

kick *n.* **pot** *m.* **+yow:** *v.* **potya**

kid *n.* (goat) **mynn** *m.* **+ow;** little kid
(goat) **mynnik** *m.*

kiddleywink *n.* **gwirotti** *m.* **-ow**

kidney *n.* **loneth** *f.* **-i** *dual*
diwloneth

kill *v.* **ladha;** kill oneself **omladha;**
kill time **delatya an termyn**

killed *v.* **ledhys**

kiln *n.* **forn** *f.* **+ow, oden** *f.:* *v.* tend
a kiln **fornya**

kilogram *n.* **kilogramm** *m.* **+ow**

kind *n.* **par** *m.* **+ow, eghenn** *f.*,
sort *m.* **+ow:** *adj.* **hweg, kuv,**
deboner

kindergarten *n.* **floghva** *f.* **+ow**

kindest *adj.* **hwegoll**

kindle *v.* (intrans.) **dewi**

kindling *n.* **skommynn** *m.*

kindly *adj.* **kolonnek, hegar**

kindness *n.* **hwekter** *m.*, **kuvder** *m.*

king *n.* **myghtern** *m.* **+edh,**
maghtern *m.* **+yow, ryw** *m.;* ruler
of kings **penn-vyghternedh** *m.*

kingdom *n.* **gwlaskor** *f.*
-kordhow, myghternans *m.*,
rywvaneth *f.*, **ternas** *m.;* United
Kingdom **Rywvaneth Unys** *f.*

kingly *adj.* **ryal**

kingship *n.* **myghternses** *m.*

kinsman *n.* **kar** *m.* **kerens**

kinsmen *plur.* **neshevin**

kiss *n.* **amm** *m.* **+ow, bay** *m.* **+ow,**
kussynn *m.* **+ow, pokk** *m.* **+ow:**
v. **amma, baya**

kitchen *n.* **kegin** *f.* **+ow**

kitchen-garden *n.* **erber** *m.* **+ow,**
losowek *f.* **-egi**

kitchen-range *n.* **slaba** *m.* **slabow**

kite *n.* (bird) **skoul** *m.;* (toy) **sarf-**
nija *f.* **serf-nija**

kitten *n.* **kathik** *f.* **-igow**

knave *n.* **drogwas** *m.* **-wesyon,**
jowdyn *m.* **+s,** knava *m.*

knead *v.* **mola, toesa**

knee *n.* **glin** *m.* **+yow** *dual* **dewlin;**
(ship-building) **esker** *f.* **+yow** *dual*
diwesker

knee-cap *n.* **krogen an glin** *f.*,
pennglin *m.* **+yow**

knell *n.* death knell **klogh an**
marow *m.*

knife *n.* **kollell** *f.* **kellylli;** carving
knife **kollell gervya** *f.;* curved
knife **kollell gamm** *f.;* pocket knife
(U.S.) **kollell bleg** *f.*

knife-handle *n.* **karn kollan** *m.*

knight *n.* **marghek** *m.* **-ogyon;**
Knight Templar **Marghek an**
Tempel *m.;* order of knights
chevalri *m.*

knighthood *n.* **chevalri** *m.*,
marghogieth *f.*

knightly n. knightly service **ago-marghogyon** f.
knit v. **gwia**
knob n. **begel** m. **+yow, talbenn** m.
+ow
knock n. **bonk** m. **+ys, knouk** m.
+ys: v. **bonkya, frappya, gweskel, knoukya;** knock oneself
omgnoukya
knoll n. **godolgh** m.; small knoll
godolghynn m.
knot n. **kolm** m. **+ow;** slip knot
kolm re m.: v. **kelmi**
knotgrass n. **kans kolm** m.,
milgolm m.
knotty adj. **kolmek**
knotwork n. **kolmweyth** m.
know v. **godhvos;** (persons or places) **aswonn;** I know **gonn**
knowledge n. **aswonnvos** m.,
dyskans m. **+ow, godhvos** m.,
skians m. **+ow, skentoleth** f.: v.
have knowledge of **godhvos**
knowledgeable adj. **skentel**
known adj. **aswonnys:** v. it is
known **godhor, gos;** make known
avisya, notya

L

label n. **libel** m.
laborious adj. **lavurus**
labour n. **lavur** m.; Labour Party
Parti Lavur m.; unskilled labour
lavur digreft m.: v. **gonis,
lavurya**
labourer n. mine labourer **spalyer**
m. **+s**
labyrinth n. **milhyntall** m.
lace n. **las** m. **+ow, +ys**
lacerate v. **skwardya**
laceration n. **skward** m. **+yow**
lack n. **fowt** m. **+ow:** v. **fyllel dhe**
lackey n. **paja** m. **pajys**

lacking adj. lacking in energy
difreth: prep. **heb:** v. be lacking
to **fyllel dhe**
ladder n. **skeul** f. **+yow;** rope
ladder **skeul lovan** f.: v. climb by
ladder **skeulya**
ladle n. **lo** f. **loyow, lo-ledan** f.
loyow-ledan
lady n. **arloedhes** f. **+ow, benyn
jentyl** f., **madama** f. **madamys**
ladybird n. **bughik-Dyw** f.
bughesigow-Dyw
ladyship n. **arloedhesedh** m.
lag v. **treynya**
lair n. **godegh** m., **gorwedhva** f.
+ow
laity n. **lekses** m.
lake n. (close to sea) **logh** m. **+ow;**
(inland) **lynn** m. **+ow**
lamb n. **oen** m. **eyn, devesik** f.
-igow; little lamb **oenik** m.
eynigow
lambkin n. **oenik** m. **eynigow**
lamb-skin n. **oengenn** m.
lame adj. **klof, kloppek:** v. go
lame **klofi**
lameness n. **klefni** m.
lament v. **galari, kyni;** (trans.)
oela
lamentation n. **drem** m., **kynvann**
m., **oelva** f.
lamina n. **lown** m. **+yow**
laminated adj. **lownek, skansek**
lamp n. **lugarn** m. **lugern,
golowlester** m. **-lestri**
lamp-chill n. **chylla** m. **chyllys**
lamp-post n. **golowbrenn** m. **+yer**
lamprey n. **mornader** f.
mornadrys
lamp-wick n. **bubenn** f. **+ow**
lance n. **gyw** m. **+ow**
lancet n. **gywik** m. **-igow**
land n. **bro** f. **+yow, gwlas** f. **+ow,
tir** m. **+yow, tiredh** m.; arable land
havrek f. **-egi;** arid land **krindir**
m.; cultivated land **mesek** f.; ley

land **gwynndonn** *f.;* ploughed land
ar *m.: v.* **tira:** *adv.* on land **war dir**
landing *n.* **tirans** *m.*
landrail *n.* (bird) **kregyar** *f.* **-yer**
Land's End *place* **Penn an Wlas**
landscape *n.* **tirwel** *m.* **+yow**
land-surveyor *n.* **tirvusuryas** *m.* **-ysi**
lane *n.* **bownder** *f.* **+ow**; (in town) **stretynn** *m.* **+ow**; traffic lane **hyns** *m.* **+yow**
langoustine *n.* **legestik** *m.* **-igow**
language *n.* **taves** *m.* **tavosow**, **yeth** *f.* **+ow**; native language **mammyeth** *f.*
lanky *adj.* **eseliek**
lantern *n.* **lugarn** *m.* **lugern**
lap *n.* **barlenn** *f.* **+ow**: *v.* **lapya**; hold in lap **barlenna**
lappet *n.* **lappa** *m.* **lappys**
lapse-rate *n.* **kevradh difyk** *m.*
lapwing *n.* **kornhwilenn** *f.* **kernhwili**
larceny *n.* (in general) **ladrynsi** *m.;* (individual crime) **ladrans** *m.*
lard *n.* **blonek** *m.*
larder *n.* **spens** *m.* **+ow**
lardy *adj.* **blonegek**
large *adj.* **bras, meur**
large-footed *adj.* **troesek**
lark *n.* (bird) **ahwesydh** *m.* **+es**
laryngitis *n.* **fagel-vryansenn** *f.*
larynx *n.* **aval-bryansenn** *m.*
lash *n.* **lash** *m.* **+ys**: *v.* **kelmi**
last *adj.* **diwettha:** *v.* **pesya, durya, pargh:** *adv.* at last **wostiwedh:** *phr.* to the last man **yn kettep gwas**
latch *n.* **kacha** *m.* **kachys, klyket** *m.: v.* **latthya**
late *adj.* **diwedhes, a-dhiwedhes, helergh**
lately *adv.* **a-gynsow**
later *adj.* **diwettha**

lath *n.* **lattha** *m.* **latthys**
lathe *n.* **troell** *f.* **+ow**
lather *v.* (with soap) **seboni**
Latin *n.* Latin language **Latin** *m.;* Latin master **latimer** *m.* **+s**
latitude *n.* (abst.) **efander** *m.;* geographical latitude **dorhys** *m.*
latitudinal *adj.* **dorhysel**
lattice *n.* **kloes** *f.* **+yow**
laud *v.* **gormel, kanmel**
laugh *v.* **hwerthin**; laugh at **hwerthin orth**
laughable *adj.* **hwarthus**
laughter *n.* **hwarth** *m.*
launce *n.* **lavyn** *m.* **+yon**
Launceston *place* **Lannstefan**
laurels *n.* **lowr** *coll.*
laurel-tree *n.* **lowrwydhenn** *f.* **+ow** *coll.* **lowrwydh**
law *n.* **lagha** *f.* **laghys, laghow**
law (act) *n.* **reyth** *m.* **+yow**
law clerk (U.S.) *n.* **laghwas** *m.* **-wesyon**
lawful *adj.* **herwydh an lagha, lafyl, laghel**
lawn *n.* **glesin** *m.* **+yow**
lawn-mower *n.* **jynn-glesin** *m.* **jynnow-glesin**
law-suit *n.* **ken** *m.*
lawyer *n.* **laghyas** *m.* **-ysi, laghyades** *f.* **+ow**
lax *adj.* **logh**
lay *adj.* **leg:** *v.* lay eggs **dedhwi**
lay-by *n.* **rypsav** *m.* **+ow**
layer *n.* **gweli** *m.* **+ow**; layer of clothing **gwiskas** *m.* **+ow**; soft layer on hard rock **kudhenn** *f.*
layman *n.* **leg** *m.* **+yon**
lazar-house *n.* **loverji** *m.* **+ow**
laziness *n.* **diegi** *m.*, **diekter** *m.*, **sygerneth** *f.*
lazy *adj.* **diek, syger**
lead *n.* (electrical) **led** *m.* **+yow:** *v.* **hembronk, ledya**
lead *n.* (metal) **plomm** *m.*

leader *n.* gedyer *m.* -oryon, gwalader *m.*, gwlesik *m.*, hembrenkyas *m.* -ysi, ledyer *m.* ledyoryon

leading *n.* leading people gwelhevin *m.*

lead-pencil *n.* pynsel plomm *m.*

leaf *n.* (of paper) lyvenn *f.* +ow; (of plant) delenn *f.* delyow *coll.* del: *v.* collect leaves delyowa; put forth leaves delya, glasa; sweep up leaves delyowa

leaflet *n.* folennik *m.* -igow

leafy *adj.* delyek, delyowek

leak *n.* dowrfols *m.* +yow: *v.* leak slowly sygera

leaky *adj.* syger

lean *v.* poesa

leap *n.* lamm *m.* +ow: *v.* lamma, lappya, lemmel

learn *v.* dyski; learn from dyski gans

learned *n.* the learned klerji *c.*: *adj.* dyskys, lettrys, skentel

learning *n.* lyenn *m.*

lease *n.* gobrenans *m.* +ow

leash *n.* lesh *m.* +ow, syg *f.*: *v.* leash hounds leshya

least *adj.* lyha

leather *n.* ledher *m.*

leave *n.* kummyas *m.*, gront *m.* +ow, +ys: *v.* gasa, avodya; leave by will kemmynna; leave off gasa; leave out gasa yn-mes

lectern *n.* lennva *f.* +ow

lectionary *n.* lennlyver *m.*

lecture *n.* areth *f.*

lecturer *n.* arethor *m.* -oryon

ledger *n.* lyver-akontow *m.* lyvrow-akontow

leech *n.* gel *f.* +es

leek *n.* porenn *f.* +ow *coll.* por

left *adj.* (opposite of right) kledh: *v.* (remaining) gesys: *adv.* on the left hand a-gledh

left-handed *adj.* kledhek

left-overs *plur.* gesigow

leg *n.* garr *f.* +ow *dual* diwarr, esker *f.* +yow *dual* diwesker, fer *f.* +ow

legacy *n.* kemmynn *m.* +ow, kemmynnro *m.* -rohow

legal *adj.* laghel

legend *n.* henhwedhel *m.* -dhlow

leggy *adj.* garrek

legion *n.* lyjyon *m.*

legitimate *adj.* herwydh an lagha

lemon *n.* lymmaval *m.* +ow

lend *v.* koela

length *n.* hys *m.*, hirder *m.*: *adj.* of equal length kehys; of the right length ewn-hys: *adv.* at length dhe-hys; full length a-hys: *phr.* the same length as kehys ha

lengthen *v.* hirhe

lengthy *adj.* hir

lenience *n.* kuvder *m.*

leniently *v.* treat leniently favera

Lent *n.* Korawys *m.*

leopard *n.* lewpard *m.* +es

leper *n.* klavorek *m.* -ogyon, lover *m.* lovryon, lovrek *m.* -ogyon; separated leper klav diberthys *m.*

leper-hospital *n.* loverji *m.* +ow

leprosy *n.* klavor *m.*, kleves bras *m.*, kleves meur *m.*, lovryjyon *m.*

leprous *adj.* klavorek, lovrek

less *adj.* le: *adv.* the less byttele

lessen *v.* lehe

lesser *adj.* le

lesson *n.* dyskans *m.* +ow

let *v.* (allow) gasa

letter *n.* (epistle) lyther *m.* +ow; (of alphabet) lytherenn *f.* +ow; covering letter kenlyther *m.* +ow

letter-box *n.* kyst-lyther *f.* kystyow-lyther

lettered *adj.* lettrys

lettuce *n.* letus *coll.* +enn

level *n.* nivel *m.* +yow: *adj.*
kompes, leven, suant: *v.*
levenhe, levna
lever *n.* kolpes *m.* +ow
levite *n.* dyagon *m.* +yon, Levyas
m. -ysi
levy *v.* levy tax tolli
ley *n.* ley land gwynndonn *f.*
ley-land *n.* tonn *coll.* +enn
liability *n.* kendon *f.*
liable *adj.* gostyth
liaise *v.* keskelmi; liaise with
keskelmi orth
liaison *v.* keskolm
liar *n.* gowek *m.* gowogyon;
inveterate liar gowleveryas *m.* -ysi
LibDem (i.e. Liberal Democrat)
adj. LivWer
liberal *adj.* larj; (politically) livrel;
(with money) hel
liberality *n.* helder *m.*
liberate *v.* livra
liberation *n.* livreson *m.*
liberty *n.* frankedh *m.*, rydhses
m.: *adj.* at liberty digabester,
frank
library *n.* lyverva *f.* +ow
licence *n.* kummyas *m.*, leshyans
m.; driving licence kummyas-
lywya *m.* kummyasow-lywya
license *n.* driver's license (U.S.)
kummyas-lywya *m.*
kummyasow-lywya
lichen *n.* barv gwydh *f.*, kywni
coll. +enn
lick *v.* lapya
lid *n.* gorher *m.* +yow: *v.* put a lid
on gorheri
lie *n.* gow *m.* +yow; teller of lies
gowleveryas *m.* -ysi: *v.* lie down
gorwedha, growedha
liege *n.* lij *m.* +ys, sojet *m.* +s: *adj.*
lij
life *n.* bywnans *m.* +ow; earthly life
trogel *m.:* *v.* bring to life bywhe

lifeboat *n.* skath-sawya *f.*
skathow-sawya
life-style *n.* bywedh *m.* +ow
lift *n.* (elevator) jynn-yskynn *m.*
jynnow-yskynn; (in car) gorrans
m. +ow: *v.* give a lift to someone
gorra nebonan; lift up drehevel
light *n.* golow *m.* +ys, lugarn *m.*
lugern: *adj.* skav: *v.* light up
enowi
light-bulb *n.* bollenn *f.* +ow
lighten *v.* (reduce weight) skavhe;
(shine) golowi
light-house *n.* golowji *m.* +ow
lightness *n.* skavder *m.*
lightning *n.* lughes *coll.* +enn;
lightning stroke lughesenn *f.* +ow
coll. lughes
lights *plur.* (lungs) skevens
like *adj.* hevelep: *v.* kara: *adv.*
avel, kepar; just like that yn
kettella; just like this yn
kettellma; like that yndella; like
this yndellma: *phr.* I like da yw
genev
likely *adj.* gwirhaval
liken *v.* hevelebi
likeness *n.* hevelep *m.*
hevelebow, hevelenep *m.*,
hevelepter *m.*
likewise *adv.* keffrys, ynwedh, yn
kepar maner
lily *n.* lili *m.;* lily of the valley
losowenn an Hav *f.*
limb *n.* esel *m.* eseli, lith *m.* +yow
lime *n.* (fruit) limaval *m.* +ow;
(mineral) kalgh *m.*, lim *m.*
lime-juice *n.* sugen limaval *m.*
lime-kiln *n.* oden-galgh *f.*
limit *n.* finwedh *f.:* *v.* finwedha
limp *n.* one who limps kloppek *m.*
-ogyon: *v.* kloppya
limpet *n.* brennigenn *f.* +ow *coll.*
brennik
limpid *adj.* ylyn
limpidity *n.* ylynder *m.*

limping *adj.* **kloppek**
line *n.* **linenn** *f.* **+ow, lin** *m.* **+enn,**
   res *f.* **+yow, rew** *m.* **+yow:** *v.*
   gwiska
lineage *n.* **linaja** *m.,* **linyeth** *f.*
line-drawing *v.* **linennans**
linen *n.* **lin** *coll.* **+enn;** fine linen
   sendal *m.;* linen cloth **lien** *m.*
   +yow
ling *n.* **grug** *m.* **+ow, mynkek** *m.*
ling-fish *n.* **lenes** *f.* **+ow**
linguist *n.* **yethonydh** *m.* **+yon,**
   yethor *m.* **+yon**
linguistics *n.* **yethonieth** *f.*
lining *n.* lining of clothes **ispann** *m.*
   +ow
link *n.* **kevrenn** *f.* **+ow**
linnet *n.* **linoges** *m.* **+ow**
lion *n.* **lew** *m.* **+yon;** lion cub **lewik**
   m. **lewigow**
lioness *n.* **lewes** *f.* **+ow**
lip *n.* **gwelv** *f.* **-ow, gwelvenn** *f.*
   +ow, min *m.* **+yow;** (human)
   gweus *f.* **+yow** *dual* **diwweus**
liquid *n.* **lin** *m.* **+yow**
liquor *n.* **gwires** *f.* **gwirosow, las**
   m. **+ow**
Liskeard *place* **Lyskerrys**
lisp *v.* **stlevi**
lisper *n.* **stlav** *m.* **stlevyon**
lisping *adj.* **stlav, stlavedh**
list *n.* **rol** *f.* **+yow, lystenn** *f.* **+ow;**
   list for jousting **list** *m.* **+ys**
listen *v.* **goslowes;** listen to
   goslowes orth
literary *adj.* **lyennek**
literate *adj.* **lettrys**
literature *n.* **lyenn** *m.*
litigation *n.* **kenans** *m.*
litter *n.* (for carrying) **gravath** *m.*
   +ow; (of animals) **torras** *m.;*
   (rubbish) **strol** *m.*
litter-bin *n.* **strolgyst** *f.* **+yow**

little *n.* **boghes** *m.: adj.* **byghan,**
   boghes, munys: *adv.* a little
   nebes; so little **mar nebes**
live *v.* **bywa;** (at a place) **triga;** live
   again **dasvywa;** live on **bywa**
   orth; live together **kesvywa**
livelihood *n.* **pygans** *m.*
liveliness *n.* **bywder** *m.*
lively *adj.* **buan, bywek, dyllo,**
   jolif
liver *n.* **avi** *m.*
liver-fluke *n.* **eyles** *m.*
living *n.* living together
   kesvywnans *m.*
lizard *n.* **pedresyf** *f.,* **pedrevan** *f.*
   -es, peswar-paw *m.* **+es**
lo *int.* **ott**
load *n.* **begh** *m.* **+yow, karg** *m.*
   +ow: *v.* **beghya, karga**
loaf *n.* **torth** *f.* **+ow;** loaf tin **kanna-**
   torth *m.;* small loaf **torthell** *m.*
   +ow
loan *n.* **koelans** *m.* **+ow:** *v.* **koela**
loathsomeness *n.* **last** *m.*
lobster *n.* **gaver vor** *f.,* **legest** *m.* **+i**
local *n.* **teythyek** *m.* **teythyogyon:**
   adj. **leel, teythyek**
locate *v.* **desedha**
lock *n.* (of door) **florenn** *f.* **+ow,**
   klow *m.;* (of hair) **kudynn** *m.*
   +ow: *v.* **alhwedha, prenna**
locker *n.* **amari** *m.* **+ow, +s**
lode *n.* caunter lode **troenn** *f.* **+ow;**
   cross lode **konter** *m.* **+s**
lodestone *n.* **tennven** *m.* **tennveyn**
lodge *v.* **ostya**
lodger *n.* **gwestyas** *m.* **-ysi,**
   gwestyades *f.* **+ow, triger** *m.*
   -oryon
lodging *n.* **gwest** *f.,* **harber** *m.* **+ys,**
   ostel *f.* **+yow**
loft *n.* **soler** *m.* **+yow**
lofty *adj.* **ughel, ardhek**
log *n.* **yttew** *m.* **+i;** sawn log **prenn**
   m. **+yer**

logic *n.* reson *m.* +s
loiter *v.* krowdra
Lombardy *place* Lombardi
London *place* Loundres
lonely *n.* lonely place tyller
    kernhwili *m.*
long *n.* long time hirneth *f.: adj.*
    hir, pell: *v.* long for hwansa,
    yeuni war-lergh: *adv.* how long
    pes termyn
long-beaked *adj.* gelvinek
longboat *n.* skath-hir *f.* skathow-
    hir
long-distance *n.* hirbellder *m.*
long-eared *adj.* skovarnek
longer *adv.* no longer na fella
longevity *n.* hiroes *m.*
longing *n.* hwans *m.* +ow, hireth
    f.: adj. hirethek, hwansek
longitude *n.* geographical longitude
    dorles *m.*
longitudinal *adj.* dorlesel
long-lasting *adj.* duryadow
long-limbed *adj.* eseliek
long-muzzled *adj.* minyek
long-nosed skate *n.* minyek *m.*
    minyoges
long-sight *n.* hirwel *m.*
long-standing *adj.* hen
long-stone *n.* menhir *m.* -yon
long-tongued *adj.* tavosek
Looe *place* Logh
look *n.* golok *f.,* tremm *f.,*
    tremmynn *m.;* (appearance) mir
    m.: adj. look out bydh war: *v.*
    mires; look after oneself
    omdhyghtya; look at aspia orth,
    hwithra orth, mires orth; look
    upon mires war: *int.* look here
    ottomma; look there ottena
looking-glass *n.* gweder-mires *m.*
    gwedrow-mires
look-out *n.* brennyas *m.* -ysi;
    look-out place goelva *f.* +ow,
    pennoelva *f.*

loop *n.* gwydenn *f.,* kabester *m.*
    -trow, sygenn *f.*
loophole *n.* tardhell *f.* +ow
loose *adj.* lows
loosen *v.* lowsel
looseness *n.* lowsedhes *m.*
lop *v.* dibenna, skethra
lopping *n.* skethrenn *f.* +ow
lord *n.* arloedh *m.* arlydhi
lordship *n.* arloettes *m.*
lorry *n.* kert *m.* +ow, +ys;
    breakdown lorry kert torrva *m.*
lose *v.* kelli
loss *n.* koll *m.,* kolles *m.* +ow;
    danger of loss argoll *m.;* state of
    loss kollva *f.*
Lostwithiel *place* Lostwydhyel
lot *n.* chons *m.* +yow: *adj.* a lot of
    meur a; a lot of houses lies chi,
    meur a jiow
lots *v.* cast lots tewlel prenn
lottery *n.* gwari-dall *m.* gwariow-
    dall
loud *adj.* (of sound) ughel
loudspeaker *n.* ughelgowser *m.*
    +yow
louse *n.* lowenn *f.* +ow *coll.* low
lousy *adj.* lowek
lout *n.* losel *m.* +s
lovable *adj.* karadow
lovableness *n.* karadewder *m.*
lovage *n.* gilles *coll.*
love *n.* kerensa *f.: v.* kara
loved *n.* loved one karadow *m.,* kuv
    kolonn *m.: adj.* much loved
    meurgerys
lover *n.* karer *m.* -oryon, kares *f.,*
    keryades *f.* +ow, keryas *m.* -ysi
loving *adj.* karadow, kuv,
    kerensedhek
loving-kindness *n.* karadewder
    m.
low *n.* low water iselvor *m.: adj.*
    isel: *v.* (of cows) bedhygla

lower *v.* iselhe: *adv.* a-woeles, a-
is: *pref.* is-
lowering *n.* iselheans *m.*
lowland *n.* iseldir *m.* +yow
lowliness *n.* iselder *m.*
lowly *adj.* isel
loyal *adj.* lel
Loyalist *n.* Lelyas *m.* Lelysi
loyalty *n.* lelder *m.*, lelduri *m.*,
lowta *m.*
lubricant *n.* loub *m.*, uras *m.*
lubricate *v.* louba, ura
luck *n.* chons *m.* +yow, fortun *m.*
+yow, happ *m.* +ys; good luck
chons da *m.;* ill luck anfeus *f.;*
rotten luck hager dowl *m.*
lucky *adj.* feusik
luggage *n.* fardell *m.* +ow
luggage-rack *n.* roes-fardellow *f.*
lukewarm *adj.* godoemm, mygyl
lull *n.* spavenn *f.*, spavnell *f.* +ow:
v. spavennhe
luminosity *n.* splennyjyon *m.*
luminous *adj.* golowek
lump *n.* bothenn *m.*, pellenn *f.*
+ow
lunar *adj.* loerel
lunatic *n.* loerek *m.* -ogyon: *adj.*
badus, loerek
lunch *n.* picnic lunch kroust *m.*
+yow: *v.* livya
lunch(eon) *n.* li *f.* livyow, liv *f.*
+yow
lungs *plur.* skevens
lure *v.* dynya, traynya
lurk *v.* omgeles, skolkya
lust *n.* lust *m.* +ys
luxuriance *n.* gordevyans *m.*
luxuriate *v.* gordevi
luxurious *adj.* fethus
lye *n.* lisiw *m.*
lying *n.* lying posture growedh *m.:*
adj. gowek, mingow
lyric *adj.* telynnek

M

ma'am *n.* madama *f.* madamys
machine *n.* jynn *m.* +ow, +ys
machine-gun *n.* gonn-jynn *m.*
gonnow-jynn
machinery *n.* jynnweyth *f.*
mackerel *n.* brithel *m.* brithyli,
bri'el *m.* br'yli; head of boiled
mackerel skogynn *m.* +ow
mad *n.* mad woman foles *f.* +ow:
adj. fol, gorboellek, mus; mad
(U.S.) konneryek
madam *n.* madama *f.* madamys
made *v.* gwrug
madman *n.* fol *m.* felyon, mus *m.*
+yon, muskok *m.* -ogyon
madness *n.* muskokter *m.*
magazine *n.* lyver-termyn *m.*
lyvrow-termyn
maggot *n.* kontronenn *f.* +ow *coll.*
kontron
maggoty *adj.* kontronek: *v.*
become maggoty kentreni
magic *n.* pystri *m.:* *v.* work magic
pystria
magical *adj.* hudel
magician *n.* huder *m.* -oryon,
hudores *f.* +ow, pystrier *m.*
-oryon
magistrate *n.* justis *m.* +yow
magnanimity *n.* meurgolonn *f.*
magnanimous *adj.* meur y
golonn
magnet *n.* tennven *m.* tennveyn
magnetic *adj.* tennvenek
magnificence *n.* meuredh *m.*,
ryalder *m.*
magnify *v.* brashe, meurhe,
moghhe
magpie *n.* piesenn *f.* +ow *coll.*
pies
Mahomet *name* Mahomm
maid *n.* gwyrghes *f.* +i, maghteth
f. +yon

maiden *n.* **gwyrghes** *f.* **+i,**
maghteth *f.* **+yon, moren** *f.* **+yon**
maidservant *n.* **maghteth** *f.* **+yon**
mail *n.* coat of mail **kaspows** *f.*
maimed *adj.* **mans**
mainland *n.* **tir meur** *m.*
mainstream *adj.* **pennfrosek**
maintain *v.* **mentena**
maintenance *n.* **mentons** *m.:*
plur. maintenance costs **kostow-
mentons**
majesty *n.* **meuredh** *m.*
make *v.* **gul**; make Cornish
Kernewekhe; make shoes **kerya**;
make up for **astiveri**; make use of
gul devnydh a
maker *n.* **gwrier** *m.*
makings *n.* **devnydh** *m.* **+yow**
malady *n.* **kleves** *m.* **+ow**
malaria *n.* **kleves seson** *m.*
male *n.* **gorreydh** *m.;* adult male
person **gour** *m.* **gwer**: *adj.*
gorow
malediction *n.* **molleth** *f.*
mollothow, mollethyans *m.* **+ow**
malice *n.* **atti** *m.,* **drogedh** *m.,*
mikenn *f.,* **spit** *m.*
malicious *adj.* **spitus**
malignant *adj.* **kammhynsek**
mallard *n.* **mallart** *m.* **-s**
mallet *n.* **morbenn** *m.* **+ow**
mallow *n.* **malow** *coll.* **+enn**
malt *n.* **brag** *m.*
malthouse *n.* **bragji** *m.* **+ow,**
bragva *f.*
maltster *n.* **brager** *m.* **-oryon**
mammal *n.* **bronnvil** *m.* **+es**
man *n.* **den** *m.* **tus**; (as opposed to
woman) **gour** *m.* **gwer**; (fellow)
gwas *m.* **gwesyon**; good man
demmas *m.,* **densa** *m.;* man and
woman **dewdhen** *m.;* man of the
house **gorti** *m.* **gwerti**; old man
koth *m.;* young man **bacheler** *m.*
+s, yonker *m.* **+s**: *phr.* to the last
man **yn kettep gwas**

Man *n.* Isle of Man **Manow** *f.*
manage *v.* **dyghtya**
management *n.* **rewl** *f.* **+ys**
manager *n.* **dyghtyer** *m.* **-yoryon**
mandible *n.* **awen** *f.,* **challa** *m.*
challys
mane *n.* **mong** *f.* **+ow**; coarse hair
of mane **reun** *f.*
manger *n.* **presep** *m.* **presebow**
manifest *adj.* **hewel**
mankind *n.* **denses** *m.,* **mab-den**
m.
manliness *n.* **gouroleth** *f.*
manly *adj.* **gourel**
manner *n.* **fordh** *f.* **+ow, gis** *m.,*
kor *m.* **+ow, maner** *f.* **+ow**
manners *n.* good manners **kortesi**
m., **norter** *m.*
manor *n.* **maner** *m.*
manor-house *n.* **manerji** *m.* **+ow**
mansion *n.* **plas** *m.* **plassow**
manslaughter *n.* **denladh** *m.*
mantelpiece *n.* **astell an oeles** *f.*
mantle *n.* **pall** *m.* **+ow**
manual *n.* **kowethlyver** *m.*
-lyvrow
manufacture *n.* **gwrians** *m.* **+ow**
manure *n.* **teyl** *m.,* **karrdeyl** *m.,*
mon *m.*
manuscript *n.* **dornskrif** *m.* **+ow**;
original manuscript **mammskrif** *m.*
+ow
Manx *n.* Manx language **Manowek**
m.: *adj.* **Manowek**
many *pron.* **lies**; as many as **myns**;
how many **pyseul**: *adj.* **lies,**
meur, nameur, lower, meur a;
as many **keniver**; as many as
kemmys; many houses **lies chi,**
meur a jiow; not many **neb lies**;
so many **keniver**: *adv.* as many as
kekemmys; how many **pes**;
many times **lieskweyth, nameur**
map *n.* **mappa** *m.* **+ow**
maple-tree *n.* **gwinwelenn** *f.* **+ow**
coll. **gwinwel**

mar *v.* **difasya**
marauder *n.* **preydher** *m.* **-oryon,**
    ravner *m.* **-oryon**
Marazion *place* **Marghasyow**
marble *n.* **marbel** *m.;* (sphere)
    marblenn *f.* **+ow**
march *n.* (border district) **ordir** *m.*
    +yow; (tune) **ton kerdh** *m.;*
    (walk) **keskerdh** *m.: v.*
    keskerdhes
March *n.* **Meurth** *m.,* **mis-Meurth**
    m.
marcher *n.* (female) **keskerdhores**
    m. **+ow;** (male) **keskerdher** *m.*
    -oryon
mare *n.* **kasek** *f.* **kasegi**
margarine *n.* **margarin** *m.*
marigold *n.* **les an gog** *m.*
marijuana *n.* **kewargh** *coll.* **+enn**
mariner *n.* **marner** *m.* **marners,**
    marnoryon
maritime *adj.* **morek**
mark *n.* **merk** *m.* **+yow, sin** *m.*
    +ys, +yow: *v.* **merkya:** *phr.* as a
    mark of **yn tokyn**
market *n.* **fer** *m.* **+yow, marghas** *f.*
    +ow; stock market **marghas**
    stokk *f.: v.* **marghasa**
marketable *adj.* **marghasadow**
marketeer *n.* **marghador** *m.*
    +yon, marghadores *f.* **+ow**
market-house *n.* **chi marghas** *m.,*
    marghatti *m.* **+ow**
market-place *n.* **marghasla** *m.,*
    marghasva *f.* **+ow, plen an**
    varghas *m.*
market-stall *n.* **stall-marghas** *m.*
marmalade *n.* **kyfeyth owraval** *m.*
marram *n.* marram grass **morhesk**
    coll. **+enn**
marriage *n.* **demmedhyans** *m.*
    +ow; state of marriage **priosoleth**
    f.
married *adj.* **pries**
marry *v.* **demmedhi**
Mars *n.* **Meurth** *m.*

marsh *n.* **hal** *f.* **halow, gwern** *coll.*
    +enn, heskynn *m.;* (reedy)
    keunek *f.* **-egi;** rush-grown marsh
    broennek *f.* **-egi**
marshy *adj.* **gwernek**
marten *n.* **yewgenn** *m.*
martian *n.* **meurthwas** *m.*
    -wesyon
martyr *v.* **mertherya**
martyrdom *n.* **mertherynsi** *f.*
marvel *n.* **aneth** *m.* **+ow, marthus**
    m. **+yon**
marvellous *adj.* **barthusek,**
    marthys
marvellously *adv.* **marthys**
Mary *name* **Maria;** Blessed Mary
    Maria Wynn
masculine *adj.* **gourel;**
    (grammatical gender) **gorow**
masculinity *n.* **gouroleth** *f.*
mash *v.* **brewi**
mask *n.* **visour** *m.*
mason *n.* **mason** *m.* **+s, ser men**
    m. **seri men**
masonry *n.* **menweyth** *m.*
mass *n.* **bush** *m.* **+ys;** (church
    service) **oferenn** *f.* **+ow;** (heap)
    gronn *m.,* **tysk** *f.* **+ow;** (in
    physics) **gronnedh** *m.* **+ow;** mass
    destruction **distruyans** *m.;* mass
    for the dead **seren** *f.;* midnight
    mass **pellgens** *m.;* requiem mass
    seren *f.:* *adj.* **yn rew:** *v.*
    celebrate mass **oferenni**
mast *n.* **gwern** *f.* **+ow**
master *n.* **arloedh** *m.* **arlydhi,**
    mester *m.* **mestrysi;** Latin master
    latimer *m.* **+s**
masterpiece *n.* **pennober** *m.* **+ow**
masterwork *n.* **pennober** *m.* **+ow**
mastery *n.* **maystri** *m.,*
    mestrynses *m.*
mastiff *n.* **gwylter** *m.*
mastless *adj.* **diwern**

mat *n.* **strel** *m.* **+yow**; bedside mat **strel gweli** *m.;* beer or table mat **strelik** *m.* **-igow**

match *n.* (equal) **par** *m.* **+ow**; (game) **fit** *m.* **+ys**; (matchstick) **tanbrenn** *m.* **-yer**

mate *n.* **koweth** *m.* **+a, par** *m.* **+ow**; (married person) **kespar** *m.* **+ow**; (pal) **kila** *m.,* **mata** *m.* **matys**

matelot *n.* **morwas** *m.* **-wesyon**

materfamilias *n.* **mamm-teylu** *f.*

material *n.* **devnydh** *m.* **+yow**: *adj.* **materyel**

materialism *n.* **materyoleth** *f.*

materialistic *adj.* **materyolethek**

maternal *adj.* **mammel**

maternity *n.* **mammoleth** *f.*

mathematically *v.* divide mathematically **disranna**

mathematician *n.* **kalkor** *m.* **+yon**

mathematics *n.* **awgrym** *m.*

matriarch *n.* **mamm-teylu** *f.*

matrimonial *adj.* **priosel**

matron *n.* **gwreg** *f.* **gwragedh**

matter *n.* **mater** *m.* **+s, +ow**; delicate matter **mater tykkli** *m.: phr.* it does not matter **ny vern**; it does not matter to me **ny'm deur**; it need not matter to us **ny res dhyn fors**; no matter **na fors**

matters *v.* **deur**

Matthew *name* **Matthew**

Maundy *n.* **Kablys** *m.;* Maundy Thursday **dy' Yow Hablys** *m.*

maw *n.* **glas** *m.,* **penngasenn** *f.*

maximum *n.* **ughboynt** *m.* **+ow**: *adj.* **moyha**

May *n.* **Me** *m.,* **mis-Me** *m.;* May Day **Kala' Me** *m.*

maybe *adv.* **martesen**

mayor *n.* **mer** *m.* **+yon**; home of mayor **merji** *m.* **+ow**

mayoress *n.* **meres** *f.* **+ow**

maze *n.* **milhyntall** *m.*

me *pron.* **my, vy, vy, -evy, -ma**; (emphatic) **-mevy**

mead *n.* (drink) **medh** *m.;* mix of ale and mead **bragas** *m.;* spiced mead **medhyglynn** *m.*

meadow *n.* **pras** *m.* **+ow, budhynn** *m.* **+yow**

meal *n.* **boes** *m.;* meal taken to work **kroust** *m.* **+yow**

meal-time *n.* **prys** *m.* **+yow, prys boes** *m.*

mean *adj.* (average) **mayn**: *v.* **styrya**

meander *n.* **kogrenn** *f.* **+ow**: *v.* **kogrenna**

meaning *n.* **styr** *m.* **+yow**

meaningless *adj.* **distyr**

means *n.* **mayn** *m.* **+ys, pygans** *m.: prep.* by means of **der, dre**

measles *n.* **brygh rudh** *f.;* German measles **brygh almaynek** *f.*

measure *n.* **musur** *m.;* (tool) **musurell** *f.* **+ow**: *adj.* of full measure **da**: *v.* **musura**

measurement *n.* **musurans** *m.* **+ow**

meat *n.* **kig** *m.* **+yow**; roast meat **goleyth** *m.;* tough bit of meat **skennynn** *m.* **+ow**

mechanic *n.* **jynnweythor** *m.* **+yon**

mechanical *adj.* **jynnweythek**

mechanism *n.* **jynnweyth** *f.*

meddle *v.* **mellya**; meddle with **attamya**

meddling *n.* **mellyans** *m.*

medical *n.* medical centre **medhygva** *f.* **+ow**; medical science **fisek** *f.:* *adj.* **medhygel**

medicine *n.* (as remedy) **medhygneth** *f.;* (as science) **medhygieth** *f.*

meditation *n.* **preder** *m.* **+ow**

medlar *n.* **merys** *m.*

medley *n.* **kabol** *m.,* **kabolva** *f.*

meek *adj.* **klor, hwar**

meet *v.* **dyerbynna, metya, omguntell**; (one another) **omvetya**; meet with **dos erbynn, mos erbynn**

meet *adj.* (suitable) **gwiw**

meeting *n.* **kuntell** *m.* **+ow, kuntelles** *m.* **+ow, kuntellyans** *m.* **+ow, metyans** *m.* **+ow**; meeting of bards **gorsedh** *f.* **+ow**; meeting of waters **kendevryon** *m.*

melancholy *n.* **moredh** *m.: adj.* **moredhek**

mellow *adj.* **adhves**

melody *n.* **ilow** *f.*, **ton** *m.* **+yow**

melon *n.* **melon** *m.* **+yow**

melt *v.* **teudhi**

melted *adj.* **teudh**

melter *n.* **teudher** *m.* **-oryon**

melting *adj.* **teudh**

member *n.* (part of body) **esel** *m.* **eseli, lith** *m.* **+yow**; member of trade-guild **mysterden** *m.* **+s**

membership *n.* **eseleth** *f.*

memento *n.* **kovro** *m.* **kovrohow**

memorial *n.* memorial stone **men-kov** *m.* **meyn-kov**

memory *n.* **kov** *m.* **+yow, kovva** *f.* **+ow**

men *plur.* (human beings) **tus**

menace *n.* **godros** *m.* **+ow**: *v.* **bragya, degynsywa, godros**

menagerie *n.* **milva** *f.* **milvaow**

mend *n.* **ewnheans** *m.* **+ow**: *v.* **ewnhe**; mend shoes **kerya**

mention *n.* **kampoell** *m.* **+ow, menek** *m.* **-egow**: *v.* **kampoella, meneges**

mentioned *adj.* **kampoellys**; already mentioned **ragleverys**

menu *n.* **rol-voes** *f.* **rolyow-boes**

merchandise *n.* **gwara** *c.*, **marchondis** *m.*

merchant *n.* **marchont** *m.* **-ons, marghador** *m.* **+yon, marghadores** *f.* **+ow**

merciful *adj.* **mersiabyl, tregeredhus**

mercury *n.* **arghans byw** *m.*

Mercury *n.* **Mergher** *m.*

mercy *n.* **mersi** *m.;* (compassion) **truedh** *m.;* (loving kindness) **tregeredh** *f.* **+ow**: *phr.* have mercy **kemmeres truedh**

mercy-seat *n.* **tregeredhva** *f.*

merge *v.* **kesunya, omjunya**; (intrans.) **omgelli**

merger *n.* **kesunyans** *m.* **+ow**

mermaid *n.* **morvoren** *f.* **+yon, morwyrghes** *f.* **+i**

merry *adj.* **digeudh, heudh, lowenek, meri**

mesh *n.* **magel** *f.* **maglow, maglenn** *f.* **+ow**

mesmerism *n.* **huskosk** *m.*

mess *n.* (meal) **sand** *m.* **+ys**; (untidiness) **strol** *m.*

message *n.* **messach** *m.* **messajys**

messenger *n.* **kannas** *f.* **+ow, messejer** *m.* **+s**

messy *adj.* **strolyek**

metal *n.* **alkan** *m.*, **metol** *m.*

meteorology *n.* **keweronieth** *f.*

meter *n.* **musurell** *f.* **+ow**

metheglin *n.* **medhyglynn** *m.*

Methodist *n.* **Methodyas** *m.* **-ysi**; Methodist Church **Eglos an Vethodysi** *f.: adj.* **Methodek**

metre *n.* (unit) **meter** *m.* **metrow**

metric *adj.* **metrek**

metricate *v.* **metregi**

metrication *n.* **metregieth** *f.*

mew *v.* **miowal**

Michael *name* **Mighal**

Michaelmas *n.* **dy'goel Mighal** *m.*

micro- *pref.* **korr**

microbe *n.* **korrbryv** *m.* **+es**

microphone *n.* **korrgowser** *m.* **+yow**

microwave *n.* microwave oven **forn-gorrdonn** *f.* **fornow-korrdonn, korrdonner** *m.*

midday *n.* **hanterdydh** *m.*

midden *n.* **byjyon** *m.* **+s**

middle *n.* **mysk** *m.*

middle-class *n.* **renkas kres** *m.*

midget *n.* **korrik** *m.* **-igow**

midnight *n.* **hanternos** *f.*

midst *n.* **mysk** *m.*

Midsummer *n.* **Goelowann** *m.*

midwife *n.* **gwelivedhes** *f.* **+ow**

mien *n.* **cher** *m.*

might *n.* **galloes** *m.,* **nerth** *m.* **+yow, krevder** *m.*

mighty *adj.* **galloesek, krev, nerthek, kevoethek**

milady *n.* **madama** *f.* **madamys**

mild *adj.* **klor, hwar**

mildew *n.* **kywni** *coll.* **+enn:** *v.* become covered in mildew **kywnia**

mildness *n.* **klorder** *m.*

mile *n.* **mildir** *m.* **+yow**

milfoil *n.* **minfel** *m.*

militia *n.* **trevlu** *m.*

milk *n.* **leth** *m.;* cow's first milk **godrek** *m.,* **leth boesa** *m.;* sweet milk **levrith** *m.:* *v.* **godra;** lose milk **heski**

milkless *adj.* (of cow) **hesk**

milky *n.* milky place **lethek** *m.* **-egow:** *adj.* **lethek**

mill *n.* **melin** *f.* **+yow**

millennium *n.* **milvlydhen** *f.* **+yow;** Millennium Commission **Desedhek an Vilvlydhen** *m.*

miller *n.* **meliner** *m.* **-yon**

mill-house *n.* **chi melin** *m.,* **melinji** *m.* **+ow**

million *n.* **milvil** *m.* **+yow**

millionaire *n.* **milvilwas** *m.* **-wesyon**

millipede *n.* **mildroes** *m.*

millpond *n.* **poll melin** *m.*

mill-pool *n.* **kreun melin** *m.*

mince *v.* **divynya**

mincemeat *n.* **brewgik** *m.*

mind *n.* **brys** *m.* **+yow;** state of mind **cher** *m.:* *v.* **gwaytya, gorwitha**

mine *n.* **bal** *m.* **+yow;** dug mine on a lode **koghynn** *m.* **+ow**

mineral *adj.* **moenek**

mineral-house *n.* **moendi** *m.*

mine-shaft *n.* **shafta** *m.* **-ys**

mine-waste *n.* **atal** *coll.*

mine-working *n.* **hwel** *m.* **+yow;** opencast mine-working **moengleudh** *m.* **+yow**

mingle *v.* **kemmyska, myska;** (oneself) **omgemmyska**

minify *v.* **lehe**

minimum *n.* **ispoynt** *m.* **+ow:** *adj.* **lyha**

minister *n.* **menyster** *m.* **+yon, -trys;** Foreign Minister **Menyster Estrenyek** *m.;* Minister for Highways **Menyster a-barth Fordhow;** *m.*

ministry *n.* **kloeregieth** *f.,* **menystrans** *m.;* Ministry of Agriculture **Menystrans Ammeth** *m.*

minstrel *n.* **mynstral** *m.* **+s**

mint *n.* (for money) **batti** *m.* **+ow;** (plant) **menta** *f.*

minute *n.* (a single record) **kovnotenn** *f.* **+ow, kovnotyans** *m.* **+ow;** (of time) **mynysenn** *f.* **+ow:** *adj.* **munys**

miracle *n.* **marthus** *m.* **+yon, merkyl** *m.* **merklys**

mire *n.* **leysyek** *f.* **-egi, stag** *m.*

mirror *n.* **gweder-mires** *m.* **gwedrow-mires, mirour** *m.* **+s**

mirth *n.* **lowender** *m.*

misadventure *n.* **droglamm** *m.* **+ow**

misbehave *v.* **kammomdhoen**

miscellany *n.* **kemmysk** *m.*

mischance *n.* gwall *m.* +ow,
meschons *m.*
mischief *n.* dregynn *m.*
miscreant *n.* drogoberer *m.*
-oryon
misdeed *n.* drogober *m.* +ow,
gwann-ober *m.* +ow,
kammweyth *m.*, kammweythres
m., kammwrians *m.* +ow
miser *n.* erbysyas *m.* -ysi, kraf *m.*
krefyon
miserable *adj.* truan, poenvosek
misery *n.* kas *m.*, anfeus *f.*, anken
m. +yow, gew *m.* +ow, poenvos
m.; state of misery poenvotter *m.*
misfortune *n.* anfeus *f.*
misjudge *v.* kammvreusi
mispronounce *v.* kammleverel
miss *n.* damsel *f.* +s;
Miss *n.* (of adult women); Mestres *f.*
(of girls) Mestresik *f.*
missel-thrush *n.* tresklenn *f.* +ow
coll. treskel
missile *n.* deghesenn *f.* +ow
mission-house *n.* kannatti *m.* +ow
mist *n.* niwl *m.* +ow; thick mist
kowas niwl *f.*
mistake *n.* kammgemmeryans
m.; mistake in writing kammskrif
m.: *v.* myskemmeres; make a
mistake kammwul; make a mistake
in writing kammskrifa
Mister *n.* Mester *m.*
mistletoe *n.* ughelvarr *coll.* +enn
mistress *n.* arloedhes *f.* +ow,
mestres *f.* +ow; mistress of the
house mamm-teylu *f.*
Mistress *n.* Mestres *f.*
mistrust *n.* mystrest *m.:* *v.*
mystrestya
misty *adj.* niwlek
misunderstand *v.*
kammgonvedhes
misunderstanding *n.*
myskemmeryans *m.*
miswrite *v.* kammskrifa

mite *n.* mita *m.* mitys, myjenn *m.*,
temmik *m.* temmigow
mitigate *v.* sewajya
mitre *n.* miter *m.* +s
mix *v.* kemmyska, kaboli
mixture *n.* kemmysk *m.*
mix-up *n.* kabol *m.*, kabolva *f.*
mobile *adj.* gwayadow
moccasin *n.* pawgenn *m.* +ow
mock *v.* gesya, gul ges a,
skornya
mockery *n.* ges *m.*, skorn *m.*
model *n.* patron *m.* +yow: *v.*
shapya
moderate *v.* musura, tempra
moderation *n.* musur *m.*
moderator *n.* temprer *m.* -oryon
modern *adj.* arnowydh
modest *adj.* isel, klor
modesty *n.* klorder *m.*
moist *adj.* glyb, gwlygh, leyth
moisten *v.* leytha
moisture *n.* glybor *m.*, gwlygha *m.*
molar *n.* dans a-dhelergh *m.;*
molar tooth kildhans *m.* -dhens
molasses *n.* molas *m.*
mole *n.* godh *f.* +ow, godhor *f.;*
mole on skin plustrenn *f.*
molest *v.* disesya, mellya, trobla
molestation *n.* mellyans *m.*
molten *adj.* teudh
moment *n.* pols *m.* +yow, kors *m.*,
prysweyth *m.*, toch *m.*
mommy (U.S.) *n.* mammik *f.*
monarch *n.* myghtern *m.* +edh
monastery *n.* managhti *m.* +ow
monastic *adj.* managhek
Monday *n.* dy' Lun *m.;* Maze
Monday dy' Lun Mus *m.*
monetary *adj.* monesek
money *n.* arghans *m.*, mona *c.*,
owr *m.*

money order (U.S.) *n.*
arghadow-post *m.*
arghadowyow-post
money-box *n.* kofrik-erbys *m.*
-igow-erbys
money-lender *n.* okerer *m.*
-oryon
money-order *n.* arghadow-mona
m. arghadowyow-mona
monitor *n.* gorwoelyas *m.* -ysi:
v. gorwoelyas
monk *n.* managh *m.* menegh
monkey *n.* sim *m.* +es
monkeyish *n.* monkeyish person apa
m. appys
monk-fish *n.* morvanagh *m.*
-venegh
monochrome *adj.* unnliw
monolingual *adj.* unnyethek
monosyllabic *adj.* unnsyllabek
monotone *n.* monotonous noise
drylsi *m.*
monotonous *adj.* unnton
monotony *n.* unntoneth *f.*
monster *n.* euthvil *m.* +es
month *n.* mis *m.* misyow; first of
month Kalann *m.;* month's end
pennvis *m.* +yow; period of a
month miskweyth *m.;* three
months trymis *m.*
monthly *adj.* misyek
Moon *n.* loer *f.* +yow
moonlight *n.* loergann *m.*
moonstruck *adj.* badus, loerek
moor *n.* hal *f.* halow, ros *m.* +yow;
(upland) goen *f.* +yow
Moor *n.* Sarsyn *m.* +s
moorhen *n.* lagyar *f.* -yer
moor-house *n.* goendi *m.* +ow
Moorish *adj.* Sarsynek
mop *n.* skubell-wolghi *f.*
skubellow-golghi, skubyllenn *f.;*
squeegee mop gwaskubyllenn *f.*
+ow
mope *v.* moutya

moral *n.* dyskas *m.*
more *adj.* moy; any more nahen:
adv. bydh moy; once more arta,
hwath; what's more ha gensi
moreover *conj.* gans henna: *adv.*
keffrys
morn *n.* bora *m.*
morning *n.* myttin *m.* +yow,
myttinweyth *m.: adv.* during the
morning myttinweyth; in the
morning diworth an myttin,
myttin +yow
morphia *n.* koskles *m.*
morrow *n.* morow *f.: adv.* on the
morrow ternos
morsel *n.* pastell *f.* +ow
mortal *n.* sojet ankow *m.: adj.*
marwel
mortality *n.* marwoleth *f.*
mortgage *n.* marwystel *m.*
marwystlow; land mortgage
gwystel-tir *m.* gwystlow-tir: *v.*
marwystla
mortise *n.* mortes *m.* +ys
mosaic *n.* brithweyth *m.*
Moses *name* Moyses
moss *n.* kywni *coll.* +enn
mossy *adj.* kywniek: *v.* become
mossy kywnia
most *adj.* moyha, moggha: *adv.*
for the most part dre vras
mote *n.* brygh *f.* +i
motel *n.* karrostel *m.* +yow
motes *plur.* mottys
moth *n.* goedhan *m.* +es
mother *n.* mamm *f.* +ow, dama *f.*
damyow; nursing mother
mammeth *f.* +ow
motherhood *n.* mammoleth *f.*
mother-in-law *n.* dama dre lagha
f., hweger *f.* hwegrow
motherland *n.* mammvro *f.* +yow
motherly *adj.* mammel
mother-tongue *n.* mammyeth *f.*
motive *n.* acheson *m.* +yow, +ys

motocross *n.* **resegva jynn-
diwros** *f.*
motor *n.* **jynn** *m.* **+ow, +ys**
motor-bike *n.* **jynn-diwros** *m.*
jynnow-diwros
motor-boat *n.* **skath-tan** *f.*
skathow-tan
motor-car *n.* **karr-tan** *m.*
motor-cycle *n.* **jynn-diwros** *m.*
jynnow-diwros
mottle *v.* **britha**
mould *n.* (fungus) **kosk** *m.*
mould *n.* (for casting) **furv** *f.* **+ow,
kowynn** *m.* **+ow, pri** *m.:* *v.*
furvya, mola
mould *n.* (soil) **gweres** *m.* **+ow**
mouldy *adj.* **loes:** *v.* go mouldy
koska
moult *v.* **moutya**
mound *n.* **knegh** *m.* **+yow, krug** *m.*
+ow, pil *m.* **+yow;** little mound
krugell *f.* **+ow, krugynn** *f.* **+ow:**
v. pile up in a mound **krugya**
mount *n.* **mont** *m.:* *v.* **yskynna**
mountain *n.* **menydh** *m.* **+yow**
mountain-ash *n.* **kerdhin** *coll.*
+enn
mountaineer *n.* **menydhyer** *m.*
menydhyoryon
mountainous *adj.* **menydhek**
mounting-block *n.* **marghven** *m.*
-veyn
mourn *v.* **galari, kyni**
mourner *n.* **kyner** *m.* **-oryon**
mournful *adj.* **trist**
mourning *n.* **kynvann** *m.*
mourning-dress *n.* **galarwisk** *m.*
mouse *n.* **logosenn** *f.* **+ow** *coll.*
logos: *adj.* abounding in mice
logosek: *v.* catch mice **legessa**
moustache *n.* **minvlew** *coll.* **+ynn**
mouth *n.* **ganow** *m.* **+ow, min** *m.*
+yow; roof of mouth **gorheras** *m.:*
phr. shut your mouth **syns dha vin**
mouthful *n.* **ganowas** *m.*

move *v.* (intransitive) **gwaya;**
(spiritually) **movya;** (trans.)
removya; move about **sommys**
movement *n.* **movyans** *m.* **+ow;**
(political) **omsav** *m.* **+ow**
mow *v.* **falghas**
mowhay *n.* **yslann** *f.* **+ow**
Mr *n.* **Mester** *m.*
Mrs *n.* **Mestres** *f.*
Ms *n.* **Mestres** *f.*
much *pron.* as much as **myns;** how
much **pyseul:** *adj.* lower; as
much as **kemmys;** so much
kemmys: *adv.* (with neg.)
nameur; as much as **kekemmys;**
how much **pygemmys**
mucus *n.* nasal mucus **pur** *m.*
mud *n.* **leys** *m.* **+yow, stag** *m.*
muddle *n.* **tervysk** *m.* **+ow:** *v.*
tervyska; muddle up **tervyska**
muddy *adj.* **leysyek**
mugwort *n.* **loesles** *m.*
mule *n.* **mul** *m.* **+yon, mules** *f.*
+ow
mullet *n.* **meyl** *m.* **+i:** *v.* catch
mullet **meylessa**
multi-national *adj.*
lieskenedhlek
multiple *adj.* **liesek**
multiplicity *n.* **liester** *m.*
multiply *v.* **kressya, lieshe;**
(intrans.) **palshe**
multitude *n.* **routh** *f.* **+ow**
mummy *n.* **mammik** *f.*
mumps *n.* **penn-sagh** *m.*
munificence *n.* **helder** *m.*
munificent *adj.* **hel**
murder *n.* **ladhva** *f.:* *v.* **ladha,
moldra**
murdered *v.* **ledhys**
murderer *n.* **denledhyas** *m.* **-ysi,
moldrer** *m.* **-oryon**
murky *adj.* **tewal, tewl**
murmur *n.* **hanas** *m.* **+ow:** *v.*
hanasa

muscle *n.* **keher** *m.* **+ow**

muscular *adj.* **keherek**

muse *n.* **awen** *f.*

museum *n.* **gwithti** *m.*

mushroom *n.* **skavell-groenek** *f.* **skavellow-kroenek**

music *n.* **ilow** *f.;* instrumental music **menestrouthi** *m.*

musician *n.* **ilewydh** *m.* **+yon**

mussel *n.* **mesklenn** *f.* **+ow** *coll.* **meskel**

must *phr.* we must **bysi yw dhyn, res yw dhyn**

mustard *n.* **kedhow** *m.*

musty *adj.* **messent**

mute *adj.* **avlavar**

mutilated *adj.* **evredh**

mutiny *n.* **gustel** *m.*

mutual *n.* mutual interest **kesles** *m.*

my *pron.* **am:** *adj.* **ow:** *phr.* and my **ha'm, ha'w;** to my **dhe'm, dh'ow**

myopia *n.* **berrwel** *m.*

myrrh *n.* **myrr** *m.*

myrtle-tree *n.* **myrtwydhenn** *f.* **+ow** *coll.* **myrtwydh**

mysterious *adj.* **kevrinek**

mystery *n.* **kevrin** *m.* **+yow, rin** *m.* **+yow**

N

nag *n.* **ronsyn** *m.;* ambling nag **hakney** *m.* **+s**

nail *n.* **kenter** *f.* **kentrow, ebil** *m.* **+yow, ebil horn** *m.;* small headless wedge-shaped iron nail **sparbyl** *m.;* small nail **kentrik** *f.* **-igow:** *v.* **takkya, kentra;** nail to **kentra orth, takkya orth;** nail with many nails **kentrewi**

naive *adj.* **anfel**

naked *adj.* **noeth, lomm;** half naked **ternoeth**

nakedness *n.* **noetha** *f.*

naker *n.* naker shell **askell** *f.* **eskelli**

name *n.* **hanow** *m.* **henwyn;** false name **fukhanow** *m.* **-henwyn:** *prep.* in the name of **a-barth:** *v.* **henwel;** name before **rakhenwel**

nap *n.* **gogosk** *m.,* **koskas** *m.:* *v.* **gogoska, nappya**

nape *n.* **gwarr** *f.* **+ow**

napkin *n.* **kwethynn** *m.* **+ow, lien** *m.* **+yow, lien diwla** *m.*

narcissi *n.* **fion** *coll.* **+enn**

narrow *adj.* **kul, ynn**

narrow-boat *n.* **skath-ynn** *f.* **skathow-ynn**

narrowness *n.* **kulder** *m.,* **ynnder** *m.*

nastiness *n.* **last** *m.*

nation *n.* **kenedhel** *f.* **-dhlow:** *adj.* United Nations **Kenedhlow Unys**

national *adj.* **kenedhlek**

nationalist *n.* **kenedhloger** *m.* **-oryon**

nationality *n.* **kenedhlogeth** *f.*

nationalize *v.* **kenedhlegi**

native *n.* **genesik** *m.* **-igyon, teythyek** *m.* **teythyogyon**

native-born *adj.* **genesik**

natural *n.* natural affection **natureth** *f.:* *adj.* **genesik, naturel**

naturalist *n.* **naturor** *m.* **+yon**

nature *n.* **natur** *f.;* (character) **gnas** *f.* **+ow, nas** *f.;* human nature **natureth** *f.*

naughty *adj.* **drog**

nave *n.* **korf eglos** *m.;* (of wheel) both *f.* **+ow**

navel *n.* **begel** *m.* **+yow**

navvy *n.* **paler** *m.* **-oryon**

navy *n.* **lu lestri** *m.,* **morlu** *m.*

neap *n.* neap tide **marowvor** *m.*

near *adj.* **ogas;** draw near **dos nes**

nearer *adj.* **nes:** *adv.* **yn-nes**

nearest *adj.* **nessa**

nearly *adv.* **ogas, nammna, ogatti**

nearness *n.* **nester** *m.*
neat *adj.* **kempenn, glanyth**
neatherd *n.* **bugel lodhnow** *m.*
neatness *n.* **glanythter** *m.*,
  kempennses *m.*
nebula *n.* **niwl-ster** *m.*
necessary *phr.* it is necessary for us
  bysi yw dhyn, res yw dhyn
necessities *n.* **pygans** *m.*
necessity *n.* **res** *m.: adv.* of
  necessity **porres**
neck *n.* **konna** *m.* **+ow**
neck-chain *n.* **torgh** *f.* **tergh**
necklet *n.* **delk** *m.*
necktie *n.* **kolm konna** *m.*
need *n.* **edhomm** *m.* **+ow, res** *m.*,
  esow *m.*
needle *n.* **naswydh** *f.* **+yow**; eye of
  needle **kraw naswydh** *m.*
needy *n.* needy person **edhommek**
  m. **edhommogyon**: *adj.*
  edhommek
negative *adj.* **negedhek**
neglect *n.* **gwall** *m.* **+ow, skoell** *m.*
  +yon: *v.* **dispresya**
negligence *n.* **lowsedhes** *m.*
negligent *adj.* **logh**
negotiate *v.* **negysya**
negotiator *n.* **negysydh** *m.* **+yon**
neigh *v.* **gryghias**
neighbour *n.* **kentrevek** *m.*
  -ogyon, kentrevoges *f.* **+ow**
neighbourhood *n.* **kentreveth** *f.*
  +ow
neighbouring *adj.* **kentrevek**
neighbourliness *n.* **kentrevogeth**
  f.
neither *pron.* **naneyl**: *conj.*
  naneyl; neither ... nor **naneyl ...
  na**: *adv.* **na ... na**
nephew *n.* **noy** *m.* **noyens**
nerve *n.* **nervenn** *f.* **+ow** *coll.* **nerv**
nervous *adj.* **es y vovya, nervus**
nest *n.* **neyth** *m.* **+ow**: *v.* **neythi**;
  build a nest **neythi**

nesting-place *n.* **neythva** *f.* **+ow**
net *n.* **roes** *f.* **+ow**; small net
  roesenn *f.* **+ow**
Netherlands *plur.* **Iseldiryow**:
  adj. pertaining to the Netherlands
  Iseldiryek
nett *adj.* **ylyn**
nettle *n.* **linasenn** *f.* **+ow** *coll.* **linas**
nettle-bed *n.* **linasek** *f.* **-egi**
network *n.* **roesweyth** *m.* **+yow**:
  v. **roesweytha**
neuter *adj.* **nebreydh**
neutral *adj.* **heptu, heb tu**: *adv.*
  nep-tu
neutralize *v.* **dinertha**
never *adv.* **bynner, byttele,
  jammes**; (in neg. phrases) **nevra**
nevertheless *adv.* **byttegyns,
  byttiwettha**
new *adj.* **nowydh**; brand new
  nowydh flamm
New Zealand *place* **Mordir
  Nowydh**
Newlyn *place* **Lulynn**
newness *n.* **nowydhses** *m.*
Newquay *place* **Tewynn Pleustri**
news *n.* **nowedhys** *m.: plur.*
  nowodhow; bad news **hager
  nowodhow, yeyn nowodhow**
newspaper *n.* **paper-nowodhow**
  m.
newt *n.* **pedresyf** *f.*, **peswar-paw**
  m. **+es**
next *plur.* next of kin **neshevin**:
  adj. **nessa**
nice *adj.* **hweg**
nickname *n.* **les-hanow** *m.*
  -henwyn: *v.* **les-henwel**
niece *n.* **nith** *f.* **+ow**
nigh *adv.* well nigh **nammna**
night *n.* **nos** *f.* **+ow**: *adv.* at night
  nosweyth; by night **d'wor' an
  nos**; by night and by day **mo ha
  myttin**; last night **nyhewer**;
  through the night **dre nos**: *phr.*
  good night **durnostadha**

nightingale *n.* eos *f.* +ow; little
nightingale eosik *f.*
nightjar *n.* churra-nos *m.*
nightmare *n.* hulla *m.*, hunlev *m.;*
(in which one is fixed) stag *m.*
nightshirt *n.* krys nos *m.*
night-time *n.* nosweyth *f.* +yow
nil *n.* mann *m.*
nimble *adj.* skav, strik, uskis
nine *num.* naw
ninepin *n.* kil *m.* +ys, +yow
nineteen *num.* nownsek
nineteenth *num.* nownsegves
ninth *num.* nawves
nits *n.* nedh *coll.* +enn
no *adv.* in no way kammenn; in no
way at all kammenn vydh; no
longer na fella: *int.* na
Noah *name* Noy
nobility *n.* pennsevigyans *m.*,
pennsevigeth *f.*
noble *n.* ughelor *m.* +yon; (coin)
nobyl *m.* noblys: *adj.* bryntin,
nobyl
nobody *n.* denvydh *m.*, den y'n
bys *m.*
nod *v.* penn-droppya
noise *n.* son *m.* +yow, tros *m.*
+yow; monotonous noise drylsi *m.*
noiseless *adj.* didros, dison
noisily *phr.* tys-ha-tas
noisome *adj.* disawor
noisomeness *n.* last *m.*
noisy *adj.* trosek
nom-de-plume *n.* fukhanow *m.*
-henwyn
nominate *v.* apoyntya, henwel
nomination *n.* hanwesigeth *f.*
+ow
nominee *n.* hanwesik *m.* -igyon
non-clerical *adj.* leg
nonconformist *n.* dissentyer *m.*
-oryon
nonconformity *v.* dissentyans

nonsense *n.* flows *m.*, treus *m.*
+yon: *plur.* hwedhlow: *int.*
tetivali
nook *n.* bagh *f.* +ow, kil *m.* +yer,
kilenn *f.* +ow, kornell *f.* +ow,
kornet *m.* +yow, korrvagh *f.*,
sorn *m.* +ow
noon *n.* hanterdydh *m.;* noon to
sunset dohajydh *m.*
no-one *pron.* nagonan
noose *n.* gwydenn *f.*, kabester *m.*
-trow, *f.*, kroglath *f.* +ow
nor *conj.* na, nag; neither ... nor
naneyl ... na: *adv.* na ... na; nor
yet bydh moy
Norman *adj.* Normanek
North *n.* kledh *m.*, gogledh *f.*,
kledh-barth *m.*, north *m.:* *adv.* on
the north side a-gledhbarth
north-east *n.* Borlewen *f.*, north-
est *m.*
northern *n.* northern side kledh-
barth *m.*
north-west *n.* north-west *m.*
nose *n.* troen *m.* -yow
nostalgia *n.* hireth *f.*
nostril *n.* frig *m.* +ow *dual* dewfrik
not *pron.* not one nagonan: *conj.*
that not na: *ptl.* ny, nyns; that
not nag: *adv.* a-der; not at all
kammenn; not yet na hwath; she
loves you not me hi a'th kar a-der
my
notary *n.* noter *m.* -oryon
note *n.* notenn *f.*, notyans *m.* +ow:
v. notya, avisya; take note of
attendya
notebook *n.* lyver notennow *m.*,
skriflyver *m.* skriflyvrow
nothing *n.* mann *m.*, lasvydh *m.*,
travydh *f.*
notice *n.* argemmynn *m.* +ow,
avisyans *m.* +ow: *v.* attendya,
medra
notification *n.* gwarnyans *m.* +ow
notify *v.* gwarnya

notion *n.* **tybyans** *m.* **+ow, devis**
m. **+yow, konsayt** *m.* **+s**

noun *n.* **hanow** *m.* **henwyn**

nourish *v.* **maga**

nourishing *n.* **meth** *m.*

nourishment *n.* **pask** *m.*

novel *n.* **romans** *m.:* *adj.* **nowydh**

November *n.* **Du** *m.,* **mis-Du** *m.*

now *ptl.* (in phrase) **nans:** *adv.* **y'n
eur ma, lemmyn;** (only in poetry)
now; just now **a-gynsow,
degynsow, kynsow;** now and
then **war euryow**

no-wise *adv.* **kammenn**

nuclear *adj.* **nuklerek**

nude *adj.* **noeth, lomm**

nudity *n.* **lommder** *m.,* **noetha** *f.*

nuisance *n.* **pla** *m.* **+ow**

number *n.* **niver** *m.* **+ow, riv** *m.*
+ow; random number **happriv** *m.:*
v. **nivera**

number-plate *n.* **plat-niver** *m.*
platyow-niver

numbness *n.* **ewinrew** *m.,*
gwynnrew *m.,* **klamder** *m.*

numeral *n.* **niverenn** *f.* **+ow**

numeration *n.* **niverieth** *f.*

numerous *adj.* **pals, niverus**

numskull *n.* **klopenn** *m.* **+ow**

nun *n.* **lenes** *f.* **+ow, managhes** *f.*
+ow

nunnery *n.* **lenji** *m.* **+ow**

nurse *n.* female nurse **klavjiores** *f.*
+ow; male nurse **klavjior** *m.* **+yon;**
staff nurse **pennklavjiores** *f.;* wet
nurse **magores** *f.* **+ow**

nursery *n.* (for children) **floghva** *f.*
+ow; nursery school **skol
veythrin** *f.*

nursery-rhyme *n.* **gwers
meythrin** *f.*

nurture *n.* **magereth** *f.,* **meth** *m.,*
norter *m.*

nut *n.* (Bot.) **knowenn** *f.* **+ow** *coll.*
know; Brazil nut **knowenn basti**
f.

nutcrackers *n.* **gevel know** *f.*

nut-grove *n.* **kellignowwydh** *coll.,*
knowek *f.* **-egi**

nutriment *n.* **megyans** *m.*

nuts *n.* **know** *coll.* **+enn:** *v.* gather
nuts **knowa**

nutty *adj.* **knowek**

nuzzle *v.* **minya**

O

O *int.* **A**

oak *n.* evergreen oak **glastanenn** *f.*
+ow *coll.* **glastan**

oak-place *n.* **darva** *f.* **+ow**

oaks *n.* place abounding in oaks
derwek *f.* **-egi:** *adj.* abounding in
oaks **derwek**

oak-tree *n.* **derwenn** *f.* **+ow** *coll.*
derow, dar *m.* **deri**

oar *n.* **rev** *f.* **+ow**

oasis *n.* **dowran** *m.*

oat-field *n.* **kerghek** *f.* **-egi**

oat-grass *n.* **kerghwels** *m.*

oath *n.* **li** *m.* **+ow, ti** *m.* **+ow;** false
oath **gowli** *m.* **+ow:** *v.* take an oath
lia

oatlands *n.* **kerghdir** *m.*

oatmeal *plur.* **brunyon**

oats *n.* **kergh** *coll.* **+enn;** bald oats
pilas *coll.;* naked oats **pilas** *coll.*

obdurate *adj.* **avleythys**

obedience *n.* **obayans** *m.*

obedient *adj.* **gostyth**

obese *adj.* **berrik**

obesity *n.* **berri** *m.*

obey *v.* **obaya**

objective *n.* **amkan** *m.* **+ow**

oblation *n.* **ro dhe Dhyw** *m.*

oblivion *n.* **ankov** *m.*

oblong *n.* **hirbedrek** *m.*
hirbedrogow: *adj.* **hirbedrek**

oboe *n.* **salmus** *m.*

obsequious *adj.* **goruvel**

observatory *n.* **mirji** *m.* **+ow**

observe *v.* **mires, aspia, avisya, medra, merkya**

observer *n.* **aspier** *m.* **-oryon**

obsessed *adj.* **gorgemmerys**

obstinate *adj.* **penn-kales**

obstreperous *adj.* **direwl**

obstruct *v.* **lettya**

obstruction *n.* **lett** *m.* **+ow, +ys**

obtain *v.* **kavoes**

obtrude *v.* **omherdhya**

obtuse *n.* obtuse angle **elin avlymm** *m.*: *adj.* **avlymm**

obvious *adj.* **apert, hewel**

occasion *n.* (cause) **acheson** *m.* **+yow, +ys**; (time) **gweyth** *f.* **+yow, prysweyth** *m.*, **treveth** *m.*: *adv.* on a future occasion **arta**

occasional *adj.* **treweythus**

occasionally *adj.* **treweythyow**

occult *adj.* **kevrinek**

occupation *n.* **soedh** *f.* **+ow**; occupation requiring manual skill **kreft** *f.* **+ow**

occupied *adj.* **bysi**

occupy *v.* **kevannedhi**

occur *v.* **dos ha, hwarvos**

occurred *adj.* **hwarvedhys**

ocean *n.* **downvor** *m.*, **gweylgi** *f.*, **keynvor** *m.*; Atlantic Ocean **Keynvor Atlantek** *m.*; Indian Ocean **Keynvor Eyndek** *m.*; Pacific Ocean **Keynvor Hebask** *m.*

oceanography *n.* **moronieth** *f.*

ochre *n.* red ochre **meles** *m.*

o'clock *n.* **eur** *f.* **+yow**

October *n.* **Hedra** *m.*, **mis-Hedra** *m.*; first of October **Kala' Hedra** *m.*

octopus *n.* **kollell-lesa** *f.*

odd *adj.* (of numbers) **dibarow**; (strange) **koynt**

odour *n.* **ethenn** *f.* **+ow, odor** *m.*

of *prep.* **a**: *adv.* of her **anedhi**; of him **anodho**; of me **ahanav**; of thee **ahanas**; of them **anedha**; of us **ahanan**; of you **ahanowgh**: *phr.* of her **a'y**; of his **a'y**; of its **a'y, a'y**; of my **a'm**; of our **a'gan**; of the **a'n**; of their **a'ga**; of thy **a'th**; of your **a'gas**

offence *n.* **offens** *m.* **+ys**; (sin) **peghes** *m.* **peghosow**; (trespass) **treuspass** *m.* **+ow**

offend *v.* **divlasa, offendya**

offer *n.* **kynnik** *m.* **-igow, profyans** *m.*: *v.* **kynnik, offra, profya**; offer onself **ombrofya**; offer up **offrynna**

offering *n.* **offrynn** *m.* **+ow**

office *n.* (abst.) **offis** *m.* **offisys**; (job) **soedh** *f.* **+ow**; (work-place) **soedhva** *f.* **+ow**; register office **soedhva govskrifa** *f.*: *v.* hold office **soedha**

officer *n.* **soedhek** *m.* **-dhogyon**; officer on watch **brennyas** *m.* **-ysi**

official *adj.* **soedhogel**

officialdom *n.* **soedhogoleth** *f.*

offspring *n.* **agh** *f.* **+ow, askorr** *m.*

often *conj.* as often as **peskweyth** may: *adv.* **menowgh, lieskweyth**

oh *int.* **ogh, out**

oil *n.* **oyl** *m.* **oylys**; lubricating oil **loub** *m.*

ointment *n.* **eli** *m.* **+ow, unyent** *m.*, **uras** *m.*

old *n.* old age **henys** *m.*, **kothni** *m.*: *adj.* **koth, hen**: *v.* grow old **kothhe**: *phr.* hundred years old **kans bloedh**; thousand years old **milvloedh**

older *adj.* **kottha**

olive-oil *n.* **olew** *m.*

olive-tree *n.* **olewbrenn** *m.* **-yer, olewenn** *f.* **+ow, olivenn** *f.* **+ow** *coll.* **oliv**

omelette *n.* **omlet** *m.* **+ow**

omen *n.* **koel** *f.*

omit *v.* **gasa yn-mes**

omnibus *n.* **kyttrin** *m.* **+yow**
omnipotence *n.* **ollgalloes** *m.*
on *prep.* **war**; (occasl.) **yn**; on her
  warnedhi; on him **warnodho**; on
  me **warnav**; on thee **warnas**; on
  them **warnedha**; on us **warnan**;
  on you **warnowgh**: *adv.* on the
  (used only in numbers to 9) **warn**
once *adv.* **unnweyth**; at once
  desempis, hware, yn unn lamm,
  skon
one *pron.* **huni**; not one **nagonan**;
  one of two **eyl**; ones **re**: *adj.* **unn**:
  num. **onan**
one-eyed *adj.* **unnlagasek**
one-piece *adj.* **unnrann**
onion *n.* **onyonenn** *f.* **+ow** *coll.*
  onyon; string of onions **plethenn**
  onyon *f.*
only *adj.* **unn, unnik**: *conj.* if only
  mar, unnweyth a: *adv.*
  unnweyth, hepken, unnsel
onward *adv.* **yn-rag**: *int.* **war yew**
ooze *v.* **sygera**
oozing *adj.* **syger**
open *adj.* **igor, rydh, apert**: *v.*
  igeri
opener *n.* **igerell** *f.* **+ow**
openly *adv.* **yn igor**
opera *n.* **gwari-kan** *m.* **gwariow-**
  kan
operate *v.* **oberi**
operating room (U.S.) *n.* **stevell-**
  oberyans *f.*
operation *n.* **oberyans** *m.*
opinion *n.* **kusul** *f.* **+yow, tybyans**
  m. **+ow, avis** *m.,* **konsayt** *m.* **+s,**
  prederyans *m.* **+ow**; mistaken
  opinion **kammdybyans** *m.* **+ow**:
  v. bring to same opinion **unnverhe**;
  hold an opinion **tybi**
opium *n.* **koskles** *m.*
opportunity *n.* **spas** *m.*
oppose *v.* **enebi**
opposed *adj.* **gorth, kontraryus**
opposer *n.* **kontrari** *m.*

opposite *adj.* **konter**: *prep.* **a-dal**
opposition *n.* **enebieth** *f.,* **gorthter**
  m., **offens** *m.* **+ys**
oppress *v.* **gwaska, arwaska,**
  beghya
oppression *n.* **arwask** *m.,*
  poesyjyon *m.*
oppressive *adj.* **beghus**
optional *adj.* **a-dhewis**
optionally *adv.* **a-dhewis**
opus *n.* **obereth** *f.*
or *conj.* **po**; or else **boken, poken**
oral *n.* **der anow** *m.*
orange *n.* (fruit) **owraval** *m.* **+ow**;
  Orange Order **Urdh Rudhvelyn** *f.*:
  adj. (colour) **rudhvelyn**
orange-juice *n.* **sugen owraval** *m.*
oration *n.* **areth** *f.*
orator *n.* **arethor** *m.* **-oryon,**
  dadhlor *m.* **+yon**
oratory *n.* **oratri** *m.* **+s**
orbit *n.* **resegva** *f.* **+ow**
orchard *n.* **avalennek** *f.* **-egi**
orchestra *n.* **bagas ilewydhyon**
  m.
ordain *v.* **apoyntya, ordena,**
  sakra, urdhya
order *n.* **gorhemmynn** *m.* **+ow,**
  rewl *f.* **+ys, reyth** *m.* **+yow**;
  (arrangement) **aray** *m.;* (command)
  arghadow *m.* **+yow**;
  (organization) **urdh** *f.;* mail order
  arghadow dre bost *m.;* order of
  knights **chevalri** *m.;* postal order
  arghadow-post *m.*
  arghadowyow-post; religious
  order **ordyr** *m.* **ordyrs**: *prep.* in
  order to **rag**: *v.* **erghi**;
  (command) **gorhemmynn**; order
  about **kontrolya**; order oneself
  omdhyghtya; order Tamsin to
  come home **erghi dhe Damsin**
  dos tre; put in order **ordena**; set
  in order **araya, kempenna**
Order *n.* Orange Order **Urdh**
  Rudhvelyn *f.*

orderly *adj.* **kempenn**

orders *plur.* holy orders **ordys**

ordinance *n.* **ordenans** *m.*

ordinary *adj.* **sempel**

ore *n.* **moen** *m.;* iron ore **kallenn** *f.*
+ow; thin seam of ore **gwri** *m.* **+ow**

ore-bearing *n.* ore-bearing ground
moenek *f.* **moenegi**

organ *n.* (Mus.) **organ** *m.* **+s**

organic *adj.* **organek**

organist *n.* **organydh** *m.* **+yon**

organization *n.* (abst.) **restrans** *m.*

organize *v.* **ordena**

organizer *n.* **ordenor** *m.* **-yon**

orienteer *n.* **hwilreseger** *m.*
-oryon

orienteering *n.* **hwilresek** *m.*

origin *n.* **dalleth** *m.,* **dallethvos** *m.,*
devedhyans *m.*

originality *n.* **ynjinieth** *f.*

originate *v.* **dalleth**

orphan *n.* (female) **omdhivases** *f.;*
(male) **omdhivas** *m.:* *v.*
omdhivasa

orphanage *n.* **omdhivatti** *m.* **+ow**

orpine *n.* (plant) **kansewin** *m.* **+es**

orthography *n.* **lytherennieth** *f.*

oscillation *n.* **daromres** *m.,* **lesk**
m. **+ow**

osier *n.* **heligenn** *f.* **+ow** *coll.* **helik**

ostrich *n.* **strus** *m.* **+yow**

other *n.* the other (f.) **hy ben** *f.:*
pron. the other (m.) **y gila:** *adj.*
arall, ken; any other **nahen**

others *plur.* **erell**

otherwise *adj.* (with neg.) **nahen:**
conj. **poken:** *adv.* **ken, kontrari**

otter *n.* **dowrgi** *m.* **dowrgeun**

ought *v.* I ought **y tal dhymm:** *phr.*
I ought to go **y koedh dhymm**
mos

ounce *n.* **ouns** *m.* **+yow**; fluid
ounce **ouns devrek** *m.*

our *pron.* **agan:** *phr.* and our
ha'gan; to our **dh'agan**

out *adv.* **yn-mes:** *int.* **out**

outcast *n.* **gal** *m.* **+yon**

outcome *n.* **diwedh** *m.*

outcry *n.* **garm** *f.* **+ow**

outfit *n.* **aparel** *m.;* (clothes)
gwiskas *m.* **+ow**

outlandish *adj.* **ankoth**

outlaw *n.* **outlayer** *m.* **+s**

outlet *n.* **tardhell** *f.* **+ow**

outline *v.* **linenna**

outlook *n.* **gologva** *f.*

outrage *n.* **outray** *m.*

outrageous *n.* outrageous action
outray *m.*

outside *adj.* **a-ves:** *prep.* **a-der:**
adv. **yn-mes**

outstretched *adv.* **a-hys, a-les**

oval *n.* **hirgylgh** *m.* **+yow:** *adj.*
hirgylghyek

ovate *n.* **ovydh** *m.* **+yon**

oven *n.* **forn** *f.* **+ow**; microwave
oven **forn-gorrdonn** *f.* **fornow-**
korrdonn, korrdonner *m.;* tender
of oven **forner** *m.* **-oryon**

over *prep.* **a-ugh, dres**

overbalance *v.* **omdhisevel**

overcast *adj.* **kommolek**

overcoat *n.* **surkot** *m.*

overcome *v.* **fetha**

overdo *v.* **gorwul**

overeat *v.* **kwoffi**

overflow *v.* **fenna**

overfly *v.* **treusnija**

overgrow *v.* **gordevi**

overgrowth *n.* **gordevyans** *m.*

overhead *adv.* **a-vann**

overheat *v.* **gordoemma**

overlap *v.* **gorgudha**

overload *v.* **gorharga, gorveghya**

overlord *n.* **gwarthevyas** *m.* **-ysi**

overseas *adj.* **tramor**

oversee *v.* **gorweles**

overspent *adj.* **du**

overtake *v.* **tremena dres**

overthrow *v.* **domhwel**
over-trousers *n.* **raglenn** *f.* **+ow**
overturn *v.* **domhwel**
owe *v.* **tyli**
owl *n.* **kowann** *f.* **+ow, oula** *m.*
oulys
own *n.* **honan** *m.: v.* **perghenna,
piw**; the children own the dogs **an
fleghes a biw an keun**: *adv.* all
on his own **y honan oll**; on his
own **y honan**
owner *n.* **perghenn** *m.* **+ow,
perghennek** *m.* **-ogyon**
ownership *n.* **perghennogeth** *f.,*
perghennieth *f.*
ox *n.* **ojyon** *m.;* wild ox **bual** *m.*
+yon
Oxford *n.* **Rysoghen** *f.*
ox-goad *plur.* **garthow**
oyster *n.* **estrenn** *f.* **+ow** *coll.* **ester**

P

pace *n.* **kamm** *m.* **+ow, pas** *m.* **+ys**
Pacific *n.* Pacific Ocean **Keynvor
Hebask** *m.*
pacify *v.* **hebaskhe, koselhe**
pack *v.* **troessa**
package *n.* **fardell** *m.* **+ow**: *v.*
fardella
paddle *n.* **rev dhewbennek** *f.*
pagan *n.* **ankredor** *m.* **+yon,
pagan** *m.* **+ys, +yon**
page *n.* (boy) **paja** *m.* **pajys**; (of
book) **enep** *m.* **enebow, folenn** *f.*
+ow, lyvenn *f.* **+ow**
paid *v.* **pes**
pail *n.* **kelorn** *m.* **kelern**
pain *n.* **payn** *m.* **+ys**; pain of spirit
poen *m.* **+ow**: *phr.* on pain of
death **war bayn mernans**
paint *n.* **paynt** *m.: v.* (a surface)
payntya; (of a picture) **lymna**
paint-box *n.* **kystenn liwyow** *f.*

paint-brush *n.* **skubyllenn baynt**
f.
painter *n.* (artist) **lymner** *m.* **-oryon**;
(of surfaces) **payntyer** *m.*
payntyoryon
painting *n.* **liwyans** *m.* **+ow,
lymnans** *m.* **+ow**
pair *n.* **dewdhen** *m., kopel* *m.*
koplow: *v.* **parya**
palace *n.* **lys** *f.* **+yow, palys** *m.*
palesyow
palaeozoology *n.* **henvilonieth** *f.*
palate *n.* **stevnik** *f.*
palfrey *n.* **palfray** *m.*
palisade *n.* **peulge** *m.* **+ow**
pall *n.* **pall** *m.* **+ow**
palm *n.* (of hand) **palv** *f.* **+ow**
palm-branch *n.* **palm** *m.* **+ow,
+ys**
palmer *n.* **palmer** *m.* **-oryon**
palm-frond *n.* **palm** *m.* **+ow, +ys**
palm-tree *n.* **palmwydhenn** *f.*
+ow *coll.* **palmwydh**
pan *n.* **padell** *f.* **+ow**; frying pan
padell fria *m.;* iron pan **padell-
horn** *f.;* preserving pan **chekk
kyfeyth** *m.*
pancakes *n.* **krampoethenn** *f.*
+ow *coll.* **krampoeth**: *v.* beg for
pancakes **krampoetha**
panda *n.* **panda** *m.* **+s**
pane *n.* pane of glass **kwarel** *m.* **+s**
panel *n.* (of people) **pannell** *m.* **+ow**
pang *n.* **gloes** *f.* **+ow**
panicky *adj.* **penn-fol**
pannier *n.* pannier basket **kowell** *m.*
+ow
pant *v.* **dyewa**
pantry *n.* **talgell** *f.* **+ow, spens** *m.*
+ow
pants (U.S.) *n.* **lavrek** *m.*
lavrogow
pap *n.* **yos** *m.*
paper *n.* **paper** *m.* **+yow**;
greaseproof paper **paper**

gorthsaym *m.;* sheet of paper
folenn *f.* **+ow, pythyonenn** *f.*
+ow *coll.* **pythyon;** writing paper
paper skrifa *m.*
paper-work *n.* **paperweyth** *m.*
parable *n.* **parabolenn** *f.* **+ow**
parabola *n.* **parabolenn** *f.* **+ow**
parachute *n.* **lammlenn** *f.* **+ow**
parade *n.* **kerdhva** *f.* **+ow**
paradise *n.* **paradhis** *f.*
parallel *adj.* **kettuel**
paralyse *v.* **palsya**
paralysed *n.* paralysed person **palsi**
m. **palsyon:** *adj.* **palsyes**
paralysis *n.* **palsi** *m.*
parasites *n.* **teurek** *coll.*
teuregenn
parasitology *n.* **teuregonieth** *f.*
parasol *n.* **howllenn** *f.* **+ow**
parboil *v.* **govryjyon, lesvryjyon**
parch *v.* **krasa**
parched *adj.* **kras, sygh, krin**
parchment *n.* **parchemin** *m.*
pardon *n.* **gevyans** *m.:* *v.* **gava;**
pardon me **gav dhymm**
parish *n.* **plyw** *f.* **+ow;** seaward
portion of a parish in Cornwall
morrep *m.*
parishioner *n.* **plywek** *m.*
plywogyon
park *n.* **park** *m.* **+ow:** *v.* **parkya**
parking lot (U.S.) *n.* **park-kerri**
m.
parliament *n.* **senedh** *m.* **+ow;**
European Parliament **Eurosenedh**
m.; Houses of Parliament **Chiow**
an Senedh *m.*
parlour *n.* **hel** *f.* **+yow, parledh** *m.*
+ow
parochial *adj.* **plywek**
parrot *n.* **papynjay** *m.* **+s**
parsley *n.* **persil** *coll.* **+enn**
parsnip *n.* **panesenn** *f.* **+ow** *coll.*
panes
parson *n.* **pronter** *m.* **+yon**

parsonage *n.* **pronterji** *m.* **+ow**
part *n.* **rann** *f.* **+ow, darn** *m.* **+ow;**
lowest part **goeles** *m.* **+ow;** second
part in plain-song **diskant** *m.;*
second part in singing duet **diskan**
f.: *plur.* spare parts **sparyon:** *v.*
diberth, ranna
participating *adj.* **kevrennek**
participator *n.* **kevrenner** *m.*
-oryon
particle *n.* **temmik** *m.* **temmigow:**
plur. small particles **manylyon**
particles *plur.* small particles
manylyon
parting *n.* **dibarth** *f.*
partner *n.* **kowethyades** *f.* **+ow,**
kowethyas *m.* **-ysi**
partridge *n.* **grugyar** *f.* **-yer,**
korryar *f.* **-yer;** young partridge
grugyerik *f.* **-igow**
party *n.* (feast) **kevywi** *m.* **+ow;**
(political) **parti** *m.* **+s, +ow;** party-
goer **kevywyas** *m.* **-ysi:** *v.* hold a
party **kevywya**
pass *n.* (gap) **aswa** *f.* **+ow;**
(topographical) **bolgh** *m.* **+ow:**
adj. come to pass **hwarvedhys:** *v.*
tremena, passya; come to pass
hwarvos; pass by **tremena dres;**
pass over **treusi**
passage *n.* **skochfordh** *f.* **+ow;**
passage over water **treth** *m.* **+yow**
passenger *n.* female passenger in
ferry **trethyades** *f.* **+ow;** male
passenger in ferry **trethyas** *m.* **-ysi**
passer-by *n.* **tremenyas** *m.* **-ysi**
passing *n.* **tremenyans** *m.;* passing
away **tremenvann** *f.*
passing-place *n.* **tremensorn** *m.*
+ow, tremenva *f.*
passion *n.* **passhyon** *m.*
passive *adj.* **godhevus, hwar**
passport *n.* **tremengummyas** *m.*
+ow
past *prep.* **dres:** *adv.* the past **an**
termyn eus passys

paste *n.* **glus** *m.* **+ow, past** *m.:* *v.*
glusa
pastoral *adj.* **bugelek**
pastry *n.* baked pastry **hogenn** *f.;*
dinner-cake made of pastry
hwiogenn *f.* **+ow**
pasture *n.* **peur** *m.;* common
pasture **pras** *m.* **+ow;** revived
pasture **aswels** *m.;* unenclosed
pasture **goen** *f.* **+yow**
pasty *n.* **pasti** *m.* **+ow**
pat *v.* **handla**
patch *n.* **klout** *m.* **+ys;** patch of blue
in clouded sky **lagas** *m.* **+ow** *dual*
dewlagas; sandy patch **trethenn**
f. **+ow:** *v.* **kloutya**
pate *n.* **pat** *m.;* scabby pate **penn-
kreghi** *m.* **pennow-kreghi;**
shaven pate **penn-blogh** *m.*
pennow-blogh: *adj.* broken pate
penn-kogh
paten *n.* **gorher** *m.* **+yow**
patent *n.* **lyther apert** *m.*
pater *n.* **pader** *m.* **+ow**
paternal *adj.* **tasek**
paternity *n.* **tasoleth** *f.*
path *n.* **hyns** *m.* **+yow**
pathetic *adj.* **truedhek**
pathos *n.* **truedh** *m.*
patience *n.* **perthyans** *m.*
patient *n.* (female) **godhevyades** *f.*
+ow; (male) **godhevyas** *m.* **-ysi**
patriarch *n.* **ugheldas** *m.* **+ow**
patriot *n.* **gwlaskarer** *m.* **-oryon**
patriotism *n.* **gwlaskerensa** *f.*
patronage *n.* **tasogeth** *f.*
patronal *adj.* **tasek**
patroness *n.* **tasoges** *f.*
patter *v.* **gerya**
pattern *n.* **patron** *m.* **+yow,**
skantlyn *m.* **+s**
paunch *n.* **borr** *f.*
pauper *n.* **boghosek** *m.* **-ogyon**
pause *v.* **hedhi, powes**
pave *v.* **konsya**

pavement *n.* **kons** *m.* **+ow**
paw *n.* **paw** *m.* **+yow**
pawn *n.* **gwystel** *m.* **gwystlow**
pay *n.* (income) **gober** *m.* **gobrow:**
v. **pe;** pay for **pe, prena;** pay off
akwitya; pay tithes **degevi;** pay
wages to **gobra;** pay with pitch
stanchura: *phr.* you'll pay for it
ty a'n pren
payee *n.* **talesik** *m.* **-igyon**
payer *n.* **taler** *m.* **-oryon**
payment *n.* **talas** *m.* **+ow;** advance
payment **ragdal** *m.*
pea *n.* **pysenn** *f.* **+ow** *coll.* **pys**
peace *n.* **kres** *m.:* *int.* **pes**
peaceful *adj.* **hebask**
peach *n.* **aval-gwlanek** *m.* **avalow-
gwlanek**
peacock *n.* **payon** *m.* **+es**
peahen *n.* **paynes** *f.* **+ow**
peak *n.* **bleyn** *m.* **+yow, pigorn** *m.*
pigern, topp *m.* **+ys**
peaked *adj.* **bannek**
peanut *n.* **knowenn dhor** *f.*
pear *n.* **perenn** *f.* **+ow** *coll.* **per;**
pear orchard **perlann** *f.* **+ow**
pearl *n.* **perl** *m.* **+ys**
pear-tree *n.* **perbrenn** *m.* **+yer**
peasepod *n.* **kodh pys** *f.*
peat *n.* **towargh** *coll.* **+enn**
peat-bog *n.* **towarghek** *f.* **-egi**
peaty *adj.* **towarghek**
pebble *n.* **bilienn** *f.* **+ow** *coll.* **bili**
peck *n.* (small kiss) **kussynn** *m.*
+ow: *v.* **piga, pigas**
pedagogy *n.* **adhyskonieth** *f.*
pedal *n.* **troesell** *f.* **+ow, troesla** *m.*
troesleow: *v.* **troesella**
peddler *n.* **gwikor** *m.* **+yon,**
troesyer *m.* **-oryon**
pedestrian *n.* **kerdher** *m.* **-oryon**
pedigree *n.* **aghskrif** *m.* **+ow**
peel *n.* **kenn** *m.,* **pil** *coll.* **+enn,**
rusk *f.* **+enn:** *v.* **diruska, pilya**
peep *v.* **gyki**

peer *n.* **koweth** *m.* **+a**; (nobleman)
gwahalyeth *m.* **+ow**: *plur.* peers
hynsa

peewit *n.* **kornhwilenn** *f.*
kernhwili

peg *n.* **ebil** *m.* **+yow, pynn** *m.* **+ow**;
(iron) **ebil horn** *m.;* (wooden) **ebil
prenn** *m.;* iron peg **henkyn** *m.*

pelican *n.* **pelikan** *m.* **+es**

pelt *v.* **pyltya**

pen *n.* **pluvenn** *f.* **+ow** *coll.* **pluv**

penance *n.* **ankenek** *m.,* **penans**
m., **penys** *m.;* long penance
hirbenys *m.:* *v.* do penance
penys

pencil *n.* **pluvenn blomm** *f.*
pluvennow plomm

penetrable *adj.* **dewanus**

penetrate *v.* **dewana, kropya**

penetrating *adj.* **glew**

penguin *n.* **penn-gwynn** *m.*
pennow-gwynn

peninsula *n.* **konna-tir** *m.*
konnaow-tir

penis *n.* **kalgh** *m.* **+yow**

penitential *adj.* **ankenek**

penknife *n.* **kellyllik** *f.* **-igow**

pen-knife *n.* **kollell bleg** *f.*

penny *n.* **diner** *m.* **+ow**

penny-piece *n.* **dinerenn** *f.* **+ow**

pennywort *n.* **krampoeth mowesi**
coll.

Penryn *place* **Pennrynn**

pension *n.* **penshyon** *m.* **+ow**;
disability pension **penshyon
evredh** *m.*

Pentecost *n.* **dy' Fenkost** *m.,*
Penkost *m.*

Penwith *place* **Pennwydh**

Penzance *place* **Pennsans**

people *n.* **pobel** *f.* **poblow**;
common people **gwerin** *f.:* *plur.*
tus: *v.* **pobla**

pepper *n.* **puber** *m.*

perceive *v.* **gweles, konvedhes,**
persevya

percentage *n.* **kansrann** *f.* **+ow**

perch *n.* (for birds) **treusprenn** *m.*
+yer

perchance *adv.* **martesen**

perdition *n.* **koll** *m.,* **argoll** *m.*

perfect *adj.* **flour, perfeyth**

perfection *n.* **keweras** *m.*

perfidious *adj.* **fekyl**

perforation *n.* **kraw** *m.* **+yow**

perform *v.* **gul, oberi, performya**

performance *n.* **gwryth** *f.,*
gwrythyans *m.,* **obereth** *f.*

performer *n.* **gwrythyer** *m.*
-oryon, oberer *m.* **-oryon**

perfume *v.* **perfumya**

perhaps *adv.* **martesen**

peril *n.* **peryll** *m.* **+ow**

perilous *adj.* **peryllus**

period *n.* (of time) **oes** *m.* **+ow,**
seson *m.* **+yow, +s, spys** *m.,*
termyn *m.* **+yow, trank** *m.:* *plur.*
(menstrual) **amseryow**

periodical *n.* **lyver-termyn** *m.*
lyvrow-termyn

peripatetic *adj.* **gwandrek**

peripheral *adj.* **amalek**

peripherality *n.* **amalogneth** *f.*

perish *v.* **perysshya**

perishable *adj.* **podradow**

periwinkle *n.* **gwighenn** *f.* **gwigh**;
periwinkles **gwigh** *coll.* **+enn**

perjury *n.* **gowli** *m.* **+ow**: *v.*
commit perjury **gowlia**

permeable *adj.* **dewanus**

permeate *v.* **dewana**

permissible *adj.* (legally) **lafyl,**
laghel

permission *n.* **kummyas** *m.,* **gront**
m. **+ow, +ys**

permit *n.* **kummyas** *m.:* *v.* **gasa,**
lavasos

perpendicular *adj.* **serth**

perpetually *adv.* **bys vykken, hogen**

perplex *v.* **amaya, penndaga**

perplexed *adj.* **penndegys**

Perran *name* **Pyran**

Perranporth *place* **Porthpyran**

persecute *v.* **persekutya**

persecutor *n.* **helghyas** *m.* **-ysi**

persicaria *n.* spotted persicaria **lagas du** *m.*

person *n.* **den** *m.* **tus, korf** *m.* **+ow,** person *m.* **+s;** monkeyish person **apa** *m.* **appys;** well-born person **jentyl** *m.* **+s;** young person **chett** *m.* **+ys**

personal *adj.* **personel**

persons *plur.* **tus**

perspiration *n.* **hwys** *m.*

perspire *v.* **hwysa**

persuade *v.* **dri,** perswadya

pert *adj.* **tont**

pertain *v.* **pertaynya**

perturb *v.* **amovya**

perverse *adj.* **gorth**

pest *n.* **ball** *f.,* **pla** *m.* **+ow:** *int.* **mal**

pet *n.* **enyval dov** *m.,* **hwegenn** *f.* **+ow:** *adj.* **dov**

Peter *name* **Peder**

petition *n.* **petyshyon** *m.*

petrify *v.* **menhe**

petticoat *n.* **goelesenn** *f.*

pheasant *n.* **fesont** *m.* **fesons**

philologist *n.* **yethonydh** *m.* **+yon**

philology *n.* **yethonieth** *f.*

phoney *adj.* **fug**

phosphorescence *n.* **mordan** *m.*

photocopy *v.* **liesskrifa**

photograph *n.* **skeusenn** *f.* **+ow**

photographer *n.* **skeusenner** *m.* **-oryon**

photography *n.* **skeusennweyth** *f.*

physic *n.* **fisek** *f.*

physically *n.* **kig yn kneus** *m.*

physician *n.* **medhyk** *m.* **medhygyon**

physicist *n.* **fisegydh** *m.* **+yon**

physics *n.* **fisegieth** *f.*

piano *n.* **piano** *m.* **+s**

pick *n.* **pigell** *f.:* *v.* (e.g. flowers) **kuntell, terri;** pick strawberries **sevia;** use a pick **pigellas**

picnic *n.* picnic lunch **kroust** *m.* **+yow**

picture *n.* **liwyans** *m.* **+ow, lymnans** *m.* **+ow**

pie *n.* **hogenn** *f.*

piece *n.* **tamm** *m.* **temmyn, darn** *m.* **+ow;** little piece **dyjynn** *m.* **+ow**

pierce *v.* **gwana, pechya, pychya**

piercing *n.* **gwan** *f.* **+yow, pych** *m.*

pig *n.* **hogh** *m.* **-es;** barrow pig **torgh** *m.* **+es;** young pig **porghell** *m.* **+i:** *plur.* pigs **mogh**

pigeon *n.* **kolomm** *f.* **+es, kolommenn** *f.* **+ow** *coll.* **kolommes**

pigeon-house *n.* **kolommji** *m.* **+ow**

piggy-bank *n.* **kofrik-erbys** *m.* **-igow-erbys**

piglet *n.* **porghellik** *m.* **-igow**

pigmy *n.* **korr** *m.* **+yon, korres** *f.* **+ow**

pignut *n.* **kelerenn** *f.* **+ow** *coll.* **keler**

pigsty *n.* **krow mogh** *m.*

pike *n.* (fish) **densek dowr** *m.;* (weapon) **pik** *m.* **+ys**

pilchard *n.* **hernenn** *f.* **+ow** *coll.* **hern;** salted pilchard **fumado** *m.*

pilchard-oil *n.* **saym** *m.*

pilchards *n.* bulk of pilchards **barkado** *m.* **+s**

pile *n.* **graghell** *f.,* **pil** *m.* **+yow;** (post) **peul** *m.* **+yow:** *v.* pile up **bernya;** pile up in a mound **krugya**

pilfer *v.* **ladra**

pilferer *n.* **lader** *m.* **ladron, brybour** *m.* **+s**

pilgrim *n.* **pergherin** *m.* **+yon,**
pryerin *m.;* (from the Holy Land)
palmer *m.* **-oryon**

pilgrimage *n.* **pergherinses** *f.*

pill *n.* **pellennik** *f.* **-igow**

pillage *v.* **pylla**

pillar *n.* **peulvan** *m.* **+ow, post** *m.*
+ow

pillory *v.* **karghara**

pillow *n.* **pluvek** *f.* **pluvogow**

pilot *n.* **lywyader** *m.* **-oryon,**
lywyer *m.* **-yoryon**

pimpernel *n.* **brathles** *m.*

pimple *n.* **kuryek** *m.* **-ogyon**

pin *n.* **pynn** *m.* **+ow;** bowling pin
(U.S.) **kil** *m.* **+ys, +yow;** drawing
pin **pynn meus** *m.;* electrical pin
ebil *m.* **+yow:** *v.* pin together
pynna

pincers *n.* **gevel** *f.;* pair of pincers
pynser *m.* **+yow**

pinch *n.* **myjenn** *m.:* *v.* **pynchya**

pine *v.* pine away **omwetha**

pine cone (U.S.) *n.* **aval-sabenn**
m. **avalow-sabenn**

pineapple *n.* **pinaval** *m.* **+ow**

pine-tree *n.* **pinenn** *f.* **+ow** *coll.*
pin, sabenn *f.* **+ow** *coll.* **sab**

pin-game *n.* **penn-ha-min** *m.*

pining *adj.* **moredhek**

pink *adj.* **gwynnrudh**

pinnacle *n.* **pynakyl** *m.* **pynaklys**

pint *n.* **pinta** *m.* **+ow**

pious *adj.* **erwir, grassyes, sansel**

pip *n.* **sprusenn** *f.* **+ow** *coll.* **sprus**

pipe *n.* **pib** *f.* **+ow, pibell** *f.* **+ow;**
(Mus.) **hwib** *f.:* *v.* **piba**

pipe-clay *n.* **pri pib** *m.*

pipe-fish *n.* **mornaswydh** *f.* **+ow,**
pryv malan *m.*

pipeline *n.* **goeth** *f.* **+ow**

piper *n.* **piber** *m.* **-oryon, pibydh**
m. **+yon**

pipit *n.* meadow pipit **bonnik** *m.*
-iges

pippy *adj.* **sprusek**

pirate *n.* **morlader** *m.* **-ladron,**
preydher *m.* **-oryon**

pit *n.* **poll** *m.* **+ow, pytt** *m.* **+ys;** pit
of water-wheel **poll ros** *m.;* small
pit **dyppa** *m.* **dyppys**

pitch *n.* (point) **prykk** *m.* **+ow;** (tar)
pyg *m.:* *v.* pay with pitch
stanchura

pitcher *n.* (jug) **pycher** *m.* **+s**

piteous *adj.* **truedhek**

pitiful *adj.* **pytethus**

pitiless *adj.* **dibyta**

pity *n.* **pyta** *m.,* **truedh** *m.:* *phr.*
have pity **kemmeres truedh;** have
pity on **kemmeres pyta orth;** I
have pity **truedh a'm beus**

place *n.* **le** *m.* **leow, tyller** *m.* **+yow;**
(mansion) **plas** *m.* **plassow;** lonely
place **tyller kernhwili** *m.;* place at
table **plas** *m.* **plassow;** place of
employment **soedhva** *f.* **+ow:** *adj.*
taken place **hwarvedhys:** *prep.* in
place of **yn le:** *v.* **gorra, settya;**
take place **hwarvos:** *adv.* at that
place or time **ena;** from what place
a-ble; to that place **dhi, di**

plague *n.* **ball** *f.,* **pla** *m.* **+ow, plag**
m. **+ys:** *v.* **plagya:** *int.* plague
take **malbew**

plain *n.* **plen** *m.* **+ys:** *adj.* **plen,**
sempel; (obvious) **playn**

plain-song *n.* second part in plain-
song **diskant** *m.*

plaint *n.* **plenta** *m.* **plentys**

plaintiff *n.* (female) **plentyades** *f.*
+ow; (male) **plentyas** *m.* **-ysi:** *v.*
be plaintiff **plentya**

plaintive *adj.* **truedhek**

plait *n.* plait of hair **pleth** *f.* **+ow,**
plethenn *f.* **+ow:** *v.* **pletha**

plaited *n.* plaited work **plethweyth**
m.

plaiter *n.* **plether** *m.* **-oryon**

plan *n.* **towl** *m.* **+ow;** drawn plan
desin *m.* **+yow:** *v.* **devisya,**
tewlel towl

plane *n.* (tool) **rask** *f.* **+ow**;
carpenter's plane **playn** *m.* **+ys:** *v.*
playnya, raska
planet *n.* **planet** *m.* **+ys, +ow**
planetarium *n.* **sterji** *m.* **+ow**
plank *n.* **astell** *f.* **estyll, plank** *m.*
plenkys, +ow: *adj.* abounding in
planks **kebrek**
plant *n.* **les** *m.* **+yow, plans** *m.*
+ow; (equipment) **daffar** *m.;*
power plant **tredanva** *f.:* *v.*
plansa
plantain *n.* **hynledan** *m.,*
ledanenn *f.* **+ow, ledanles** *m.*
plantation *n.* (of trees) **gwydhlann**
f. **+ow**
plaster *n.* **plaster** *m.;* small plaster
plestrynn *m.* **+ow:** *v.* **plastra**
plate *n.* **plat** *m.* **+yow, +ys**; plate
metal **plat** *m.* **+yow, +ys**
plate-rack *n.* **kloes-platyow** *f.*
kloesyow-platyow, lestrier *m.*
+yow
platform *n.* **arethva** *f.* **+ow, bynk**
f. **+yow**; (of railway station) **kay** *m.*
kayow
plausibility *n.* **gwirhevelepter** *m.*
plausible *adj.* **gwirhevelep**
play *n.* **gwari** *m.* **+ow**; play a trick
gul pratt *m.;* play having a folk-
tale plot **drolla** *m.* **drollow:** *v.*
gwari; (of a wind instrument)
hwytha; (of an instrument) **seni**;
play a harp **telynnya**; play unfairly
fugya
play hookey (U.S.) *v.* **mynchya**
player *n.* **gwarier** *m.* **-oryon**
playful *adj.* **gwariek**
playground *n.* **garth-gwari** *m.*
garthow-gwari
play-group *n.* **bagas-gwari** *m.*
bagasow-gwari
playing-place *n.* **plen an gwari** *m.*
plead *v.* **pledya**
pleader *n.* **pledyer** *m.* **-oryon**
pleasant *adj.* **hweg**

pleasantness *n.* **hwekter** *m.*
please *n.* **mar pleg** *m.:* *v.* **plesya:**
adv. **dell y'm kyrri**
pleased *v.* **pes da**
pleasing *adj.* **hweg, didhan,**
jentyl, plegadow: *v.* be pleasing
to **plegya dhe, plegya gans**
pleasure *n.* **delit** *m.,* **fansi** *m.,*
plesour *m.* **+s**
pledge *n.* **arwystel** *m.,* **gaja** *m.*
gajys, gwystel *m.* **gwystlow:** *v.*
gwystla
plentiful *adj.* **pals**
plenty *n.* **palster** *m.:* *adv.* in plenty
lowr
pliable *adj.* **gwedhyn**
pliers *plur.* **geveligow**
plight *n.* **plit** *m.*
plod *v.* **troesya**
plot *n.* (conspiracy) **bras** *m.;* (of
ground) **splatt** *m.* **+ow:** *v.* **brasa**
plotter *n.* **braser** *m.* **-oryon**
plough *n.* **arader** *m.* **ereder**; frame
for the moulding of a wooden plough
branell *m.* **+ow:** *v.* **aras**; plough
together **kevaras**
ploughed *ptl.* **erys**
ploughman *n.* **aradror** *m.* **+yon**
ploughshare *n.* **sogh** *m.* **+yow**
plough-staff *n.* **karthprenn** *m.*
plug *n.* **stoppyer** *m.* **+s**; (electrical)
ebilyer *m.* **+ow**
plum *n.* **ploumenn** *f.* **+ow**
plummet *n.* **plemmik** *m.*
plemmigow
plump *adj.* **berrik**
plum-tree *n.* **ploumbrenn** *m.* **+yer**
plunder *n.* **preydh** *m.:* *v.* **ladra,**
pylla, ravna
plunge *v.* **troghya**; plunge under
water **gorthroghya**
plural *n.* **liesplek** *m.* **-egow:** *adj.*
liesek
plurality *n.* **liester** *m.*
Plymouth *place* **Aberplymm**

pocket *n.* **poket** *m.* **+ow**; fold
forming pocket **askra** *f.*
pockmark *n.* **pokk** *m.* **pokkys**
pockmarked *adj.* **tellek**
pod *n.* **gwisk** *m.*, **kodh** *f.* **+ow,**
maskel *f.* **masklow, pliskenn** *f.*
+ow *coll.* **plisk**
poem *n.* **kan** *f.* **+ow, bardhonek** *m.*
-ogow
poesy *n.* **bardhonieth** *f.*
poet *n.* **bardh** *m.* **berdh, bardhes** *f.*
+ow, prydydh *m.* **+yon**
poetess *n.* **prydydhes** *f.* **+ow**
poetic *adj.* **awenek, bardhonek,**
prydydhyek
poetry *n.* **bardhonieth** *f.*,
prydydhieth *f.:* *v.* compose poetry
prydydhi
poinard *n.* **kledha byghan** *m.*
point *n.* **bleyn** *m.* **+yow, kolgh** *m.*
+ow, pig *m.* **+ow, poynt** *m.* **+ys,**
prykk *m.* **+ow**; point of land **rynn**
m. **+ow, troen** *m.* **-yow**; point of
view **gwelva** *f.* **-ow**; sharp point
bros *m.* **+ow**; turning point
troboynt *m.:* *v.* **bleynya,**
poyntya: *phr.* there's no point in
ny amont
pointed *adj.* **minyek**
poise *n.* **kespoes** *m.:* *v.* **omberthi**
poised *adj.* **omborth**
poison *n.* **gwenon** *m.*, **venim** *m.:*
v. **posna, venimya**
poisoner *n.* **gwenonriyas** *m.* **-riysi**
poisonous *adj.* **gwenonek**
poke *n.* **pok** *m.* **+yow**: *v.* **pokya**
Poland *place* **Poloni**
pole *n.* **gwelenn** *f.* **gwelynni** *coll.*
gwel, lorgh *f.* **+ow, peul** *m.* **+yow**
polecat *n.* **yewgenn** *m.*
police *n.* **kreslu** *m.;* police car **karr**
kreslu *m.;* police station **soedhva**
greslu *f.;* riot police **kreslu**
gustel *m.*
policeman *n.* **gwithyas kres** *m.*
gwithysi gres

policy *n.* insurance policy **ambos**
surheans *m.*
Polish *n.* Polish language **Polonek**
m.: *adj.* **Polonek**
polite *adj.* **kortes**
politeness *n.* **kortesi** *m.*
political *adj.* **gwlasek, politek**
politician *n.* **politeger** *m.* **-oryon**
politics *n.* **politegieth** *f.*
poll *n.* **poll** *m.*
pollack *n.* young pollack **dojel** *m.*
pollen *n.* **bleus bleujyow** *m.*
poll-tax *n.* **toll-benn** *f.*
pollute *v.* **defola**; pollute water
stronka
pollution *n.* **defolans** *m.*
polygamy *n.* **lieswregeth** *f.*
polyglot *n.* **liesyethek** *m.* **-ogyon:**
adj. **liesyethek**
pomegranate *n.* **greunaval** *m.*
+ow
pomp *n.* **meuredh** *m.*, **ryalder** *m.*
pond *n.* **lagenn** *f.* **+ow, lynn** *m.*
+ow, stagen *m.;* artificial pond
kreun *m.* **+yow**; cattle pond **poll**
lo'n *m.;* dammed-up pond **poll**
greun *m.;* pond for livestock
grelynn *f.* **+ow**; salt pond **poll**
hoelan *m.;* tadpole pond **poll**
pennynnow *m.:* *adj.* abounding in
ponds **lynnek**
ponder *v.* **prederi, ombrederi**
pond-weed *n.* **dowrles** *m.*
pony *n.* **hobi** *m.* **+s, merghik** *m.*
-igow
pool *n.* **poll** *m.* **+ow, logh** *m.* **+ow,**
lynn *m.* **+ow**; dirty pool **poll**
stronk *m.;* little pool **pollenn** *f.*
+ow; swimming pool **poll neuvya**
m.
poop *n.* **aros** *m.* **+yow**
poor *adj.* **boghosek, truan**
poor-cod *n.* **gwiber** *m.*
pope *n.* **pab** *m.* **+ow**
poplar-grove *n.* **edhlek** *f.* **-egi**

poplar-tree *n.* **edhlenn** *f.* **+ow**
  coll. **edhel**
populace *n.* **gwerin** *f.*
populate *v.* **pobla**
populated *adj.* **peblys**
population *n.* **poblans** *m.* **+ow**
populous *adj.* **poblus**
porch *n.* **porth** *m.* **+ow**
pork *n.* **kig mogh** *m.*
porker *n.* **porghell** *m.* **+i**
porpoise *n.* **morhogh** *m.* **+es,**
  pyffyer *m.* **-s**
port *n.* **porth** *m.* **+ow**; cargo port
  port *m.* **+ys**; entry port **port** *m.*
  +ys
portent *n.* **ragarwoedh** *f.* **+yow**
porter *n.* **porthores** *f.* **+ow**
porthole *n.* **port** *m.* **+ys**
portion *n.* **rann** *f.* **+ow, darnas** *m.*
  +ow
portly *adj.* **korfek**
portmanteau *n.* **portmantell** *m.*
  +ow
portrait *n.* **hevelep** *m.* **hevelebow**
portray *v.* **delinya**
Portugal *place* **Portyngal**
Portuguese *n.* Portuguese language
  Portyngalek *m.:* *adj.*
  Portyngalek
position *n.* **gre** *m.* **+ys, offis** *m.*
  offisys, savla *m.* **savleow, trig** *m.*
positive *adj.* **poesedhek**
possess *v.* **piw**
possession *n.* **kerth** *f.* **+ow,**
  perghennogeth *f.*, **pyth** *m.* **+ow**:
  v. take possession of **degemmeres**
possessor *n.* **perghennek** *m.*
  -ogyon
possible *adj.* **possybyl**
possibly *adv.* **martesen**
post *n.* **peul** *m.* **+yow, stykkenn** *f.*
  +ow; (mail) **post** *m.;* (pole) **post**
  m. **+ow**; observation post
  pennoelva *f.;* post office
  soedhva an post *f.*

postage *n.* **lytherdoll** *m.*
postage-stamp *n.* **stamp** *m.* **+ys,**
  +ow
post-card *n.* **kartenn-bost** *f.*
  kartennow-post
posterior *n.* **tin** *f.*
posterity *n.* **henedh** *m.* **+ow**
post-horn *n.* **trybedh** *m.* **+ow**
postman *n.* **lytherwas** *m.* **-wesyon**
post-mark *n.* **merk-post** *m.*
  merkyow-post
post-master *n.* **postvester** *m.*
  -vestrysi
post-office *n.* **lytherva** *f.* **+ow**
postpone *v.* **delatya, hokya**
pot *n.* **pott** *m.* **+ys, +ow**;
  earthenware pot **pott pri** *m.;* iron
  pot **pott horn** *m.;* large round
  earthenware pot **boessa** *m.;* two-
  handled pot **perseth** *m.*
potato *n.* **aval-dor** *m.* **avalow-dor,**
  patatysenn *f.* **+ow** *coll.* **patatys**
pot-bellied *adj.* **krothek, torrek**
potent *adj.* **galloesek, nerthek**
pottage *n.* **iskell** *m.*, **kowl** *m.* **+ow**
potter *n.* **priweythor** *m.* **+yon**
pottery *n.* **priweyth** *m.*,
  priweythva *f.* **+ow**
pound *n.* **peuns** *m.* **+ow**; hundred
  pound weight **kanspeuns** *m.;*
  pound weight **peuns** *m.* **+ow**
pour *v.* **skoellya, dinewi, diveri**;
  pour back **astiveri**
pout-fish *n.* **bothek** *m.* **-oges**
poverty *n.* **boghosogneth** *f.*
powder *n.* **polter** *m.*
Powder *place* (name of a hundred in
  Cornwall) **Powder**
power *n.* **galloes** *m.*, **nerth** *m.*
  +yow, kevoeth *m.* **+ow, nell** *m.*,
  power *m.* **+s**
powerful *adj.* **galloesek, nerthek,**
  kevoethek
powerless *adj.* **dialloes, difreth,**
  dinerth

pox *n.* **brygh** *f.* **+i**; chicken pox
  brygh yar *f.*
practicable *adj.* **hewul**
practice *n.* **praktis** *m.* **+yow**
practise *v.* **omassaya, praktisya**
praise *n.* **gormeula** *m.,* **lawa** *m.,*
  prays *m.* **+ys**: *v.* **gormel,**
  praysya; praise highly **kanmel**:
  phr. praise him ! **dh'y lawa** !
pram *n.* **pramm** *m.* **+ow**
prank *n.* **pratt** *m.* **+ys**
prate *v.* **gerya**
pray *v.* **pysi**; I pray thee **my a'th**
  pys; pray for **pysi rag**; pray to
  God **pysi war Dhyw**; repeat
  prayers **padera**
prayer *n.* **gologhas** *m.,* **pysadow**
  m.; Lord's Prayer **pader** *m.* **+ow**
preach *v.* **pregowtha**
preacher *n.* **pregowther** *m.*
  -oryon
pre-arrange *adj.* **ragrestra**
precede *v.* **bleynya**
precept *n.* **presept** *m.* **+ys**
precinct *n.* **klos** *m.* **+yow, +ys**
precious *adj.* **drudh**
precipice *n.* **kleger** *m.* **+ow,**
  lammleder *f.*
precipitous *adj.* **deserth,**
  klegerek
precise *adj.* **kewar**
precision *n.* **kewerder** *m.*
preclude *v.* **keas mes, rakkeas**
precursor *n.* **ragresegydh** *m.*
  +yon
predate *v.* **ragresek**
predator *n.* **preydher** *m.* **-oryon**
predecessor *n.* **ragresegydh** *m.*
  +yon
predicament *n.* **plit** *m.,* **studh** *m.*
  +yow
predict *v.* **dargana, darleverel**
predictable *adj.* **darganadow**
prediction *n.* **dargan** *f.* **+ow**

preface *n.* **raglavar** *m.* **+ow,**
  ragskrif *m.*
prefer *adj.* I prefer **gwell yw genev**
prefix *v.* **ragworra**
prehistoric *adj.* **kynsistorek**
pre-judge *v.* **ragvreusi**
prejudicate *v.* **ragvreusi**
prejudice *n.* **ragvreus** *m.*
prelate *n.* **parlet** *m.*
preparation *n.* **darbar** *m.*
prepare *v.* **pareusi, araya,**
  darbari, dyghtya; prepare oneself
  ombareusi, omdharbari
prepared *adj.* **parys**
prescribe *adj.* **ragsettya**
presence *n.* **lok** *m.,* **presens** *m.:*
  prep. in the presence of **a-rag,**
  derag
present *n.* (offering) **ro** *m.* **rohow**:
  adj. **a-lemmyn**: *v.* **ri,**
  kommendya: *adv.* at present
  lemmyn
presentiment *n.* **ragown** *m.*
presently *adv.* **y'n eur ma**
preservation *n.* **gwithyans** *m.,*
  sawder *m.*
preserve *n.* **kyfeyth** *m.* **+yow**: *v.*
  gwitha, kyfeythya, sawya,
  preservya
preside *v.* **kaderya**
president *n.* **lywydh** *m.* **+yon**
press *n.* **gwask** *f.;* The Press **An**
  Wask *f.:* *v.* **gwaska, hornella**;
  (of clothes) **levna**
pressure *n.* **poes** *m.* **+ow, ynni** *m.*
  +ow; pressure on one's head before
  a thunderstorm breaks **poester** *m.*
presume *v.* **bedha**
presumption *n.* **bolder** *m.*
presumptious *adj.* **bedhek**
pretence *n.* **fayntys** *m.*
pretend *v.* **omwul, dolos, fasya,**
  fekla
pretext *n.* **ragskeus** *m.* **+ow**: *adv.*
  on the pretext of **war skeus**

prettier *adj.* **tekka**
pretty *adj.* **teg, kader**
prevail *v.* **prevaylya**
prevent *v.* **lettya, lesta, stoppya**;
  prevent from **lettya rag**
previous *adj.* **kyns**
prey *n.* **preydh** *m.:* *v.* prey on
  preydha
price *n.* **pris** *m.* **+yow**: *v.* **prisya,**
  talvesa
pricey *adj.* **kostek**
pricing *n.* **prisyans** *m.*
prick *n.* **bros** *m.* **+ow, gwan** *f.*
  +yow: *v.* **brosa, gwana, piga,**
  pigas
prickle *n.* **dren** *m.* **dreyn,**
  eythinenn *f.* **+ow** *coll.* **eythin**
pride *n.* **goeth** *m.*
priest *n.* **pronter** *m.* **+yon, oferyas**
  m. **oferysi**; high priest
  arghoferyas *m.* **-ysi**
priesthood *n.* **prontereth** *f.*
priestly *adj.* **oferyasek**
primate *n.* (cleric) **gwerthevin** *m.*
prime *n.* prime minister
  pennmenyster *m.* **+yon**
primrose *n.* **briallenn** *f.* **+ow** *coll.*
  brialli
prince *n.* **pennsevik** *m.* **-igyon,**
  pryns *m.* **+ys, ughelor** *m.* **+yon**
princess *n.* **pennseviges** *f.* **+ow,**
  prynses *f.* **+ow**
principality *n.* **prynseth** *f.* **+ow**
print *n.* **prynt** *m.* **+ow**; (e.g. of foot)
  ol *m.* **+ow**: *v.* **pryntya**
printer *n.* (machine) **jynn-pryntya**
  m. **jynnow-pryntya**; (person)
  prynter *m.* **-oryon**
printing-office *n.* **pryntji** *m.* **+ow**
print-run *n.* **pryntyans** *m.* **+ow**
priority *n.* **ragwir** *m.*
prison *n.* **prison** *m.* **+yow**
prisoner *n.* (female) **prisnores** *f.*
  +ow; (male) **prisner** *m.* **+s,**
  -oryon

prithee *v.* I prithee **my a'th pys**
privacy *n.* **privetter** *m.*
private *n.* private matter **privyta** *m.:*
  adj. **priva, privedh**
privation *n.* **esow** *m.*
privet *n.* **skeuswydh** *coll.* **+enn**
privy *n.* **kawghla** *m.,* **kawghti** *m.*
  +ow
probe *n.* **tavell** *f.* **+ow**: *v.* **hwithra,**
  kropya, tavella
problem *n.* **kudynn** *m.* **+ow,**
  problem *m.:* *v.* solve a problem
  digelmi: *phr.* no problem **heb**
  grev
proceed *v.* **mos yn-rag**
process *n.* **argerdh** *m.* **+ow**: *v.*
  argerdhes
procession *n.* **keskerdh** *m.*
processor *n.* **argerdhell** *f.* **+ow**
proclamation *n.* **gwarnyans** *m.*
  +ow
procure *v.* **gwaynya, kavoes,**
  provia
produce *n.* **askorr** *m.*
producer *n.* **askorrer** *m.* **-oryon**
product *n.* **askorras** *m.*
production *n.* **askorrans** *m.*
profanation *n.* **disakrans** *m.*
profane *adj.* **ansans, diras**: *v.*
  disakra
profanity *n.* **ansansoleth** *f.*
profess *v.* **professya**
profession *n.* **galwesigeth** *f.* **+ow**
professional *n.* (man) **galwesik** *m.*
  -igyon; (woman) **galwesiges** *f.*
  +ow: *adj.* **galwesik**
professor *n.* **professor** *m.* **+yon**
proffer *v.* **profya**
profit *n.* **les** *m.,* **budh** *m.,* **gwayn**
  m., **prow** *m.:* *v.* **gwaynya**
profitability *adj.* **budhadewder**
profitable *adj.* **budhadow**
profitless *adj.* **diles**
profound *adj.* **down**
profundity *n.* **downder** *m.* **+yow**

profuse *adj.* **gorfals**
profusion *n.* **gorfalster** *m.*
progeny *n.* **has** *coll.* **+enn, linyeth** *f.*
program *v.* **towlenna**
programme *n.* **towlenn** *f.* **+ow**
programmer *n.* **towlenner** *m.* **-oryon, towlennores** *f.* **+ow**
progress *v.* **avonsya, spedya**
progressive *adj.* **a-gammow**
progressively *adv.* **a-gammow**
prohibit *v.* **defendya, difenn**
prohibition *n.* **difenn** *m.,* **difennadow** *m.*
projection *n.* **balek** *m.* **balogow**
proletariat *n.* **gwerin** *f.*
promenade *n.* **kerdhva** *f.* **+ow, rosva** *f.* **+ow**
prominent *n.* prominent place **bann** *m.* **+ow**: *adj.* **bannek**
promise *n.* **ambos** *m.* **+ow, dedhewadow** *m.:* *v.* **ambosa, dedhewi;** keep a promise **kewera;** promise to someone **ambosa orth nebonan**
promontory *n.* **garth** *m.* **+ow, pennardh** *m.* **+ow, pennrynn** *m.* **pennrynnow, ros** *m.* **+yow;** little promontory **rosynn** *m.;* rough promontory **garros** *m.*
promote *v.* **avonsya**
promotion *n.* **avonsyans** *m.*
prompt *adj.* **tromm**
promptly *adv.* **a-boynt**
prong *n.* **forgh** *f.* **fergh**
pronoun *n.* **rakhanow** *m.* **rakhenwyn**
pronounce *v.* **prononsya**
pronunciation *n.* **gis-leveryans** *m.,* **leveryans** *m.* **+ow**
proof *n.* **prov** *m.*
prop *n.* **jist** *m.* **+ys**
propaganda *n.* **plontyans** *m.*
propagate *v.* **plontya**
propel *v.* **rakherdhya**

propeller *n.* **rakherdhell** *f.* **+ow**
proper *adj.* **ewn, gwiw, onest**
properly *adv.* **yn fas**
property *n.* **kerth** *f.* **+ow, pyth** *m.* **+ow**
prophecy *n.* **dargan** *f.* **+ow**
prophesy *v.* **dargana, profoesa**
prophet *n.* **profoes** *m.* **+i**
proportion *n.* **kemusur** *m.*
proposal *n.* **kynnik** *m.* **-igow, profyans** *m.*
propose *v.* **profya**
proposition *n.* **kynnik** *m.* **-igow**
propriety *n.* **glander** *m.,* **kompoester** *m.,* **onester** *m.*
prose *n.* **yeth-plen** *f.*
prosecute *v.* **darsywya**
prosecutor *n.* **darsywyas** *m.* **-ysi, kuhudhor** *m.* **+yon**
prospect *n.* **gwel** *m.* **+yow**
prosper *v.* **seweni**
prosperity *n.* **sewena** *f.,* **sewenyans** *m.*
prosperous *adj.* **sewen**
protect *v.* **difres;** protect from **gwitha rag;** protect oneself from **omweres rag**
protector *n.* **difresyas** *m.* **-ysi**
protectress *n.* **difresyades** *f.* **+ow**
protest *v.* protestya
Protestant *n.* **Protestant** *m.* **-ans**
protuberance *n.* **borr** *f.*
proud *n.* proud man **orgelous** *m.:* *adj.* **goethus, orgelous, stout**
prove *v.* **previ, gul prov;** prove oneself **ombrevi**
proverb *n.* **henlavar** *m.* **+ow, lavar koth** *m.*
provide *v.* **dyghtya, provia**
provider *n.* **proviyas** *m.* **-ysi**
province *n.* **pow** *m.* **+yow**
provision *n.* **daffar** *m.,* **darbar** *m.*
provisional *adj.* **servadow**
provoke *v.* **serri**

prow *n.* flour-rag *m.*

proximity *n.* nester *m.*

prudence *n.* doethter *m.*

prudent *adj.* doeth

prune *v.* skethra

psalm *n.* salm *m.* +ow

psalter *n.* sowter *m.*

psaltery *n.* sowtri *m.*

pseudonym *n.* fukhanow *m.* -henwyn

psychological *adj.* brysoniethel

psychology *n.* brysonieth *f.*

puberty *n.* kedhorieth *f.*

pubic *n.* pubic hair kedhor *m.*

public *adj.* poblek

publication *n.* dyllans *m.* +ow

publish *v.* dyllo

publisher *n.* dyller *m.* -oryon

pudding *n.* podin *m.* +s; bread pudding podin bara *m.;* Christmas pudding podin Nadelik *m.*

puddle *n.* lagenn *f.* +ow, pollenn *f.* +ow

puerile *adj.* floghel

puff *n.* hwyth *m.* +ow: *v.* hwytha, pyffya

puffin *n.* nath *m.* +es, popa *m.* popys

pull *n.* tenn *m.* +ow: *v.* tenna; pull back kildenna

puller *n.* tenner *m.* -oryon

pullet *n.* mabyar *f.* -yer

pulpit *n.* gogell *f.* +ow

pulsate *v.* polsa

pulse *n.* pols *m.* +yow

pump *n.* pomp *m.* +yow: *v.* pompya

pumpkin *n.* pompyon *m.* +s

punch *n.* hwaff *m.* +ys: *v.* boksusi, dorna

punctual *adj.* a-boynt

punctually *adv.* a-dermyn

puncture *n.* gwanas *m.* +ow: *v.* gwana

punish *v.* kessydhya, paynya

punishment *n.* kessydhyans *m.*

punk *n.* penn-pilus *m.* pennow-pilus

pup *n.* little pup kelynik *m.*

pupil *n.* dyskybel *m.* dyskyblon; (of the eye) byw an lagas *m.*

puppet *n.* popet *m.* +ow

puppy *n.* kenow *m.*, kolyn *m.* kelyn

purchase *n.* prenas *m.* +ow: *v.* prena

purchaser *n.* prener *m.* -oryon; (professional) prenyas *m.* -ysi

pure *adj.* kler, pur

purge *n.* karth *m.* +yon: *v.* kartha, purjya

purification *n.* purheans *m.*

purify *v.* purhe

purity *n.* glander *m.*, puredh *m.*

purple *adj.* glasrudh, purpur, rudhlas

purpose *n.* entent *m.* +ys, mynnas *m.*, porpos *m.:* *prep.* for the purpose of rag: *v.* porposya

purse *n.* pors *m.* +ys, yalgh *f.* +ow

pursue *v.* helghya, pursywya

pus *n.* gor *m.*

push *n.* pok *m.* +yow: *v.* herdhya, pokya

push-chair *n.* kador-herdhya *f.* kadoryow-herdhya

put *v.* gorra; put aside gorra a-denewen; put in a bag sagha; put out a fire difeudhi; put together keskorra: *phr.* put to death gorra dhe vernans

putridity *n.* podredhes *m.*

puzzle *n.* jigsaw puzzle gwari mildamm *m.*

pylon *n.* peul *m.* +yow

Q

quack *v.* kwakkya
quack-doctor *n.* pomster *m.* +s
quackery *n.* pomstri *m.*
quail *n.* rynk *f.* +i
quake *n.* kren *m.* +yow
quaker *n.* krener *m.* -oryon
quaking *n.* krys *m.*
quaking-grass *n.* kryswels *coll.*
qualities *plur.* teythi
quality *n.* gnas *f.* +ow
quandary *n.* transyek *m.*
quantity *n.* myns *m.*
quarrel *n.* kedrynn *f.*, trynn *f.: v.*
    kedrynna, omdhal
quarry *n.* (stone-pit) mengleudh *m.*
    +yow: *v.* mengleudhya
quart *n.* kwart *m.* +ys
quarter *n.* kwartenn *f.* +ow,
    kwarter *m.* kwartrys, kwartron
    m. +ys; (of a year) trymis *m.: v.*
    cut in quarters kwartrona
quarterly *adj.* trymisyek
quartermaster *n.* erberjour *m.*
quartz *n.* kanndir *m.*
quay *n.* kay *m.* kayow
queen *n.* myghternes *f.* +ow,
    rywvanes *f.* +ow
quench *v.* difeudhi; quench thirst
    disygha
quern *n.* brow *f.* +yow
question *n.* govynn *m.: v.*
    govynn
questionnaire *n.* govynnek *m.*
    -egi
queue *n.* lost *m.* +ow: *v.* gul lost,
    lostya
quick *adj.* byw, buan, snell, uskis
quicken *v.* bywhe
quickly *adv.* skon, dihwans,
    prest, snell, uskis
quicksand *n.* lonktreth *m.*
quicksilver *n.* arghans byw *m.*

quiet *n.* taw *m.*, kosoleth *f.;* quiet
    interval spavenn *f.: adj.* kosel,
    hebask: *phr.* be quiet gas dha
    son; keep quiet taw taves
quieten *v.* koselhe
quietude *n.* hebaska *m.*
quill *n.* pluvenn *f.* +ow *coll.* pluv,
    kwyllenn *f.* +ow
quilt *n.* kolghes *f.* +ow
quit *v.* kwitya
quite *adv.* glan, poran, teg
quiver *v.* krysya
quivering *n.* krys *m.*
quota *n.* klosniver *m.* +ow
quotation *n.* devynn *m.* +ow;
    price quotation towlgost *m.* +ow
quote *v.* devynna
quoth *v.* yn-medh

R

rabbit *n.* konin *m.* +es
rabbiting *v.* go rabbiting koninessa
rabbit-skin *n.* koningenn *m.*
rabble-rouser *n.* predheger *m.*
    -oryon
rabid *adj.* konneryek
rabies *n.* konnar *f.*
race *n.* res *m.;* (ethnic) agh *f.* +ow
racer *n.* resegydh *m.* +yon, reser
    m. -oryon
racial *adj.* aghel
racing-car *n.* karr-resek *m.* kerri-
    resek
rack *n.* kloes *f.* +yow, rastell *f.*
    restell; (mach.) rastell dhensek
    f.; airing rack kloes-ayra *f.*
    kloesyow-ayra
raconteur *n.* rakker *m.* -oryon
radar *n.* radar *m.*
radiance *n.* golowder *m.*,
    golowyjyon *m.*
radiate *v.* dewynna
radical *adj.* gwreydhyel

radio *n.* diwiver *m.*, radyo *m.*
+yow

radish *n.* redigenn *f.* +ow *coll.*
redik

raffle *n.* gwari-dall *m.* gwariow-
dall, gwari-sagh *m.* gwariow-
sagh

raft *n.* skath-kloes *f.* skathow-
kloes

rafter *n.* keber *f.* kebrow, styl *m.*
+yow

ragamuffin *n.* tellek *m.* tellogyon

rage *n.* koler *m.*, konnar *f.*

ragged *n.* ragged fellow skethrek *m.*
-ogyon: *adj.* pilennek

raggedy person (U.S.) *n.* fregys
m.

rags *n.* pil *coll.* +enn

raid *n.* omsettyans *m.* +ow: *v.*
omsettya; raid on horseback
ehwias

rail *n.* kledher *coll.* kledhrenn: *v.*
raylya

railing *n.* peulge *m.* +ow

railway *n.* hyns-horn *m.*
hynsyow-horn

raiment *n.* dillas *coll.* +enn,
gwiskas *m.* +ow

rain *n.* glaw *m.:* *v.* gul glaw

rainbow *n.* kammneves *f.*

rainstorm *n.* kowas *f.* kowasow

raise *v.* drehevel; (of a child)
meythrin; (of children or animals)
maga; raise again dastrehevel;
raise oneself up omdhrehevel;
raise up sevel

rake *n.* garden rake rakan *m.* +ow:
v. rakana

rally *n.* (of cars, etc.) ralli *m.*

ram *n.* hordh *m.* +es: *v.* herdhya,
kornya

ramp *n.* ledrynn *f.*

rampart *n.* fos *f.* +ow

ramsons *n.* kennin *coll.* +enn

ranatra *n.* (water-insect) peswar-
paw *m.* +es

random *n.* random number happriv
m.: *adv.* at random war amkan

range *n.* (of missile etc.) towl-hys *m.*

rank *n.* degre *m.* degrys, gre *m.*
+ys, ordyr *m.* ordyrs, renk *m.*
+ow: *v.* rank in order renka

ransom *n.* daspren *m.:* *v.*
dasprena

rant *n.* predhek *m.:* *v.* predheges

ranter *n.* predheger *m.* -oryon

rap *v.* frappya

rapture *n.* ravshyans *m.*

rare *adj.* tanow

rarely *adv.* nammenowgh

rarity *n.* tanowder *m.*

rascal *n.* drokpolat *m.* +ys,
jowdyn *m.* +s, lorel *m.* +s, losel
m. +s

rash *adj.* diswar

rasp *n.* liv *f.* +yow, rathell *f.* +ow:
v. ratha

raspberry *n.* avanenn *f.* +ow *coll.*
avan, morenn-rudh *f.*
morennow-rudh *coll.* mor-rudh

rat *n.* rath *m.* +es

rate *n.* kevradh *m.* +ow; (on
property) toll-annedh *f.;* rate of
exchange kevradh chanj *m.;* rate
of interest kevradh oker *m.;* rate
of tax kevradh toll *m.;* water rate
toll-dhowr *f.* tollow-dowr

rather *adv.* kyns; rather than a-
der; she loves you rather than me hi
a'th kar a-der my

rattle *n.* ruglenn *f.* +ow: *v.*
kryghylli, rugla

ravage *v.* ravna

rave *v.* muskegi

raven *n.* bran vras *f.*, marghvran
f. -vrini

ravine *n.* kownans *m.* +ow

raw *adj.* (uncooked) kriv

rawness *n.* (uncooked state) krivder
m.

ray *n.* (e.g. of light) dewynn *m.* +ow;
(fish) rogha *m.* roghys; cuckoo

ray **kalamajina** *m.;* smooth ray
karleyth *f.* **+ow, karleyth trylost**
f.; starry ray **grija** *m.*
razor *n.* **altenn** *f.* **+ow**
razor-fish *n.* **kyllik** *coll.* **+enn**
razor-shell *n.* **kyllik** *coll.* **+enn**
reach *v.* **drehedhes, hedhes**
read *v.* **redya**; read aloud **lenna**;
read banns **bannya**
reader *n.* **lennor** *m.* **+yon, redyer**
m. **-oryon, redyores** *f.* **+ow**
readily *adj.* **prest**: *adv.* **heb**
ahwer, yredi
readiness *prep.* in readiness for
erbynn
reading *n.* **redyans** *m.*
reading-matter *n.* **mater-redya**
m.
re-adjust *v.* **dastesedha**
ready *adj.* **parys**; ready to serve
servabyl: *v.* make ready **darbari,**
fyttya, pareusi
real *adj.* **gwir**
reality *n.* **gwirvos** *m.*
realize *v.* **aswonn, konvedhes**
really *adv.* **dhe wir, surredi, yn**
tevri
realm *n.* **gwlaskor** *f.* **-kordhow,**
ternas *m.*
reap *v.* **mysi**
reaper *n.* **myser** *m.* **-oryon,**
myswas *m.* **-wesyon**; (machine)
jynn-mysi *m.* **jynnow-mysi**
rear *n.* **delergh** *m.:* *adj.* in the rear
helergh: *v.* **maga, meythrin**
reared *v.* **megys**
rearer *n.* **mager** *m.* **-oryon,**
magores *f.* **+ow**
reason *n.* **acheson** *m.* **+yow, +ys,**
ken *m.,* **poell** *m.,* **praga** *m.,* **reson**
m. **+s, skila** *f.* **skilys**: *v.* **argya,**
resna
rebate *n.* **daskorr** *m.*
rebellion *n.* **rebellyans** *m.* **+ow**
rebound *n.* **aslamm** *m.* **+ow**: *v.*
aslamma

rebuild *v.* **dassevel, dastrehevel**
rebuke *n.* **keredh** *f.:* *v.* **keredhi**
re-buyer *n.* **dasprenyas** *m.* **-ysi**
recall (remember) *v.* **perthi kov**
recede *v.* **kila**
receipt *n.* **akwityans** *m.*
receive *v.* **degemmeres,**
kemmeres, resseva
recent *adj.* **a-dhiwedhes**
recently *adv.* **a-gynsow,**
degynsow
receptacle *n.* **kib** *f.*
reception *n.* **kemmeryans** *m.,*
ressevans *m.;* reception room
degemmerva *f.*
recess *n.* **kil** *m.* **+yer**
recession *n.* **kilans** *m.*
recipe *n.* **resayt** *m.* **+yow**
recitation *n.* **dyth** *m.* **+ow**
recite *v.* **dythya**
reckless *adj.* **diswar**
reckon *v.* **nivera, akontya, rekna**
reckoning *n.* **akont** *m.* **+ys, +ow,**
akontyans *m.* **+ow, reken** *m.*
reknow
reclaim *v.* **daswaynya**
recline *v.* **growedha**
recluse *n.* **ankar** *m.* **ankrys**
recognize *v.* **aswonn**
recognized *adj.* **aswonnys**
recoil *n.* **kildenn** *m.:* *v.* **ergila,**
kildenna, trebuchya
recollection *n.* **kov** *m.* **+yow,**
kovva *f.* **+ow**
recommend *v.* **kommendya**
recompense *n.* **attal** *m.:* *v.* **tyli,**
attyli
reconcile *v.* **akordya, unnverhe**
reconciled *adj.* **unnverhes**
reconciliation *n.* **akord** *m.,*
unnverheans *m.* **+ow**
record *n.* **kovadh** *m.,* **rekord** *m.*
+ys; (a single record) **kovnotenn**
f. **+ow**; (sound-recording) **plasenn**
f. **+ow**: *v.* **rekordya, sonskrifa**

recorder *n.* kovadhor *m.* +yon;
(Mus.) tollgorn sowsnek *m.*
recording *n.* (sound, etc.) plasenn *f.*
+ow, rekordyans *m.* +ow
recover *v.* daskavoes
re-creation *n.* daswrians *m.* +ow
rectangle *n.* hirbedrek *m.*
hirbedrogow
rectangular *adj.* hirbedrek
rectory *n.* pronterji *m.* +ow
red *adj.* rudh
redbreast *n.* rudhek *m.* -ogyon
redden *v.* rudha
reddish *adj.* rudhik
redeem *v.* dasprena, prena;
redeem oneself ombrena
redeemer *n.* dasprenyas *m.* -ysi
redemption *n.* daspren *m.*,
dasprenans *m.*
re-development *n.*
dastisplegyans *m.*
Redruth *n.* Rysrudh *f.*
redstart *n.* tingogh *m.* +es
reduce *v.* byghanhe
redundancy *n.* dresnivereth *f.*
redundant *adj.* dresniver
redwing *n.* sevellek *f.* -oges
reed *n.* korsenn *f.* +ow *coll.* kors
reed-bed *n.* kersyek *f.*,
keunegenn *f.* +ow, keunek *f.*
-egi, korsek *f.* -egi
reeds *n.* kors *coll.* +enn: *adj.*
abounding in reeds kersyek
reedy *adj.* korsek
reef *n.* (of rocks) krib *f.* +ow
reek *n.* mog *m.*
reel *n.* (dance) plethenn *f.* +ow;
(wooden) rolbrenn *m.* +yer
re-entrant *n.* (large) pans *m.* +ow;
(small) gobans *m.* +ow
refer *v.* kampoella
referee *n.* breusydh *m.* +yon; (for
character) dustunier *m.* -oryon

reference *n.* (e.g. in a letter)
kampoellans *m.* +ow; (for
character) dustuni *m.* dustuniow
references *n.* (for potential
employees) lytherow kresys *m.*
refined *adj.* fin
reflect *v.* prederi, ombrederi; (of
light) dastewynnya
reform *v.* dasfurvya
reformation *n.* dasfurvyans *m.;*
The Protestant Reformation An
Dasfurvyans *m.*
refrain *n.* principal refrain in plain
chant pennpusorn *m.* +ow
refresh *v.* disygha
refrigerator *n.* yeynell *f.* +ow
refuge *n.* harber *m.* +ys, meneghi
m., skovva *f.* +ow
refusal *n.* nagh *m.*
refuse *v.* nagha, denagha,
skonya; refuse to do something
skonya a wul neppyth
regain *v.* daskemmeres
regal *adj.* ryal
regard *n.* govis *m.*, reowta *m.: v.*
mires orth
regenerate *v.* dastineythi
regeneration *n.* dastineythyans
m.
regiment *n.* kaslu *m.* +yow
region *n.* pow *m.* +yow, ranndir
m., rannvro *f.* +yow
regional *adj.* ranndiryel
register *n.* kovlyver *m.* -lyvrow,
kovskrifenn *f.* +ow; register office
soedhva govskrifa *f.: v.*
kovskrifa
registry *n.* kovskrifla *m.* -leow
regret *n.* edrek *m.*, edrega *m.*,
govijyon *m.*, keudhesigeth *f.*,
moredh *m.;* cause for regret
dihedh *m.: phr.* I regret edrek
a'm beus
regretful *adj.* edregus
regular *adj.* reyth
regulate *v.* governya, rewlya

regulation *n.* rewl *f.* +ys
regulator *n.* (elect.) rewlerynn *m.*
  +ow
rehearsal *n.* assay *m.* +s, ragober
  m. +ow
rehearse *v.* omassaya, ragoberi
reign *n.* reyn *m.* +ys: *v.* reynya;
  reign together kesreynya
reigning *adj.* reynys
reindeer *n.* karow ergh *m.*
rejected *v.* neghys
rejoice *v.* lowenhe, omlowenhe
rejoicing *n.* heudhder *m.*
rejuvenate *v.* yowynkhe
relate *v.* leverel, derivas; relate to
  derivas orth
related *adj.* related by blood
  unnwoes
relative *n.* near relative kar ogas *m.*,
  neskar *m.* neskerens
relax *v.* diskwitha, lowsel,
  omdhiskwitha
release *v.* dyllo, delivra, livra,
  rydhhe; (from trap) divagla
relent *v.* diserri
reliance *n.* fydh *f.*, kyfyans *m.*,
  trest *m.*
relic *n.* (of saint) krer *m.* +yow
relief *n.* difres *m.*, difresyans *m.*,
  solas *m.*; tax relief difresyans
  toll *m.*
relieve *v.* difres, sewajya, sokra
religious *adj.* kryjyk
relinquish *v.* hepkorr
reliquary *n.* krerva *f.* +ow
relish *n.* blas *m.*, fansi *m.*: *v.*
  blasa
relocate *v.* daslea
reluctance *n.* anvodh *m.*,
  anvodhogeth *f.*, danjer *m.*
reluctant *adj.* anvodhek, hell:
  phr. I am reluctant dihedh yw
  dhymm
remain *v.* gortos, triga
remainder *n.* remenant *m.* +s

remake *v.* daswul
remark *v.* notya
remedy *n.* kur *m.*, medhygieth *f.*,
  remedi *m.*
remember *v.* perthi kov a, kovhe,
  perthi kov
remembrance *n.* kovadh *m.*,
  kovva *f.* +ow
remind *v.* kovhe
remiss *adj.* logh
remission *n.* gevyans *m.*
remit *v.* gava
remnant *n.* pennynn *m.* +ow,
  remenant *m.* +s
remorse *n.* edrek *m.*
removal *n.* removyans *m.*
remove *v.* dilea, kemmeres yn-
  mes, removya, tenna yn-mes
remover *n.* remover of charms peller
  m. -oryon
remunerate *v.* gobra
rend *v.* skwardya
render *v.* ri
rendezvous *n.* kuntellva *f.* +ow
renew *v.* nowydha, nowydhhe
renewable *adj.* nowydhadow
rennet *n.* godroeth *m.*: *v.* curdle
  with rennet godroetha
renounce *v.* gasa, nagha,
  hepkorr
renounced *v.* neghys
renovate *v.* nowydhhe
rent *n.* rent *m.* +ow, +ys, skward
  m. +yow
rental car (U.S.) *n.* karr gobrena
  m.
rent-to-own (U.S.) *v.* hirbrena
renunciation *n.* hepkorrans *m.*
reorganize *v.* dasordena
repair *n.* ewnheans *m.* +ow: *v.*
  ewnhe
repay *v.* attyli
repayment *n.* attal *m.*
repeat *v.* dasleverel

repeatedly *adv.* **menowgh**
repent *v.* **kavoes edrek;** cause to repent **keudhesikhe**
repentance *n.* **edrek** *m.,* **keudhesigeth** *f.*
repentant *adj.* **edregus, keudhesik**
replenish *v.* **lenwel**
repletion *n.* **gorlanwes** *m.,* **gwalgh** *m.,* **kwoff** *m.*
reply *n.* **gorthyp** *m.* **gorthybow:** *v.* **gorthybi;** reply impertinently **kammworthybi**
repopulate *v.* **daspobla**
report *n.* **ger** *m.* **+yow,** derivas *m.;* false report **hwedhel** *m.* **hwedhlow:** *v.* **dannvon, derivas, meneges**
reporter *n.* **derivador** *m.* **+yon**
repose *n.* **powes** *m.:* *v.* **diskwitha**
representative *n.* **negysydh** *m.* **+yon**
reprint *v.* **daspryntya**
reproach *n.* **keredh** *f.,* **mewl** *m.:* *v.* **keredhi**
reproof *n.* **keredh** *f.*
reprove *v.* **keredhi**
reptile *n.* **kramvil** *m.* **+es**
republic *n.* **repoblek** *f.*
re-publication *n.* **dastyllans** *m.* **+ow**
re-publish *v.* **dastyllo**
repulsive *adj.* **kasadow, disawor, hegas**
reputation *n.* **bri** *f.,* **gerda** *m.,* **pris** *m.* **+yow**
repute *v.* **gerya**
request *n.* **desir** *m.* **+ys, gorholedh** *m.,* **govynnadow** *m.:* *v.* **dervynn**
request-stop *n.* **savla-govynn** *m.* **savleow-govynn**
requiem *n.* requiem mass **seren** *f.*
require *v.* **erghi, dervynn;** require of someone **mynnes orth nebonan**

requisites *n.* **pygans** *m.*
requisition *n.* **gorholedh** *m.*
requittal *n.* harsh requittal **drog ras** *m.*
re-read *v.* **dasredya**
resale *n.* **daswerth** *f.* **+ow**
resay *v.* **dasleverel**
rescue *v.* **sawya, selwel**
research *n.* **hwithrans** *m.* **+ow:** *v.* carry out research **hwithra**
researcher *n.* **hwithrer** *m.* **-oryon, hwithrores** *f.* **+ow**
resemblance *n.* **hevelep** *m.* **hevelebow**
resemble *v.* **favera, bos haval dhe**
resembling *adj.* **haval**
reservation *n.* **ragarghas** *m.* **+ow**
reserve *n.* **gwithva** *f.* **+ow;** (of land) **gwithlann** *f.* **+ow;** (of money or materials) **kreun** *m.* **+yow;** nature reserve **gwithva natur** *f.:* *v.* **gwitha, gorra a-denewen;** (e.g. a room) **ragerghi**
reservoir *n.* **kreun** *m.* **+yow**
resettle *adj.* **dasannedhi**
residence *n.* **treveth** *f.;* imparked residence **kenkidh** *m.* **+yow**
residual *n.* **pennynn** *m.* **+ow**
residue *n.* **remenant** *m.* **+s**
resist *v.* **offendya, settya orth, sevel orth**
resistance *n.* **defens** *m.*
resolve *v.* **ervira**
resound *v.* **dasseni**
respect *n.* **reowta** *m.,* **revrons** *m.*
respectively *adv.* **a-gettep**
respite *adv.* without respite **anhedhek**
respond *v.* **gorthybi**
response *n.* **gorthyp** *m.* **gorthybow**
responsibility *n.* **charj** *m.* **+ys, omgemmeryans** *m.* **+ow**

responsible *v.* become responsible for **omgemmeres**

rest *n.* **powes** *m.;* state of rest **powesva** *f.:* *v.* **hedhi, powes, diskwitha**

re-start *n.* **dastalleth** *m.:* *v.* **dastalleth**

restate *v.* **dasleverel**

restaurant *n.* **boesti** *m.* **+ow**

resting-place *n.* **powesva** *f.*

restitution *n.* **daskorrans** *m.*

restless *adj.* **dibowes**

restore *v.* **daswul, restorya**; (fig.) **asver**

restrain *v.* **chastya, fronna**

restraint *n.* **fronn** *f.* **+ow**: *plur.* wage restraints **fronnow-gober**

result *n.* **sywyans** *m.* **+ow**: *v.* **sywya**

resurrection *n.* **dasserghyans** *m.*

retain *v.* **gwitha, dalghenna**

retainer *n.* **den koskor** *m.,* **omajer** *m.* **+s**

retake *v.* **daskemmeres**

retinue *n.* **koskor** *m.*

retire *v.* **omdenna**

retiring *adj.* **gohelus**

retract *v.* **denagha**

retranslate *v.* **dastreylya**

retreat *n.* **argel** *f.* **+yow, fo** *m.,* **godegh** *m.,* **kildenn** *m.,* **tegh** *m.:* *v.* **kildenna**

retrench *v.* **erbysi**

retribution *n.* **dial** *m.,* **kessydhyans** *m.*

return *n.* **dehwelans** *m.:* *v.* **dehweles, restorya**; return to giver **daskorr**: *adv.* by return **war nuk, war nuk**

reunion *n.* **dasunyans** *m.* **+ow**

reunite *v.* **dasunya**

reveal *v.* **diskudha**

revel *n.* **goel** *m.* **+yow**

revenge *n.* **drog-gras** *m.*

revenue *n.* **rent** *m.* **+ow, +ys**; Inland Revenue **Tollva an Wlas** *f.*

reverberate *v.* **dasseni**

reverberation *v.* **dassenyans**

reverence *n.* **revrons** *m.*

reverse *n.* reverse gear **maglenn dhelergh** *f.:* *v.* **kildenna**

review *n.* **daswel** *m.* **+yow**: *v.* **dasweles**

revival *n.* **dasvywnans** *m.*

revive *v.* **dasvywa**

revolution *n.* (in mechanics) **hweldro** *m.* **+yow**; (political) **domhwelans** *m.*

revolutionary *adj.* **domhwelus**

reward *n.* **gober** *m.* **gobrow, gwerison** *m.,* **piwas** *m.* **+ow**: *v.* **gobra, ri piwas dhe**

rheumatism *n.* **remm** *m.*

rhinoceros *n.* **troengornvil** *m.* **+es**

rhubarb *n.* **trenkles** *m.*

rhyme *n.* **rim** *m.* **+yow**: *v.* **rimya**

rhythm *n.* **resyas** *m.* **+ow**

rib *n.* **asowenn** *f.* **+ow** *coll.* **asow, asenn** *f.* **+ow**

ribbed *adj.* **asennek**

ribbon *n.* **snod** *m.* **+ow, +ys**

rice *n.* **ris** *coll.;* grain of rice **risenn** *f.* **+ow** *coll.* **ris**

rich *n.* rich man **golusek** *m.* **golusogyon**: *adj.* **golusek, rych**

riches *n.* **rychys** *m.:* *plur.* **pythow**

richness *n.* (e.g. of a culture) **rychedh** *m.*

rick *n.* **bern** *m.,* **das** *f.* **deys**

rickets *n.* **legh** *m.*

rick-yard *n.* **yslann** *f.* **+ow**

rid *v.* **kartha**

riddle *n.* (strainer) **kroeder** *m.* **kroedrow, rider** *m.* **ridrow**

riddled *adj.* **tellek**

ride *v.* **marghogeth**; ride forth **ehwias**

ride (U.S.) *n.* **gorrans** *m.* **+ow**

rider *n.* **marghoges** *f.* **+ow**; (on horseback) **marghek** *m.* **-ogyon**

ridge *n.* **keyn** *m.* **+ow, drumm** *m.* **+ow, garth** *m.* **+ow, mujovenn** *f.,* **trumm** *m.* **+ow**; long ridge **hirdrumm** *m.,* **hiryarth** *f.;* ridge of a house **krib chi** *f.;* ridge of corn-mow **pleth** *f.* **+ow**

ridge-pole *n.* **nenbrenn** *m.* **+yer**

ridicule *v.* **gul ges a, skornya**

ridiculous *adj.* **hwarthus**

riding-hood *n.* **huk** *f.* **+ys**

rift *n.* **fols** *m.* **+yow**

right *n.* **gwir** *m.* **+yow, reyth** *m.* **+yow**; legal right **ewnder** *m.* **+yow, titel** *m.* **titlow, titlys**; right angle **elin pedrek** *m.;* right of way **gwir dremen** *m.:* *adj.* **gwir, reyth**; (opposite to left) **deghow**; of the right length **ewn-hys**; right hand **deghow**: *v.* set right **amendya**: *adv.* on the right hand **a-dheghow**; right away **hware**

righteous *adj.* **gwiryon**

rightly *adv.* **poran**

rights *plur.* **gwiryow**; civil rights **gwiryow kemmyn**

rigid *adj.* **diwedhyn**

rigidity *n.* **diwedhynder** *m.*

rigorously *adv.* **dour**

rim *n.* **amal** *m.* **emlow, kammek** *f.* **-ogow**

rind *n.* **rusk** *f.* **+enn**

ring *n.* **kylgh** *m.* **+yow**; (for finger) **bysow** *m.* **bysowyer**; large ring for mooring **lagasenn** *f.* **+ow**: *v.* (of a bell) **seni**

ringmaster *n.* **mester syrk** *m.*

ring-road *n.* **kylghfordh** *f.* **+ow**

ring-worm *n.* **darwes** *coll.* **+enn, kenek** *m.*

riot *n.* **gustel** *m.:* *v.* **gustla**

rip *n.* **skward** *m.* **+yow**: *v.* **frega, skwardya**

ripe *adj.* **adhves**

ripen *v.* **adhvesi**; (of corn) **gwynnhe**

ripeness *n.* **adhvetter** *m.*

ripple *n.* **krygh** *m.* **+yow, tennik** *f.* **-igow**: *v.* **krygha**

rise *v.* **drehevel, sevel**; (of tide) **morlenwel**; rise again **dasserghi**; rise sharply **serthi**; rise straight up **serthi**; rise up **drehevel, omsevel**

risk *n.* **peryll** *m.* **+ow**: *v.* incur risk **peryllya**: *phr.* at any risk **awos peryll**

risky *adj.* **peryllus**

rite *n.* **devos** *m.* **+ow**

ritual *adj.* **devosel**

rive *v.* **folsa**

river *n.* **avon** *f.* **+yow, dowr** *m.* **+ow**

river-mouth *n.* **aber** *m.* **+yow**; (estuary) **heyl** *m.* **+yow**

rivet *n.* **gorthkenter** *f.* **-kentrow**: *v.* **gorthkentrewi**

rivulet *n.* **gover** *m.* **+ow**

roach *n.* (fish) **talek** *m.* **taloges**

road *n.* **fordh** *f.* **+ow, hyns** *m.* **+yow**; main road **fordh-veur** *f.* **fordhow-meur**; no through road **fordh dhall** *f.,* **fordh-dhall** *f.* **fordhow-dall**; single-track road **fordh unnlergh** *f.*

road-block *n.* **fordhlett** *m.* **+ow**

road-junction *n.* road-junction (T or Y) **fordh-dhibarth** *f.*

road-sign *n.* **arwoedh-fordh** *f.* **arwoedhyow-fordh**

road-works *plur.* **hwelyow fordh**

roam *n.* **rosyas** *m.:* *v.* **gwandra**

roamer *n.* **gwandryas** *m.* **-ysi**

roar *v.* **bedhygla, grommya, tarena**

roaring *adj.* **hwyflyn**

roast *v.* **rostya**

roasted *v.* **restys**

roasting pan (U.S.) *n.* **kanna-rostya** *m.*

roasting-tin *n.* **kanna-rostya** *m.*

rob *v.* **ladra**

robber *n.* **lader** *m.* **ladron, gwyll** *m.* **+yow**

robbery *n.* (in general) **ladrynsi** *m.;* (individual crime) **ladrans** *m.*

robe *n.* **gon** *m.*

robin *n.* **rudhek** *m.* **-ogyon**

robust *adj.* **nerthek**

rock *n.* **karrek** *f.* **kerrek, karregi;** rock altar **karrek sans** *f.;* small cavity in rock **fog** *f.;* soft layer on hard rock **kudhenn** *f.;* underlying rock **karn** *m.* **+ow:** *v.* **leska**

rockery *n.* **meynek** *f.* **-egi**

rocking-horse *n.* **margh-leska** *m.* **mergh-leska**

rockling *n.* three-bearded rockling **penn-barvus** *m.* **pennow-barvus, ploumsugen** *m.,* **ploumsugesenn** *f.*

rock-pile *n.* **karn** *m.* **+ow**

rock-pool *n.* **pollenn** *f.* **+ow**

rocky *n.* rocky ground **karnek** *f.* **-egi;** rocky place **meynek** *f.* **-egi:** *adj.* **karnedhek, karnek, meynek**

rod *n.* **gwelenn** *f.* **gwelynni** *coll.* **gwel, lath** *f.* **+ow;** fishing rod **gwelenn-byskessa** *f.* **gwelynni-pyskessa**

roedeer *n.* **yorgh** *f.* **+es**

rogue *n.* **adla** *m.* **adlyon, drogwas** *m.* **-wesyon, sherewa** *m.* **sherewys**

roguery *n.* **sherewneth** *f.*

roll *n.* **rol** *f.* **+yow;** (bread) **bara byghan** *m.:* *v.* **rolya;** roll into a ball **pellenni**

roller *n.* stone roller **rolven** *m.* **rolveyn;** wooden roller **rolbrenn** *m.* **+yer**

roller-skate *n.* **roskis** *m.* **+yow**

rolling-pin *n.* **rolbrenn** *m.* **+yer**

Roman *n.* **Roman** *m.* **+yon:** *adj.* **Romanek**

romantic *adj.* **romansek**

romanticism *n.* **romansogeth** *f.*

romanticist *n.* **romanseger** *m.* **-oryon**

Rome *place* **Rom**

rood *n.* **krows** *f.* **+yow**

roof *n.* to *m.* **tohow:** *v.* **ti**

roofless *adj.* **dido**

roof-tree *n.* **nenbrenn** *m.* **+yer**

rook *n.* **bran dre** *f.* **brini tre**

room *n.* **stevell** *f.* **+ow;** (chamber) **roum** *m.* **+ys;** (space) **spas** *m.;* reception room **degemmerva** *f.*

roost *n.* **klus** *m.* **+yow:** *v.* **klusya**

root *n.* **gwreydhenn** *f.* **gwreydhyow** *coll.* **gwreydh:** *v.* **gwreydhya;** (of pigs) **terghya;** take root **gwreydhya**

rootle *v.* **terghya**

root-stock *n.* **kyf** *m.*

rope *n.* **lovan** *f.* **+ow;** long rope **fun** *f.* **+yow**

rope-maker *n.* **lovaner** *m.* **lovanoryon**

roper *n.* **lovaner** *m.* **lovanoryon**

rose *n.* **rosenn** *f.* **+ow** *coll.* **ros**

roses *n.* **brilu** *coll.* **+enn**

rostrum *n.* **arethva** *f.* **+ow**

rot *n.* **breynder** *m.;* rot in timber **kosk** *m.:* *v.* **pedri, breyna;** get dry rot **koska;** rot through damp **leytha**

rotary (U.S.) *n.* **fordh-a-dro** *f.*

rotor *n.* **rosell** *f.* **+ow**

rotor-arm *n.* **bregh-rosell** *f.*

rotten *adj.* **breyn, pesek, poder**

rotter *n.* **pesek** *m.* **pesogyon, podrynn** *m.* **+ow**

rough *adj.* **garow, smat;** (of sea) **tonnek**

rough-barked *adj.* **ruskek**

rougher *adj.* **garwa**

roughness *n.* **anhwekter** *m.,* **garowder** *m.*

roulette *n.* roulette wheel **rosell** *f.* **+ow**

round *n.* **kylgh** *m.* **+yow**: *adj.*
krenn, kylghyek, rond
roundabout *n.* (at fair) **res-a-dro**
m. **resow-a-dro**; (for traffic)
fordh-a-dro *f.*
rounders *n.* (disease of sheep) **penn-
dro** *f.*
roundness *n.* **krennder** *m.*
route *n.* alternative route **gohelfordh**
f. **+ow**
rove *v.* **gwandra**
rover *n.* **gwandryas** *m.* **-ysi**
row *n.* (disturbance) **habadoellya**
m., **habadrylsi** *m.*
row *n.* (objects in a line) **res** *f.* **+yow,
rew** *m.* **+yow**
row *v.* (a boat) **revya**
rower *n.* **revador** *m.* **+yon**
rowing *n.* **revyans** *m.*
rowing-boat *n.* **skath-revya** *f.*
skathow-revya
royal *adj.* **ryal**
rub *v.* **rutya**
rubber *n.* (eraser) **rutyer** *m.* **+yow**
rubbing *n.* **rutyans** *m.*
rubbish *n.* **atal** *c.,* **plosedhes** *m.*
rubbishy *adj.* **skubellek**
rubella *n.* **brygh almaynek** *f.*
rudder *n.* **lyw** *m.* **+yow**
ruddle *n.* **meles** *m.*
rude *adj.* **diskortes**
rue *n.* (herb) **ruta** *m.*
ruffian *n.* **avleythys** *m.* **+yon**
ruffle *v.* **distempra**
rugged *adj.* **garow**
ruin *n.* **magor** *f.* **+yow, meschyf**
m.; ruin of ancient dwelling **kryllas**
m.: *v.* **diswul, meschyvya,
shyndya**
ruinate *v.* **distrui**
ruined *adj.* **shyndys**
rule *n.* **rewl** *f.* **+ys**: *v.* **governya**;
(trans.) **rewlya, routya**
ruler *n.* **router** *m.* **+s, ryw** *m.;*
(head of state) **rewler** *m.* **-oryon,**

rewlyas *m.* **-ysi**; (tool) **rewlell** *f.*
+ow; ruler by force **turant** *m.*
turans; ruler of kings **penn-
vyghternedh** *m.*
ruling *n.* ruling class **gwelhevin** *m.*
rumble *v.* **grommya**
ruminate *v.* **dasknias**
rummage sale (U.S.) *n.* **basar** *m.*
rumour *n.* **kyhwedhel** *m.*
kyhwedhlow
rump *n.* **tin** *f.*
run *v.* **poenya**; (of liquids and
people) **resek**; run away **diank**;
run before **ragresek**; run through
berya
runaway *n.* **fowesik** *m.* **-igyon**
rune *n.* **run** *m.* **+yow**
runner *n.* **resegydh** *m.* **+yon,
reser** *m.* **-oryon**; swift runner
belaber *m.*
running *n.* running of water **res** *m.*
runt *n.* **pyg byghan** *m.*
runway *n.* **hyns-tira** *m.* **hynsyow-
tira**
rupture *n.* **torr** *m.* **+ow, torrva** *f.*
+ow
ruse *n.* **kildro** *f.* **+yow**
rush *n.* **porvenn** *f.* **+ow** *coll.* **porv;**
(hurry) **fysk** *m.;* (plant) **broenenn**
f. **+ow** *coll.* **broenn, keunenn** *f.*
+ow *coll.* **keun:** *v.* **fyski**
rush-head *n.* (insult) **penn-
broennenn** *m.* **pennow-
broennenn**
rushy *adj.* **broennek**
russet *adj.* **rudhloes**
Russia *place* **Russi**
Russian *n.* Russian language
Russek *m.:* *adj.* **Russek**
rust *n.* **gossen** *f.:* *v.* **gosseni**
rustic *n.* **trevesik** *m.* **-igyon**
rusty *adj.* **gossenek:** *v.* go rusty
gosseni
rye *n.* **sugal** *coll.* **+enn**; rye ground
sugaldir *m.*
rye-field *n.* **sugalek** *f.* **-egi**

S

Sabbath *n.* **Sabot** *m.*
sacerdotal *adj.* **oferyasek**
sack *n.* **sagh** *m.* **seghyer:** *v.*
(dismiss) **gordhyllo**
sackcloth *n.* **saghlenn** *m.* **+ow,**
yskar *m.;* (garments) **saghwisk** *f.*
sacrament *n.* **sakrament** *m.* **+ys:**
v. take the Sacrament **komunya**
sacred *adj.* **sans**
sacrifice *n.* **sakrifis** *m.* **+ow:** *v.*
offrynna, sakrifia; sacrifice
oneself **omsakrifia**
sacrilege *n.* **disakrans** *m.:* *v.*
commit sacrilege **disakra**
sad *n.* sad state of affairs **truedh** *m.:*
adj. **trist, truesi**
sadden *v.* **tristhe**
saddle *n.* **diber** *m.* **dibrow:** *v.*
dibra
saddle-horse *n.* **palfray** *m.*
saddler *n.* **dibrer** *m.* **-oryon**
sadness *n.* **tristans** *m.,* **tristyns** *m.*
safe *n.* **kofer horn** *m.:* *adj.* **saw,**
salow
safety *n.* **diogeledh** *m.,* **sawder** *m.*
safety-belt *n.* **grogys diogeledh**
m. **grogysyow diogeledh**
saffron *n.* **goedhgennin** *coll.,*
safron *m.*
sage *n.* **doeth** *m.* **+yon**
said *v.* **yn-medh**
sail *n.* **goel** *m.* **+yow:** *v.* **goelya**
sailing-boat *n.* **skath-woelya** *f.*
skathow-goelya
sailor *n.* **marner** *m.* **marners,**
marnoryon
saint *n.* **sans** *m.* **sens, demmas**
m., **den Dyw** *m.,* **dremas** *m.;* (as
title) **Sen** *m.;* (female) **sanses** *f.*
+ow; patron saint **tasek** *m.*
tasogyon; saint's grave **merther**
m. **+yon**
saintliness *n.* **sansoleth** *f.*

saintly *adj.* **sansel**
Saints *plur.* All Saints **ollsens**
sake *prep.* for the sake of **a-barth:**
conj. **awos:** *phr.* for Christ's sake
awos Krist
salad *n.* **salad** *m.*
salary *n.* **gober** *m.* **gobrow, waja**
m. **+ys**
sale *n.* (act of selling) **gwerthas** *m.*
+ow; (the event) **gwerth** *f.;* jumble
sale **basar** *m.;* sale price
gwerthbris *m.* **+yow**
saleable *adj.* **marghasadow**
salesman *n.* **gwerther** *m.* **-oryon**
saleswoman *n.* **gwerthores** *f.* **+ow**
salient *adj.* **pennardhek**
saline *adj.* **hoelanek**
salinity *n.* **hoelanedh** *m.*
saliva *n.* **trew** *m.*
salmon *n.* **eghek** *m.* **eghogyon**
salt *n.* **hoelan** *m.;* salt once used
hoelan koth *m.;* salt water **hyli**
m.: *v.* to salt **salla**
Saltash *place* **Essa**
salt-cellar *n.* **sallyour** *m.*
salted *adj.* **sall, sellys**
salter *n.* **hoelaner** *m.* **-oryon**
salting-pot *n.* large salting-pot
boessa *m.*
salt-maker *n.* **hoelaner** *m.* **-oryon**
salty *adj.* **hoelanek**
salute *v.* **dynnerghi, salusi**
salvation *n.* **selwyans** *m.*
salve *n.* **eli** *m.* **+ow, sawment** *m.*
sawmens, unyent *m.,* **uras** *m.*
same *adj.* **keth:** *adv.* in the same
way **kepar:** *phr.* the same length as
kehys ha
sample *n.* **sampel** *m.* **samplow:**
v. **sampla**
sanctify *v.* **sanshe**
sanctimonious *adj.* **sansolethus**
sanctity *n.* **sansoleth** *f.*
sanctuary *n.* **meneghi** *m.,*
meneghiji *m.* **+ow, sentri** *m.*

sand *n.* **tewes** *coll.* **+enn**; coarse
sand **grow** *coll.;* scouring sand
growdir *m.*
sandal *n.* **sandal** *m.* **+yow, +ys**
sand-eel *n.* **lavyn** *m.* **+yon**
sand-hopper *n.* **morhwynnenn** *f.*
+ow *coll.* **morhwynn**
sand-pit *n.* **poll tewes** *m.*
sandspire *n.* **morhesk** *coll.* **+enn**
sandstone *n.* **krag** *coll.* **+enn**
sandwich *n.* **baramanenn** *m.*
sandy *adj.* **tewesek, trethek**
sanitary *adj.* **yeghesel**
sanitation *n.* **yeghesweyth** *m.*
sap *n.* **sugen** *m.* **+yow**
saponaceous *adj.* **sebonus**
Saracen *n.* **Sarsyn** *m.* **+s**
sarcophagus *n.* **bedh men** *m.*
sardine *n.* **fumado** *m.,* **hernenn** *f.*
+ow *coll.* **hern**
sartorial *adj.* **tregheriethek**
Satan *name* **Satnas**
satellite *n.* artificial satellite **loerell** *f.*
+ow
satiate *v.* **gwalgha**
satiety *n.* **gwalgh** *m.*
satire *n.* **ges** *m.*
satisfy *v.* **pe**
satrap *n.* (Persian official of high
rank) **gwahalyeth** *m.* **+ow**
saturate *v.* **souba**
Saturday *n.* **dy' Sadorn** *m.,*
Sadorn *m.*
Saturn *n.* (planet or god) **Sadorn** *m.*
sauce *n.* **sows** *m.* **+ow**
saucepan *n.* **padell-dhorn** *f.*
padellow-dorn
saucer *n.* **padellik** *f.* **-igow, skala**
m. **+ys, sowser** *m.* **+yow**
saucy *adj.* **tont**
sausage *n.* **selsigenn** *f.* **+ow** *coll.*
selsik
savage *adj.* **gwyls**

save *conj.* **marnas**: *v.* **difres**;
(amass money) **erbysi**; (from
danger) **sawya, selwel**; save
oneself **omsawya**
savings *plur.* **erbysyon**
Saviour *n.* **Selwador** *m.,* **Selwyas**
m.
savour *n.* **sawer** *m.* **+yow**: *v.*
sawra
savoury *adj.* **sawrek**
saw *n.* (tool) **heskenn** *f.* **+ow** *coll.*
hesk; band saw **heskenn vond** *f.;*
bow saw **heskenn warak** *f.;* chain
saw **heskenn gadon** *f.:* *v.*
heskenna
sawdust *n.* **bleus heskenn** *m.*
saxifrage *n.* **mendardh** *coll.,* **torr-
men** *m.*
Saxon *n.* **Sows** *m.* **+on**
say *v.* **leverel, medhes**; say before
ragleverel
saying *n.* **ger** *m.* **+yow, lavar** *m.*
+ow
says *v.* **yn-medh**
scab *n.* **kragh** *m.* **kreghi, krevenn**
f. **+ow, troskenn** *f.;* scab over
sores **krammenn** *f.* **+ow** *coll.*
kramm
scabbard *n.* **goen** *f.*
scabby *n.* scabby pate **penn-kreghi**
m. **pennow-kreghi:** *adj.* **kragh,
lovrek**
scabious *n.* (plant) **penn-glas** *m.*
pennow-glas
scald *v.* **skaldya**
scale *n.* **skeul** *f.* **+yow**; (of fish)
skansenn *f.* **+ow** *coll.* **skans:** *v.*
skeulya
scales *n.* (for weighing) **mantol** *f.*
+yow
scalpel *n.* **kollell gravya** *f.*
scaly *n.* scaly creature **skansek** *m.*
-ogyon: *adj.* **skansek**
scandal *n.* **bysmer** *m.,* **sklander** *m.*
scapegoat *n.* **bogh-diank** *m.*
scar *n.* **kreyth** *coll.* **+enn**

scarce *adj.* **skant, tanow, treweythus**
scarcely *adv.* **skant**
scarcity *n.* **fowt** *m.* **+ow, tanowder** *m.*
scarecrow *n.* **boekka** *m.* **+s**
scarf *n.* **lien konna** *m.:* *v.* **skarfa**
scarify *v.* **tergravas**
scarlatina *n.* **kleves kogh** *m.*
scarlet *adj.* **rudh, kogh**
scatter *v.* **keskar**
scatter-brained *adj.* **penn-skav**
scattered *adj.* **keskar**
scattering *n.* **keskar** *m.*
scent *n.* **ethenn** *f.* **+ow**
sceptic *n.* **diskryjyk** *m.* **-ygyon**
sceptre *n.* **ternwelenn** *f.* **+ow**
schedule *n.* **towlenn** *f.* **+ow**; schedule of work **towlenn ober** *f.*
scheme *n.* scheme of work **towlenn ober** *f.*
schism *n.* **fols** *m.* **+yow**
scholar *n.* **skoler** *m.*, **skolores** *f.* **+ow**
scholarship *n.* (learning) **skolheygieth** *f.*, **skolheygses** *m.*
scholastic *adj.* **dyskansek**
school *n.* **skol** *f.* **+yow**; (of whales) **hes** *f.* **+ow**; elementary school **skol elvennek** *f.*; grammar school **skol ramer** *f.*; high school **skol nessa** *f.*; night school **skol nos** *f.*; nursery school **skol veythrin** *f.*; primary school **skol gynsa** *f.*; secondary school **skol nessa** *f.*; Sunday school **skol Sul** *f.*
school-house *n.* **skolji** *m.* **+ow**
schoolmaster *n.* **skolvester** *m.* **skolvestri**
science *n.* **skians** *m.* **+ow, godhonieth** *f.*; medical science **fisek** *f.*
scientific *adj.* **godhoniethek**
scientist *n.* **godhonydh** *m.* **+yon**

Scilly *place* **Syllan**; Isles of Scilly **Ynysek Syllan**
scimitar *n.* **kledha kamm** *m.*
scissors *plur.* **gwelsigow**
scold *n.* **tavosa** *m.:* *v.* **deraylya, godros**
scorching *n.* **poethvann** *m.:* *adj.* **poeth**
score *n.* (in game) **kevriv** *m.* **+ow, skor** *m.* **+yow**; tavern score **skot** *m.* **+ys**: *num.* eight score **eth-ugens**; nine score **naw-ugens**; seven score **seyth-ugens**; six score **hwegh-ugens**: *v.* (in game) **skorya**
scot-free *adj.* **dispal**
Scotland *place* **Alban**
Scots *adj.* **Albanek**
Scotsman *n.* **Alban** *m.* **+yon**
Scotswoman *n.* **Albanes** *f.* **+ow**
Scottish *adj.* **Albanek**
scour *v.* **kartha**
scourge *n.* **skorja** *m.* **+ys**: *v.* **skorjya**
scouring *n.* **karth** *m.* **+yon**
scout *n.* **aspier** *m.* **-oryon**
scowl *n.* **talgamm** *m.* **+ow**: *v.* **talgamma**
scramble *v.* **krambla**
scrap *n.* **dral** *m.*, **pastell** *f.* **+ow, tekkenn** *f.*
scrape *v.* **kravas, ratha**; scrape mechanically **kravellas**; scrape off skin **diruska**
scraper *n.* **kravell** *f.* **+ow**
scratch *v.* **kravas, skravinyas**
scree *n.* **radell** *m.*
screech *v.* **skrija**
screw *n.* **trogenter** *f.*
screw-driver *n.* **trogentrell** *f.*
scribe *n.* **skrifwas** *m.* **-wesyon, skrifyas** *m.* **-ysi**
Scribe *n.* (Biblical) **Skriba** *m.* **Skribys**
Scripture *n.* **Skryptor** *m.* **+s**

scrofula *n.* **kleves an myghtern**
m.
scrub *n.* **krann** *coll.*
scrubby *adj.* **pryskek**
scrubland *n.* **kranndir** *m.* **+yow**
scrupulously *adv.* **dour**
scrutinize *v.* **hwithra**
scullery *n.* **kegin-geyn** *f.* **+ow-
keyn**
sculptor *n.* **gravyer** *m.* **-yoryon,
imajer** *m.* **-oryon**
sculpture *n.* (in abst. sense) **imajri**
m.
scum *n.* **lastedhes** *m.*
scummy *adj.* **kennek**
scurf *n.* **kragh** *m.* **kreghi:** *plur.*
kreghi
scurvy *adj.* **kragh**
scythe *n.* **falgh** *f.* **fylghyer, fals** *f.*
+yow: *v.* **falghas, falsa**
sea *n.* **mor** *m.* **+yow;** deep sea
downvor *m.:* *v.* put to sea **mora**
sea-area *n.* **rannvor** *m.* **+yow**
sea-board *n.* **morrep** *m.*
sea-eagle *n.* **morer** *m.* **+es**
sea-fort *n.* **merdhin** *m.*
sea-holly *n.* **kelynn mor** *coll.,*
kelynn treth *coll.,* **morgelynn**
coll. **+enn**
seahorse *n.* **morvargh** *m.* **-vergh**
sea-kale *n.* **morgowl** *m.*
seal *n.* **sel** *f.* **+yow;** (mammal) **reun**
m. **+yon:** *v.* **selya, stanchura**
sealing-wax *n.* **koer selya** *coll.*
seam *n.* **gwri** *m.* **+ow;** thin seam of
ore **gwri** *m.* **+ow**
seaman *n.* **den mor** *m.,* **morwas** *m.*
-wesyon
sea-marsh *n.* **morva** *f.* **+ow**
seamew *n.* **goelann** *f.* **+es**
sea-mist *n.* **lugh** *m.*
seamless *adj.* **diwri**
seamstress *n.* **gwriadores** *f.* **+ow,
sewyades** *f.* **+ow**
sea-pink *n.* **bryton** *m.*

search *v.* search for **hwilas**
sea-serpent *n.* **morsarf** *f.* **morserf**
sea-shore *n.* **treth** *m.* **+ow, morrep**
m.
seaside *n.* **morrep** *m.*
sea-slug *n.* **morvelhwenn** *f.* **+ow**
sea-smoke *n.* **lugh** *m.*
season *n.* **prys** *m.* **+yow, seson** *m.*
+yow, +s
seasoned *adj.* **sawrys**
seasoning *n.* **sawrans** *m.*
sea-swallow *n.* **morwennol** *f.*
-wennili
seat *n.* **kador** *f.* **+yow, chayr** *m.*
+ys, esedh *f.* **+ow, esedhva** *f.*
+ow, kevysta *f.,* **se** *m.* **seow;**
chief seat **pennplas** *m.;* judge's
seat **barr** *m.* **+ys**
sea-voyage *n.* **trumach** *m.*
trumajow, trumajys
seaward *n.* seaward portion of a
parish in Cornwall **morrep** *m.*
sea-water *n.* **hyli** *m.*
sea-wave *n.* **mordonn** *f.* **+ow**
seaweed *n.* **goemmon** *m.*
sea-wrack *n.* **morwels** *coll.*
secede *v.* **distaga**
second *n.* (of time) **eylenn** *f.* **+ow;**
second home **kenkidh** *m.* **+yow:**
adj. **nessa:** *num.* **sekond:** *v.*
eyla
second-hand *adj.* **wor'tasworth**
secrecy *n.* **keladow** *m.*
secret *n.* **kevrin** *m.* **+yow, rin** *m.*
+yow; secret matter **privyta** *m.:*
adj. **kevrinek, priva, privedh:** *v.*
keep secret **keles:** *adv.* in secret
yn-dann gel
secretary *n.* **skrifennyades** *f.*
+ow, skrifennyas *m.* **-ysi**
section *n.* **tregh** *m.* **+ow**
secure *adj.* **diogel:** *v.* **diogeli,
krafa**
security *n.* **diogeledh** *m.,* **gaja** *m.*
gajys, sawder *m.*
sedate *adj.* **hebask:** *v.* **hebaskhe**

sedation *n.* hebaskheans *m.*
sedentary *adj.* sedhek
sedge *n.* elestrenn *f.* +ow *coll.*
elester; (one individual plant)
heskenn *f.* +ow *coll.* hesk
sediment *n.* godhes *m.*
seduce *v.* ardhynya
see *v.* gweles: *int.* ott
seed *n.* has *coll.* +enn; (an
individual seed) hasenn *f.* has: *v.*
run to seed hasa
seedbed *n.* hasek *f.* -egi, sprusek
f. -egi
seed-plot *n.* hasek *f.* -egi
seed-pod *n.* bolghenn *f.* +ow *coll.*
bolgh
seedy *adj.* hasek
seek *v.* hwilas; seek something from
someone hwilas neppyth orth
nebonan
seem *v.* heveli
seemly *adj.* onest
seems *adv.* as it seems dell hevel
seer *n.* dargenyas *m.* -ysi
seesaw *n.* astell-omborth *f.* estyll-
omborth
seethe *v.* tythya
seething *n.* bryjyon *m.*
segregation *n.* dibarth *f.*
seine-boat *n.* skath-roes *f.*
skathow-roes
seize *v.* dalghenna, kachya, sesa,
sesya
seizin *v.* take seizin of a freehold
sesa
seizure *n.* shora *m.* shorys
seldom *adv.* boghes venowgh,
nammenowgh
selection *n.* dewis *m.*
self *n.* honan *m.*
self-adhesive *adj.* omlusek
self-awareness *n.* omwodhvos *m.*
self-confidence *n.* omgyfyans *m.*
self-consciousness *n.*
omwodhvos *m.*

self-determination *n.*
omervirans *m.*
self-indulgent *adj.* omvodhek
self-rule *n.* omrewl *f.*
selfsame *adj.* kethsam
sell *v.* gwertha
semester *n.* hweghmis *m.*
semicircle *n.* hanterkylgh *m.*
+yow
semi-detached *n.* semi-detached
house gevellji *m.* +ow
sempiternal *adj.* duryadow
senate *n.* senedh *m.* +ow
senator *n.* senedher *m.* -oryon
send *v.* dannvon; send far away
pellhe; send for dannvon
warlergh; send in order to
dannvon a
seneschal *n.* rennyas *m.* -ysi
senior *adj.* henavek, kottha
sensation *n.* omglywans *m.* +ow
sense *n.* skians *m.* +ow; sense of
hearing klyw *m.:* *v.* omglywes
senses *adj.* out of one's senses
gorboellek
sensitive *adj.* kroghendanow
sensual *adj.* omglywansel
sensuous *adj.* omglywansus
sentence *v.* breusi
separate *adj.* diblans: *v.* diberth
separately *adv.* dibarow
separation *n.* dibarth *f.,* diberthva
f.
September *n.* Gwynngala *m.,*
mis-Gwynngala *m.*
septennial *adj.* seythblydhenyek
sepulchre *n.* bedh *m.* +ow
sequence *n.* kevres *m.* +ow
sequencer *n.* kevresell *f.* +ow
sequential *adj.* kevresek
sequester *v.* argeles
sequestered *n.* sequestered place
argel *f.* +yow
sequestrate *v.* sesa

sequins *plur.* **golowylyon**
seraph *n.* **serafyn** *m.*
serenade *n.* **noskan** *f.* **+ow**
serf *n.* **keth** *m.* **+yon**
serge *n.* light fine serge **saya** *m.*
serial *adj.* **a-gevres, kevresek**
serially *adv.* **a-gevres**
series *n.* **kevres** *m.* **+ow, steus** *f.*
  +ow
serious *adj.* **sad, sevur, truesi**
seriously *adv.* **devri**
seriousness *n.* **sevureth** *f.*
sermon *n.* **pregoth** *m.* **+ow**
serpent *n.* **sarf** *f.* **serf**
serpentine *n.* (rock) **sarfven** *m.:*
  adj. **sarfek**
servant *n.* **gwas** *m.* **gwesyon,**
  maw *m.,* **den koskor** *m.,* **gonisek**
  m. **-ogyon, servyas** *m.* **-ysi;** civil
  servant **gonisyas** *m.* **-ysi**
serve *v.* **dyghtya, menystra,**
  servya; (in employment) **soedha**
server *n.* **servyas** *m.* **-ysi**
service *n.* **gonis** *m.,* **gonisogeth** *f.,*
  gwryth *f.,* **servis** *m.* **+yow;**
  knightly service **ago-marghogyon**
  f.; religious service **oferenn** *f.*
  +ow: *adj.* of service **'vas:** *v.*
  Health Service **Gonis Yeghes;**
  Youth Service **Gonis Yowynkneth**
serviceable *adj.* **servabyl,**
  servadow
service-book *n.* **ordenal** *m.* **+ys**
service-station *n.* **edhommva** *f.*
  +ow
servile *adj.* **keth**
serving-boy *n.* **paja** *m.* **pajys**
serving-dish *n.* **tallyour** *m.* **+s**
servitude *n.* **kethneth** *f.*
session *n.* **esedhvos** *m.* **+ow**
set *n.* (group of people) **parsel** *m.* **+s;**
  set of opponents **parti** *m.* **+s, +ow:**
  v. **gorra, settya;** (of Sun) **sedhi;**
  set back up **dassevel;** set before
  ragworra; set in line **resa;** set in

order **kempenna;** set in place
  desedha; set oneself **omsettya**
set free *v.* **livra**
setback *n.* **pervers** *m.*
set-square *n.* **skwir** *m.* **+ys**
settee *n.* **gweli-dydh** *m.*
setting *n.* **sedhes** *m.;* (location)
  desedhans *m.,* **settyans** *m.* **+ow**
settle *v.* **ervira;** (on new land)
  trevesiga; settle accounts with **pe**
settlement *n.* **trevesigeth** *f.,*
  unnverheans *m.* **+ow**
seven *num.* **seyth:** *adv.* seven times
  seythgweyth
sevenfold *adj.* **seythplek**
seventeen *num.* **seytek**
seventeenth *num.* **seytegves**
seventh *num.* **seythves**
sever *v.* **distaga**
severe *adj.* **kales, ahas, sevur**
severity *n.* **sevureth** *f.*
Severn *place* **Havren**
sew *v.* **gwrias, sewya**
sewage *plur.* **karthyon**
sewer *n.* **pibenn-garth** *f.*
  pibennow-karth; foul sewer
  kawghbib *f.* **+ow, pibenn-gawgh**
  f. **pibennow-kawgh**
sewer-pipe *n.* **karthpib** *m.* **+ow**
sex *n.* **reydh** *f.*
sexton *n.* **den an klogh** *m.*
sexual *adj.* **reydhel**
shackle *n.* **karghar** *m.* **+ow, sprall**
  m.: *v.* **karghara**
shad *n.* (fish) **keynek** *m.* **-oges;**
  allis shad **dama'n hern** *f.*
shade *n.* **goskes** *m.,* **goskotter** *m.,*
  skovva *f.* **+ow:** *v.* **goskeusi**
shadow *n.* **skeus** *m.* **+ow**
shadowed *adj.* **goskeusek**
shadowy *adj.* **skeusek**
shady *adj.* **goskeusek, skeusek**
shaft *n.* **gwelenn** *f.* **gwelynni** *coll.*
  gwel
shag *n.* (bird) **spilgarn** *m.*

shaggy *adj.* **blewek**

shake *n.* **kren** *m.* **+yow**: *v.* **krena, kryghylli, shakya**

shaking *n.* **krys** *m.*

shale *n.* **kyllas** *m.*

shallow *adj.* **bas**: *v.* grow shallow **basya**

shallowness *n.* **baster** *m.*

sham *adj.* **fug**

shame *n.* **meth** *f.* **mothow, sham** *m.:* *v.* **shamya**; put to shame **shamya**

shameful *adj.* **methus**

shameless *adj.* **diveth**

shank *n.* **berr** *f.* **+ow, fer** *f.* **+ow, garrenn** *f.* **+ow**

shape *n.* **furv** *f.* **+ow, roth** *m.* **+ow, shap** *m.* **+ys**: *v.* **furvya, shapya**

share *n.* **rann** *f.* **+ow, kevrenn** *f.* **+ow, part** *m.* **+ys**: *v.* **kevrenna, ranna**

shared *adj.* **rennys**

shareholder *n.* **kevrenner** *m.* **-oryon, kevrennek** *m.* **-ogyon**

shark *n.* **morvleydh** *m.* **+i**; blue shark **morast** *f.* **moristi**; bottle-nosed shark **porbugel** *m.*

sharp *adj.* **glew, hwerow, tynn**; (of taste or smell) **trenk**; (pointed) **lymm**

sharpen *v.* **bleynya, lymma**

sharpness *n.* **lymmder** *m.;* (of taste) **trenkter** *m.*

sharp-sighted *n.* sharp-sighted one **lagasek** *m.* **-ogyon**

shaven *n.* shaven pate **penn-blogh** *m.* **pennow-blogh**

shavings *plur.* **reskyon**

shawl *n.* **gwarrlenn** *f.* **+ow**

shawm *n.* **salmus** *m.*

she *pron.* **hi**

sheaf *n.* **manal** *f.* **+ow, tysk** *f.* **+ow, tyskenn** *f.* **+ow**: *v.* put in sheaves **manala**

shear *v.* **knyvyas**

shears *plur.* **gwelsow**

shearwater *n.* Manx shearwater **skuthenn** *m.*

she-ass *n.* **kasek asyn** *f.*

sheath *n.* **goen** *f.*

sheath-knife *n.* large sheath-knife **kollan** *f.* **+ow**

she-bear *n.* **orses** *f.* **+ow**

she-cat *n.* **kathes** *f.* **+ow**

shed *n.* **krow** *m.* **+yow, skiber** *f.* **+yow**: *v.* **dinewi**; shed tears **dagrewi, devera**

she-devil *n.* **dyowles** *f.* **+ow**

sheep *n.* **davas** *f.* **deves**; sheep shed (U.S.) **krow deves** *m.;* wether sheep **mols** *m.* **mels**: *v.* chase sheep **devessa**

sheep-cot *n.* **devetti** *m.* **+ow, krow deves** *m.*

sheep-dipping *v.* **troghya deves**

sheepdog *n.* **ki-deves** *m.* **keun-deves**

sheep-rot *n.* **podh** *m.*

sheepskin *n.* sheepskin coat **pellyst** *m.* **+ow**

sheep-track *n.* **kammdhavas** *m.*

sheep-worrier *n.* **devyder** *m.* **-oryon**

sheer *adj.* **serth**

sheet *n.* (for a bed) **lien gweli** *m.;* sheet of paper **folenn** *f.* **+ow, pythyonenn** *f.* **+ow** *coll.* **pythyon**; winnowing sheet **nothlenn** *f.* **+ow**

shelf *n.* **estyllenn** *f.* **+ow** *coll.* **estyll**

shell *n.* **krogen** *f.* **kregyn**; (explosive) **tanbellenn** *f.* **+ow**: *adj.* having a shell **krogenek**: *v.* **pliskenna**

shellfish *n.* shore-gathered shellfish **boes tryg** *m.*

shelter *n.* **glawji** *m.* **+ow, goskes** *m.,* **harber** *m.* **+ys, kel** *m.* **+yow, kowatti** *m.,* **skotter** *m.,* **skovva** *f.*

+ow: *adj.* without shelter **digloes**:
v. **goskeusi, klysa**
shelter-belt *n.* **klyswydh** *coll.*
+enn
sheltered *adj.* **goskeusek, klys**
shepherd *n.* **bugel deves** *m.*
shepherdess *n.* **bugeles** *f.* **+ow**
sheriff *n.* high sheriff **ughelver** *m.*
she-wolf *n.* **bleydhes** *f.*
shield *n.* **skoes** *m.* **+ow**; human
shield **skoes byw** *m.;* small shield
bokler *m.* **+s**
shield-bearer *n.* **skoeswas** *m.*
-wesyon
shieling *n.* **havos** *f.*
shift *n.* (shirt) **krys** *m.* **+yow**; (work)
kor *m.* **+ow**
shift down (U.S.) *v.* **magla 'nans**
shift up (U.S.) *v.* **magla 'bann**
shilling *n.* **sols** *m.* **+ow**
shine *n.* **kann** *m.:* *v.* **splanna,**
dewynnya, golowi; shine back
dastewynnya
shingle *n.* (timber) **astell** *f.* **estyll,**
plenkynn *f.* **+ow**
shining *adj.* **splann**
ship *n.* **gorhel** *m.* **-holyon**
shirk *v.* **kavanskeusa**
shirt *n.* **krys** *m.* **+yow**; (rough)
hevis *m.* **+yow**
shiver *v.* **degrena, rynni**
shoal *n.* (of fish) **hes** *f.* **+ow**;
(topographical) **bas** *m.:* *v.* (of fish)
hesya
shoaling *n.* **hevva** *f.*
shock *n.* **skruth** *m.;* electric shock
jag tredan *m.*
shocked *adj.* **dyegrys**
shock-headed *adj.* **penn-bagas**
shocking *adj.* **skruthus**
shoe *n.* **eskis** *f.* **+yow**; shoes
arghenas *m.:* *v.* **arghena**; mend
shoes **kerya**; put shoes on **arghena**
shoemaker *n.* **keryer** *m.* **-oryon**

shoot *n.* **egin** *m.* **+yow, lows** *m.;*
(of plant) **skyllenn** *f.* **+ow** *coll.*
skyll: *v.* **tenna**; (of plants)
egina, tevi
shop *n.* **gwerthji** *m.* **+ow**; baker's
shop **popti** *m.;* butcher's shop **kikti**
m. **+ow**
shopping *plur.* **prenasow**: *v.* go
shopping **prenassa**
short *adj.* **berr, kott**
short-cut *n.* **skochfordh** *f.* **+ow**
shorten *v.* **berrhe, kotthe**
shortly *adv.* **a verr spys, a verr**
dermyn
shorts *n.* (clothing) **lavrek berr** *m.*
short-sight *n.* **berrwel** *m.*
shoulder *n.* **skoedh** *f.* **+ow** *dual*
diwskoedh; hard shoulder **glann**
gales *f.*
shoulder-piece *n.* linen shoulder-
piece **skoedh-lien** *m.*
shout *n.* **garm** *f.* **+ow**: *v.* **garma,**
leva
shove *n.* **pok** *m.* **+yow**: *v.*
herdhya
shovel *n.* **pal** *f.* **+yow**
shoveller *n.* **paler** *m.* **-oryon**
show *n.* **diskwedhyans** *m.:* *v.*
diskwedhes; show off
ombraysya
shower *n.* **kowas** *f.* **kowasow**: *v.*
kowesi
showery *adj.* **kowasek**
shred *v.* **frega, skethenna**
shredded *adj.* **skethennek**
shredder *v.* **fregell**
shrew *n.* (mouse) **hwistel** *f.*
hwistlow
shriek *n.* **us** *m.:* *v.* **usa**
shrimp *n.* **bibyn-bubyn** *m.*
bibynes-bubyn
shrine *n.* **krerva** *f.* **+ow**
shrive *v.* **yes**
shrivel *v.* **krygha**
Shrovetide *n.* **Ynys** *m.*

shrug *n.* **skruth** *m.*
shudder *n.* **kren** *m.* **+yow, skruth**
m.: *v.* **degrena, skrutha**
shun *v.* **avoydya, goheles**
shut *adj.* **klos**; shut out **digloes:** *v.*
degea, keas
shuttle *n.* **gwerthys** *f.* **+ow**;
weaver's shuttle **gwennel** *f.*
gwennili
shy *adj.* **gohelus:** *v.* be shy of
goheles
sick *n.* sick person **klav** *m.* **klevyon:**
adj. **klav**
sickle *n.* **krommenn** *f.*
sickness *n.* **kleves** *m.* **+ow**
side *n.* **tu** *m.* **+yow, amal** *m.*
emlow, parth *f.* **+ow, tenewenn**
m. **tenwennow**; (in a conflict)
parti *m.* **+s, +ow**; opposite side
gorthenep *m.* **-ebow**; reverse side
gorthenep *m.* **-ebow:** *v.* take the
side of **assentya gans:** *adv.* to
one side **a-denewenn**
side-lamp *n.* **lugarn-byghan** *m.*
lugern-byghan
sidelong *adv.* **dhe-denewen**
sideways *adv.* **a-denewenn**
siege *n.* **esedhva** *f.* **+ow**
sieve *n.* **rider** *m.* **ridrow**; coarse
sieve **kroeder** *m.* **kroedrow**; large
sieve **kasyer** *m.:* *v.* **ridra**
sift *v.* **kroedra, ridra, sidhla**
sigh *n.* **hanas** *m.* **+ow, hanasenn** *f.*
+ow: *v.* **hanasa**
sight *n.* **gwel** *m.* **+yow, golok** *f.,*
tremm *f.,* **vu** *m.:* *adj.* without sight
dall: *adv.* in sight of **a-wel dhe**
sign *n.* **arwoedh** *f.* **+yow, sin** *m.*
+ys, +yow; sign of the cross **sin**
an grows *m.:* *v.* **sina**; make a
sign **arwoedha:** *phr.* as a sign of
yn tokyn
signal *n.* **sin** *m.* **+ys, +yow, sinell**
f. **+ow:** *v.* **arwoedha, sina,**
sinella
signalman *n.* **arwoedhor** *m.* **+yon**

significance *n.* **styr** *m.* **+yow**
signify *v.* **arwoedha, styrya**
sign-post *n.* **post arwoedh** *m.*
silage *n.* **goera glas** *m.*
silence *n.* **taw** *m.*
silent *adj.* **didros, tawesek:** *v.* be
silent **tewel**
silk *n.* **owrlin** *m.;* glossy silk fabric
pali *m.*
silkworm *n.* **pryv owrlin** *m.*
silly *adj.* **gokki**
silt *n.* **leys** *m.* **+yow**
silver *n.* **arghans** *m.;* ground rich in
silver **arghansek** *f.* **-egi**
silversmith *n.* **gweythor arghans**
m.
silvery *n.* silvery stream **arghantell**
f.
similar *adj.* **haval, hevelep,**
kehaval; similar to **haval dhe:** *v.*
make similar **hevelebi**
similarity *n.* **havalder** *m.* **+yow,**
hevelepter *m.*
similarly *adv.* **yndella, yn kepar**
maner
simmer *v.* **govryjyon**
simple *adj.* **sempel:** *v.* make
simple **sempelhe**
simpleton *n.* **boba** *m.*
simplicity *n.* **sempledh** *m.*
simplify *v.* **sempelhe**
simultaneously *adv.* **war not, yn**
kettermyn
sin *n.* **pegh** *m.,* **peghes** *m.*
peghosow: *v.* **pegha**
since *prep.* **a-dhia**; since Christmas
a-dhia Nadelik: *conj.* **a-ban:**
adv. **dell**; long since **seuladhydh**
sincerely *adv.* **heb gil**
sincerity *n.* **gwiryonses** *m.,*
lenduri *m.*
sinew *n.* **giowenn** *f.* **+enn** *coll.*
giow, skenna *m.* **skennys,**
skennow
sing *v.* **kana**

singe *v.* goleski

singer *n.* kaner *m.* -oryon, kanores *f.* +ow; professional female singer kenyades *f.* +ow; professional male singer kenyas *m.* -ysi

singing *n.* kenys *m.*

single *pron.* single person onan; single thing onan: *adj.* unnik: *adv.* single file yn rew

singular *adj.* (not plural) unnplek

singularity *n.* unnikter *m.*

sink *n.* new *f.* +yow: *v.* sedhi

sink-basket *n.* kowellik *m.* -igow

sinking *n.* sedhes *m.*

sinner *n.* peghador *m.* +yon, peghadores *f.* +ow

sinning *n.* peghadow *m.*

sip *n.* lommenn *f.* +ow: *v.* eva

sir *n.* syrr *m.* +ys, syrra *m.*

sire *n.* sira *m.* sirys

sirrah *n.* syrra *m.*

sister *n.* hwoer *f.* hwerydh; little sister hwerik *f.*

sit *v.* sit down esedha

sitting-room *n.* esedhva *f.* +ow

situate *v.* desedha

situated *v.* be situated omgavoes

situation *n.* le *m.* leow, desedhans *m.*

six *num.* hwegh

sixpence *n.* hwedner *m.*

sixteen *num.* hwetek

sixteenth *num.* hwetegves

sixth *num.* hweghves

sixty *num.* tri-ugens

size *n.* myns *m.*, braster *m.*

sizzle *v.* tythya

skate *n.* karleyth *f.* +ow, morgath *f.* +es; (fish) talverr *m.* +es: *v.* skesya

skate-board *n.* rostell *f.* +ow

skein *n.* kudynn *m.* +ow

skeleton *n.* korf eskern *m.*

sketch *v.* linenna, linennans

skewer *n.* kigbrenn *m.* +yer, kigver *m.* +yow

ski *v.* skia

skilful *adj.* sley

skill *n.* sleyneth *f.;* occupation requiring manual skill kreft *f.* +ow

skim *v.* (in mining) gobalas

skin *n.* kroghen *f.* kreghyn, kenn *m.*, kneus *coll.* +enn: *v.* scrape off skin diruska

skinner *n.* kroener *m.* -oryon

skinny *adj.* kroenek

skirt *n.* lostenn *f.* +ow

skit *n.* (wanton girl) skout *f.* +ys

skittle *n.* kil *m.* +ys, +yow

skua *n.* great skua gwagel *f.* +es

skulk *v.* skolkya

skull *n.* klopenn *m.* +ow, krogen *f.* kregyn, krogen an penn *f.;* horse's skull penn-glas *m.* pennow-glas; skull of animal penn-pral *m.* pennow-pral

sky *n.* ebrenn *f.*

skylark *n.* (bird) ahwesydh *m.* +es

slab *n.* legh *f.* +yon

slack *adj.* lows

slacken *v.* lowsel

slackness *n.* lowsedhes *m.*

slain *v.* ledhys

slake *v.* slake thirst terri syghes

slander *n.* sklander *m.: v.* sklandra

slap *n.* hwatt *m.* +ys, hwettya *m.*, stiwenn *m.: v.* boksusi, stiwenna

slapdash *adv.* hwymm-hwamm

slash *n.* lash *m.* +ys: *v.* hakkya

slate *n.* kyllas *c.*, leghenn *f.* +ow: *v.* ti

slater *n.* tior *m.* +yon

slaughter *n.* ladhva *f.*

slaughter-house *n.* latti *m.* +ow

slave *n.* (female) kethes *f.* +ow; (male) keth *m.* +yon

slavery n. kethneth f.
slay v. ladha
sledgehammer n. sloj m. slejys
sleep n. kosk m., hun m., hunes m.,
   koskas m.: v. koska, huna
sleeper n. koskador m. +yon
sleepless adj. digosk
sleeplessness n. difunedh m.
sleet n. erghlaw m.
sleeve n. breghel m. bregholow
sleeved adj. bregholek
sleigh n. draylell f. +ow
sleight n. sotelneth f.
slender adj. moen, ynn
sleuth n. helerghyas m. -ysi
slice n. lownyans m. +ow, tregh m.
   +ow: v. lownya, skethenna
slide n. slynk m. +ow: v. slynkya
slight n. skorn m.: adj. ydhyl
slim adj. moen
slime n. leys m. +yow, loub m.;
   green slime on stones linos coll.
slip n. (woman's undergarment)
   goelesenn f.: v. slynkya; slip
   out skapya
slipper n. pawgenn m. +ow
slippery adj. slynk
slip-road n. rybfordh f. +ow
sliver n. lown m. +yow, skether
   m.: v. lownya
slobber n. glavor m.: v. glaveri
sloes n. eyrin coll. +enn
slope n. leder f. ledrow, riw f.: v.
   ledra
sloping adj. ledrek
slops plur. golghyon, skoellyon
sloth n. diegi m., sygerneth f.
slothful adj. diek
slough n. lagenn f. +ow
slow adj. lent, hell, syger
slow-witted adj. penn-sogh
slow-worm n. anav m. +es
slug n. gluthvelhwenn f. +ow,
   melhwenn f.

sluggish adj. syger
sluggishness n. sygerneth f.
sluice n. ladres f. +ow
slumber n. hun m., hunes m.: v.
   huna
slush n. dowrergh m., teudhergh
   m.
smack n. hwatt m. +ys, hwettya m.
small adj. byghan: v. make smaller
   byghanhe
smaller adj. le
smallest adj. lyha
smallholding n. pastell-dir f.
smallpox n. brygh f. +i
smart v. gloesa
smell n. blas m.; bad smell fler m.
   +yow: v. blasa; (stink) flerya
smelt v. teudhi
smile n. minhwarth m.: v.
   minhwerthin
smith n. gov m. +yon
smithy n. govel f. +i
smock n. hevis m. +yow
smocking n. hevisweyth m.
smoke n. mog m.: v. megi
smoked adj. megys
smooth adj. gwastas, leven: v.
   kompoesa, levenhe, levna
smoothing-iron n. hornell f. +ow
smother v. megi
smoulder v. goleski
smuggler n. noswikor m. +yon
smuggling n. noswikorieth f.
smut n. hudhygel m.
snack n. kroust m. +yow
snail n. bulhorn m. +es,
   melhwesenn f. +ow coll.
   melhwes: v. catch snails
   melhwessa
snail-like adj. melhwesek
snake n. sarf f. serf
snap n. krakk m. +ys: v. krakkya:
   int. knakk

snare *n.* **antell** *f.* **antylli, krogenn**
 f., **maglenn** *f.* **+ow**
snarl *v.* **deskerni, grysla,**
 skrynkya; snarl at **deskerni orth**
snatch *v.* **kachya, kibya**
sneak *n.* **kilgi** *m.* **kilgeun, skolk** *m.*
 +yow: *v.* **skolkya**
sneeze *n.* **striw** *m.* **+yow:** *v.* **striwi,**
 rahaya
snipe *n.* **gaver hal** *f.,* **kiogh** *f.* **+yon**
snivel *v.* **mera**
sniveller *n.* **merek** *m.* **-ogyon**
snivelling *adj.* **goverek, merek,**
 purek
snore *n.* **ronk** *m.:* *v.* **hwyrni, renki**
snorer *n.* **renkyas** *m.* **-ysi**
snort *n.* **ronk** *m.:* *v.* **pyffya, renki**
snorter *n.* **renkyas** *m.* **-ysi**
snotty *adj.* **purek**
snout *n.* **troen** *m.* **-yow**
snow *n.* **ergh** *coll.*
snowdrift *n.* **tommenn ergh** *f.*
snowflake *n.* **erghenn** *f.* **+ow** *coll.*
 ergh
snowy *adj.* **erghek**
snuffers *n.* **gevel** *f.*
snuffling *adj.* **goverek**
snug *adj.* **klys:** *v.* make snug **klysa**
so *adj.* **kemmys;** so many **keniver;**
 so much **kemmys:** *conj.* **ytho;** so
 that **ma, may;** so that (before
 vowels) **mayth:** *adv.* **dell, mar**
soak *v.* **gwlyghi, segi, souba**
soap *n.* **sebon** *m.:* *v.* **seboni**
soap-opera *n.* **gwari-sebon** *m.*
soapwort *n.* **sebon-les** *f.*
soapy *adj.* **sebonus**
sober *adj.* **divedhow**
soccer *n.* **peldroes** *f.*
sociable *adj.* **kowethyadow**
society *n.* **kowethas** *m.* **+ow;** one
 of a society **esel** *m.* **eseli**
sock *n.* **lodrik** *m.* **-igow**

socket *n.* **kraw** *m.* **+yow;** eye socket
 kraw lagas *m.*
soda *n.* **soda** *m.*
soft *adj.* **medhel, blin, bludh;** (of
 sound) **isel**
soften *v.* **bludhya, medhelhe**
softness *n.* **medhelder** *m.*
software *n.* **daffar medhel** *m.,*
 medhelweyth *m.*
soil *n.* **dor** *m.,* **gweres** *m.* **+ow;** the
 soil **an dor** *m.:* *v.* **mostya**
soiled *adj.* **los**
sojourn *v.* **triga**
solace *n.* **hebaska** *m.,* **solas** *m.*
solder *n.* **soder** *m.:* *v.* **sodra**
soldier *n.* **marghek** *m.* **-ogyon,**
 souder *m.* **-oryon, soudrys**
sole *n.* (fish) **gorleythenn** *f.* **+ow**
 coll. **gorleyth;** (of foot) **godhen**
 m. **godhnow:** *adj.* **unn**
solemn *adj.* **solempna**
solemnity *n.* **solempnyta** *m.*
 -nytys
solicitor *n.* **laghyas** *m.* **-ysi,**
 laghyades *f.* **+ow, noter** *m.*
 -oryon
solicitous *adj.* **prederus**
solicitude *plur.* **fienasow**
solidarity *n.* **unnveredh** *m.;*
 Cornish Solidarity **Unnveredh**
 Kernewek *m.*
solitude *n.* **unnigedh** *m.*
solution *n.* **digolm** *m.,* **remedi** *m.*
solve *v.* **assoylya;** solve a problem
 digelmi
sombre *adj.* **du, tewl**
some *n.* **nebes** *m.:* *pron.* **neb, re**
someone *pron.* **nebonan**
somersault *n.* **kryghlamm** *m.*
 +ow: *v.* **kryghlemmel**
Somerset *place* **Gwlas an Hav**
something *pron.* **neppyth**
sometime *adv.* **nep-prys**
somewhat *adv.* **nebes;** somewhat
 long **nebes hir**

somewhere *adv.* **nep-tu**
son *n.* **mab** *m.* **mebyon**; mother's
son **mab bronn** *m.;* small son
meppik *m.* **-igow**; Sons of
Cornwall **Mebyon Kernow** *m.*
song *n.* **kan** *f.* **+ow**; choral song
keurgan *f.* **+ow**
son-in-law *n.* **deuv** *m.* **+yon**
soon *adv.* **skon**; as soon as **kettell**,
kettoeth
sooner *adv.* **kyns**
soot *n.* **hudhygel** *m.*
sooth *n.* **sodh** *m.*
soothe *v.* **hebaskhe, koselhe**
soothing *n.* **hebaska** *m.*
soothsayer *n.* **koelyek** *m.* **-ogyon**,
koelyoges *f.* **+ow**
sooty *adj.* **hudhyglek**
soprano *n.* **trebyl** *m.*
sorcerer *n.* **huder** *m.* **-oryon**,
pystrier *m.* **-oryon**
sorceress *n.* **hudores** *f.* **+ow**,
pystriores *f.* **+ow**
sorcery *n.* **pystri** *m.*
sore *n.* **goli** *m.* **+ow, gwennenn** *f.*
+ow; festering sore **podredhes**
m.: *adj.* **klav**; full of sores
podrek
soreness *v.* **brewvann**
sorrel *n.* **bara an gog** *m.*
sorrow *n.* **galar** *m.* **+ow, keudh** *m.*,
ahwer *m.*, **dughan** *m.*, **govijyon**
m., **moredh** *m.*, **tristans** *m.*,
tristyns *m.:* *plur.* **kavow**
sorry *adj.* **keudhesik**: *v.* make
sorry **keudhi**: *phr.* be sorry
kemmeres dughan; I am sorry
drog yw genev
sort *n.* **par** *m.* **+ow, eghenn** *f.*, **sort**
m. **+ow**: *v.* **digemmyska, sortya**
soul *n.* **enev** *m.* **+ow**
sound *n.* (noise) **son** *m.*
m. **+yow**; sound of surf **mordros**
m.: *adj.* (healthy) **yagh**; (safe)
saw: *v.* (of an instrument) **kana**,
seni

sounding *n.* (of instruments) **kenys**
m.
soundless *adj.* **dison**
soundness *n.* **sawes** *m.*
sound-recording *n.* **sonskrif** *m.*
+ow: *v.* make a sound-recording
sonskrifa
soup *n.* **iskell** *m.*, **kowl** *m.* **+ow**,
soubenn *f.* **+ow**
soup-bowl *n.* **skudell** *f.* **+ow**
source *n.* (of stream) **pennfenten** *f.*
-tynyow, penngover *m.* **+yow**
sourness *n.* **trenkter** *m.*
South *n.* **deghow** *m.*, **Soth** *m.:*
adv. on the South side **a-**
dheghowbarth
southernwood *n.* **deghowles** *f.*
souvenir *n.* **kovro** *m.* **kovrohow**
sovereign *n.* **myghtern** *m.* **+edh**,
maghtern *m.* **+yow, sovran** *m.:*
adj. **sovran**
sovereignty *n.* **myghternses** *m.*,
sovranedh *m.*
sow *n.* (pig) **banow** *f.* **bynewi, gwis**
f. **+i**: *v.* **hasa**
sower *n.* **gonador** *m.* **+yon**
sow-thistle *n.* **lethegenn** *f.* **+ow**
coll. **lethek**
space *n.* **spas** *m.;* (Astron.)
efanvos *m.;* (in general) **efander**
m.
spacious *adj.* **efan**
spade *n.* **pal** *f.* **+yow**
spaghetti *n.* **spagetti** *coll.*
Spain *place* **Spayn**
span *n.* (unit of length) **dornva** *f.*
dornvedhi
spangles *plur.* **golowylyon**
Spaniard *n.* **Spayner** *m.* **-oryon**
spaniel *n.* **spaynel** *m.* **+s**
Spanish *n.* Spanish language
Spaynek *m.:* *adj.* **Spaynek**
spanner *n.* **alhwedh-know** *f.*
alhwedhow-know
sparable *n.* **sparbyl** *m.*

spare *plur.* spares **sparyon**: *v.*
  sparya
spark *n.* **elvenn** *f.* **+ow,**
  gwryghonenn *f.* **+ow** *coll.*
  gwrygh
sparkle *v.* **sterenni**
sparkler *n.* (firework) **elvennell** *f.*
  +ow
spark-plug *n.* **kantol** *f.* **+yow**
sparrow *n.* **golvan** *m.* **+es**
spasm *n.* **skwych** *m.* **+ys, gloes** *f.*
  +ow
spatter *v.* spatter with filth **kagla**
spatterdashes *n.* **polltrigas** *m.*
spatula *n.* **lo** *f.* **loyow, spadell** *f.*
  +ow
spay *v.* **spadha**
spayed *adj.* **spadh**
speak *v.* **kewsel, medhes**; speak
  hoarsely **hosi**; speak to **kewsel**
  orth; speak under one's breath
  hanasa
speaker *n.* **leveryas** *m.* **-ysi,**
  medher *m.* **-oryon**; public speaker
  arethor *m.* **-oryon**
speaking *n.* **kows** *m.* **+ow**; way of
  speaking **yeth** *f.* **+ow**: *v.* cease
  speaking **tewel**
spear *n.* **gyw** *m.* **+ow**: *v.* **gywa**
special *adj.* **arbennik**
specialism *n.* **arbennikter** *m.*
specialist *n.* **arbenniger** *m.* **-oryon**
speciality *n.* **arbennikter** *m.*
specialize *v.* **arbennigi**
specially *adj.* **yn arbennik**
species *n.* **eghenn** *f.*
specimen *n.* fine specimen **flourenn**
  f. **+ow**
speckled *adj.* **brygh**
speckled hen *n.* **spekkyar** *f.*
spectacles *n.* **dewweder**
spectral *adj.* (of ghosts)
  tarosvannus; (of spectra)
  kammnevesel
spectre *n.* **tarosvann** *m.* **+ow**

spectrum *n.* **kammneves** *f.*
speculate *v.* **aventurya, desevos**
speech *n.* **kows** *m.* **+ow, lavar** *m.*
  +ow, areth *f.;* formal speech
  pregoth *m.* **+ow**; manner of speech
  kowsans *m.:* *v.* make a noisy
  speech **predheges**; make a speech
  arethya
speechless *adj.* **avlavar**
speed *n.* **toeth** *m.;* high speed **toeth**
  bras *m.,* **toeth da** *m.;* high speed
  train **tren toeth bras (T.T.B.)** *m.:*
  adv. at full speed **toeth men**: *phr.*
  God speed **Dyw gweres**
speed-limit *n.* **finwedh-doeth** *f.*
speedometer *n.* **musurell-doeth** *f.*
  musurellow-toeth
spell *n.* (period of time) **kors** *m.:* *v.*
  lytherenna
spelling *n.* **lytherennans** *m.* **+ow**
spend *v.* **spena**
spendthrift *n.* **skoellyek** *m.*
  -ogyon
sperm *n.* **has** *coll.* **+enn**
sphere *n.* **pel** *f.* **+yow**
spice *n.* **spis** *m.* **+ys, +yow**
spicer *n.* **spiser** *m.* **-oryon, +s**
spider *n.* **kevnisenn** *f.* **+ow** *coll.*
  kevnis, gwiader *m.* **-oryon**
spider-crab *n.* **gevrik** *f.* **-igow,**
  gryll *m.* **+es, krygell** *f.,* **pilyek** *m.*
  pilyogyon
spigot *n.* **kanell** *m.*
spike *n.* **kenter** *f.* **kentrow, kolgh**
  m. **+ow**: *v.* drive in a spike **kentra**
spikenard *n.* **spiknard** *m.*
spill *v.* **skoellya**
spin *n.* **troyll** *m.* **+yow**: *v.* **rosella**;
  (of yarn) **nedha**; spin around
  troyllya; spin out time **strechya**
spinach *n.* **spinach** *m.*
spine *n.* **dren** *m.* **dreyn**
spinner *n.* **nedher** *m.* **-oryon,**
  nedhores *f.* **+ow**
spinney *n.* **dreynek** *f.* **-egi,**
  dreyngoes *m.* **+ow**

spiral *n.* **korhwyth** *m.* **+ow**
spire *n.* **peul** *m.* **+yow**
spirit *n.* **spyrys** *m.* **+yon**
spirits *n.* ardent alcoholic spirits
  gwires *f.* **gwirosow**
spit *n.* roasting spit **ber** *m.* **+yow:** *v.*
  trewa, berya
spite *n.* **atti** *m.,* **spit** *m.:* *conj.* in
  spite of **awos, yn despit dhe, spit**
  dhe: *v.* **despitya, spitya**
spiteful *adj.* **spitus**
spittle *n.* **trew** *m.*
splash *v.* **kaboli, lagenna, lagya;**
  make a great splash **plowghya**
splay *v.* **displewyas**
spleen *n.* **felgh** *f.*
splendid *adj.* **splann, bryntin**
spline *n.* **skarf** *m.:* *v.* **skarfa**
splint *n.* **astell** *f.* **estyll**
splinter *n.* **askloesenn** *f.* **+ow** *coll.*
  askloes, skether *m.,* **skethrenn** *f.*
  +ow, skommynn *m.,* **skyrenn** *f.*
  +ow *coll.* **skyr;** little splinter
  skethrik *m.:* *v.* **askloesi**
splintered *adj.* **skethrek**
split *n.* **fols** *m.* **+yow:** *adj.* **felsys:**
  v. **folsa;** split fragments **kriba**
spoil *n.* (plunder) **preydh** *m.:* *v.*
  diswul, pylla
spoke *n.* spoke of wheel **asenn** *f.*
  +ow
spoken *n.* **der anow** *m.:* *adj.* well
  spoken of **geryes da**
spokeshave *n.* **raskel** *f.* **rasklow**
sponge *n.* **spong** *m.* **+ow:** *v.*
  spongya
spoon *n.* **lo** *f.* **loyow**
spoonful *n.* **loas** *f.* **+ow**
sport *n.* **sport** *m.* **+ow, +ys:** *v.*
  sportya
spot *n.* (location) **tyller** *m.* **+yow;**
  (pimple) **namm** *m.* **+ow;** red spot
  on skin **kuryek** *m.* **-ogyon;** white
  spot on forehead **ball** *m.:* *adv.* on
  the very spot **stag**
spot (location) *n.* **le** *m.* **leow**

spotless *adj.* **kler, dinamm**
spouse *n.* **kespar** *m.* **+ow, pries** *m.*
  priosow
spout *n.* **pistyll** *m.* **+ow:** *v.*
  pistylla
sprat *n.* **hernenn vyghan** *f.* **hern**
  byghan
spread *n.* **lesans** *m.:* *v.* **lesa;**
  (intrans.) **omlesa**
spring *n.* (coil) **torgh** *f.* **tergh;**
  (season) **gwenton** *m.;* (water)
  fenten *f.* **fentynyow;** spring tide
  reverthi *f.*
springe *n.* **krogenn** *f.,* **kroglath** *f.*
  +ow
sprinter *n.* **belaber** *m.*
sprout *n.* **egin** *m.* **+yow, lows** *m.;*
  (Brussels) **kowlennik** *f.* **-igow,**
  kowlik *m.* **-igow;** (of plant)
  skyllenn *f.* **+ow** *coll.* **skyll**
spue *v.* **hwyja**
spur *n.* (for boot) **kentrynn** *m.* **+ow;**
  (topographic) **ros** *m.* **+yow:** *v.*
  kentrynna
spur-dog *n.* (fish) **drenek** *m.*
  -ogyon
spurge *n.* **flammgoes** *m.*
spur-shaped *adj.* **kentrek**
sputum *n.* **trewyas** *m.*
spy *n.* **aspier** *m.* **-oryon, aspiyas**
  m. **aspiysi:** *v.* **aspia;** spy on
  aspia orth
squad *n.* **para** *m.* **parys, parsel** *m.*
  +s
squalid *adj.* **los**
squall *n.* **kowas gwyns** *f.*
squander *v.* **skoellya, wastya**
square *adj.* **pedrek, pedrek -ogow**
squash *v.* **skwatya**
squat *v.* **plattya**
squeak *n.* **gwigh** *m.* **+yow, mik** *m.:*
  v. **gwighal**
squeegee *n.* squeegee mop
  gwaskubyllenn *f.* **+ow**
squeeze *v.* **gwaska, gwrynya,**
  strotha

squid *n.* **stifek** *m.*

squirm *v.* **gwynnel**

squirrel *n.* **gwiwer** *m.* **-ow**

squirt *n.* **skit** *m.,* **stif** *f.* **+ow**: *v.*
skitya, stifa

St Austell *place* **Sen Ostell**

St Ives *place* **Porthia**

St John's wort *n.* **losowenn Sen
Yowann** *f.*

stab *n.* **gwan** *f.* **+yow, pych** *m.:* *v.*
gwana, pychya; stab oneself
omwana

stability *n.* **faster** *m.*

stable *n.* **marghti** *m.* **+ow**

stable-lad *n.* **paja mergh** *m.*

stack *n.* **bern** *m.,* **das** *f.* **deys**: *v.*
bernya, dasa

stadium *n.* **sportva** *f.* **+ow**

staff *n.* (group of workers) **meni** *m.;*
(rod) **lath** *f.* **+ow, lorgh** *f.* **+ow**;
pastoral staff **bagel** *f.* **baglow**

stag *n.* **karow** *m.* **kerwys**

stage-coach *n.* **kocha** *m.* **kochow,
kochys**

stair *n.* **gradh** *m.* **+ow, gris** *m.*
+yow, +ys

stake *n.* **peul** *m.* **+yow, stykkenn** *f.*
+ow: *v.* **stykkenna**

stake-net *n.* **kidell** *m.* **+ow**

stakes *n.* enclosure of stakes to trap
fish **kores** *f.* **+ow**

stalk *n.* **garr** *f.* **+ow**

stall *n.* **stall** *m.* **+ow**

stallion *n.* **margh** *m.* **mergh,
margh kellek** *m.*

stalwart *adj.* **men**

stamina *n.* **nerthegeth** *f.*

stamp *n.* (of foot) **stank** *m.:* *v.*
stampya; (with foot) **stankya,
trettya**

stamping-mill *plur.* **stampys**

stance *n.* **sav** *m.*

stand *n.* **sav** *m.:* *v.* **sevel**; stand
against **sevel orth**; stand as a
candidate **ombrofya**; stand bail

mewghya; stand by **mentena**;
stand upright **serthi**

stand up *phr.* **sa'bann**

standard *n.* **nivel** *m.* **+yow, savon**
f. **+ow**; (basis of comparison) **skwir**
m. **+ys**: *adj.* **savonek**

standard-bearer *n.* **baneror** *m.*
+yon

standardise *v.* **savonegi**

stand-off *n.* **stagsav** *m.* **+ow**

standpoint *n.* **savla** *m.* **savleow**

standstill *n.* **gorsav** *m.* **+ow**

stannous *adj.* **stenus**

star *n.* **sterenn** *f.* **+ow** *coll.* **ster**;
little star **sterennik** *f.* **-igow**: *v.* (in
film) **sterenni**

stare *v.* **lagatta**

starer *n.* **lagatter** *m.* **-oryon**

starfish *n.* **pympbys** *m.*

starlight *n.* **stergann** *m.*

starling *n.* **troes** *m.,* **troesenn** *f.*

starry *adj.* **sterennek**

start *n.* **dalleth** *m.,* **derow** *m.*

startle *v.* **amovya**

starvation *n.* **nown** *m.,* **divoetter**
m., **famyans** *m.*

starve *v.* (intrans.) **famya**

state *n.* **studh** *m.* **+yow**; (political)
stat *m.* **+ow, +ys**: *v.* **derivas**

station *n.* **degre** *m.* **degrys**;
(railway or bus) **gorsav** *m.* **+ow**;
police station **soedhva greslu** *f.;*
power station **tredanva** *f.;*
underground station **gorsav yn-
dann dhor** *m.*

statue *n.* **delow** *m.* **+yow**

status *n.* **gre** *m.* **+ys, savla** *m.*
savleow

staunch *adj.* **stanch**

stave *n.* stave of barrel **asenn** *f.* **+ow**

stay *n.* **trigas** *m.* **+ow**; short stay
godrik *m.* **-igow**: *v.* **gortos,
sevel, triga**; (at a hotel, etc.)
ostya; stay for a short time
godriga

steadfast *adj.* **fyrv, sad**

steal *v.* **ladra**
steam *n.* **ethenn** *f.* **+ow**
steam-boat *n.* **gorhel-tan** *m.*
  gorholyon-tan
steam-engine *n.* **jynn-ethenn** *m.*
  jynnow-ethenn
steam-roller *n.* **jynn-rolya** *m.*
  jynnow-rolya
steel *n.* **dur** *m.*
steep *adj.* very steep **deserth, krakk**
  y gonna
steep *adj.* **serth**
steep *v.* **segi, souba**
steeple *n.* **tour** *m.* **+yow, kleghtour**
  m. **+yow, peul** *m.* **+yow**
steepness *n.* **serthter** *m.*
steer *n.* **lodhen** *m.* **lodhnow, lo'n**
  m. **+ow;** inadequately castrated
  steer **ryjer** *m.:* *v.* **lywya**
steering *n.* steering wheel **ros lywya**
  f.
steersman *n.* **lywyader** *m.* **-oryon**
stem *n.* **garr** *f.* **+ow**
stench *n.* **fler** *m.* **+yow, flerynsi** *m.*
step *n.* **gradh** *m.* **+ow, gris** *m.*
  +yow, +ys, kamm *m.* **+ow, pas**
  m. **+ys**
step-brother *n.* **les-vroder** *m.*
  -vreder
step-child *n.* **les-flogh** *m.* **-fleghes**
step-daughter *n.* **elses** *f.* **+ow,**
  les-vyrgh *f.* **+es**
step-father *n.* **altrow** *m.* **+yon,**
  les-tas *m.* **+ow**
step-mother *n.* **altrewan** *f.,* **les-**
  vamm *f.* **+ow**
step-sister *n.* **les-hwoer** *f.*
  -hwerydh
step-son *n.* **els** *m.* **+yon, les-vab**
  m. **-vebyon**
sterile *adj.* **gownagh**
sterility *n.* **anvabas** *m.*
sterling *n.* **sterlyn** *m.:* *adj.* **sterlyn**
stern *n.* **delergh** *m.:* *adj.* **asper**
stern-deck *n.* **aros** *m.* **+yow**

stew *n.* **bros** *m.* **+ow:** *v.* **bryjyon**
  yn kosel
steward *n.* **mer-boes** *m.* **meryon-**
  boes, rennyas *m.* **-ysi**
stewardship *n.* **gwithyans** *m.*
stick *v.* **glena, glusa, klyjya;** stick
  to **glena orth**
sticker *n.* **glenysenn** *f.* **+ow**
stickleback *n.* **keyndreynek** *m.*
  -oges
sticky *adj.* **glusek**
stiff *adj.* **diwedhyn**
stiffness *n.* **diwedhynder** *m.*
stifle *v.* **megi, taga**
stile *n.* **kammva** *f.* **+ow**
still *adv.* **hwath, hogen;** still more
  bydh moy
stillness *n.* **kalmynsi** *m.,* **kosoleth**
  f.
stimulant *n.* **piger** *m.* **+yow**
stimulus *n.* **bros** *m.* **+ow**
sting *n.* **bros** *m.* **+ow:** *v.* **brosa,**
  gwana, piga, pigas
stingy *adj.* **pith**
stink *n.* **fler** *m.* **+yow:** *v.* **flerya,**
  mosegi
stinkard *n.* **flerys** *m.*
stinking *adj.* **flerys, mosek**
stir *v.* **kaboli, treylouba;** (move)
  gwaya; stir up **sordya**
stirrer *n.* **kaboler** *m.* **-oryon**
stirrup *n.* **gwarthol** *f.* **-yow**
stitch *n.* **gwri** *m.* **+ow;** (of land) **len**
  m.: *v.* **brosya, gwrias, sewya;**
  stitch roughly **krafa**
stitcher *n.* **brosyer** *m.* **-oryon,**
  brosyores *f.* **+ow, gwriador** *m.*
  +yon, sewyas *m.* **-ysi**
stoat *n.* **yewgenn** *m.*
stock *n.* **iskell kig** *m.,* **stokk** *m.*
  +ys, +ow
stocking *n.* **loder** *m.* **lodrow,**
  hosenn *f.* **+ow** *coll.* **hos**

stocks *n.* **karghar-prenn** *m.:* *v.* put
in stocks **karghara**: *adv.* in the
stocks **y'n stokkys**

stoker *n.* **foger** *m.* **-oryon**

stole *n.* **stol** *f.* **+yow**

stolen *adj.* **ledrys**

stomach *n.* **torr** *f.* **+ow, glas** *m.*,
penngasenn *f.;* (of animal)
agenn *f.*

stone *n.* **men** *m.* **meyn**; (in body)
mantedhenn *f.* **+ow** *coll.*
mantedh; flat stone **legh** *f.* **+yon**;
foundation stone **selven** *m.*
selveyn; holed stone **tollven** *m.*
tollveyn; loose stones **radell** *m.;*
splashing stone **kabolenn** *f.;*
standing stone **menhir** *m.* **-yon**,
peulvan *m.* **+ow**; stone circle
dons meyn *m.;* thin flat stone
leghenn *f.* **+ow**: *plur.* individual
stones **menow**; the stones **an
veyn**: *v.* **labydha**; turn to stone
menhe

stonechat *n.* **chekker** *m.* **chekkres**

stone-house *n.* **meyndi** *m.*

stone-mason *n.* **ser men** *m.* **seri
men**

stonework *n.* **menweyth** *m.*

stool *n.* **skavell** *f.* **+ow**

stoop *v.* **gwarrgromma**

stooping *adj.* **gwarrgromm**

stop *v.* (intrans.) **hedhi**; (trans.)
stoppya; stop a cheque **lettya
chekkenn**; stop oneself **omlettya**:
int. **hedh, ho**

stoppage *n.* stoppage of work **astel-
ober** *m.*

stopper *n.* **ebil** *m.* **+yow, stoppyer**
m. **+s**

store-cellar *n.* **talgell** *f.* **+ow**

storehouse *n.* **gwithva** *f.* **+ow**

storey *n.* **leur** *m.* **+yow**

stork *n.* **hwibon** *m.*

storm *n.* **tewedh** *m.;* storm damage
arnow *m.*

story *n.* **hwedhel** *m.* **hwedhlow,
drolla** *m.* **drollow**; amusing story
rakka *m.* **rakkow**: *plur.* stories
hwedhlow

story-teller *n.* **rakker** *m.* **-oryon**

stove *n.* **forn** *f.* **+ow**

straddle *v.* **garrgamma**

straight *adj.* **ewn**: *adv.* straight
away **distowgh**

straight-edge *n.* **linennell** *f.* **+ow**

straighten out *v.* **digamma**

straightway *adv.* **dison, sket**

strain *v.* **sidhla**

strainer *n.* **sidhel** *m.* **sidhlow**

strait *n.* **kulvor** *m.*

strand *n.* **treth** *m.* **+ow**

strange *adj.* **estren, koynt,
ankoth, astranj, revedh**

stranger *n.* **estren** *m.* **+yon,
estrenes** *f.* **+ow, den ankoth** *m.*

strangle *v.* **taga**

strangulation *n.* **tag** *m.*

strap *n.* **kroen** *m.* **+ow**; leather
strap **ledhrenn** *m.*

stratum *n.* **gweli** *m.* **+ow**

straw *n.* **gwelenn-gala** *f.*
gwelynni-kala, kalavenn *f.* **+ow**
coll. **kala**; (in bulk) **kala** *coll.;*
straw bedding **kala-gweli** *coll.*

strawberry *n.* **sevienn** *f.* **+ow** *coll.*
sevi: *v.* pick strawberries **sevia**

strawberry-bed *n.* **seviek** *f.* **-egi**

stray *v.* **gwandra, sowdhanas**

straying *n.* **sowdhan** *m.*

streak *n.* **linenn** *f.* **+ow, ribin** *m.*
+ow

streaked *adj.* **brith**

stream *n.* **fros** *m.* **+ow, gover** *m.*
+ow, goeth *f.* **+ow, stredh** *f.*
+ow; place abounding in streams
goethek *f.* **-egi**; silvery stream
arghantell *f.;* winding stream
koger *m.:* *v.* **frosa**

streamlet *n.* **goverik** *m.* **-igow**

streamwork *n.* streamwork for tin
hal *f.* **halow**

street *n.* **stret** *m.* **+ow, +ys**; little
street **stretynn** *m.* **+ow**

strength *n.* **nerth** *m.* **+yow, fors**
m., **krevder** *m.,* **nell** *m.*

strengthen *v.* **krevhe**; (a person)
nertha

strenuous *adj.* **nerthek**

stress *n.* **gwask** *f.;* (emphasis)
poeslev *m.* **+ow**; (quantity in
physics) **gwaskedh** *m.: v.*
poesleva

stretch *v.* stretch apart **displewyas**;
stretch oneself **omystynna**

stretcher *n.* (for carrying) **gravath**
m. **+ow**; (wooden beam) **tenn** *m.*
+ow

strict *adj.* **straght, stroth, tynn**

stride *n.* **braskamm** *m.* **+ow**: *v.*
braskamma

strife *n.* **bresel** *f.* **+yow, strif** *m.*
+ow

strike *n.* **astel-ober** *m.;* (suspension
of work) **astel** *m.:* (hit) *v.*
gweskel; *v.* strike oneself
omweskel

striker *n.* **astelyer** *m.* **-yoryon**

string *n.* **kordenn** *f.* **kerdyn,
linenn** *f.* **+ow, funenn** *f.* **+ow**;
string of onions **plethenn onyon** *f.*

stringent *adj.* **stroth**

stringently *adv.* **dour**

strip *n.* **ribin** *m.* **+ow, sketh** *m.*
+ow, skethenn *f.* **+ow**; (of land)
len *m.;* narrow strip of land **konna**
m. **+ow**: *v.* **destrypya, pilya**;
strip bare **lommhe**

striped *adj.* **brith, labol**

stripling *n.* **glaswas** *m.* **-wesyon**

strive *v.* **omdhal, strivya**; strive
against **offendya**

stroke *n.* **boemmenn** *f.* **+ow,
kronk** *m.* **+ys, lash** *m.* **+ys,
strekys** *f.* **strokosow**; (of hand)
palvas *m.* **+ow**: *v.* **tava, handla,
palva**

stroll *n.* **rosyas** *m.: v.* stroll around
rosya

stroller *n.* **roser** *m.* **-oryon**

strong *adj.* **krev, men**: *v.* make
strong **krevhe**

strong-backed *adj.* **keynek**

strong-box *n.* **kofer horn** *m.*

strongly *adv.* **yn fen**

strop *n.* **raw** *f.* **+yow**

structure *n.* **framweyth** *m.*

struggle *v.* **gwynnel**

strut *v.* **payoni**

stub *n.* **kyf** *m.,* **stokkynn** *f.* **+ow**;
(of ticket) **gorthdhelenn** *f.* **+ow**

stubble *n.* **arys** *m.;* stubble field
sowlek *f.* **-egi**

stubbly *adj.* **sowlek**

stubborn *adj.* **gorth, penn-kales**

stubbornness *n.* **gorthter** *m.,* **her**
m.

stud *n.* (animals) **gre** *f.* **+ow**; collar
stud **garrvoth** *f.* **+ow**

student *n.* **studhyer** *m.*
studhyoryon, skolheyk *m.*
skolheygyon

studio *n.* **studhla** *m.* **-leow**

studious *adj.* **studhyus**

study *n.* (room) **studhva** *f.* **+ow**: *v.*
studhya

stuff *n.* **devnydh** *m.* **+yow, stoff**
m.: v. **gwalgha, stoffya**

stumble *v.* **omdhisevel,
trebuchya**

stump *n.* **ben** *m.* **+yow, kyf** *m.,*
stokk *m.* **+ys, +ow**

stun *v.* **basa**

stupefaction *n.* **sowdhan** *m.*

stupendous *adj.* **gorvarthys**

stupid *adj.* **gokki, penn-sogh, tal-
sogh**

stupidity *n.* **gokkineth** *f.,* **muskogneth** *f.*

sturdy *adj.* **stordi**

sty *n.* **krow** *m.* **+yow**

style *n.* **gis** *m.,* **kor** *m.* **+ow**; (literary) **gis-skrifa** *m.*

suave *adj.* **melgennek**

sub- *pref.* **is-**

sub-committee *n.* **iskessedhek** *m.* **-ogow**

subdue *v.* **tempra**

subject *n.* **mater** *m.* **+s, +ow**; (e.g. of a king) **sojet** *m.* **+s**; (of study) **testenn** *f.* **+ow**: *adj.* **keth**: *v.* subjektya

sublime *adj.* **gorughel**

submarine *n.* **lester-sedhi** *m.* **lestri-sedhi**

submerge *v.* **sedhi**

submissive *adj.* **gostyth, hwar**

submit *v.* **obaya, omblegya,** submyttya

subscribe *v.* **ragbrena**

subscriber *n.* **ragbrener** *m.* **-oryon**

subscription *n.* **ragbren** *m.*

subservient *adj.* **gostyth**

subside *v.* **omsedhi**

subsistence *n.* **sosten** *m.*

subsoil *n.* undug subsoil **kothenn** *f.*

substance *n.* **stoff** *m.,* **substans** *m.*

sub-standard *adj.* **issavonek**

substructure *n.* **isframweyth** *m.*

subterfuge *n.* **kavanskeus** *m.,* **keladow** *m.,* **wrynch** *m.*

subtilize *v.* **sotla**

subtitle *n.* **istitel** *m.* **istitlow**: *v.* istitla

subtle *adj.* **sotel**

sub-tropical *adj.* **istrovannel**

suburb *n.* **mestra** *f.* **+ow, ranndra** *f.*

suburban *adj.* **mestrevek**

subversive *adj.* **domhwelus**

subvert *v.* **domhwel**

subway *n.* **kowfordh** *f.* **+ow**; (underground walkway) **konvayour** *m.*

subway station (U.S.) *n.* **gorsav yn-dann dhor** *m.*

succeed *v.* **seweni, spedya**

success *n.* **sewena** *f.,* **sewenyans** *m.*

successful *adj.* **sewen**

succession *n.* **rew** *m.* **+yow**

successor *n.* **sywyas** *m.* **-ysi**

succour *n.* **sokor** *m.:* *v.* **sokra**

succulent *adj.* **sugnus**

such *phr.* such people **tus a'n par na**

suck *v.* **dena, sugna**

sucking-pig *n.* **porghellik** *m.* **-igow**

suckle *n.* **ri bronn** *f.:* *v.* **bronna**

suction *n.* **sugnans** *m.*

sudden *adj.* **desempis, tromm**

suddenly *adv.* **a-dhesempis,** **distowgh**

suddenness *n.* **trommder** *m.*

suds *plur.* **golghyon**

suet *n.* **soev** *m.*

suffer *v.* **godhav, godhevel**

sufferer *n.* (female) **godhevyades** *f.* **+ow**; (male) **godhevyas** *m.* **-ysi**

suffering *n.* **dughan** *m.,* **godhevyans** *m.*

sufficiently *adv.* **lowr**

sugar *n.* **sugra** *m.:* *v.* **sugra**; sweeten with sugar **sugra**

suggest *v.* **profya**

suggestion *n.* **profyans** *m.*

suicide *v.* commit suicide **omladha**

suit *n.* suit of cards **sewt** *m.*

suitability *n.* **gwiwder** *m.* **+yow**

suitable *adj.* **gwiw, 'vas**: *v.* is suitable **delledh**

suitor *n.* **tanter** *m.* **-oryon**

sulk *v.* **moutya**

sullen *adj.* **talgamm**

sulphur *n.* **loskven** *m.*

sulphuric *adj.* **loskvenek**
sulphurous *adj.* **loskvenus**
Sultan *n.* **sodon** *m.* **+ys**
sultry *adj.* **poes, tesek**
sum *n.* **somm** *m.*, **sommenn** *f.* **+ow**
summarize *v.* **berrskrifa**
summary *n.* **berrskrif** *m.* **+ow**
summer *n.* **hav** *m.* **+ow**: *v.* pass
the summer **havi**
summer-fallow *n.* **havar** *m.*
summer-time *n.* **havas** *m.*
summery *adj.* **havek**
summit *n.* **gwartha** *m.*, **penn** *m.*
+ow, barr *m.* **+ow, topp** *m.* **+ys;**
summit conference **keskusulyans
barrek** *m.*
summon *v.* **gelwel**
summons *n.* **galow** *m.*
sumptuous *adj.* **rych**
Sun *n.* **Howl** *m.*
sunbathe *v.* **omhowla**
Sunday *n.* **dy' Sul** *m.*, **Sul** *m.*
+yow; (time) **Sulweyth** *m.;* Low
Sunday **Pask Byghan** *m.: adv.* on
a Sunday **Sulweyth**
sundew *n.* **eyles** *m.*
sun-glasses *plur.* **howlwedrow**
sunlight *n.* **Howl** *m.*, **howlsplann**
m.
sunny *adj.* **howlyek**
Sunrise *n.* **Howldrevel** *m.*,
Howldrehevel *m.*
Sunset *n.* **howlsedhes** *m.;* noon to
sunset **dohajydh** *m.*
sunshade *n.* **howllenn** *f.* **+ow**
sunshine *n.* **Howl** *m.*, **howlsplann**
m.
sunstroke *n.* **towl-howl** *m.*
sup *n.* **lommenn** *f.* **+ow**: *v.* **eva,
sopya, soubenna**
superabundance *n.* **gorfalster** *m.*
superabundant *adj.* **gorfals**
superior *adj.* **trygh**
superiority *n.* **ughelder** *m.* **+yow**

supermarket *n.* **gorvarghas** *f.*
+ow
superstition *n.* **euvergryjyans** *m.*,
hegoeledh *m.*
superstitious *adj.* **euvergryjyk,
hegoel**
superstructure *n.* **ughframweyth**
m.
supper *n.* **boes soper** *m.*, **soper** *m.*
supple *adj.* **gwedhyn, hebleth**
supplement *n.* **ystynnans** *m.* **+ow;**
literary supplement **ystynnans
lyennek** *m.*
suppleness *n.* **gwedhynder** *m.*
supplication *n.* **pysadow** *m.*
supplier *n.* **proviyas** *m.* **-ysi**
supply *v.* **darbari, provia**
support *n.* **konfort** *m.;* (abst.)
skoedhyans *m.: v.* **skoedhya,
konfortya**
supporter *n.* **mentenour** *m.* **-s,
skoedhyer** *m.* **-oryon**
suppose *v.* **tybi, desevos**
suppress *v.* **suppressya**
suppurate *v.* **gori**
suppuration *n.* **gor** *m.*
supreme *adj.* **gorughel**
sure *adj.* **sur, kowgans**: *v.* be sure
to **gwaytya, gwitha**
surely *adv.* **sur;** most surely
surredi
surety *n.* **gwystel** *m.* **gwystlow**
surf *n.* **mordardh** *m.;* sound of surf
mordros *m.: v.* **mordardha**
surface *n.* **enep** *m.* **enebow,
bejeth** *f.* **+ow**
surfeit *n.* **gorfalster** *m.*
surge *n.* surge of sea **hwythfians** *m.*
surgery *n.* (place) **medhygva** *f.*
+ow
surly *adj.* **deskernus**
surpass *v.* **passya**
surplice *n.* **kams** *f.* **+ow**
surprise *n.* **marth** *m.* **+ow**: *v.*
sowdhanas

surreal *adj.* **gorwir**

surrender *v.* **hepkorr, obaya, omdhaskorr, omri**

surroundings *n.* **kyrghynn** *m.*

surveyor *n.* (for map-making) **musuryas** *m.* **-ysi**

susceptibility *n.* **gostythter** *m.*

susceptible *adj.* **gostyth**

suspend *v.* **kregi, astel**

suspension *n.* **kregyans** *m.*, **krog** *f.* **+ow**

suspicion *n.* **gogrys** *m.*

sustain *v.* **sostena**

sustenance *n.* **megyans** *m.*, **sosten** *m.*

suzerain *n.* **gwarthevyas** *m.* **-ysi**

suzeraine *n.* **gwarthevyades** *f.* **+ow**

swaddling-band *n.* **lystenn** *f.* **+ow**

swagger *v.* **payoni**

swallow *v.* **lenki**; swallow down **daslenki, kollenki**

swallow *n.* (bird) **gwennel** *f.* **gwennili**

swamp *v.* **liva**

swan *n.* **alargh** *m.* **elergh**

swarm *n.* **hes** *f.* **+ow**; first swarm **kyns-hes** *f.*; second swarm **tarow-hes** *f.*; third swarm **lost-hes** *f.*: *v.* **hesya**

swarming *n.* **hevva** *f.*

swarthy *adj.* **mindu**

swathe *n.* **dramm** *f.* **+ow**: *v.* **maylya**

swear *v.* **ti**

sweat *n.* **hwys** *m.*: *v.* **hwysa**

sweatshirt *n.* **krys hwys** *m.*

sweat-shop *n.* **hwysti** *m.* **+ow**

sweep *v.* **skuba**; sweep up leaves **delyowa**

sweepings *n.* **skubyon** *coll.*

sweet *n.* **hwegynn** *m.* **+ow**: *adj.* **hweg**; very sweet **melys**

sweetest *adj.* **hwegoll**

sweetheart *n.* **keresik** *m.* **-igyon, kuv kolonn** *m.*

sweeting *n.* **hwegenn** *f.* **+ow**

sweetness *n.* **hwekter** *m.*, **melder** *m.*

swell *v.* **hwythfi, ynkressya**; swell up **kwoffi**

swelling *n.* **bothenn** *m.*, **hwythfians** *m.*

swerve *v.* **swarvya**

swift *adj.* **skav**

swig *n.* **swynnenn** *f.* **+ow**

swim *v.* **neuvya**

swimmer *n.* **neuvyer** *m.* **-yoryon**

swimwear *n.* **neuvwisk** *m.*

swindle *n.* **fug** *m.*, **hyg** *f.*

swindler *n.* **faytour** *m.* **+s**

swine *n.* **hogh** *m.* **-es**: *plur.* swine (pl.) **mogh**

swineherd *n.* **bugel mogh** *m.*

swing *n.* **lesk** *m.* **+ow**; (plaything) **lesk-lovan** *m.* **leskow-lovan**: *v.* **leska**; (e.g. one's arms, or a golf club) **swaysya**

switch *n.* (electric) **skwychell** *f.* **+ow**: *v.* **skwychya**; switch off **ladha, skwychya yn farow**; switch on **skwychya yn fyw**

sword *n.* **kledha** *m.* **kledhedhyow**: *v.* wield a sword **kledhya**

sword-dance *n.* **dons-kledha** *m.*

swordsman *n.* (amateur) **kledhevor** *m.* **+yon**; (professional) **kledhevyas** *m.* **-ysi**

sycamore-tree *n.* **skawenn-wragh** *f.* **skawennow-gwragh** *coll.* **skaw-gwragh**

syllable *n.* **syllabenn** *f.* **+ow**

syllabus *n.* **dyskevres** *m.* **+ow**

symbol *n.* **arwoedh** *f.* **+yow**

symbolic *adj.* **arwoedhek**

symbolism *n.* **arwoedhogeth** *f.*

symmetrical *adj.* **kemusur**

symmetry *n.* **kemusur** *m.*

sympathize *v.* **keskodhevel**

symptom *n.* **arwoedh** *f.* **+yow,**
   tokyn *m.* **toknys, tokynyow, sin**
   m. **+ys, +yow**
synagogue *n.* **synaga** *m.* **synagys**
synod *n.* **senedh** *m.* **+ow**
synthetic *adj.* **synthesek**
syringe *n.* **skitell** *f.* **+ow:** *v.* **skitya**

T

tabernacle *n.* (dwelling-place)
   skovva *f.* **+ow;** (tent) **tylda** *m.*
   tyldow, tyldys
table *n.* **moes** *f.* **+ow**
table-cloth *n.* **lien moes** *m.*
tablespoon *n.* **lo-veur** *f.* **loyow-**
   meur
tablespoonful *n.* **loas-veur** *f.* **+ow**
tablet *n.* **legh** *f.* **+yon**
table-tennis *n.* **tennis moes** *m.*
table-top *n.* **bord** *m.*
tabor *n.* **tabour** *m.* **+s, +yow**
taciturn *adj.* **tawesek**
taciturnity *n.* **tawesigeth** *f.*
tack *n.* (nail) **kentrik** *f.* **-igow**
tadpole *n.* **pennynn** *m.* **+ow**
tail *n.* **lost** *m.* **+ow**
tail-back *n.* (traffic) **treynas** *m.*
   +ow
tailor *n.* **tregher** *m.* **-oryon**
tailoring *n.* **tregherieth** *f.*
take *v.* **kemmeres, tann;** take an
   oath **lia;** take Communion
   komunya; take late dinner **koena;**
   take place **hwarvos;** take seizin of
   a freehold **sesa;** take someone
   gorra nebonan; take the chair
   kaderya; take the Sacrament
   komunya; take the side of
   assentya gans; take with one **dri**
tale *n.* **hwedhel** *m.* **hwedhlow,**
   drolla *m.* **drollow, kyhwedhel** *m.*
   kyhwedhlow, romans *m.;*

amusing tale **rakka** *m.* **rakkow:** *v.*
   tell tales about **kuhudha**
talented *adj.* **roasek**
talk *n.* **kows** *m.* **+ow;** idle talk
   flows *m.:* *v.* **kewsel, kows;** talk
   about **kyhwedhla;** talk noisily
   klattra; talk nonsense **flowsa**
talkative *n.* talkative person
   klappyer *m.* **+s:** *adj.* **tavosek**
talker *n.* **leveryas** *m.* **-ysi**
tall *adj.* **hir**
tallow *n.* **soev** *m.;* wax tallow
   candle **kantol goer** *f.,* **kantol soev**
   f.
talon *n.* **ewin** *m.* **+es**
Tamar *n.* (name of river) **Tamer** *m.*
tame *adj.* **dov:** *v.* **dova, dovhe,**
   tempra
tameness *n.* **dovedh** *m.*
tamer *n.* **dover** *m.* **-oryon,**
   temprer *m.* **-oryon;** lion tamer
   dover lewyon *m.*
tan *adj.* (brown) **gell**
tangent *n.* **tavlinenn** *f.* **+ow**
tank *n.* **tank** *m.* **tankow;** fish tank
   tank puskes *m.*
tankard-bearer *n.* **botler** *m.* **+s**
tanker *n.* **tanker** *m.* **+yow;** oil
   tanker **tanker oyl** *m.*
tannery *n.* **kreghynva** *f.* **+ow**
tap *n.* (e.g. of bath) **tapp** *m.* **+ow,**
   +ys: *v.* **bonkya;** tap a barrel
   tardra
tape *n.* **snod** *m.* **+ow, +ys**
tappet *n.* **mortholynn** *m.* **+ow**
tar *n.* **pyg** *m.*
tardy *adj.* **hell**
tares *n.* **gwyg** *coll.* **+enn, ivra** *m.*
target *n.* **kostenn** *f.* **+ow:** *plur.*
   key targets **pennkostennow;**
   primary targets **pennkostennow:**
   v. **kostenna**
tarpaulin *n.* **pyglenn** *f.* **+ow**
tartan *n.* **brithenn** *f.* **+ow** *coll.*
   brith
task *n.* **oberenn** *f.* **+ow**

tassel *n.* kribell *f.* +ow, toes *m.*
+ow: *v.* form a tassel kribella
taste *n.* blas *m.,* sawer *m.* +yow,
sawrenn *f.* +ow, tast *m.:* *v.*
previ, blasa, sawra, tastya
tasteless *adj.* anvlasus
tastelessness *n.* anvlas *m.*
tasty *adj.* sawrek
tatter *n.* pil *coll.* +enn, sketh *m.*
+ow, skethenn *f.* +ow: *v.* frega,
skethenna
tatterdemalion *n.* fregys *m.,*
skethrek *m.* -ogyon
tattered *adj.* skethennek,
skethrek
tattle *plur.* hwedhlow
taut *adj.* tynn, yn tenn
tavern *n.* tavern *m.* +yow
tawny *adj.* gell, melyn
tax *n.* toll *f.* +ow; income tax toll-
wober *f.;* land tax toll-dir *f.*
tollow-tir; property tax toll-
annedh *f.;* purchase tax toll-
brenas *f.;* super tax gordoll *m.;*
tax collector toller *m.* -oryon; tax
inspector tellyas *m.* -ysi; tax relief
difresyans toll *m.;* wealth tax
toll-gevoeth *f.:* *v.* tolli; levy tax
tolli
taxation *n.* tollans *m.*
tax-free *adj.* didoll
taxi *n.* taksi *m.* +ow
tax-office *n.* tollva *f.* +ow
tax-payer *n.* taler toll *m.*
tea *n.* te *m.*
teach *v.* dyski
teacher *n.* dyskador *m.* +yon,
dyskadores *f.* +ow
teaching *n.* dyskas *m.*
tea-leaves *n.* godhes *m.*
team *n.* para *m.* parys
teapot *n.* tebott *m.* +ow, pott-te *m.*
tear *n.* skward *m.* +yow; (weeping)
dager *m.* dagrow, dagrenn *f.*
+ow: *v.* skwardya; shed tears

dagrewi; tear down a house terri
chi; tear up frega
tease *v.* hyga; tease out rope
kribella
teaspoon *n.* lo-de *f.* loyow-te
teaspoonful *n.* loas-te *f.* +ow
teat *n.* teth *f.* +ow, tethenn *f.* +ow
teddy-bear *n.* orsik *m.* -igow
tedium *n.* hirder *m.*
tee-shirt *n.* krys T *m.*
telecommunication *n.*
pellgomunyans *m.* +ow
tele-cottage *n.* pellbennti *m.* +ow
telegram *n.* pellskrifenn *f.* +ow
telegraph *v.* pellskrifa
telephone *n.* pellgowser *m.* +yow;
telephone call galwenn bellgows
f.: *v.* pellgewsel
telephony *n.* pellgows *m.*
telescope *n.* pellweler *m.*
television *n.* pellwolok *f.*
pellwologow
tell *v.* leverel, derivas; tell jokes
gesya; tell off keredhi, keski;
tell tales leverel anethow; tell
tales about kuhudha
teller *n.* (of tales) leveryas *m.* -ysi;
teller of the truth gwirleveryas *m.*
-ysi
temper *v.* tempra
temperate *adj.* temprek
temperature *n.* tempredh *m.* +ow
tempest *n.* annawel *f.*
template *n.* skantlyn *m.* +s
temple *n.* tal *m.* +yow, tempel *m.*
templow, templa *m.* templys;
(head) er *m.* +yow
tempt *v.* temptya
temptation *n.* temptyans *m.*
tempter *n.* tempter *m.* -oryon
ten *adj.* ten times dekkweyth: *num.*
deg +ow
tenacious *adj.* kraf
tenancy *n.* delghyaseth *f.,*
gobrenans *m.* +ow

tenant *n.* delghyas *m.* -ysi,
gobrener *m.* -oryon

tendency *n.* plegyans *m.,* tuedh
m. +ow

tender *adj.* medhel, bludh, tender

tenderize *v.* bludhhe

tenderness *n.* medhelder *m.*

tendon *n.* giowenn *f.* +enn *coll.*
giow, skenna *m.* skennys,
skennow

tenfold *adj.* degplek

tennis *n.* tennis *m.*

tenor *n.* tenor *m.* +yon

tense *n.* (of verb) amser *f.* +yow

tension *n.* tennva *f.,* tynnder *m.*

tent *n.* tylda *m.* tyldow, tyldys

tentative *adj.* a-gynnik

tentatively *adv.* a-gynnik

tenth *num.* degves

tenure *n.* feudal tenure ago-
marghogyon *f.*

tepid *adj.* mygyl

term *n.* termyn *m.* +yow; school
term trymis *m.*

terminate *v.* gorfenna; (kill)
ladha; terminate employment of
gordhyllo

termly *adj.* trymisyek

tern *n.* morwennol *f.* -wennili,
skrawik *m.* -igow

terrace *n.* terras *m.* +ow

terrible *adj.* euthek

terribly *adv.* euthek

terrier *n.* dorgi *m.* dorgeun

terrified *adj.* dyegrys

territory *n.* tir *m.* +yow, tiredh *m.*

terror *n.* browagh *m.,* euth *m.*

terrorist *n.* (female)
broweghyades *f.* +ow; (male)
broweghyas *m.* -ysi

terrorize *v.* broweghi

test *n.* apposyans *m.,* prevyans *m.*
+ow, prov *m.: v.* previ; test by
questions apposya; test oneself
omassaya

testament *n.* (Biblical) testament
m.; New Testament Testament
Nowydh *m.;* Old Testament
Testament Koth *m.*

testicle *n.* kell *f.* +ow *dual* diwgell

testify *v.* desta, dustunia

testimonial *n.* dustunians *m.*
+ow, testskrif *m.* +ow

testimony *n.* dustuni *m.*
dustuniow, rekord *m.* +ys

tether *n.* stag *m.: v.* staga

text *n.* tekst *m.;* original text
mammskrif *m.* +ow

texture *n.* gwias *m.* +ow,
gwiasedh *m.* +ow

than *conj.* ages, es

thank *v.* grassa; thank someone
grassa dhe nebonan: *phr.* thank
you durdallodhy'hwi, meur ras

thanks *n.* gras *m.* grassys,
grassow: *v.* give thanks for
grassa

that *pron.* (f.) honn; (m.) henn;
that one (f.) honna; that one (m.)
henna: *conj.* that not na: *ptl.*
nag: *adv.* na

thatch *n.* sowl *coll.;* bundle of
thatch orrenn *f.* +ow: *v.* ti

thatcher *n.* tior *m.* +yon

thaw *v.* teudhi

the *art.* an: *phr.* and the ha'n; in
the y'n; to the dhe'n

theatre *n.* gwariva *f.* +ow; open-air
theatre plen an gwari *m.;*
operating theatre stevell-oberyans
f.

thee *pron.* jy; (emphatic) tejy

theft *n.* (in general) ladrynsi *m.;*
(individual crime) ladrans *m.*

their *pron.* aga: *phr.* and their
ha'ga; to their dh'aga

them *pron.* i: *phr.* a's

themselves *pron.* ynsi

then *conj.* ha, ytho; well then ytho:
adv. ena, y'n eur na

thence *adv.* alena

thenceforth *conj.* **wosa henna**
thenceforward *adv.* **alena rag**
there *adv.* **ena, eno**; from there
alena: *int.* there is **otta**
thereby *adv.* **dredhi**
therefore *conj.* **rakhenna, ytho**
they *pron.* **i**; (emphatic) **ynsi**: *phr.*
y's
thick *adj.* **tew**
thicken *v.* **tewhe**
thicket *n.* **dreynek** *f.* **-egi, goedhel**
m. **goedhyli, kaswydh** *m.,* **perth**
f. **-i, pryskenn** *f.* **+ow** *coll.* **prysk**
thick-head *n.* **penn-bras** *m.*
pennow-bras
thick-lipped *adj.* **gwelvek**
thickness *n.* **tewder** *m.*
thick-shelled *adj.* **krogenek**
thief *n.* **lader** *m.* **ladron**
thigh *n.* **mordhos** *f.* **-osow** *dual*
diwvordhos
thimble *n.* **byskoen** *f.* **+yow**; silver
thimble **byskoen arghans** *f.*
thin *adj.* **moen, tanow**
thing *n.* **tra** *f.* **+ow, pyth** *m.* **+ow**;
smallest thing **gik** *m.:* *plur.* material
things **taklow**
things (abst.) /thing *plur.* **traow**
think *v.* **prederi, tybi**
thinking *n.* way of thinking **brys** *m.*
+yow
third *num.* **tressa, trysa**; Third
World **Tressa Bys**
thirst *n.* **syghes** *m.:* *v.* quench
thirst **disygha**
thirsty *n.* I am thirsty **yma syghes**
dhymm *m.*
thirteen *num.* **trydhek**
thirteenth *num.* **trydhegves**
this *pron.* **ma**; (f.) **homm**; (m.)
hemm; this one (f.) **homma**; this
one (m.) **hemma**
thistle *n.* **askallenn** *f.* **+ow** *coll.*
askall
thistly *adj.* **askallek**

thither *adv.* **bys di, dhi, di**
Thomas *name* **Tommas**
thong *n.* **kroen** *m.* **+ow**
thorn *n.* **dren** *m.* **dreyn, dreynenn**
f. **+ow** *coll.* **dreyn, spernenn** *f.*
+ow *coll.* **spern**
thornback *n.* **rogha** *m.* **roghys**
thornbrake *n.* **spernek** *f.* **-egi**
thorny *adj.* **drenek, spernek**
thoroughfare *n.* **fordh-lan** *f.*
fordhow-glan
thoroughly *adv.* **purra**
those *adv.* **na**
thou *pron.* **ty**; (emphatic) **dhejy**
though *conj.* **awos, kyn, kynth**:
phr. though I die **awos mernans**
thought *n.* **tybyans** *m.* **+ow,**
preder *m.* **+ow**; inward thought
kowses *m.:* *v.* err in thought
kammdybi
thoughtless *adj.* **dibreder**
thousand *n.* **mil** *m.* **+yow**: *adv.*
thousand times **milweyth**: *phr.*
thousand years old **milvloedh**
thousandfold *adj.* **milblek**
thousandth *num.* **milves**
thrash *v.* **dorna, fusta, kastiga,**
kronkya, skorjya
thread *n.* **linenn** *f.* **+ow, lin** *m.*
+enn; (in general) **neus** *coll.;*
(individual) **neusenn** *f.* **+ow** *coll.*
neus: *v.* **neusenna**
threat *n.* **godros** *m.* **+ow**
threaten *v.* **bragya, degynsywa,**
godros
three *num.* (f.) **teyr**; (m.) **tri**; three
hundred **trihans**
three-bearded *n.* three-bearded
rockling **penn-barvus** *m.*
pennow-barvus, ploumsugen
m., **ploumsugesenn** *f.*
three-dimensional *adj.*
trymynsek
threescore *num.* **tri-ugens**
thresh *v.* **drushya**
thresher *n.* **drushyer** *m.* **+yoryon**

threshold *n.* **treudhow** *m.*
thrice *adv.* **teyrgweyth**
thrift *n.* (plant) **bryton** *m.;* (saving money) **erbys** *m.* **+yow**
thrifty *adj.* **erbysek**
throat *n.* **bryansenn** *f.*
throne *n.* **gorsedh** *f.* **+ow, esedh** *f.* **+ow, se** *m.* **seow, tron** *m.* **+ys, +yow**
throng *n.* **routh** *f.* **+ow**
through *prep.* **der, dre;** through the course of **dres**
throw *n.* **towl** *m.* **+ow:** *v.* **tewlel;** throw out **estewlel, tewlel yn-mes;** throw stones at **labydha;** throw up **hwyja**
thrush *n.* **molgh** *f.* **+i**
thrust *n.* **pych** *m.:* *v.* **pokya**
thumb *n.* **meus** *m.*, **bys bras** *m.:* *v.* thumb a lift **meusya**
thump *n.* **boemm** *m.* **+yn, kronk** *m.* **+ys:** *v.* **dorna, kronkya**
thunder *n.* **taran** *f.:* *adj.* like thunder **taranek:** *v.* **tarena**
thunderer *n.* **taraner** *m.* **-oryon**
thundery *adj.* **taranek**
Thursday *n.* **dy' Yow** *m.*, **Yow** *m.;* Maundy Thursday **dy' Yow Hablys** *m.*
thy *pron.* **dha:** *phr.* and thy **ha'th;** to thy **dhe'th**
thyme *n.* **tim** *m.;* wild thyme **koesfinel** *coll.*
ticket *n.* **tokyn** *m.* **toknys, tokynyow;** return ticket **tokyn mos-ha-dos** *m.*
ticket-office *n.* **tokynva** *f.* **+ow**
tickle *v.* **debreni, kosa**
tickling *n.* **debron** *m.*, **kos** *f.*
ticklish *adj.* **hegos**
tide *n.* **mordid** *m.*, **tid** *m.;* high tide **lanow** *m.*, **morlanow** *m.;* low tide **mordryk** *m.*, **tryg** *m.;* neap tide **marowvor** *m.;* spring tide **reverthi** *f.*

tidiness *n.* **glanythter** *m.*, **kempennses** *m.*
tidings *n.* **kyhwedhel** *m.* **kyhwedhlow, nowedhys** *m.:* *plur.* **nowodhow**
tidy *adj.* **kempenn, glanyth:** *v.* **kempenna;** make tidy **restra**
tie *n.* (clothing) **kolm konna** *m.;* (link) **kolm** *m.* **+ow, stagell** *f.*, **syg** *f.:* *v.* **kelmi;** tie to **kelmi orth;** tie together **fasthe**
tiger *n.* **tiger** *m.* **tigri**
tight *adj.* **stroth, tynn**
tighten *v.* **fastya**
tightness *n.* **tynnder** *m.*
tightrope *n.* **lovan tynn** *f.*
tights *plur.* **tynnow**
tigress *n.* **tigres** *f.* **+ow**
tile *n.* **prileghenn** *f.* **+ow**
till *n.* (in shop) **rekenva** *f.* **+ow:** *conj.* **erna, ernag**
tilth *n.* **ar** *m.*
timber *n.* **prenn** *m.* **+yer;** squared timber **plenkynn** *f.* **+ow**
time *n.* **eur** *f.* **+yow, prys** *m.* **+yow, termyn** *m.* **+yow, seson** *m.* **+yow, +s;** long time **hirneth** *f.;* short time **pols** *m.* **+yow;** time of birth **genesigeth** *f.;* time to go **prys mos** *m.:* *prep.* by the time that **erbynn:** *v.* kill time **delatya an termyn;** waste time **gwibessa:** *adv.* all the time **pub eur oll;** at any time **nep-prys;** at some time **war neb tro;** at that place or time **ena;** at that time **y'n eur na;** at this time **y'n eur ma, y'n tor' ma, y'n tor' ma;** at what time **p'eur;** from time to time **a dermyn dhe dermyn;** in good time **a-brys;** in time **a-dermyn;** on time **a-brys, a-dermyn**
timely *adv.* **a-brys**
times *adv.* how many times **peskweyth**
timetable *n.* **euryador** *m.*

time-waster *n.* **termynek** *m.*
-**ogyon**

timpano *n.* **naker** *m.* **nakrys**

tin *n.* (container) **kanna** *m.* **kannow**;
(metal) **alkan** *m.*, **sten** *m.;* baking
tin **kanna-pobas** *m.;* fine mealy
tin **florenn** *f.;* ground rich in tin
skovenn *f.;* smelted tin **sten**
gwynn *m.;* tin ground **stenek** *f.*
-**egi**; unsmelted tin **sten du** *m.:*
plur. low-grade tin **manylyon**,
relystyon: *adj.* containing tin
stenus

tin working *n.* **hwel-sten** *m.*

tin-bounds *plur.* **bounds**

tinder *n.* tinder box **korn tan** *m.*

tine *n.* **dans** *m.* **dens**

tingle *v.* **kosa**

tinkle *v.* **tynkyal**

tinner *n.* **stenor** *m.* +**yon**

tin-ore *n.* rich tin-ore **skov** *m.*

tin-pit *n.* **poll sten** *m.*

tinsel *plur.* **golowylyon**

tinstone *n.* **pryl** *m.*

tint *n.* **liw** *m.* **liwyow**

Tintagel *place* **Dintagell**

tinted *adj.* **liwek**

tin-working *n.* area of tin-working
bal *m.* +**yow**

tip *n.* (end) **bleyn** *m.* +**yow, min** *m.*
+**yow, toppynn** *m.* +**ow**; (for
rubbish) **skoellva** *f.;* (money)
grastal *m.:* *v.* tip over **omhweles**;
tip up **omhweles**

tipsy *adj.* **govedhow**

tire *v.* **annia, skwitha, skwithhe**

tired *adj.* **skwith**; dead tired **skwith**
marow: *v.* make tired **skwithhe**

tiredness *n.* **skwithter** *m.*,
skwithans *m.*

tiring *adj.* **skwithus**

tit *phr.* tit for tat **tys-ha-tas**

tithe *n.* **dega** *m.;* rectorial tithes
manal *f.* +**ow**: *v.* pay tithes
degevi

title *n.* **titel** *m.* **titlow, titlys**

titmouse *n.* **penn-glow** *m.*

to *prep.* **dhe**; (occasl.) **yn**; to her
dhedhi; to him **dhodho**; to me
dhymm, dhymmo; to thee **dhis**,
dhiso; to them **dhedha**; to us
dhyn; to you **dhy'hwi**,
dhy'hwyhwi, dhywgh; *phr.* to
our **dh'agan**; to the **dhe'n**; to their
dh'aga; to your **dh'agas**

toad *n.* **kroenek** *m.* -**ogow, lyfans**
m. +**es**; dark toad **kroenek du** *m.;*
light toad **kroenek melyn** *m.;* little
toad **kroenegynn** *m.* +**ow**; ugly
black little toad **kroenegynn**
hager du *m.:* *v.* hop like a toad
kroenogas, lyfansas

toadpool *n.* **poll kroenogow** *m.*,
poll lyfans *m.*

toadstool *n.* **skavell-groenek** *f.*
skavellow-kroenek

toast *n.* (food) **kras** *coll.* +**enn**;
piece of toast **krasenn** *f.* +**ow**: *v.*
(food) **krasa**

toasted *adj.* **kras**

toast-rack *n.* **kloes-kras** *f.*
kloesyow-kras, rastell gras *f.*

today *n.* **y'n jydh ma** *m.:* *adv.*
hedhyw

toddle *v.* **gogerdhes**

toddler *n.* **gogerdher** *m.* -**oryon**

toe *n.* **bys troes** *m.*

toffee *n.* **klyji** *m.*

together *adv.* **warbarth**

toil *n.* **lavur** *m.*, **lavuryans** *m.:* *v.*
gonis, lavurya

toilets *plur.* **privedhyow**

toilsome *adj.* **lavurus**

token *n.* **tokyn** *m.* **toknys,**
tokynyow, nos *m.* +**ow**

tolerate *v.* **perthi, godhav,**
godhevel

toleration *n.* **perthyans** *m.*

toll *n.* (of flour) **arval** *m.;* (tax) **toll** *f.*
+**ow**

toll-booth *n.* **tollva** *f.* +**ow**

toll-bridge *n.* **tollbons** *m.*

toll-gate *n.* **tollborth** *m.* **+ow**

toll-house *n.* **tollji** *m.* **+ow**

toll-road *n.* **tollfordh** *f.* **+ow**

tomato *n.* **aval-kerensa** *m.*
avalow-kerensa

tomb *n.* **bedh** *m.* **+ow**; stone-built
tomb **bedh men** *m.*

tom-cat *n.* **gorgath** *m.* **+es**

tomorrow *adv.* **a-vorow**;
tomorrow morning **ternos vyttin**

ton *n.* **tonnas** *m.* **+ow**

tone *n.* **ton** *m.* **+yow**

tongs *n.* **gevel** *f.*; iron tongs
gevelhorn *f.*

tongue *n.* **taves** *m.* **tavosow**: *phr.*
hold thy tongue **syns dha glapp**

tonight *adv.* **haneth**

tonne *n.* **tonnas** *m.* **+ow**

too *n.* too many **re** *m.*; too much **re**
m.: *adv.* **keffrys, re**

tool *n.* **toul** *m.* **+ys, +ow**; garden
tool **toul-lowarth** *m.* **toulow-
lowarth**

tooth *n.* **dans** *m.* **dens**; back tooth
dans a-dhelergh *m.*; front tooth
dans a-rag *m.*; molar tooth
kildhans *m.* **-dhens**: *v.* show
one's teeth **grysla**

tooth-brush *n.* **skubyllenn dhens**
f.

tooth-paste *n.* **past dens** *m.*

toothy *adj.* **densek**

top *n.* **gwartha** *m.*, **topp** *m.* **+ys**:
adv. on top **a-wartha**

tor *n.* **karn** *m.* **+ow, kastell** *m.*
kastylli, torr *f.* **+ow**

torch *n.* **faglenn** *f.* **+ow**

torment *n.* **payn** *m.* **+ys, torment**
m. **tormens**: *v.* **tormentya**

tormentil *n.* (herb) **seythdelenn** *f.*

tormentor *n.* **tormentor** *m.* **+ys**

tornado *n.* **gwyns a-dro** *m.*,
korwyns *m.* **+ow**

Torpoint *place* **Penntorr**

torque *n.* **torgh** *f.* **tergh**; (physical
quantity) **torghedh** *m.*

torrent *n.* **keynres** *m.*

tortoise *n.* **kroenek ervys** *m.*,
melhwyoges *f.*

tortuous *adj.* **gwius**

torture *n.* **payn** *m.* **+ys, torment**
m. **tormens**: *v.* **paynya,
tormentya**

torturer *n.* **tormentor** *m.* **+ys**

toss *v.* **tewlel**

total *n.* **somm** *m.*, **sommenn** *f.*
+ow

touch *v.* **tava**; touch accidentally
tochya

tough *n.* tough guy **smat** *m.* **+ys**;
tough nut **avleythys** *m.* **+yon**

tour *n.* **torn** *m.* **+ow**

tourism *n.* **tornyaseth** *f.*

tourist *n.* **tervyajor** *m.* **+yon,
tornyas** *m.* **-ysi**; summer tourist
havyades *f.* **+ow, havyas** *m.* **-ysi**

towards *prep.* **war-tu, troha, tu
ha**: *adv.* **trohag**

towel *n.* **towell** *m.* **+ow**

tower *n.* **tour** *m.* **+yow**; control
tower **tour routya** *m.*

town *n.* **tre** *f.* **trevow**: *adv.* in town
y'n dre

town-hall *n.* **hel an dre** *f.*, **burjesti**
m. **+ow**

townsman *n.* **burjes** *m.* **burjysi**

toy *n.* **gwariell** *f.* **+ow, tegynn** *m.*
+ow: *v.* toy with **trufla**

trace *n.* (as in art) **tresenn** *f.* **+ow**;
(link) **kadon** *f.* **+yow**; (of a
harness) **syg** *f.*; (track) **lergh** *m.*, **ol**
m. **+ow, tres** *m.* **+ow**: *v.* **tresya**;
(as in art) **tresa**

trachaeotomy *n.* **trogh-
bryansenn** *m.*

tracing *n.* **tresas** *m.* **+ow**

track *n.* **lergh** *m.*, **ol** *m.* **+ow, tres**
m. **+ow**; ancient track **henfordh** *f.*:
v. **helerghi**

tracker *n.* **helerghyas** *m.* **-ysi**

trackless *adj.* **heb fordh**

track-rod *n.* (mach.) **lorgh-resa** *m.* **lorghow-resa**

tractor *n.* **jynn-tenna** *m.* **jynnow-tenna**

trade *n.* **kenwerth** *m.*, **myster** *m.;* Department of Trade **Asrann Genwerth** *f.:* *v.* **kenwertha, marghasa**

trade-guild *n.* member of trade-guild **mysterden** *m.* **+s**

trader *n.* **gwikor** *m.* **+yon, marchont** *m.* **-ons;** bad trader **gwann-wikor** *m.* **+yon**

tradesman *n.* **kenwerther** *m.* **-oryon**

tradition *n.* **hengov** *m.* **+yow**

traditional *adj.* **hengovek**

traffic *n.* **daromres** *m.:* *phr.* through traffic **dhe bub le**

traffic circle (U.S.) *n.* **fordh-a-dro** *f.*

trailer *n.* **draylyer** *m.* **-oryon**

trailer (U.S.) *n.* **karavan** *m.* **+s**

train *n.* goods train **tren fres** *m.;* high speed train **tren toeth bras** (T.T.B.) *m.;* railway train **tren** *m.* **+ow:** *v.* **dyski;** train Peter to sing **dyski dhe Beder kana**

trainer *n.* (shoe) **eskis sport** *f.* **eskisyow sport**

train-oil *n.* **saym** *m.*

traitor *n.* **traytour** *m.* **+s**

tramp *n.* **loselwas** *m.* **-wesyon, skajynn** *m.* **+ow**

trample *v.* **stankya, trettya;** trample wet soil **pochya**

tranch *n.* **tregh** *m.* **+ow**

tranquil *adj.* **kosel**

tranquillity *n.* **diagha** *m.*, **kalmynsi** *m.*, **kosoleth** *f.*

transaction *n.* **negys** *m.* **+yow**

transcribe *v.* **treusskrifa**

transcription *n.* **treusskrif** *m.* **+ow**

transept *n.* **krows eglos** *f.*

transfer *n.* **treusporth** *m.* **+ow:** *v.* **treusperthi, treusworra**

transfigure *v.* **treusfurvya**

transfix *v.* **berya, pychya**

transform *v.* **treusfurvya**

transformation *n.* **treusfurvyans** *m.* **+ow, treylva** *f.*

transfuse *v.* **treustroetha**

transfusion *n.* **treustroeth** *m.*

transgress *v.* (intrans.) **kammdremena**

transgression *n.* **peghadow** *m.*, **treuspass** *m.* **+ow**

transit *n.* **tremen** *m.*

translate *v.* **treylya**

translation *n.* **treylyans** *m.* **+ow**

translator *n.* **treylyer** *m.* **+yon**

translucent *adj.* **boll, glew**

transom *n.* **treusprenn** *m.* **+yer**

transparency *n.* **klerder** *m.*

transparent *adj.* **boll, ylyn**

transplant *v.* **treusplansa**

transport *n.* **karyans** *m.*, **treusporth** *m.* **+ow;** (of delight) **ravshyans** *m.;* Department of Transport **Asrann Garyans** *f.:* *v.* **doen, karya, treusperthi**

transverse *adj.* **treus**

transversely *adv.* **a-dreus**

trap *n.* **antell** *f.* **antylli, maglenn** *f.* **+ow:** *v.* **bagha, magla**

trap-stile *n.* **trapp** *m.* **+ys**

trash (U.S.) *n.* **atal** *c.:* *v.* **strolya**

trash can (U.S.) *n.* **atalgyst** *f.* **+yow**

trashy (U.S.) *adj.* **skubellek**

travail *n.* **keudh** *m.*

travel *n.* travel *m.:* *v.* **lavurya, travalya, vyajya**

traveller *n.* **tremenyas** *m.* **-ysi**

tray *n.* **servyour** *m.* **+s**

treacherous *adj.* **fals**

treachery *n.* **trayson** *m.*, **trayturi** *m.*

treacle *n.* **molas** *m.*

tread *n.* (of tyre) **godhen** *m.*
 godhnow; heavy tread **stank** *m.*
treadle *n.* **troesla** *m.* **troesleow**
treason *n.* **trayson** *m.*
treasure *n.* **tresor** *m.* **+yow, +ys:**
 v. **tresorya**
treasurer *n.* **alhwedhor** *m.* **+yon**
treasury *n.* **tresorva** *f.* **+ow**
treat *v.* **dyghtya;** treat badly
 tebeldhyghtya; treat kindly
 chershya: *phr.* treat wantonly
 tewlel dhe skoell
treatment *n.* **dyghtyans** *m.*
treaty *n.* **kevambos** *m.* **+ow**
treble *n.* (Mus.) **trebyl** *m.*
tree *n.* **gwydhenn** *f.* **+ow** *coll.*
 gwydh; evergreen tree **sabenn** *f.*
 +ow *coll.* **sab, sybwydhenn** *f.*
 +ow *coll.* **sybwydh;** hollow tree
 kowbrenn *m.* **+yer;** shady tree
 goskeuswydhenn *f.* **+ow** *coll.*
 goskeuswydh; sheltering trees
 klyswydh *coll.* **+enn**
tree-trunk *n.* **kyf** *m.*
trefoil *n.* bird's foot trefoil **mellyon**
 melyn *coll.*
trellis *n.* **kloes** *f.* **+yow**
tremble *n.* **kren** *m.* **+yow:** *v.*
 degrena, krena
trembling *adj.* **dyegrys**
trench *n.* **kleudh** *m.* **+yow, kleys**
 m. **+yow;** (for warfare) **kaskleudh**
 m. **+yow:** *v.* dig a trench
 kleudhya
trencher *n.* **tallyour** *m.* **+s**
trend *n.* **tuedh** *m.* **+ow**
trespass *n.* **kamm** *m.* **+ow,**
 kammweyth *m.,* **treuspass** *m.*
 +ow: *v.* **kammdremena,**
 treuspassya
trial *n.* **prov** *m.;* (legal) **trial** *m.* **+s**
triangle *n.* **trihorn** *m.* **trihern**
triangular *adj.* **trihornek**
tribe *n.* **kordh** *m.* **+ow, loeth** *m.*
tribunal *n.* **barr** *m.* **+ys, sedhek** *m.*
 -ogow

trice *adv.* in a trice **yn unn lamm**
trick *n.* **kast** *m.* **+ys, pratt** *m.* **+ys,**
 wrynch *m.;* confidence trick
 kammfydhweyth *m.* **+ow;** play a
 trick **gul pratt** *m.:* *v.* **kestya**
trickle *v.* **devera**
trickster *n.* confidence trickster
 kammfydhwas *m.* **-wesyon**
tricycle *n.* **teyrros** *f.* **+ow**
trifle *n.* **truflenn** *f.* **+ow:** *v.* **trufla**
trifling *adj.* **trufel**
trim *v.* **dyghtya, godreghi**
trinity *n.* **trynses** *f.;* The Trinity
 An Drynses *f.*
trinket *n.* **tegenn** *f.* **+ow, tegynn**
 m. **+ow**
trip *v.* **trebuchya;** trip and fall
 omdhisevel; trip up **disevel**
tripe *n.* **klout bolghenn** *m.*
tripod *n.* **trybedh** *m.* **+ow**
triumph *n.* **gormeula** *m.,* **trygh** *m.:*
 v. **gormeuledha, tryghi**
triumphant *adj.* **gormeuledhek,**
 trygh
trivet *n.* **trybedh** *m.* **+ow**
trolley *n.* (e.g. in supermarket)
 karrigell *f.* **+ow;** (for food)
 rosvoes *f.* **+ow**
troop *n.* **bagas** *m.* **+ow, meni** *m.*
tropic *n.* **trovann** *m.* **+ow**
tropical *adj.* **trovannel**
trouble *n.* **ahwer** *m.,* **anken** *m.*
 +yow, kedrynn *f.,* **poenvos** *m.,*
 trobel *m.,* **trynn** *f.;* state of trouble
 poenvotter *m.:* *plur.* **kavow:** *v.*
 grevya, trobla; trouble someone
 grevya dhe nebonan
troubled *adj.* **anes, poenvosek,**
 troblys
trough *n.* **new** *f.* **+yow**
trousers *n.* **lavrek** *m.* **lavrogow**
trout *n.* **truth** *m.* **+es**
trowel *n.* **lo-balas** *f.* **loyow-balas**
truant *v.* play truant **mynchya**
truce *n.* **powes** *m.*

truck *n.* truck (U.S.) **kert** *m.* **+ow,
+ys**
trudge *v.* **travalya, troesya**
true *adj.* **gwir, gwiryon**
truly *adv.* **devri, yn hwir, dhe wir,
heb wow**
trump *n.* **trompa** *m.* **trompys**
trumpet *n.* **hirgorn** *m.* **hirgern,
trompet** *m.;* large trumpet **trompa**
m. **trompys**
trumpeter *n.* **hirgernyas** *m.* **-ysi,
trompour** *m.* **+s**
truncheon *n.* **fust** *f.* **+ow**
trunk *n.* (box) **trog** *m.* **+ow**; (of
animal) **troen** *m.* **-yow**
Truro *place* **Truru**
truss *v.* **troessa**
trust *n.* **fydh** *f.,* **fydhyans** *m.,*
kresys *m.,* **kyfyans** *m.,* **trest** *m.;*
Cornwall Heritage Trust **Trest
Ertach Kernow** *m.;* Healthcare
Trust **Trest Gwith-Yeghes** *m.:* *v.*
**fydhya, koela, koela orth, Trest
Gwith-Yeghes**
trustful *adj.* **hegoel**
trusty *adj.* **lel, len**
truth *n.* **gwir** *m.* **+yow, gwirder** *m.,*
gwiryonedh *m.,* **sodh** *m.;* teller of
the truth **gwirleveryas** *m.* **-ysi:**
adv. in truth **dhe wir, dhe-wir**
try *v.* **assaya, hwilas, previ;** (in
court) **tria**
tub *n.* **beol** *m.,* **keryn** *f.* **+yow,
kibell** *f.* **+ow**
tube *n.* **pibenn** *f.* **+ow**; capillary
tube **korrbibenn** *f.* **+ow**; the Tube
an Bib *f.*
tucker *n.* **troghyer** *m.* **-oryon**
Tuesday *n.* **dy' Meurth** *m.,* **Meurth**
m.
tuft *n.* **kribell** *f.* **+ow, toes** *m.* **+ow:**
v. **kribella**
tufted *adj.* **toesek**
tug *n.* **krog** *f.* **+ow, tenn** *m.* **+ow;**
(boat) **tennlester** *m.* **-lestri**
tug-of-war *n.* **tennstrif** *m.*

tumbler *n.* **gwedrenn** *f.* **+ow**
tumbler (U.S.) *n.* **lappyer** *m.*
-yoryon
tumour *n.* **kalesenn gig** *f.*
tump *n.* small tump **godolghynn** *m.*
tumult *n.* **fros** *m.* **+ow, tervans** *m.:*
v. make a tumult **terva**
tumulus *n.* **krug** *m.* **+ow**
tun *n.* **tonnell** *f.* **+ow**
tune *n.* **ilow** *f.,* **ton** *m.* **+yow**
tungstate *n.* tungstate of iron **kall** *m.*
tunnel *n.* **kowfordh** *f.* **+ow**
turban *n.* **tulyfant** *m.*
turbary *n.* **towarghek** *f.* **-egi,
towarghweyth** *m.*
turf *n.* **tonn** *coll.* **+enn;** (for
burning) **towargh** *coll.* **+enn**
turfwork *n.* **towarghweyth** *m.*
Turk *n.* **Turk** *m.* **+ys, +yon**
turkey *n.* **yar Gyni** *f.*
turn *n.* **tro** *f.* **+yow, kor** *m.* **+ow,
tor'** *m.,* **torn** *m.* **+ow, troenn** *f.*
+ow; backward turn **kildro** *f.*
+yow; good turn **torn da** *m.:* *v.*
treylya, stumma; turn oneself into
omwul
turncoat *n.* **negedhys** *m.* **+yon**
turning *n.* **stumm** *m.* **+ow**
turning-point *n.* **treylva** *f.*
turnip *n.* **ervinenn** *f.* **+ow** *coll.*
ervin
turnstile *n.* **kammva-dro** *f.*
kammvaow-tro
turret *n.* **tourik** *m.* **-igow**
turtle-dove *n.* **turenn** *f.* **+ow**
tush *int.* **tetivali**
tut-tut *int.* **tetivali**
tweak *n.* **krog** *f.* **+ow**
twelfth *num.* **dewdhegves**
twelve *num.* **dewdhek**
twentieth *num.* **ugensves**
twenty *num.* **ugens**
twentyfold *adj.* **ugensplek**
twice *adv.* **diwweyth**

twig *n.* **barrenn** *f.* **+ow**
twiggy *adj.* **barrek**
twilight *n.* **mo** *m.*
twin *n.* (female) **gevelles** *f.* **+ow;**
(male) **gevell** *m.* **+yon:** *v.*
gevella
twine *n.* **lovanenn** *f.* **+ow:** *v.* **gwia**
twinkle *v.* **terlentri, dewynnya,**
sterenni
twinkling *adv.* in a twinkling **war**
unn plynch
twinning *n.* **gevellans** *m.* **+ow**
twist *n.* **tro** *f.* **+yow:** *v.* **treylya;**
(of yarn) **nedha**
twitch *n.* **skwych** *m.* **+ys:** *v.*
skwychya
two *num.* (f.) **diw;** (m.) **dew**
twofold *adj.* **dewblek**
two-score *num.* **dew-ugens**
type *v.* **jynnskrifa**
typewriter *n.* **jynn-skrifa** *m.*
jynnow-skrifa
tyrant *n.* **turant** *m.* **turans**
tyre *n.* **bondenn** *f.* **+ow, bond-ros**
m. **bondow-ros**

U

udder *n.* **sagh bugh** *m.*
ugh *int.* **agh**
uglier *adj.* **hakkra**
ugliness *n.* **hakter** *m.*
ugly *adj.* **hager**
ulcer *n.* **goli** *m.* **+ow**
umbelliferous *n.* umbelliferous plant
kegis *coll.* **+enn**
umbrella *n.* **glawlenn** *f.* **+ow**
unabashed *adj.* **diveth**
unable *adj.* **dialloes**
unacceptable *adj.*
ankemmeradow
unalarmed *adj.* **diagha**

unanimous *adj.* **keskolonn,**
unnver
unarmed *adj.* **diarv**
unattached *adj.* **distag**
unavoidable *adj.* **anwoheladow**
unbeatable *adj.* **antryghadow**
unbelief *n.* **diskryjyans** *m.*
unbelievable *adj.* **ankrysadow**
unbeliever *n.* **ankredor** *m.* **+yon,**
diskryjyk *m.* **-ygyon**
unbelieving *adj.* **ankryjyk,**
diskryjyk
unbending *adj.* **diwedhyn**
unburden *v.* **diveghya**
unbutton *v.* **divotonya**
uncastrated *adj.* **kellek, lawen**
uncertainty *n.* **ansurneth** *f.* **+ow**
unchained *adj.* **digabester**
uncle *n.* **ewnter** *m.* **ewntres**
unclean *adj.* **avlan**
unclothe *v.* **diwiska**
uncoil *v.* **diderghi**
unconcealed *adj.* **digudh**
unconstrained *adj.* **digabester**
uncover *v.* **diskudha**
uncultivated *adj.* **goedh**
under *prep.* **yn-dann, is**
Underground *n.* the Underground
an Bib *f.*
underpants *n.* **islavrek** *m.* **-ogow,**
lavrek byghan *m.*
underpass *n.* **kowfordh** *f.* **+ow**
under-seal *v.* **isstanchya**
under-secretary *n.* **isskrifennyas**
m. **-ysi**
underskirt *n.* **goelesenn** *f.*
understand *v.* **konvedhes;**
understand each other
omgonvedhes
undertake *v.* **omgemmeres**
underworld *n.* **annown** *m.*
undo *v.* **diswul, distrui,**
diswruthyl, diswuthyl
undone *v.* **diswrys**

undress *v.* **diwiska**; undress oneself **omdhiwiska**

uneasiness *n.* **anes** *m.*

unemployed *adj.* **diweyth**

unemployment *n.* **diweythieth** *f.;* unemployment benefit **gober dilavur** *m.*

unequalled *adj.* **dibarow, somper**

uneven *adj.* **ankompes**

unfairly *v.* play unfairly **fugya**

unfaithful *adj.* **dislen**

unfasten *v.* **difastya**

unfavoured *adj.* **diskrassyes**

unfit *adj.* **anwiw**; (out of condition) **anyagh**

unfold *v.* **displegya, lesa**

unfortunate *adj.* **anfeusik**

unfortunately *adv.* **yn gwettha prys**

unfurl *v.* **displetya**

unguent *n.* **unyent** *m.,* **uras** *m.*

unhappily *adv.* **yn gwettha prys**

unharmonious *adj.* **digesson**

unhealthy *adj.* **anyagh**

unholy *adj.* **ansans**

unicorn *n.* **unnkorn** *m.* **unnkern**

unicycle *n.* **unnros** *f.* **+ow**

unified *adj.* **unys**

unify *v.* **unya**

uninhabitable *adj.* **anannedhadow**

union *n.* **kesunyans** *m.* **+ow, unyans** *m.;* trade union **kesunyans lavur** *m.*

unique *adj.* **dibarow, unnik**

uniqueness *n.* **unnikter** *m.*

unit *n.* **unnses** *m.*

unite *v.* **kesunya, kesya, unya**

united *adj.* **unys**

unity *n.* **unnses** *m.*

university *n.* **pennskol** *f.* **+yow**

unjust *adj.* **kammhynsek**

unkind *n.* unkind action **droktro** *f.:* *adj.* **diguv**

unkindly *adj.* **dignas**

unknown *n.* unknown thing **ankothvos** *m.,* **anwodhvos** *m.:* *adj.* **ankoth, anwodhvos**

unleash *v.* **dileshya**

unless *conj.* **marnas, saw, mar's, ma's**

unlike *adj.* unlike others **dibarow**

unload *v.* **diskarga, diveghya**

unlock *v.* **dialhwedha**

unlocked *adj.* **dialhwedh**

unloose *v.* **lowsya**

unluckily *adv.* **yn gwettha prys**

unlucky *adj.* **anfeusik**

unmarried *adj.* **andhemmedhys**

unmatched *adj.* **dibarow**

unnatural *adj.* **dignas, dinatur**

unofficial *adj.* **ansoedhogel**

unpleasant *adj.* **anhwek**

unprotected *adj.* **diwith**

unravel *v.* **digemmyska**

unreal *adj.* **tarosvannus**

unreality *n.* **anwirvos** *m.*

unrighteous *adj.* **kammhynsek**

unripe *adj.* **anadhves, kriv**

unroll *v.* **dirolya**

unruly *adj.* **direwl**

unsavoury *adj.* **disawor**

unseat *v.* **disedha**

unseemly *adj.* **anwiw**

unskilled *adj.* **digreft**

unstable *adj.* **dyantell**

unsteadily *adv.* **hwymm-hwamm**

unstructured *adj.* **anstrethys**

unsuitable *adj.* **anwiw**

unswathe *v.* **dismaylya**

untaught *adj.* **didhysk**

untether *v.* **distaga**

untethered *adj.* **distag**

untidy *n.* untidy person **skubellek** *m.* **-ogyon, skubelloges** *f.* **+ow:** *adj.* **ankempenn:** *v.* make untidy **strolya**

untie *v.* **digelmi, lowsel, lowsya**

until *prep.* **bys**: *conj.* **erna, ernag**:
  adv. **bys may, bys pan**
untilled *adj.* **anerys**; long untilled
  koth
unto *adv.* **bys yn**
untruth *n.* **gow** *m.* **+yow**
unusual *n.* unusual thing **koyntys** *f.*:
  adj. **koynt, anusadow**
unwary *adj.* **diswar**
unwelcome *adj.* **didhynnargh**
unwell *adj.* **anyagh**
unwillingness *n.* **anvodh** *m.*
unwise *adj.* **anfur**
unworthiness *n.* **anwiwder** *m.*
unworthy *adj.* **anwiw**
unwrap *v.* **dismaylya**
up *prep.* up to **bys**: *adv.* up from the
  ground **a-dhiwar-leur**; up to this
  point **bys omma**: *int.* **yn-sol**
upbringing *n.* **magereth** *f.*
upholding *n.* **mentons** *m.*
upon *prep.* **war**
upper *adj.* **gwartha**
upright *adj.* **ewnhynsek**
uprising *n.* **omsav** *m.* **+ow,**
  sevyans *m.*
upset *n.* **reudh** *m.*: *v.* **disevel,**
  distempra, reudhi
upward(s) *adv.* **yn-bann, ughos,**
  war-vann
urban *adj.* **trevek**
urge *n.* **debron** *m.,* **ynni** *m.* **+ow**:
  v. **ynnia**
urgency *n.* **mall** *m.,* **ynniadow** *m.*
urgent *adj.* **ter, ynniadow**
urgently *adv.* **porres**
urinal *n.* **pisva** *f.*
urinate *v.* **pisa**
urine *n.* **pisas** *m.,* **urin** *m.;* (fig.)
  dowr *m.* **+ow**
us *pron.* **ni, nyni**
usage *n.* **usadow** *m.*
use *n.* **us** *m.*: *v.* **gul devnydh a,**
  devnydhya, usya; make use of
  gul devnydh a; use up **spena**

used *adj.* **usys**
useful *adj.* **dhe les, 'vas**
useless *n.* useless person **pilyek** *m.*
  pilyogyon: *adj.* **didhevnydh,**
  diles, euver, pilyek
uselessness *n.* **euveredh** *m.*
user *n.* **devnydhyer** *m.* **-yoryon**
usual *adj.* **usadow, usys**: *adv.* as
  usual **herwydh usadow**
usurer *n.* **okerer** *m.* **-oryon**
usurp **usurpya**
usury *n.* **oker** *m.*
utmost *n.* **eghenn** *f.*
utter *v.* **leverel**
utterance *n.* **lavar** *m.* **+ow, lev** *m.*
  +ow

V

vacancy *n.* **gwagla** *m.* **-leow**
vacant *adj.* **gwag**
vacation (U.S.) *n.* **dy'goel** *m.*
  +yow
vacuum *n.* **gwagva** *f.* **+ow**
vacuum-cleaner *n.* **skubell-**
  sugna *f.* **skubellow-sugna**
vagabond *n.* **brybour** *m.* **+s,**
  faytour *m.* **+s, skajynn** *m.* **+ow**
vagina *n.* **kons** *f.*
vagrant *n.* **brybour** *m.* **+s, gwyll**
  m. **+yow, jowdyn** *m.* **+s, lorel** *m.*
  +s, losel *m.* **+s**; worthless vagrant
  foul y berghenn *m.*
vain *adj.* **koeg**
vainglory *n.* **goeth** *m.*
valley *n.* **nans** *m.* **+ow**; deep valley
  downans *m.* **+ow**; flat valley
  stras *m.* **+ow**; large valley **glynn**
  m. **+ow**; small valley **golans** *m.*
  +ow, komm *m.* **+ow**; streamless
  valley **syghnans** *m.* **+ow,**
  syghtenow *m.*
valley-bottom *n.* **tenow** *m.* **+i,**
  tnow *m.* **-i**
valour *n.* **vertu** *f.* **+s**
valuable *adj.* **a bris, talvosek**

value *n.* bri *f.,* pris *m.* +yow,
talvosogeth *f.:* *v.* talvos,
talvesa
vandal *n.* vandal *m.* +s
vanquish *v.* fetha
vaporize *v.* ethenna
vapour *n.* ethenn *f.* +ow
variegated *adj.* brith, brygh
variety *n.* kemmysk *m.,* eghenn *f.,*
liester *m.*
various *adj.* divers, liesek
vassal *n.* omajer *m.* +s
vear *n.* porghell *m.* +i
vegetable *n.* vegetable garden
losowek *f.* -egi
vegetables *plur.* losow-kegin
veil *n.* goel *m.* +yow, kudhlenn *f.,*
vayl *f.:* *v.* lenni
vein *n.* gwyth *f.,* gwythienn *f.* +ow
coll gwythi; (of ore) skorrenn *f.*
+ow *coll.* skorr
veined *adj.* gwythiek
vellum *n.* parchemin *m.*
velocity *n.* uskitter *m.* +yow
velvet *n.* pali *m.*
vendor *n.* gwerther *m.* -oryon,
gwerthores *f.* +ow
veneer *n.* lownyans *m.* +ow: *v.*
lownya
vengeance *n.* dial *m.,* venjans *m.:*
v. wreak vengeance diala: *phr.*
wreak vengeance on tyli dial war
venom *n.* gwenon *m.,* venim *m.*
venomous *adj.* gwenonek
vent *n.* tardhell *f.* +ow
ventilate *v.* ayrella
ventilation *n.* ayrellans *m.*
ventilator *n.* ayrell *f.*
ventriloquist *n.* torrleveryas *m.*
-ysi
venture *n.* bedhas *m.* +ow, vyaj
m.: *v.* bedha, lavasos; make a
venture aventurya
venturesome *adj.* bedhek

Venus *n.* Gwener *f.;* (as morning
"star") Borlewen *f.*
verb *n.* verb *f.* +ow
verbal *n.* (spoken) der anow *m.:*
adj. (concerned with words) geryel;
(concerning verbs) verbel
verbose *adj.* gerennek, tavosek:
v. be verbose gerya
verdant *n.* verdant ground glastir *m.*
+yow
verdict *n.* breus *f.* +ow
verdure *n.* glasenn *f.* +ow,
glasneth *f.*
verily *adv.* devri, dhe wir, dhe-
wir, surredi, yredi
verisimilitude *n.* gwirhevelepter
m.
vermin *n.* lastedhes *m.:* *v.* hunt
vermin pryvessa
verminous *adj.* pryvesek
vernacular *adj.* teythyek
verse *n.* gwers *f.* +yow
versification *n.* gwersieth *f.*
vertebra *n.* mell keyn *m.*
vertical *adj.* plommwedhek
vertigo *n.* penn-dro *f.*
very *adv.* fest, pur, purra
vespers *n.* gwesper *m.* +ow
vessel *n.* (container or ship) lester *m.*
lestri; (container) kavas *m.* +ow;
(ship) gorhel *m.* -holyon
vest *n.* hevis *m.* +yow, vesta *m.*
vestry *n.* gwiskti *m.* +ow
vet *n.* milvedhyk *m.* -ygyon
veterinary *n.* veterinary science
milvedhygieth *f.*
vex *v.* serri, annia, disesya, trobla
vexation *n.* poenvos *m.*
vexed *adj.* poenvosek
viaduct *n.* ponsfordh *f.* +ow
vial *n.* fiol *f.* +yow
viands *n.* vytel *m.*
vicar *n.* pronter *m.* +yon
vicarage *n.* pronterji *m.* +ow

vice *n.* **drog** *m.*, **drogedh** *m.*, **drokter** *m.;* vice (tool) **bis** *f.* **+yow**
vice- *pref.* **is-**
vice-chairman *n.* **iskaderyer** *m.*
vice-chancellor *n.* **ischansler** *m.* **+s**
vice-president *n.* **islywydh** *m.* **+yon**
vicinity *n.* **kyrghynn** *m.;* in the vicinity of **yn kyrghynn** *m.: adv.* **yn herwydh**
victor *n.* **trygher** *m.* **-oryon**
victorious *adj.* **budhek, budhogel, trygh**: *v.* be victorious **tryghi**
victory *n.* **budhogoleth** *f.*, **trygh** *m.*
victualler *n.* **mether** *m.* **-oryon**
victuals *n.* **vytel** *m.*
video *n.* **gwydhyow** *m.*
video-cassette *n.* video-cassette **gwelgyst** *f.* **+yow**
view *n.* **gwel** *m.* **+yow, vu** *m.*
view-point *n.* **gwelva** *f.* **-ow**
vigil *n.* **goel** *m.* **+yow**
vigilant *adj.* **hewoel**
vigorous *adj.* **krev**
vigour *n.* **kris** *m.*
Viking *n.* **ankredor mor** *m.*
vile *adj.* **los, vil**
vileness *n.* **bileni** *f.*, **losni** *m.*, **vilta** *f.*
village *n.* **kastell** *m.* **kastylli, tre** *f.* **trevow, gwig** *f.* **+ow, treveglos** *f.* **+yow**
villain *n.* **gal** *m.* **+yon**
villainous *adj.* **bilen**
villainy *n.* **bileni** *f.*
vine *n.* **gwinbrenn** *m.* **+yer**
vinegar *n.* **aysel** *m.*, **gwin fellys** *m.*
vinegary *adj.* **ayselek**
vinery *n.* **gwinji** *m.* **+ow**
vineyard *n.* **gwinlann** *f.* **+ow**
viola *n.* (plant) **mellyon tryliw** *coll.*
violate *v.* **defola, ravna**

violence *n.* **freudh** *m.:* *v.* commit violence **freudhi**
violent *adj.* **freudhek**
violet *adj.* (colour) **glasrudh**
violets *n.* **mellyon** *coll.* **+enn**
violin *n.* **fyll** *m.* **+ow, krowd** *m.* **+ys**
violinist *n.* **fyller** *m.* **-oryon, fyllores** *f.* **+ow, krowder** *m.* **-oryon**
viper *n.* **nader** *f.* **nadres**
virgin *n.* **gwyrghes** *f.* **+i**
virginal *adj.* **gwyrgh**
virile *adj.* **gourel**
virility *n.* **gouroleth** *f.*
virtue *n.* **ras** *m.* **+ow, vertu** *f.* **+s:** *plur.* virtues **vertutys**
viscount *n.* **isyurl** *m.*
visible *adj.* **a-wel**; easily visible **hewel**
vision *n.* **hunros** *m.* **+ow, golok** *f.;* (apparition) **gwelesigeth** *f.* **+ow**
visit *n.* **godrik** *m.* **-igow:** *v.* **godriga**
visitation *n.* (of evil) **plag** *m.* **+ys**
visitor *n.* **godriger** *m.* **-oryon**; summer visitor **havyades** *f.* **+ow, havyas** *m.* **-ysi**
vixen *n.* **lowarnes** *f.* **+ow**
vocabulary *n.* **gerva** *f.* **+ow**
vocation *n.* **galwesigeth** *f.* **+ow**
voice *n.* **lev** *m.* **+ow**
void *n.* **gwagva** *f.* **+ow:** *adj.* **gwag:** *v.* void excrement **kagla, kawgha**
volcanic *adj.* **loskvenydhyek**
volcano *n.* **loskvenydh** *m.* **+yow**
volt *n.* **volt** *m.*
voltage *n.* **voltedh** *m.*
voluble *adj.* **gerennek**
volume *n.* (quantity in physics) **dalghedh** *m.* **+ow;** (spatial) **dalgh** *m.* **+ow**
voluntarily *adv.* **a-vodh**
voluntary *adj.* **a-vodh, bodhek**
volunteer *n.* **bodhek** *m.* **-ogyon**

vomit *v.* **hwyja**
vortex *n.* **lonklynn** *m.* **+ow**
vote *n.* **raglev** *m.* **+ow**: *v.* **ragleva, votya**
vowel *n.* **bogalenn** *f.* **+ow**
voyage *n.* **vyaj** *m.*: *v.* **vyajya**
vulgar *adj.* **isel, kemmyn**

W

waddle *v.* **rambla**
waffle *n.* **flows** *m.*: *v.* **flowsa**
wag *v.* **shakya**
wage *n.* **gober** *m.* **gobrow, waja** *m.* **+ys**: *plur.* wage restraints **fronnow-gober**
wager *n.* **kenwystel** *m.* **kenwystlow**: *v.* **kenwystla**
wages *n.* **arveth** *m.*: *v.* pay wages to **gobra**
wage-settlement *n.* **unnverheans gober** *m.*
wail *v.* **kyni**
wailing *n.* **oelva** *f.*
waist *n.* **kres** *m.*
waistcoat *n.* **kryspows** *f.*
wait *v.* wait for **gortos**; wait for someone **gortos nebonan**
wait in line (U.S.) *v.* **gul lost, lostya**
waiter *n.* **servyas** *m.* **-ysi**
waitress *n.* **servyades** *f.*
wake *n.* **goel** *m.* **+yow**: *adj.* wake up **difun**
Wales *n.* **Kembra** *f.*
walk *n.* **kerdh** *m.* **+ow, rosyas** *m.*; long walk **travel** *m.*; organized walk **keskerdh** *m.*: *v.* **kerdhes**; walk far **travalya**; walk together **keskerdhes**
walker *n.* **kerdher** *m.* **-oryon**
walker (U.S.) *n.* **fram-kerdhes** *m.*
walking-frame *n.* **fram-kerdhes** *m.*

walking-stick *n.* **lorgh** *f.* **+ow**
walk-out *n.* **eskerdh** *m.* **+ow**
wall *n.* **fos** *f.* **+ow**; (interior) **paros** *m.* **+yow**; little wall **fosynn** *f.*; low wall of earth and stone **ke** *m.* **keow**; party wall **paros** *m.* **+yow**
wallet *n.* **tigenn** *f.* **+ow, skryp** *m.* **+ys**
wallflower *n.* **bleujenn fosow** *f.*
wall-hanging *n.* **goel** *m.* **+yow, kroglenn fos** *f.*, **kudhlenn fos** *f.*
wallpaper *n.* **paper paros** *m.*
walnut *n.* **knowenn frynk** *f.*
walrus *n.* **morvugh** *f.* **+es**
wand *n.* **gwelenn** *f.* **gwelynni** *coll.* **gwel**
wander *v.* **gwandra**
wanderer *n.* **gwandryas** *m.* **-ysi**
wandering *adj.* **gwandrek**
want *n.* **edhomm** *m.* **+ow, boghosogneth** *f.*, **esow** *m.*: *v.* **mynnes**
wanton *n.* wanton person **gyglet** *m.*
war *n.* **bresel** *f.* **+yow, bel** *m.*, **kas** *f.* **+ow**: *v.* make war **breseli, gwerrya**
warden *n.* **gwithyas** *m.* **gwithysi, gwithyades** *f.* **+ow**
wardrobe *n.* **dillasva** *f.* **+ow**
war-horse *n.* **kasvargh** *m.* **kasvergh**
warlike *adj.* **breselek**
warm *adj.* **toemm**: *v.* **toemmhe, toemma**; warm in the sunshine **tesa**
warming-pan *n.* **padell-doemma** *f.* **padellow-toemma**
warmth *n.* **toemmder** *m.*, **tes** *m.*, **toemmyjyon** *m.*
warn *v.* **gwarnya**
warning *n.* **gwarnyans** *m.* **+ow**; warning to evildoers **bysna** *m.*
warp *n.* **steuv** *m.* **+ow**: *v.* **steuvi**
warrant *n.* warrant for arrest **kapyas** *m.*

warranty *n.* mewgh *m.* +yow
warren *n.* rabbit warren koneri *m.*
warrior *n.* breselyer *m.* -yoryon,
kasor *m.* -oryon; (professional)
breselyas *m.* -ysi
wart *n.* gwennogenn *f.* +ow;
cattle wart ryg *m.* +yow
wary *adj.* war
was *v.* esa, o; I was esen
wash *v.* golghi; wash oneself
omwolghi: *phr.* wash the dishes
golghi an lestri
washing *n.* washing machine jynn-
golghi *m.*
washing-powder *n.* lisiw *m.*
washing-up *n.* washing-up liquid lin
sebon *m.*
wash-place *n.* golghva *f.* +ow
washroom (U.S.) *n.* golghva *f.*
+ow
wasp *n.* goghienn *f.* +ow *coll.*
goghi
wassail *n.* wassel *m.*
wast *v.* thou wast es, eses
waste *n.* difeyth *m.*, skoell *m.*
+yon: *adj.* difeyth, wast: *v.*
skoellya; lay waste difeythya,
gwastya, wastya; waste time
gwibessa
wasteful *adj.* skoellyek
wasteland *n.* difeyth *m.*
waster *n.* skoellyek *m.* -ogyon
wastrel *n.* skoellyek *m.* -ogyon
watch *n.* (timepiece) euryor *f.;*
(vigil) goel *m.* +yow; night watch
goelyas *f.;* officer on watch
brennyas *m.* -ysi: *v.* mires
orth; keep watch goelyas; watch
out warya
water *n.* dowr *m.* +ow; filthy water
beudhowr *m.;* high water
gorlanow *m.;* inlet of water logh
m. +ow; salt water hyli *m.: v.*
dowra, dowrhe
water-channel *n.* kanel *f.*
kanolyow; (from a mine) odyt *m.*

watercourse *n.* awedh *f.* +yow,
dowrhyns *m.* +yow, goeth *f.* +ow
water-cress *n.* beler *coll.* +enn
waterfall *n.* dowrlamm *m.* +ow,
pistyll *m.* +ow
watering-can *n.* dowrer *m.*
watering-place *n.* dowran *m.,*
dowrla *m.,* dowrva *f.* +ow
waterless *adj.* sygh
water-lilies alow +enn
waters *n.* meeting of waters
kendevryon *m.*
waterside *n.* dowrlann *f.* +yow,
glann *f.* +ow
water-tank *n.* dowrargh *m.* +ow
watertight *adj.* stanch
water-wheel *n.* pit of water-wheel
poll ros *m.*
watery *n.* watery ground goethel *m.;*
watery place dowrek *f.* -egi: *adj.*
deverel, devrek, dowrek,
goethel
wattle *v.* pletha
wave *n.* tonn *f.* +ow; (in sea)
mordonn *f.* +ow; medium wave
tonnhys kres *m.: v.* gwevya
wavelength *n.* tonnhys *m.*
wavelet *n.* tennik *f.* -igow
wavy *adj.* tonnek
wax *n.* koer *coll.* +enn; cake of wax
koerenn *f.* +ow *coll.* koer; wax
tallow candle kantol goer *f.,*
kantol soev *f.: v.* koera
way *n.* fordh *f.* +ow, tu *m.* +yow,
hyns *m.* +yow, kammenn *f.,*
maner *f.* +ow; great way pellder
m. +yow: *adv.* all the way to bys
yn; in no way kammenn; in no
way at all kammenn vydh; in that
way y'n for' na; in the same way
kepar; in this way y'n for' ma,
yndellma; on the way war fordh;
this way and that hwymm-
hwamm: *phr.* in some way war
neb kor; there's no way out nyns
eus dhymmo remedi

waybread *n.* hynledan *m.*

we *pron.* ni: *v.* we are on

weak *adj.* gwann, anven, ydhyl

weaken *v.* bludhya, gwannhe, medhelhe

weakling *n.* gwann *m.* +yon

weakness *n.* gwannder *m.*, gwannegredh *m.*

wealth *n.* rychys *m.*: *plur.* worldly wealth pythow an bys

wean *v.* didhena

weapon *n.* arv *f.* +ow: *plur.* nuclear weapons arvow nuklerek

wear *v.* gwiska

wearied *adj.* anes, skwithhes

weary *adj.* skwith: *v.* annia, skwithhe

weasel *n.* konna-gwynn *m.*, lowennan *m.* -es

weather *n.* awel *f.* +yow, kewer *f.*; bad weather hager awel *f.*: *v.* tewedha

weather-beaten *adj.* tewedhek

weathercock *n.* kulyek-gwyns *m.*

weathering *v.* tewedhans

weave *adj.* easy to weave hebleth: *v.* gwia

weaver *n.* gwiader *m.* -oryon, gwiadores *f.* +ow

web *n.* gwias *m.* +ow; spider's web gwias kevnis *m.*

web.-site *n.* gwiasva *f.* +ow

wedding *n.* demmedhyans *m.* +ow

wedge *n.* iron wedge genn *m.* +ow: *v.* genna

Wednesday *n.* dy' Mergher *m.*, Mergher *m.*

weed *n.* hwynnenn *f.* +ow *coll.* hwynn; climbing weed gwyg *coll.* +enn

weed-patch *n.* hwynnek *f.* hwynnegi

weedy *adj.* hwynnek

week *n.* seythun *f.* +yow

weekday *n.* dy'gweyth *m.* +yow

weekend *n.* pennseythun *f.* +yow

weekly *adj.* seythunyek

weep *v.* oela, dagrewi

weeping *n.* oelva *f.*

weever *n.* weever fish kalkar *m.*

weigh *v.* poesa

weight *n.* poes *m.* +ow; (quantity in physics) poesedh *m.* +ow; hundred pound weight kanspeuns *m.*

weighty *adj.* poesek

weir *n.* kores *f.* +ow, kryw *m.*

welcome *n.* dynnargh *m.*: *adj.* wolkomm: *v.* dynnerghi, wolkomma

welfare *n.* sewena *f.*; welfare payment dol *m.*

welkin *n.* ebrenn *f.*

well *adv.* as well keffrys

well *adj.* well (healthy) salow; well (not ill) yagh: *conj.* as well maga ta: *adv.* yn ta; as well keffrys, kekeffrys, ynwedh; very well fest yn ta: *int.* wel

well *n.* (e.g. for water) puth *m.* +ow; surface well fenten *f.* fentynyow

well-born *adj.* jentyl

well-doer *n.* masoberer *m.* -oryon

well-formed *adj.* fethus

Welsh *n.* Welsh language Kembrek *m.*: *adj.* Kembrek

Welshman *n.* Kembro *m.* +yon

Welshwoman *n.* Kembroes *f.* +ow

wen *n.* gwennenn *f.* +ow

wench *n.* benewenn *f.* +ow

went *v.* eth

were *v.* they were esens; we were esen; you were esewgh, ewgh

west *n.* howlsedhes *m.*, West *m.*; the West gorlewin *f.*: *adj.* West

wet *adj.* glyb, gwlygh: *v.* glybya

wether *n.* wether sheep mols *m.* mels

wetness *n.* glybor *m.*, gwlygha *m.*

whack *n.* hwaff *m.* +ys, hwatt *m.*
+ys, hwettya *m.*

whale *n.* morvil *m.* +es

wharf *n.* kay *m.* kayow

what *pron.* pandra, py, pyth: *adj.*
pana, pan: *adv.* what for prag:
int. dar

whatever *pron.* kekemmys,
pynag, pypynag, pyseul

whatsoever *pron.* pynagoll

wheat *n.* gwaneth *coll.* +enn

wheatear *n.* (bird) tinwynn *f.* +yon

wheatfield *n.* gwanethek *f.* -egi

wheatland *n.* gwanettir *m.* +ow

wheedle *v.* flattra

wheedler *n.* flatter *m.* -oryon

wheel *n.* ros *f.* +ow; big wheel ros
veur *f.;* gear wheel ros dhensek
f.; spare wheel ros parys *f.;*
spinning-wheel ros nedha *f.;*
steering wheel ros lywya *f.*

wheel-barrow *n.* gravath-ros *m.*

wheel-chair *n.* kador-ros *f.*
kadoryow-ros

whelp *n.* kolyn *m.* kelyn

when *conj.* pan: *adv.* p'eur

whence *adv.* a-ble, a-byla

whenever *conj.* peskweyth may:
adv. bydh pan

where *adv.* ple: *phr.* ple'th; where
is ple'ma

wherefore *conj.* rakhemma: *adv.*
prag

wherever *conj.* plepynag

wherewithal *n.* pygans *m.*

whet *v.* lymma

whetstone *n.* igolenn *f.* +ow

whey *n.* meydh *m.;* cheese whey
keusveydh *m.*

which *pron.* py; (of two) pyneyl:
conj. that which an pyth

while *n.* a good while polta *m.:*
conj. ha, hedra

whim *n.* sians *m.*

whimsically *adv.* hwymm-
hwamm

whinny *v.* gryghias

whip *n.* hwypp *m.* +ys, skorja *m.*
+ys: *v.* fusta, hwyppya, skorjya

whirl *v.* forlya, rosella

whirlpool *n.* lonklynn *m.* +ow,
poll troyllya *m.*, troboll *m.* +ow

whirlwind *n.* gwyns a-dro *m.*,
korwyns *m.* +ow

whirr *v.* hwyrni

whiskers *n.* boghvlew *coll.*,
minvlew *coll.* +ynn

whisper *n.* hwystrenn *f.* +ow: *v.*
hwystra

whistle *n.* hwythell *f.* +ow;
(instrument) hwibanowl *f.:* *v.* (by
mouth) hwibana

whistler *n.* hwibanor *m.* +yon

whistling *n.* (by mouth) hwiban *f.*

white *adj.* gwynn; bright white
kann

white-headed *adj.* penn-gwynn

whiten *v.* gwynnhe

whiteness *n.* gwynnder *m.*

whiting *n.* gwynnek *m.* -oges

whitish *adj.* gwynnek, skyllwynn

Whitsuntide *n.* Penkost *m.*

who *pron.* piw

whoever *pron.* myns, kekemmys,
piwpynag, pynag, seul

whole *adj.* kowal, saw, dien

wholesome *adj.* da, yaghus

wholly *adv.* oll

whooping-cough *n.* pas-garm *m.*

whore *n.* gast *f.* gesti, hora *f.*
horys

whortleberry *n.* lusenn *f.* +ow
coll. lus

whosoever *pron.* pynagoll

why *adv.* prag, praga, pyraga:
int. dar

wicked *adj.* drog, tebel, treus

wide *adj.* efan, ledan

widely *adv.* a-les

widow *n.* gwedhwes *f.* +ow
widowed *adj.* gwedhow
widower *n.* gwedhow *m.* +yon
width *n.* les *m.*
wife *n.* benyn *f.* +es, gwreg *f.*
gwragedh
Wight *n.* Isle of Wight Ynys Wyth *f.*
wild *adj.* fol, gwyls, goedh
wilderness *n.* gwylvos *m.*
wild-natured *n.* wild-natured
individual heller *m.* helloryon
wilful *adj.* omvodhek: *v.* be wilful
omvodhya
will *n.* bodh *m.*, bolonjedh *m.*:
adv. against his will a'y anvodh
willing *adj.* bolonjedhek: *v.* be
willing to mynnes
willow-garden *n.* helik-lowarth
m. +ow
willow-plant *n.* heligenn *f.* +ow
coll. helik
wilt *v.* klamdera
wily *adj.* fel
win *v.* gwaynya
wince *v.* omwen
winch *n.* gwyns *f.* +ys; steam-
driven winch gwyns-ethenn *f.*
wind *n.* awel *f.* +yow, gwyns *m.*
+ow; icy wind oerwyns *m.* +ow;
(to turn) *v.* stumma
winding *n.* winding stream koger
m.: *adj.* gwius
windlass *n.* gwyns *f.* +ys
windmill *n.* melin-wyns *f.*
melinyow-gwyns
window *n.* fenester *f.* -tri
windpipe *n.* bryansenn *f.*
windy *adj.* gwynsek, awelek
wine *n.* gwin *m.*; spiced wine
pyment *m.*
wine-glass *n.* gwinwedrenn *f.*
wine-press *n.* gwinwask *f.* +ow
wine-server *n.* botler *m.* +s
wing *n.* askell *f.* eskelli
winged *adj.* askellek

wingless *adj.* diaskellek
wink *n.* (of eye) gwynk *m.*: *v.*
gwynkya
winnow *v.* gwynsa, gwynsella,
kroedra, notha
winnowing *n.* winnowing sheet
nothlenn *f.* +ow
winter *n.* gwav *m.* +ow: *v.* gwavi;
pass the winter gwavi
wintercress *n.* kasbeler *m.*
winze *n.* gwyns *f.* +ys
wipe *v.* sygha
wire *n.* (an individual wire)
gwivrenn *f.* gwiver
wireless *n.* diwiver *m.*
wisdom *n.* furneth *f.*, skentoleth *f.*
wise *adj.* fur, skiansek, skentel
wish *n.* bolonjedh *m.*, hwans *m.*
+ow, mynnas *m.*: *v.* mynnes
wishful *adj.* hwansek
wistful *adj.* hirethek
witch *n.* gwragh *f.* +es; white
witch peller *m.* -oryon
witchcraft *n.* pystri *m.*
with *prep.* gans; along with a-
barth; with her gensi; with him
ganso; with me genev; with thee
genes; with them gansa; with us
genen; with you genowgh
withal *adv.* ha gensi, kekeffrys
withdraw *v.* omdenna, avodya,
kildenna
withdrawal *n.* kildenn *m.*
wither *v.* gwedhra
withered *adj.* sygh, krebogh, krin
withhold *v.* skonya
within *prep.* a-ji dhe, a-berth:
adv. a-ji
without *prep.* heb, a-der
witless *adj.* diskians: *v.* become
witless dotya
witness *n.* rekord *m.* +ys, test *m.*
+ow; (person) dustunier *m.*
-oryon; (testimony) dustuni *m.*

dustuniow: *v.* **desta, rekordya**;
bear witness **dustunia, testa**

wits *adj.* out of his wits **mes a'y
skians**

woad *n.* **liwles** *m.*

woe *n.* **gew** *m.* **+ow**: *int.* **tru, go**;
woe is me **go-vy**; woe to him **go-
ev**

wolf *n.* **bleydh** *m.* **+es, +i**

wolves *adj.* abounding in wolves
bleydhek

woman *n.* **ben** *f.,* **benyn** *f.* **+es,
gwreg** *f.* **gwragedh, benynreydh**
f.; little woman **benewenn** *f.* **+ow**;
young woman **myrgh** *f.* **myrghes**:
pron. that woman **honna**; this
woman **homma**

womanhood *n.* **benynses** *m.*

womanly *adj.* **benynek, gwregel**

womb *n.* **torr** *f.* **+ow, brys** *m.*

women *v.* consort with women
benyna

wonder *n.* **aneth** *m.* **+ow, marth** *m.*
+ow, marthus *m.* **+yon, revedh**
m. **+ow**; state of wonder or alarm
transyek *m.: v.* **omwovynn**;
wonder at **gul aneth a**

wonderful *adj.* **barthusek,
marthys**

wonderfully *adv.* **marthys**

wondrous *adj.* **barthusek,
wondrys**

wood *n.* (as timber) **prenn** *m.* **+yer**;
(as trees) **koes** *m.* **+ow**; charcoal
burners' wood **glow-wydhek** *f.;*
wood for charcoal **glow-wydh** *f.*

woodbine *n.* **gwydhvos** *coll.* **+enn**

woodcock *n.* **kevelek** *m.* **-oges**: *v.*
shoot woodcock **kevelekka**

wood-corner *n.* **korn keunys** *m.*

wooded *adj.* **gwydhek, gwydhyel**

woodland *n.* **gwydhek** *f.* **-egi**

wood-louse *n.* **gwragh oeles** *f.*

woodpecker *n.* **kasek-koes** *f.*
kasegi-koes

wood-pigeon *n.* **kolomm koes** *f.,*
kudhon *f.*

woodwork *n.* **prennweyth** *m.*

woodworm *n.* **pryv prenn** *m.*

woody *adj.* **koesek**

wooer *n.* **tanter** *m.* **-oryon**

wooing *n.* **tantans** *m.*

wool *n.* **gwlan** *coll.*

wool-card *n.* **kribin** *f.*

woolly *adj.* **gwlanek**

word *n.* **ger** *m.* **+yow**; single word
gerenn *f.* **+ow**: *adv.* without
another word **dison**

word-processor *n.* **gerdhyghtyer**
m.

work *n.* **hwel** *m.* **+yow, lavur** *m.,*
ober *m.* **+ow, gonis** *m.,* **gweyth**
m.; major work **obereth** *f.: v.*
oberi, gonis, gweytha, lavurya;
set to work **gweytha**; work
backwards in mine **kilweytha**

worked *adj.* **gonedhys**

worker *n.* **gweythor** *m.* **+yon,
oberer** *m.* **-oryon**

work-force *n.* **lavurlu** *m.* **+yow**

working-class *n.* **renkas ober** *m.*

workman *n.* **oberwas** *m.* **-
wesyon, gonisek** *m.* **-ogyon,
gonysyas** *m.* **-ysi, gwas-hwel** *m.*
gwesyon-hwel, gweythor *m.*
+yon

work-sheet *n.* **folenn ober** *f.*

work-shop *n.* **chi hwel** *m.*

world *n.* **bys** *m.* **+ow, nor** *m.;* the
world **an nor** *m.*

worldly *adj.* **a'n bys**

worldwide *adj.* **treusvysek**

worm *n.* **pryv** *m.* **+es, +yon,
pryvenn** *f.* **+ow**

wormwood *n.* **fuelenn** *f.,* **loesles**
m.

wormy *adj.* **pryvesek**

worn *adj.* worn out **usys**

worried *adj.* **prederys**

worries *phr.* no worries **heb grev**

worry *n.* **preder** *m.* **+ow:** *v.*
despitya
worrying *adj.* **prederus**
worse *adj.* **gweth, lakka;** far worse
milweth
worsen *v.* **gwethhe**
worship *n.* **gologhas** *m.,*
gordhyans *m.:* *v.* **gordhya**
worst *adj.* **gwettha**
wort *n.* **les** *m.* **+yow**
worth *n.* **bri** *f.,* **talvosogeth** *f.*
worthiness *n.* **gwiwder** *m.* **+yow**
worthless *n.* worthless person **koeg**
m. **+yon, koegas** *m.:* *adj.* **koeg:**
phr. it's absolutely worthless **ny dal**
oy
worthwhile *adj.* **dhe les**
worthy *adj.* **gwiw, wordhi**
wound *n.* **goli** *m.* **+ow:** *v.* **golia**
wrangle *v.* **debatya**
wrangler *n.* **striver** *m.* **-oryon**
wrap *v.* **maylya**
wreath *n.* **garlont** *f.* **+ow, torgh** *f.*
tergh
wreathe *v.* **terghi**
wreck *n.* **gwrekk** *m.* **+ys**
wreckage *plur.* **skommow**
wren *n.* **gwrannenn** *f.*
wrench (U.S.) *n.* **alhwedh-know**
f. **alhwedhow-know**
wrest *v.* **wrestya**
wrestle *v.* **gwrynya, omdewlel**
wrestler *n.* **omdowler** *m.* **-oryon,**
gwrynyer *m.* **-yoryon**
wrestling *n.* **omdowl** *m.*
wretch *n.* **anfeusik** *m.* **-igyon,**
kanjon *m.* **+s**
wretched *adj.* **truan, trogh**
wretchedness *n.* **kas** *m.*
wriggle *v.* **gwynnel, omwen**
wrinkle *n.* **kris** *m.* **+yow, krygh** *m.*
+yow: *v.* **krygha**
wrinkled *adj.* **krebogh**
wrist *n.* **konna-bregh** *m.*

writ *n.* **skrifa** *m.;* writ of arrest
kapyas *m.*
write *v.* **skrifa;** write again
dasskrifa; write by hand
dornskrifa; write wrongly
kammskrifa
writer *n.* **skrifer** *m.* **+s, -oryon;**
(professional) **skrifyas** *m.* **-ysi**
writhe *v.* **gwynnel, kamma,**
omwen
writing *n.* **skrif** *m.* **+ow, skrifa** *m.,*
skrifenn *f.* **+ow**
wrong *n.* **kamm** *m.* **+ow,**
drokoleth *f.,* **kammhynseth** *f.:*
adj. **kamm**
wrongdoing *n.* **kammweythres** *m.*
wrong-headed *adj.* **penn-kamm**
wrought *adj.* **gonedhys;**
faultlessly wrought **fin gonedhys**
wrynecked *adj.* **penn-kamm**

Y

yard *n.* (enclosure) **garth** *m.* **+ow;**
(measure) **lath** *f.* **+ow**
yardarm *n.* **dela** *f.* **deledhow**
yarrow *n.* **minfel** *m.*
yawn *v.* **deleva**
ye *pron.* **hwi, hwyhwi**
yea *int.* **ye**
year *n.* **blydhen** *f.* **blydhynyow;**
year of age **bloedh** *m.:* *adv.* last
year **warlyna;** this year **hevlyna**
yearly *adj.* **blydhenyek**
yearn *v.* **yeuni;** yearn after **yeuni**
war-lergh
yearning *n.* **hireth** *f.,* **yeunadow**
m., **yeunes** *m.* **+ow:** *adj.*
hirethek
Year's *n.* New Year's Day **Kalann**
Genver *m.;* year's end
pennvlydhen *f.* **-vlydhynyow;**
year's time **bloedhweyth** *m.*
yeast *n.* **burm** *c.,* **goell** *m.*
yell *n.* **us** *m.:* *v.* **usa**

yellow *adj.* **melyn**:   *v.* make yellow
  melynhe
yellowhammer *n.* **melynek**
  eythin *m.*
yellowish *adj.* **melynik**
yellowness *n.* **melynder** *m.*
yes (normally expressed by repeating
  the verb) *int.* **ya**
yesterday *adv.* **de**; yesterday
  evening **nyhewer**
yet *adv.* **hwath, byttegyns, hogen**;
  not yet **na hwath**
yew *n.* **ywin** *coll.* **+enn**
Yiddish *n.* Yiddish language
  Yedhowek *m.*
yield *v.* **daskorr**
yoghurt *n.* **yogort** *m.* **+ow**
yoke *n.* **yew** *f.* **+ow**:   *v.* **yewa**; yoke
  together **kesyewa**
yoke-ox *n.* **eal** *m.*
yonder *adv.* **eno, enos, hons,**
  nos, yn-hons
York *place* **Evrek**

you *pron.* (pl.) **hwi, hwyhwi**:   *v.* you
  are **owgh**:   *phr.* are you **osta**; you
  are **osta, o'ta**
young *n.* young man **bacheler** *m.*
  +s, yonker *m.* **+s**; young person
  chett *m.* **+ys, flogh** *m.* **fleghes**:
  adj. **yowynk, yo'nk**:   *v.* make
  young **yowynkhe**
your *pron.* **agas**:   *phr.* and your
  ha'gas; to your **dh'agas**
yourselves *pron.* **hwyhwi**
youth *n.* **maw** *m.*, **den yowynk** *m.*,
  yowynkneth *f.*, **yowynkses** *m.*

Z

zealous *adj.* **diwysek**
zero *num.* **mann**
zimmer *n.* zimmer frame **fram-**
  kerdhes *m.*
zither *n.* **sowtri** *m.*
zoo *n.* **milva** *f.* **milvaow**